Legitimization of Religious Symbols in the Education

Europäische Hochschulschriften Recht

European University Studies in Law

Publications Universitaires Européennes de Droit

Band/Volume **6082**

Niran Hen

Legitimization of Religious Symbols in the Education – Development towards Pluralism or Secularism

A legal comparison in Germany, England and France and Introspection on the European Level

PETER LANG

Bibliografische Information der Deutschen Nationalbibliothek
Die Deutsche Nationalbibliothek verzeichnet diese Publikation in der Deutschen Nationalbibliografie; detaillierte bibliografische Daten sind im Internet über http://dnb.d-nb.de abrufbar.

Zugl.: Frankfurt (Main), Univ., Diss., 2017

D 30
ISSN 0531-7312
ISBN 978-3-631-76960-7 (Print)
E-ISBN 978-3-631-78291-0 (E-PDF)
E-ISBN 978-3-631-78292-7 (EPUB)
E-ISBN 978-3-631-78293-4 (MOBI)
DOI 10.3726/b15344

Peter Lang – Berlin · Bern · Bruxelles · New York · Oxford · Warszawa · Wien

Diese Publikation wurde begutachtet.

www.peterlang.com

Preface

This work had been accepted as a dissertation in 2017 at the Johann Wolfgang Goethe-University, Frankfurt am Main.

During the period that I have been working on my thesis, I received considerable support from various people; without their encouragement and assistance, this work would not have been productively concluded. My appreciation is dedicated to all of the people who assisted me throughout this long way, and I would like to thank them for all their meaningful and precious advice and guidance.

First and foremost, I would like to thank my Ph.D. supervisor, Prof. Dr. Rainer Hofmann, who accepted me as his Ph.D. student and was an extraordinary supportive and patient supervisor. His constant understanding and encouragement during the entire process had an immense impact on my motivation. I cordially thank him for his prompt and continuous support that was always there when I needed it. It was a great honour to work for him.

I would also like to thank Prof. Dr. Diana zu Hohenlohe, for accepting and preparing her second opinion.

A huge word of thanks is devoted to my mother for all the love and guidance during my entire education; for her endless encouragement and great values she always endowed upon her children, especially in recognizing the significance of high education, dedication to hard work, and self-discipline. I will always cherish her selfless dedication to my personal success.

My husband, Dr. Tobias Brors, who was always there for me during all highs and lows, who provided orientation and conveyed guidance. I would also like to thank Dr. Kyrill Farbmann who dedicated his precious time to support me on my way and for his constant honest opinion. Both contributed significantly to the success of my work.

I dedicate this work to my parents, who encouraged me to have aspirations and enabled me to follow my ambitions with their endless love and support. Last but definitely not least, I would like to dedicate my work for my lovely children, Aurelia and Jonathan, to whom I hope I will provide the support and guidance that I have received myself.

Contents

List of Abbreviations

ACS	Administrative Court of Stuttgart
Admin	Administrative Court
All ER	All England Law Reports
AGG	Allgemeines Gleichbehandlungsgesetz
AJDA	Actualité Juridique Droit Administratif
Am.J.Comp.L.	American Journal of Comparative Law
Am.U.Int'l L.Rev.	American University International Law Review
App	Application
ArbG	Arbeitsgericht
BAG (FLC)	Bundesarbeitsgericht
BBG	Bundesbeamtengesetz
BayEUG	Bayerisches Gesetz über das Erziehungs- und Unter-richtswesen
BayGVBl	Bayerisches Gesetz- und Verordnungsblatt
BayVerf	Bayerische Verfassung
BayVerfGH	Bayerischer Verfassungsgerichtshof
BayVBl	Bayerische Verwaltungsblätter
B.C. Inte'l & Comp. L. Rev.	Boston College International and Comparative Law Review
BGBl. (Federal law Gazette)	Bundesgesetzblatt
BlnLV	Berlin Verfassung
BremSchulG	Bremer Schulgesetz
BSR	Bavarian Elementary School Ordinance
BVerfG (FCC)	Bundesverfassungsgericht
BVerfGG (FCCA)	Bundesverfassungsgerichtsgesetz
BVerwG (FAC)	Bundesverwaltungsgericht
BW	Baden-Württemberg
BWVerf	Landesverfassung Baden-Württemberg
BYU L. Rev.	Brigham Young University Law Review
CA	Court of Appeal
Cardozo J. Int'l & Comp. L.	Cardozo Journal of International and Comparative Law
Cardozo J.L. & Gender	Cardozo Journal of Law & Gender
Cardozo L. Rev.	Cardozo Law Review

Christian common schools (CGS)	Christliche Gemeinschaftsschule
CE	Conseil d'Etat
CEHR	Committee for Equality and Human Rights
Colum. J. Gender & L.	Columbia Journal of Gender & Law
Comp. Lab. L. & Pol'y J.	Comparative Labor Law & Policy Journal
Cons. const.	Conseil constitutionnel
CRE	Commission for Racial Equality
CREA	Childrens' Religious Education Act
CSU	Christlich Soziale Union
Dick.J.Int'l L.	Dickinson Journal of International Law
DÖV	Die Öffentliche Verwaltung
DRC	Disability Right Commission
Drs.	Drucksache
DW	Deutsche Welle
EAT	Employment Appeal Tribunal
ECHR = (EMRK)	European Convention of Human Rights
ECtHR = (EGMR)	European Court of Human Rights
ECJ	European Court of Justice
ed	Edition
eds	Editors
e.g.	exempli gratia
EOC	Equal Opportunities Commission
Emory Int'l L.Rev.	Emory International Law Review
Et. Seq.	Et Sequentes
EuGRZ	Europäische Grundrechte-Zeitschrift
EWCA	England and Wales Court of Appeal
EWHC	England and Wales High Court
FDP	Freie Demokratische Partei
FS	Festschrift
GBl.	Gesetzblatt
GC	Grand Chamber
GG (Basic Law)	Grundgesetz
GVBl.	Gesetz-und Verordnungsgesetzblatt des Bun-des
GV NRW	Gesetz-und Verordnungsblatt Nordrhein-Westfale
HAC	High Administrative Court
HdbStR	Handbuch des Staatsrechts

HdbStKirchR	Handbuch des Staatskirchenrechts der Bundesrepublik
HL	House of Lords
HRA	Human Rights Act
HRC	Human Rights Committee
Hum. Rts. Q.	Human Rights Quarterly
i.e.	in example
Int'l & Comp. L.Q.	International and Comparative Law Quarterly
ICCPR	International Convention for Civil and Political Rights
CERD	International Convention on the Elimination of all Forms of Racial Discrimination
IZM	Islamic Centre of Munich (Islamisches Zentrum in Mün-chen)
J.L. & Relig.	Journal of Law and Religion
JuS	Juristische Schulung
JZ	Juristen Zeitung
KritV	Kritische Vierteljahresschrift für Gesetzgebung und Rechtswissenschaft
KuR	Kirche und Recht
Law & Soc'y Rev.	Law and Society Review
LEA	Local Education Authority
LVerfNRW	Landesverfassung Nordrhein-Westfalen (NRW Constitution)
LT	Landtag
MS	Member States
NJW	Neue Juristische Wochenschrift
NRW	North Rhine-Westphalia
NSchG	Niedersächisches Schulgesetz
N.Y.L. Sch. L. Rev.	New York Law School Law Review
NZA	Neue Zeitschrift für Arbeitsrecht
NVwZ	Neue Zeitschrift für Verwaltungsrecht
OJLS	Oxford Journal of Legal Studies
OVG	Oberverwaltungsgericht
ÖARR	Österreichiches Archiv für Recht und Religion
Para	Paragraph
Paras	Paragraphs
PDS	Partei des Demokratischen Sozialismus
QB	Quenns Bench
RDJB	Recht der Jugend und des Bildungswesens
RGBl.	Reichsgesetzblatt

S.	Sentence
SACRE	Standing Advisory Council on Religious Education
SchG BW	Schulgesetz für Baden-Württemberg
SchulG-Berlin	Schulgesetz für das Land Berlin
SchulG NRW	Schulordnungsgesetz NRW
SchoG	Schulordnungsgesetz Saarland
Sec.	Section
SPD	Sozialdemokratische Partei Deutschlands
SSFA	School Standard and Framework Act
TEU	Treaty on European Union
Tul. L. Rev.	Tulane Law Review
UDHR	Universal Declaration of Human Rights
U.Det. Mercy L. Rev.	University of Detroit Mercy Law Review
VBlBW	Verwaltungsblätter für Baden-Württemberg
VG	Verwaltungsgericht
VGH	Verwaltungsgerichtshof
VGH BW	Verwaltungsgerichtshof Baden-Württemberg
VSO	(Bayerische) Volksschulordnung
VVDStRL	Veröffentlichungen der Vereinigung der Deutschen Staatsrechtslehrer
WRV	Weimarer Reichsverfassung (The Constitution of Wei-mar)
Yale J. Int'l L.	Yale Journal of International Law
ZAR	Zeitschrift für Ausländerrecht und Ausländerpolitik
ZevKR	Zeitschrift für evangelisches Kirchenrecht

I Introduction

The period following the Second World War was characterized by decline of religious influence in European public life. Nonetheless, during the mid-1990s political and legal discussions raised and caught public attention with respect to the role of religion in society; the position of the state in ensuring endorsement of religion and religious influence in its public institutions has become relevant again. Whereas debates during the 1960s and 1970s concentrated mainly on the power and influence of the Christian churches on the states and their population against the background of growing cultural diversity, large immigration influx from predominantly Islamic countries, increasing tendency towards secularization of the states, and disentanglement of religion from the public sphere, the change in the legal discourse has become noticeable towards the end of the twentieth century. This can be attributed to the fact that Europe had to challenge abruptly with its transformation from a homogenous, Christian population to a multi-cultural, multi-pluralistic society that had to accommodate to changing social-religious needs of foreign, alienated immigration that did not fit or could be settled with the spirit of the so called 'Christian-Western tradition and culture', i.e., '*Geist der christlich-abendländischen Kultur*', as was already imprinted in 1949 with the famous pronouncement of Konrad Adenauer, the then presiding Chancellor of Germany. The change in the legal discourse marked also the outset of a period that threatened to tumble down state-religion interplay in the European countries that had to accommodate to the religious needs of its minorities, incurred by its transformation to a religious-pluralistic society. In addition, the contention raised in social and even legal literature is that a pivotal factor for the change in the legal discourse is the lack of willingness among Muslim immigrants to integrate or assimilate, and their expectation that their religious needs and practices should be accommodated by the hosting countries. The reason why the fierce debates engaged Europe, especially in regard to manifestation of symbols like the Islamic headscarf in public education, is strongly interlinked with the perception of society with respect to its public schools system. State schools are viewed to be institutes that convey its future citizens with moral and values as they will eventually form their societies. This task is to be achieved through fostering and preservation of the Christian-Western tradition that seem to conform with the ideal presiding among the majority of the European nations. The fear of the European countries was mainly of losing their national identities and was reflected in particular in France due to the special significance it imparts to the notion of nationalism and its entrenched Jacobin notion of Republicanism. Nonetheless, the fear of loss of national identity, though not starkly observed in England and Germany, remained relevant even if featured in another form. In Germany, the need to secure allegiance to the obligation of the state to religious neutrality, as enshrined in its constitution (*Grundgesetz*), and in England preserving liberal neutrality, the acceptance of cultural diversity and non-discrimination in the form of equality offered to all religions in its society. The tense controversy had been intensified due to the refusal of immigrants to acknowledge that they had to accustom themselves to a different society and recognize as well as respect diverse cultural attitudes prevalent in the Western democratic European states; this refusal contributed only to the increase of the immigrants' social marginalization and segregation. The role of Islam in Europe has become in fact the focal point in legal discussions. The intensity of the discourse has gained even further traction since the large immigration wave hit Europe and, in particular, Germany during autumn 2015. Public discussions and even election campaigns emphasized vehemently the negative influence to be expected by the role of Islam in European societies. Besides the Financial Crisis that hit Europe in 2008 and continuous large immigration waves, the impact on European societies has become of tremendous relevance for the EU and its future shape.

The question of integration and assimilation into European societies and the ability of immigrants in their majority of Muslim countries to adapt to the legal systems had been often doubted, and was raised even as a trigger for possible future conflicts in the general public debates. This recent socio-historical development can be compared to the events during the 1950s and 1960s where large influx of Muslim immigrants rushed into the European continent, and their difficulty to integrate, mirrored in the social structure of the compared states in this analysis, has been vivid up to date. For instance, the Turkish immigrants in Germany, the Pakistanis in England and in France, and the refusal of its North-African immigrants to assimilate into French society had been reflected in its extremist form. In France, this was explained as a behaviour developed by North-African immigrants based on their fear of losing their identity and was compared to a colonial situation where 'traditional' practices were invented in order to present their resistance against colonization.

Given these socio-political and historical aspects designated above, this work focuses on the legal discourse and position taken in the European countries France, England, and Germany with regard to the influence of religion in the public sphere in general, and the manifestation of religious insignias in state schools in particular. Due to their different history, constitutional traditions, cultural diversities, the socio-political structure, and the impact of religion on the state system, each of the countries developed its own approaches to face the respective challenges encountered with legal controversies surrounding the admissibility of religious insignias in public education.

Relevant aspects in this regard are the role of teachers in the school system, the state and its function as an institute responsible for providing infrastructure for the religious needs of its citizens, the position of the state towards religion, the obligation of the state to obey by the neutrality precept especially in the context of public education (though in recent years tendency has shown extension towards obligation to neutrality in the public sphere for instance: the judiciary in Germany, employment in corporations as in France and Belgium and a general ban in public spaces as in Austria), and finally the protection the states offers to fundamental human rights taken into consideration their obligations under EU law. The neutrality principle has been especially emphasized in the jurisprudence when outweighing the generally accepted principle of state's neutrality against the individual right to religious freedom. In general, the principle of religious neutrality of the state prevails in the legal systems of Germany and France and even in jurisprudence of the European Court of Human Rights if special requirements or tests are fulfilled. The principle has gained importance and was further developed in modern constitutional history of the states. The main reason for its lack of predominance in the past was absence of relevance at the time when constitutional principles had evolved in Europe (e.g., piety of the majority of the population to the Christian tradition and homogenous structure of society which was predominantly Christian in nature).

The presence of religious symbols in the premises of public institutions on the one hand, and the admissibility of religious symbols that are being individually worn or presented in state institutions on the other hand, constitute suitable examples to describe the role of religion in France, England, and Germany. Several aspects are to be taken into account as far as permissibility of religious symbols in the education system is concerned.

The administrative structure and legislative competencies with respect to education range in the three states from regionally divisiveness, as in England and Germany to strictly centralized, as in France. These different state systems lead to diverging results with regard to the interplay of colliding rights, interests, and competencies.

The conceptual state-church model is a significant factor in the perception of religious interplay with state affairs, featuring how an excessive or distinct church entanglement will predominate national controversies over the right of religious minorities to manifestation of religious symbols in the state school system. While England is known for its liberal-accommodative policy towards religious minorities minted by its multiculturalist approach, France is characterized by its stark Jacobin republican tradition enshrined by the unitary idea, loyalty to the republic, and strong obligation of its citizens to assimilate and integrate. The German approach is distinguishable in comparison to these two extreme approaches, as it adopted a mid-path which is adaptable to religion and religious needs of its society, while preserving the secular nature of the state through allegiance and observance of its constitution and prominent precept prescribing the state's obligation to religious neutrality. In England, the societal role religion plays in the public sphere and its effect on the right of public officials to manifest their religion or belief will, to a large extent, reflect the English policy endorsing multicultural diversity and encouragement of social cohesion and tolerance among its religious minorities.

The circumstances establishing the reform of introduction of religion into the public school system can be explained relatively with respect to Germany and England due to their relative moderate-accommodative approach in the context of state-church relations. However, the struggle, many controversies, and the attention surrounding the issue of practising religious right in the educational sphere have gained significance in the last years in particular due to the inseparable task of schools perceived by society as a measure to transmit the values and traditions of religion to its future generation. This had been underscored as a significant factor playing a major role in all three legal systems in this analysis.

The complexity of endorsing religious insignias in state schools can be observed also with respect to religious minorities such as Muslims and other minority faiths who wish to ensure that their religious customs and traditions will be accorded respect in state schools. Nonetheless, racial minorities, and in particular Muslims, encounter difficulties when they wish to practise their religion. This was proved to be the case in the United Kingdom especially in the field of education.[1] However, the tendency in the recent years shows an expansion of the obligation to neutrality to other fields in the public sphere, as for instance: the judiciary in Germany, employment issues relating to dress code in public corporations as in France and Belgium, and even a general ban to appear with a full-face veil in public spaces as adopted in France, Belgium and Austria.[2]

---

1 *Cumper* in *Harris/Joseph* (eds.), The International Covenant on Civil and Political Rights and UK Law, 1995, p. 380.

2 http://www.sueddeutsche.de/karriere/gerichte-robe-und-kopftuch-vertragen-sich-nicht-1.3289481; https://www.asil.org/insights/volume/21/issue/15/veil-bans-

The arguments against the presence or absence of institutional symbols in public schools is basically being discussed in three dimensions: the educative task of the state, the negative right of religious freedom of the pupils, and a potential equality or non-discrimination aspect regarding pupils who are members of a religious minority.

The discussion around individual symbols worn by teachers encompasses the positive right of religious freedom of the teacher, the potential influence on pupils which collides with their negative right of religious freedom, and the potential violation of the neutrality of the state if a state representative displays a symbol of a particular belief. In the context of the Islamic headscarf, the discussion even refers to a potential contradiction between the problematic role of women in Islam, namely of oppression and subordination, and the Western liberal understanding of gender equality, i.e., the equation between men and women. In contrast, the display of the Cross or Crucifix as an institutional symbol demonstrates the adherence of the European states to the Christian culture and tradition (*Abendland Kultur*). In that sense, the Crucifix was not perceived to contravene with Western values.

Due to the dynamics that developed around individual religious symbols, legislators and school administrators – at least in France and Germany – enacted bans on teachers to display religious symbols in the case that they are worn during their public function as civil servants. Obviously, these bans aimed at the headscarf, *niqab*, and *burqa*, even though the phrasing of the acts did not mention those garments explicitly. These legislative acts have been challenged before national courts as well before the European Court of Human Rights. Courts developed criteria and prerequisites that these bans need to comply with in order to be regarded as constitutional and lawful. These prerequisites will be elaborated in detail throughout this work.

In the first part of the examination, the legal framework in the three different states will be displayed and rated against the background of the history of the individual states. The second chapter will engage in detail in the respective school system of each of the states, and will scrutinize the application of regulations that impose a ban of religious symbols as prescribed in practice by legislators or school administrators. The assessment of the courts will be based on an outweigh between constitutional principles and fundamental rights of individuals. In addition, the sum of possible justifications and interests which are suitable

---

european-court-human-rights; https://www.telegraph.co.uk/news/2017/10/01/austrias-burka-ban-comes-force-prohibiting-face-veils-public/.

and adequate for delimitation will reflect the outweigh of the positions in favour of a compromise that provides a workable basis for living together in a pluralistic society. The third part of this work will review the influence of European jurisdiction and case laws on domestic laws of the compared states. Due to the diverging legislative layout and constitutional structures set in those states, the legal position of fundamental human rights provisions, prescribed in the ECHR and decisions of the European Court of Human Rights, have different impact and influence on the respective legal systems.

The relative dubious jurisprudence of the ECtHR in the context of individuals' right to manifestation of religious insignias in a compulsory state school system raises doubts as to the enforceability of a uniform approach applicable to all European states. This is even fortified by granting a wide margin of appreciation to the MS in consideration of their national interests, enabling a wide gap for encroachment upon minorities' rights to religious freedom.

This analysis will explore how the principle of neutrality and impartiality had been translated by the ECtHR into the legal discourse of cases involving religious manifestation in education with respect to both institutionally displayed and individually worn symbols. It was remarkable that in both prominent case laws brought before the ECtHR (i.e., The *Lautsi* concerned the display of a Crucifix in Italian state school classrooms, and *Dahlab* the wearing of Islamic headscarf by an elementary school teacher in Switzerland) the neutrality principle had been invoked; however, it has been applied differently for each case and, as a result, yielded different outcomes. In the case of a state display of the Crucifix, the ECtHR found no violation of the neutrality principle towards the minority pupils, who objected its presence claiming for their right to (secular) education and for an education corresponding with the religious conviction of their parents as guaranteed in Art. 2 of the First protocol ECHR. Whereas in the case of *Dahlab*, the neutrality principle had been given prevalence against the teacher's right to profess her religion by her religious attire. The emphasis of the ECtHR had been placed on the duty of the state to religious impartiality, especially in public education, which justified the precedence given for protection of the negative religious freedom of minor pupils. It was explained that pupils by virtue of their tender age, their lack of self-determination and inability to escape negative influence deserve special protection against a state's power to impose an influence of a particular faith or any other form of proselytising effect practiced by it. In addition, the fact that pupils were constantly confronted with looking at a teacher with a headscarf and were unable to extract themselves from the classroom can amount to coercion which is heavily criticized, especially due to the vulnerability of young children.

In Germany, the alignment of legislation in education among the different federal states in order to achieve cohesion and uniformity as far as admissibility of religious insignias into the state school system is concerned, is very difficult to achieve. This is not only by virtue of the different customs and traditions that are unique to each region, but also due to sets of law and rules and constitutional framework applicable to each of the states. The recent pronouncement from the German Federal Constitutional Court (*Bundesverfassungsgericht*) declared the general, all-inclusive headscarf ban on teachers as deployed in NRW state schools unconstitutional and void. Nevertheless, less than one year succeeding the outlawing of the ban on headscarves in NRW by the Federal Constitutional Court, a different ruling with respect to the same agenda has been delivered by the Federal Employment Court of Berlin (*Bundesarbeitsgericht*). The case is yet to be fully published; however, in this case it was announced that a general headscarf ban in the state of Berlin conforms to the constitution and the equality precept prescribed in it, as the prohibition applies to all religious symbols without segregation.

Germany has developed a moderate system of state-church separation. An absolute exclusion of any institutional link between church and state is rejected in its constitutional law; in fact, it demonstrates a strong protection of fundamental human rights by virtue of its constitution. The obligation to conform to the European Convention of Human Rights only fortifies the existing legislative fundament. The impact that the state-church model adopted in England has on the protection of minority rights to religious freedom demonstrates the efforts made by domestic courts to comply with the jurisdiction delivered by the ECtHR. In principle, the tendency accepts a liberal approach to accommodation of religious needs of its minorities.

France, as the extreme model of state-church separation, will face difficulties to align its recent enactments, especially the bans imposed by the Acts of 2004 and 2011, with the standards established on the European level and France's obligation to their precedence upon domestic legislation. Special consideration will be granted to France's obligation to its sacrosanct principle of neutrality in the public service. In addition, the neutrality principle as a legitimate aim for curtailment of teachers' and pupils' right to religious freedom will be assessed. The tendency of France indicates a stricter perception of laicism and further secularization in its public education.

It is worth to note that the tendency as demonstrated recently in judgments delivered in Germany indicates a shift in the legal discussion which draws back from the educational system to the permissibility of religious symbols when manifested within the justice system (i.e., lawyers, judges, trainee-lawyers, student-apprentices). However, the permissibility to display an ostentatious religious symbol such as the headscarf remains controversial even when its legitimacy is challenged in the justice system. The different approaches within the German juridical instances reflect the inconsistency and lack of uniformity also in this legal debate. In particular, the lack of legal basis for the prohibition of religiously motivated symbols or garments with respect to legal apprentices or trainees had been underscored by the courts; as also the observance of the duty to religious neutrality for those who work for the justice system had been subject for legal challenges. Thus, on the one hand, the Bavarian High Administrative Court decided that the ban on jurists or legal practitioners to appear with a headscarf in Bavarian courtrooms is inadmissible.[3] This was reasoned based on insufficient grounds for the ban in legal regulations. On the other hand, the German High Administrative Court in the state of Hessen decided to rule against a trainee-lawyer who appeared to court with a headscarf.[4] The main ground submitted by the Court underscored the significance of state-representatives to appear neutral and unbiased so that citizens would not feel interfered or influenced by their view and associate the conduct or outer appearance of the state-representative in any way with those of the state. The Court emphasized that any doubt raised by the citizens as to the neutral position of the trainee who appears as a state authority and acts on behalf of the state, in particular in the justice system where the safeguarding of state neutrality becomes so meaningful, would undermine the trust in the justice system to act unprejudiced and impartial. Therefore, even an abstract endangerment to the fundament of the neutrality principle incurred on part of the citizens by virtue of their confrontation with state-representatives manifesting a religious symbol and that raises doubt in regard to the impartiality of the judiciary will be sufficient for imposing a ban on religious symbols. A citizen who may feel offended by the view of a headscarf worn by a trainee within her practice will justify the ban on religiously motivated symbols, especially when performing functions that enable citizens to perceive her as acting on behalf of the state or its justice system.

In a similar manner, inconsistency exists also within the European jurisdiction as to the permissibility of conspicuous religious symbols in the public sector. While the ECJ reviews the admissibility of the headscarf in a work place based on sufficient internal standards inside an organization and declaring therefore the principle of neutrality as a legitimate aim,[5] the ECtHR remains rather reserved

3 VG Augsburg, decision from 30.6.16 – Au 2 K 15.457 = JA 2017, 78.

4 VGH decision from 24.5.17, Az.1 B 1056/17.

5 ECJ decision from 14.3.17, Az. C-157/15

and enables MS a wide margin of appreciation with respect to bans imposed on religiously orientated symbols or garments when manifested outwardly in the public sector.[6]

Nonetheless, several distinguishable grounds should be taken into account when trying to segregate the justice system and the field of education. First, no-subordinate relationship – the teacher within her educative competency is perceived by her pupils as an authoritative figure; in that sense, her outer appearance and the constant face-to-face encounter with the pupils cannot exclude any kind of impact on the pupils (as already approved in the jurisprudence). In contrast, trainee-lawyers or apprentices do not perform in a capacity of subordinate relations. Since lawyers, trainees, or law apprentices do not carry any authoritative function and due to a short temporary encounter with citizens, it is even less likely that the latter would be affected by their view. Second, willingness and voluntariness – civil servants are bound by a special relationship of subordination to the public authorities which they freely accepted. The willingness of teachers to accept this special relationship when choosing their profession justifies some restriction on the enjoyment of their public freedoms to a limited extent. In contrast to teachers, lawyers, trainee-lawyers or student apprentices (excluding judges) do not act within their function as state- representatives and are not yet privileged with public benefits as is the case with respect to civil servants. Therefore, as long as trainee-lawyers or apprentices are not acting as civil servants it is only reasonable not to incur on them a special duty which would have been relevant only if they were occupied as state representatives. Furthermore, by virtue of their performance as individuals they do not enjoy public benefits granted to civil servants; as a result, a restriction on their public freedoms, in particular of the fundamental right to religious manifestation would be excessive and would not stand the proportionality test. Third, the reason for prohibiting religious symbols in the state school system was justified often mainly on the ground of ensuring religious neutrality in education which is regarded as an essential aim for preserving the impartiality of the state and of public interests (e.g., public safety, public order). The aim of ensuring religious neutrality cannot be applied in the justice system in the same manner as in the education. Unlike pupils who may be easily influenced by the view

---

6 ECtHR Ebrahimian v France, App. no. 64846/11, decision from 26.11.2015; Dakir v Belgium, App. no. 4619/2 decision from 11.7.2017; Belcacemi and Oussar v Belgium, App. no. 37798/13 decision from 11.7.2017; S.A.S v France, App. no. 43835/11 decision from 1.7.2014.

of ostentatious religious symbols due to their constant exposure to their school teacher and who may be subject to some indoctrinating effect as a result, this cannot be the case with respect to trainee-lawyers or student apprentices who mainly encounter citizens that already established their minds and self-determination. It remains doubtful, however, whether these criteria would be equally applicable to judges who incur other duties than practitioners or trainee-lawyers by virtue of their civil servant status. In addition, the interpretation of the notion of religious neutrality is argued to be restrictive in form in a very similar manner to that argued in the public education sector. It is reasoned by proponents of the principle of religious neutrality that in particular in courts – which symbolize the hall of justice – the necessity of public servants as state representatives to appear unbiased gains even further significance.

II Legal Framework

1. Introduction

The presence and importance of religion in public life plays a different role in each of the compared states: Germany, England, and France as the institutional role of religion, in many respects, has its origins primarily in the established state-church relations. Fundamental elements underlying the relationship between state and church are inscribed in the legal order specific to each country and are indicative of the position and predominance that religion acquires in a society.

In principle, religious freedom constitutes a recognized liberty right in the legal order of all three countries in this analysis. However, the embodiment of fundamental human rights, such as religious freedom in the legal system of the countries compared in this analysis differs in terms of legislative layout, form of incorporation into the legal structure, attainment of constitutional status, and the content and scope of protection.

The establishment of religious freedom as a recognized liberty right derives its status and position from its anchorage in the constitutional order of a state. Religious freedom as an underlying right prescribed in a constitutional document or bill of rights as, e.g., in Germany, will entail compliance with special requirements so as to justify infringement. The guarantee of the right to religious freedom and its scope of protection is likely to suffer fewer infringements as long as its incorporation is made in a legally binding document, such as a constitution or bill of rights, as opposed to its implementation in simple legislation, as the case is under the English legal system.

In addition, state-church relations and the respective adopted model (strict separation, a dual, or a cooperationist model) are indicative of the extent of entanglement between state and religion. In the context of public school education, the permissibility to display religious symbols will be reviewed under the aspect of an individual-rights-based standard deriving authority from the level of protection offered to religious freedom under each of the conceptual state-church models. Consequently, the boundaries to religious freedom will be considered based on the inner dynamics developed between the fundamental right to religious freedom as inscribed in the legal order of a state and the structural state-church nexus. A rigorous or liberal approach towards endorsement of religious signs in public education will reflect the position, function, and the role religious freedom acquires in accommodation of individuals' fundamental rights based on the respective conceptual model.

Further, the protection of the right to religious freedom in employment and workplace (e.g., a teacher with a headscarf) provided for the establishment of a legal challenge to discrimination based on religious grounds. The ability to invoke the protection of religious rights which is not founded on a fundamental human rights claim but rather on equality/anti-discrimination rights is common, for instance, in England.[7] The reason for this is that the recognition of the right to religious freedom as an established fundamental right under English law was not entrenched in its legal system and took effect through interminable process; this process was successful only towards the end of the twentieth century.[8]

This chapter will provide an overview with respect to the anchorage of fundamental human rights in the respective legal framework of the compared countries in this analysis. The overview will be followed by a reference to pertinent provisions or legislation affecting the relationship between state and church, including those determining the role of religion in public education. The responsibility of parents to determine the education of their children as a dominant factor will also be given careful consideration.

Following that, the examination will focus on relevant equality rights and principles underlying the notion of religious freedom as an extended legitimate ground covered under equality/anti-discrimination laws. Finally, a designation of the predominant constitutional principles comprised as an integral part of the constitutional order in the different legal systems will provide an introspection as to the adopted state-church model and the impact conceptual differences may have on an individual's fundamental right to religious freedom. The degree of state-church separation and the structural state-church interplay will especially be taken into account as considerable factors for limitations imposed on an individual's right to religious freedom within the context of the public school system.

---

7 Even under anti-discrimination laws, the protection of ethnic or religious minorities was a matter that used to be covered on grounds of race based on the abolished Race and Relations Act 1976 till the extension in the Equality Act 2010 to include religion as grounds for discrimination. See in *Blair/Aps*, Education and the Law, 17(1–2), 2005, pp. 1, 9; *van Ooijen*, Religious Symbols in Public Functions, Unveiling State Neutrality, A Comparative Analysis of Dutch, English and French Justifications for Limiting the Freedom of Public Official to Display Religious Symbols, 2012, p. 212.

8 *Sandberg*, in: Hunter-Henin, Law, Religious Freedoms and Education in Europe, 2011, pp. 327, 332.

2. Germany

a) Sources of Law and the Constitutional Hierarchy of Norms

In Germany, the legal framework regulating state-church relations and establishing religious rights is found in the German Grundgesetz (hereinafter: Grundgesetz).[9] Other normative sources designated to regulate structural relations between the state and religious communities, as well as addressed protection of individuals' rights against the state, are specified in provisions of the 1919 Weimar Constitution (*Weimarer Reichsverfassung*), which were incorporated into the Grundgesetz.[10]

In addition, in the past history of the German nation, agreements were concluded (1924) between the state and the predominant religious communities: the Catholic and Protestant Churches. These agreements were formulated to intensify churchly positions and are known as the '*paritaetische Konkordate*'.[11]

At the state-regional level, the governance of religious rights and state-church relations are inscribed in provisions of the individual states' constitution (*Landesverfassung*) and ordinary education laws and schools' legislation legislated and promulgated at the sole discretion of each individual state.

Finally, construction of fundamental human rights is made through case laws. The development of the right to religious freedom and delineation of its scope of protection is subject to jurisprudential interpretation of the German Federal Constitutional Court (BVerfG). The BVerfG is regarded as the guardian of constitutional order and is empowered to decide on constitutional matters only in retrenched public-law controversies.[12] Apart from judicial interpretation of constitutional rights, the BVerfG, in the course of judicial review, develops constitutional values and principles. However, the BVerfG is bound by the constitutional guidelines set by itself and is not empowered to create new norms and values. It is therefore obliged to interpret statutes, when possible, in conformity with the

9 Although the German Grundgesetz constitutes in fact a form of a constitutional document, the Parliamentary Council, responsible for its drafting, was reluctant to bestow the term 'constitution' on a document that was meant to govern only a part of Germany for a transitional period until reunification. See in *Kommers/Miller*, The Constitutional Jurisprudence of the Federal Republic of Germany, 3rd ed., 2012, p. 43.

10 *Kommers/Miller*, p. 538; *Robbers*, BYU L. Rev. 2001, pp. 643, 644–645.

11 *Listl*, Die Konkordate und Kirchenverträge in der Bundesrepublik Deutschland, Vol. I, 1987, pp. 287, et seq., 508, et seq.

12 *Kommers/Miller*, p. 3.

Grundgesetz (*Pflicht zur Verfassungskonformen Auslegung*)[13] and the spirit of the constitution.

Consequently, all rulings and decisions of the BVerfG declaring the compatibility of a statute or legal provision with the Grundgesetz have the force of a law, and bind all judicial branches and levels of government.[14] This will also be the case should the BVerfG decide to nullify or strike down a statute or ordinary law.[15] This is known as the binding effect principle (*Bindungswirkung*) of the BVerfG's ruling.[16] The decision of the BVerfG, which is declaratory in nature, will bind all other judicial branches and is prospective in nature (*ex tunc*). This means that when a legal provision is sustained or declared incompatible with the Grundgesetz but not void, it will still be enforceable. Nevertheless, the effect of such a decision on lower instances is to cease procedures in pending cases, as it will be the task of the legislator to amend the statute so it will conform to the constitution according to guidelines set by the BVerfG.[17] An exception to the binding effect principle will apply with respect to the BVerfG itself, which is not bound by its own decisions (the rule of *stare decisis* does not bind the German judiciary).[18]

Throughout the historical development of the German state until 1919, the prevailing role of churches in the nation's public life – here predominantly the Catholic and Protestant Church – was undistinguishable and characterized by the close ties between state and church.[19] As a result, the protection of religious minority rights remained unfamiliar until the twentieth century, while for non-believers (atheists) the right to refrain from any religious influence was not even recognized.[20] The powerful position of the church, especially with

13 *Kommers/Miller*, p. 34.

14 The binding effect principle is prescribed in Sec. 31 para 1 BVerfGG.

15 Sec. 31 para 2 BVerfGG; *Kommers/Miller*, pp. 34–35.

16 *Kommers/Miller*, p. 37; BVerfGE 14, 1951 45, 54, et seq.

17 *Kommers/Miller*, p. 37, pp. 35–36, 38.

18 *Kommers/Miller*, p. 37.

19 *Germann/Wiesner*, RdJB 2013, pp. 399–402, 407. 'In allen Ländern außer Baden und Hessen – Darmstadt....blieb das Schulwesen bis 1918/1919 durchweg konfessionell gegliedert' a.a. 'Das Verhältnis von Schule und Religion war ein Schwerpunkt in den kulturpolitischen Auseinandersetzung während der Entstehung der Weimarer Republik 1918/1919'; *Heckel*, Tel-Aviv Uni. Studies in Law 13 (1997), pp. 187, 195; *Kommers/Miller*, pp. 539–540; *Bloss*, Cuius religio- EU ius regio? 2008, p. 33.

20 *Bloss*, 2008, p. 33.

respect to schools and educational matters, contributed to widespread religious discrimination.

In principle, the right to religious freedom as liberty right was enhanced following the long Thirty Years' War between the recognized Christian religions (Catholics and Protestants), known as '*Kulturkampf*'. Religious rights had been gradually increased and received constitutional recognition in both the WRV constitution of 1919 and in the current Grundgesetz of 1949. The constitutional rights of religious communities had been expanded so to enable their statutory recognition as public corporate, granting them the privilege of self-determination, i.e., the administration of religious and cultural affairs and running of public worships at their own discretion.[21]

b) Grundgesetz

The current constitution of the Federal Republic of Germany is the Grundgesetz.

The Grundgesetz was created under the influence of the Allied Powers who, following the Second World War, proposed a framework for establishing a German federal state to the eleven German states comprising West Germany. One of the three documents, known as the 'Frankfurt Documents', authorized the eleven prime ministers to call a constitutional convention. According to the document, the proposed constitution purported to make Germany a democratic and federal state that grants social rights and adheres to the rule of law.[22] It was conditioned to receive allied approval if it provided three things: 'democracy, federalism, and constitutional fundamental rights'.[23]

The Grundgesetz was drafted by a parliamentary council, ratified by two-thirds of the states' parliaments and became effective on 23 May 1949. However, due to lack of agreement on a new constitutional framework for the relationship between church and state, it was decided to incorporate the relevant provisions from the Weimar Constitution of 1919 (WRV) into the Grundgesetz.[24]

---

21 *Palmer*, Religious Liberty: The Legal Framework in Selected OSCE Countries, 2000, p. 40.

22 *Palmer*, p. 41.

23 *Kommers/Miller*, pp. 7, 43, 48, 79.

24 GG Art. 140 refers to the Weimar Constitution of 11 August 1919 and explicitly incorporates the following articles Art. 136, 137, 138, 139, and 141 into the German constitution. The Weimarer Reichsverfassung (Constitution of the Weimar Republic) in Reichsgesetzblatt 1919, p. 1383; *Palmer*, p. 41; *Robbers*, 2001, pp. 643, 644.

The Grundgesetz was to take effect with relation to the German nation. This actually referred more to the territorial scope rather than to the individual, personal scope, as many norms of the Grundgesetz also apply with respect to foreigners. Nowadays, the territorial scope of the Grundgesetz enfolds all the regions of the federal states, as listed in the Preamble of the Grundgesetz.[25]

Germany's Grundgesetz contains various provisions affecting the relationship between church and state. The church-state relation, as well as the role of religion in the educational system, is determined by two kinds of elements that are relevant for the given context. First, there are several written and unwritten principles which constitute the skeleton for the educational system and the role of religion therein (e.g., the principle of religious neutrality of the state). Second, the Grundgesetz contains a catalogue of human rights that explicitly safeguards the rights to religious freedom (Art. 4 GG) and includes the protection of religious freedom through other liberties (e.g., Art. 2 para 1 GG general freedom of action and Art. 12 para 1 GG freedom of profession). The latter mentioned are basic rights which determine the position of an individual in the structural constitutional system. Nevertheless, unlike the right to religious freedom, other liberty rights are not unreserved and can be confined by any regular legislation and not necessarily only by provisions prescribed in the constitution itself.

The normative source of fundamental human rights, including the right to freedom of religion deriving from the German constitution, can be basically divided into liberty rights, equality rights, and constitutional principles.

Liberty rights have the function of driving back the state's influence on the individual sphere.[26] Equality rights have the function to guarantee an equal treatment of an individual by the state, as well as by other individuals.[27] Constitutional principles are embedded in the constitution but were developed and given extensive interpretation by the German jurisprudence. Finally, the right to religious freedom is constitutionally safeguarded so its protection can succeed should a violation of the right be recognized and classified as fundamental human or equality right. It should be noted though that the examination of encroachment on the right to religious freedom would not yield any preferential advancement for substantiation of a complaint in the German legal system whether founded solely on grounds of the fundamental right to religious freedom or equality

---

25 *Jarass*, in: Jarass/Pieroth, Grundgesetz für die Bundesrepublik Deutschland Kommentar, 14th ed., 2016, Preamble p. 8.

26 *Jellineck*, System der subjektiven öffentlichen Rechte, 2nd ed., 2011, pp. 81, et seq.

27 *Giegrich*, Israel Law Review, 34 (2000), pp. 211, 242.

rights, i.e. each of the grounds will be sufficient for establishment of a claim. Under German constitutional law, equality rights would be supportive of the main claim established on the fundamental right to religious liberty.

aa) Examination Procedure of Basic Rights

When examining the role and relevance of a basic right, at first one has to define the scope of protection. The scope describes the range and extent of actions and mindsets that are protected by the basic right. In a second step, a potential infringement is being examined. The classic understanding of infringement, according to German jurisprudence, must ensure compliance with the following prerequisites: the limitation must (i) be conclusive, (ii) be direct, (iii) take place in form of legislative act; additionally, (iv) the state must have enforced its action against the individual in a coerced manner.[28]

Nonetheless, the evolvement of the modern understanding of infringement had acknowledged that also factual and indirect measures of the state may constitute as possible limitations imposed on fundamental rights.[29] This modern conceptualization of infringement applies also with respect to the right of religious freedom and will not necessarily follow the classic dogma in order to be substantiated.

The extensive comprehension of infringement and the prerequisites for limitation of fundamental rights circumvented the ability to delineate the boundaries termed also (in German) *Konturlosigkeit* or *Konturverlust* for limitations of the scope of fundamental rights.[30] Consequently, this will remain a task of the judiciary to determine on a case-by-case basis.[31]

---

28 *Lübbe-Wolff*, Die Grundrechte als Eingriffsabwehrrechte, 1998, p. 42; *Eckhoff*, Der Grundrechtseingriff, 1992, pp. 175, 230; *Sachs*, in: Stern, Staatsrecht III/2, 1994, p. 104; *Isensee*, in: Isensee/Kirchhof, HdbStR V, Sec. 191 recital 111; *Münch v/Kunig*, in: Münch v./Kunig, Grundgesetz-Kommentar, 6th ed., 2012, preliminary note, Art. 1–19, recital 34; *Dreier*, in: Dreier, Grundgesetz, Vol I, 2008, preliminary note, recital 124.

29 BVerfGE 66, 39, 60; 105, 252, 273; 105, 279, 300, et seq.; *Lübbe- Wolff*, p. 47; *Jarass*, in: Jarass/Pieroth, preliminary note before Art. 1 recital 28; *Sachs*, in: Sachs, Grundgesetz, 7th ed., 2014, preliminary note before Art. 1 recital 83; *Pieroth/Schlink*, Grundrechte, 31th ed., 2015, recital 261.

30 *Isensee*, in: Isensee/Kirchhof, HdbStR V, Sec. 191 recital 112; *Marauhn/Merhof*, in: Dörr/Grote/Marauhn, EMRK/GG Konkordanzkommentar zum europäischen und deutschen Grundrechtsschutz, 2nd ed., 2014, pp. 383, 384; *Bethge*, VVDStRL 57 (1998), 7, 40, et seq.

31 *Marauhn/Merhof, in: Dörr/Grote/Marauhn*, pp. 383, 384; Pieroth/*Schlink*, recital 265; *Isensee*, in: *Isensee/Kirchhof*, HdbStR V, Sec. 191 recital 119.

As a third step, one has to scrutinize whether grounds for a justification of the infringement are available and substantiated.

bb) Liberty Rights

The Grundgesetz contains a list of guaranteed fundamental human rights. The most relevant liberty rights with respect to religious symbols within the educational system are: general freedom of action and of personal development (Art. 2 GG), freedom of religion (Art. 4 GG), and the parental right to decide on the education of their children (Art. 6 GG). Relevant in this regard is the scope of each of these rights as well as prerequisites to their limitation when colliding or contrasting with other rights or interests.

(1) Art. 2 para 1 GG/General Freedom of Action

In principle, Art. 2 para 1 GG prescribes the general freedom of an individual to free development of his/her personality, and the right of every individual to life and general integrity. The right pursuant to Art. 2 para 1 GG enjoys a superior position in the constitutional hierarchy of norms and is even considered in legal literature as capable of limiting the right to religious freedom (Art. 4 para 1 & 2 GG).[32] The enjoyment of the right will be guaranteed as long it does not violate other constitutional rights, or offend the constitutional order or the moral code.

(a) Scope of Protection

Art. 2 para 1 GG includes a general, comprehensive liberty right of the individual to form his or her personality at his or her own discretion. According to this provision, the right protects every action or omission committed by the individual for the purpose of his or her self-development. This right includes the freedom to wear religious symbols or any garments which form part of an individual's personality and constitute personal identification with an ideological or religious creed.[33]

Art. 2 para 2 GG stipulates that the right to life and the liberty of an individual shall be inviolable. Encroachment upon these rights may be possible only pursuant to specification in law.

It is due to its all-embracing scope and the ability to invoke Art. 2 para 1 GG practically in every aspect of daily life that the right conferred under it will be

---

32 *Muckel* in: Muckel, Schriften zum Öffentlichen Recht, 2010, pp. 234, 236–237.

33 BVerfG, EuGRZ 1999, 102, 104; *Wiese*, p. 214.

subsidiary to all other liberty rights. In other words, a referral to this general right will take place in order to protect aspects of individual freedom that are not covered by special liberty rights and relate only to a specific topic.[34]

(b) Infringement

An individual will be able to exert his/her right pursuant to Art. 2 para 1 GG as long as it does not contravene other provisions in the constitution or collide with the rights or interests of others.

(c) Justification

Infringement of Art. 2 para 1 GG can be justified based on the constitutional legal order, which includes formal parliamentary regulations as well as orders or even customary law.[35] Furthermore, an infringement of Art. 2 para 1 can be justified in order to protect the rights of others. While some state that this limitation has no autonomous meaning as the definition 'rights of others' is already included in the notion 'constitutional legal order',[36] others consider this limitation as the amount of compound interests which are worth protection by virtue of the Grundgesetz.[37]

This entails that infringement of the basic right Art. 2 para 1 can be justified in order to protect the legal rights or interests of others.

(2) Art. 4 GG Freedom of Faith, Conscience, and Ideological Creed

This fundamental right is guaranteed in Art. 4 GG. The right is granted to everyone and is enjoyed by individuals including minors and adults, as well as religious groups and organizations.[38]

The significance of religious freedom as a fundamental human right has been recognized by the framers of the constitution, who, as a result, explicitly

---

34 BVerfG, NJW 1989, 2526; *Degenhart,* JuS 1990, p. 161.

35 *Münch v./Kunig*, in: Münch v/Kunig, Art. 2 recital 22, et seq; *Hofmann,* in: Schmidt-Bleibtreu/Hofmann/Hennecke, Art. 2 recital 6.

36 *Pieroth/Schlink*, recital 429.

37 *Di Fabio, in:* Maunz/Dürig, Kommentar zum Grundgesetz, Art. 2 para 1, recital 13.

38 *Muckel* in: Muckel, Schriften zum Öffentlichen Recht, 2010, p. 234. It is explained that Art. 4 para 1 & 2 GG constitutes as general fundamental right that applies to everyone, foreigners as well as German nationals can invoke their right to religious freedom in accordance with Art. 4 GG; *v. Ungern-Sternberg*, 2008, p. 241; BVerfGE 24, 236, 245, et seq.

implemented a commitment of the German state to safeguard both the right to have or own a religion as well as the freedom to practise a religion at one's own discretion, as inscribed in the constitution.

The right to religious freedom as prescribed in Art. 4 GG consists of two provisions:

> Art. 4 para 1 proclaims: "Freedom of faith, of conscience, and freedom of creed, religious or ideological *(Weltanschauung)*, shall be inviolable." Whereas Art. 4 para 2 declares that: "The undisturbed practice of religion is guaranteed".

(a) Scope of Protection

The right to religious freedom as established in Art. 4 para 1 GG is recognized and guaranteed as a positive freedom which is unreserved in the constitution.[39] However, albeit the formulation in Art. 4 para 1 GG that the right to religious freedom is guaranteed without any reservation (*vorbehaltlos*) the opinions in legal literature as to its constitutional limitation remain controversial. In this sense, the right to religious freedom has a pre-eminent position nonetheless it will not be given preference to other constitutional rights prescribed in the constitution such as Art. 1 para 1 (the right to human dignity) & Art. 2 para 1 GG (the right to freedom of action and personal development). [40] As such, the law must accommodate the religious convictions of individuals or religious groups and ensure the undisturbed practice of religion so as not to ease any interference in its scope of protection.[41]

The right to religious freedom embraces an ample scope of protection and has normally conferred by the high judicial instances an extensive interpretation due to its intertwining with the right to human dignity.[42]

It thence enfolds two spectrums of protection: First, personal scope of protection and, second, factual scope of protection.

(aa) Personal Scope of Protection

The personal scope of protection requires delimitation of the legal right holders, i.e., the individuals who would be able to invoke their right to religious freedom. The problem, however, is to define the applicability of the right to religious

---

39 *Coumont*, in: von Campenhausen/Link/Winter, Schriften zum Staatskirchenrecht 38, 2007, p. 66.

40 *Muckel* in: Muckel, Schriften zum Öffentlichen Recht, 2010, pp. 234, 236, 249.

41 *Robbers*, 2001, pp. 643, 658.

42 BVerfGE 32, 98, 106.

freedom with respect to minor children. This refers to the question of the age in which children will be considered to reach legal maturity so as to express autonomously their religious pertinence or non-pertinence.

The protection offered with respect to the right of religious freedom has also been recognized with respect to minors.[43] Nonetheless, the right to decide on the religious education of children until achievement of legal age to express independently their religion or belief (*Religionsmündigkeit*) is conferred to the parents as legitimate right-holders against the state (Art. 6 para 2 GG).[44] As soon as the child reaches maturity and is independent to decide freely on his/her faith or religion, the right of the parents to act or decide for the children's benefit in religious matters will be withdrawn as stipulated in the Children's Religious Education Act, (Gesetz über die religiöse Kindererziehung).[45] There is no determination as to the legal age considered as adequate for a child's self-determination. However, it is presumed that an adequate age for a child to decide independently on religious conviction or matters is 14 years of age at the latest, as by that time adolescents are capable of developing autonomous thinking.[46]

Moreover, Art. 4 consists of a collective dimension with respect to religious freedom. This guarantee safeguards the right of individuals to gather in the form of religious groups as well as to exert collective worship.[47] Consequently, it enables religious communities to invoke their constitutional right pursuant to Art. 4 GG if they believe an infringement in their inner sphere or right to self-determination has taken place.[48] The right to self-determination of religious

---

43 *Campenhausen* v., in: Isensee/Kirchhof, HdbStR VII, Sec. 157, recital 102; *Starck*, in: Mangoldt v./Klein/Starck, Kommentar zum Grundgesetz, 6th ed., 2010, Art. 4 recital 71; *Kokott*, in: Sachs, Art. 4 recital 7; *Coumont*, in: von Campenhausen/Link/Winter, Schriften zum Staatskirchenrecht 38, 2007, p. 66.

44 There is a presupposition that parents will act in the best interest of their child. As a result, as long as the child is minor, it is assumed he/she cannot protect his/her interest against state acts or school authority; thus, parents are legitimated to act on behalf of the minors' interest till they reach maturity. § 1 das Gesetz über die religiöse Kindererziehung vom 15.7.1921 (See in detail in Chapter II 2 (3)(a)); BVerfGE 30, 415, 424; *Herzog*, in: Maunz/Dürig, Art. 4 recital 43; *Kokott*, in: Sachs, Art. 4, recital 8; *Schmitt-Kammler, in*: Sachs, Art. 6, recital 54.

45 Gesetz über die religiöse Kindererziehung, v. 15 July 1921, RGBl. p. 939, last amended on 17 December 2008 BGBl. I. p. 2586.

46 *Wiese*, pp. 110, 145; *Sachs,* in: Sachs, before Art. 1, recital 75; § 5 das Gesetz über die religiöse Kindererziehung vom 15.7.1921 (See further details in Chapter II 2 (3)(a)).

47 *Seifert*, Comp. Lab. L. & Pol'y J, 30(3) (2009), pp. 529, 533.

48 BVerfGE 24, 236, 245, et seq.

communities has been explicitly incorporated in Art. 137 para 3 WRV through Art. 140 GG.

(bb) Factual Scope of Protection

Essentially, this comprehensive, unified scope of freedom of religion under Art. 4 para 1 and para 2 GG, guarantees not only the *forum internum* but also the *forum externum.*[49] Both parts of Art. 4 are inseparable and aligned with each other so the undisturbed right to exercise a religion according to Art. 4 para 2 cannot attain its full meaning without its conjoined part prescribed in Art. 4 para 1, which guarantees in general the right to freedom of faith, religion, and conscience.[50]

(aaa) Forum Internum

The wording of Art. 4 para 1 GG ensures the freedom of faith, conscience, religious and ideological creed. The right embraces not only the personal freedom to believe or not to believe but also includes the right to profess a faith, to keep it secret, to renounce a former belief, and uphold or adopt another, known as the *forum internum.*[51] The forum internum relates to the internal or private sphere of an individual's belief. It not only includes the (internal) freedom of choice of an individual to have or not have a faith but also the (negative) right not to be exposed to religious influence supported by the state, known as the negative right to religious freedom.[52] In that sense, the forum internum is absolute as it is subject to no limitations.[53]

(bbb) Forum Externum

Art. 4 para 2 GG supplements Art. 4 para 1 as it guarantees an individual the undisturbed right to manifest or practise a religion, belief, or ideological creed.[54] The right enfolds the freedom to worship publicly, to proselytize, and to compete openly with other religions (the forum externum). The forum externum was depicted as 'the right of an individual to align his behaviour in accordance with the precepts of his faith and to act in accordance with his internal

---

49 *Seifert*, pp. 529, 533.

50 BVerfGE 24, 236, 245, et seq.; 32, 98, 106; 41, 29, 49.

51 BVerfGE 49, 375, 376; 52, 223, 238; 65, 1, 39; *Mager*, in: Münch v./Kunig, Art. 4, recital 16; *Starck*, in: Mangoldt v./Klein/Starck, Art. 4, recital 34, et seq.

52 BVerfGE 41, 29, 49; 52, 223, 238; *Morlok*, in: Dreier, Vol I, Art. 4, recital 69; *Starck*, in: Mangoldt v./Klein/Starck, Art. 4, recital 23, et seq.; *Jarass*, in: Jarass/Pieroth, Art. 4, recital 13; *v. Campenhausen* in: *Munsonius*, p. 665.

53 BVerfGE 49, 375, 376; 52, 223, 238; 65, 1, 39; *Mager*, in: Münch v./Kunig, Art. 4 recital 16; *Starck*, in: Mangoldt v./Klein/Starck, Art. 4, recital 34, et seq.

54 BVerfGE 24, 236, 245, et seq.; 32, 98, 106; 41, 29, 49.

convictions'.[55] The question whether an individual's practice, act, or behaviour is truly motivated by a religious precept and its assessment based on a subjective test, according to the jurisprudential practice, remained controversial.[56] The presumption is that verifying the intention of the legal right-holder leaves room for abuses on part of the legal right-holder. This will be subject to judicial review by the courts that will examine whether the behaviour in question was truly religiously motivated or not.[57]

Unlike the forum internum, the right to manifest a religion or belief is not inclusive and may be subject to limitations, which will be permissible only under certain conditions. This means that a legislative confinement of the right to exercise a religion will be valid only if it is sanctioned by provisions prescribed in the Grundgesetz itself.[58]

The guarantee under Art. 4 para 2 not only includes churchly or sectarian activities and attendance in religious ceremonies but also religious education, the right to conduct religious gatherings, and other daily activities of confessional expressions.[59]

In principle, both guarantees constitute a comprehensive and uniform consistent basic right of freedom of religion and denomination, which includes also the right of exertion.[60]

Art. 4 GG is very unique in its form as it combines in the same clause an affirmative aspect (free exercise principle[61]) as well as a negative aspect

---

55 *Ganz*, Das Tragen religiöser Symbole und Kleidung in der öffentlichen Schule in Deutschland, Frankreich und England, 2009, p. 61; BVerfG, NJW 2003, 3111, 3112; BVerGE 32, 98, 106 ‚sein gesamtes Verhalten an den Lehren seines Glaubens auszurichten und seiner inneren Glaubensüberzeugung gemäß zu handeln'.; *Listl* in: Listl/Pirson, HdbStKirchR I, pp. 439, 440, et seq.; *Müller-Volbehr*, DÖV 1995, pp. 301, 304; *Hassemer/Hömig*, EuGRZ 1999, 525, 527; *Campenhausen* v., in: Isensee/Kirchhof, HdbStR VII, Sec. 157 recital 70; *Morlok*, in: Dreier, Vol 1, Art. 4 recital 66; *Starck*, in: Mangoldt v./Klein/Starck, Art. 4 recital 37; *Campenhausen* v./*de Wall*, Staatskirchenrecht, 4th edn., 2006, p. 54, et seq.; *Walter*, *Religionsverfassungsrecht* in vergleichender und internationaler Perspektive, 2006, p. 502, et seq.

56 *Walter*, p. 506, et seq.

57 BVerfGE 83, 341, 353; 47, 327, 385; BVerfG NJW 2004, 3111, 3112; *Pieroth/Schlink*, recital 576.

58 *Kommers/Miller*, pp. 543–544.; *Robbers*, 2001, pp. 643, 647.

59 BVerfGE 24, 236, 246.

60 *Jarass*, in: Jarass/Pieroth, Art. 4 recital 1; BVerfGE 24, 236, 245; *Pieroth/Schlink*, recital 572; *Morlok*, in: Dreier Vol I, Art. 4 recital 58.

61 *Alloway*, Dick.J.Int'l L. 15(2) (1997), pp. 361, 364.

(non-establishment or non-identification principle).[62] This entails that the Grundgesetz can be used as a double-edged sword. In other words, the very same clause which offers an individual the protection of the Grundgesetz to practise his/her religious beliefs can also be used to restrain others from practising their religion.[63]

The right to religious freedom as prescribed in Art. 4 para 1 enfolds two dimensions: positive and negative.

(aaaa) Positive Dimension

This aims to protect the right of individuals to religious freedom. Pursuant to this, it provides an individual an ample scope to freely choose a religion or belief including the right to live according to his/her religion or belief and adjust his/her whole life to fit to the rules of that religion.[64]

(bbbb) Negative Dimension

This safeguards not only the negative right of an individual not to choose or have a religion or belief[65] but also the right not to join a religious community or the right to abandon a certain religious belief.[66] The prevailing view in the legal literature sustain that the acknowledgement of an individual to religious events or the exposure to any kind of religious symbols or religious influence exerted by the state or within, including an action taken in contradiction to the precepts of one's religion will not be prohibited at all times by virtue of the negative right to religious freedom. It is argued that the right does not convey an unreserved freedom to orientate and deploy one's own confession without being exposed to any religious influence provided by the state on behalf of its people.[67]

---

62 Art. 4 para 2 GG together with its counterpart Art. 137 para 1 WRV; BVerfGE 52, 223.

63 *Alloway*, pp. 361, 364.

64 BVerfGE 41, 29, 49; 57, 215, 218; BayVGH, NVwZ 1987, 706, 708; BVerfGE 12, 1, 3.

65 *Zacharias*, FS Rüfner, 2003, pp. 987, 992; BVerfGE 93, 25, 32.

66 *Pieroth/Schlink*, recital 582; BVerfG, May 16, 1995,1 BvR 1087/91, 93; BVerfGE 1, 15.

67 *Coumont* in: v. Campenhausen/Link/Winter, Schriften zum Staatskirchenrecht 38, 2007, p. 96; *Muckel* in Muckel, Schriften zum öffentlichen Recht, 2010, pp. 244–245. A different opinion to the meaning and interpretation of the negative right to religious freedom is held by Zacharias, arguing that the prevalent view in legal literature perceives the negative right to religious freedom as 'forbearance' or 'omission' from the religious-philosophical context (*'... Unterlassen im religiös-weltanschaulischen Kontext'*). This, in her opinion, retrenches the meaning of the negative right to religious freedom and the guarantees thereof. In contrast, several points for assessment of the negative right to religious freedom and its scope of protection are suggested: (a) if an individual does not share a religious or philosophical belief, this does not necessarily convey him the

In this sense, the right of an individual to religious freedom includes the freedom of not having to bear any prescription on part of the state to adhere to the belief of the dominant religion or any religion advanced by it.[68]

As a general rule, claims brought by plaintiffs under Art. 4 para 1 will invoke the impairment of their (positive) right to freely exercise their religion, resulting in a specific detrimental state practice, whereas the reliance on the negative aspect will be raised in claims where the plaintiff believes that the state either advances a certain religion over other religions or advances religion generally over non-believers (atheists).[69]

In this context, the assertion that atheists are refrained from enforcing their (negative) right against that of the majority of parents and pupils and of a school's management task of providing the children with religious values is dissolved on grounds of inconsistency with the inherent nature of the Grundgesetz. In fact, Art. 4 para 1 GG offers the same protection with respect to non-believers who wish to enforce their right not to be exposed to religious themes,[70] and does not demand a reliance on substantial content of a religious writ as a condition for its application.

Evidently, this approach was even approved by the High Administrative Court determining that Art. 4 para 1 GG expands its protection also with relation to atheists,[71] thereby eliminating the argument stating that non-believers cannot invoke the protection provided under Art. 4 para 1 GG.

For instance, Art. 4 para 1 GG guarantees the right of non-believers to keep away from the educational framework of their children any religious influence to which they may be exposed while on the school premises. Nonetheless, the tendency of the court to approve such a claim will be subject to establishment of the objection on 'reasonable' and 'foreseeable' grounds.[72] It is held further that the negative right to religious freedom does not confer an individual more rights

---

right to live in a religion-free zone; (b) the right of an individual not to confess to an own religion cannot be equated with his/her right to remain silent. A denial of one's own religion or a false statement as to his/her 'true' religion or belief may be the outcome of the wish to resemble the mainstream in order not to incur disadvantages, or, otherwise, in order to get benefits or advantages; (c) Non-participation in religious events may bear more 'activism' on part of the individual than participation in those events would have incurred (e.g., keeping away from a territory of a religious event). See in *Zacharias,* FS Rüfner, 2003, pp. 987, 990–991.

68 BVerfGE 32, 98, 106; BVerfGE 93, 1, 15; BVerfGE 108, 282, 297.

69 *Alloway*, pp. 361, 363.

70 *Kommers/Miller,* pp. 567,578–579.

71 BVerwG Berlin, Urt. v. 21.4.1999, EuGRZ p. 1.

72 BayVerfGH, BayVBl. 1997, 686, 690; EuGRZ 1997, 447, et seq.

or freedoms than those comprehended under Art. 4 para 1 & 2 GG scope of protection. Moreover, the negative right to religious freedom will not precede the positive right to religious freedom.[73]

(b) Restrictive or Extensive Scope of Protection

The interpretation of Art. 4's scope of protection was subject to a controversy between the legal literature favouring a restrictive approach[74] and the jurisprudence laid down by the BVerfG and some proponents in the legal literature favouring a liberal extensive approach.[75]

Historically, German constitutionalism did not consider the right to undisturbed practice of religion to include the freedom of an individual to express his/her inner conviction based on the precepts of his/her religion or belief as self-evident. The reason for that lay in the distinction made between religious rights of the privileged dominant churches and those granted to minor religious groups or sects, which were normally disfavoured.[76]

In this context, a difficulty exists as to an interpretive definition of 'religion', 'ideological creed', and 'conscience' (Art. 4 para 1 GG). An explicit definition as to what will be regarded as 'religion' or 'ideological creed' (*Weltanschauung*) has not been fully comprised by the BVerfG, mainly due to the fact that it was not problematic to provide for a constellation that falls under the term 'religion'.[77] The problematic aspect is normally attached to the interpretation given to a specific behaviour or act determining whether it will be regarded as a 'practice of religion' entitled to be safeguarded under Art. 4 para 2 GG.

This directs to an additional interpretive difficulty with respect to the scope of protection of an action or behaviour which is contended to be conscientiously (*gewissenhaft*) motivated.[78] A delineation of a practice or behaviour as derived

---

73 *Zacharias*, FS Rüfner, 2003, pp. 987, 991–992.

74 *Kästner*, JZ 1998, 974; *Classen*, recital 155; *Mager*, in: Münch *v.*/Kunig, Art. 4 recital 17.

75 BVerfGE 93, 1; 33, 23 (30 f.); 44, 33 (49); 52, 223 (246 f.); 91,1 (21); 102, 370 (387); 108, 282 (297). Supporters of the liberal approach in legal literature See, *v. Campenhausen/de Wall*, Staatskirchenrecht, 4th ed. 2006, p. 68; *Maunz/Dürig*, Grundgesetz Kommentar, Art. 140/Art. 136 WRV, Rn. 54; *Kokott*, in: Sachs, Art. 4, recital 36 ff.

76 *Kommers/Miller*, p. 540.

77 BVerfGE 83, 341, 353; *Robbers*, 2001, pp. 643, 647.

78 It was upheld in the German jurisprudence that freedom of conscience scopes of protection enfolds not only in the inner form of an individual's own conscience but also in the right to act or behave in accordance with one's conscientious belief. See in BVerfGE 12, 45, 55; 78, 391, 395.

by an individual personal belief or consciousness is very difficult to be drawn as in real life the compliance with a religious or ideological precept will be mostly directed by a person's inner conscience.[79]

The main contention in legal literature supporting a restrictive approach claims that an extensive interpretation of the right to religious freedom will induce free interpretation of religious rights, which is dependent on subjective discretion of the individual who invokes the right pursuant to Art. 4 GG.[80] This runs the risk that an extensive interpretation of Art. 4's scope of protection will be subject to abuse made by every unreasonable demand of an individual to recognize his/her behaviour or practice as guaranteed under the right to religious freedom. This is known in legal literature as an overestimation of the right to religious freedom (hypertrophy of the right to religious freedom).[81]

(c) Infringement

It is due to the significance of religious freedom in the German constitution that it is guaranteed as outlined in the constitution itself, practically without any explicit reservation or caveat.[82] However, the limitation of Art. 4 is not excluded and it may be possible to confine the right to religious freedom only against other constitutional rights prescribed in the constitution itself and insofar the limitation complies with certain pre-requisites that justify such a confinement.

The prerequisites for limitation of Art. 4 are not explicitly mentioned in the words of the provision itself, but are actually mentioned indirectly in other provisions of the Grundgesetz (e.g., Art. 2 para 2 GG).

Unlike other freedoms, which can be limited by any regular statutory law on grounds of incompliance with other constitutional standards (e.g., public interest), religious freedom can only be limited against other colliding rights or interests laid down in the constitution itself.[83]

However, as a general principle, the existence of a constitutional provision purporting to protect the legitimate interest of others will be interpreted

---

79 *Starck*, in: Mangoldt v./Klein/Starck, Art. 4 recital 13; *Walter*, in: Dörr/Grote/Marauhn, p. 972.

80 *Muckel* in: Muckel, Schriften zum Öffentlichen Recht, 2010, pp. 234,,248–249;

81 *Kästner*, JZ 1998, 974.

82 *v. Ungern-Sternberg*, 2008, p. 241; *Muckel* in: Muckel, Schriften zum Öffentlichen Recht, 2010, pp. 234, 242; *Coumont*, in: v. Campenhausen/Link/Winter, 2007, p. 78.

83 *Pieroth/Schlink*, recital 605; BVerfGE 28, 243, 260, et seq.; 41, 29, 50, et seq.; 41, 88, 107; 44, 37,49, et seq.; 52, 223, 247; 83, 130, 142; 93, 1, 21; 32, 98, 107; 33, 23, 29; *Robbers*, 2001, pp. 643, 647; *Seifert*, pp. 529, 532; BVerfGE 32, 98, 107.

narrowly so as to ensure that unnecessary limitation of religious freedom would not take place.

As a possible interference in religious or denominational freedom, one may refer to any event where the right of thought, speech, or action of the individual relating to the practice or exertion of his religious freedom was influenced or impaired by the state.[84]

(d) Justification

Similar to the element of infringement, no specification exists in Art. 4 GG as to what would be regarded as possible justification for interference of the right to religious freedom. Art. 4 para 2 determines that the right to religious freedom is unreserved and undiminished.

Nonetheless, the jurisprudence acknowledged interference in guaranteed liberty rights such as the right to religious freedom. However, such an encroachment or confinement will be justified only if its restriction is necessary for: first, the protection of other constitutional rights and values and, second, satisfying the proportionality test.

(aa) The Protection of Other Constitutional Rights and Values

Since the BVerfG prefers a liberal and extensive method of interpretation with respect to the right of religious freedom, it is not sufficient that religious freedom will be limited by other competing constitutional rights or values; rather, such a limitation must comply with special requirements.[85] The result is that due to the significance attributed to religious freedom in German constitutional law, its limitation cannot be justified by any law purporting to protect any public interest. A limitation can be justified only if prescribed by a law that enforces public interests or constitutional value recognized and laid down in the constitution itself.[86]

The BVerfG declined to accept the prevailing view in legal literature favouring confinement of Art. 4's scope of protection. In this context, the German constitution enables specific fundamental rights prescribed in the constitution[87] such as the right to freedom of personality and life under Art. 2 para 2 GG to superimpose

84 *Pieroth/Schlink*, recital 593, et seq.

85 *Pieroth/Schlink*, recital 605.

86 *Robbers*, 2001, pp. 643, 647; BVerfGE 28, 243, 261; 93, 1,21; 32, 98, 107; 33, 23, 29; *Sachs*, in: Sachs, before Art. 1 recital 120, et seq.

87 Other rights which may obtain precedence over the right to religious freedom are: Art. 1 (the right to human dignity) and Art. 3 (The equality principle) GG.

Art. 4 GG.[88] However, the same limitations designated in Art. 2 para 1 (the rights of others, constitutional order or moral code) cannot be assigned as possible limitations with respect to Art. 4's scope of protection.[89] That means that limitations prescribed in one of the Grundgesetz provisions cannot be assigned to retrench another provision in the Grundgesetz. Accordingly, the confinement of Art. 2 para 1's scope of protection through regular parliamentary legislation cannot be assigned to confinement of Art. 4 scope of protection. The same refrainment of the BVerfG exists with respect to the notion relating to the caveat prescribed in Art. 136 para 1 of the WRV. It was upheld that this provision, which dictates the enjoyment of civil rights and duties irrespective of the right to practise religious freedom, should not prevail simply as it cannot outweigh a central fundamental right like the right to religious freedom.[90]

(bb) The Test of Proportionality

The test must prove that a limitation or infringement imposed on a constitutional right is justified only if it fulfils the proportionality test.[91] The proportionality test must prove fulfilment of several requirements. (i) The infringement is an adequate pursuant of the aim it seeks to achieve. The legislator must establish that an infringement imposed by a law on a fundamental right for the purpose of protecting another constitutional right is suitable or adequate for the purpose of the aim it seeks to achieve. (ii) Moreover, the limitation must be necessary in order to achieve the aim. The measure that is taken is necessary in order to achieve the pursued aim. In this respect, it must provide that no other, less cumbersome measures exist for the achievement of the desired aim.[92]

(iii) In the end there must be a careful outweighing of the competing rights ('practical concordance') which will have to demonstrate that the gravity of the infringement and its necessity can ensure an effective protection of the

---

88 *Robbers*, 2001, pp. 643, 644.

89 BVerfGE 32, 98, 107; *Listl*, in: Listl/Pirson, HdbStKirchR I, pp. 439, 466, et seq; *Jarass*, in: Jarass/Pieroth, Art. 4, recital 28.

90 BVerfGE 33, 23, 30 et seq.; 44, 37, 49 et seq.; 93,1, 21; *Isak*, Selbstverständnis der Kirchen und Religionsgemeinschaften und seine Bedeutung für die Auslegung staatlichen Rechts, 1994, p. 255; *Müller-Volbehr*, pp. 301, 306; *Hemmrich*, in: Münch v./Kunig, Art. 140, recital 7; *Morlok*, in: Dreier Vol I, Art. 4, recital 124; *Korioth*, in: Maunz/Dürig, Grundgesetz, Art. 136 WRV recital 54; BVerwG, NJW, 2002, 3344, 3345.A different opinion is held by Muckel, see in *Muckel* in: Muckel, Schriften zum Öffentlichen Recht, 2010, pp. 234, 248–249;

91 BVerfGE 89, 69, 84; 90, 145, 173; 113, 63, 80.

92 BVerfGE 30, 292, 316; 67, 157, 176; 102, 197, 217, et seq.

conflicting interest or right as well as its proportionality. The perception of the German judicator is to seek for a compromise that will grant all of the colliding interests due regard.[93] In this respect, the legislator is privileged with a wide scope of discretion as to the list of objectives it pursues to achieve.[94]

(cc) Individual Religious Freedom Rights Established Under the WRV

Additional prescription of the fundamental right to religious freedom can be found in the provisions of the WRV. The WRV provisions determine the duties the state may enforce vis-à-vis the individual's right to religious freedom (Art. 136 WRV). Moreover, the provisions encompass institutional guarantees for churches and religious communities.

Thus, the right to religious freedom under Art. 4 GG is not the only constitutional provision regulating state-church affairs. It is rather supplemented and attenuated by Art. 136–141 of the German Reich's Weimar constitution of 1919 (WRV). These were incorporated from the Weimar constitution into the Grundgesetz by Art. 140 GG and comprise an inseparable part of German constitutional law.[95]

The provisions are also known as the 'Church-articles' due to the friendly church attitude and the privileged status granted to the big Christian churches in Germany.[96] These articles mainly constitute valid and binding constitutional provisions that evenly rank alongside the Grundgesetz and form an integral part of it.[97]

In principle, the aforementioned articles of the Weimar constitution refer not only to the individual freedom of religion (Art. 136 WRV), but also to religious freedom of the collective (Art. 137 WRV). This means that religious communities will also be able to invoke their constitutional right to religious freedom based on the guarantee provided under Art. 4 GG together with its complementary provision Art. 137 WRV.

---

93 BVerfGE 93,1 = NJW 1995, 2477; VG BerlinNVwZ-RR 2010, 189, 190.

94 *Jarass*, in: Jarass/Pieroth, Art. 20, recital 122; The same privilege is somewhat retrenched in scope when conferred upon the executive. See in *Jarass*, in: Jarass/Pieroth, Art. 20, recital 126, et seq.

95 BVerfGE 19, 206, 219; 226, 236; *Seifert*, pp. 529, 534.

96 *Seifert*, pp. 529, 532, 534; *Robbers*, 2001, pp. 643, 644.

97 Art. 136 WRV: Individual freedom of religion and the prohibition of discrimination on religious grounds; Art. 137 WRV: Collective freedom of religion and recognition of religious communities as statutory corporations; Art. 138: Benefits conferred by the state and property of religion; Art. 139 WRV the guarantee of Sundays and feast days; Art. 141 WRV chaplainry in public institutions.

Additionally, due to the fact that the provisions of the WRV enabled the major religions existing in 1919 (particularly the Catholic and Protestant churches) to retain their status and autonomy as public corporations and granted them extensive institutional guarantees, it in fact affirmed the constitutional, legitimate function of the state to fulfil its obligation in the religious sphere. Consequently, several articles of the Weimar constitution may be used as a valid justification for the confinement of religious freedom.[98]

The most important and relevant elements underlying the fundaments of the constitutional relationship between state and religion under the complementary framework of the Weimar Constitution have their basis in Art. 136 and 137 of the WRV.

Essentially, Art. 136 WRV prohibits discrimination on religious grounds and enables individuals the right not to disclose their religious affiliation. Art. 136 para 1 WRV prescribes that civil and political rights and duties laid down by law shall be neither dependent on nor restricted by the exercise of religious freedom. Art. 136 para 4 goes further and declares the right of every citizen not to be coerced to participate in religious festivities.[99] However, Art. 136 para 3 includes a reservation for statutory powers (*Gesetzesvorbehalt*) for interferences in the negative freedom of religion and denomination. This enables the government or state authorities the right to inquire as to an individual's religious affiliation, only if rights or duties are dependent thereon or if a statutory statistical inquiry demands it.[100]

Nonetheless, a judicial determination of the BVerfG with respect to this matter upheld that a simple reservation for statutory powers does not sufficiently respect the essential meaning of Art. 4 of the Grundgesetz and its unlimited protection. Art. 136 is therefore completely superimposed by Art. 4 GG, so that the simple reservation for statutory powers does not come into effect.[101] This

---

98 For instance, according to Art. 136 para 3 WRV, no one is obliged to disclose his religious denomination, and discrimination on religious grounds is prohibited. Albeit the right granted to individuals to keep silent with respect to their religious affiliation, authorities still have the right to inquire for the pertinence of individuals as to their religious affiliation as far as rights or obligations are dependent thereon or a statutory inquiry demands it.

99 Art. 136 para 4 WRV determines that: 'no one may be compelled to perform any religious act or ceremony, to participate in religious exercises or to take a religious form of oath'.

100 *Palmer*, p. 41.

101 BVerfGE 33, 23, 31; *Pieroth/Schlink*, recital 600.

emanates that every statutory enactment interfering with the scope of Art. 4 GG must be evaluated and interpreted in order to reconcile with the inherent purport of Art. 4 GG.

(3) Art. 6 GG – The Parental Right to Education

The provision of the Grundgesetz that was designed to protect family relations in the context of the school system and guarantee parental rights with respect to the education of their children is secured in Art. 6 GG. The most important provisions legitimating the protection afforded to a parent's natural right to decide on the education of their children are established in Art. 6 para 2 as well as Art. 7 para 2 GG.

(a) Scope of Protection

Parents' right to take care of the education of their children is prescribed under Art. 6 para 2 GG which proclaims that the 'care and upbringing of children are the natural right of and a duty primarily incumbent on parents'. Art. 6 para 2 further stipulates that the duty of education is primarily (*zuvorderst*) a task of the parents. This priority implies that the educational task belongs also to the state, at least in the second degree.[102]

This natural right of parents (Art. 6 paras 1 and 2 GG) conjoined with the right to religious freedom (Art. 4 para 1 GG) extends parents' right to determine the education of their children in religious and philosophical matters.[103] This implies also their right to keep the children away from religious convictions that seem wrong or harmful to the parents.[104] In order to prevent a conflict between the mandate of parents on the religious education of their children and the right of children to self-determination of their religion, reference should be made to stipulations in the Children's Religious Education Act 1921 (CREA). The CREA prescribes different ages of maturity for children to determine their religious adherence (*Grundrechtsmündigkeit*).[105] As a result, parents are entitled to decide

102 Bay VGH, NVwZ 1992, 1224; Pieroth/Schlink, recital 749, et seq.

103 BVerfGE 41, 88, 107; 41, 29, 44, 47, et seq; BVerfG 2 BvR 1693/04 = BayVBl. 2006, 633; *Mager*, in: Münch v./Kunig, (2000), Art. 4, recital 33; *Kokott*, in: Sachs, (2014), Art. 4, recital 8.

104 BVerfGE 1436/02 Judgement of 24 September 2003–2 BvR 1436/02 para 45 – NJW 2003, 3111, 3113;

105 Art. 5 of the CREA stipulates diverging ages to which children are legally entitled to determine their religious pertinence or non-pertinence, the so called '*Religionsmündigkeit*' of the child. It determines that when reaching the age of 12 years a child cannot be professed to another religion than the one he was brought

on the participation of their children in religious lessons in school (Art. 7 para 2 GG) or to demand their omission.[106] In addition, participation in other lessons is subject to the demands of the parents that their children should not be influenced or exposed to a religion or faith that is different than the faith they hold.[107]

The educational right of parents pursuant to Art. 6 para 2 GG appears, thence, in two dimensions: as an institutional guarantee and as a classic, basic liberty right. The institutional guarantee stipulates the parental right to decide on the education of their children. The classic liberty right aims to defend against respective restrictions of the educational right by the state.[108]

(b) Infringement

Tension points may emerge in the public school system in two ways: (i) the conveyance of educational aims within the framework of a school's curriculum that collide with or run counter to a parent's right for their children not to be exposed to religious education or content they perceive as harmful or wrong; (ii) the exposure of pupils to religious dress or symbols worn by the teacher may invigorate unease or tension among pupils as well as their parents.

Art. 6 para 2 GG does not accord parents the exclusive right to educate their children. According to the educational mandate granted to the state under Art. 7 para 1 GG 'the entire school system shall be under the supervision of the state'. This entails that the public education task and the parental education right stand equally side-by-side.[109] Nonetheless, the educational task of the state does not conclude to the mere organization of public schools but also includes the

---

up with against his/her will. When reaching the age of 14 years a child has the right to decide as to his/her religious adherence. § 5 das Gesetz über die religiösereligöse Kindererziehung vom 15 July 1921: 'Nach der Vollendung des vierzehnten Lebensjahrs steht dem Kinde die Entscheidung darüber zu, zu welchem religiösen Bekentnnis es sich halten w*ill. Hat das Kind das zwölfte* Lebensjahr vollendet, so kann es nicht gegen seinen Willen, in einem anderen Bekenntnis als bisher erzogen werden'.; *Coumont*, in: von Campenhausen/Link/Winter, Schriften zum Staatskirchenrecht 38, 2007, pp. 67–68.

106 Art. 1 of the CREA prescribes that the right to decide on the religious education of the child is an agreed decision of the parents. § 1 das Gesetz über die religiöse Kindererziehung vom 15 July 1921: 'Über die religiöse Erziehung eines kindes bestimmt die freie Einigung der Eltern, soweit ihnen das Recht und die Pflicht zusteht, für die Person des Kindes zu sorgen…'.

107 BVerfGE 52, 223, 235, et seq.; 41, 29, 47, et seq.; 41, 88, 107.

108 BVerfGE 68, 176, 190; BVerfGE 24, 119, 143.

109 *Hemmerich* in: Münch v./Kunig, Art. 7, recital 3.

establishment of educational goals and content of lessons. It is only reasonable that the specific educational design of school lessons cannot take into account and respect all the demands of all parents at all times. Thus, Art. 7 para 1 GG grants the school administration a broad freedom of design regarding school curriculum. The parental education right is not permitted to influence the school curriculum in the sense of co-determination and, moreover, the parental right may not be enforced by majority decisions.[110]

To that extent, the state's discretion with respect to educational matters is independent of parents, and it is inevitable that those two interests will be regularly in conflict. Consequently, a balance between the parental education right and the public education task needs to be achieved by applying the principle of 'practical concordance' (*das Prinzip der 'Praktischen Konkordanz'*).[111] The tension between the educative task of the state and the religious interests of pupils and their parents obliges school authorities to find an acceptable settlement that is agreed on by all parties. Hand in hand, pupils and their parents must also take into consideration other reasonable alternatives for practising their right to religious freedom. The necessity to find a solution or a compromise dictates that within application of the practical concordance each party will have to set back so that one right will not override the other unnecessarily.[112]

---

110 BVerfGE 47, 46, 78; BVerwGE 47, 94, 197; *Pieroth/Schlink*, recital 756.

111 *Germann Wiesner*, p. 420. See more detail on the principle of 'practical concordance' in this chapter under headline 2 c) dd).

112 The daily tension in public schools stemming from the legal right of the state to form and establish its school system by virtue of the educative task conferred to it in the constitution (Art. 7 para 1 & 2 GG) and the obligation of the state to accommodate to varying religious needs in a pluralistic society had been recognized by the judiciary which, in response, developed and applied the principal of practical concordance, for example, in cases involving the request of a pupil to be exempted from swimming lessons or sport classes. BVerwGE 94, 82 (89–94) = NVwZ 1994, 578; BayVGH, decision from 6 May 1987 – 7 B 86.01557= NVwZ 1987, 706–708; HessVGH, decision from 8 September 1987= NVwZ 1988, 951; OVG Lüneburg decision from 26 April 1991 – 13 M 7618/91 = NVwZ 1992, 79–81; OVG Bremen, decision from 13 June 2012 – 1 B 9912 = NVwZ-RR 2012, 842; OVG NRW, Decision from 15 November 1991 – 19 A 2198/91; VG Düsseldorf, decision from 7 May 2008 – 18 K 301/08; VG Aachen, decision from 12 January 2011 – 9 L 518/10. The problems in achieving a uniform formula when applying the principle of practical concordance has also been demonstrated in the case of a school-prayer taken outside the classroom. The case had been challenged in several instances with varying outcomes resulting in different application of the principle of practical concordance. The ban on a pupil in the state of Berlin to refrain from publicly praying during school breaks was justified

Further infringement on the parental right to education may be imposed by the exposure of pupils to religious dress or symbols worn by the teacher. Art. 7 para 2 GG ensures parents the right to have their children educated in accordance with the faith of their choice.

(4) Overview Liberty Rights

The centrepiece of the right to religious freedom is guaranteed in Art. 4 GG. Its unrestrained provision underlines the fundamental commitment of the German state to religious freedom.

Art. 2 GG has a supplementary function and does not fulfil a specific function in the core field of religious freedom.

Whereas Art. 4 and Art. 2 GG aim at driving back the state's influence in favour of religious freedom of the individual and its practice, Art. 6 GG guarantees parents the authority to keep their children away from harmful influence.

This combination of the abovementioned basic rights ensures the individual's free choice to either practise his/her religious beliefs or to refrain from this.

cc) Equality Rights/Anti-Discrimination Rights

Equality rights ensure equal treatment of every individual by the state inter alia with regard to religious issues. Thus, the following analysis will deal with the guarantee of the general principle of equal treatment as depicted in Art. 3 para

---

by school authorities on grounds of its disturbance and unease to other pupils and infringement of their negative right to religious freedom. While the administrative court of Berlin had taken all competing interests into account through careful consideration of the precept of practical concordance, it decided eventually that the pupil should be permitted to hold his prayer as long as it does not occur during lesson time and does not form any detraction to the ordinary school operation. The Administrative Court stated explicitly that it does not share the view that religious neutrality of the state implies a strict segregation between state and religion (see in VG Berlin, decision from 29 September 2009 – VG 3 A 984/07 = NVwZ-RR 2010, 189, 191). In contrast, the High Administrative Court adopted a very secular ('laizistisch') interpretation of the right to religious freedom upholding that the guarantee of the freedom to practise religion within school premises poses a violation of the state to abide by its duty to religious neutrality (OVG Berlin, decision from 27 May 2010 – 3 B 29/09 = LKV 2010, 422, 426); a different verdict was delivered by the BVerwG which concluded that the right to religious freedom can be limited only in special circumstances which are necessary for danger prevention, the so called '*Gefahrenabwehrrecht*'. See in BVerwG, decision from 30 November 2011 – 6 C 20/10).

3, as well as the guarantee of equality of access to the public service as prescribed in Art. 33 para 2 GG.

These provisions are known as the equality provisions and comprise the equality principle. The principle of equality has established its importance in the German jurisprudence and evolved its relevance with respect to religious symbols when their admissibility had been questioned within the context of public servants' dress code. For instance, the permissibility of a Muslim teacher to appear with a headscarf in school was often challenged in legal literature using the example of the eligibility granted to a nun to wear a habit or a necklace with a cross during lessons, and the consequent exposure of pupils to her religious dress code.[113] The distinction made in the same profession where teachers had two different religions drew criticism as it infringes against the equality precept and equal treatment in the public service, granting other religious minorities the right to affiliation of religion by wearing a religious symbol or garment.[114] Should Christian symbols worn by a teaching nun be admitted as a sign of the Christian faith, whereas the headscarf of a Muslim teacher should be rejected by virtue of its manifestation of the Islamic faith, this would constitute an infringement of the state to adhere by its obligation to religious neutrality and the equality precept.

The absence of a unified civil servant code that equally applies to all federal states enables major discrepancies between the states as to permissibility of religious symbols in the public school system and to a lack of consistency in the German jurisprudence. In fact, the religious determination of civil servants and, consequently, their eligibility to appear with religious dress or symbols plays a distinctive role with respect to different office holders in the public service (e.g., police force, judges). The significance of a unified dress code rule, especially with respect to teachers, was subject to fierce controversies and debates as it was contended that the wearing of ostentatious religious symbols or garments in classrooms may have an effect on the pupils. It is due to this potential influence on pupils that teachers as public servants are much more exposed to public

---

113 *Brenner*, VVDStRL 59 (2000), pp. 264, 283–284; *Mahrenholz*, in: FS Badura, 2004, p. 749.

114 *Brenenr* refers to other case laws dealt in the German jurisprudence with respect to admissibility of a teacher to appear with the typical Bhagwan garments to school, see p. 284 in Fn. 77–78 in VGH München, NVwZ 1986, p. 405. In addition, the right of a teacher, a member of the Mala, to wear the traditional dressing was subject to judicial review as delivered in the following instances – BVerwG, NVwZ 1988,937/938; OVG Hamburg, DVBl.1985, p. 456; BayVGH, BayVBl.1985, p. 721; VG München, BayVbl. 1985, p. 284.

scrutiny and, as a result, also justifies their abidance with a different set of dress code rules. Nonetheless, the equality precepts as outlined in the Grundgesetz mandate the application of equal treatment with respect to all civil servants and such a segregation in the same profession contrasts starkly with it.

(1) Art. 3 GG/Guarantee of Equality before the Law

Art. 3 para 1 GG establishes the general guarantee of equality before the law, whereas para 3 of it specifically prohibits discrimination and preference on account of gender, ethnic origin, race, language, religion, or religious/political opinions. Art. 3 para 3 GG specifies: 'nobody shall be disadvantaged or favoured due to his/her gender, nationality, race, language, country, origin, faith, religion, or political view'. This equality imperative mainly addresses the state as a legislator and prohibits any differentiation which relates to the aforementioned criteria.[115]

Moreover, Art. 3 para 3 GG bears a supportive function with respect to religious freedom as it supplements the unreserved guarantee prescribed in Art. 4 para 1 GG with the prohibition of discrimination based on religious grounds. In this respect, the definition of 'religious opinion' (*religiöse Anschauung*) will be interpreted so as to correspond with the identical term enfolded under Art. 4's scope of protection.

Actually, Art. 3 para 3 is realized as an unconditional or absolute differentiation prohibition aiming to ensure that no violation of the equality principle takes place on part of the state with respect to its individuals. This general prohibition of discrimination was expanded by jurisdiction of the BVerfG to cover not only acts of direct but also of indirect discrimination.[116] That means that any differentiation of treatment induced by the state with respect to an individual and

---

115 *Pieroth/Schlink*, recital 503.

116 Direct discrimination occurs when a person is treated less favourably based on a specified ground forbidden by law (e.g., gender, race, ethnicity etc.). Indirect discrimination, on the other hand, is less obvious and arises when a criterion seemingly applies equally to all, but in fact creates an explicit distinction between individuals, simply as they are not able to comply with this specific criterion or practice; as a result, it produces identical or almost identical discriminatory effects. The inclusion of indirect discrimination under Art. 3 scope of protection was a submission of the German Federal Constitutional Court to the transposition of European anti-discrimination law into German law. See in this respect BVerfG, 27 November 1997; 97 BVerfGE 35, 43; 104 BVerfGE 373, 393.

presumed to establish direct or indirect discrimination according to the above-mentioned criteria will be regarded as unlawful.

(2) Art. 33 GG/Equal Access to Public Service

Essentially, both the principle of equality and the prohibition of discrimination are enfolded and complemented in Art. 33 GG. In fact, Art. 33 para 1 GG guarantees every German the enjoyment of civil and political rights. Art. 33 para 2, on the other hand, provides that every German is eligible for application to the public service, which will be permissible according to his aptitude, qualifications, and professional achievements.[117]

Furthermore, the strict obligation determining that eligibility for a post in the public service shall be independent from a person's religious denomination is pursuant to Art. 33 para 3 GG. This constitutional guarantee determines also that no one may suffer any disadvantage by reason of his/her adherence or non-adherence to a specific denomination or ideology.[118]

This means that, principally, individuals would be able to retain their adherence to their religion even when observed through wearing of religious garments, and would not be exposed as a result to unfavourable treatment in the application process or to exclusion from the public service. A common presumption in this respect suggests that religion or belief is normally not relevant for the performance and qualification of an individual at a work place, therefore recognizing any discrimination or violation by the state of its obligation for equal treatment as unlawful.[119]

In practice, controversies surrounding the admissibility of a teacher to wear religious symbols in the public education system usually invokes Art. 33 para 3 GG when complemented and conjoined by the following: Art. 3 para 1 (equality of all citizens before the law) and Art. 3 para 3 S. 1 (general prohibition of discrimination), Art. 4 (religious freedom), Art. 33 para 2 (equal access to the public service) as well as Art. 136 WRV in association with Art. 140 GG (prohibition of discrimination on religious grounds). However, it is due to the distinctive feature and specificity of Art. 33 para 3 GG that German courts have inclined to give it priority over the aforementioned rights.[120]

---

117 *Giegrich*, Freedom of Religion and Equality, Israel Law Review 34 (2000), p. 231.

118 Art. 33 para 3 GG holds that: 'enjoyment of civil and political rights, eligibility for public office, and rights acquired in the public service shall be independent of a person's religious denomination'.

119 *Seifert*, pp. 529, 554–555.

120 BVerwGE, 81, 22, 24.

This means that albeit the explicit prohibition of religious discrimination in the public service, Art. 33 para 3 does not supersede the general qualification requirement prescribed under Art. 33 para 2 GG. This constitutional guarantee provides that every German is eligible for any public office according to his/her aptitude, qualifications, and professional achievements.

The reason that the 'aptitude' or qualification requirement (Art. 33 para 2) reinforces the general prohibition of discrimination (Art. 33 para 3) can be justified in view of the German constitution to serve as a general safety mechanism. Simply, the constitution does not wish to grant protection to individuals or religious extremists induced by a wrong motive, such as the fostering of an ideology which is incompatible with the fundamental constitutional values.[121]

(3) Anti-Discrimination Legislation (AGG)

Germany's obligation under European law to transform several EU anti-discrimination directives into domestic law triggered the German parliament to act for the implementation of the new rules. The German General Equal Treatment Act (*Allgemeines Gleichbehandlungsgesetz*, AGG) was enacted on 14 August 2006.[122] The AGG was intended to integrate the EU Directives[123] which cover equal treatment and anti-discrimination in hiring and employment practice as well as provide for special protection against discrimination established on religious grounds. The AGG prohibits in Sec. 1 any discrimination that may occur based on the following grounds: race, ethnical origin, gender, religion, ideological creed, disability, age, and sexual identity. The AGG was enacted

---

121 The insertion of the 'aptitude' requirement in the German jurisdiction was originally meant to serve indeed as a safety mechanism in order to exclude political extremists who do not support the fundamental values of the constitution from applying to the public service. On the same token, this may be used as a restriction to the prohibition prescribed in Art. 33 para 3 in case of religious extremists. See in that case: BVerfGE 39, 334; *Giegrich*, pp. 211, 231.

122 BGBl. I, p. 1897, came into force on 14 August 2006.

123 The AGG purported to transpose the following directives into German Law: Council Directive 2000/43/EC of 29 June 2000 implementing the principle of equal treatment between persons irrespective of racial or ethnic origin; Council Directive 2000/78/EC of 27 November 2000 establishing a general framework for equal treatment in employment and occupation in force since 2 December 2000; Directive 2002/73/EC on the implementation of the equality treatment principle for men and women as regards access to employment, vocational training, promotion, and working conditions; Council Directive 2004/113/EC of 13 December 2004 implementing the equality treatment principle between men and women in the access to and supply of goods and services.

in order to prevent discrimination in the private sector or any selection criteria occurring in relation to a person's professional life, in particular in employment relations. Nonetheless, Sec. 24 of the AGG determines its validity also for civil servants in the public sector.

In principle, the anti-discrimination commands inscribed in the AGG are identical in content and aim to the basic equality principle prescribed in Art. 3 para 3 GG. However, the AGG offers at the outset an explicit, codified legislation that prohibits any discrimination or unequal treatment in the daily professional life of employees. Thence, the scope of protection under the AGG is much more extensive and ample than the basic principle outlined in Art. 3 para 3 GG;[124] it covers large numbers of participants in the employment sector (applicants, employees, freelancers, apprentices, etc.) and includes different discriminatory features.

c) Religious Aspects in the Grundgesetz and Constitutional Principles

The safeguard of religious rights is not confined merely to the specific provisions of the Grundgesetz that explicitly relate to it (e.g., Art. 4, Art. 7 para 2 & para 3 GG). Religious rights obtain protection also through the shield (*Schirm*) of several distinguishable constitutional principles, like the principle of practical concordance. The formulation of constitutional principles assisted the judicator in application and assessment of clashing fundamental rights when trying to balance them against each other. The significance of these principles becomes relevant as especially the discussion surrounding the permissibility of state institutions such as common public schools to display or present religious symbols within their premises is subject to many conflicts and is known to be highly controversial. As a result, it was in many cases the judicator that through interpretive approach attempted either to elaborate existing principles based on the explicit words of the constitution and adapt them to the particular legal controversy, or, evaluate the legitimacy of the scrutinized law and the interests it affects through a pragmatic approach. This method of interpretation took place even to the extent of deducing a formal principle based on the constitutional text, eventually establishing a recognized judicial practice.

Since the right to religious freedom acquires a pre-eminent place in the German constitution it is not surprising that the commitment to safeguard this

---

124 *Heinrichs*, in: Palandt, Introduction, before Sec. 1 AGG, recital 7.

right is also alluded to in the preamble to the German constitution. Thence, a brief reference to the preamble of the German Grundgesetz will be provided in the following. Thereafter, an overview of the following principles is indispensable for the apprehension of the doctrinal analysis of the German jurisprudence with respect to religious liberty rights, and the efforts made to disentangle church and state especially in the educational context. Considerable emphasis will be conferred to the following aspects: first, the preamble, second, the principle of neutrality, and, third, the principle of practical concordance.

aa) Preamble

The meaning and scope of the preamble constitute an integral part of the Grundgesetz.

The preamble explicitly declares that the Grundgesetz acquires its legal validity not through reference to a different constitution, but rather from empowerment given to the legislator through sovereignty of the German people.[125] Thus, the significance of such an empowerment emanating from sovereignty of the German people may confine itself only with respect to the present Grundgesetz. As a result, the German legislator is not able to exchange the constitution with another, as it was not authorized to do so by the German nation.

In the preamble to the German constitution there is a reference to God and humankind. The preamble includes an 'invocatio dei' which is mainly meant as a reference to Germany's Christian tradition.[126] The 'invocatio dei' has often been criticized for its disintegrating function for atheists.[127] The reference to God actually acknowledges a confined sphere which the state cannot transcend. This formula is supposed to serve as a rejection of totalitarian ideologies,[128] but should not challenge the neutrality with respect to an ideological creed.[129] At the same time, the 'invocatio dei' opposes a state's ideology which completely denies any kind of religious denomination.[130]

---

125 *Jarass*, in: Jarass/Pieroth, preamble, recital 2.

126 *Sachs*, in Sachs, preamble, recital 38.

127 Bericht Gem VerfKom-Dr 37, 72; Bericht Gem VerfKom, BR Dr 800/93, p. 217, et seq.

128 *Robbers*, 2001, pp. 643, 645; Bericht Gem VerfKom, BR Dr 800/13, p. 211.

129 BVerfGE 33, 23, 28; 41, 29, 50.

130 BVerfGE 19, 206, 216; *Mückl*, in Isensee/Kirchhof, HStR VII, Sec. 159 recital 20, et seq.; *Münch v./Kunig*, preamble recital 12, et seq.; *Sachs*, in Sachs, preamble, recital 38.

bb) *The Principle of State Neutrality*

The most central constitutional pillar prescribing the relationship between state and religion, inter alia the designation of state's supervision with respect to religious matters in the education is the principle of neutrality. In general, the principle underlies the concept of separation between state and religion insofar as it prohibits the establishment of a state-church system.

In this respect, it is worth noting that the constitutional concept of separation has been significantly modified throughout the constitutional and legal history of Germany.[131] Thus, the principle of neutrality deserves a thorough introspection of meaning, nature, source, structure, and implementation in the constitution. Yet, though the concept of separation has gained general acceptance regarding its existence, several aspects relating to the neutrality principle remain controversial, namely, the normative source upon which this principle derives authority, its dogmatic structure, and its content. These aspects and the legal debates surrounding them will be thence discussed further in detail.

(1) Notion of Neutrality

The neutrality principle is not explicitly guaranteed in the constitution. It is rather a development of the judiciary and the legal literature deducing its existence from the embodiment of different constitutional provisions.[132]

Due to the lack of some written source ascertaining the existence of such a principle – which could have provided a clue as to its content – the controversies around this principle are quite ample and have even increased in the past few years mainly as a counter response to the growing plurality of religions in the public education system.

As a practical matter, this principle depicts the position of the state with relation to religious communities and ecclesiastical matters, and embraces two diverging prongs: the principle of non-identification and non-intervention.[133] It follows that the state should in fact stay neutral and must not identify itself with a

131 *Ladeur*, 30 Cardozo L. Rev. (2009), pp. 2245, 2246.

132 The prohibition of state-church establishment (Art. 137 para 1 WRV); the guarantee of civil and political rights irrespective of an individual's religion or belief (Art. 136 para 1 WRV); equal access to public office irrespective of religious denomination (Art. 33 para 3 GG); prohibiting discrimination on account of religious belief (Art. 3 para 3 GG); the constitutional protection granted to freedom of religion and belief (Art. 4 GG).

133 *Robbers*, 2001, pp. 643, 649; *Heckel*, 1997, pp. 187, 190.

particular religion and prefer or support it to the detriment of other religions. In plain words, this notion suggests a complete segregation in all aspects between those two entities: state and church. The idea is to sever religion from public institutions. Consequently, the state is prohibited from any initiation of a state-church educational model, as well as the granting of privileges to a certain religious group or interfering in their inner-affairs (non-intervention).[134]

(2) Normative Source

In the legal doctrine and German jurisprudence it is presumed that the anchorage of the neutrality principle has its roots in Art. 137 para 1 WRV, as its precept declares that 'there is no state-church', i.e., prohibition of cooperation between these two institutions, state and religion. It should be noted that although Art. 137 para 1 WRV and Art. 140 GG prescribe that 'there shall be no established state-church', the assumption is that it refers only to the obligation of the state and the church to act independently from each other on the basis of mutual cooperation. Yet this does not insinuate a radical separation thereof.[135]

The principle of state neutrality, its interpretation, and the position it maintains in jurisprudence of the courts and legal literature rests in various underlying structures and relationships rooted in Germany's constitution.

Notably, one aspect that remained undisputed by the judiciary and the legal literature is the fact that this principle should be regulated by the state in order

134 *Robbers*, ÖARR, 2003, pp. 405, 413; BVerfGE 24, 236, 246; 33, 23, 28; 93, 1, 17; 30, 415, 422; 19, 1, 8; 19, 206, 216 (*Kirchenlohnsteuer II*). In the last decision the court declared the constitutional right of churches to deduct taxes from their members according to the prerogative conferred to it by power of the state (*Hoheitsrechts*). It was explained that this form of tax deduction through the state does not insinuate of any state-church cooperation but rather it is derived from power of the state to charge taxes on behalf of the church. The duty of the state to abide by the precept of religious neutrality and non-favoritism of a particular religion bars the introduction of institutional entanglement between state and church. This was expressed as follows: ‚*Das Grundgesetz legt durch Art. 4 para 1, Art. 3 para 3, Art. 33 para 3 GG sowie durch Art. 136 para 1 und 4 und Art. 137 para .1 WRV in Verbindung mit Art. 140 GG dem Staat als Heimstatt aller Staatbürger ohne Ansehen der Person weltanschaulich-religiöse Neutralität auf. Es verwehrt die Einführung staatskirchlicher Rechtsformen und untersagt auch die Privilegierung bestimmter Bekentntnisse*'.

135 *Heckel*, 1997, pp. 187, 197; *Heckel*, Emory Int'l L.Rev. 10 (1996), pp. 107, 108; *Seifert*, pp. 529, 534.

to achieve more conformity and establish understanding between church-state relations and religious freedom in Germany.[136]

(a) Designation in Grundgesetz (Basic Law)

As mentioned before, the principle of religious neutrality of the state is not explicitly stipulated in the German Grundgesetz. However, jurisprudence and legal literature inferred its existence based on various constitutional provisions which specify or imply an obligation of the state to comply with the neutrality principle regarding religious matters, and acknowledges it as an inseparable constitutional principle.

In particular, the Grundgesetz relates to and indicates the existence of the neutrality principle based on the following constitutional guarantees: the safeguarding of equality before the law and the prohibition of preferential treatment based on religious grounds as determined in Art. 3 para 3 GG. The explicit commitment is to ensure the inviolable protection of freedom of religion and belief as prescribed under Art. 4 para 1 GG and the guarantee of equal access to the public service independent of religious denomination as affirmed in Art. 33 para 3 GG.

This is further supplemented by articles of the Weimar Constitution, such as the prominent Art. 137 para 1 WRV which establishes the principle of separation between state and church,[137] Art. 136 para 1 WRV, which sustains the guarantee of civil and political rights of the citizens irrespective of pertinence to a certain religion or denomination, and Art. 136 para 4 that ensures the right of every citizen not to participate in religious festivities or worships.

The provisions mentioned heretofore are only a compound of the most distinguishable elements connoting and identifying the duty of the state to religious neutrality. However, it does not constitute a confined list of provisions as elements of the neutrality principle are alluded from other provisions in the Grundgesetz.

(b) Designation in Jurisprudence

In accordance with the foregoing constitutional provisions, the BVerfG has coined the famous term that the state is the 'homeland of all its citizens'.[138] This

---

136 *Wiese*, p. 146; *Huster*, Die ethische Neutralität des Staates: Eine liberale Interpretation der Verfassung, 2002, p. 680 (10).

137 *Czermak*, in: FS Rüfner 2003, pp. 79, 90.

138 BVerfG, Judgement of 14 December 1965; BVerfGE 19 206, 216 = NJW 1966, 147.

demonstrates above all that it is the duty of the state to maintain religious neutrality so it will be averted from identifying itself with a certain religion or sect or aiming to influence in its favour, and at the same time deny similar privileges from other religious groups.

Strikingly, it was only in 1960 that a judgement delivered by the BVerfG mentioned the term 'religious neutrality of the state' for the first time.[139]

Admittedly, the state carries the duty to treat all religions or denominations equally and cannot favour a specific religion, thus eventually amounting to its identification with it. The fact that Germany is no longer a homogenous but rather a pluralistic society supports the sense of an altered concept of neutrality which will be more open and liberal towards different religious confessions and promote them equally.[140] This apprehension was finally affirmed even by the BVerfG in one of its most famous decisions, the Crucifix case.[141]

A far-reaching implementation of the neutrality principle had established the ground for the decision of the BVerfG in *Ludin's* case, determining that the obligation of the state to religious neutrality may collide with the religious freedom of the teacher to wear the headscarf.[142] The criticism with respect to the judgement delivered in Ludin's case raised the claim that the Court has limited this exalted right of religious freedom not against other legal provisions laid down in the constitution itself, but rather in favour of an unwritten principle, (i.e., the principle of religious neutrality). It was disputed that a pre-eminent right such as the right to religious freedom cannot be restricted by the neutrality principle that in itself can be inferred only from sets of norms rooted in the German constitution and is not explicitly designated in it.[143]

---

139 BVerfGE 19, 206, 216 = NJW 1966, 147; BVerfGE 12, 1, 4.

140 BVerfG, Dec. 14, 1965, 1 BvR 413/60, 1 BvR 416/60; BVerfGE 24, 236, 246; BVerfGE 33, 23, 28; BVerfGE 93, 1, 17; BVerfGE 108, 282, 309, 310.

141 BVerfG, May 16, 1995, 1 BvR 1097/81, 93 BVerfGE, 1.

142 BVerfGE 108, 282; BVerfG, NJW 2003, 3111, 3112.

143 *Ganz*, explains that religious neutrality as a precept is not stipulated explicitly in the German constitution pp. 40-41 and refers to the interpretation provided to this precept by the BVerfG in the case of Ludin pp. 206- 207; *Wiese*, pp. 146, 148- 149. A different approach to the neutrality precept and its interpretation holds *Huster* (2002), p. 682. Due to the significance of religious freedom, the Grundgesetz stipulates that the laws that limit religious freedom must comply with special requirements. BVerfGE 32, 98, 107.

(c) Designation in Legal Literature

In legal literature a critic approach was held contending that the neutrality principle had been bloated so that it transcends even those constitutional sets of norms from which it acquires its validity.

Those who dispute the existence of the neutrality principle in the constitution fear that the judiciary will independently initiate further construction of its content and of other similar unwritten principles till they are so embodied by the courts, therewith transcending over other specifications in the constitution. This perception maintains that the optimal balance for restrictions or conflicts between religious freedoms and other constitutional rights or interests needs to be found within the provisions and specifications mentioned explicitly in the constitution itself.

(d) Designation in Common Law

The definition of common law can be understood as the formation of unwritten law which evolved through interpretation of case laws and statutes in the past and which was recognized as common law through its general acceptance and observance over a period of time. The question whether the existence of the state neutrality principle can be inferred from the common law is disputable and in any case there is no indication as to its content and scope.[144]

The contention held partially in the legal constitutional literature[145] proclaims that the driving force behind the establishment of the neutrality principle was the historical development of state-church separation. Similarly, the approach held by the judicator perceived the obligation of the state to remain neutral in aspects of religion as mandatory, since only in such a manner can the state guarantee the co-existence of the different religions in its society.[146] This perception underpinned the notion of state-church separation as it has its roots in the historical evolvement of the German state and its attempts to segregate the church from administrative-organizational affairs. This idea also advocates that the state must refrain from any favouritism of a particular religion so as not to endanger the peaceful co-existence in its society, which is known in the German constitutional terminology as '*Friedensgefährdungsverbot*'.[147]

---

144 Wiese, pp. 156, 158.

145 *Böckenförde*, Staat, Gesellschaft, Freiheit, 1976, pp. 92, et seq.; *Huster* 2002, pp. 47, et seq.; *Wiese*, p. 155.

146 BVerfGE 93, 1, 16.

147 BVerfGE 105, 279, 295; BVerfGE 102, 370, 383; BVerfGE 93, 1, 16; BVerfGE 19, 206, 216.

The question whether the existence of the state neutrality principle can be implicitly inferred from unwritten law and provide a clue as to its substance, i.e., strict or liberal apprehension of the state-neutrality principle, will be examined here briefly. For that purpose, several historical aspects will be considered in order to provide an overview of the grounds for the evolvement of the state neutrality precept and in particular taking into perspective the long lasting political-religious battles to obtain power over state education.

First, as previously mentioned, the church has been playing a leading role in the history of the German state since the Middle Ages,[148] taking control of education, demanding influence over public schooling, and accommodating schools with a salient confessional orientation.[149] Disagreements between the church and the state arose in the early nineteenth century and escalated up to the twentieth century.[150] The controversies focused on the endorsement of religion into public education, whether the nature and character of schools should be confessional or denominational, and lasted even in the modern age; for example, following national unification, it was debated whether religious affairs should be left to the sole discretion of the Federation or lands' parliaments to decide on such matters.[151]

Second, until reformation took place in 1517 the predominant religion in most of the regions of the German state was Catholicism, under the authority of the Holy Roman Empire (*Heiliges Römisches Reich*). However, in the course of the reformation many areas in west, north, and central Europe became protestant. This historical development broke down the religious unity of Christian Catholics that prevailed till the time of the Reformation and presented under German realm (*Reich*) the formal state religion (*Staatsreligion*). In order for the Protestant population not to be excluded from control of the German regime, the state was divided into territories dominated either by the Catholic or Protestant Church. This arrangement was imprinted at a later stage with the famous phrase known as the '*cuius regio, eius religio*' principle. The principle was meant to signify at that time that the rulers of a region are entitled to determine the religion for its population.[152] Each territory was completely controlled by the church, which accordingly had the authority to decide, determine, and administrate its

148 *Heckel*, 1997 pp. 187, 187–188; *Kommers/Miller*, pp. 539–540.

149 *Ladeur*, pp. 2445, 2449;

150 *Kommers/Miller*, pp. 575–576.

151 *Hennecke*, Jahrbuch zur Staats- und Verwaltungswissenschaft 8 (1995), pp. 83, 84–87; *Spotts*, Journal of Church and State 18 (1976), p. 208.

152 *v. Ungern-Sternberg*, 2008, p. 7; *Bloss*, 2008, pp. 29–30.

inner religious affairs on sole discretion and without any disturbance from the central state. In that sense the state kept itself away from religious matters and did not interfere in the functions of the church.

Third, during the era of the German Empire (*Königreich Preußen*),[153] there were different forms of cooperation between the church and its domination over state schools. While at the beginning of the nineteenth century priests and clergy still took active positions with their supervisory authority in almost all educational matters, this privileged position took a turn as of mid-nineteenth century.[154] The attempts to disentangle the church from its supervision over state schools and disempower its interference in educational matters were noticeable and have taken gradually a form; this historical development is known as '*die Entkirchlichung der Schulaufsicht*'.[155] This tendency escalated especially within the period 1871–1878 when the Reich Chancellor, Otto von Bismarck, embarked upon a bitter battle with the Catholic Church in order to confine its political power. A ray of reforms which were introduced not only in the administrative-organizational structure of schools had also taken place in various forms and reached its peak towards the end of the nineteenth century with the famous Cultural War (*Kulturkampf*) between the German Empire (*Kaiserreich*) and the Catholic Church lasting from 1871 to 1887.

Notably, during the time of the Cultural War no mechanism existed to safeguard the right of religious freedom, not to mention its lack of recognition as a personal, individual right. Citizens had no choice of self-discretion and, as a result, were actually practising their religious right in conformity with the determination of the prevalent religion.

This situation was reversed for the first time only in the twentieth century under the Weimar Regime, which had established the secular character of the German state under the Weimar Constitution.[156]

To conclude, the historical evolvement of this state-church separation theory does not deliver a satisfactory content depiction nor does it imply the normative source of this state neutrality principle is to be found in the common law practice.

---

153 The era of the monarchy of Prussia (*Preußen*) was a long one and stretched over the period of time from 1701–1918.

154 *Germann/Wiesner*, pp. 400–401.

155 *Germann/Wiesner*, pp. 400–401.

156 *Kommers/Miller*, pp. 539–540; *Wiese*, p. 157.

The arguments used in the legal literature to negate the existence of a common law practice suggest: first, the fact the Federal Republic of Germany carries a secular nature is the outcome of interminable conflicts between secular and ecclesiastic powers which consequently inscribed the secular state system.[157] Second, even if it would have been regarded as common law practice it still does not provide sufficient ground for the existence of a substantial theory of religious neutrality or its nature (strict or liberal application).[158]

Third, it was purported that famous model of 'cuius regio, eius religio', which was dominating during the confessional wars in the sixteenth century bears no analogy to the fundamental principle of state-church separation as stipulated in the German constitution nowadays.[159] As a result, it remains doubtful whether this form of religious neutrality should be comprehended as common law.

Ultimately, the notion of the neutrality principle in the interpretation of the BVerfG aimed mainly to bring religious-confessional conflicts to an end and prevent their reiteration.[160]

(e) Conclusion

In the Grundgesetz, no explicit stipulation exists of the principle of state neutrality.[161] Nonetheless, this principle was recognized in jurisdictions of the courts[162] and legal literature, which sustained its endorsement in various provisions of

---

157 *Böckenförde*, Staat, Gesellschaft, Freiheit, 1976, pp. 42, et seq.; *Schlaich*, Neutralität als verfassungsrechtliches Prinzip, 1972, pp. 26, et seq.

158 *Huster*, 2002, pp. 51, 679. et seq.; *Müller*, in: Ethel Leonore Behrendt: Rechtsstaat und Christentum, Vol. I, 1982, pp. 443–484.

159 *Huster*, Die etische neutralität des Staates: Eine liberale interpretation der Verfassung, 2017, p. 52; *Schlaich*, p. 31.

160 *Magen*, Staatskirchenrecht als symbolisches Recht, 2003, pp. 35–37. Here Magen brings for support of his contention two exemplary, significant judgements delivered by the BVerfG: 1. The Crucifix and 2. The Headscarf ('*Kopftuch*') to demonstrate the use made under German constitutional law with respect to the interpretation of the neutrality principle as a justifying ground for avoidance of conflicts in the public sphere; *Häußler*, ZAR, 2000, pp. 255, 256; *Morlok*, Selbstverständnis als Rechtskriterium – Vorkommen, Funktionen und dogmatische Bedeutung, 1993, pp. 331, et seq; *Mahlmann*, German Law Journal 4(11) (2004), pp. 1099, 1114.

161 However, this theory of state's neutrality was explicitly pre-determined in the constitution of some of the federal states (Länder), e.g. Art. 131 BayVerf.; Art. 26 BremenVerf.; Art. 56 III HessVerf.; *Wiese*, p. 146.

162 BVerwGE 42, 346, 347.

the Grundgesetz.[163] The most prominent provision in the Grundgesetz which embodies the notion of state neutrality is considered to be Art. 137 para 1 WRV.

It was due to the fact that the state neutrality principle was a creation of the judiciary, gradually developed and implemented by its various instances and mainly the BVerfG, that there is demand among scholars to dispose of the neutrality principle as it is alleged to be simply redundant and deceptive.[164]

Accepting this perception, however, would not only contradict general rules of jurisprudence but would also be inappropriate, as the neutrality principle is not the only constitutional order exclusively inferred from various relationships and sets of values created by the constitution.[165]

A complete disposal would probably merely stymie the further construction and development of the constitution and would not necessarily contribute to a decrease in controversies around this topic. Albeit a parochial view, there is an acceptance of the principle by all various jurisdictions. The controversies surrounding the principle relate more to its content and way of implementation.

Finally, even though the neutrality principle is understood differently and construed by the judiciary in contradiction to the legal literature, there is no ground to ask for its disposal only due to lack of unity in its interpretation.[166]

(3) Different Approaches to the Application of the Neutrality Principle

After the principle of neutrality had been generally recognized as a fundamental and integral precept, which is embedded in the constitution and has an established stand in the legal practice, different approaches and interpretations on its particular application have been developed by the legal literature and judiciary.

The range of positions on the adequate application of the state's neutrality principle is extensive and offers a diverse range of opinions. The approaches

---

163 For the endorsement of neutrality principle in the constitutional discussion and interpretations theories see *Huster (2017)*, p. 29 ff.; *Czermak*, NVwZ 2003, p. 949, et seq.; one of the earliest debates with relation to embodiment of the state's neutrality principle *Papier*, in: FS Scholz (2007), pp. 1123, et seq.; *Ladeur/Augsberg*, Toleranz – Religion – Recht. Die Herausforderung des "neutralen" Staates durch neue Formen der Religiosität in der postmodernen Gesellschaft, 2007, pp. 12, et seq.

164 *Holzke*, NVwZ, 2002, pp. 903, et seq.

165 For example, the rule of law principle inferred from Art. 20 para 3 and Art. 19 para 4 GG.

166 For example, the rule of law 'Rechtsstaatsprinzip' derived from Art. 20 para 3 and Art. 19 para 4 GG; *Wiese*, p. 153.

range from a stricter application on the one hand to the liberal approach on the other hand and some midway positions.[167]

(a) Strict Application of the State's Neutrality Principle

According to the strict approach, any form of cooperation between the state and religion is forbidden. This kind of strict application bans any identification of the state with a particular religion or religious communities in general and, consequently, disposes of its adhesion to all religious-confessional communities.[168] In other words, the separation of state and church must be understood as distancing of the state with respect to religious matters.[169] In this sense, the state must not advance any form of religion.[170] Those in favour of such a narrow interpretation of the law decline any administrative or political entanglement of the state over religious activities and negate the inseparable bond of these joint activities (e.g., church services or worship in hospitals or prisons, religious instruction in public schools).[171]

Such a model of a strict separation between state and church which applies equally to all other religions, beliefs, or denominations is comparable to the French principle of *laïcité*.[172]

---

167 Besides the strict and the liberal approach, other attempts for a structural and dogmatic analysis have been made. The most relevant approaches are (i) an explanation of the neutrality principle by implementing a separation principle, see in: *Huster*, 2017, pp. 635-636; and (ii) a limitation on the guarantee of the right religious freedom will be considered only if it involves limits that are prescribed for fundamental rights of the Grundgesetz, the so called 'limitation of the limits' (i.e.,. *Schranken-Schranke*). Any statutory limitation will be valid if it is sanctioned by other provisions prescribed in the Grundgesetz itself. For instance, the neutrality principle as a legitimate ground for encroachment upon individuals' right to free exercise of religious freedom. See in *Mückl*, Der Staat, 2001, pp. 96, 123–124.

168 BVerwG, NJW 1999, 3063, 3064; *Pottmeyer*, Religiöse Kleidung in der öffentlichen Schule in Deutschland und England, 2011, p. 39; *Huster* (2017), p. 35–37; *Krüger*, Allgemeine Staatslehre, 2nd edn., 1966, pp. 179, 184, 282; *Renck*, JuS (1989), pp. 451, 453, et seq.; *Schlaich*, p. 21, et seq.; 134, et seq., 220, 255, et seq.; *Wiese*, p. 147.

169 *Gerstenberg*, International Journal of Constitutional Law 3(1) (2005), pp. 94, 96.

170 *Krüger*, p. 36; Zezschwitz von, JZ (1966), pp. 337, 340.

171 *Magen*, pp. 37–38; *Morlok* in: Dreier Vol III, Art. 137, WRV, recital 16, et seq.; *Czermak*, NvWZ (2003), pp. 949, 950, et seq; BVerfGE 93, 1, 16; 105, 279, 294.

172 *Brenner*, pp. 264, 270;

(b) Liberal Application of the State's Neutrality Principle

The liberal approach to this principle requires that the state should not obtain any concrete position in favour or to the detriment of a particular religion. Nonetheless, it must take into consideration the right of its citizens or communities to freely develop their religion or confession through a rigorous conveyance of the equality treatment theory to be conceptualized through religious pluralism and diversity.[173] In principle, the liberal approach does not primarily negate that reasonable and adequate room will be conferred to the freedom of religion in public schools. It determines simply the obligation of the state not to practise a concerted influence to the benefit of a confessional or ideological organization/group, nor to assign explicit or implied measures that will lead to its identification with a particular religion or confession.[174]

(c) Discussion of Approaches

Naturally, those notions and views were trying to underpin their stand based on recourse to legal sources, such as provisions in the constitution, common law practice, sets of norms, social-philosophical paradigms, and judgements of the BVerfG.

Accordingly, it needs to be evaluated whether the constitution holds elements supporting the strict approach on neutrality.

(aa) Arguments in Support of the Strict Approach

(aaa) Equality in an Increasingly Pluralistic Society

Supporters of the strict approach conclude its application from the equality treatment principle and, respectively, the state's duty to stay impartial (non-identification theory) when applying the law.[175]

---

173 *Czermak*, in: FS Rüfner 2007, pp. 79, 91; *Gerstenberg*, pp. 94, 96.

174 *Robbers*, ÖARR 2003, pp. 405, 412; BVerfGE 93, 1, 16, et seq.

175 VG Stuttgart, NVwZ 2000, 959; VGH Mannheim, NJW 2001, 2899; BVerwG NJW 2002, 3343; *'Deshalb gewinnt das Neutralitätsgebot mit wachsender kultureller und religiöser Vielfalt – bei einem wachsenden Anteil bekenntnisloser Schüler – zunehmend an Bedeutung und ist nicht etwa im Hinblick darauf aufzulockern, dass die kulturelle, ethnische und religiöse Vielfalt in Deutschland inzwischen auch das Leben in der Schule prägt, wie die Klägerin meint'.* English Translation: *'The principle of religious neutrality gains significance especially in a growing pluralistic society as in particular in public education the state is obliged to demonstrate impartiality, also with respect to its non-believers, and it* cannot *remain indifferent with respect to its duty (i.e., to act neutral and unbiased). The cultural-ethnical and religious diversity which exists in Germany*

This theory fosters the notion that the state itself has neither religion nor does it identifies itself with an ideological denomination or creed. Its 'ideology' yields actually from constitutional rules and principles, which constitute central prerequisites for the state's existence.[176]

Neutrality does not mean that the constitution can be understood or interpreted as favouring Christianity or other religions or non-confessional groups. Plainly, the state should not ascribe itself a religious or anti-religious aura. Moreover, the meaning of neutrality does not even ascribe to it indifference or secularism in the sense of ignoring all other religions.[177] In principle, according to the strict approach, there is a demand for a general ban of all religious symbols from school premises.[178] However, such selective favouring of a strict application of the neutrality principle only focusses on the Muslim headscarf leading to tensions with the principle of equality.[179]

This argument has been recognized by the administrative courts when vindicating its rigid judgement prohibiting headscarves in schools. The courts redefined the neutrality principle with reference to an increasing pluralism in a society which will give rise to the necessity of detraction of the role religion will play in school.

Integration is a key issue in German law on religion nowadays. It is probably the foremost challenge that German jurisdictions and legal literature have had to encounter over the past few years, mainly due to Germany's increasing

---

nowadays has imprinted also its state school system, as stated by the complainant'. (my translation: therefore the state should keep its neutrality also in educational matters).

176 *Czermak*, in: FS Rüfner 2007, pp. 79, 90 (e.g., The Grundgesetz, the right to a free, non-biased process, Art. 79 para 3 GG which guarantees the inviolable principle of the federation division into states).

177 *Renck*, BayVBl (1999), pp. 70, 77, a critic of the traditional application of the law on religion emphasizes the misapprehension of the state's neutrality definition which may be confused with the principle of laicism, indifference, and strict separation; *Czermak*, in: FS Rüfner 2007, pp. 79, 90, et seq., 91.

178 *Mahrenholz*, pp. 749, 755; *Goerlich*, NJW (1999), pp. 2929, 2933; *Janz/Rademacher*, NVwZ (1999), pp. 706, 711.

179 It is, however, remarkable that among supporters of a stricter implementation of the state's neutrality principle there are several who demand the explicit general ban of the headscarf as a religious symbol. BVerwG, JZ 2004, 1178, 1179, et seq.; BVerwG, ZBR 2003, 37, 38, et seq.

Islamic population, but also due to the growth of other religious groups and non-religious philosophical organizations.[180]

This dilemma was even highlighted in Ludin's case delivered by the BVerfG, and indirectly raised the question regarding the capability of the Grundgesetz to adapt itself to ongoing social changes. The Court held the view that an increase in religious pluralism in a society occurring due to a social change (i.e., demographic dispersal, volume of certain religious organizations and their composition, etc.) can serve as sufficient grounds for a new stipulation determining the permissible scope of religious emblems in state schools.[181]

It was mainly due to this overgrowing plurality of religions that in Ludin's case even the Administrative Court declared a new definition of the term religious neutrality, which is respectively to be comprehended as the obligation of the state to a strict application of the neutrality principle.

In fact, the lower instances considered the diversity of religious or confessional groups and even of non-religious, philosophical organizations as a factor impairing the role of religious symbols in state-supported schools, thus justifying their approach for a stricter application of the neutrality principle.[182]

Meanwhile, there has been an attempt to construe religious pluralism as a dogma with roots already entrenched in the constitution through a re-course to social-philosophical perception. This perception makes a reference with relation to the debate regarding integration of religious minorities in a democratic state. In fact, this notion establishes the bond between religion and integration through this social-philosophical perception.

It determines that the extent of protection offered to religious minorities who wish to keep their religious identity should be evaluated based on a balance of prospects that such an integration will eventually be successful.[183]

Correspondingly, this perception holds the view that integration of the individual and its success are of major significance and are a crucial condition for

180 *Anger*, KritV (2005), pp. 52, 65; *Mahrenholz*, p. 143; *Mann*, Das Kopftuch der muslimischen Lehrerin (Lehramtsanwärterin) als Eignungsmangel im Beamtenrecht, 2004, p. 143; *Weber*, ZAR (2004), pp. 53, 54.

181 BVerfG, NJW 2003, 3111, 3115 '*Der mit zunehmender religiöser Pluralität verbundene gesellschaftliche Wandel kann Anlass zu einer Neubestimmung des zulässigen Ausmaßes religiöser Bezüge in der Schule sein*'.

182 BVerwG, ZBR 2003, 37, 38.

183 *Wiese*, p. 159.

the chances of better integration of the whole (a particular) religious group in a society.[184]

In other words, should the state prohibit the admittance of a teacher with a headscarf into school, this would have the negative effect of failure of integration, not only on the individual level but also on a community level for the entire religious group.

(bbb) The Constitutional Prohibition of State-Church Relations

The fact that Germany retains no established church-state relations strengthens proponents in the legal literature who sustain that this constitutional state of affairs of strict separation between state and church form the source from which the neutrality principle derives its existence.[185]

Art. 137 in tandem with 141 WRV prohibit the establishment of a state-church and prescribes in Art. 137 para 1 the 'no-state-church principle'. In fact, this constitutes the legal source for the principle of state neutrality and the notion of separation of the state from interference in religious matters. This institutional separation between state and church can be inferred from other provisions in the constitution. Art. 137 para 3 WRV guarantees the autonomy of religious societies and enables religious communities the right to maintain and regulate their inner administration without any governmental interference. Moreover, the constitutional autonomy of religious societies and their special status obtain significance especially due to their ability to ask for recognition as a public corporation and, as a result, benefit from all privileges attached to it (Art. 137 para 5).

(bb) Arguments in Support of the Liberal Approach

The preamble of the German constitution describes Germany's commitment to religious freedom.[186] As a result and in contrast to the notion shared by supporters of the strict application approach underlying their contention based on the words of Art. 137 para 1 WRV, supporters of the liberal approach contend that the Grundgesetz's primary effect must neither advance (in the sense of its identification with a particular religion) nor inhibit religion. It is rather a comprehensive liberal form of neutrality which enables and encourages the self-determination and development of the different religions in society.[187]

---

184 *Wiese*, p. 159; *Langenfeld*, Integration und kulturelle Identität zugewanderter Minderheiten, 2001, p. 575.

185 *Fischer*, Volkskirche Ade! Trennung von Staat und Kirche, 4th ed, p. 18; *Janz/Rademacher*, NVwZ 1999, pp. 706, 707.

186 *Robbers*, 2001, pp. 643, 645.

187 *Böckenförde*, NJW (2001), pp. 723, 725; *Robbers*, RdJB 51. Jahrgang, 1/2003, pp. 11, 19.

To exemplify, based on the equality precept the Grundgesetz permits every religious community to provide for religious instruction in state-supported schools[188] and permits churches as public corporations[189] to tax their members.[190] Apart from that, the state is obligated to provide for subventions for clergy's teachers' education including theology faculties in universities.[191] Likewise, the aspect of education and further educational training (*Aus – und Fortbildung der Geistlichen*) for dissemination university chairs in particular theology for their clergy had been perceived as a central activity of the Church. Therefore, for the studies of science of religion and pedagogic studies of religion, clergy are supported by the church so they are not nominated merely by the state but rather with the consent of the church and in accordance with its ethical rules.[192]

Indeed, the task of public education does not end with the conveyance of specific knowledge to children. School authorities have the task of developing and cultivating the personality of the children and this includes forming a personality within a religious life. The confrontation of children with different ideas, confessions, or beliefs will make them more open, integrative, and tolerant. As such, the state must also accommodate the religious needs of children.

Thus, it is only evident that the introduction of those provisions into the Grundgesetz does not necessarily indicate their contradiction to the explicit state-church prohibition as stated in Art. 137 para 1 of the WRV. In fact, Art. 137 WRV is the only explicit regulation supporting a strict approach of the state's neutrality.

---

188 Art. 7 para 3 GG provides: 'Religious instruction shall form part of the curriculum in state schools except non-denominational schools. Without prejudice to the state's right of supervision, religious instruction shall be given in accordance with the doctrine of the religious community concerned. Teachers may not be obliged to give religious instruction against their will'. *Heckel*, 1997, pp. 187, 198–200.

189 Art. 140 GG, Art. 137 para 5 WRV.

190 *Palmer*, pp. 40, 46, 47; Art. 140 GG, Art. 137 para 6 WRV.

191 *Ladeur*, pp. 2445, 2449; *Spotts*, p. 192.

192 *Bloss*, 2008, pp. 198–199. It was argued that Art. 173 para 3 WRV prescribes that religious communities administer and organize their own activities 'eigenen Angelegenheiten'. It was explained that although it is highly controversial to decide which activities are included within the competency of religious communities a reference is made to a list suggested by von *Campenhausen* in order to reach some guidance and support. An activity which is regarded to be a main task of the church is the propagation of clergy for teaching and further vocational training; *Heckel*, 1997, pp. 187, 193, 198; *Heckel*, Emory Int'l L. Rev. 10 (1996), pp. 107, 108; *Hennecke*, p. 83, 86.

Furthermore, in no case could such a strict separation of state and church be inferred from the plain words of the Grundgesetz and, apart from that, no substantial evidence had been presented in its support.

The key issue upheld by supporters of the liberal implementation of the neutrality principle emphasizes rather the obligation of the state to remain neutral in its acts in the sense that it will allow its individuals to freely exercise their religious freedom and, at the same time, in order to preserve its unbiased position it should apply equal measures to all religions and confessions.[193]

The supporters of the liberal approach argue that fundaments of this religious neutrality principle are to be found in the various provisions of the Grundgesetz, which respectively takes its implementation into consideration whenever competency or act of the state collide with other competing religious/anti-religious rights or interests (Art. 4 para 1, Art. 3 para 3, Art. 6 para 2, Art. 33 para 3 GG).

In comparison to the overriding stricter approach, which was dominant among the administrative courts, the BVerfG preferred the adoption of an ample, forthright comprehension of the state's neutrality principle and did not demand a strict separation between state and church.[194]

That means the BVerfG follows the liberal approach.

To exemplify, the establishment of confessional schools (Christian denominated) and the endorsement of prayers in schools were admitted by the BVerfG.[195] This position of the BVerfG was espoused further in two other famous decisions which, however, resulted in a different outcome. In the famous Crucifix decision[196] it approved removal of the crucifix only following an objection from parents or pupils, eventually deciding for removal of the crucifix from the appellants' classroom due to the non-identification precept which mandates the duty of the state to appear neutral in its actions. A similar approach was later affirmed in the judgement of Ludin's case delivered in 2003.[197] The BVerfG found no reason to prohibit the teacher from wearing a headscarf while on duty; however, due to absence of authorization by law it avoided the delivery of a final verdict on the matter. Pursuant to this liberal attitude, it was asserted in Ludin's case that the state should stay impartial and not identify itself with a particular

193 *Robbers*, ÖARR 2003, pp. 405, 412; *Czermak*, in: FS Rüfner 2007, pp. 79, 91; BVerfG, NJW 2003, 3111, 3113; *Wiese*, p. 148.

194 BVerfGE 52, 223, 238, et seq.; BVerwG, NJW 1999, 3063, 3064.

195 BVerfGE 52, 223, 238, et seq., 240, et seq.; 41, 29, 46, et seq., 49.

196 BVerfGE 93, 1, et seq.

197 BVerfG, NJW 2003, 3111, 3113.

religion or confession.[198] Nevertheless, the state should at least foster incorporation and development of the different confessions or religions of its citizens, based on a stricter enforcement of the equal treatment principle.[199]

The BVerfG elaborated the risk it foresees should the neutrality principle not be implemented in accordance with the liberal approach. It determined that the state must not practise a concerted influence in favour of a particular political, religious, or confessional organization, nor must it take measures that may appear as an explicit or implied identification with a particular religion. It was explained that it may bear the inevitable consequence of endangering the peaceful co-existence of various religions in the German society[200] (e.g., the state must not jeopardize highly valued norms like public safety or public order).

This approach is coherent to the decision of the Lüneburg Administrative Court, which presumed no obligation of the state to the adherence of a stricter application of the neutrality principle, hence allowing a teacher to wear the headscarf during school time.[201] This approach was even subsequently fostered by the BVerfG when delivering its verdict on the matter.

As a matter of fact, one can consequently say that an overall, abstract ban on a teacher from wearing the headscarf will not avail without distinguishing between the exceptional circumstances particular to each case. Such a determination stipulates a separate individual introspection, adjustable according to the exceptional characteristics of each case. Despite this liberal position, it was underscored by the BVerfG in Ludin's case that although a general ban on the teacher from wearing the headscarf cannot be comprehensively accepted without reviewing the circumstances particular to each case, this does not inevitably necessitate that plurality of cultures and confessions in school will permanently pursue a liberal implementation of the state's neutrality principle.

---

198 More with respect to the non-identification theory of the state in: BVerfGE 105, 279, 295; *Debus*, Das Verfassungsprinzip der Toleranz unter besonderer Berücksichtigung der Rechtsprechung des Bundesverfassungsgerichts, 1999, p. 114; *Isak*, p. 195; *Krüper*, Jahrbuch des öffentlichen Rechts 53 (2005), pp. 79, 109; *Morlok*, in: Dreier Vol III, Art. 140, recital 36; *Morlok*, p. 332; *Püttner*, Toleranz als Verfassungsprinzip – Prolegomena zu einer rechtlichen Theorie des pluralistischen Staates, 1976, p. 17; *Schlaich*, p. 236.

199 *Isak*, pp. 197, et seq.; *Meyer-Teschendorf*, ZevKR 23, pp. 216, et seq.; *Schlaich*, p. 242; *Wiese*, p. 149.

200 BVerfG, NJW 2003, 3111, 3113.

201 VG Lüneburg, NJW 2001, 767, 769.

Remarkably, when determining in Ludin's case the lower courts implemented a creative interpretation of the liberal approach which stood in contrast to the view held later on by the BVerfG. The administrative courts of Stuttgart[202] and Mannheim,[203] though in principle adopting the comprehensive, liberal approach of the neutrality principle in Ludin's case, still determined that an abstract prohibition on the teacher from appearing with a headscarf would be allowed without even the need to refer to the distinctive, specific relevant details of the particular conflict.[204]

(cc) Consideration of Approaches

At the time of delivery of Ludin's judgement, it still remained doubtful whether the BVerfG would purport to straighten line with this new principle of neutrality and follow a similar approach to that of the lower instances when coming to determine the case. Yet, in the legal literature there was an assertion expressing a hope that the conflict around the headscarf would rather be differently addressed by the BVerfG when outweighing competing rights based on the principle of '*praktische Konkordanz*'.[205]

This view yielded as a resonance to the rigid implementation of this principle made by the Administrative Court in the Ludin's case.[206] The Court had to outweigh the (negative) rights of pupils and parents against the (positive) right of the teacher to wear the headscarf during school time and decided that a general acceptance of the headscarf when a teacher applies for a vacancy in the public sector until the pupils or parents raise an objection is unacceptable. The Court made no attempt to find out whether an inadmissible influence was exerted by the teacher, and finally decided to negate the right of the teacher to wear the headscarf based on the principle of '*praktische Konkordanz*'.[207]

For this reason, critics reproached the BVerfG for its favourable approach towards the liberal implementation of the neutrality principle. It was argued that the BVerfG was mistaken when admitting its endorsement into the Grundgesetz through an amplified construction enabling it to prevail a constitutional right

---

202 VG Stuttgart, DÖV 2000, 561, 562.

203 VGH Mannheim, NJW 2001, 2899.

204 VG Stuttgart, NVwZ 2009, 959, 961; *Brenner*, pp. 264, 284; *Kästner*, in: FS Heckel (1999), pp. 359, 365; *Mückl*, pp. 96, 124; *Marre*, in: FS Rüfner (2003), pp. 552, 567.

205 *Mahrenholz*, pp. 749, 752; more on the principle of *praktische Konkordanz* in this chapter under II c) dd).

206 VG Stuttgart, NVwZ 2000, 959.

207 VG Stuttgart, NVwZ, 2000, 959, 960.

(the right of a teacher to exercise her religious freedom) explicitly guaranteed in the constitution (Art. 4 GG).[208]

Essentially, such a strict construction of the law is incompatible with the spirit of the constitution. In particular, Art. 137 para 1 WRV cannot be read so narrowly as such a conception stands predominantly contrary to Art. 7 para 3 and para 5 GG and the rest of the provisions in the Weimar constitution. Otherwise, a compliance with such an interpretation will make those provisions unconstitutional.

Finally, this kind of confined cooperation between two institutions, namely, the state facilitating religious instructions in public schools and the relevant religious communities enabled to define their content and remain within their competency, does not contravene the constitution in its conclusive form. The state is merely obliged to make religious instruction adequately available and guarantee the children's free participation in it.

This way, there is nothing to provide or indicate the inseparable bond between state and church or the endangering of their existence as independent institutions. It is, as a matter of fact, a two-institution system.

In that sense, the presumption that some provisions in the Grundgesetz are unconstitutional or exceeding the scope of state neutrality would be regarded as erroneous.

Despite the explanation delivered in support of the liberal approach, those who opine the liberal perception claim that the Grundgesetz cannot establish the definition of neutrality principle based on a social-philosophical perception derived from a social-philosophical interpretation of the constitution. The reason for that emanates from the need to establish the neutrality principle based on constitutional norms. These constitutional norms are normally characterized by nature with a protective approach, meaning a higher impact in favour of the rights safeguarded in the constitution (e.g., religious freedom).

Eventually, this social-philosophical perception did not present a solid ground established on imprinted constitutional norms, so as to enable the state to confine religious freedom based on plurality of religions in a society.

By no means can this perception justify its legitimacy in the legal literature if it cannot establish an affinity to an explicit provision or norm inscribed in the constitution.

An increasing plurality of religions and the consequence it bears cannot be completely out-factored from the educational sphere in a modern, globalized society. However, due to a lack of explicit reference in the constitution it cannot

208 BVerfG, NJW 2003, 3111, 3112.

be read into the constitution through conferment of new interpretation to the definition of state neutrality (see Ludin's case) nor through a re-course to a social-philosophical perception as suggested by some scholars.

Naturally, religious pluralism can be regarded by the courts as a factor to be outweighed against other constitutional values when coming to determine on issues of religious freedom in the educational system. Nevertheless, a consistent implementation of religious pluralism combined utterly with the narrow, strict definition of religious neutrality will not only be disproportionate but also unconstitutional to the aim it sought to achieve (i.e., the free exercise of positive religious freedom).

To sum up, the judgements delivered by the various instances with relation to neutrality of state provide no clear estimation as to the desired approach to be adopted by the jurisprudence. This results in lack of consistency and inability to align the case laws in accordance with an established judicial interpretation of the state neutrality principle. This leads further to vagueness which already exists with respect to controversies surrounding the admissibility of religious symbols in public education.

cc) The Principle of Practical Concordance/Das Prinzip der Praktischen Konkordanz

The principle of practical concordance prescribes that constitutionally protected legal principles and values must be harmonized with each other when they come into conflict.[209] Since all constitutional principles emerge from the Grundgesetz, there is a need to outweigh competing values against each other so that no constitutional value will override another competing constitutional value.[210] The preservation of constitutional values and their outweighing against each other is a specific mechanism developed by the BVerfG for that purpose, and is known as the principle of 'practical concordance' (*praktische Konkordanz*). This term has been taken from the German constitutional law. It was coined in the legal system by a Federal Constitutional Court Justice, Konrad Hesse, and has been established in the prevailing constitutional debate.

The meaning of the principle is to be read as follows: 'Constitutional protected values must be assigned to each other while trying to provide a solution to a problem, so that each of them will accomplish its objectives. … every principle

---

209 *Kommers/Miller*, p. 67.

210 *Kommers/Miller*, pp. 67–68.

will have to set its boundaries in order for them both to attain maximum efficaciousness'.[211]

In fact, the principle is an interpretive creation of the judiciary purporting to solve conflicts between competing rights or interests in order to find an adequate settlement that will benefit and conform to the interests of all parties to the greatest possible extent.[212] It is based on a proportionality measure test, which tends to review the aims, means, and effects of a reviewed state practice that impairs relevant protected interests (e.g., religious freedom of the teacher (Art. 4 GG) against the educative supervision of the state (Art. 7 para 1 GG).

When the courts encounter issues relating to the impingement of religious liberty rights they need to define on the first level what the interests protected under the Grundgesetz are and whether the infringement is adequate in order to achieve the purported aim, or if it is only a preferential practice. On the second level, the courts will strive to reach a settlement between the conflicting interests while ensuring that no disproportionate and excessive solutions take place while giving one right or interest preference over the other.[213] In that sense, the proportionality test requires that the limitation of one value will not exceed that which is necessary to maintain a concordance of both legal values.

The implementation of the practical concordance has been sustained in several significant judgements delivered by the BVerfG dealing with prominent conflicts relating to church-state relations.[214] The purpose of the principle of practical concordance is to ensure a proper evaluation and reconciliation of the competing interests so that both will be adequately and maximally implemented (an 'optimization rule').[215] However, at the same time it is the task of the court to observe whether an infringement of a constitutional protected interest will not

---

211 *Hesse*, Grundzüge des Verfassungsrechts der Bundesrepublik Deutschland 20 ed. 1999, p. 30; *Kommers/Miller*, p. 68. Translation in German: '*Verfassungsrechtlich geschützte Rechtsgüter müssen in der Problemlösung einander so zugeordnet werden, dass jedes von ihnen Wirklichkeit gewinnt. …beiden Gütern müssen Grenzen gesetzt werden, damit beide zu optimaler Wirksamkeit gelangen können*'.

212 *Zacharias,* Neuere Entwicklungen im Religionsrecht europäischer Staaten 61 (2013), pp. 859, 872–873.

213 *Beatty*, Am. J.Comp.L., 49 (2001), pp. 79, 81.

214 The School prayers case, BVerfGE 52, 223, the Crucifix case, BVerGE 93, 1.

215 'Konflikte zwischen der Glaubensfreiheit und anderen verfassungsrechtlichen geschützten Gütern sind nach dem Grundsatz praktischer Konkordanz zu lösen, der fördert, dass nicht eine der wiederstreitenden Rechtspositionen bevorzugt und maximal behauptet wird, sondern alle einen möglichst schönenden Ausgleich erfahren'. See in BVerfGE 93,1 = NJW 1995, 2477; *Stern*, in: Stern, Staatsrecht I, p. 133; *Hesse*,

exceed the necessary measure required in order to achieve effectiveness of the other competing interest.

In this context, the BVerfG has already determined that a constitution has an inner logical unity and that no clause or provision may be interpreted independently, but rather with relation to all other clauses and provisions of the constitution as a whole.[216]

Taken as a unit, where the meaning of one part is linked to that of the other provisions, a constitution reflects certain overarching principles and fundamental precepts to which individual provisions are subordinate. In this sense, the judiciary acknowledged the existence of a higher law transcending positive law which consequently binds even the framers of the constitution and legislators.[217] The designation of predominant provisions and their special transcendent status even finds its support in Art. 79 para 3 GG. It demonstrates the absolute supremacy of the Grundgesetz over ordinary law and even international treaties.[218]

The BVerfG declared[219] that from this rule of interpretation (i.e., structural unity of the Grundgesetz) it follows that even a particular constitutional provision or constitutional amendment which is found to be in conflict with higher law or those overarching fundamental principles of the Grundgesetz may be judged as unconstitutional.[220]

Consequently, the Court does not decline the possibility of declaring a constitutional provision to be null and void only because it is a part of the constitution. The Court determines that there are constitutional principles that are so fundamental and so much an expression of a law that they obtain precedence even over other constitutional precepts. Those pre-eminent provisions, due to their highly ranked positions, bind also the framers of the constitution, while

---

Grundzüge des Verfassungsrechts der Bundesrepublik Deutschland, 20th edn., 1999, recital 72, 317, et seq.

216 *Kommers/Miller*, pp. 56–57, 63, 68, 82; The structural unity of the Grundgesetz (Basic Law) as a judicial interpretive method had been established by the BVerfG in the Southwest State Case (*Südweststaat*) BVerfGE 1, 14 paras. 76, 79. See in http://www.servat.unibe.ch/dfr/bv001014.html

217 *Kommers/Miller*, pp. 63, 82.

218 *Kommers/Miller*, pp. 58–59, 76, 82.

219 See the Southwest State Case (*Südweststaat*) BVerfGE 1, 14 paras 91, 92.

220 *Kommers/Miller*, pp. 56–57, 82, 84; *Youngs*, English, French and German Comparative Law, 3rd. edn. 2014, p. 6.

other constitutional provisions which do not rank so high may be null and void because they contravene these pre-eminent principles.

This emanates that any constitutional provision must be interpreted in a manner that is compatible with those distinguished principles and with the fundamental decisions of the framers of the constitution.[221]

d) Assessment of the Legal System

In Germany, the legal source providing the guarantee of fundamental rights and regulation of state-church affairs is to be found in its constitution, the Grundgesetz. The most significant provision in the Grundgesetz safeguarding the freedom of religion, belief, and conscience is laid down in Art. 4. By virtue of its protection in the highest rank of a constitutional document, the right to religious freedom obtains the status of a pre-eminent protected right. Though the right to religious freedom is specified in other legal sources, it will not be conferred the same protection as provided in the constitutional text.

The right to religious freedom constitutes a fundamental human right which is not only laid down in a constitutional document but has its origins in other normative sources, such as the individual states' constitutions and ordinary legislation of the individual federal states, and the common law developed through interpretational jurisprudence of the BVerfG. Due to the unique federative structural system in Germany, the federal legislators of the individual states are bound by the precepts of Art. 4 when enacting laws affecting religious rights. By virtue of their obligation to obey the wording of the Grundgesetz (Art. 83 GG), it is the task of the individual states' legislators to ensure compliance of ordinary laws and legislation with Art. 4 GG, which otherwise may be considered incompatible (*unvereinbar*) by the BVerfG.

The German approach perceives religious freedom as a positive freedom. This implies the obligation of the state to grant its citizens adequate room for the practice of their religion and provide all religions sufficient space to flourish. Therefore, the constitutional guarantee of religious freedom is granted not only to individuals; rather, it has a far-reaching scope which confers institutional guarantees and privileges for churches and other religious communities incorporated mainly through provisions of the 1919 Weimar Constitution.

It is due to its pre-eminent position in the Grundgesetz that the constitutional safeguarding of the right to religious freedom is made without any reservations. This unreserved (*vorbehaltlos*) characteristic does not allow the limitation of

221 *Kommers/Miller*, pp. 63, 82.

religion by ordinary law. The absence of a reservation clause mandates that it can be limited only by other rights and values prescribed in the constitution itself. The infringement of the right to religious freedom can, thence, be justified only if it contravenes specific freedoms anchored in the German constitution (e.g., human dignity,[222] freedom of general action,[223] equal protection[224] etc.). A contradiction between Art. 4 and other values of constitutional rank will be resolved through outweighing of the conflicting interests, which will be assessed based on the value system of the Grundgesetz so as to eventually merit prevalence over the right to religious freedom ('practical concordance').

The German legislator safeguards religious freedom through its embodiment as a liberty right in the Grundgesetz (Art. 4). Liberty rights aim at driving back the state's influence on the individual sphere. This defensive approach has been favoured by the legislator as a reaction to Germany's totalitarian history and is intended to prevent its reoccurrence.

Therefore, religious freedom is also guaranteed and mostly supplemented through other constitutional provisions, thus fortifying further the right as comprised in Art. 4. These provisions underlie considerable principles which are entrenched in Germany's constitutional system and establish the obligation of the state to non-identification; in addition, they ensure even-handed treatment of all religious communities within its geographical scope. In practice, Art. 4 GG will be discussed in the jurisprudence mainly in correlation with equality rights (Art. 3 and Art. 33 GG) as well as provisions from the Weimar Constitution prohibiting the establishment of an official church (Art. 140 in tandem with 136 para 1 and 137 para 1 WRV).

The protection of equality rights (Art. 3 and 33 GG) in the Grundgesetz has a supplementary and supportive function to individuals' claims invoking the right to protection of their religious freedom. In principle, the equality provisions do not constitute the main path when substantiating a claim for violation of religious freedom. However, they indirectly guarantee religious freedom by prohibiting discrimination of specific beliefs or religions in relation to the majority's faith.

Alongside this, there are constitutional principles, such as the principle of neutrality and the principle of practical concordance, which have been in part established by the legislator, have found their anchorage in several provisions of the Grundgesetz, and were developed in part by the BVerfG.

222 Art. 1 GG.
223 Art. 2 GG.
224 Art. 3 GG.

In principle, the neutrality principle was termed to depict the separation between state and church. It underlies the prohibition of the establishment of a state-church system and, though not explicitly mentioned in the Grundgesetz, it is to be inferred from it. Though there is no specific embodiment of the neutrality principle in the constitution, its existence has not been negated in the jurisprudence and legal literature; rather, its normative source, content, and ways of interpretation have been the subject of controversy. This yielded the core for controversies surrounding the application and interpretation of the neutrality principle that was either to comply with a strict form of state-church separation or embody the liberal approach that finds anchorage not only in the Grundgesetz but also adapts itself to new challenges the German state had encountered over the last centuries (i.e., confrontation with majority of (non-Christian) immigrants, plurality of religions etc.).

According to German jurisprudence, as well as the legal literature, the principle has its roots in Art. 137 para 1 WRV which constitutes the counterpart to Art. 4 GG. This provision establishes the 'no state-church precept', and as such is considered to found the basis for the regulation of the relations between state and church, which incorporates the notion of strict separation. This means, according to proponents of the strict separation approach, that the state must comply with two other precepts emanating from it: first, *non-identification* – the state must not identify itself with a specific religion; second, *non-intervention* – the state must not advance a particular religion and should guarantee the right of religious communities to self-determination.

In favour of the strict implementation of the neutrality principle in practice were the administrative courts, which perceived the task of the state as remaining neutral in its approach and not demonstrating any affinity to a particular religion nor the advancement of it in any form. This approach established itself based on Art. 137 para 1 WRV that prohibits the institutional incorporation between state and church as well as the constitutional demand for equality of all citizens and the demand for equality treatment in the civil service (Art. 3 para 3 and 33 para 3 GG). This apprehension translated into the controversy surrounding the endorsement of religious emblems into the public school system, as exemplified in the Ludin's case. The admissibility of a Muslim teacher to appear with a headscarf in school was held by the administrative courts to collide with the obligation of the state to appear neutral in its actions. In that view, the teacher is perceived as a state representative and bears special obligations emanating from his/her duty as a civil servant to appear neutral and unbiased. This requires that no introduction of ostentatious symbols like the headscarf should be allowed into school premises.

Proponents of the liberal approach, on the other hand, perceive at the outset the admittance of an adequate and reasonable room for religion and its exercise in public education. In principle, the liberal approach does not foster any identification with a specific religion, but it also does not require to inhibit religion. This notion enfolds a comprehensive liberal apprehension of neutrality in the sense that enables religion a sphere to flourish and guarantees religious communities the right to self-determination as safeguarded in the constitution. It lays its fundament in various provisions in the Grundgesetz which recognize the inseparable bond between state and religion, namely, the obligatory religious instruction (Art. 7 para 3 GG) in state schools which are to be conducted by the responsible religious community, and the recognition of religious communities as public corporations (Art. 173 para 5 WRV).

The liberal approach recognizes the task of the state to enable an individual to freely exercise his/her religion and obey the precepts prescribed by his/her faith so that he/she can act and behave in accordance with his/hers internal conviction. This includes the obligation of the state to foster the cultural personality of pupils, including the accommodation of their religious needs within the framework of public education. By that the state should apply equal measures with respect to all religions in order to maintain its unbiased position.

The liberal approach was adopted and fostered by the BVerfG in many case laws. For instance, the establishment of Christian confessional schools and the endorsement of religious prayers in state schools were admitted by the BVerfG. In the Ludin's case it affirmed the right of a Muslim teacher to appear with a headscarf in school in the absence of specific legislation prohibiting manifestation thereof. However, in the Crucifix decision the BVerfG upheld that the state should refrain from practising a concerted influence in favour of a particular religion or any identification with religion that may jeopardize the existence of other pre-eminent values (e.g., peaceful co-existence in school, public order, or safety). This was followed by application of the practical concordance, i.e., weighing the competing constitutional values against each other.

One can say that the arising debate with respect to the application of the neutrality principle in context of the admissibility of religious emblems into public education has evolved around its interpretation and application (strict or liberal). As demonstrated above, the opinion in the jurisprudence and of legal scholars as to its strict or liberal implementation seems to be divided. Albeit diverging opinions, supporters of either the strict or liberal approaches base their positions on reference to specific provisions in the constitution itself.

German courts were particularly eager to maintain compliance with Art. 4 GG. Therefore, Art. 4 is very unique in its application as it may be invoked in order to protect positive as well as negative religious freedom. This is known as the 'double-edged sword' effect, as the same precept may be used to safeguard religious rights of one party on the one hand, while, on the other hand, it accepts an encroachment on the religious rights of others. Given the case that the courts are approached with constitutional disputes, they are under obligation to confer an interpretation to the contradicting statutes so as to conform as much as possible to the Grundgesetz.

This was established by the BVerfG as the fundamental tenet of interpretation (*Verfassungskonforme Auslegung*). Germany's highest constitutional court prefers the interpretive model when asked to elaborate and extend the meaning of the constitution. A very eminent illustration is the elaboration of constitutional principles, such as the 'practical concordance' or state neutrality, which are a judicial creation of the BVerfG and inherent in the constitutional jurisprudence.[225]

To sum up, the legal framework establishing the fundament for the role of religion in the education system derives at the federal-national level mainly from the Grundgesetz, including provisions incorporated from the German Weimar constitution of 1919.

The right to religious freedom is unreserved, which means that it cannot be limited by any regular law, but rather only against another constitutional law purporting to protect public interests inscribed in the constitution itself. The Grundgesetz acknowledges and respects as a protected interest the institution of marriage and family and as a result safeguards parental right to determine on the religious education of their children (Art. 6 and 7 para 2 GG). The encroachment of other constitutional rights must enfold a protected legal value. The reconciliation of the competing rights at stake is subject to constitutional interpretation of the BVerfG (practical concordance) in order to justify the overriding of a protected interest over another (e.g., the fundamental right of a teacher to wear a religious garb or symbol (Art. 4 GG) while in class against the parental right to decide on the education of their children (Art. 6 para 2 GG)).

In practice, claims invoking violation of Art. 4 GG will generally tend to incorporate the equality principles (Art. 3 or Art. 33) or other provisions from the Weimar Constitution such as the 'no state-church' precept (Art. 137 para 1 WRV) as attentive and supplementary to each other.

All this demonstrates the eminent and distinguishable position religious freedom has attained in Germany's constitutional law.

---

225 See in detail the principle of neutrality in this chapter under headline 2c)bb)(b) and the principle of practical concordance under headline 2c)cc).

3. England

Like many other European countries, the United Kingdom,[226] predominantly a Christian nation, had undergone considerable social, ethnical, and cultural changes incurred due to waves of immigration in the 1990s which brought into Europe a growth of religious pluralism in general and of Islam in particular.[227] These sociological changes induced liberal immigration policies launched by the British government since the 1950s and eventually affected the law [228] in formation and promulgation of future legislation that had to correspond to a new legal situation. The British legislator could not ignore a necessary adaption of the anachronistic legislation that still conformed to the Christian character of the state[229] and, as a result, delved into increase of new laws intended to protect religion and to expand the regulation on religion.[230]

The contemporary extensive ethnic, cultural, and religious diversity of the population of England and Wales has posed a major challenge for the government in developing a new legal framework that will accommodate those religious differences,[231] especially under education law. This involved not only aspects relating to curriculum content, for instance in regulating religious education and collective worship in state supported schools, but also the legal position of teachers and school staff with regards to religious dress and symbols sought response under English law. The issue of displaying the Islamic veil detracted public debates from all parts of society,[232] in particular when worn by Muslim

---

226 Though sovereignty merged Wales, Scotland, and Northern Ireland to form the United Kingdom, each territory has its own constitutional arrangements and separate jurisdictions so the text in this analysis will refer solely to England and Wales.

227 *Sandberg*, in: Hunter-Henin, Law, Religious Freedoms and Education in Europe, 2011, pp. 327, 330; *Davie*, The Hedgehog Review 8 (2006), pp. 5, 33.

228 *Fetzer/Soper*, Muslims and the State in Britain, France, and Germany, 2005, p. 30.

229 See in detail in Chapter III 3. C) aa). For instance, The Education Act 1944; The Education Reform Act 1988.

230 This trend was referred to in legal literature as the 'juridification of religion' see, *Sandberg*, in: Hunter-Henin, Law, Religious Freedoms and Education in Europe, 2011, pp. 327, 330; and more extensively elaborated in *Sandberg*, Law and Religion, Chapter 10, 2011.

231 Meredith, Yearbook of the European Association for Education Law and Policy 6 (2006), pp. 155, 156.

232 *Liederman-Molokotos*, Islam and Christian – Muslim Relations 11(1) (2000), p. 105; *Meredith*, in: Lopez-Muniz/De Groof/Lauwers, Religious Education in Public Schools, 2006, p. 155.

pupils (*jilbab, niqab*)[233] as this involved the accommodation of religious garments or symbols in school uniform policies. However, teachers, unlike pupils, are not subject to school uniform policies and, in addition, are subject to different set of rules; therefore, they are offered different legislative protection in terms of their right to display their religious belief. This provides an explanation as to why there are barely case laws found under English law with respect to the legal position of teachers to religious manifestation.

The fact that Britain is no longer a homogeneous Christian nation, but has rather transformed into a multi-faith society which has to guarantee religious liberty to all its citizens[234] made it no easy task for the legislator who had to adjust legal regulations to the dynamics of a pluralistic society.

Albeit the fact that freedom of religion and worship is a fundamental feature of Britain's constitutional traditions and constitutes an integral part of its legal system as a democracy, it began to acknowledge recognition only in the seventeenth and eighteenth centuries.[235] During the late eighteenth- and early nineteenth century, legal restrictions on Christian groups were gradually removed and, as of this point, religious freedom was maintained in Britain.[236] It is, however, striking that it was only till the middle of the twentieth century that observance and acknowledgement of the right to religious freedom as a legal right took place[237] within England's obligation to respect treaties on the international level. The British state retained an obligation to respect this right already in 1948, as it was a supporter and a signatory of the Universal Declaration of Human Rights (UDHR). Art. 18 of the declaration which established the universal right to freedom of thought, conscience, and religion was literally transformed almost

---

233 The term *jilbab* refers to a long loose fit garment or coat worn by Muslim women, which covers the entire body except for hands, face and head. The term *niqab* refers to a form of a headcovering worn by Muslim women, which covers the whole face leaving a space for the eyes to be seen. Noteworthy, because of the variety in head coverings (i.e. *hijab*) existing in the Muslim world, the terms *niqab* and *burqa* are often used interchangeably. However, the *burqa* is a garment worn by Muslim women that covers the whole body from head to toe.

234 *Cumper* in Harris/Joseph (eds.) , p. 357.

235 *Palmer*, p. 159.

236 *McGoldrick*, Human Rights and Religion: The Islamic Headscarf Debate in Europe, 2006, p. 12.

237 *Poulter*, Ethnicity, Law and Human Rights, 1998, pp. 293, 297, 321; *van Ooijen*, p. 216

word for word into Art. 9 of the European Convention on Human Rights (ECHR or Convention) and has remained unaltered in this form.[238]

The formal guarantee of the right to religious freedom was substantiated with the signing of the ECHR in 1950 as the UK took upon itself within the framework of an international treaty to protect a list of basic rights including the right to religious freedom (Art. 9 ECHR) which comprised a set of 'fundamental human rights'. Nonetheless, this guarantee as a fundamental right within the catalogue of International convention rights did not suffice to form the basis for an enforcement mechanism that would enable a legal challenge before domestic courts.[239]

This legal system that was supposed to guarantee protection of fundamental rights under the Convention suffered criticism as it failed to provide a powerful enforcement mechanism under English law that had thus far safeguarded fundamental individual rights within the boundaries of normal laws.[240] The right to freedom of religion was not effectively protected as a fundamental legal right in the constitutional system of Britain till the end of the twentieth century[241] when rights enshrined in the ECHR were incorporated into the 1998 Human Rights Act (HRA 1998). A distinctive feature of the incorporation of Convention rights into the HRA 1998 is that it has a direct enforcement mechanism in English courts.

This shift from a tradition of religious tolerance to religious liberty as a positive right[242] can be demonstrated in developments of human rights and discrimination law that were affected by these sociological changes and were reflected in changes of the legal framework, taking place from the middle of the twentieth century onwards.[243] This trend has accelerated the active advancement of religious liberty as a recognized fundamental right in laws of the twenty-first century.[244] Thence, the significant step towards recognition of religious freedom and

---

238 *McGoldrick*, 2006 p. 12; *Mawhinney* in Cranmer, Hill, Kenny ua. (eds.), The Confluence of Law and Religion, 2016, pp. 205, 208; Ian Brownlie and *Guy S. Goodwin-Gill*, Basic Documents on Human Rights, 4th ed. 2002, p. 258.

239 *Ward/Wragg*, Walker & Walker's English Legal System, 9th ed., 2005, pp. 148–149.

240 *Edge*, Legal Responses to Religious Difference, 2002, pp. 77–78; *van Ooijen*, p. 211; *Ward/Wragg*, p. 149.

241 *v. Ungern – Sternberg*, p. 21.

242 *Sandberg*, Law and Religion, 2011, p. 192.

243 For instance, the Employment Act 1989, the incorporation of the Declaration (Art. 18).

244 *van Ooijen*, p. 213; *Sandberg*, in: Hunter-Henin, Law, Religious Freedoms and Education in Europe, 2011, pp. 327, 330–331.

other fundamental rights was accomplished when the HRA 1998 came into force in 2000 as it transposed in full the ECHR provisions.[245]

In relation to the place of religion in the public sphere the right of teachers and school staff to wear religious symbols or dress while at work, the protection of the right to religious freedom is normally litigated under anti-discrimination law. For this reason, religion law is scattered in English law and can be found both in human rights and discrimination law statutes.[246]

The following section will outline the legal structure and sources of law upon which individual rights, including religious rights, derive their validity under English law. It will also provide an overview of the current legal framework available for school staff in protection of their religious freedom. As will be explained, the law on religion was achieved and developed in piecemeal measures and was characterized by the fact that it was lightly regulated.[247] Accordingly, the focus of this analysis will be directed to the most relevant legislative instruments demonstrating the legal shift made under English law with respect to the position of religious freedom. This includes state initiative to facilitate religion in the public sphere achieved through intensified regulation on its guarantee as a basic right and under anti-discrimination laws. Though state-church relations in England do not fit to a model of a complete separation, the shift is marked by the gradual evolvement of a fundamental human right guaranteed by unwritten rules of common law to a positive right regulated by laws and statutes. The shift has been titled in the legal literature a transfer from a tolerance-based approach to a right-based approach.[248] The first step can be attributed to incorporation fundamental rights including of Art. 9 (religious freedom) and Art. 10 (freedom of expression) of the ECHR to the HRA 1998. Their relevance for the ensuing discussion gains further effect especially following their incorporation into domestic law. For the purpose of the present examination taking the legitimacy of religious symbols in public education into context it will be interesting to demonstrate the significance these articles draw in the development of the English jurisprudence, in

245 *Ward/Wragg*, p. 149; *Edge*, p. 77; *van Ooijen*, p. 211; *Oliva*, BYU L. Rev. 2008, pp. 877, 883–884.

246 *Sandberg*, in: Hunter-Henin, Law, Religious Freedoms and Education in Europe, 2011, pp. 327, 328.

247 *Sandberg*, in: Hunter-Henin, Law, Religious Freedoms and Education in Europe, 2011, pp. 327, 329, 330.

248 *van Ooijen*, pp. 210, 212; *Sandberg*, in: Hunter-Henin, Law, Religious Freedoms and Education in Europe, 2011, pp. 327, 329, 330; *Freedland/Vickers*, Comp. Lab. L. & Pol'y J., 30 (2009), pp. 597, et seq.

particular due to ease of access to courts. The incorporation of the Conventions' articles into domestic law enabled for individuals in complaints of religious interference in the education context a direct application against schools and education authorities and provided an easy access to national courts, without having to make a recourse to the Strasbourg jurisdictions.

An emphasis will be given also to discrimination law provisions which are of relevance under English law in order to evaluate the protection of religious rights offered for teaching staff employed in state schools. In England, aspects concerned with the wearing of religious dress and symbols by teachers are interlinked with general statutory prohibition of discrimination in employment prescribed in the consolidating Equality Act 2010. These considerable enactments are regarded as the legal pillars for the evaluation of the protection of religion as a fundamental right; the legal position offered to teaching staff to exercise their right to religious freedom will be evaluated in accordance with these two pieces of legislation. Eventually, an assessment of the system will be elucidated, taking into consideration the constitutional position and reference, in particular to the available mechanisms guaranteeing religious rights in Britain.

a) Sources of Law and Legal Hierarchy of Norms

In respect to this view, it is worth to underscore special characteristics that are unique to England's constitutional order as these will serve a key element for understanding the legal position of religious freedom as a fundamental liberty right. The British legal system has a distinctive composition as its constitutional order is based on a variety of sources. Since England has no written constitution in the form of a written document establishing state power relations, its constitutional precepts is regarded to derive from various legal and extra-legal rules and practices.[249] Essentially, the main historical sources of English law are to be found in common law and equity, legislation made by parliament (Acts of Parliament and Orders made under such Acts) and taken a focus on international law the UK has entered into several international conventions which have influence on the interaction between English Law and the guarantee of human rights including enforcement of religious rights embodied and governed by these international agreements. Some treaties did not intend to create a legal document that binds the states upon international standards but were more declaratory in nature, such as for instance the Universal Declaration of Human Rights (UDHR). Other international agreements intended to

249 *Edge*, p. 75; *van Ooijen*, p. 210.

strongly enforce responsibility of the participating states to international standards on human rights and compel observance through immediate application of their provisions in their domestic law (e.g., the European Convention on Human Rights).

In addition, in the absence of a written Bill of rights the protection of fundamental rights originated formerly from a diverse origin of constitutional rules as well as judicial review of courts and tribunals.[250] It is therefore, practically still possible to find that protection of fundamental rights derive authority based on Acts of Parliament and doctrine of common law developed by the courts.[251]

b) Individual Rights

In principle, in the legal system of Britain fundamental rights such as religious freedom are not identifiable in a single overarching legal document that guarantees their protection.[252] This distinctive characteristic, conjoined with the constitutional order in the English legal system which entails the constitutional principle of Parliament supremacy and which has no written constitution increases the danger of disregarded or abused fundamental rights, especially given the lack of an effective mechanism enforcing their protection.

Instead of a codified legislation responsible for the protection of fundamental human rights, a variety of mechanisms is available. Fundamental individual rights can be guaranteed by: first, *formal British legislation* – encompassing mainly Acts of Parliament and constitutional principles embedded in the text of English law, as well as jurisprudence of the courts (common law); second, *international treaties or conventions* – the protection of basic rights, including religious freedom rights, is ensured through international treaties and commitments to which England is signatory. Several conventions were even incorporated into the British legal system and, as a result, the courts are obliged to keep in line with their precepts when delivering their judgements interpretation to statutes of parliament.[253]

---

250 *Edge*, p. 76.

251 Since the administration of justice was historically a prerogative power of the Crown, the basis of the common law is found in royal commands of the Monarch. In fact, it reflects the law that was administered by the King's courts and developed by judges through decisions in individual cases and supplemented and administered the local custom existing at that time. See in: *Ward/Wragg*, pp. 4–5; *Edge*, p. 30.

252 *Edge*, p. 76.

253 *Hill*, Religious Liberty and Human Rights, 2002, p. 6.

The United Kingdom is a party to international treaties which contain guarantees of freedom of religion, most notably the International Convention on Civil and Political Rights (ICCPR) and the European Convention on Human Rights (ECHR).[254] Taking the legal perspective of a sizeable enforcement mechanism on domestic law, the ICCPR provides a weaker enforcement mechanism attributed to its global application on the international level and, a result, is left as a symbolic statement rather than a treaty with strong enforceable rights. The guarantee of the right to religious freedom is outlined in Art. 18 ICCPR. Albeit the fact that the wording of Art. 18 para 1 and para 3 ICCPR are similar in content and nature to the guarantee prescribed in Art. 9 ECHR, its lack of direct application makes it of no real relevance to complaints brought before the Strasbourg instances. Further, due to the availability of an effective human right instrument on the European level, namely the ECHR, further elaboration will concentrate only on Art. 9 and its scope of application as it is anyway subject to a different set of rules and interpretative methods evolved by the European jurisdiction. In sharp contrast to the ICCPR the ECHR as an international treaty intended to have a direct application on human rights and fundamental freedoms under domestic law of the signing states and as a result implemented successfully strong enforcement mechanism for observance and their guarantee.

In the UK, the protection of individual rights falls mainly within the responsibility of Parliament and the courts, and can be identified under two different legislative grounds: (i) liberty; and (ii) anti-discrimination/equality rights. This legal system enables aggrieved individuals to opt between two alternative tracks when submitting a claim for infringement of their right to religious manifestation. While the guarantee of fundamental rights such as religious liberty rights was incorporated into domestic law following ratification of international conventions (e.g., the incorporation of the ECHR), equality rights yielded mainly as Acts of Parliament.

aa) Origins of Basic Rights

Fundamental rights in England derive their subsistence from divergent sources: 1. domestic law – includes statutes and legal rules encompassing Acts of Parliament, legislation by other bodies authorized by parliament, doctrines of Common law where it is possible to detect specific rights[255] practices and custom (i.e., early common law developed through application by the courts), and in

254 *Palmer*, p. 161.
255 *Edge*, p. 76.

decisions and judgements of national courts. 2. International law – obligations to ratify or incorporate human rights treaties on the international level (e.g., ECHR, ICCPR).[256]

(1) Domestic Law

Since fundamental rights were not explicitly ensured in an over-arching constitutional document, such as a Bill of Rights, they were protected and restricted by regular legislation.[257]

The legal system in England enables enactments regulating religious affairs through statutes or regulations that will be published subsequently as Acts of Parliament. Even the issuance of administrative regulations as statutory instruments will need to get approved by the British Parliament.

The entrenched constitutional principle of parliament supremacy enables the British legislator to promulgate Acts of Parliament that are apt to change any law and prevail other statutes or regulations.[258] In fact, this supremacy can be used in order to curb, detract, or disregard fundamental rights or other constitutional values, simply as they cannot be challenged on legal grounds.

(2) Common Law

Historically, there was no legal recognition of the right to religious freedom and no substantial protection was offered to individuals and other denominational groups (including Roman Catholics) opposing the Anglican faith. Therefore, the protection on grounds of religious discrimination was subject to common law tradition. Accordingly, the legal framework relied on the integrity of the Common Law system to provide religious communities protection against the infraction of their fundamental right to freedom of religion and belief.[259]

(3) Ratification and Incorporation of International Treaties

International treaties can be directly applicable in the UK given that they are ratified by parliament. Until the Constitutional Reform and Governance Act 2010, the ratification of international treaties was a royal prerogative. Since the enactment of the Governance Act in 2010, parliamentary approval is required for the

256 See in detail in this Chapter under headline 3b) bb) (1) & (2).
257 *Edge*, p. 78.
258 *Edge*, p. 77.
259 *Oliva*, 2008, pp. 877, 878.

ratification of international treaties.[260] There are occasions, however, where ratification of a treaty by the United Kingdom would suffice and no incorporation would be necessary if certain rights mentioned in the treaty are already protected under domestic law. In principle, international treaties will not gain precedence over domestic law; this can be achieved only through statutory interpretation.[261]

Under English law, the incorporation of an international treaty generally requires its approval by the British Parliament through the passing of an enabling statute.[262] This was the case with the ECHR, which due to constant refusal of the UK has not become part of the domestic legal order in the UK until its final incorporation by Parliament.[263] The intention was to ensure an effective mechanism for enforcing the rights protected under the Convention. Though the UK was among the first states to ratify the ECHR (in 1951), it has been incorporated into the Human Rights Act 1998 only after a long struggle in the British Parliament,[264] taking effect only in 2000.[265]

In practice, the incorporation of the ECHR into domestic law bears several significant effects: first, *commitment of the state* – governmental institutions are more committed to respect and guarantee the rights protected under the Act;[266] second, *expansion of judicial review* – citizens seeking remedy may find it easier to enforce their infringed religious rights through direct redress to an Act of Parliament, as violations of religious freedom rights will be submitted directly to national courts rather than to the European Court of Human rights (ECtHR);[267] third, *reducing likelihood for contradicting legislation* – the position of the ECHR will benefit from an improved status in the British jurisprudence. According to the HRA, the interpretation of statutory instruments (primary and subordinate legislation) would incline British courts to subordinate and give effect to domestic legislation (whether passed before or after the HRA) so it will conform as much as possible with the spirit of the Convention and the rights safeguarded in it.[268]

---

260 Sec. 20 of the Constitutional Reform and Governance Act 2010, see in http://www.legislation.gov.uk/ukpga/2010/25/section/20

261 *Saxena*, U.Det. Mercy L. Rev., 84(5) (2007), pp. 765, 784.

262 *Ward/Wragg*, p. 149; R v Chief Immigration Officer, Heathrow Airport, ex parte Bibi (Salamat) (1976) 3 All ER 843, (1976) 1 WLR 979.

263 *Hill*, 2002, p. 2, Fn. 216; *Edge*, p. 77, Fn. 202; *van Ooijen*, p. 211, Fn. 202.

264 *Edge*, p. 78.

265 *Oliva*, 2008, pp. 877, 883–884, Fn. 211; *Edge*, p. 78, Fn. 202; *van Ooijen*, p. 211, Fn. 202.

266 *Edge*, p. 78; Fn. 202; Straw/Boateng para 1.17.

267 *Edge*, p. 78; *Straw/Boateng* para 1.17.

268 HRA 1998 Section 3 para 1; *Hill*, 2002 p. 6; *van Ooijen*, p. 211.

bb) *Liberty/Fundamental Human Rights*

Liberty rights have been a consistent part of the British history of human rights. Civil liberty rights in England exist as a norm and are not encompassed under codified legislation. For this reason, infringements of liberty rights will be permissible only through legislative acts or judicial decisions.[269] Since the function of liberty rights is to protect an individual from abuse of power by the state, it is rather surprising that the right to freedom of thought, conscience, and religion in the legal tradition of England was not explicitly guaranteed in any statute until the enactment of the HRA 1998.[270]

(1) *Human Rights Act 1998*

The Human Rights Act (HRA) passed in 1998 came into effect only in 2000.[271] It is regarded as the first explicit declaration committed to protection of fundamental rights within the UK.[272] The notion behind the enactment of the HRA was an impetus within British parliament – in light of a lack of British Bill of Rights – to seek and incorporate the European Convention on Human Rights into domestic law.[273] In the absence of a proper mechanism for the protection of fundamental rights and liberties, a consultation paper suggested the incorporation of the ECHR into English law. This was intended to bypass the procedure of the enforcement of the Conventions' rights into domestic law, which would have been time-consuming and costly, providing an easier and more beneficial alternative to individuals' grievances on the one hand, and, on the other hand, demonstrating commitment of the British Government to protect the rights safeguarded in the ECHR.[274]

The prevailing legal situation prior to the enactment of the HRA served as an incentive for incorporation of the Conventions' rights into domestic law by the British Parliament. The legal situation was characterized primarily: (1) by lack of codification with respect to fundamental rights and effective enforcement mechanism to secure their position and inhibit their unnecessary abuse by the state; (2) no recognition of the right to religious freedom as a positive right.

269 *Palmer*, p. 159.

270 *Howard*, Law and the wearing of Religious Symbols, 2012, p. 9; *Edge*, p. 77.

271 The reason for the elapse of time till the HRA has come into force was attributed to the period required for training of state officials, see *Edge*, p. 100.

272 *Ward/Wragg*, p. 149; *Oliva*, 2008, pp. 877, 883, 884; *Edge*, p. 77.

273 *Edge*, p. 78; Straw/Boateng *(bringing rights home)*, p. 100; *van Ooijen*, p. 211.

274 *Edge*, p. 78.

Earlier doctrines of the common law which were developed prior to the enactment of the HRA recognized the right to religious freedom primarily as a negative right.[275]

Eminently, the HRA provided a domestic fundament for the protection of basic human rights enshrined in the ECHR. The desirable aim of the HRA was to guarantee the protection of individual rights, including the freedom of thought, conscience, and religion, thus enabling individuals seeking redress to initiate a claim through a rapid procedure by applying directly in domestic courts.[276]

The importance attributed to the enactment of the HRA relates mainly to its contribution to the protection of civil liberty rights in the legislation of British history. This explicit acknowledgement enfolds two main aspects: (i) constitutional level – the state holds no longer a prevailing role with respect to religion as the individual becomes the centre of this framework; (ii) conceptual level – this legislation acknowledged religious freedom not only as a fundamental right; rather, it was finally recognized and guaranteed as a positive right instead of a negative right as had been the case thus far.[277]

It is worth to note that despite the legal significance attributed to the enactment of the HRA, its impact on the development of British jurisprudence concerning manifestation of religious symbols has eventually remained minor.[278]

(a) The Provisions of the ECHR

The HRA 1998 declares allocation of 'the convention rights' through para 1;[279] insertion of procedural stipulations to amendments of the act itself are specified in para 1, 4 and 6. It prescribes, likewise, that the underlying articles of the ECHR are set out in Schedule 1 of the HRA 1998 (para 1 (3).[280] The focus of this analysis will be directed to significant provisions which are of relevance for the discussion.

---

275 *Oliva*, 2008, pp. 877, 883, 879; *Alder*, Constitutional and Administrative Law 444, 6th ed., 2007, p. 444.

276 *van Ooijen*, p. 211; *Edge*, p. 78.

277 *Oliva*, 2008, pp. 877, 882; *van Ooijen*, p. 211; *Edge*, p. 77.

278 *van Ooijen*, p. 211.

279 Para 1, (1), (a), (b), (c) determine correspondingly the incorporation of Art. 2 to 12 and 14 of the ECHR; Art. 1 to 3 of the First Protocol; Art. 1 of the Thirteenth Protocol.

280 Art. 1 para 3 of the HRA 1998. The articles are numerically identical to those designated in the ECHR.

(aa) Art. 9 ECHR Freedom of Religion

The wording of Art. 9 HRA[281] prescribes in para 1 the general guarantee of religious freedom to everyone, and this is regarded to be an absolute right, which means that the right is unconfined and the state cannot restrict or limit it.[282] This paragraph provides the guarantee that aims to protect the *forum internum*. However, para 2 of Art. 9 deals with manifestation of religion, i.e. the *forum externum*. Unlike the guarantee ascribed to the *forum internum*, *forum externum* issues allow restrictions on the qualified right to religious freedom subject to limitations as set out in Art. 9 para 2 HRA (the protection of rights and freedoms of others or protection of certain public interests).[283]

The right to religious freedom prescribed in Art. 9 ECHR is clearly defined and elaborated; it encompasses the freedom to hold or adopt a religion or belief as well as the right to have it self-determined on a free will basis. This includes the right of an individual to manifest one's religion or belief in public or private. In fact, the HRA gives further effect to the rights mentioned in the ECHR.

Albeit Art. 9 carries no unambiguous formulation prima facie, the guarantee of religious freedom conferred under Art. 9 has not always enabled complainants an easy establishment in claims of interference of their religious rights. In addition, since English courts are obliged to interpret domestic law so as to accord with the Convention,[284] they need to take account of several distinguishable pre-requisites of Art. 9 as already identified by the ECtHR. This was naturally followed by English courts, even if reluctantly to some extent. It is due to the importance of these pre-requisites for the following analysis that these will be briefly specified below:

First, according to the jurisprudence of the ECtHR with respect to interpretation of Art. 9, it was acknowledged that the protection of freedom of religion

---

281 1. Everyone has the right to freedom of thought, conscience, and religion; this right includes freedom to change one's religion or belief and freedom in community with others and in public or private, to manifest one's religion or belief in worship, teaching, practice, and observance.
2. Freedom to manifest one's religion or beliefs shall be subject only to such limitations as are prescribed by law and are necessary in a democratic society in the interests of public safety; for the protection of public order, health, or morals or for the protection of the rights and freedom of the others.

282 *Senyonjo*, International Journal of Constitutional Law, 2009, pp. 275, 280.

283 *Mawhinney*, pp. 205, 208.

284 *Hill*, A New Dawn for Freedom of Religion: Grounding the Debate in Religious Liberty and Human Rights, 2002, pp. 6–8.

extends itself also with respect to organizations and institutes and is not confined solely to natural persons.[285]

Second, further, the right to freedom of religion and belief is regarded as absolute. However, the right to 'manifest a religion or belief' is not unlimited, as the words of Art. 9 para 2 clearly indicate. The ECtHR acknowledged in its judgements that confinement of the right to religious freedom may be justified upon fulfilment of several requirements.[286]

Third, though it was common that complaints under Art. 9 included also allegations of interference in the right to religious expressions according to Art. 10 of the ECHR, the tendency of both British courts as well as the ECtHR was to consider and evaluate only the relevant right that stood in question and deliver a decision merely with reference to this specific right.[287]

Fourth, in addition, Art. 2 of the first protocol ECHR relates to the pre-eminent right of every person to education.[288] It was for that reason that applicants (mainly pupils or students) relied in practice on Art. 9 conjoined with Art. 2 of the first protocol when establishing the ground of their allegations against school authorities claiming for interference of their religious rights.[289]

Fifth, since the right to wear religious symbols is regarded as a 'manifestation of fundamental religious freedom', it clearly provided a fertile ground for claims brought in front of the ECtHR also on grounds of religious discrimination.

---

285 *Martínez-Torrón*, in: Hill, Religious Liberty in European Jurisprudence in Religious Liberty and Human Rights, 2002, pp. 99, 101. It should be noted that the ECtHR was drawing a differentiation between the terms 'religious freedom' and 'freedom of thought and conscience' as mentioned in para 1 of Art. 9 ECHR, as the latter can only be attributed with respect to individuals. (e.g., Company X v. Switzerland, 1981, 16 DR 85); for other case laws recognizing religious rights of sectarian or religious organizations to act on behalf of their members see X and Church of Scientology v. Sweden, 1979, 16 DR 68; Chappell v. UK, 1987, 53 DR 241; *Addison*, Religious Discrimination and Hatred Law, 2007, p. 13.

286 Leyla Sahin v. Turkey application no. 44774/98, 10 November 2005; Kokkinakis v. Greece, 1993, 17 EHRR 397.

287 Leyla Sahin v. Turkey application no. 44774/98, 10 November 2005; Hammond v. DPP, 2004, EWHC 69 (Admin).

288 http://www.hri.org/docs/ECHR50.html#P1. Art. 2; '*No person shall be denied the right to education. In the exercise of any functions which it assumes in relation to education and to teaching, the state shall respect the right of parents to ensure such education and teaching in conformity with their own religious and philosophical convictions*'.

289 Begum v. Denbigh High School, 2006, UKHL 15; Sahin v. Turkey ECtHR Application no. 44774/98

Essentially, the jurisprudence of the ECtHR with respect to Art. 9 and its interpretation laid significant restrictions on the right to religious freedom. This approach of the ECtHR was criticized by English courts, which often abide its implementation unwillingly. However, since the intention behind the HRA 1998 was to encourage British courts to assert and enforce Convention's rights in accordance with parameters established by the ECtHR, then the British judicator was under obligation to follow the same path as well.[290]

(bb) Art. 10 ECHR Freedom of Expression

The guarantee of the right to freedom of expression is ascertained in Art. 10 ECHR. The right includes the freedom to express one's religion openly, to hold opinions, as well as receive and impart information and ideas.[291] Similarly to Art. 9, there are designated reservations with respect to Art. 10.

Therefore, the right to freedom of expression is not absolute and may be confined subject to the following restrictions: first, it is in accordance with the law; second, it is necessary in a democratic society; and, third, it aims to protect a legitimate aim (similarly to those specified in Art. 9 para 2 ECHR).

It is worth to note that experience in legal practice demonstrated that due to the proximity of Art. 9 and Art. 10 ECHR it was often the case that claims brought by individuals alleging a breach of the right to religious manifestation according to Art. 9, will also establish their claim in conjunction with the right to freedom of expression, pursuant to Art. 10 of the ECHR.[292]

(b) Limitation of Scope

The HRA 1998, though purporting to safeguard religious freedom, is not unreserved in its scope and therefore may be subjected to the following limitations:

(i) *Direct application on public bodies* – since the Convention is an international instrument, it has a direct effect on public authorities; however, this is not the case with respect to individuals and private corporations that are not likely to be bound by it. They will be excluded from the remit of the HRA, especially if they do not exercise any public function. In that case, the state would

290 *Oliva*, 2008, p. 877.

291 Art. 10 para 1 HRA 1998 provides that: 'Everyone has the right to freedom of expression. This right shall include freedom to hold opinions and to receive and impart information and ideas without interference by public authority and regardless of frontiers'.

292 Sahin v Turkey 10 November 2006; Hammond v DPP, 2004, EWHC 69 (Admin).

presume to be liable if it had permitted an individual or private organization to violate the religious rights of another or even omitted from doing so.

(ii) *Declaration of incompatibility with the Convention* – the HRA enables English courts to make a declaration of incompatibility of a state action or administrative decision with respect to the Convention.[293] However, it is due to sovereignty of Parliament and non-interference in Parliament's inner affairs that it is very likely that English courts will feel reluctant to declare incompatibility of parliament legislation with the ECHR. Consequently, state courts will enjoy a wider discretion with respect to application of the margin of appreciation doctrine when asked to review the compatibility of offending legislation or administrative decision.[294]

(iii) *Parliament supremacy* – ultimately, the constitutional order in Great Britain conferring unfettered legal powers to British parliament enables it practically to legislate contrary to the ECHR.[295]

(2) The International Covenant on Civil and Political Rights

The international covenant on civil and political rights (ICCPR)[296] is one of the most essential legal instruments existing on the international level for the protection of substantial human rights.

The ICCPR is a multilateral treaty agreed by the general assembly of the United Nations. Under this treaty, the states are obliged to guarantee civil and political rights of individuals, inter alia the freedom of religion prescribed in

---

293 The HRA prescribes a new rule of statutory interpretation with respect to Parliament's legislation so as to indicate whether incompatibility with the ECHR exists. The declaration of incompatibility with the convention may be a statement of either a Minister of Parliament or of the courts. This mechanism aims to substantially restrain state organs from infringements of fundamental liberty rights, i.e., religious rights.

294 The doctrine of margin of appreciation was developed by the European Court of Human Rights and was intended to grant latitude of discretion to individual states within the European region in conflicts arising between state organs and individuals and resulting in restrictions or violations of human rights. This means serves as a balance between individual rights and national interests where the existence of margin of appreciation will depend on the justification delivered by the state in order not to be held liable for violation of human rights. This will be discussed in more detail in Chapter IV.

295 *Edge*, p. 87.

296 https://treaties.un.org/doc/Publication/UNTS/Volume%20999/volume-999-I-14668-English.pdf

Art. 18 ICCPR.[297] The United Kingdom ratified the ICCPR on 20 August 1976.[298] The ICCPR was originally thought to be a comprehensive instrument that would give effect to all of the rights included in the Universal Declaration of Human Rights,[299] only that this document would have the effect of a legal binding document upon all member states of the United Nations.[300] The significance of the ICCPR as an international convention with a declaratory nature of human rights' guarantee as opposed to other global instruments of human rights protection is distinguishable in several respects: first, *legal binding document* – its binding force enables it to bind the states that are its signatories to observe its guarantees through implementation in the legislation of their national systems or other enforceable mechanisms under domestic law; second, *enforcement mechanism* – the ICCPR established the Human Rights Committee (HRC) which constitutes as an institution to support its values in the form of observing that member states respect its guarantees;[301] third, *detailed description of freedoms* – enables a better guarantee of the rights prescribed in the ICCPR since a violation by a state would be easy to recognize. Insofar, the rights and their scope of protection are specified in the treaty itself it will be easy to establish infringement of the rights guaranteed in it.[302]

Albeit the commitment of England to ensure human rights within the international law framework (e.g., UDHR, ICCPR), the difficulty these global instruments raise is distinctive, in particular due to their global reach which detracts them from becoming influential tools for enforcement of human rights. This lack of ability to impose an international standard should be considered with regard to the human rights treaties mentioned above: first, their weakness

---

297 *Harris* in Harris/Joseph (eds.), p. 1, 2-3; Art. 18 ICCPR in *Brownlie*, Basic Documents in International Law, 2002, p. 211.

298 *Harris* in *Harris*/ Joseph (eds.), p. 1, 41; International Covenant on Civil and Political Rights together with the International Covenant on Economic, Social and Cultural Rights was adopted and opened for signature, ratification, and accession by General Assembly resolution 2200A (XXI) of 16 December 1966. Both documents came into force in 1976.

299 The Universal Declaration of Human Rights was adopted by the UN General Assembly on 10 December 1948. *McGoldrick*, The Human Rights Committee: Its Role in the Development of the International Covenant on Civil and Political Rights, 1994, p. 5. As to the significance of the ICCPR as an international treaty for protection of human rights see in *McGoldrick*, 1994, pp. 13-14.

300 *McGoldrick*, 1994, pp. 13-14, 20; *Edge*, p. 35.

301 *Adrian*, Religion, State and Society, 37(4) (2009), pp. 345, 357.

302 *Edge*, p. 35.

to offer a strong enforcement mechanism in the sense that states should be made accountable for violations of human rights. A powerful enforcement mechanism is significant since the states took upon themselves to guarantee the catalogue of human rights specified in them within the global context of international law.[303] This requires strengthening the mechanism of control and supervision at the regional level in order to ensure that obligations are met by domestic decision makers; second, they have no immediate application for complainants claiming to be the victims of human rights violations. Even the HRC, which was established by the ICCPR to receive complaints from aggrieved individuals and is authorized to evaluate reports submitted by state parties through periodic state report mechanism as to the measures (i.e. legislative form, manner, or initiative) taken to secure their obligations under the ICCPR, did not prove to be efficient as its views were not legally enforceable.[304]

Eventually, a considerable effect on the protection of human rights in the British legal system was not perceived to be incurred by virtue of commitments made on the international level, but rather was proved to be more effective and binding when imposed at the regional level, as can be testified by a treaty like the ECHR.[305]

(3) Implementation of Art. 9 HRA 1998

(a) Scope of Protection

Art. 9 para 1 HRA[306] distinguishes between: (i) the freedom to have or adopt a religion or belief; and (ii) the right to manifest a religion or belief.

The freedom to have or adopt religion is considered to be an 'inner freedom' which includes private religious activities, such as inner faith, prayer, and personal devotion. This freedom is absolute and by no means subject to restrictions.

In contrast, the right to manifest a religion is perceived as an 'external freedom'[307] which is subject to the restrictions prescribed in the provision itself.

---

303 ICCPR, Art. 40; *McGoldrick*, 1994, p. 504.

304 *Mawhinney*, pp. 205, 208; *Opsahl*, in: *Alston*, The United Nation and Human Rights: A critical Appraisal, 1995, pp. 369, 421; *Edge*, p. 37.

305 *Edge*, p. 32.

306 'Freedom to manifest one's religion or beliefs may be subject only to such limitations as are prescribed by law and are necessary to protect public safety, order, health, or morals or the fundamental rights and freedom of others'.

307 *Casin*, in: Kanger, Human Rights in the UN Declaration, 1984, p. 119; *Cumper* in *Harris/Joseph* (eds.), p. 373.

The reason for differentiation is rational, as an individual manifestation of a religion or belief is likely to delimit the privacy of others, and may directly affect the society or public interests such as public order, safety, or welfare.[308] This is unlikely to happen when interference in the inner freedom of an individual takes place, as the right involves the individual himself.

It is claimed that Art. 18 ICCPR is broader in its scope of protection than Art. 9 ECHR.[309] This can be explained based on two grounds: (i) as case laws show the headscarf ban on Muslim students to refrain from appearing with head coverings or identical garments while attending public university gains a higher protection on the international level (Art. 18 ICCPR) as opposed to the minimum standard offered on the European level (Art. 9 ECHR);[310] (ii) Art. 18 para 3 ICCPR, which is the equivalent of Art. 9 para 2 ECHR, goes even further than the wording of the ECHR, as Art. 4 para 2 ICCPR includes a reservation with respect to several ICCPR provisions. Art. 4 para 2 ICCPR stipulates that the right to freedom of religion or belief is non-derogable even in time of war or public emergency.[311]

(b) Restrictions on Freedom of Religion or Belief

The right to manifest a religion may only be restricted in compliance with the restrictions laid down in Art. 9 para 2 ECHR. According to this regulation, there are three conditions to be met:

(i) The restriction must be prescribed by law; (ii) it must establish that it is 'necessary in a democratic society'; and (iii) it must be proportionate to the protection of the legitimate aim pursued.

---

308 *Cumper* in *Harris/Joseph* (eds.), p. 373.

309 *v. Ungern-Sternberg*, p. 74.

310 The reference is made with respect to two case laws. In the case of Sahin, the ban on a Turkish student to abstain from wearing a headscarf in a public university had been accepted and justified by the ECtHR, whereas the same prohibition on a Muslim student from Uzbekistan to refrain from wearing the hijab while at university had been declared by the HRC to be unlawful. See for comparison: *Leyla Sahin v Turkey* 2005, ECtHR, no. 44774/98 and Communication. no. 931/2000 *Raihon Hudoyberganova v Uzbekistan* decision from 18 January 2005.

311 ICCPR Art. 4 para 2. Art. 4 para 1. ICCPR declares: 'In time of public emergency which threatens the life of the nation and the existence of which is officially proclaimed, the State Parties to the present Covenant may take measures derogating from their obligations under the present Covenant…'. Art. 4 para 2 ICCPR states: 'No derogation from articles 6, 7, 8 … and 18 may be made under this provision'.

The conditions are accumulative and must be justified by relevant, sufficient reasons. As a principle, the contracting states[312] enjoy a certain discretion in deciding to which extent an interference in the fundamental right to religious freedom is needed and what measure to adopt at the national level (known as 'margin of appreciation'). Nonetheless, the final determination identifying whether the requirements prescribed in Art. 9 para 2 ECHR were fulfilled and appeared to be relevant and sufficient so as to justify an interference in the right to freedom of religious manifestation is subject to supervision of the European jurisdiction.

(aa) Prescribed by Law

The requirement for a restriction on the right to religious freedom to be prescribed by law had been explained in the legal literature to serve the purpose of a citizen's certainty with regard to the consequences of his/her acts and to the knowledge that restrictions would not be imposed arbitrarily by the state but would have a legal basis in a state's domestic law.[313] The explanation provided by the ECtHR with respect to the interpretation of the expression 'prescribed by law' suggests two requirements to be inferred from it. First, accessibility of the law to the citizen so that he/she can have an indication as to the legal rules that would apply under certain circumstances. Second, the law must be sufficiently precise. Within the meaning of a law, a norm can be included only if it is formulated with such a precision which enables the citizen to regulate his/her conduct and to foresee what the consequences of a given action may entail.[314]

These requirements, as laid down by the ECtHR, demonstrated in other case laws that the concept 'prescribed by law' was not intended to undertake a rigid form in the sense of a 'formal' law, but acknowledged that it must be understood in its 'substantive' sense. For instance, in the case of *Kervanci v France* and *Dogru v France* the expulsion of two schoolgirls due to their refusal to take their headscarves off during sport lessons was justified even if the ban was not explicitly established in a legislative enactment. The ECtHR confirmed two main

---

312 The states that are members in the Council of Europe and are signatories to the ECHR. See in detail in Chapter IV.

313 *Howard* (2012), p. 104; *Evans*, Manual on the Wearing of Religious Symbols in Public Areas, 2008, p. 125; *Murdoch*, Freedom of Thought, Conscience and Religion. A Guide to the implementation of Art. 9 of the European Convention on Human Rights; Human Rights Handbooks, no. 9, Strasbourg; Council of Europe, 2007, p. 27.

314 The ECtHR refers altogether to the term 'prescribed by law' as stipulated in several provisions: Art. 9 para 2, 10 para 2 and 11 para 2 ECHR in Sunday Times v. United Kingdom App. no. 6538/74 (1979–80) 2 EHRR 245, para 49.

purposes in this regard: foreseeability and accessibility of the law. It was explained that these purposes flow from the concept 'prescribed by law'. Firstly, a citizen should be able to calculate his actions so as to foresee his liability according to the law. Secondly, the ability of a citizen to access the law should include any written form of enactments even of lower ranks than statutes.[315] It was explained that as long as the schoolgirls and their parents were made aware of the school's dress code rules and even undertook to comply with these school rules upon registration to school then the consequence of expulsion from school could be reasonably anticipated in case of disregard of these rules.

Essentially, the requirement that a limitation or restrictions on an individual's right to manifest religious symbols in the context of public education must be 'prescribed by law' did not constitute for state parties a hurdle which was difficult to establish.[316]

Though the HRC abstains from disclosing in its General Comment how the term 'prescribed by law' should be comprehended, it has been suggested that the words extend to unwritten norms of common law which are clearly expressed, as well as to formal enactments or statutes. This view has been embraced also by the ECtHR.[317]

The HRC has also provided a clarification stating that restrictions on freedom of religion or belief must 'be directly related and proportionate to the specific need on which they are predicated'.[318]

(bb) Necessary in a Democratic Society

The second requirement for a restriction on the fundamental right to manifest one's religion is essentially a matter left within the 'margin of appreciation' of the contracting states. The ECtHR explained in this respect that since the ECHR leaves each state the task to secure in their national systems the rights and liberties it enshrines, it becomes inevitable that each respective domestic law may change by time, era, and region.[319] It states further that

315 Kervanci v France (Kervanci) App. no. 31645/04 para 52; Dogru v France *(Dogru)* App. no. 27058/05, 4 December 2008, paras. 49 - 52.

316 *Kervanci and Dogru,* para 59.

317 *Cumper* in *Harris/Joseph* (eds.), p. 373; *Nowak*, UN Covenant on Civil and Political Rights. CCPR Commentary, 2nd ed., 2005, pp. 310, 325; Sunday Times v United Kingdom, Series A No 30 (1979).

318 ICCPR, General Comment 22, para 8.

319 Handyside v United Kingdom App. no. 5493/72 (1979–80) 1 EHRR 737, para 48. It is worth to note that though this case involved Art. 10(2) ECHR, the test relating to the concept of 'necessity' has been established in other articles of the ECHR using this requirement, such as 8 para 2, 9 para 2, and 11 para 2.

states' authorities are in a better position than the international judge to state an opinion on the exact content of the requirements prescribed in the Convention's articles as well as on the 'necessity' of a 'restriction' intended to meet them. It is for the national authorities to make an initial assessment of the reality of a pressing social need implied by the notion of 'necessity' in this context.[320] It must be proven that the interference is 'necessary in a democratic society' in order to pursue one of the legitimate aims prescribed in Art. 9 ECHR and that the measure adopted by the state is proportionate to the aim it was sought to achieve. The ECtHR emphasizes that this margin granted to the states is not unlimited and that the final ruling will remain within its jurisdiction.[321]

(cc) Legitimate Aim

As a legitimate aim, reference is made to one of the specific categories mentioned in Art. 9 para 2 ECHR, such as public safety, public order, morals health, or fundamental rights and freedoms of others.

(aaa) Public Safety

The notion behind legitimating this aim was the importance to establish a person's identity for safety and security purposes.[322] The problem raised in the legal literature, especially with respect to Islamic religious clothing such as *hijab*, *niqab*, and *burqa* is that they make it impossible to identify a person.[323] It is for this reason that the wearing of these religious garments can be considered as a threat to public safety and security. Other than the identification problem, which remains disputable as to a legitimization of a general ban of the full veil, it should be underscored that Islamic religious clothing are often associated with a threat to Western values and democracy, and are perceived in Western society as symbols representing fundamentalism, terror, and religious extremism. The fear in Western society to promote such an 'Islamic fundamentalist network' through acceptance of the strict religious ideology of Muslims with respect to headcoverings or even other full body coverings (e.g. Burqa), contributed to the fact that these symbols have been often identified as a threat to public safety and

---

320 Handyside v United Kingdom App. no. 5493/72 (1979–80) 1 EHRR 737, para 48.

321 Handyside v United Kingdom App. no. 5493/72 (1979–80) 1 EHRR 737, para 49.

322 *Howard* (2012), pp. 31–32, 107–108;

323 *Howard* (2012), p. 31; *Idriss*, Legal Studies 25(2) (2005), pp. 260, 275; See *McGoldrick*, 2006, p. 20 '*For Western observers perhaps the most frightening image is of the veiled Muslim woman hiding terrorist bombs or on a suicide mission*'.

security.[324] This was even recognized in judgements delivered by the European jurisdictions, as will be specified below.

The public safety argument was often successful in other cases than those particularly engaged in the education context (e.g., a request directed during airport security check to a Sikh man to remove his turban,[325] a woman who was asked to take off her veil for identification reasons while attending the French Consulate).[326] In public schooling, the significance known to the ability to identify the persons who enter school premises can be objectively justified based on public safety grounds even if it is discriminatory in nature.[327] It is provided that restrictions may be placed on the right of peaceful assembly (Art. 21) and freedom of association (Art. 22 para 2) in the interests of 'national security or public safety'.

However, the limitation clause of Art. 18 ICCPR includes only 'public safety'. It was therefore raised that the fine line between the terms 'public safety' and 'national security' may lead to misuse by some of the states attempting to justify restrictions on religious freedom by claiming that religious groups are engaged in political activities, as a result endangering public safety, while they are in fact motivated by considerations of national security.[328]

(bbb) Public Order

In general, the terms public safety and public order will be used in conjunction as they are mostly regarded to protect the same interests.[329] In the context of

---

324 *Howard* (2012), pp. 31 - 32. Howard also refers to parliamentary debates in some European states, such as Belgium, France, and Netherland debating the ban of the headscarf and other face coverings like the niqab in public for the protection of public safety and security, p. 177 (Fn. 8, 9, 10, 11). Conseil d'Etat, Study of Possible Legal Grounds for Banning the Full Veil, Report adopted by the Plenary General Assembly of the Council d'Etat, 25 March 2010, 40–5, http://www.counseil-etat.fr/cde/media/document/RAPPORT%20ETUDES/etude_voile_integral_anglais.pdf.

325 Phull v France App. no. 35753/03, 11 January 2005.

326 El Morsli v France App. no. 15585/06, 4 March 2008.

327 A ban on pupils to abstain from wearing a *niqab* during their attendance in occupational training college was justified by the Dutch authorities, Equal Treatment Commission (Commissie Gelijke Behandeling, CGB) on public safety grounds, although constituted indirect discrimination against Muslim pupils as clearly disadvantaged as opposed to other pupils. See in Commisie Gelijke Behandeling, Judgement 2003–40, 4.10.

328 *Cumper* in *Harris/Joseph* (eds.), p. 374.

329 *Howard* (2012), p. 108.

public education, it was often the case that the ban on either pupils or teachers to abstain from wearing religious garments while on school premises was justified on ground of a state's abidance to the neutrality principle, and the necessity of preserving its secular nature especially in a growing pluralistic society.

Any admissibility of religious symbols in public schooling runs the danger of adhesion to a particular religion that indicates a state's favouritism towards religion, thus violating its duty to neutrality.

The public order argument has been successful as a legitimate aim in several cases brought before the ECtHR involving bans on religious symbols in schools (e.g., *Kervanci* and *Dogru*)[330] and higher education. In the majority of cases the applicants were pupils and the argument for justification of the ban was legitimized by the protection of public order as the ECtHR was considered to be endangered due to wearing of religious symbols that are associated with 'extremist political movements' (e.g., the ban on a Turkish student to refrain from appearance with the Islamic headscarf when at university had considered the protection of public order as one of the legitimate aims recognized by the ECtHR in the case of *Sahin*).[331]

However, It was criticized in the legal literature, that the term 'public order' could be interpreted broadly and provide member states the potential power to circumvent the rights of minority religious groups merely due to their lack of conformity with the dominating religion.[332]

In negotiations of the HRC it was suggested that 'public order' should be interpreted so 'to avoid disturbance to the order in the narrow sense'.[333] This appears to have been the approach taken by the drafters of the ECHR.[334]

(ccc) Morals

All of the limitation clauses in the Covenant recognize morality as a basis for restrictions. However, since this term is ambiguous and leaves uncertainty as to

---

330 Dogru v France, no. 27058/05, 4 December 2008; Kervanci v France, no. .31645/04, 4 December 2008, para 60.

331 Leyla Sahin v Turkey App. no. 44774/98, (2005) 41 EHRR 8, para 108–109 and (2007) 44 EHRR 5, para 115.

332 *Howard* (2012), p. 108; *Evans* (2001), p. 150.

333 Due to the fact that the English term 'public order' is fundamentally different from its French equivalent, there had been many proposals as to its interpretation in the context of Art. 18 of the Covenant. Finally, it was decided to adopt a narrow interpretation of the expression 'public order' that will not expand beyond what is considered to be necessary for the protection of public order. *Nowak*, pp. 310, 327.

334 *Humphrey*, in Meron, Human Rights International Law, p. 181.

its interpretation, the ECtHR has struggled to agree upon a common European concept of 'morals' that will fit the domestic law of the European states.[335]

The Court concluded that notions of morals and its perception may vary by society, place, and time.[336]

However, in its General Comment, the Committee agreed that 'the concept of morals derives from many social, philosophical, and religious traditions' and that 'morals must be based on principles not deriving exclusively from a single tradition'.[337]

(ddd) Health

The restrictions on the grounds of 'public health' enable the state to confine individuals' wearing of religious symbols even if this runs counter to their belief. Such a restriction will be justified if the aim is to protect the health and safety of the individual believer himself. The restriction on an individual's right to manifest his/her religious freedom may sometimes apply in order to correspond with safety rules or regulations. For instance, in the famous British case of *Begum* (Begum), a female pupil who was wearing the headscarf and subsequently wished to wear a religious garment covering from head to toe (the *jilbab*), the HL found that no breach of her right to religious freedom pursuant to Art. 9 ECHR took place and if there was an infringement it was justified. It was underscored that the pupil Begum knew from the schools' uniform requirements and these did not include the jilbab. As a result the wearing of the jilbab violated the schools' uniform policy. In contrast, the schools' dress code requirements were detailed with respect to the shalwar kameeze as well as the headscarf. Thence the wearing of the headscarf under the detailed requirements of school (i.e. lightweight fabric, headscarf ends should be tucked in, etc.) could be legitimized in order to conform with public health and safety requirements and as a result had been permitted in school.[338] On the same token, the ban on

---

335 *Harris/Joseph*, 62.8 (42) p. 375.

336 *Harris/Joseph*, 62.8 (42) p. 375; *Handyside v UK*, Series A No 24 (1976), a case concerning freedom of expression;

337 General Comment 22, para 62.

338 R (on the application of Begum (by her litigation friend, Rahman)) (Respondent) v. Headteacher and Governors of Denbigh High School (Appellants) [2006] UKHL 15, para 76 (See the explanation provided by Lord Scott rejecting the claim of unlawful exclusion of the pupil Begum since there was nothing unreasonable or unlawful in the school's uniform policy. The claim of Begum that the school's refusal to allow her to attend school with the jilbab denied her right to education pursuant to Art. 2 of the First Protocol to the Convention and violated her right to religious manifestation according to Art. 9 ECHR was dismissed by the majority of the HL).

French schoolgirls to appear with a headscarf to sport lessons in school was justified by the need to ensure the health and safety of the pupils as schools are entrusted with this duty.[339]

Although restrictions on religious freedom based on grounds of health can be objectively verified, as one need not rely on the subjective approach of the individual in order to evaluate the benefits emanating from the practice of his/her religious freedom, difficulties still arise when the state has to decide whether an individual's health outweighs his/her religious convictions.

Finally, some find it necessary to draw a distinction between a restriction on religious practice of an individual which aims to protect 'public health' and a restriction intending to keep the safety of an individual.[340]

(eee) Fundamental Rights and Freedom of others

The necessity to curtail individuals' right to wear a religious a garment was often legitimized in order to protect the rights and freedoms of others. This aim has been used sometimes on its own or in combination with other aims mentioned in Art. 9 para 2 ECHR, and was very successful in claims brought before the ECtHR. For instance, in the case of *Begum*, the restriction of school authorities on the pupil to appear with a *jilbab* was motivated, among other considerations, by the need to protect the rights and freedoms of others (Art. 9 para 2 ECHR). It was sustained in court that other female Muslim pupils feared of being pressured into wearing the jilbab and the prohibition helped other schoolgirls from being exposed to religious peer pressure in their community. It was acknowledged that different Muslim communities impose pressure on Muslim women to accord with strict dress codes for social and religious reasons and if the head teacher had allowed Begum to appear with the *jilbab* to school this would encourage its acceptance as a permissible variant of the school uniform.[341] This same interest

---

339 Dogru v. France, no. 27058/05, 4 December 2008 para 73; Kervanci v. France, no. 31645/04, 4 December 2008.

340 *Cumper* in *Harris/Joseph* (eds.), p. 376.

341 Begum UKHL 15, See Lord Bingham (para 18) and of Baroness Hale (paras 95–98); R (on the Application of X) v Headteacher and Governors of Y School (2007) EWHC 298 (Admin.) (2008) 1 ALL ER 249, para 64. In this case, the claimant – a Muslim schoolgirl (X) – submitted an application by her father since she was excluded from school due to her refusal to abide by the school's uniform policy and take off her niqab. The court decided that the school's refusal to allow her to wear the niqab did not constitute a breach of her right to manifest her religion under Art. 9 ECHR; even if it had been interfered, this had been justified in the interests of public safety and for the protection of the rights and freedoms of others.

of protecting the rights and freedoms of other students from exposure to any kind of pressure exerted by religious political movements to conform to religious precepts they do not adhere or share has been acknowledged by the ECtHR in the case of Sahin.[342] The ECtHR accepted the right of secular universities to impose restrictions on the manifestation of religious symbols for the purpose of ensuring the peaceful co-existence between students, since this would ensure the protection of religious minorities which is recognized as a legitimate aim.

Likewise, the protection of beliefs and rights of schoolchildren as a legitimate aim was considered also in the context of curtailment of a schoolteacher's right to manifest her religious belief. The prohibition on a teacher to refrain from appearing with the Islamic headscarf in elementary school classrooms was justified under Art. 9 para 2 ECHR. The teachers' right to obey the religious precept of her faith should be set against the right of pupils and their parents not to be influenced or offended in their own beliefs. The ECtHR raised the need to protect the religious rights and freedoms of the schoolchildren, especially those of younger age (since they are more impressionable), to be free from any proselytising influence that may be incurred by the view of a headscarf worn by a teacher.[343] Finally, the fear of an indoctrinating effect was seen as falling under the protection of the rights and freedom of others.

Notably, taking a brief recourse to international law, the equivalent counterpart of Art. 9 para 2 ECHR is found in Art. 18 para 3 ICCPR which does not merely permit restrictions for the protection of the rights and freedoms of others, but rather limits it to 'their fundamental rights and freedoms'.[344]

(4) Parental Right to Determine Religious Influence on Their Children

(a) Art. 2 of the First Protocol ECHR

The first sentence of Art. 2 of the First Protocol ECHR proclaims in general the right to education. The second sentence of Art. 2 of the First Protocol relates to the right of parents to decide on the education of their children and to ensure that education and teaching conform to their religious or philosophical belief.[345]

---

342 Sahin App. no. 44774/98, (2005) 41 EHRR 8 para 50, 57.

343 Dahlab v Switzerland App. no. 42393/98, 15 February 2001, para 13.

344 The criticism with relation to this term suggests that there is no real difference between the terms 'rights' and 'fundamental rights'. However, state parties may prohibit religious practice if they are to deny from others the right to life, or impose cruel, inhuman, or degrading treatment or punishment; *Harris/Joseph*, 62.8 (42), p. 377.

345 'No person shall be denied a right to an education. In the exercise of any functions which it assumes in relation to education and to teaching, the State shall respect the

In principle, the view of the ECtHR with respect to parental right to decide on the education of their children (the second sentence of Art. 2 of the First Protocol ECHR) is that it is not an own standing right, but is an adjunct of the fundamental right of their children to education. The ECtHR explained that it is in the discharge of the primary obligation of parents to take care of the education of their children that enables them to request from the state to respect their convictions, as parents share a responsibility which enables them the enjoyment of the right to education.[346] In addition, the European judicator perceives the natural parental duty towards their children to act in correlation with the educative task of the state. It held that Art. 2 of the First Protocol applies to each of the state's function in relation to education and teaching and is binding upon all MS.[347] In this respect, the function of the state assumed in relation to education extends itself also to planning of the school curriculum and the state should ensure respect for parents' religious and philosophical convictions. However, it does not prevent the state from imparting through teaching or education religious information of any kind, as otherwise the state school system would run the risk of proving impracticable.

Notably, the reservation made by the Court with respect to fulfilment of the state's educative task is that it must ensure within the setting and planning of the curriculum that information will be conveyed in an objective, critical, and pluralistic manner. The Court, thence, sets a limit that must not be exceeded by the MS while fulfilling their educative function, that is to pursue an aim of indoctrination.[348]

(b) Parental Choice and Religious Schools in England and Wales

Similarly to the case in Germany, the inherent right of parents to take account of their religious and denominational preferences was acknowledged by the British legislator as a determining factor with respect to the parental choice of school.

---

right of parents to ensure such education and teaching in conformity with their own religious and philosophical convictions'.

346 ECtHR *Kjeldsen, Madsen and Pedersen v Denmark* Case no. 5095/71 para 52.

347 ECtHR *Kjeldsen, Madsen and Pedersen v Denmark* Case no. 5095/71 para 50: 'The second sentence of Art. 2 (P1-2) aims in short at safeguarding the possibility of pluralism in education which possibility is essential for the preservation of "a democratic society" as conceived by the Convention. In view of the power of the modern State, it is above all through state teaching that this aim must be realised'. Also with respect to interpretation of Art. 2 of the First Protocol ECHR see the case of *Folgero and Others v Norway* Case no. 15472/02, para 84.

348 ECtHR *Kjeldsen, Madsen and Pedersen v Denmark* Case no. 5095/71 para 53.

The right of parents to decide on the education of their children was prescribed in Section 76 of the Education Act 1944. This right of the parents that the education of their child will accord to their wish was pre-conditioned: first, it must be compatible with the provision of efficient instruction and, second, the avoidance of unreasonable public expenditure.[349]

(c) Religious Education in Light of Art. 18 para 4 ICCPR

Art. 18 para 4 of the ICCPR guarantees children's 'religious and moral' education as long as this accords with the convictions of their parents or legal guardians.[350]

The HRC considers that public education which includes instruction in a particular religion or belief is inconsistent with Art. 18 para 4 ICCPR, unless exemption is provided that would accommodate the wishes of other parents.[351] The HRC held that parents have the right to withdraw their children from compulsory religious education. Nonetheless, alternative instructions on the history of religion and ethics were permissible if 'given in a neutral and objective way' and provided there was nothing in the content of those instructions to collide with the views of the parents who had no religious affiliations.[352] In the United Kingdom, parents have considerable influence on what is taught in the classroom. The School Standards and Framework Act 1998 provides that state-funded schools (community, foundation, or voluntary) must ensure that all children attend a daily act of collective worship.[353]

The nature of this collective worship is also stipulated in Schedule 20 of the SSFA 1998 and ordains that in community- and foundation schools without a religious character this must be 'wholly or mainly of a broad Christian character',[354]

349 *Cumper* in *Harris/Joseph* (eds.) , p. 380.

350 'The States Parties to the present Covenant undertake to have respect for the liberty of parents and, when applicable, legal guardians to ensure the religious and moral education of their children in conformity with their own convictions'.

351 General Comment 22, para 6.

352 *Cumper* in *Harris/Joseph* (eds.), p. 380. In *Hartikainen v Finland* (40/1978).

353 Sec. 70 and 71 The School Standards and Framework Act 1998. Sec. 71 prescribes exceptions and special arrangements for parents who wish their children to be exempted from religious education or attendance in collective religious worship of school. It is worth to note that Sec. 55 of the Education Act 2006 amended Sec. 71 of the School Standards and Framework Act in such a manner as to ensure the right of sixth-form pupils (between sixteen and eighteen years of age) in secondary education to be excused from attendance at religious worship if they request so.

354 Sec. 3 para 2 of Schedule 20 of the SSFA 1998.

reflecting the 'broad tradition of Christian belief without being distinctive of any particular Christian denomination'.[355]

Since children cannot be compelled to attend Christian school assemblies, there exists an alternative in schools where the majority of pupils are non-Christians.

In such a case, the principal will apply to the Local Standing Advisory Council on Religious Education (SACRE), on the grounds that these Christian school assemblies are inappropriate for some of the pupils.[356] Consequently, an 'alternative' daily worship must be provided for this group of pupils.

If the parents are Atheists (non-believers) and object to participation of their child in collective worship or religious education, they enjoy the right to withdraw their children from these school events.[357]

Similarly, parents have a legal right to withdraw their children from religious education lessons.[358] Religious education is taught in maintained schools according to a locally agreed syllabus. Any coercion on minority-faith children to attend Christian assemblies and religious education lessons is illegal. In addition, it was affirmed by the Department for Education that in case parents seek to withdraw their children from religious education lessons, the school must comply.[359] Therefore, if minority-faith children opt out of religious education, they may either be set an alternative, or may receive religious lessons from a teacher of their own faith without the need to bear any financial burden.[360] Furthermore, it was concluded that sex education lessons fall within the scope of Art. 18 para 4 ICCPR.[361] In this respect, the HRC even stipulates that 'moral education' must respect the wishes of the parents.[362]

---

355 Sec. 3 para 3 of Schedule 20 of the SSFA 1998. These paragraphs were found in Sec. 6 of the former Education Reform Act 1988. Sec. 7 para 1 and 2 of the Education Reform Act 1998 prescribe that County schools take care for the education of 75 % of pupils in England and Wales.

356 Education Reform Act 1988 Sec. 11 para 1 b, Sec. 12 para 1. The SACRE's function is to advise the LEA on religious worship and religious education in county schools (Education Reform Act 1988 Sec. 11 para 1a); Cumper in *Harris/Joseph* (eds.), p. 383.

357 Education Act 1944 Sec. 25, re-enacted in the Education Reform Act 1988, Sec. 9, Sec. 71 para 1 of the School Standards and Framework Act 1988.

358 Education Act 1944, Sec. 25 para 4.

359 DoE Draft Circular on Religious Education and Collective Worship, 11 October 1993, Sec. 73 para 2, 75, 79.

360 Education Act 1944, Sec. 26; *Cumper* in *Harris/Joseph* (eds.), p. 385.

361 *Cumper* in *Harris/Joseph* (eds.), p. 385; ICCPR/C/SR. 1207.

362 General Comment 22, para 6.

It is therefore the case that parents in Britain may withdraw their children from schools endorsing sex education lessons, unless it forms part of the national curriculum.[363]

cc) Equality Rights/Anti-Discrimination Rights

According to English Law, there is no broad non-discrimination principle.[364] In fact, the evolvement of anti-discrimination laws in England occurred similarly to the development of fundamental rights in a fragmentary manner.[365] The recognition of their importance in the context of protection of religious minority rights emerged only due to pressing societal resentment within the British people directed especially against their Muslim immigrants.[366] In similar, to the prevailing legal situation of absent established legislation recognizing religious freedom as a fundamental right, the recognition of 'religion' as a discriminatory ground took a turn only in the last two decades. The development of anti-discrimination laws acknowledging discrimination in employment on grounds of 'religion or belief' were an initiative of the British legislator realized only in the early years of the preceding decade.[367]

In fact, prior to the divergent legislation of the recent years regarding anti-discrimination and equality rights, conflicts in the workplace on occurring on the background of religious discrimination were subject to a very limited regulation in the UK.[368] This with the exception of Northern Ireland which already espoused separate legislation on religious discrimination.[369]

---

363 Education Act 1993, Sec. 241 para 3.

364 *van Ooijen*, p. 212; *Blair/Aps*, pp. 1, 9.

365 *Sandberg* in: Hunter-Henin, Law Religious Freedoms and Education in Europe, 2011, pp. 327, 329; *van Ooijen*, p. 213.

366 Intolerance and repugnance directed especially towards Muslim immigrants in England was notable in particular following the events of 9/11 in New York and of 7/7 in London. See *van Ooijen*, p. 233.

367 *van Ooijen*, p. 212.

368 *van Ooijen*, p. 212; *Sandberg* in: Hunter-Henin, Law, Religious Freedoms and Education in Europe, 2011, pp. 327, 332.

369 Northern Ireland had introduced legislation protecting against discrimination on grounds of religion and belief already in 1976. The protection against religious discrimination in employment and occupation is established currently by the Fair Employment and Treatment (Northern Ireland) Order 1998, SI 1998/3162 (N. Ir. 21); *Freedland/Vickers*, pp. 597, 601.

The first act was the Race Relation Act 1976 which provided the basis for the prohibition of discrimination. However, the focus of this legislation was directed towards discrimination based on racial or ethnic grounds rather than on religion.

The next step was the promulgation of the Employment Equality Regulations 2003 (religion or belief) which provided claimants in allegations of religious discrimination with the option to exhaust the scope of available legislation against their employers and, in fact, integrate anti-discrimination laws and the right to religious freedom which was protected under international ECHR or domestic legislation protecting religious rights (e.g., the HRA). This was followed by the enactment of the Equality Act 2006, which aimed at the implementation of equal treatment standards primarily in the public sector.

Eminently, both the 2003 Religion or Belief Regulations and the Equality Act 2006 incorporated and implemented the EU Directives prescribing a general prohibition of unequal treatment in employment and occupation.[370]

Finally, the Equality Act 2010 was put into force and at first level, joined together the provisions on religion and belief discrimination.[371] At second level, it streamlined and extended the existing anti-discrimination standards and norms.

The implementation of the Anti-discrimination Directives into domestic law had a considerable effect on the traditional legislative framework in England, which was known to be tolerance-orientated rather than right-based associated.[372]

The significance of implementing EU Directives into domestic law is distinguishable in two respects: first, *consistency and reliability of the legislative framework* – until the implementation of the EU Directives, the challenge of discrimination based on religion has not existed in English law. This provided a solid ground for grievances of individuals that would enable to challenge discrimination based on religious grounds. Second, *extension of discriminatory grounds* – previously, the challenge of discriminatory acts against religious or ethnic minorities focused on the racial as opposed to the religious aspect. Accordingly, it was not unusual that some religious minorities were recognized as protection worthy, not because of their religious character but rather due to their recognition as an ethnic group (e.g., Jews and Sikhs) which was recognized by the law.

---

370 *Freedland/Vickers*, pp. 597, 601; *Blair/Aps*, pp. 1, 15; *van Ooijen*, p. 212. Reference is made specifically to Council Directive 2000/78/EC of 27 November 2000. To be found in eur-lex.europa.eu.

371 *Sandberg*, in: Hunter-Henin, Law, Religious Freedoms and Education in Europe, 2011, p. 327; *van Ooijen*, p. 212.

372 *Sandberg*, Law and Religion, 2011, p. 192; *van Ooijen*, p. 212.

(1) Race Relation Act 1976

The enactment of the Race Relations Act 1976[373] was undoubtedly an important step towards the protection of minorities. This act made it unlawful to discriminate on racial grounds in fields such as employment and education.[374]

The Race Relations Act was amended to oblige schools to conduct a race equality policy. In practice, this obligation compelled school administrates to assess the impact of their policies, in particular those relating to uniform dress codes.[375]

In accordance with the Equality Act 2010 that came into force in 2000, the Race Relation Act 1976 was completely repealed.

(2) Employment and Equality (Religion or Belief) Regulations 2003

Previously, the protection against discrimination at work on grounds of religion and belief had been provided in the Employment Equality (Religion or Belief) Regulations 2003, (Religion or Belief Regulations 2003).[376]

In this respect, it is worth to note that the Equality Act 2010 revoked the Religion or Belief Regulations in whole.[377] An overview with respect to its prominent provisions and related legislation will be provided, since it has a considerable significance for apprehending the background of the judicial decisions delivered prior to promulgation of the Equality Act 2010.[378] Basically, substantial provisions which had already been included in the Religion or Belief Regulations 2003 have been maintained, transferred into the Equality Act 2010, and partially extended.

---

373 Race Relations Act, 1976, c. 74, Sec. 4–9, 17–19 (Eng).

374 *Oliva*, 2008, p. 877.

375 The new Sec. 1 provided by the Race Relations Act 1976 (Amendment) Regulations 2003, applies to discrimination on grounds of race or ethnic or national origins. See Race Relations Act, 1976, Sec. 1 (b)(ii) the protection against discrimination will be on account of 'colour, race, nationality or ethnic or national origins' and not by religion; *Oliva*, 2008, pp. 877, 879; Nonetheless, due to the fact that this act aimed to protect only religious groups which were perceived as individual races as well, it was in a fact deploying its scope of protection only with relation to distinct racial bodies such as Sikhs and Jews who were able to enjoy the benefits of this legislation.

376 http://www.legislation.gov.uk/uksi/2003/1660/pdfs/uksi_20031660_en.pdf.

377 Schedule 27 of the Equality Act 2010 provides a list of revoked and repealed Acts and Regulations substituted by the new legislation.

378 A detailed examination of English jurisprudence relating to manifestation of religious symbols in public schools will be provided under Chapter III (below).

The significance of the Religion or Belief Regulations 2003 can be summarized as follows:

First, the 2003 Regulations were meant to prohibit four different types of discrimination against an employee or potential employee on grounds of religion and make them unlawful. These were: 1. Direct discrimination. 2. Indirect discrimination. 3. Harassment 4. Victimization.

Second, in general, the 2003 Regulations were meant to regulate the position of teaching staff in non-faith schools as well as of other public officials in the public sector.[379] In the case that the employment of a teacher was governed by the Regulations, then the extent to which schools could place religious requirements on its teaching staff was significantly restricted.[380]

The employment of teachers in faith schools is subject to a different set of rules, namely, the Schools Standards and Framework Act (1998). This enables voluntary aided schools to impose religious requirements on teaching staff without being subject to an unlawful discrimination claim.

Third, a limitation of any kind on a teacher prohibiting or confining his/her right to visibly display a religious symbol or the appearance with a conspicuous garment has to conform with a triple-requirement test. The prohibition should be objectively justified (i.e., genuine and determining element of the job),[381] it should be proportionate to the aim sought to be achieved, and it should serve a legitimate aim.[382]

Fourth, genuine occupational requirements – the 2003 Regulations include provisions which constitute as exceptions to the general prohibition of discrimination on religious ground in employment and acceptance to work. This enables employers to discriminate employees in acceptance and admittance for work if genuine occupational requirements for unequal treatment are at hand (known also as GOR).[383] In addition, they allow clear discrimination also with respect to vocational training required for a particular religious post under certain prerequisites.[384]

---

379 *Vickers*, Religion and Human Rights 4 (2009), pp. 137, 147.

380 *Vickers*, 2009, pp. 137, 149.

381 Sec. 7 para 2 (a) of the Religion or Belief 2003 Regulations prescribed: '…*having regard to the nature of the employment or the context in which it is carried out -being of a particular religion or belief is a genuine and determining occupational requirement…*'.

382 Sec. 7 para (b) of the Employment Equality Religion or Belief 2003

383 Under the 2010 Act these are known as 'Occupational Requirement' prescribed in Schedule 9.

384 Sec. 17 para 1 Employment Equality Religion or Belief Regulations 2003; *Addison*, p. 99.

In short, the 2003 Regulations allow two-tier GOR exceptions: first, found in Regulation 7 para 2, prescribes that an employment requirement should be genuine and a determining element for pursue of the job in question; second, Regulation 7 para 3 enables a broader exception for organizations with a religious ethos. Organizations of religious ethos were exempted from the regulations' scope having regard to the nature of employment or the context in which it is carried.

(a) Genuine and Determining Element

Regulation 7 para 2 establishes exceptions that will not be regarded as discriminatory against an employee, while taking into consideration the nature of the employment or the context in which it is carried out:

It establishes several pre-requisites to be sustained in order to be regarded as non-discriminatory act or practice for the purpose of employment and occupation.

Accordingly, the exception in employment requirements prescribed in regulation 7 para 2 will be permissible and relevant only with respect to schools which support religion or involve its teaching.[385] This means that an exception under Regulation 7 para 2 would not be permissible if it is made in order to satisfy the wish of a particular religious group to work with others of the same faith or religion.[386]

(b) Exception for Organization with Religious Ethos

An employment requirement prescribed by an organization with a religious ethos is regarded permissible if it satisfies solely the element of being genuine. This allows a greater scope of freedom for religious organizations, as they would be able to employ personnel even when the religious requirement is not necessarily a determining element for practising the job (i.e., when the personnel is not engaged directly in religious work).[387]

(3) The Equality Act 2006

The Equality Act 2006 (2006 Act), which came into force in April 2007, was intended to achieve more equality, transparency, and compliance with general equality duties, mainly in the public sector. This situation was a direct

---

385 *Vickers*, 2009, pp. 137, 148.
386 *Freedland/Vickers*, pp. 597, 603.
387 *Vickers*, 2009, pp. 137, 148.

consequence of absent adequate legislation regulating anti-discrimination laws at that time, subsequently urging the British legislator to clarify the vagueness and ensure better enforcement of acknowledged discriminatory grounds. The 2006 Act made public authorities, bodies, and institutes accountable for unlawful discriminatory conduct, and obliged them to conform to general duties advancing equality of opportunities towards individuals based on grounds designated in the Act itself.

Interestingly, the notion behind the 2006 Act when passed in the British parliament was to provide response to several unregulated topics[388]: (i) the perception held among several religious or denominational groups (e.g., Muslims) that unlike other religious minorities (Jews and Sikhs) they could not seek protection under the Race Relations Act 1976 and, as a result, demanding the extension of anti-religious discrimination laws on grounds of 'religion or belief';[389] (ii) due to the entangled church-state relations in England, the establishment of faith-based education was not perceived as unusual but rather as desirable. Therefore, in debates over passing the Bill through Parliament it was underscored that faith and denominational schools should be granted special exemptions so that they will not be regarded as incompatible with the ECHR due to their discriminatory character.[390]

Essentially, the distinctiveness of the 2006 Act can be summarized as follows: first, the establishment of legislation recognizing discrimination law embracing different grounds in order to protect individual rights from unfair treatment; second, its pivotal impact with respect to public authorities as they are committed to comply with their duties in forbearance of any kind of discrimination as stipulated in the 2006 Act. Naturally, the ensuing Equality Act 2010 (to be discussed below) derived consequences also with respect to the 2006 Act in the form of abolition of some of its provisions; nonetheless, although it repealed

388 The Act was also said to achieve the most significant change in gender equality legislation and laid a more restrictive duty on public sector authorities and institutes impacting their capacities as employers.

389 *Addison*, p. 27; It is worth to note in this context that discrimination on grounds of 'religion or belief' in the employment sector was already covered at that time under the Employment Equality (Religion or Belief) Regulations 2003; therefore, the intention was to provide a broader scope of protection that will cover all aspects of discrimination on account of religious grounds.

390 See opinions of the then Home Office Minister Baroness Scotland in Hansard, 13 July 2005, col 1136; as well as Home Office Minister Paul Goggins in Hansard, 6 December 2005, col 171; *Addison*, pp. 92–93.

the provisions of Part 2 of the 2006 Act (relating to discrimination on grounds of religion and belief),[391] it has made no meaningful alterations to the obligations existing already under the 2006 Act.[392]

(a) Scope of Protection

Mainly, it is Part 2 of the 2006 Act that introduced a new concept into the British legal system of 'discrimination on grounds of religion or belief' since it acknowledged the necessity to expand its scope of application to cover diverse areas other than employment.[393] In a sense, Part 2 of the Equality Act 2006 is regarded to be complementary to the Employment Equality (Religion or Belief) Regulations 2003. However, it was responsible for several changes relating to the definitions and scope of protection set out under the Religion or Belief Regulations. Accordingly, a brief overview of the main aims the 2006 Act purported to achieve with reference to discrimination on grounds of 'religion or belief' will be outlined:[394]

First, *establishment of the CEHR* – the 2006 Act orders the founding of the Committee for Equality and Human Rights (CEHR)[395] whose task it will be to promote understanding of equality and human rights as well as challenging acts

---

391 Para 80 of Schedule 26 in the Equality Act 2010 orders the omission of Part 2 of the Equality Act 2006. The amendments to the 2006 Act are prescribed in para 61–85 of Schedule 26 to the Equality Act 2010.

392 Notably, while the Equality Act 2010 made merely several amendments to the 2006 Act, it revoked other anti-discrimination legislation which was closely related to issues covered under the 2006 Act; for instance, the Employment Equality (Religion or Belief) Regulations 2003 and the Race Relations Act 1976, as they were substituted through the new provisions in the 2010 Act.

393 *Addison*, p. 27.

394 Further distinguishable intent of the 2006 Act was to strengthen enforcement of discrimination on grounds of gender and, as a result, incurred a duty on public authorities to foster equality of opportunity on account of gender as well as prohibited sex discrimination in the exercise of public functions (this made public authorities accountable for their actions as they were subjected to review with respect to all their practices, starting with recruitment and ending with dismissal).

395 The CEHR was supposed to take over the function of several commissions and merge them under a single body. These were, prior to establishment of the 2006 Act, the responsibility of the following commissions: the Equal Opportunities Commission (EOC), the Commission for Racial Equality (CRE), and the Disability Right Commission (DRC). In principle, the CEHR will be responsible for advancing human rights and supervising observance of equality in respect of religion and belief, sexual orientation, and age. Among its tasks are: the publishing of plans for its activities, commencing investigations, publishing reports relating to progress and establishment

of unlawful discrimination, especially in the public sector but also with respect to the private sector (though not directly included in the 2006 Act but may still be regarded subject to its effect).

Second, *interpretation of religion and belief* – the definition of 'religion and belief' as determined in the 2006 Act[396] altered the definition of religion or belief as stipulated under the abolished 2003 Regulations.[397] The widened definition was transferred from the 2006 Act to the Equality Act 2010 so that the definition of 'belief' means 'any religious or philosophical belief'.[398]

Third, *extension of scope of application* – the 2006 Act extended unlawful discrimination on grounds of religion or belief to cover more fields other than employment, thus different than stipulated under the 2003 Regulations. These were all covered under the Equality Act 2010 and include: any aspect of employment,[399] goods, facilities, and services,[400] the disposal and management of premises,[401] the exercise of public functions,[402] and education.[403]

Fourth, *education* – the impact of a general ban imposed on institutions of education to refrain from any acts of discrimination based on religious grounds included private schools as well as state-supported schools.[404] In addition,

---

of the legislation in the society, and even applying to a county court in order to inhibit act of discrimination.

396 The definition of religion and belief was stipulated formerly in para 44 (b) of the 2006 Act.

397 The definition of 'religion and belief' according to the former 2003 Regulations were prescribed in Regulation 2 (1) and used the term 'any religion, religious belief, or similar philosophical belief'. By omitting the word 'similar' from the abolished Sec. 44(b) of the 2006 Act it created a change, widening the scope to cover any belief and they do not have to be philosophically 'similar' to religious beliefs.

398 The definitions of 'religion and belief', as used to be inscribed in the former section 44 of the 2006 Act, nowadays in Sec. 10 of the Equality Act 2010, stipulate as follows: (a) "religion" means any religion; (b) "belief" means any religious or philosophical belief; (c) a reference to religion includes a reference to lack of religion; (d) a reference to belief includes a reference to lack of belief.

399 Former Sec. 77 of the 2006 Act.

400 Sec. 46 of the 2006 Act.

401 Sec.s 47–48 of the 2006 Act.

402 Sec. 52 of the 2006 Act.

403 Former Sec. 49–51 of the 2006 Act.

404 School authorities were prohibited to discriminate against pupils based on religious grounds and covered an extensive scope of educational aspects: from admission and terms of admission to school to denial of access to benefit, service, or facility of school

a general prohibition to refrain from impingement of individuals' religious rights was imposed also on local education authorities while exercising their functions.[405]

Fifth, *forms of discrimination* – the 2006 Act intended to capture within its scope all forms of 'unlawful discrimination' carried out on grounds of religion or belief.[406] Several types of discrimination were recognized and re-inserted within the scope of the 2010 Act, for instance: (i) *direct discrimination* – occurs where a person is treated on grounds of his/her religion of belief less favourably than others in equivalent circumstances;[407] (ii) *indirect discrimination* – the application of a practice, provision, or criteria though applied equally to everyone places people of a particular religion at disadvantage to others;[408] (iii) *victimization* – treating someone less favourably given that there is a knowledge or even suspicion that this person submitted a complaint or proceedings under the 2010 Act.[409] The other two heads were repealed by the 2010 Act and included the following heads: (iv) *discriminatory advertisements*;[410] and (v) *instructing or causing discrimination*.[411]

(b) Limitation of Scope

The list of exceptions to which the scope of the 2006 Act does not apply is captured also under the Equality Act 2010. The exceptions are very similar in content and the objects the British legislator wished to exclude from their scope of protection so they will not fall within the general prohibition of discrimination on religious grounds. An overview of the exceptions listed in the 2010 Act will be mentioned briefly:

---

as well as pupils' exclusion from school. The provisions were covered by Part 2 (Sec. 49(1) of the 2006 Act) which was abolished and are now covered by Part 6 of the 2010 Act.

405 Sec. 85 of the Equality Act 2010 (formerly Sec. 51 of the 2006 Act).

406 Formerly, Sec.s 45–55 of the 2006 Act.

407 Sec. 13 of the Equality Act 2010 (Formerly, Sec. 45 para 1 of the 2006 Act).

408 Sec. 19 of the Equality Act 2010 (Formerly, Sec. 45 para 3 of the 2006 Act).

409 Sec. 27 of the Equality Act 2010 (Formerly, Sec. 45 para 4 of the 2006 Act).

410 Discriminatory advertisement was formerly captured under Sec. 54 of the 2006 Act and was designated – the publishing or causing an advertisement to be published if it indicates to discriminate in any way to be regarded unlawful under the 2006 Act.

411 Instructing or causing discrimination was formerly captured under Sec. 55 of the 2006 Act that prescribed – instructing or causing another person to discriminate in a way regarded unlawful under the 2006 Act.

First, *designated schools* – by that, the legislator intended to grant protection to schools with a religious character. A list of various schools which were exempted from the general prohibition of unlawful discrimination applied with respect to educational institutions and included mainly schools with a religious character or religious ethos.[412] The provisions which have now been re-introduced under the 2010 Act and include state-supported schools as well as private denominational schools remained unaltered.[413]

Second, *faith schools* – together with schools of a religious ethos were considered to be exempted from compliance with the general ban of religious discrimination to ensure that the tenets of faith schools are not in conflict.[414]

Third, *curriculum and collective worship* – in order to prevent a misuse of the practices observed in denominational schools, an exception was endorsed with respect to:[415]

(i) The content of curriculum in schools, and

(ii) Acts of worship or other religious observance organized by or on behalf of an educational establishment (whether or not forming part of the curriculum).

Fourth, *religions or belief organizations* – the law meant to capture organizations with a religious ethos within its scope. The exception applied also if the purpose of a religious organization was to educate, practise, or advance persons of the same religion if they were to carry an activity given that it conformed to the framework of that religion or belief.[416]

---

412 Educational establishments which were governed by the former Sec. 49 and its prohibition of discrimination were granted exemption under Sec. 50 of the 2006 Act.

413 Now prescribed under Part 2 of Schedule 11 of the Equality Act 2010. Formerly under Sec. 49, 50, 59, and 61 of the Equality Act 2006.

414 Formerly, Sec. 59 of the 2006 Act. It should be underscored that despite the list of exceptions provided to faith or religious schools in Sec. 50 (1) of the 2006 Act, it provided no defence to claims brought under Sec. 49 (c) (iii) relating to exclusion of a pupil from the establishment or (iv) the subjecting of a pupil to any other detriment as this was condemned to be a discriminatory practice if occurred prior to school admission. It was explained that religious schools could discriminate a pupil prior to application; however, no justification to acceptance of exception will avail school authorities if the pupil or his/her parents subsequently have changed or lost their faith. See in this respect *Addison*, p. 94.

415 The 2006 Act prescribed in Sec. 50 (2) this exception to the discrimination prohibition that was set out in the former Sec. 49 (1) (c) (i), (ii), or (iv) and excluded its application with respect to school's curriculum and acts of worship or religious observance.

416 Sec. 3 of Schedule 9 of the Equality Act 2010; Formerly, Sec. 61 of the 2006 Act.

Fifth, *proportionality and reasonableness* – as a general rule, indirect discrimination would not be unlawful if it can be justified. So basically, any complaint of indirect discrimination[417] conducted on grounds of religion or belief by reason of any the exceptions prescribed by the 2006 Act[418] is to be regarded permissible if the discriminator was able to demonstrate the existence of a legitimate aim[419] and stand the tests of reasonableness and proportionality.

(4) Equality Act 2010

The Equality Act 2010 (Equality Act 2010 or 2010 Act), which came into force on 1 October 2010 purported to strengthen and streamline anti-discrimination legislation in Great Britain.[420] In fact, the Equality Act 2010 conjoined the provisions on religious and belief discrimination that up to that time were scattered over the Religion or belief Regulations 2003 and the Equality Act 2006.[421] It therefore incorporated the existing compilation of acts and regulations establishing the fundaments of anti-discrimination laws, and provided a comparable extended protection for an ample array of equality rights consolidated in one single piece of legislation.

The equality Act 2010 aimed to create a new public sector equality duty which offers extension of the protection to new equality grounds, such as religion and belief, age, sexual orientation, maternity, and pregnancy.[422] It imposes an equality duty on public authorities, including governing bodies of maintained schools.[423]

---

417 Formerly, Sec. 54 para 3 of the 2006 Act.

418 Formerly, Sec.s 46–52 of the 2006 Act.

419 This statutory demand for 'legitimate aim' was provided and incorporated in the former Sec. 45 para 3 (d) of the 2006 Act.

420 http://odi.dwp.gov.uk/disabled-people-and-legislation/equality-act-2010-and-dda-1995.php.

421 Though the Religion or Belief Regulations 2003 were abolished by the Equality Act 2010 and therefore are no longer of any relevance for future complaints, this does not make them redundant, especially given the modifications created by the 2006 Act and its distinctiveness in comparison to the Religion or Belief Regulations 2003.

422 The extension of the public sector equality duty to other equality heads is contained in Sec. 149 of the Act which came into effect only in April 2011. The new duties were added to the duties already existing under different statutes with regard to race, gender, and disability.

423 Sec. 150 para 3, Equality Act 2010 refers to the list of '*public authorities*' as prescribed under the Equality Act 2010, Schedule 19. The list includes '*governing bodies of an educational establishment maintained by an English local authority*' within the definition of 'public authorities'. What will be regarded as '*English Local Authority*' is taken

Sec. 149 para 1 imposes a duty on public authority in the exercise of its functions to have due regard to the need to:

(a) eliminate discrimination, harassment, victimization, and any other conduct that is prohibited by or under this Act.
(b) advance equality of opportunity between persons who share a protected characteristic and persons who do not share it.
(c) foster good relations between persons who share a relevant protected characteristic and persons who do not share it.

The new Religion and Belief public sector equality duty was intended to apply in the education context both to faith and non-faith schools.[424] Although the law remains silent as to the form or manner in which public authorities are supposed to comply with the new equality duty, a reference can be inferred from other equality policies introduced in the education system (e.g., the duty imposed on schools to promote community cohesion).[425] The duty to eliminate discrimination and promote equality had been recognized especially in schools as a key element for promotion of good relations between communities in a society. Schools are perceived as an appropriate place to achieve equality on a wider range other than religion and belief, tackle discrimination, and foster community cohesion. It is due to this fact that different initiatives taken on part of schools and governing bodies to promote equal opportunity, such as the well-established community cohesion agenda and active, positive promotion of the equality duty had been introduced long before the new equality duty went into force; in some sense those initiatives had already provided protection to the new equality grounds added by the 2010 Act.[426]

The criticism raised with respect to the equality duty on grounds of religion and belief in the form of its active promotion in state schools views the conflict of interests between different religious groups as well as those of no faith. The difficulties arise due to lack of a clear definition of the term 'religion and belief' in the legislation as well as problems to evaluate which religion or belief should be protected and deserve accommodation of its needs.[427] It is considered that

within the meaning prescribed in Sec. 162 para 6 of the Education and Inspections Act 2006.

424 *Vickers*, in: Hunter-Henin, Law, Religious Freedoms and Education in Europe, 2011, pp. 97, 101.

425 Education and Inspection Act 2006, Sec. 38.

426 *Vickers*, in: Hunter-Henin, 2011, p. 97.

427 The conflicts that may arise due to inclusion of the equality of religion and belief duty to the public sector duty can be demonstrated already when school authorities decide

full participation of all religious groups is identified and recognized in school as endorsement of religion. Thence, it is contended that this understanding of equality together with an active initiative to foster good relations and community cohesion can be perceived as an official endorsement of religion into the educational system. This is regarded inappropriate by those who believe that religion should be left out of the educational context or the public sphere.[428] It is criticized that the obligation to active promotion of equality and the fostering of good relations between religious groups in form of positive steps risks the extension of public sector equality duty which aimed in its formal sense, as set out in Sec. 149 Equality Act 2010, merely to eliminate discrimination and promote equality in schools.

This reflects the weakness of the Equality Act 2010, since full equality that acknowledges and recognizes all religious identities in a society may pose danger to promotion of community cohesion in state schools. The reason for this is that the focus on religion in schools might emphasize and draw attention to religious differences.[429] This may eventually increase tensions in school between different religious groups including between those with a religion or faith and those of no faith.

In practice, compliance with the new equality duty has not led to a great change as it did not add much to the earlier public sector duties which were already protected in a range of policies and initiatives undertaken in schools. These formal equality policies had been introduced by schools and governing bodies as part of the well-known community cohesion agenda to which schools are committed. However, according to the Equality Act 2010, no duty is incumbent on schools to take active steps to promote equality, maintain social cohesion,

---

that the religious needs of the majority of mainstream religions will be accommodated (e.g., days of rest and holidays, religious dietary requirements, religious dress code etc.), as opposed to that of minority religious groups or those who share no belief at all. In that sense, equality for non-religious persons demands also their protection through a complete exclusion of religion from school or maybe a separate assembly or celebration the same as allowed to other religions in schools would promote the equality duty. In addition, even between the same religious groups there may be different streams and opinions. The difficulty will be to establish or value which voice within that group represents a reliable voice of the religion or the predominating stream within this religious group.

428 *Vickers*, in: Hunter-Henin, 2011, pp. 97, 101.

429 *Vickers*, in: Hunter-Henin, 2011, pp. 97, 100.

and foster good relations. Instead of an active duty to promote equality, schools are only expected to abide by the equal treatment principle.

Primarily, the 2010 Act aims at extension of the public sector and the introduction into schools of new equality grounds such as religion and belief duty. This can be achieved by tackling discrimination at school, advancing equal opportunities, and fostering good community cohesion.[430]

(a) Scope of Protection

In principle, the declaratory aim of the Equality act 2010 is to ban unfair treatment and foster the achievement of equal opportunities in the workplace in British society. This was meant to be achieved through the introduction of 'general equality duty' on public authorities.[431]

The 2010 Act mirrors the EU Equality Directives;[432] it demands equal treatment in access to workplaces in the private as well as in the public sector and forbids discrimination on account of various grounds. In this view, a reference will be given to the key elements constituting the Equality Act 2010.

(aa) Addition of New Equality Grounds

The major change was the endorsement of nine grounds designated under Chapter 1 of Part 2 of the 2010 Act which are defined as 'protected characteristics' and no longer as discriminatory grounds. Hence, 'protected characteristics' include the following: age, disability, gender reassignment, marriage and civil partnership, race, religion, or belief, sex, and sexual orientation. Each of the aforementioned grounds is specified in a separate provision so that the rest of the

---

430 The suggestion in legal literature is that a successful implementation of the new equality religion and belief duty can be achieved through focus on social inclusion and equality that is based on full participation in society for all. This will detract the attention from a notion of a quantitative equal treatment for each religious or belief group that may increase tension between different religion groups in schools as they will all wish to be protected and in addition will run the danger of endorsement of religion into schools. See *Vickers*, in: Hunter-Henin, 2011, pp. 97, 100–102.

431 Sec. 149 of the Equality Act 2010.

432 These are the following: European Community Council Directive 2000/78/EC, known as the Employment Equality Directive, provides a general framework for equal treatment in employment and occupation and prohibits discrimination based on religion or belief, gender, disability, age, or sexual orientation; and The Racial Equality Directive, Council directive 2000/43/EC that implements the principle of equal treatment of persons irrespective of ethnic or racial origin.

2010 Act provisions apply to all of the 'protected characteristics' unless an exception is specifically designated with respect to one or several of them.

(bb) Definition Religion and Belief

The definition of 'religion and belief' as set out under the 2010 Act is of no substantial difference to the definition of 'religion and belief' as prescribed under the 2006 Act. In fact, they are similar and include the right to hold every religion as well as every form of philosophical belief, including atheism and other non-denominational forms or lack of belief.[433] This in itself may provide a fertile ground for controversies between different identity groups that may rise due to religious endorsement in state schools.

The terms 'religion' and 'belief' are defined as 'any religion, religious belief' or 'philosophical belief'.[434] This elaborated the scope of what will normally be regarded as 'philosophical belief' to include genuine philosophical belief and political belief. These vague definitions in the legislation create two combined problems as they: first, make protection under the 2010 Act uncertain and dubious; second, schools as employers will remain unclear about the scope of their new employment duty. Guidance, though, can be drawn from jurisprudence of the ECtHR which determines that the term 'belief' must have sufficient 'cogency, seriousness, cohesion and importance' to warrant protection.[435]

(cc) Discrimination on Religious Grounds in Employment

Discrimination on religious grounds in employment is governed by Chapter 1 of Part 5 of the 2010 Act.[436] The 2010 Act covers any discriminatory act or behaviour on part of the employer aiming to prejudice or disadvantage employees of other religion or belief. The scope of protection extends to cover discriminatory practices in employment and occupation, making it unlawful to discriminate on grounds of religion or belief in acceptance to work, in terms of employment, and by refusing to offer employment.[437] When employment takes place, it will be forbidden to discriminate in the afforded terms of employment, in opportunities for promotion, by dismissal, and by ending the employment relationship.[438]

433 Sec. 10 para 1 and & para 2 Equality Act 2010.

434 Equality Act 2010, Sec. 10. See in http://www.legislation.gov.uk/ukpga/2010/15/section/10

435 X, Y and Z v. UK, (1982) 31 DR 50 (U.K.); Campbell and Cosans v UK, 4 Eur. H.R. Rep 293 (1982) (U.K.).

436 In particular, Sec.s 39–41 of the 2010 Act.

437 Sec. 39 of the Equality Act 2010.

438 Sec. 39 para 2 of the Equality Act 2010.

According to the 2006 Act which established the categorization of different forms of discrimination (acknowledged also under the abolished Religion or Belief Regulations 2003), it is apparent that the 2010 Act followed that path and made at large no segregation with respect to their main substance, apart from the fact that these discrimination forms will apply to all 'protected characteristics' with the relevant exceptions applicable respectively. As they are equivalent to their former counterparts in the 2006 Act, a repetition here will be surplus so that a reference to the relevant provisions underscoring merely essential changes should suffice.[439]

(aaa) Direct Discrimination

Direct discrimination is defined as discrimination that occurs when a person is treated less favourably than others in similar circumstances on grounds of a person's actual religion or belief.[440] This includes discrimination based on association with people of a particular religion and which does not accord with the employer's religion.

However, discrimination on grounds of the employer's religion remains outside the scope of the 2010 Act and would be regarded as legal (e.g., an institution with a religious ethos, such as a church, may demand that employees will be members of the same religion as their employers).[441]

(bbb) Indirect Discrimination

Indirect discrimination will occur in case a provision, criterion, or practice applied equally to those not of the same religion, but in fact places persons of the religion in question at a distinguishable disadvantage compared to others. Such a detrimental practice is to be regarded illegal if it cannot be proved to constitute a proportionate mean for achieving a legitimate aim.[442]

---

439 The following forms of discrimination were recognized by the 2010 Act: 1. Direct Discrimination (Sec. 13). 2. Indirect Discrimination (Sec. 19). 3. Harassment (Sec. 26). 4. Victimization (Sec. 27).

440 This discrimination on grounds of religion or belief is the least favourable of all forms of discrimination and is much easier to detect. It is set out in Sec. 13 of the Equality Act 2010.

441 The exception is prescribed in Sec. 3 of Schedule 9 to the Equality Act 2010; previously the same exception was prescribed under the Religion or Belief Regulations 2003 in Regulation 7 para 3 and was known as the so called 'religious ethos employer exception'. Nonetheless, now and then these exceptions had to bear limitations and were subject to scrutiny (i.e., the demand to comply with a religious demand had to be proportionate and serve a legitimate aim).

442 The Equality Act 2010, Sec. 19.

In order to establish a claim of indirect discrimination, the claimant must prove that neutral work requirements operate to his disadvantage due to his pertinence to a religious (or non-religious) or belief- based group.

Notably, it is of no relevance that an employee can in fact comply with a requirement, but rather whether it is harder for him to comply with the requirement in practice such that it works to his detriment in comparison to others of different faiths or religions.[443]

It will then be the task of the employer to show that the requirement is justified as a proportionate means of achieving a legal aim. If the requirement cannot be justified, it will be regarded as unlawful indirect discrimination.[444]

(ccc) Victimization

The unlawful discrimination of victimization had incurred no changes as opposed to its former counterpart under the Equality Act 2006; as a result, it remained similar in content.[445]

Apart from the discriminatory forms as known and replicated from the 2006 Act, there has been an extension to a new form of unlawful discrimination introduced by the Equality 2010 Act. It has actually extended the protection offered to employees under former equality legislations with respect to several aspects as follows:

(ddd) Harassment on Grounds of Religion and Belief

An additional form of discrimination was introduced in the 2010 Act and included the unlawful offence, harassment. Harassment is depicted in Sec. 26 of the 2010 Act and constitutes an '…unwanted conduct related to a relevant protected characteristic…' such as religion or belief, and has the purpose or effect of violating, first, an 'individual's dignity' or, second, 'creating of an intimidating, hostile, degrading, humiliating or offensive environment…' for the complainant.[446] The 2010 Act goes further to extend and supplement liability of employers to cover 'third party harassment' related to a 'protected characteristic' such as religion or belief, as clearly indicated in Sec. 40. This actually extends liability of employers with respect to the offence of harassment conducted by a third party (e.g., other teachers in school) and imposes a higher burden on employers.

---

443 *Freedland/Vickers*, pp. 597, 608.

444 *Freedland/Vickers*, pp. 597, 608.

445 Sec. 27 of the Equality Act 2010.

446 Sec. 26 para 1 of the 2010 Act.

(dd) Combined Discrimination

As a practical matter, a complainant will be able to submit allegation against an employer or any public authority comprehended by the 2010 Act by virtue of a dual characteristic discrimination (e.g., religion or belief together with race).[447] This, undoubtedly, will ease the access of complainants in discrimination claims to court as they can establish a combined equality claim relying on a single enactment.

(ee) Discrimination on Religious Grounds in Education

Discrimination on religious grounds in education is covered under Chapters 1 and 2 of Part 6 of the 2010 Act (in particular sections 85, 86, 91, and 92). The 2010 Act concludes compliance of schools and institutes of higher education, such as universities and colleges with the 'general equality duty' imposed with respect to the 'protected characteristics' stipulated in the 2010 Act.[448] The legislation captures educational institutions, local authorities, and education authorities.[449] Since educational establishments are recognized as public bodies under the 2010 Act,[450] it may affect educational institutions in the following matters:

- Employment, recruitment, and dismissal of teaching staff (Sec. 39 Equality Act 2010)
- Teaching (Sec. 39 and 40 Equality Act 2010)
- Admission of students (Sec. 85 para 1 Equality Act 2010)
- Accessibility to facilities and services of educational institutes (Sec. 85 para 2 (b) Equality Act 2010).

The prohibition of discrimination of pupils in educational institutes by arrangement for admission, terms of admission, and refusal of a pupil's admission were literally transferred from the former provisions specified in the 2006 Act and re-inserted in Sec. 85 paragraphs 1 and 2 of the 2010 Act.[451]

---

447 Sec. 14 of the Equality Act 2010.

448 Chapter 1 of Part 6 of the 2010 Act relating to the educational system and the general ban of discrimination imposed on the different educational institutes provided in Sec. 84 for an exception with respect to the following 'protected characteristics': 1. age. 2. marriage and civil partnership.

449 Sec. 85 para 7 and para 8 of the Equality Act 2010.

450 The status of educational establishments as public authorities and their obligation to comply with the 2010 Act is confirmed in Sec. 150 para 1 which refers to the listing of public bodies as specified in Schedule 19 of the 2010 Act.

451 The former equivalent was found in Sec. 49 para 1 of the 2006 Act. Sec. 85 (1) of the 2010 Act dealing with admission and treatment of pupils to schools determines that: ' *The responsible body of a school to which this section applies must not discriminate*

In case unlawful discrimination should take place, a complainant can seek redress by applying for judicial proceedings. The 2010 Act points out the legal proceedings that a claimant needs to carry out prior to submission of a claim against education authorities.[452]

(b) Limitation of Scope

Under the 2010 Act exceptions are appointed in the relevant schedule for each chapter. Mostly, they are similar in notion and content to provisions prescribed in former equality legislations (i.e., Religion and Belief Regulations 2003 and Equality Act 2006), and will constitute an exception to the general non-discrimination rule if proved necessary and proportionate to the aim the legislator sought to achieve.[453] The following will apply with exception of minor changes underlined below:

(aa) General Occupational Requirement

In confined circumstances, an employer will be able to specify that job applicants must acquire a specific 'protected characteristic' designated under the 2010 Act. If the employer will prove that this 'protected characteristic' constitutes an inherent requirement for the nature or context of work and is proportionate for achieving a legitimate aim, it will not be considered as unlawful discrimination captured under the 2010 Act.[454] Therefore, occupational requirement[455] of an

---

against a person – '(a) in the arrangements it makes for deciding who is offered admission as a pupil; (b) as to the terms in which it offers to admit the person as a pupil; (c) by not admitting the person as a pupil'. Sec. 85 (2) prescribes that: *'The responsible body of such a school must not discriminate against a pupil – (a) in the way it provides education for the pupil; (b) in the way it affords the pupil access to a benefit, facility or service; (c) by not providing education for the pupil; (d) by not affording the pupil access to a benefit, facility or service; (e) by excluding the pupil from the school; (f) by subjecting the pupil to any other detriment'*. Sec. 91 of the 2010 Act relates to admission and treatment of a student to a university or an institute of higher education. In that sense, the wording of Sec. 91 para 1 and para 2 constitutes a repetition of the requirements announced with regard to school pupils in Sec. 85 para 1 and para 2 as quoted above, but with the necessary reference to university or high-education students.

452 Sec. 114 para 1 (c) para 2, para 3, and para 4 of the Equality Act 2010 (formerly Sec. 66 para 2 and para 3 of the Equality Act 2006).

453 *Freedland/Vickers*, pp. 597, 617.

454 Para 1 (1) and 1 (2) of Schedule 9 of the 2010 Act.

455 Previously under the 2003 Regulations, the specification in Regulation 7 para 2 was for Genuineness Employment Requirement so the employer had to bear the burden of proof demonstrating that the demand for an employee to comply with a work requirement was indeed a genuine one for that specific job.

employer referring to a particular 'protected characteristic' will not be regarded as contravening specific provisions under Chapter 1 of Part 5 of the 2010 Act prohibiting discrimination in employment as long as they comply with specific requirements outlined in para 1(1) of Schedule 9 of the 2010 Act.[456]

(bb) Denominational and Faith Schools

In principle, the exceptions to the general prohibition of religious discrimination in schools of religious ethos or character as reviewed under the 2006 Act are replicated in the 2010 Act. Thus, the corresponding exceptions under the 2010 Act are set out respectively in Part 2 of Schedule 11 (Sec. 5).[457] These provisions were inserted as the government believed that denominational schools have the right to discriminate on religious grounds, and that it is better to keep faith schools undisturbed as it was alleged that they carry an important contribution to the diversity of education.

---

456 The provisions regulating the exception of 'Occupational Requirements' within Employment (Chapter 5) are described in Schedule 9 of the 2010 Act.

457 Sec. 5 in Part 2 of Schedule 11 of the 2010 Act makes a list of schools with a religious character to which an exception will apply so that no discriminatory act on religious grounds will be accounted to them; it declares that Sec. 85 para 1 and para 2 (a) to (d) will not be applicable with respect to them. These are the following.

(a) A school designated under Sec. 69 para 3 of the School Standards and Framework Act 1998 (foundation or voluntary school with religious character) (Formerly Sec. 50 para 1 (a) Equality Act 2006).
(b) A school listed in the register of independent schools for England or for Wales designating that the school carries a religious ethos (Formerly Sec. 50 para 1 (b) Equality Act 2006)
(c) A school transferred to an education authority under Sec. 16 of the Education (Scotland) Act 1980 (transfer of certain schools to education authorities) which is conducted in the interest of a church or a denominational body (Formerly Sec. 50 para 1(c) and (d) Equality Act 2006).
(d) A school provided by an education authority under Sec. 17 para 2 of the Act (denominational schools).
(e) A grant-aided school which is conducted in the interest of a church or a denominational body (Formerly Sec. 50 para 1(e) Equality Act 2006).
(f) A school registered in the register for independent schools in Scotland if the school: admits only pupils who belong, or whose parents belong, to one or more particular denominations (Formerly, Sec. 50 para 1(f) Equality Act 2006).
(g) A school registered in that register if the school is conducted in the interest of a church or denominational body. http://www.legislation.gov.uk/ukpga/2010/15/schedule/11

By excluding faith schools from of the scope of the Equality Act 2010, it allows in fact discrimination by faith schools in order to ensure that they retain their religious character.[458] Therefore, in case a school falls within the list of exceptions (designated in para 5 of Part 2 of Schedule 11 to the 2010 Act), its application will provide school authorities a complete defence against any claim of discrimination brought under Sec. 85 para 1 and 2(a)–(d) of the 2010 Act.

(cc) Organizations with a Religious Ethos

Para 3 of Schedule 9 of the 2010 Act enables organizations with religious ethos to impose an occupational requirement[459] of pertinence to a particular religion 'having regard to the ethos and nature of the work'.[460] In such a case, the requirement must be proportionate and serve a legitimate aim so as not to contravene the equality duty and be deemed a prohibited discrimination.[461]

(dd) Curriculum and School Practices

Similarly to the rule in the above-mentioned subsection, an exception to the general prohibition of discrimination on religious grounds will be applicable also with respect to the content of curriculum or collective worships. This is stipulated in Part 2 of Schedule 11 (Sec. 6).

In other words, a pupil or his parents wishing to establish a claim against school administrative due to their refusal to the content of school curriculum or acts of worship, such as school prayers organized by school authorities, will not succeed as such a claim would most likely be repelled (Para 6 of Schedule 11 to the 2010 Act).

(ee) Pursue of a Legitimate Aim

Conceivably, some workplaces will impose a dress code policy and expect their employees to keep compliance accordingly. The demand of a public authority

---

458 *Addison*, p. 99.

459 Para 3(a) Schedule 9, Equality Act 2010.

460 Para 3(b) Schedule 9, Equality Act 2010.

461 Previously, specific exceptions to the non-discrimination rules were prescribed in regulations 7 para 2 and 7 para 3 of the Religion or Belief Regulations 2003. Nonetheless, even under the Regulations these exceptions were subject to limitations. Accordingly, Regulation 7 para 3, known as the 'religious ethos employer exception' took into consideration the nature of the employment where the employer has a religious ethos in order to examine the genuineness and proportionality of the requirement to be of a particular religion before allowing such religious discrimination to be justified. See also in: *Freedland/Vickers*, pp. 597, 604.

from its employees to conform to rules on dress or appearance at work would be regarded as permissible given that they do not give rise to unlawful discrimination.

In principle, employees have to comply with dress codes imposed by their employers. The requirements of the employer to comply with a particular dress code may include the obligation to wear a uniform, may consist of rules on hair length, and may even include the ban to wear religious symbols such as crosses, headscarves, or turbans during working time.[462]

These requirements may place religious individuals at a particular disadvantage and, as a result, need to prove that the restriction is proportionate and achieves a legitimate aim in order to be justified.[463] Unjustified policies can substantiate a claim of indirect discrimination, unless the employer would be able to prove that imposition of such a dress code serves a proportionate mean to achieve a legitimate aim. The requirement of a legitimate aim would suffice for the courts if they fall into the category of a legitimate aim recognized as one of the following: national security,[464] health regulations, public safety, and the preservation of a professional image of the employer.

In addition, a person will not be regarded as contravening the provisions specified in the 2010 Act (e.g., Employment and Education Chapters) given that the provisions relate to the protected characteristic, 'religion or belief' contained therein, and so far as the person acts in pursuant to a requirement specified in an enactment or a requirement or condition imposed by virtue of an enactment.[465] In that sense, an employer will not be deemed to contravene the 2010 Act with respect to the relevant 'protected characteristic' if the practice or conduct in question are pursuant to a requirement or grounds for justification stipulated in an enactment. This accords with the exception of statutory provisions administered under Schedule 22 of the 2010 Act that specifies which chapters in the 2010 Act apply to each specific 'protected characteristic' and to which the general prohibition of discrimination would not apply if their contravention takes place

462 See a Guide for Employers relating to religion and belief in the workplace published by the Equality and Human Rights Commission http://www.equalityhumanrights.com/sites/default/files/publication_pdf/GD.12.411-2 %20Religion%20belief%20workplace%20employers%2026-03-14b.pdf.

463 Para 1(1) (b) of Schedule 9 to the Equality Act 2010.

464 The Equality Act 2010, Sec. 192.

465 Para 1(1) of Schedule 22 (Statutory Provisions) to the Equality Act 2010.

by virtue of a statutory requirement prescribed by an enactment (either the 2010 Act or another enactment).[466]

Many discussions involved the issue of religious dress codes at work with relation to the headscarves or veils of female Muslims and whether its prohibition would be regarded as lawful or not.[467]

As the 2010 Act deals with equality rights and the protection of individual's religious interests, it is inevitable that competing interests exist and generate conflicts and controversies, especially in the context of education and employment within the educational system. It is therefore inevitable that accommodation to special religious needs of an individual (pertaining to a minority religious group) will always trigger and undermine the negative freedom of others (in that case other employees pertaining to the majority religious group or to non-believers group employed in the same educational institute).

c) Constitutional and Legal Principles

aa) Parliament Supremacy

In the absence of a written constitution or analogous legal document carrying a pre-eminent legal status in England, the constitution is comprised of extra-legal rules and practices, some of which obtain a distinctive feature.[468] The legal rule of parliament supremacy, like other rules of the English constitution, is an unwritten constitutional principle; however, it is distinguishable in its uniqueness since it regards the supremacy of parliament and not of the constitution,[469] as the case would presumably be in other constitution-based systems (e.g., Germany and France).

The principle prescribes basically that an Act of Parliament can change any law, produce any result, and cannot be challenged on legal grounds even to the extent that it infringes fundamental rights or run counter to other constitutional values.

---

466 Para 4 of Schedule 22 to the Equality Act 2010 permits schools to contravene the equality duty prescribed in Art. 149 of the Equality Act 2010 by virtue of a statutory requirement prescribed in other educational legislation. For instance, dismissal of a teacher for failure to deliver religious education efficiently according to the School Standards and Framework Act 1998 (para 4(a) of Schedule 22).

467 *Freedland/Vickers*, pp. 597, 613.

468 *Edge*, p. 75.

469 *Edge*, p. 77.

bb) Principle of Neutrality

Albeit the fact that England has an established church, there is a strong approach in Britain favouring the notion that the state should remain neutral on religious issues.[470] This approach is based on the accommodative[471] and accepting attitude England demonstrated towards its religious minorities in the course of its history. In addition, the acknowledgement that it has become an increasing multi-cultural society with divergent ethnic and religious backgrounds,[472] carrying legitimate expectations from the state to grant them with adequate space to practise their religious manifestation and guarantee the legal protection thereof, has contributed to the adaption of a neutral-state approach.[473]

Especially in public education, where establishment, recruitment of teaching staff, and dress code rules are subject to regional governance, it was easier to adjust to the neutrality principle as conflicts on religious matters were not left to central administration but were resolved between school authorities and involved parents.

In principle, there is no formal separation between state and religion. However, the notion of state neutrality is used in the public and legal discussion. It is due to the lack of a written constitution that there is neither express enunciation of the principle of neutrality,[474] nor an explicit codification of the state neutrality principle in a legislative act. The principle is rather derived from other constitutional principles, such as the rule of law and the equality treatment principle.

The reasons for which the principle of neutrality was not explicitly defined in the legal framework of England can be attributed to the following:

First, *no codification of rules and legal principles* – a distinctive characteristic of the legal tradition and practice in England is that its constitutional rules and legal principles are not established in a single comprehensive legal document,[475] but are rather scattered throughout the body of the English law. Therefore, no efforts were made to legislate or codify the neutrality principle as a legal rule.

Second, *no legal definition of public service*[476] – this presents challenges and difficulties the state may encounter in its attempt to accommodate the needs of its

470 *Vickers*, 2009, pp. 137, 144; *Hill*, Church Autonomy in the United Kingdom, p. 274.
471 *van Ooijen*, pp. 215, 216.
472 *Vickers*, 2009, pp. 137,144.
473 *van Ooijen*, p. 214; *Fetzer/Soper*, p. 38.
474 *Hill*, Church Autonomy in the United Kingdom, p. 274.
475 *van Ooijen*, p. 220.
476 *van Ooijen*, p. 220.

religious minorities given that there is a need to impose limitations on fundamental rights in a sphere which remains undefined.

The state neutrality principle in England takes form through:

First, *implication from other constitutional principles* – the obligation of the state to remain neutral in its acts without demonstration of favouritism to a specific religion, especially in the public sphere, can be inferred from other constitutional principles, such as the rule of law and the principle of equality.[477] The principle of the rule of law confines state power, so it is unable to interfere with freedom or liberties of individuals without legitimate grounds embodied in legislation. The equality before the law prescribes that all citizens are equal before the law and prohibits the state from discriminatory acts founded on different grounds, such as race, ethnic, religion, gender, etc.

Second, *public service ethos* – in principle, although it is difficult to conceptualize the definition of the British public service ethos, one can say that it is a congregation of specific ethic rules. One of the most prominent and recognized is the duty of the state to impartiality in its actions.[478]

In the context of state-church interplay and the position religion should accommodate in the public sphere, the tendency indicates explicitly towards religious neutrality. This applies to the public sector as a whole including specific public functions such as in the educational sphere.[479]

It is notable that the notion of state neutrality and the importance attributed to it in the English legal were subject to criticism framework when considered as a legitimate ground to curtail rights of religious minorities to manifest their religion in the public sphere. This criticism was mainly directed to the lack of consistency of the British state to maintain a coherent secular or neutral approach towards its versatile religious groups.[480]

d) Assessment of the Legal System

The British legal system within the context of its state-church relations and the position religion acquires in the public sphere features at large a direct outcome of the place religion had known in the history of England. On a legal level, the right to freedom of religion was not recognized as a positive right,

---

477 *van Ooijen*, p. 220; *Vickers*, 2009, pp. 137, 145.

478 *van Ooijen*, p. 220; *Rayner/Williams/Lawton/Allinson*, p. 28.

479 *Vickers*, 2009, pp. 137, 144.

480 *Bloß*, p. 58; *Fetzer/Soper*, p. 38.

and surprisingly remained an unprotected right in England's legislative system until mid-twentieth century. Following a review of the evolution the British legal system had historically undergone with respect to the freedom of religious rights, it is rather overwhelming to discover that only in the last decades this freedom was acknowledged as a fundamental right. In retrospect, it becomes apparent how this development turned indispensable while it was transferring from a general notion of religious tolerance to an explicit acknowledged basic right of religious freedom.

The reason the right to religious freedom was not recognized as fundamental liberty right can be attributed in large part to the lack of a written constitution and the absence of a legal mechanism set for the protection of fundamental human rights in the UK. In addition, since no legal recognition existed, it is more staggering to reveal that due to the lack of a set of fundamental guarantees protected under a single document, like a British Bill of Rights, the protection of individuals' rights in England remained secured in practice by the legislator (British Parliament) and the judiciary which previously evolved under the doctrine of the common law system.

Originally, since the right to religious freedom was not recognized in the British legal system as a protected liberty right, the protection of religious rights of minority groups took place through different equality legislations, such as The Race and Relations Act 1976 and the Religion or Belief Regulations 2003 which were abolished later by the Equality Act 2010. It is worth to note that the established position of the Anglican faith and themes relating to the Christian religion (with the exception of Catholicism) remained solely within the discretion of the Church of England by virtue of its privileged status granted to it by law.

In principle, the sources of law in England's legal system had their origins mainly on domestic level, from parliament legislation and the evolvement of common law through the British judicature which developed legal rules that acquired significance under substantive law. On the international level, the obligation of England to respect and abide fundamental human rights, based on global standards facilitated to ensure their guarantee, took place through the ratification or incorporation of international treaties which have become increasingly significant as a traditional source of English law.

The British legislator contributed significantly to the growth of legislation. In particular, anti-discrimination and education laws have constantly changed and expanded in the last two decades. Due to the development of the rule of legislative supremacy of Parliament it remains within the power of the British legislator to change or abolish existing legislation as well as common law principles so that it basically transcends common law and is apt to encroach on fundamental human rights.

The evolution of common law by the judicature is confined nowadays to development and application of existing legal rules and principles; however, the creation and evolvement of new principles is rather retrenched and is considered to be a part of Parliament's task.[481]

Though the UK is a signatory to several international human rights treaties aiming to achieve a global standard for the promotion and observance of fundamental rights through agreement of states to be bound by international obligations, a considerable influence of international law within the English legal system is to be ascribed especially to the incorporation of the ECHR into domestic law. This yielded in its outcome a major piece of legislation, the HRA 1998, that marked its importance as the first written document establishing the guarantee of fundamental human rights. This incorporation of European law into the English legal system is a direct source of English law.

The historical development of the law on religion was longsome and protracted and, in fact, its evolvement took place in a piecemeal measure. This is relevant for the development of the fundamental right to religious freedom under its twofold categories, i.e., the guarantee of individual rights had been captured under two different legislative heads: equality rights and liberty rights.

At the outset, the protection of religious rights has been dealt to a considerable extent through anti-discrimination/equality legislation. Activities of the legislator in the area of liberty rights protection were limited to ratification and transformation of international treaties into British Law.

The respective treaties (e.g., UDHR and ICCPR) contained various religion-related liberty rights enabling religious minorities to raise claims in term of securing their individual fundamental freedoms. Nonetheless, the weaknesses of their enforcement mechanisms were proved non-beneficial for the promotion and guarantee of human rights in the context of achievement of a powerful common standard under international law, and they remained general statements of religious rights. However, a major turnover relating to enforcement of human rights inter alia religious rights can be ascribed to the enactment of the Human Rights Act 1998. The transformation of the ECHR into domestic law constituted the first written document that guaranteed religious freedom in the UK. In addition, the HRA 1998 had made a shift acknowledging the right to

481 *Ward/Wragg*, p. 5.

religious freedom as a positive right and no longer in its former retrenched scope as a negative right.

The distinctive significance of the HRA 1998 can be attributed to ease of access to courts that is made possible due to a direct and binding effect under domestic law. This also simplifies the process for individuals who no longer need to redress a remedy under international law but are able to seek for remedy with a simple submission to national courts.

Prior to the endorsement of the HRA 1998 the only path left to aggrieved individuals who claimed for violation of their religious rights was mostly dependent on the existing anti-discrimination legislation. In the aftermath of the introduction of the HRA 1998 into Britain's legislative system, the observance and guarantee of fundamental human rights were not only enforceable within domestic law but also compelled the judiciary to interpret domestic legislation as far as possible in a manner compatible with the Convention rights. The English judicature was bound as well to follow decisions delivered by the European jurisdictions.

Another major achievement to be underscored with respect to the enactment of the HRA 1998 relates to interpretation of all domestic legislation, whether future or existing, to be construed in a manner compatible with the rights as safeguarded in the ECHR. This had a considerable impact in the English legal system that thus far had been characterized by rather a tolerance-based as opposed to a rights-based approach.

Alongside the evolvement of the right to religious freedom to recognition of its statutory position as a legal right and increase of regulation on part of the state, a similar process has taken place with the widening and facilitating of regulation on religion through equality laws, a process titled as the 'juridification of religion'.

Despite the fact that, historically, the safeguarding of religious rights were hardly recognized under domestic law as a fundamental human right but rather more as a commitment on England's part to respect international human rights standards, the opposite can be said with regard to the evolvement of its anti-discrimination legislation. In fact, the British legal system focussed on anti-discrimination and equality regulations in order to guarantee religious rights. Though equality rights had also been developed over the years in a fragmentary manner, they were established under domestic law and can be traced long back before the recognition of religious freedom as a fundamental human right.

The ample array of anti-discrimination laws was scattered over different statutes and regulations. Some of them were repealed with the major legislative work of British parliament to codify equality legislations under one single Act, i.e., The Equality Act 2010.

The 2010 Act replaced several primary anti-discrimination laws in particular; the most relevant for the purpose of this analysis are: the Employment Equality (Religion or Belief) Regulations 2003, the Equality Act 2006 (several provisions), and the Race Relations Act 1976.

The Race Relations Act 1976 did prohibit discrimination; nonetheless, this covered only two equality grounds, namely race and ethnic, but not religion. The major criticism this Act has suffered was that it did not provide real protection against religious discrimination. Thence, religious minority groups such as Muslims or Sikhs, which do not fall into the definition of race or ethnicity, remained unprotected.[482] It was only following pressure of the Muslim community on British Parliament to introduce necessary legislative amendments to accommodate to their special religious needs that the British legislator was urged to respond and introduce a new enactment. This took effect with the endorsement of the Religion or Belief Regulations 2003. Prominent features of the 2003 Regulations can be ascribed to its attempt to interlink between anti-discrimination laws and different equality grounds such as religious freedom. This legislation paved the path for protection offered to religious minorities in employment and terms of admission to a workplace that were to be covered under different forms of discrimination specified in the enactment itself.[483] In addition, taken the perspective of employment in education, it should be underscored that the employment of teaching staff and their discrimination in admission to employment in non-faith schools based on religious grounds were significantly restricted.

The following legislative step was the introduction of the Equality Act 2006 whose main purpose was the achievement of equality and transparency especially in the public sector, making it accountable for unlawful discrimination. This was directed especially to public authorities and institutions, including public and private schools without religious ethos, obliging them to comply with general equality duties. It was meant to guarantee better enforcement of recognized discriminatory grounds as prescribed in the enactment itself, in particular the extension of the protection against religious discrimination. Its scope of application extends itself beyond employment relations and vocational training to providers of goods and services.[484] In general, it contributed

482 *v. Ungern-Sternberg*, 2008, p. 173.

483 *v. Ungern-Sternberg*, 2008, p. 168.

484 *v. Ungern-Sternberg*, 2008, pp. 175–176.

to promotion and advancement of equality of opportunities of individuals employed in employment.

The last step in the evolvement of anti-discrimination laws in the English legal system was the introduction of the Equality Act 2010. Its major importance can be ascribed to the fact that it is primarily a consolidating act meant to codify the array of equality legislations and regulations that were in fact scattered till that time in compilation and together formed the basis of anti-discrimination laws in Great Britain. It further aimed at extending the protection offered under former legislation to an ample array of equality grounds, and intended to create a new public sector equality duty. In general, the main purpose of the new public sector equality duty envisaged the obligation of public authorities to take active steps in ensuring the elimination of all discrimination forms. In addition, it was meant to advance equality of opportunities that would apply in a large scale to an elaborated list of equality grounds than was thus far known under former legislation. It also implemented the goals viewed under the different EU Equality Directives aiming to combat discrimination on different equality grounds.[485]

While the scope of previous equality enactments had been limited to certain and specific equality grounds applied in designated sectorial fields (e.g., employment or education), the Equality Act 2010 provided for the first time an extensive scope of protection that included not only various equality grounds, inter alia religious freedom, but in addition covered diverse fields as for instance, the supply of goods and services.[486] Those field were not prescribed under the Equality Act 2006 or the former abolished Religion or Belief 2003 Regulations. It is worth to mention that though the 2010 Act had conducted several amendments with respect to several provisions in the Equality Act 2006, by no means was it intended to serve as its substitute.

The Equality Act 2010, as a significant legislative instrument, raises complex problems with respect to the extent of scope that should be given to religious interests at work, especially given the vagueness of the definition of the term 'religion and belief'.

The implementation of the duty to promote equality of opportunities, in particular with respect to religion and belief in the educational context, can enfold a variety of difficulties. For instance, when school authorities are left with the task to 'value' religions or beliefs and to estimate whether certain faith

---

485 The Employment Equality Framework Directive 2000/78/EC, The Racial Equality Directive 2000/43/EC and the Equal Treatment Directive 2006/54/EC.

486 *Hale* in: Cranmer/Hill/Kenny, The Confluence of Law and Religion, 2016, pp. 218, 221.

or religious groups are worth protecting, and if so to which extent. In such a case, any decision of school authorities regarding a denial of special religious needs of a minority group or their accommodation may initiate proceedings against the school authorities by virtue of violation of its equality duty (Sec. 149 Equality Act 2010). In case of a denial, school authorities bear the risk of infringement of their equality duty towards that religious minority group. In case of accommodation to their religious needs it may violate its equality duty towards another religious group, non-believers, or even individuals pertaining to the same minority groups. Since schools cannot practically accommodate to the religious needs of each individual, a positive obligation to accord with the equality duty prescribed under the Equality Act 2010 offers a proper and adequate solution. In addition, an attempt of school authorities to comply with every religious need of every individual or a minority religious group runs the risk of violating the neutrality principle which prohibits endorsement of religion into schools.

Similar conflicts are addressed in the Equality Act 2010 through a specific requirement of the equality duty, which may retreat in exceptional cases (the list of exceptions mentioned above, e.g., faith schools, organizations with a religious ethos, etc.). Even-handedly to previous equality legislation, the inclusion of exceptions to the general equality duty remained an integral part of the Equality Act 2010. Nonetheless, in order to ascertain the validation of an exception to the non-discrimination principle it must fulfil the requirements of being necessary and proportionate to meet a legitimate aim.

To sum up, the Equality Act 2010 did not deviate substantially from the obligations imposed on employers under the abolished Religion or Belief Regulations 2003 nor from their former counterparts prescribed under the Equality Act 2006, so that at large they remained the same.

Due to the relative rapid development of discrimination laws in recent years, the success of the new equality duties will be measured based on implementation of equality policies and initiative of schools to eliminate discrimination and promote equal opportunities. Notably, criticism raised in the legal literature suggests that many of the new grounds added in the Equality Act 2010 will be surplus. The reason provided is that in particular with regard to the specified issue of exercising religious rights in the fields of employment and education, protection is covered by the obligation of schools to promote community cohesion prescribed already by other education legislation.[487] It should be noted

487 Education and Inspections Act 2006, p. 38; *Vickers*, in: Hunter-Henin, 2011, p. 87.

that analogous to the relative minor impact which the incorporation of the Employment Chapter had with respect to its introduction into the 2010 Act, the same can be said as to the inclusion of the Education Chapter. The application of the Education Chapter for most part of the legislation had shown no significant effect in comparison to previous legislation.

In a similar fashion, the same claim can be directed to the shift the HRA 1998 marked with respect to the positive legal recognition of the right to religious freedom as a fundamental human right, as in the same manner an impact is recognized with respect to the implementation of the EU Equality Directives prohibiting discrimination founded on various equality grounds into the 2010 Act. The new equality duty aiming to combat unlawful discrimination and foster equal treatment in employment and occupation indicated as well the distinguishable shift the English legal system had undergone from passive tolerance, identified by the common law doctrine, to a prescriptive regime of regulation on religion law. These together are recognized as key legal changes that have led to the juridification of religion in England.

To a large extent, the initial lightness of religion that has been characterized by a lack of prescriptive regulatory regime on part of the state aiming to administer the place of religion in England's legislative system can be interlinked to several factors: first, *the absence of a written constitution that guarantees fundamental freedoms such as religious rights*. Since fundamental freedoms are not recognized and safeguarded in a legislative constitutional document, potential violations or interferences on fundamental rights can be easily made on part of the state. This is also a direct outcome of the unwritten parliament supremacy principle that enables an Act of Parliament to amend or repeal any law even to the extent that it may infringe upon fundamental rights or run counter to their constitutional value. The same supremacy that qualifies parliament to create new safeguards for particular rights affords it to carry its own abuses. Moreover, if rights are not legally recognized, then it becomes difficult to ascertain their scope and determine whether infringement took place.

Second, *no formal separation of state-church relations* – the fact that England does not adopt a formal model of state-church separation enables it to keep its liberal accommodating approach towards religious minorities. Albeit the deference demonstrated by the judiciary towards religion, there is nothing to indicate that England adopts a clear church and state separation. Though it is commonly perceived that England's tendency is towards separation of state and church, and although to a large extent the judiciary plays a significant role in transformation of this notion due to a discerned approach demonstrated towards religion, this separation does not in fact convey the real situation. In that respect, the House of Lords did not develop independent constitutional principles with regard to religious freedom and the neutrality of state.

Third, *no codification of the neutrality principle as a legal rule* – in the legal tradition of England constitutional rules and legal principles were not comprised under a comprehensive single document. As a result, there is no defined term of 'state neutrality'. Due to the fact that it remains an unwritten principle with unclear boundaries, there exists no strict obligation on part of the state to abide by it if not entrenched in its constitutional system. It is worth to note that the term neutrality is not unfamiliar in the legal discussion and there is a strong approach favouring the notion that the state should remain neutral, especially in its acts in the public sphere. However, since it is not codified as a legal principle, it enables the state to adjust the neutrality principle. This, for instance, can be exemplified by the liberal approach adopted by the British legislator towards its religious minorities that is interlinked with the acknowledgement that Britain has become a multi-cultural nation. Thence, the increase of regulation on religion came as a response to sociological changes that have taken place in the last two decades and have affected the law and place of religion in the public sphere.

Finally, the importance which the constitutional principles carry in the context of the guarantee offered to fundamental human rights in the legislative framework of England can be summarized in brief: first, even though there is no written constitution in the English legal system, there are principles that still qualify the British legislator to ensure that fundamental rights are guaranteed, i.e., the principle of Parliament Supremacy. Another mechanism set for enforcement of fundamental rights is provided by the judiciary. Courts and tribunals have the power to supervise abuses made by state organs and are subject to their judicial review. Second, though the principle of neutrality does not exist in England's constitutional system as a codified legal principle, its implication can be inferred from other legal principles, such as the rule of law and the principle of equality of treatment. The rule of law confines state power so that no abuses of individual rights will be possible without legitimization by law. The equality treatment prohibits favouritism towards a particular religion on part of the state since all citizens are equal before the law. This principle naturally declines any discriminatory act established by the state on different grounds; in addition, the public service ethos imposes a duty on the state to be impartial in its actions.

4. France

The constitutional system of France and its secular nature constitute a salient feature of the French republic and its sacrosanct ideology. The distinctiveness of

French republican ideology is underscored by the notion of secularism and individualism, which was meant to perpetuate the ideal of a unified and indivisible state.[488] This dates back to the politics of the French revolution of 1789 and the First Republic that was marked by the abolition of the monarchy and a strong wish to diminish the political power of the Catholic Church.[489]

Nonetheless, the period ensuing the outbreak of the French Revolution was not characterized by an absolute strained approach towards religion and the church. The developments were rather inconsistent as, on the one hand, Concordat between Napoleon and Pope Pius VII to establish peace between France and the Catholic Church was signed in 1801.[490] Napoleon signed a Concordat with the Holy See under which the position of the three established religions (Catholic, Protestant, and Jewish) was secured as they became part of the civil service. This was part of civil religion where clergy or priests were to receive salary from the state and religious buildings were publicly owned and maintained.[491] On the other hand, Republican proponents of the separationist model promoted endorsement of legislation on the separation between state and church (the 1905 Law).[492]

In addition, an inner introspection on the organizational-constitutional model in France is essential for the French perception of state-individual relations. This aspect, together with the French approach towards citizenship will provide an explanation as to the way it treats its religious minorities and the accommodation of their religious needs.[493]

The uniqueness of the organizational structure is interlinked with the conception of the state, which is founded in France on the republican values and ideology.[494] Several paramount elements underlie the notion of French Republicanism. These will be set forth and provide a descriptive delineation of its main features.

---

488 *Scott*, The Politics of the Veil, 2010, p. 12.

489 *Wick* in von Campenhausen/Frisch/Heckel, Beiträge zum evangelischen Kirchenrecht und zum Staatskirchenrecht, 2007, pp. 29–31.

490 *Wick* in von Campenhausen/Frisch/Heckel, Beiträge zum evangelischen Kirchenrecht und zum Staatskirchenrecht, 2007, pp. 29, 32; *Fetzer/Soper*, p. 69; *McGoldrick* (2006) , p. 35.

491 *Troper* in Sajo, The Law of Religious Identity: Models for Post - Communism, 1999, pp. 89, 90.

492 *Fetzer/Soper*, p. 70.

493 *van Ooijen*, p. 169.

494 *Poulter*, OJLS, 17(43) (1997), pp. 43, 50.

First, the republic considered the relations between the state and the citizens to be regulated on an individualized base without interference of religion, race, class, or gender.[495] Hence, the purpose was not only to ensure allegiance of all citizens to the republic but also to achieve a sameness in order to eliminate differences on account of various grounds. This compelled citizens to assimilate to the norms of its cultures and adhere to the republican values[496] so as to achieve national cohesion.[497] Second, the republic does not recognize the perception of minorities, whether conceptually, politically, or legally.[498] Third, France recognizes in the aspect of citizenship construction the concept of religious identity as opposed to ethnic identity. This connotes that within the French discourse no questions surrounding ethnicity will be raised and indicates French uneasiness with the notion of race and ethnicity.[499]

Accordingly, in a first step it will be necessary to deliver a brief review of the legal and constitutional background existing in the past, then refer to the current constitutional provisions establishing and safeguarding the right to religious freedom, following with a list of all international treatments and agreements France has adopted.

a) Sources of Law and the Constitutional Hierarchy of Norms

In order to understand the right to religious freedom and the position it holds in the constitutional tradition of France, it is necessary to understand the constitutional hierarchy of laws guaranteeing protection of fundamental rights, and the available constitutional sources upon which they are established.

---

495 *Auslander*, Cultural Dynamics 12(3) (2000), pp. 283, 294.

496 *Scott*, p. 13.

497 *Poulter*, 1997, pp. 43, 50; *McGoldrick* (2006), p. 42.

498 *van Ooijen*, p. 170; *McGoldrick* (2006), pp. 43, 47–48. This provides an explanation as to France's refusal to declare Art. 27 of the International Covenant on Civil and Political Rights as eligible. The text of the reservation proclaims: 'In the light of article 2 of the Constitution of the French Republic, the French government declares that article 27 is not applicable so far as the Republic is concerned'. To be found on the website of the UN Treaty Collection treaties.un.org

499 *Liederman-Molokotos*, p. 112. Such a confinement to religious identity will not be adequate at all times when having regard to Muslim immigrants in France. Since French Muslims originate from various countries (North Africa and Turkey), they all may share the same religion but do not perceive themselves as one group due to ethnicity differences.

It is common to divide the constitutional development into two periods: first, until 1958 – a period distinguished by the importance attributed to legislative primacy (the term '*loi*' refers to statutory legislation passed by parliament).[500] These legislative enactments passed by parliament ('*loi*'), combined with two other constitutional sources: the written Constitution of 1946 and administrative decisions delivered by French courts comprised altogether a tripled level of hierarchy of norms.[501] Second, following 1958 – the stage marked by the introduction of the 1958 Constitution aimed at strengthening the constitutional authority and supervision over its provisions. This period envisaged the supremacy of constitutional rules and principles over legislative enactments. This naturally shifted the emphasis within the constitutional hierarchy of norms, where ordinary statutes lost their primacy; instead, prevalence was given to the written constitution of 1958, international treaties, and European legislation. In addition, the sphere of parliamentary intervention had been substantially retrenched.[502]

Another element that will be considered within the process of creation of sources of law includes French court institutions upon their distinctive structural system: public law and private law courts, *Conseil d'Etat* (Council of State) which acts as the legal advisor of the French government and Supreme Court of the Administrative, and the *Conseil constitutionnel* (Constitutional Council) which acts as the highest constitutional authority.

Thence, the hierarchy of regulations in France can be depicted as follows:[503]

*aa) Constitution and Constitutional Laws (*Lois Constitutionnelles*)*

France is known for its long legacy of written constitutions. The latest of all was the constitution of 1958 of the Fifth Republic. Though it mainly comprised rules governing the competence and functioning of governmental organs, the enactment of legislation, and the guarantee of judicial independence, it affirms in addition a few fundamental values stipulated in former constitutions. Since the

500 The importance attributed to parliamentary legislation at that time was interlinked with the view that it reflected the expression of the will of the nation; in French: '*l'expression de la volonté générale*', as underlied in the Declaration of Human and Civic Rights of 26 August 1789. Art. 6 establishes: '*The Law is the expression of the general will. All citizens have the right to take part, personally or through their representatives, in its making*'. English translation found in: http://www.conseil-constitutionnel.fr/conseil-constitutionnel/root/bank_mm/anglais/cst2.pdf

501 *Bell/Boyron/Whittaker*, Principles of French Law, 2nd edn., p. 15.

502 *Bell/Boyron/Whittaker*, p. 15.

503 *Bell*, French Constitutional Law, 1992, pp. 10–14.

1958 Constitution does not constitute in itself an exhaustive statement of constitutional provisions, the reference given in the legal literature to the whole of constitutional rules identifies it as the 'block of constitutional provisions' (*le bloc de constitutionnalité*).[504] This term was explained by the Conseil constitutionnel to designate fundamental principles having a constitutional status. The fact that there is no definitive, indicative list of constitutional rules and principles poses a problem to the definition of a 'fundamental principle' and leaves in practice its interpretation subject to jurisdiction of the ordinary courts. In any case, constitutional values and principles will always be given precedent over ordinary legislation.[505]

bb) Treaties and International Agreements

France accepted upon itself an integrated system acknowledging both national and international law. Therefore, the commitment of France towards international human rights treaties to which it is a signatory, will have a binding force on the French government.[506] Fundamental human rights are given effect by international human rights conventions and agreements, which have a self-executing force by virtue of Art. 55 of the French Constitution 1958.[507] This means that international law is directly applicable for individuals that can rely on an international treaty without due delay, and invoke their right before national courts given that it has been published in the Official Journal. Art. 55 stipulates that: 'Treaties or agreements duly ratified or approved shall, upon publication,

---

504 The phrase 'bloc de constitutionnalité' refers to three constitutional documents: the Constitution of 1958, the preamble of the Constitution of 1946 and the Declaration of Rights of Man from 1789 and constitute altogether a set of fundamental liberties. The will serve as a yard-stick according to which ordinary laws will be assessed and evaluated, see in, *v. Ungern-Sternberg*, 2008, p. 91; *Bell/Boyron/Whittaker*, p. 16.

505 *Bell/Boyron/Whittaker*, p. 17. The constitutional council (*Conceil Constitutionnel*) had to decide whether the preamble of the 1958 Constitution constitutes an integral part of the constitution and shall enjoy in itself a constitutional rank. It was affirmed in two decisions delivered by the constitutional council in the seventies and as a result conferred by the attachment in the preamble of the 1958 Constitution an equal constitutional rank to the preamble of the 1946 Constitution and the Declaration of Rights of Man from 1789. See in, *v. Ungern-Sternberg*, 2008, p. 91.

506 *Saxena*, pp. 765, 767.

507 The limitation on the self-executing force of international human rights treaties is that they must be subject to ratification or approval by the French Government, See *Saxena*, pp. 765, 767, 784; *van Ooijen*, p. 166.

prevail over Acts of Parliament, subject, in regard to each agreement or treaty, to its application by the other party'.[508]

The courts have the sole authority to decide whether an international treaty is directly applicable in case an individual invokes its right in accordance to it, subject to the condition that the treaty had been ratified or approved by the French government. In case an ordinary court encounters incompatibility of a statute with a treaty provision, the latter should be given prevalence. The Constitutional Court can verify whether an international treaty is consistent with the French Constitution.[509] European and international human rights instruments prevail over national legislation, whether enacted before or even subsequent to inconsistent legislation.[510]

cc) Legislation

The law (*loi*) in France established its superiority under French constitutional law since enactments of parliament are considered to reflect the wish of the people and are democratically legitimized. However, legislation derives from different sources and obtain in itself an inner hierarchical structure. Thence, legislation will be subsequent to other formal sources of law termed as 'supereminent principles' [511] namely: the Constitution and international treaties. The latter will succeed in rank Organic laws, legislation and regulations ratified by parliament (*réglements*).

dd) Organic laws

Organic laws are regarded as laws which affect the power and cooperation of constitutional authorities. They are designated to provide the government an authority to amend Acts of Parliament. The use of organic laws originated in practice due to political necessity during the period of the Third Republic to facilitate the legislative process. The need to pass legislation in a rush was enabled by a statute (*décret loi*) delegating powers to the government.[512] This

508 Art. 55 of the 1958 Constitution available at http://www.conseil-constitutionnel.fr/conseil-constitutionnel/english/constitution/constitution-of-4-october-1958.25742.html

509 *van Ooijen*, p. 166.

510 Art. 55 of the 1958 Constitution.

511 *David*, pp. 194, 207; *Bell/Boyron/Whittaker*, p. 14.

512 *Bell/Boyron/Whittaker*, p. 20.

statutory procedure, which was rejected in the 1946 Constitution, was replaced by the law of 17 August 1948 (*la loi André Marié*) that was meant to assign clear separation between powers of the executive and the legislator. The 1958 Constitution, acknowledging the importance of clear designation of legislative powers between governmental and parliament domain, introduced similar procedural provisions, thus enabling the government to override parliament in a list of subject matters.[513] This procedural division of legislative powers between the executive and the legislator granted the government a considerable advantage as opposed to parliament, since the latter was limited in topics left to its legislative authority. It enabled the government with extensive legislative power with respect to all other areas not specified under the list.[514] As a result, Acts of Parliament (*loi*) are equal in rank to regulations (*réglements*) adopted by the executive.

ee) Ordinary Laws and Ordinances Ratified by Parliament

Art. 38 of the 1958 Constitution endorsed a third category of ordinary legislation – ordinances, in French (*ordonnances*). According to this legislative procedure prescribed in Art. 38, a law can define several criteria that will assist the government in exhausting its powers and promoting legislation: the area of intervention delegated to Parliament, the principles of the legislation, and a certain period of time to be submitted for Parliament's approval. If no objection on part of the Parliament is raised within this period of time, the legislation will become final and conclusive. This delegated legislation according to Art. 38, referred to as ordinances, is on the same level in the hierarchy of norms as ordinary laws (*lois ordinaires*) and regulations (*réglements*).[515]

ff) Custom

The practice of Custom is not that entrenched as a binding source in modern French law. The reasons for which customary practices were not regarded as an essential element of law can be attributed to several factors. First, insufficient

513 Art. 34 of the 1958 Constitution provides a list of topics that will be within the legislative domain of parliament, whereas Art. 37 refers to all other subject matters delegated to the governmental legislative sphere.

514 *Bell/Boyron/Whittaker*, p. 21.

515 *Bell/Boyron/Whittaker*, p. 22.

fulfilment of the necessary requirements to be regarded an established customary practice.[516] Second, its practice by users of law was regarded rather redundant. Third, French judiciary declared customary practices which were inconsistent with law to have no binding force.[517]

gg) Jurisprudence (Development of Case Laws)

Development of case laws by French jurisdictional institutions are not regarded legally binding but are perceived rather as an influential source of law. The reason for that is the legal perception that French law is mostly codified, and since codification is meant to cover all possible situations and is drafted in a clear text manner, then judge-made law is considered to be surplus. Since the judiciary does not create legal rules – and even if they did, those rules would not be regarded binding – judges are rather curtailed in their discretion of legislative interpretation. They mostly apply pre-existing statutes or customs and, in the absence of those, judges are allowed to make reference to principles of equity, reason, justice, or tradition. Criticism has been raised in the legal literature as to whether this entrenchment of the judiciary role is desirable, especially due to the fact that French Civil Code does not cover all other areas of law and, in addition, does not reflect societal and periodical changes and developments.[518]

hh) General Principles of Law

General principles of law pertain a source of jurisprudence creation. The need for creation of general principles of law emanated from lack of codification or legislation of administrative law. This explains why they have been mostly in use by the CE as opposed to other divisions of courts. Some general principles were created for the purpose of development of rules governing the action of the administration, such as the general principle of the right to a fair hearing (*le droit de la défense*). Other general principles were taken from constitutional texts protecting rights and freedoms and include, for instance, the principle of equality.[519]

---

516 The prerequisites are: (1) practice of long duration (2) a belief that a practice is obligatory, and (3) consistency with fundamental principle of law.

517 *David*, p. 170; *Bell/Boyron/Whittaker*, p. 25.

518 *Bell/Boyron/Whittaker*, p. 25.

519 *Bell/Boyron/Whittaker*, pp. 32, 33.

ii) *Legal Writing*

This refers to writing of academics known as '*la doctrine*' either of individual scholars or university jurists as a community which took upon themselves: first, the task to provide theories as to the nature and manner of legal interpretation when these are not clear or in case of existence of a legislative gap; second, provide with specific judicial solutions when the judiciary encountered new situations to which no solution was provided in the legal text.[520] Judges were also able to assess the influence of their jurisprudence through publications of comments and reviews provided in the legal academic writings. It should be noted that judges in France are curtailed with their right of statutory interpretation mainly due to strong codification that provided a clear text and left no room or necessity for judiciary interpretation. Though they do not really count as a law under its official meaning, these legal writings are regarded as a direct influential source on jurisprudential development, and assist judges in many cases to have an extensive understanding of a complex issue which may eventually be adopted in their case laws.[521] Judges are not committed to adopt some of these academic positions, but are many times influenced by the views and positions reflected in them.[522]

b) Individual Rights

The development of individual religious liberty rights in France had been starkly inflected by several historical milestones that imprinted a cultural perception of religion. The long battle with the Catholic Church, which had lasted till the nineteenth century with the concordats concluded between Napoleon Bonaparte and the Pope, the division of the Catholic Church into two parts, the 'Civil Constitution of Clergy' and the 'refractory clergy' (only the latter considered legitimate in the eyes of the Catholic church in Rome), the French Enlightenment, the 1789 French Revolution and in its efforts to impose the notion of 'civil religion' had all left profound impression on the development of France's modern constitutionalism.[523]

Religious liberty right is regarded foremost as an individual liberty right since it enables a person to decide individually whether to have or adopt a religion

520 *Bell/Boyron/Whittaker*, pp. 33, 34.

521 *Bell/Boyron/Whittaker*, p. 33.

522 *Bell/Boyron/Whittaker*, p. 35.

523 *Baubérot,* in: Lindholm/Durham/Tahzib-Lie, Freedom of Religion or Belief: A Deskbook, 2004, pp. 442–443; *Gunn*, BYU L. Rev. 2004, pp. 419, 435.

or reject any pertinence to a religious group. Recognition of the right to religious freedom as a basic right has been acknowledged through its embodiment in several of France's constitutional documents and legislations. Nonetheless, its constitutional position as an indispensable right among the list of fundamental individual liberty rights is not indicative of France's state-church relations and the perception of its salient republican ideology imprinted by the historical antagonistic approach towards religion. In fact, religious rights in France, though embodied in a constitutional document, are not adequately safeguarded as one would have assumed taking into consideration their prominent position in the hierarchy of norms.

aa) Liberty Rights/Freedom of Conscience

The legal position in France is that civil liberty rights are not consolidated under an overarching document or equating codified 'bills of rights'.[524] These are scattered over several legislative instruments and constitutional principles developed from ordinary legislation by the judiciary.[525] Thence, in France fundamental rights and civil guarantees are not only safeguarded and affirmed by the Constitution, but they are also recognized by ordinary laws and statutes of the republic.[526]

---

524 *van Ooijen*, p. 166.

525 For further explanation with respect to the development of constitutional principles see Chapter III 4 d) below.

526 Art. 34 of the 1958 Constitution. It is worth to note that the French constitutional terminology with respect to the definition of 'fundamental rights' is indefinite and ambiguous rather than unequivocal and explicit since it was appropriated analogous perceptions. In part, it is referred to as '*libertés publiques*' that can only partially be translated into English as 'civic liberties' as there exists no word-to-word translation in the English legal terminology. The analogy to German terminology is more accurate and can be described as 'öffentliche Freiheiten'. An equivalent term that resembles most the English and German (Grundrechte) terminology for fundamental rights is designated in French as 'droits fondamentaux'. Principally, though these definitions are used analogously in France's constitutional system, there are several commentators who presume that 'droit *fondametaux*' can be used only in order to designate rights that are imprinted in the European constitution or public international law. *Ganz*, p. 46; *Morange*, Droits de l'Homme et libertés publiques. – PUF – Droit fondamental, 5th ed. 2000, p. 131. Furthermore, the right to religious freedom is integrated in an array of human right conventions and declarations to which France is a party. The most significant human rights conventions, namely the ECHR, the ICCPR, the Convention

The protection of liberty rights is outlined in the 1789 Declaration of Human and Civil Rights, which marked the French Revolution (*De´claration des droits de l'homme et du citoyen*, hereinafter: 1789 Declaration).[527]

The commitment of the French people to fundamental liberty rights as established in the 1789 Declaration is also reaffirmed in the 1946 and present constitution of 1958.[528]

Nonetheless, the protection of fundamental rights, including the right to religious freedom, is not unconfined. The rights may be restricted or confined in their scope in the case one of the following should be invoked:

First, a curtailment of one of the fundamental liberty rights safeguarded under the 1789 Declaration which was adopted into the current 1958 Constitution, fortifying its binding force, takes place. Second, a collision with other competing interests, such as public safety, public order, or the principle of neutrality given that they are established by law. Notably, the legislative text in French law refers explicitly to infringement of 'public order' as long as statutory provision is established by law. Other grounds justifying curtailment of the right to religious freedom will be permissible if they accord with the requirements enumerated in Art. 9 para 2 ECHR by virtue of France's obligation to accord with international treaties and their self-executing force.

Eminently, the French constitutional model, as already established above, does not convey a clear dogmatic structure of rights protection which outlines a distinctive segregation with respect to scope of protection, limitations or infringements, and justification of limitations on fundamental rights. This incurs legal uncertainty when trying to exhaust a fundamental right such as religious

---

on the Elimination of Discrimination Against Women, and the Convention Against Discrimination in Education.

Following an authorization to ratify is given by the parliament, the treaties have then the authority superior to that of a law.

The incorporation of international treaties into domestic law is prescribed in Art. 55 to the 1958 Constitution as set forth: 'Treaties or agreements duly ratified or approved shall, upon publication, prevail over Acts of Parliament, subject, with respect to each agreement or treaty, to its application by the other party'.

527 An English Translation can be found on e.g., the website of the Conseil Constitutionnel www.conseil-constitutionnel.fr/conseil-constitutionnel/root/bank_mm/anglais/cst2.pdf.

528 The Preamble of the Constitution states: 'Le peuple francais proclame solennellement son attachement aux Droits de l'Homme et aux principes de la souverainete nationale tels qu'ils ont e'te' definis par la Declaration de 1789….'. 'The 1789 Declaration has been granted constitutional status by the Constitutional Council'

freedom, since the mechanism of judicial review with respect to its implementation and application remains absent.

In addition, in order to evaluate the position the right to religious freedom possesses in the constitutional tradition of France, it is not only necessary to understand the constitutional hierarchy of laws, but also consider the impact other factors had on its evolvement. Following factors should be taken into account for the purpose of this assessment and will be dealt with in the forthcoming chapter: the historical development of religion, the manner in which it inculcated state-church relations (the adopted separationist model), the system and functions of the judiciary including the role of France's constitutional courts, and the powers and interrelationship between constitutional authorities, such as parliament, the constitutional council, and the judiciary.

Freedom of conscience enables every citizen to choose whether to have or reject a religion or belief, adopt any religion or spiritual life, and live in accordance to its precepts.

The French perception of religion is that it is an individual matter that should remain within the boundaries of the private sphere. This apprehension of remoteness to religion is so salient that it was even described in the legal literature as the desired relation French citizens seek to adopt as far as the place religion should acquire in its public space. It is depicted at best in the following quintessence:

Organized, bounded, orderly, contained in its buildings, and defined by worship practices in those buildings. If it strays into the street, selling tracts, or proselytising, it is out of bounds, and even when it is tolerated it is no longer protected by the French constitution and can easily be quashed in the name of protecting public order.[529]

Freedom of conscience is also identified as a value of laïcité and had been several times repeated in the Stasi report to constitute one of three interconnected values of the principle of secularity, 'liberty of conscience, equality of rights in spiritual and religious choices and neutrality of political power'.[530]

---

529 *Bowen*, Why The French Don't Like Headscarves: Islam, The State, and Public Space, 2007, p. 18. An interview with Vianney Sevaistre, formerly Chief of the Central Office of Organized Religions between 2002–2004. *Davis*, B.C. Inte'l & Comp. L. Rev. 34 (2011), pp. 117, 122.

530 *Gunn*, BYU L. Rev. 2004, pp. 419, 466; *Poggeschi*, European Yearbook of Minority Issues, 3 (2003/2004), pp. 263, 270; Rapport Au President De La Republique (Stasi Report) (2003), p. 9. see at http://www.ladocumentationfrancaise.fr/var/storage/rapports-publics/034000725.pdf (last visited March 28, 2016).

(a) Scope of Freedom of Conscience

In order to understand the position freedom of conscience acquires in the constitutional hierarchy, it is necessary to have a recourse to its development in the history of France and, naturally, to the modern French approach with respect to the importance and place religion acquires in public life.

In principle, freedom of religion is recognized and established as a constitutional right. The acknowledgement of freedom of conscience has been confirmed by the Cons. Const. to be a fundamental principle accredited by the laws of the French Republic.[531]

However, since the constitutional system in France has its fundaments entrenched in various constitutions and legal principles minted in regular enactments, this emanates that the right to religious freedom draws existence from diverse judicial sources and legislative origins.[532]

In the French terminology, reference to the definition of freedom of conscience will enfold mainly the forum internum of the freedom of religion.[533] This is mainly due to the French perception that religion and belief are matters consigned solely to the private sphere. In general, the guarantee of religious freedom is interpreted as a negative rather than a positive right.[534]

Notably, the French concept of religious freedom did not grow out of an existing pluralism of religions, but rather has its roots historically bound with dominant Catholicism as the single official religion of the nation.[535]

However, this situation had lasted until the French revolution (1789), which signifies the far-reaching de-confessionalization of the French state[536] and brought to an end the period of the French state-church model (*Staatskirchentums*). This separation of the secular state from religion was further marked by a subsequent event that took place in the aftermath of the French revolution. It was the establishment of the right to religious freedom in one of the most significant constitutional documents in France's history regarding the safeguarding of individuals' liberty rights, namely, the Declaration of 1789.[537]

---

531 *van Ooijen*, p. 166: Conseil Constitutionnel, 23 November 1977, Decision no. 77–87 DC www.conseil-constitutionnel.fr

532 *Baubérot*, pp. 441, 445.

533 *van Ooijen*, p. 166.

534 *McGoldrick* (2006), p. 36

535 *Baubérot*, pp. 441, 442; *Gunn*, BYU L. Rev. 2004, pp. 419–506.

536 *Wick*, Die Trennung von Staat und Kirche, 2007, p. 38.

537 *Wick*, p. 30. 'Die Erklärung der Menschen und Bürgerrechte führte zu einer Trennung der säkularen von der religiösen Ebene und zu einer tief greifenden

(aa) Freedom of Religion in the Declaration of Rights of Man 1789

Freedom of religion in France is guaranteed by the constitutional rights set forth in the 1789 Declaration. This document is considered by legal authorities to have equal legal standing with the 1958 Constitution of France as it is explicitly mentioned and integrated in the preamble of the 1958 Constitution.[538]

The 1789 Declaration enfolds the French apprehension towards individual liberty rights. Firstly, already in its first provision the declaration establishes the individual's right to liberty and equality before the law.[539] This serves a clear indication as to the significance attached to these rights. Second, the rights in the 1789 Declaration do not refer to the existence of a divine source.[540] Third, civil liberty rights are guaranteed by the state and are not recognized as legal guarantees against the state. This special characteristic reflects the general will of the French people, thence, making the state subject to this will.[541]

The right to religious freedom is laid down in Art. 10 of the 1789 Declaration of Rights of Man declaring that:[542]

Entkonfessionalisierung des französischen Staates. Dies bedeutete ...das Ende des französischen Staatskirchentums'.

538 *v. Ungern-Sternberg*, 2008, p.91, See further as explained above in Chapter II 4 a)aa); *Wick*, p. 62. The constitutional legal standing of the 1789 Declaration and its application by the French judicator in an equal manner to the 1958 Constitution was demonstrated in the legal practice. For instance, in the Al Kherouaa decision the Conseil d'Etat referred to the constitutional principle of Laizität prescribed in Art. 2 of the 1958 Constitution and contested it against the freedom of religion and belief stipulated in Art. 10 of the 1789 Declaration. See also in 4b)a)(cc) the 1958 Constitution proclaiming in its preamble the attachment of the 1789 Declaration.

539 Art. 1 of the 1789 Declaration reads: 'Les Hommes naissent et demeurent libres et e´gaux en droit...'.

540 *van Ooijen*, p. 165; A reference to a divine source within the context of fundamental rights and their origin was rather a common matter at that time, see *Baubérot*, pp. 441, 442.

541 *van Ooijen*, p. 165; *Troper*, in: Bermann/Picard, Introduction to French Law, 2008, p. 16.

542 *Troper*, Cardozo L. Rev. 30(6) (2009), pp. 2561, 2571. The original text of Art. 10: '*Nul ne doit être inquiété pour ses opinions, même religieuses, pourvu que leur manifestation ne trouble pas l'ordre public établi par la Loi*'. '*No one may be questioned on account of his opinions, including his religious views, provided that their manifestation does not disturb the public order established by the law*'.

No one may be disturbed on account of his opinions, even religious ones, as long as the manifestation of such opinions does not interfere with public order as established by Law.[543]

The right to religious freedom as established by the Declaration of 1789 makes clear that the right is not unreserved. It is guaranteed as long as religious activities do not infringe on public order or act in ways detrimental to society.[544]

Further, the 1789 Declaration captures the notion of religious neutrality, consisting of a negative and positive dimension. The negative dimension of neutrality is presumed to be an element of Art. 10 of the 1789 Declaration. It enfolds the negative notion of neutrality since it presupposes the duty of the state to allow diverse manifestations of thought and opinions, including religious opinions; however, at the same time it must ensure that no person shall be exposed to any pressure due to his religious opinion or any attempt made by a religious group or the state to impose its preferences on other individuals or on its citizens.[545] It does not proclaim outright the liberty of religious freedom but rather as a reserved right that can be practised as long as it does not interfere with another interest such as public order, and given that it is stipulated by law.

(bb) Freedom of Conscience in the Constitution of 1946

The sanctity of religious freedom and the prohibition on account of religion or other grounds was even further asserted and underscored in the preamble of the 1946 Constitution.

The preamble of the 1946 Constitution proclaims that 'any human being possesses inalienable and sacred rights, without distinction as to race, religion, or beliefs'.[546]

Notably, the preamble of the 1946 Constitution pertains pursuant to a decision of the Cons. Const. from 1971 – a viable and valid constitutional legal source in French law, inscribing the protection of freedom of conscience as a prominent fundamental right.[547]

---

543 English translation see at, http://www.conseil-constitutionnel.fr/conseil-constitutionnel/root/bank_mm/anglais/cst2.pdf

544 'The law has the right to ward [i.e., forbid] only actions [which are] harmful to the society. Anything which is not warded [i.e., forbidden] by the law cannot be impeded, and no one can be constrained to do what it [i.e., the law] does not order'.

545 *Robert*, BYU L. Rev. 2003, pp. 637, 642.

546 *Troper*, 2009, pp. 2561, 2571; *Palmer*, p. 29.

547 Further consideration of the inclusion of the Preamble of the 1946 Constitution into the 1958 Constitution will be provided in Chapter III.

(cc) Freedom of Conscience in the Constitution of 1958

Strikingly, the 1958 Constitution focuses primarily on the function and the relations between organs of the state rather than on safeguarding fundamental rights.[548] However, the guarantee of liberty rights is made through reference in the preamble of the 1958 Constitution to several legal sources. Its preamble proclaims, first, the attachment of the French people to the Rights of Man as defined in the Declaration of 1789 and, second, to the preamble of the 1946 Constitution.[549]

Art. 1 of the 1958 Constitution declares the laic character of the Republic. Apart from that, it designates the unequivocal guarantee of religious freedom to all citizens of the French Republic and the assurance to treat all religions or belief equally, without any distinction founded on different grounds.[550]

Art. 1 of the 1958 Constitution establishes that: 'France shall be an indivisible, secular, democratic and social Republic. It shall ensure the equality of all citizens before the law, without distinction of origin, race or religion. It shall respect all beliefs'.[551] This emanates that the French state should provide all of its citizens an equal access to its public schools regardless of their religious adherence.[552]

---

548 *Palmer*, p. 26. Religious Liberty: The Legal Framework in Selected OSCE Countries, a report prepared by the law library of Congress at the request of the Commission on Security and Cooperation in Europe, Washington 2000, p. 26.

549 *'The French people solemnly proclaim their attachment to the Right of Man and the principles of national sovereignty as defined by the Declaration of 1789, confirmed and complemented by the* Preamble *to the Constitution of 1946…'.* http://www.conseil-constitutionnel.fr/conseil-constitutionnel/english/constitution/constitution-of-4-october-1958.25742.html#PREAMBLE
The French text as well as its translated English version can be looked up also in: http://www.assemblee-nationale.fr/english/8ab.asp. 'Le peuple français proclame solennellement son attachement aux Droits de l'Homme et au principe de la souveraineté nationale tels qu'ils ont été définis par la Déclaration de 1789 confirmée et complétée par la Préambule de la Constitution de 1946…'.

550 Art. 1, original text: *'La France est une Republique indivisible, laique, democratique et sociale. Elle assure l'égalité devant la loi de tous les citoyens sans distinction d'origine, de race ou de religion. Elle respecte toutes les croyances. Son organisation est decentralisee'.*

551 http://www.conseil-constitutionnel.fr/conseil-constitutionnel/english/constitution/constitution-of-4-october-1958.25742.html#PREAMBLE.

552 *Wick* in: von Campenhausen/Frisch/Heckel, Beiträge zum evangelischen Kirchenrecht und zum Staatskirchenrecht, 2007, pp. 29, 58.

(dd) Freedom of Conscience in the Act of 1905

As explained previously, since there is no compilation of fundamental rights under one single document, these may be found not only in several constitutional documents but can be traced in ordinary laws created by the French Parliament. It falls under the responsibility of the French Parliament to create new safeguards for fundamental guarantees and determine rules for the exercise of civil liberties.[553]

The strained approach to religion and the church had reached its peak with the enactment of the 1905 Law, which marked legislation designating the separation between church and state (hereinafter: 1905 law). [554]

In this context, it is worth to mention a momentous and probably the most significant legislation implementing the assurance of the French Republic to respect and regard the right to religious freedom. This guarantee, as prescribed in Art. 1 of the 1905 Law, comprises recognition of the French Republic of its task to protect freedom of conscience as well as acts of religious worship.[555] Albeit the guarantee provided for the right to religious freedom under Art. 1 of the 1905 Law, its enactment was meant to restrict religion as an individual right solely to the private sphere.[556]

However, Art. 2 of the 1905 Law prescribes that the guarantee of religious freedom corresponds to its negative aspect rather than to its positive one.[557]

The guarantee of freedom of conscience by the French Republic enfolds an obligation of the state not only to respect and ensure the practical operation of religious freedom, but also to place sanctions in case of its violation. Indeed, even courts recognized that any act or practice tending to create discrimination based on religious belief will be regarded as unlawful.[558] As a result, if the

---

553 http://www.assemblee-nationale.fr/english/8ab.asp#V. Art. 34 of the 1958 Constitution appoints that: '*Statutes shall determine the rules concerning: civic rights and the fundamental guarantees granted to citizens for the exercise of their civil liberties…*'.

554 Loi du 9 decmbre 1905 concernant la separation des Eglises et de l'Etat.

555 Art. 1, original text: '*La République assure la liberté de conscience. Elle garantie le libre exercice des cultes sous les seules restrictions édictées ci-après dans l'intérêt de l'ordre public. La République ne reconnaît, ne salarie ni ne subventionne aucum culte*'. In translation: '*The Republic assures freedom of conscience. It guarantees the free exercise of religious worship under the sole restrictions hereafter in the interest of public order. The republic does not grant recognition nor pay no subsidies to any church*'. *Messner/Prélot/Woehrling*, pp. 404, 405.

556 *Troper*, Cardozo L. Rev. 21(6) 2000, pp. 1267, 1276.

557 'The Republic does not recognize, remunerate, or subsidize any religious denomination'.

558 *Robert*, 2003, pp. 637, 643–644.

discriminating act, practice, or proviso is encroached by public authorities, then the individual may enforce his/her right to respect this freedom before the administrative courts.

Accordingly, Art. 31 of the 1905 Law created the offence of harming liberty of conscience. It is prescribed as a criminal offense to pressure an individual into practising or refraining from practising a religion by using threats or violence against the individual or his/her family or by fear that he/she will lose his/her workplace.[559]

(b) Limitation of Scope

The possible limitation of the right to religious freedom will be justified in order to protect interests of the public order and is established already in Art. 10 of the 1789 Declaration. It substantially prescribes the right of an individual to religious freedom without any interdiction on part of the state given that the religious behaviour or act does not disturb the public order.

The same notion had been affirmed already in the first French Constitution of 1791 which albeit conferring upon all French citizens the right to exercise their religious belief, and considers it to be a 'natural and civil right', expressed the possibility of its confinement. The Constitution of 1791 declared in its first article that liberty and other fundamental provisions guaranteed by the constitution should be applied in a manner that does not pose endangerment or a threat to public safety or that may interfere or collide with other individual rights.[560]

The French courts will consider an infringement of the right to religious freedom simply based on an affirmation or denial that such an impingement has actually taken place; given that a violation is confirmed, this will necessitate an establishment of a lawful justification so as to determine its validity.

Nonetheless, a pronouncement of a lawful justification will not suffice in itself, as the violating act or practice will be subject to a proportionality test. Both the administrative courts and the constitutional council will apply in practice the proportionality test.[561] In addition, in the past few years it has become noticeable as a tendency that French jurisprudence implements in its case laws the principle of 'practical concordance' adopted from the German jurisprudence. The

559 *Robert*, 2003, pp. 637, 643–644; *McGoldrick* (2006), p. 39; JO, 11 December 1905, Art. 31, at 7206.

560 *Robert*, 2003, pp. 637, 644.

561 The proportionality test will be explained in further detail in Chapter IV 3.b)(2)(g) below.

outweigh of competing rights, for instance, the obligation of the state to remain secular in its actions, which may collide with the right to religious freedom, will be conducted by the appropriate jurisdictional authority in these matters, the Conseil d'Etat.[562]

bb) Equality Rights/Anti-Discrimination Rights

In principle, the right to equality before the law has been considered an integral part of the French constitutional and legal doctrine.[563] Though development and importance of anti-discrimination laws have increased in the last years, the protection of the right to religious freedom through anti-discrimination laws has not much developed under French Law. Equality rights are guaranteed mainly through: first, various norms scattered throughout different sources, essentially criminal and employment law;[564] second, as a member state in the EU, France is bound to implement the EU Equality Directives.[565]

Prescriptions banning discrimination on account of different grounds, including religion, are to be found in the different constitutional texts. In addition, there are also several enactments determining a general prohibition of discrimination triggered due to pertinence or non-pertinence to a particular race, religion, ethnic group, or nation.[566]

An overview of the legal precepts appointing a ban of discrimination on religious grounds will be set forth as follows:

(1) The 1789 Declaration

The equality of individuals before the law is outlined already in the first provision of the 1789 Declaration. The principle that all people are equal before the law originates from the notion that the law reflects the general will of the people and,

---

562 *Poggeschi*, pp. 263, 270.

563 *van Ooijen*, p. 164; *McGoldrick* (2006), p. 41.

564 *v. Ungern-Sternberg*, 2008, p. 147; *Curtit,* in: Hill, Religion and Discrimination Law in the European Union, 2012, pp. 145, 150; as well as the implementation of the Racial Equality Directive Loi no 2008–496 from 27 May 2008.

565 Council Directive 2000/43/EC from 29 June 2000 (Racial Equality Directive).

566 *v. Ungern- Sternberg*, 2008, p. 149; Law no. 72–546 dated 1 July 1972, contains provisions concerning specific acts of discrimination, JO (Journal Officiel), 2 July 1972, at 6803–6804; Law no. 90–615 dated 13 July 1990, contains a general ban of all types of discrimination based on pertinence or absence of membership to an ethnic group, a nation, or a religion and compels the state to ensure compliance with this principle, JO, 14 July 1990, at 8333.

as a result, must be similar for everyone.[567] The right to equality implies also the right to equal eligibility in application to public functions.[568]

(2) The Constitution of 1946

The prohibition of discrimination on account of religious grounds is to be found in the preamble of the 1946 Constitution[569] which appoints that no one should be impaired at work or in occupation on grounds of ethnicity, religion, and belief.[570]

(3) The Constitution of 1958

The constitution of 1958 establishes in Art. 1 the principle of equality of all French citizens irrespective of their origin, race, and religion. The provision goes further and guarantees to respect and observe all beliefs.[571]

A more detailed depiction of the equality principle and dispersion of its elements in divergent legal sources will be provided under subheading 4 C) cc) of this chapter.[572]

(4) Recognition of Equality Rights

(a) Pupils

The obligation to ensure equal treatment on account of religious freedom is guaranteed with respect to pupils in the educational system of the French

567 Art. 6 of the 1789 Declaration reads: 'La loi est l'expression de la volonte generale... Elle doit etre la meme pour tous...'.

568 Art. 6 of the 1789 Declaration reads: 'Tous les citoyens, etant egaux a ses yeux, sont egalement admissibles a toutes dignites, places et emplois publics...'.

569 Though the Constitution of 1958 replaced the 1946 Constitution, it was decided by the Constitutional Council in 1971 to incorporate the preamble of the 1946 Constitution into the new constitution; thus, the basic rights encompassed in the 1946 constitution still remain a valid constitutional source of law. Id. Art.s 56–53; Conseil Constitutionnel [CC] [Constitutional Court] decision no. 71–44DC, 16 July 1971, J.O. 7114 (Fr.); See *Davis*, pp. 117, 124.

570 Art. 5 of the 1946 Constitution declares: *'Each person has the duty to work and the right to employment. No person may suffer prejudice in his work or employment by virtue of his origins, opinions or beliefs'*. The French text: *'Nul ne peut être lésé, dans son travail ou dans son emploi, en raison de ses origines, de ses opinions ou de ses croyances'*.

571 Art. 1 of the 1958 Constitution determines that: *'France... shall ensure the equality of all citizens before the law, without distinction of origin, race or religion. It shall respect all beliefs'*. http://www.assemblee-nationale.fr/english/8ab.asp

572 Subheading 4. C)cc).

Education Code (*Code de l'Education*). It declares that in accordance with the guarantee of fundamental rights as prescribed in the constitution, it will be the task of the state to ensure and take consideration of pupils' religion or belief.[573] Notably, the legal system in France perceives the right not to be discriminated on religious grounds as an inseparable part of the fundamental right to religious freedom and as closely related to it.

(b) Teachers

The precept prohibiting discrimination with respect to office holders in the public sector is provided in Art. 6 of the law from 1983, which bans direct and indirect discrimination on religious grounds. The law in Art. 6 para 2 inhibits any form of direct or indirect discrimination conducted in the public sector on account of political, commercial, philosophical, or religious grounds.[574]

In fact, Art. 6 of the 1983 Law integrated the prohibition of discrimination in employment and occupation on grounds of religion and belief as stipulated in Directive 2000/78 of the European Union.[575]

(5) International Agreements

France is a signatory to several agreements on the international level. Some, like the UDHR, have no legal binding force; others, like the ICCPR, ECHR,

---

573 Code de l' Education L. 141–2: *'Following the principles defined in the Constitution, the state provides to children and adolescents in public schools the opportunity to receive an education in conformity with their skills in equal respect for all faiths'*. Original French Text cites: '*Suivant les principes définies dans la Constitution, l'État assure aux enfants et adolescents dans les établissements publics d'enseignement la possibilité de recevoir un enseignement conforme à leurs aptitudes dans un égal respect de toutes les croyances*'. *See in* https://www.legifrance.gouv.fr/affichCode.do;jsessionid=254784F5CD9DA63A388FDF5313069988.tpdila23v_1?idSectionTA=LEGISCTA000006166566&cidTexte=LEGITEXT000006071191&dateTexte=20160302.

574 Law no. 83–634 from 13 July 1983, which was modified by legal ordinance no. 2005–901 from 2 August 2005 declares in Art. 1 para 1 that: *'La liberté d'opinion est garantie aux fonctionnaires*. Para 2: *Aucune distinction, directe ou indirecte, ne peut être faite entre les fonctionnaires en raison de leurs opinions politiques, syndicales, philosophiques ou religieuse…'*. In translation: *'Freedom of opinion is guaranteed to civil servants. No distinction, direct or indirect, can be made between civil servants because of their political opinions, trade union, philosophical or religious, their origin, their sexual orientation, or gender identity, their age, their name, their status health, physical appearance, disability or* membership *or non-membership, real or supposed, of an ethnic group or* race'.

575 *Ganz*, p. 53.

and other international human rights instruments, are not only binding for the French government due to France's consent to accede to international law and the human rights system prescribed in them, but even obtain prevalence over national law.[576]

The right to religious freedom is recognized and safeguarded under many international agreements ratified by France.[577] Religious freedom constitutes a significant, pivotal profound liberty within human rights law. The need to ensure its effective guarantee as a profound legal norm dates back to the founding of the UN which within an adoption of a universal set of declaratory norms wished to provide minorities protection against discrimination for manifestation of religion in public.[578] The importance of religious freedom as established under international law can serve as a yardstick to evaluate France's commitment to respect religious rights. Taking into consideration limitations incurred by domestic law over manifestation of religious symbols in public schools leaves a great doubt as to France's willingness to confer international treaties' priority over national law.

It is claimed that the French debate is complicated especially as far as application and compliance with international human right law is concerned.[579] In practice, French courts encounter difficulties to prioritize international law, and have provided inconsistent decisions when international treaties were invoked so to declare incompatibility of French law.[580]

The reasons why French courts are hesitant and unclear as to French constitutional commitment to grant international treaties legislative prevalence over national law are various and ample and will be set out briefly.

---

576 *Adrian*, pp. 345, 356.

577 Convention Against Discrimination in Education (CADE) see in JO, Nov. 7, 1961, at p. 10166; The International Convention on the elimination of all forms of Racial Discrimination (CERD) JO, 10 November, 1971, Art. 5, at 11100; *Brownlie/Goodwin-Gill*, p. 284.

578 *Adrian*, pp. 345, 356.

579 Bernard Stasi Report (11 December 2003) Para. 2.1; *Saxena*, pp. 788, 789; *Adrian*, pp. 345, 353–358, 360. Adrian examines the legal legitimacy provided by the Stasi Commission Report for introducing the Law of 2004 that was drawn up to prohibit all religious and political symbols in public schools and their recommendation for its adoption affirming conformity of French Law and its principles with international human rights standards espoused to the right of religious freedom.

580 *Saxena*, pp. 765, 785;

First, France's unwillingness to recognize the status of religious minorities under international human rights instruments.[581] The opinion held in legal literature supports the notion of respect and acceptance of religious and cultural pluralism in a democratic society.[582] So even if restrictions are imposed on minorities' right to manifest their religious belief, the state is under obligation to approach this fundamental right with tolerance and careful diligence. However, the French perception of citizenship takes no differentiation on any ground into account and favours neutrality to promote equality, liberty, and solidarity among its citizens.[583]

Second, the legal position France upholds to religious freedom in the long-standing history of French law. In particular, taken its separationist approach towards religion imprinted by its chosen model of church-state relations and stark adherence to the concept of laïcité.

Third, general interpretation rules of the ECHR dictates that the fundamental right of religious freedom as prescribed in Art. 9 ECHR should be comprehended in its widest sense, whereas limitations should remain narrowly formulated. In fact, the scope of restrictions imposed through Art. 9 para 2 ECHR should be narrowly confined in interpretation compared to other provisions safeguarded under the ECHR.[584] Despite this interpretative principle, the French approach was proved to be reversed.[585] This is mainly due to the doctrine of margin of appreciation allowing member states discretion when outweighing individual rights and national interests against universal values.

Fourth, the assessment of restrictions imposed on religious freedom and its application, taking into account their formulation and phrasing in international human rights treaties becomes complicated and contributes to inconsistencies in adjudication, mainly due to lack of precise guidance as to interpretation of

---

581 For instance, France announced the inapplicability of Art. 27 of the ICCPR with Art. 2 of the 1958 Constitution. The same declaration was provided with respect to Art. 30 of the UN Convention on the Rights of the Child.

582 *Martinez-Torron*, Emory Int'l L.Rev. 19(2) (2005), pp. 578, 599; *Evans*, Religious Liberty and International Law in Europe, 1997, pp. 195, 226.

583 It was claimed that France demonstrated no will to provide affirmative protection to its religious minorities, especially Muslims, with the promulgation of the headscarf ban. See *Saxena*, pp. 765, 788.

584 *Evans*, Freedom of Religion under The European Convention on Human Rights, p. 137.

585 *Adrian*, pp. 345, 360.

special terms, such as 'religious belief', 'legitimate aim', 'margin of appreciation', 'public order', and 'necessary in a democratic society'.[586]

(a) ECHR

The ECHR is considered to be a legal binding agreement in France's constitutional hierarchy of norms. France has approved the ECHR in 1974,[587] and by that accepted the European human rights regime prescribed by it. Fundamental rights prescribed under the ECHR are self-executing and can be invoked directly before national courts by virtue of a constitutional prevalence (Art. 55 1958 Constitution).

The protection of the right to religious freedom within this European system of human rights is established in Art. 9 ECHR. The limitation clause of Art. 9 ECHR established a three-tier test in order to assist national judicators in establishing whether restrictions imposed on religious freedom are justifiable. The three-principle test prescribes that any limitation on religious freedom must fulfil the following: first, it must be prescribed by law; second, it must be necessary in a democratic society; and, third, it must correspond to one of the legitimate aims outlined in Art. 9 para 2 ECHR and proportionate to the specific need on which they are predicated.

Several tension points may arise between restrictions imposed on the right to religious manifestation in public education and the ability to reconcile with the limitation clause of Art. 9 ECHR. Some may relate to the fact that the list of legitimate aims prescribed in Art. 9 para 2 ECHR should remain entrenched in scope and not allow insertion of a broader limitation clause and new purposes justifying interferences. Other conflicts may relate to vague definitions of important phrasings as listed above. For instance, the definition of 'public order', which has been often used and invoked by French authorities as a legitimate aim for interdiction of religious symbols in state schools.[588] As mentioned above, under French law confinement of religious rights, especially when occurring in the context of education, will often be justified on ground of the threat it poses to public order, and as long as it is established by law. Nonetheless, compliance of French education laws and bans imposed on manifestation of religious symbols

---

586 *Saxena* pp. 765, 788; *Adrian*, pp. 345, 358.

587 France ratified the ECHR on 3 May 1974. See at http://www.coe.int/en/web/conventions/full-list/-/conventions/treaty/155.

588 *Adrian*, pp. 345, 359, 360.

in the public school system that form violation of the right to religious freedom as enshrined in Art. 9 ECHR will be discussed profoundly in the next chapter.

(b) International Covenant on Civil and Political Rights (ICCPR)

This international agreement concluded within the UN framework for the purpose of establishment of a strong enforceable mechanism of fundamental human rights. The ICCPR was meant to be a powerful enforcement mechanism than the one offered under the UDHR which remains declaratory in nature[589]. The right to manifest religious belief and its scope of protection is set out in Art. 18 of the ICCPR.[590] The ICCPR is classified under the legal status of a binding legal agreement upon France, to which it is obliged under international human rights constitutional position. France has acceded its obligation to the ICCPR on 4 November 1980.[591]

The HRC was established as a supervisory institute for monitoring the implementation of the ICCPR, and its protocols can be accredited for considerable contributions made in two aspects:

First, Art. 18 ICCPR – provided in General Comment 22[592] that limitations on the right to religious freedom must be strictly interpreted so as not to impair the rights guaranteed in Art. 18 ICCPR. In addition, they must be applied only for purposes for which they are prescribed, and they must be directly related and proportionate for the specific need on which they are predicated. Restrictions are not allowed on grounds not specified in Art. 18 itself, even if they are allowed with respect to other rights prescribed in the ICCPR.[593]

---

589 *Harris* in Harris/Joseph (eds.), pp. 1-2; *Brownlie*, p.192.

590 *Brownlie/Goodwin-Gill*, p. 284.

591 The ICCPR came into force on 23 March 1976, while France has ratified it only on 4 November 1980 and entered into force on 4 February 1981. https://en.wikipedia.org/wiki/International_Covenant_on_Civil_and_Political_Rights.

592 General Comment, 1993. Para. 8 to General Comment 22 outlines that *'Limitations imposed must be established by law and must not be applied in a manner that would vitiate the rights* guaranteed *in Art. 18… Limitations may be applied only for those purposes for which they were prescribed and must be directly* proportionate *to the specific need on which they are predicated. Restrictions may not be imposed for discriminatory purposes or applied in a discriminatory manner'* U.N. International Human Rights Instruments, Compilation of General Comments and General Recommendations Adopted by Human Rights Bodies, p. 37, U.N. Doc. HRI/GEN/1/Rev.1 (29 July 1994).

593 *Adrian*, pp. 345, 357.

Second, the ruling of the HRC was in favour of an individual's right to religious freedom holding that the national law of a member state (Uzbekistan) did infringe upon Art. 18 para 2 ICCPR. The importance of the case was highlighted not only because a member state was expected to amend its domestic legislation for its failure to comply with the ICCPR provisions, but also for the formal recognition of religious freedom as a vital fundamental right.[594]

c) Constitutional and Legal Principles (Lois Constitutionnelles)

In the course of the constitutional history of France, some elementary principles have been developed out of regular enactments, but were ranked high to a level of a constitutional law in the French jurisprudence.[595] In particular, there are historically fundamental and important values of secularity, democracy, social inspiration, and decentralization. These principles have an equal status and establish the constitutional pillars upon which the French system is based.

aa) The Principle of Neutrality

The notion of neutrality in the French context is exclusive in its application since it derives validity from another constitutional fundament, the principle of laïcité. Neutrality is identified as a value of laïcité.[596] The notion of neutrality suggests that the state should refrain from any favouritism towards a specific religion or demonstrate any deterrence towards another religion.

In other words, the state adopts an official policy of non-recognition and simply negates a system of 'recognized religions' by eliminating any distinction between the largest recognized religious groups and by placing them on the same political level.[597]

---

594 Communication. no. 931/2000 *Raihon Hudoyberganova v Uzbekistan* dealt with a submission of a complaint to the HRC by a student who was prohibited from wearing the Islamic headscarf at her institute of studies. In 1998, following endorsement of a national law prohibiting all citizens from wearing religious dress in public schools she was even excluded from her institute. The complainant's application was successful as the HRC ruled in her favour. See at http://www.ohchr.org/Documents/Publications/SDecisionsVol8en.pdf

595 *Morange*, p. 84; *Heun*, ZevKR 49, 2004, pp. 273, 274.

596 *Gunn*, BYU L. Rev. 2004, pp. 419, 466.

597 *Robert*, 2003, pp. 637, 640.

The principle of neutrality enfolds the notion that public service should be neutral.[598]

The negative aspect of the neutrality principle bars public officials from manifestation of their religion or belief by any kind of expression: either verbally, by attire, or conduct.

Under this aspect, neutrality affords double protection: on the one hand, it protects public officials from the state, and, on the other hand, it protects citizens which make use of a public service against public officials.[599]

The state should actually adopt neutrality of political power, abstain from display of religious symbols in the public space, and forbear any religious influence in public school system.[600] The observance of the neutrality principle is therefore of high importance, especially within the public service.[601] Though the principle of neutrality is not codified in France's legal system, it confers the notion that the state should observe neutrality towards religion in all its public services.[602] France implemented the neutrality principle in a strict manner, and perceives the duty of state to neutrality by way of diminishing any visibility of religion from its public sphere. Therefore, within the context of public service and state relations, it is incumbent on a public official to conform with the image of the state as this absolute obligation is inherent to his duty. Thence, the interaction of a public official with citizens obliges him to renounce his/her freedom to manifest a religion or belief, and incur the duty of neutrality since he/she appears as a representative of the state. As a result, taking the triangle of relations between state-public official and citizen it is concluded that public officials are expected to align their personal view with the state, and forego their position as an individual bearing rights. The personification of the state, necessitating a public official to vanish any individuality or personal right create a straight line between state and citizen that makes the public official a redundant actor within this triangle of actors. Moreover, taking into account the context of relations between the state and the citizen, it is known that citizens have a direct connection with the state. This makes any intermediary parties, such as public officials, irrelevant in this triple equation reshaping the triangle of actors to a straight line operating solely between state and citizen.[603]

598 *van Ooijen*, p. 178.
599 *van Ooijen*, p. 178.
600 *Gunn*, BYU L. Rev. (2) 2004, pp. 419, 465; *van Ooijen*, p. 178.
601 *Bell/Boyron/Whittaker,* p. 171.
602 *Poulter*, 1997, pp. 43, 58.
603 McGoldrick (2006), pp. 38–42; *van Ooijen*, p. 200.

Since the principle of neutrality applies in uniformity with respect to all functions of the public service, it will be valid also with respect to public school teachers. This assumes the teachers' responsibility to refrain from any manifestation of religion or belief, as it will contrast their obligation to neutrality incumbent upon them by virtue of their voluntary function as public officials.

bb) The Principle of Laïcité

The principle of laïcité is a special term imparting its significance as a unifying and founding principle of the French Republic. Legal literature entails vast and numerous attempts to identify the real definition of laïcité.[604] The main difficulty to establish the exact term is the inability to find a translatable definition in any other language; this is attributed to its lack of existence in any other constitutional system as part of its specialness and superiority of French republicanism.[605]

Prior to delivery of an overview of its evolvement in French history and the fact that it became one of the significant cornerstones of its constitutional system, a brief depiction of the notion is necessary for further discourse.

The French understanding of the term '*laïcité*' explains that its purport comes to suggest the adequate place and function that religion acquires within the state.[606] Laïcité is meant to be a system of public order under which religion should be excluded from public space, including civil affairs and public education.[607] However, unlike its English counterpart 'secularism', it does not mean a radical rejection of religion, but rather captures the notion of separation of church and state through the state's protection of individuals from the claims of religion (i.e., proselytism).[608]

---

604 *McGoldrick* (2006), pp. 38–39, 41–42; *van Ooijen*, pp. 175–178; *Scott*, p. 15; *Gunn*, BYU L. Rev. (2) 2004, pp. 419, 420, 465, 466; *Davis*, pp. 117, 119; Delmas, Das Kopftuchverbot in Frankreich, Ein Streit um die Definition von Laizität, Republik und Frauenemanzipation, 2006, p. 35.

605 *Fetzer/Soper*, pp. 69–76; *McGoldrick* (2006), p. 38; *van Ooijen*, p. 175; *Saxena*, pp. 765, 769; *Scott*, p. 15.

606 *McGoldrick* (2006), p. 38; *van Ooijen*, p. 175.

607 See *Gunn*, BYU L. Rev. (2) 2004, pp. 419, 420 (Fn. 2) as he traces attempts in French legal literature to provide definition to the term laïcité. Gunn refers to the definition of laïcité depicted in the *Le Grand Robert* dictionary as a: 'political notion involving the separation of civil society and religious society, the state exercising no religious power and the churches exercising no political power', as cited from Alain Rey and Paul Robert, 5 Le Grand Robert DE LA LANGUE FRANCAISE 915 (2nd edn. 1992).

608 *Scott*, p. 15.

(1) Historical Development

Laïcité originally emanated in a period of time in French history where the republic developed hostility towards religion and wished to cease the control of the Catholic Church over its inner affairs.[609] The modern French conception of laïcité acquired a different meaning as it developed during two distinct periods in French history. The first period, the five years following the Revolution of 1789, was marked by a strong anti-clericist approach with hostility targeted towards the Roman Catholic Church. The second period is considered during the time of the Third Republic (1879–1905).[610] The second period is identified by strong separationist approach, which eventually led to the enactment of the 1905 Law and aimed at limiting religion to the private sphere.[611] It had even reached a higher level towards the end of the nineteenth century when the first stage of laicization in the context of public education took place. From a French constitutional perspective, the notion of laïcité was safeguarded through a laicizing process incurred on the state.[612]

It was the French government following the French Revolution in 1789 that decided to aggravate relations with the Catholic Church by seizure of church property and by severing relations with the Vatican, in efforts to dismantle any power it had over the state.[613]

So in principle, the term '*laïcité*' was envisaged as a two-way process: state-political powers should not exercise religious powers, and religious powers should not exercise state-political powers.

Later, the interpretation of the laïcité principle was meant to exclude any religious affinity from public spaces, including civil affairs and public education.[614]

(2) Notion of Laïcité

The concept of *laïcité* comes to represent a philosophy, or notion, which describes the appropriate relationship that should exist between church and state in France.[615]

In fact, the term *laïcité* is often interlinked with the neutrality principle, though they differ in terms of definition and conceptualization.[616] Essentially, the translation

---

609 *McGoldrick* (2006), pp. 34–35, 38, 40–41.

610 *Gunn*, BYU L. Rev. (2) 2004, pp. 419, 432,433.

611 *Franzke*, DöV Vol 57.1, 2004, p. 384.

612 *van Ooijen*, p. 200.

613 *Davis*, pp. 117–119; *McGoldrick* (2006), pp. 34–35, 40–41.

614 *Chelini-Pont*, BYU L. Rev. 2005, pp. 611–627; *McGoldrick* (2006), p. 39; *Levine*, Cal. W. Int'l L.J. 40 (2009) pp. 33, 37.

615 *Gunn*, BYU L. Rev. (2) 2004, pp. 419, 420 (describing laïcité as much more than a word and as a concept not easily defined); *McGoldrick* (2006), p. 38.

616 *van Ooijen*, p. 175.

of the word laïcité refers to its English counterpart 'secularism', though it does not transfer in full the purport of this principle.[617] In addition, the term *laïcité* does not have an identical equivalent in other international constitutional systems.[618] Due to the absence of a precise definition of the term *laïcité*[619] by the French legislator the opinions differs as to its interpretation and application.[620]

Indeed, the principle of laïcité is not to be attributed the general universal synonym of secularism but, rather, must be apprehended in its special France version, which is unique to French history and national character (*une singularité francaise*).[621] The secular nature of France is one of its salient features and is known as the fundament of the French unicité (*uniqueness*).[622] The notion of secularity was inherent in the ideals of enlightenment of the French revolution and embodies a concept revered in France's history.[623]

In fact, many French politicians and legal scholars uphold a proud approach to the definition of laïcité and impart its uniqueness to the fact that it can only transfer its true meaning in the French language[624] and thorough knowledge of the development of French history.[625]

---

617 *McGoldrick* (2006), p. 38; *Gunn*, 46 Journal of Church and State, 2004, pp. 1, 8; Baubérot suggests the term laicism as an equivalent to the French term laïcité, See *Baubérot*, p. 441; *van Ooijen*, p. 175.

618 Though the principle of laïcité is very unique to the French system, other countries (e.g. Turkey) have made acquaintance with the principle either by adoption or export. See in *van Ooijen*, pp. 175, 176.

619 *Fetzer/Soper*, p. 71.

620 *McGoldrick* (2006), p. 41; *Idriss*, pp. 260, 261.

621 *Scott*, p. 97.

622 *Poggeschi*, pp. 263, 264.

623 *Poggeschi*, pp. 263, 264; *Ségur*, Annales de l'Université des Sciences Sociales de Toulouse, 1996, pp. 117–134.

624 President Jacques Chirac in his speech from the Elysée Palace delivered on 17 December 2003, http://www.jacqueschirac-asso.fr/archives-elysee.fr/elysee/elysee.fr/anglais/speeches_and_documents/2003/fi004414.html

Former Prime Minister Jean-Pierre Reffarin in his speech to the CRIF on 25 January 2003, http://www.crif.org/fr/lecrifenaction/Diner-du-CRIF-du-25-janvier-2003-en-l-honneur-de-M-Jean-Pierre-RAFFARIN---Premier-Ministre-Discours-de-M-Roger-CUKIERMAN---President659, Nicolas Sarkozy and Jean Gaeremynck a counselor of state (a conseiller d'Etat) see in *Gunn*, BYU L. Rev. 2004, pp. 419, 429.

625 *Bowen*, pp. 17–18. The author refers to the general political approach in France regarding state-church affairs and key terms specific to French republicanism, such

An affirmation of this prominent position of laïcité was delivered even in a 2003 speech by President Chirac depicted as the 'cornerstone' (*pierre angulaire*) of French Republicanism.[626] Since the term is unique to France's national identity and symbolizes the superiority of its republican ideology, it can obtain its full meaning only in the French language.

It is said that the values underpinning the principle of laïcité are 'liberty of conscience, equality of rights in spiritual and religious choices, and neutrality of political power'.[627]

Hence, the principle conjoins two fundamental elements emanating from it: first, the negative aspect attached to the plain notion of separation between church and state[628] which dictates: no exercise of religious power, no acknowledgement or financial funding of religion,[629] and confinement of churches in the exercise of political power;[630] second, the positive aspect that perceives the task of the state to protect the right of individuals to free exercise of religion.[631] In this regard, the right to freedom of conscience is considered as inherent to the principle of laïcité.[632]

The third prominent judicial pillar of the laïcité principle is the notion of religious neutrality of the state, which means that the state neither favours a recognized religion nor works to the detriment or disadvantage of other religions.[633]

---

as laïcité, by quoting the political philosopher Blandine Kriegel, former advisor to President Jacques Chirac, and Vianney Sevaistre, former Chief of the Central Office of Organised Religion within the Ministry of Interior.

626 *Gunn*, Journal of Church and State, 2004, pp. 1, 10; Conseil d'Etat report (2004).

627 *Gunn*, BYU L. Rev. (2) 2004, pp. 419, 466.

628 Laïcité is even explained as a model of separationism between state and religion, see *Fetzer/Soper*, p. 69.

629 The definition of laïcité in Le Grand Robert dictionary as referred to in *Fetzer/Soper*, p. 73 suggests that it is to be comprehended as freedom of religion where the state neither recognizes nor subsidizes any religion.

630 Laïcité could be perceived as a separation of civil society and religion. religious society. 'le principe de separation de la societé civile et de la societé religieuse, l'état n'exercant aucun pouvoir religieux et les eglises aune pouvoir politique', see *Bedouelle/Costa*, Les laïcités à la française, 1998, pp. 11, 13–14.

631 *Scott*, pp. 91, 98.

632 *McGoldrick* (2006), p. 39.

633 It was noted that the French regime is not hostile but rather tolerant with respect to other religions, see *Robert*, 2003, pp. 637, 639.

Conceivably, the fact that the republic does not recognize any religion does not mean that it ignores religion or religious belief. It simply aims to extinguish any disparities between different cults, religious or faith groups, and strives for their equal treatment in order to achieve national cohesion. Thence, the French apprehension with respect to the principle of laïcité does not necessarily negate its positive approach towards religious pluralism and tolerance.[634]

Nowadays, however, laïcité defines the public identity of the French people as a collective. Laïcité in that sense is supposed to protect French citizens from external influence of religious minority groups since they are perceived as a threat to the secular French identity.[635] It is therefore suggested that France's approach to the laïcité principle should be established upon passive neutrality in the private domain so that the state would not interfere in the religious sphere of an individual, as this is regarded permissible. This should be interlinked with a non-discrimination principle in the public sphere so as not to demonstrate any affinity to a particular religion.[636]

Another aspect of laïcité (separation of state and church) is to conclude that it was intended to provide protection for the citizens against excessive involvement of religion. In principle, religion became a private option for French citizens and is no longer a public service.[637]The idea is to offer individuals protection against any religious group's pressure or any form of proselytism, and, therefore, requiring positive protection of the state against any form of it.[638]

This approach comes near to another interpretation of the laïcité principle, suggesting a more rigorous application where the state can protect its values and maintain its religious neutrality given that boundaries can be set to religious freedom in the interests of public order.[639] It should be noted that this forms a notion of active secularism that dominates in most governmental and educational authorities since it permits justifiable state control over any religious expression

634 The diverse interpretations relating to the French principle laïcité, whether positively associated with religious pluralism or not, are various and controversial. See *Liederman-Molokotos*, p. 110.

635 *Weil*, Cardozo L. Rev. 30 (2009), pp. 2704–2705.

636 *Poulter*, 1997, pp. 43, 50; *Idriss*, pp. 260, 261.

637 *Robert*, La liberte' Religieuse, 46 R.I.D.C. 2, p. 630; *Palmer*, p. 24.

638 *Robert*, 2003, pp. 642–643; *McGoldrick* (2006), p. 39.

639 *Poulter*, 1997, pp. 43, 50.

taking place in public institutions, including on part of schoolteachers and pupils as participants in public education institutions.[640]

Accordingly, laïcité is meant to be a system of public order (*l'ordre public*) under which religious freedom can flourish, and may be restricted only when prescribed by the law and in order to protect interests of public order.

(3) Legal Sources

The meaning and implementation of the laïcité principle have changed throughout the history of France, as it was highly influenced by the prevailing regime at that time and by the political situation. France was said to raise laïcité to the level of a funding value; it therefore easily formed a fundamental part in the constitutions of the Fourth and Fifth Republics (1946, 1958) as well as in laws enacted by the parliament at that time.

(a) Laïcité in the Declaration of 1789

The recognition of liberty of conscience as a judicial pillar of laïcité had been established already in the Declaration of 1789, which pronounces the guarantee of several fundamental freedoms, among them free expression of religion and other opinions, as stipulated in Art. 10. Nonetheless, the right to liberty of conscience is confined and will remain undisturbed as long as it does not disturb established law and order.

(b) The Law of 1795

The notion of neutrality embossed as a funding judicial pillar of the laïcité principle was introduced firstly in legislation. The first law formally separating the church from the state was promulgated on 21 February 1795, and included the prohibition of wearing 'religious ornaments or clothing in public'.[641] In fact, it affirmed the fundamental principle of freedom of worship, but admitted state control over the display of religious symbols in public by virtue of implementing in practice an old decision of the constituent assembly from 1792 prohibiting priests from wearing their religious attire in public.[642]

---

640 *Idriss*, pp. 260, 261–262.

641 *Saxena*, pp. 765, 770; *Gunn*, BYU L. Rev. (2) 2004, pp. 419, 438.

642 *Saxena*, pp. 765, 770.

(c) The Notion of Laïcité in the Constitutions of 1946 and 1958

Since the principle possesses a central place in the French national identity, it has even been integrated into the preamble of the 1946 constitution[643] and reiterated in Art. 1 of the 1958 Constitution.[644]

French insistence not to integrate religion into the public service is a notable feature in the French ideal of citizenship. In fact, the notion of separation was intended to secure the allegiance of citizens to the republic, as they had to choose between their religion and the state and thus break the political power of the Catholic Church.[645]

It is, therefore, the case that apart from special regions (e.g., regions of Alsace-Moselle), which due to historical reasons were allowed to keep the former local law determining the relationship between state and church, the French government is prohibited by law from granting official recognition to religion and from subsidizing religious organizations or paying their personnel.[646]

Notably, the principle of separation of state and church and the fundamental right of religious freedom were already confirmed in the 1958 Constitution. In principle, this was already acknowledged in the 1946 Constitution and later on reproduced in Art. 1 of the 1958 Constitution.[647]

The preamble to the 1946 Constitution proclaimed that:

> … (T)he people of France proclaim anew that each human being, without distinction of race, religion or creed, possesses sacred and inalienable rights. They solemnly reaffirm the rights and freedoms of man and the citizen enshrined in the Declaration of Rights of 1789 and the fundamental principles acknowledged in the laws of the Republic (i.e., the principles of indivisibility, secularism, democracy, and equality).[648]

---

643 Art. 1 of the 1946 Constitution proclaims France as a 'laique' republic: 'France is an indivisible, lay, democratic and social state'.

644 Art. 1 of the 1958 Constitution declares that: 'France shall be an indivisible, secular, democratic and social republic'.

645 *Scott*, p. 91.

646 Art. 2 of the 1905 Law.

647 For an English translation of the 1958 Constitution, see at http://www.conseil-constitutionnel.fr.

648 For English translation of the 1946 Constitution, see at http://www.conseil-constitutionnel.fr/conseil-constitutionnel/root/bank_mm/anglais/cst3.pdf.

While Art. 1 of the 1958 Constitution prescribes that:

> France shall be an indivisible, secular, democratic and social Republic. It shall ensure the equality of all citizens before the law, without distinction of origin, race or religion. It shall respect all beliefs. It shall be organised on a decentralised basis.[649]

(d) Laïcité in the Law of 1905

The main feature of the French constitutional system is the notion of separation of state and church established in the Law of 9 December 1905[650] (1905 Law). The 1905 Law was completed and modified by the Law of 2 January 1907[651] on the public freedom of worship, and the Law of 13 April 1908.[652]

The relationship between government and religion in France is defined by the 1905 Law, which principally regulates the notion of separation between state and church (*Loi concernant la séparation des Églises et de l'Etat*).

Evidently, the general norm on which the principle of secularity was founded is the law of 9 December 1905 on the separation between churches and the state. This is often considered to be the founding base of the principle of laïcité prescribed in a formal legal status.[653]

In general, it is contended that the legal framework of the act was founded on the three overriding principles mentioned above: 'freedom of conscience, separation of state and churches, and the equal respect of all faiths and beliefs'.[654]

The 1905 Law set out two fundamental principles that essentially affirm: first, the respect for freedom of conscience and, second, the religious neutrality of the state. These are to be found in the first two articles of the law:

Art. 1 of the 1905 Law states that 'the Republic ensures the freedom of conscience. It guarantees the free exercise of beliefs, with the exception restrictions dictated in the following Articles according to the interest of public order'.[655]

---

649 1958 CONST. Art. 1 (Fr.), available at http://www.assemblee-nationale.fr/english/8ab.asp. *Poggeschi*, p. 263; *Desbach/Pontier*, Les Constitutions de la France (Editions Dalloz, 1983); '*La France est une Republique indivisible, laique, democratique et sociale. Elle assure l'egalite de tous les citoyens sans distinction d'origine, de race ou de religion. Elle respecte toutes les croyances*'.

650 JO, 11 December 1905, p. 7204.

651 JO, 3 January 1907, p. 34.

652 JO, 14 April 1908, p. 2609.

653 Law of 9 December 1905, Journal officiel, 11 December 1905, 7205; *Gunn*, BYU L. Rev., 2004, pp. 419, 441.

654 *Weil*, pp. 2699, 2704.

655 www.legifrance.gouv.fr/texteconsolide/MCEBW.htm.

Art. 2 determines that 'the republic does not recognize, remunerate pay, or financially support any religious denomination. Accordingly, from first of January following the enactment of this law, all expenses related to the exercise of religion will be removed from state budgets, departments and municipalities'.[656]

This law has gained importance in French legislation since it constitutes the legal base establishing the principle of separation between state and church as it embarked on a period following gradual development upon which France was no longer defined as a Catholic nation. This notion enfolds the following aspects which signify this historical upheaval:

First, confinement of relations between citizens and religious adherence. Second, cease of financial support for religious communities (the state neither acknowledges nor subsidizes religious communities).[657]

(4) Exceptions to the Laïcité Principle

It is contended though that there is no justification for the strict application of the principle of state-church separation in modern times.[658] The reasons are varied and will be outlined here briefly:

(a) The Alsace Lorraine exception

One of the exceptions to the Law of 1905 relates to the regions of Alsace-Lorraine and Moselle, which exceptionally adopted and maintained different regulations regarding state-church affairs. Since both had been under German control for a considerable time as a result of the Franco-German war of 1871, they stayed under the regime established by the Concordat of 1801.[659] After the return of these regions to France, they maintained their previous legislation administering their relations with the Christian churches (Catholic and Protestant) and the Jewish community.[660]

---

656 Art. 2, original text: 'La République ne reconnait, ne salarie ni ne subventionne aucun culte'. See www.legifrance.gouv.fr/texteconsolide/MCEBW.htm; *Palmer*, p. 31.

657 *van Ooijen*, p. 174.

658 *van Ooijen*, p. 174.

659 The Concordat of 1801, one of the most significant acts signed between Napoleon and the Pope in order to establish state-church relations and restore peace in France. See, *Wick* in: von Campenhausen/Frisch/Heckel, Beiträge zum evangelischen Kirchenrecht und zum Staatskirchenrecht, 2007, pp. 29, 32. Supra note 3 (OSCE), p. 31; *van Ooijen*, p. 174.

660 *Poggeschi*, pp. 263, 266; *Scott*, p. 101.

(b) The Changing Social-Demographical Context

Initially, the law was meant to tackle the social strength the Catholic Church acquired at that time in all daily aspects of the citizens, as well as the pre-eminent position it held in the public sphere.[661] It is therefore that the resonance of the law determining the secular character of the French nation is to be attributed to historical reasons reflecting the hostile separation which existed at that time between the Catholic Church and the state; this separation was intensified due to frequent conflicts over power.[662]

Undoubtedly, the historical reasons supporting the adoption of the notion of laïcité, which were relevant to the time of promulgation of the 1905 Law, are not reflective of the situation nowadays.

(c) Accommodation Faced with Immigration

The large immigration of Muslims into France forced some religious accommodation on part of the state (e.g., recognition of religious holidays). This can be interpreted as incompatible with the principle of separation. In fact, the notion of laïcité which emerged earlier due to a strong wish, mainly on part of the Protestant church, to diminish the invincible position of the Catholic church had been set a different context due to conflicts that incurred with the large immigration of the Islamic community into France.[663] The necessity to accommodate to religious needs of large immigration waves of Muslims, especially from North Africa, requires a moderate application of the laïcité principle that takes social-religious changes into account.

(d) Subsidies of Religion

The 1905 law leaves an option for financial support granted either for non-religious activities which take place in religious buildings, or for the maintenance of religious buildings including chaplainries.

---

661 *Weil*, pp. 2699, 2704; *Davis*, pp. 117, 118.

662 *Poggeschi*, pp. 263, 266.

663 The integration problems of the Muslim community in France and conflicts with female Muslim pupils on the background of their refusal to remove their Islamic headcoverings (*foulard*) while attending schools, see in *Bloss*, 2008, pp. 115–121; *Poggeschi*, pp. 263, 264.

(5) *Different Approaches*

The principle of laïcité is revered by French people, as it symbolizes the specialness of French universalism rooted in the historical development of French republicanism, and since it is distinctive in character as it forms a pivotal pillar of a unified and indivisible nation. Nonetheless, the historical variability of the notion of laïcité accrued different approaches as to its application and, in practice, has remained to this date an ardent part of public discourse. In this context, it will be interesting to examine – respective of the existing approaches (strict or liberal) – the impact the laïcité principle has over religious freedom and its place in French society.

As mentioned before, the translation of the French word '*laïcité*' into English 'secularism' enfolds only partially its true and complete meaning. There are several approaches to the interpretation of laïcité and its meaning and use have changed over history.

(a) Strict Application

Incontestably, the strong allegiance of the French Republic and its citizens to the notion of a secular state and adamant observance of its implementation is likely to inhibit religious freedom. From a historical perspective, the political shift of the secular combat line, which was associated with the traditional republican hostility to religion (*la laïcité négative*) gave way during the twentieth century to a more amicable, integrative approach towards diversity of religions that was induced in particular by a strong presence of the Islamic religion (*la laïcité positive*).[664] Hence, the principle of neutrality of state that was to determine the church-state relations in France is characterized by a negative as well as a positive aspect.

The negative aspect acknowledges two elements: the first proclaims that while the republic accepts all manifestations of thought and rejects no ideology or philosophical view in principle, it still does not have an affinity towards a certain religion.[665] This implies that in public functions, in particular in the educational context, the state should refrain from any display of religious symbols and should not take any position in favour or to the detriment of any religion or belief in schools' curricula.[666] Second, the state is abstained from taking into

---

664 *Robert*, 2003, pp. 637, 642; *Rogoff*, French Constitutional Law: Cases and Materials, 2011, p. 337.
665 *Palmer*, p. 31.
666 *van Ooijen*, p. 178.

account the opinion of its individuals, whether religious or political.[667] However, the positive aspect of neutrality incurs upon the state the responsibility to ensure that its citizens can freely exercise their religion and enjoy religious practice without disturbance. It is proclaimed that the negative and positive prongs of religious neutrality have their fundaments established in two constitutional documents: first, the negative aspect embodied in Art. 10 of the Declaration of the Rights of Man prescribes the duty of the state to uphold its discretion and not harass its citizens based on their religious opinions, since no grounds for differentiation exist nor will be taken into account. Second, the positive aspect is entrenched in Art. 2 of the 1958 Constitution that guarantees all of its citizens' equality before the law without distinction of origin, race, or religion.[668] The strict application supports the view that religion should be excluded from the public sphere, and in particular from public education. This firm view rests on the notion that freedom of religion and its exertion by individuals is a private matter that should be kept away from public interference.[669]

Intelligibly, this connotes of a strict observance of the laïcité principle. Apparently, this seems to follow the underlying notion of the heritage conferred by the Ferry laws, which believed that schools should mark the conversion from the private to the public sphere in order to achieve an extensive assimilation of pupils from different backgrounds.

In addition, salient features of the sacrosanct neutrality of the French Republic stand out for its dissociation from religion or interference in religious affairs embodied in one of the following forms: first, absence of monetary support – the French Republic is prohibited from providing financial support to any religion, faith, or cult.[670] Second, non-interference – the Republic is not interfering in the inner affairs of religious organizations so that they are free to administer their organizational affairs and act within their own sphere.[671]

The problem raised in the legal literature, namely that no justification exists nowadays with respect to a strict application of the laïcité principle establishes itself mainly on the need of French society to adapt itself to a changing social-cultural society consisting mainly of the largest religious group of Muslim immigrants. The historical background and incentives, founded mainly on the

---

667 *van Ooijen*, p. 178.

668 *Robert*, 2003, pp. 637, 642.

669 *Scott*, p. 98.

670 See Art. 2 of the 1905 Law.

671 *Robert*, La liberté Religieuse, 46 R.I.D.C. (2–1994), p. 630; *Palmer*, p. 32.

wish of the French nation to dissociate itself from the influence of the Catholic Church, do not correspond any longer with the social challenges of modern times. Thence, proponents of the strict approach of the laïcité principle will probably find it difficult to align their arguments when coming to assess the impact it has on religious freedom bearing in mind that the latter is regarded a guaranteed freedom in the French legal system.[672]

(b) Liberal Application

The guarantee of the right and choice of an individual to freely practise a religion or faith is considered to include the positive aspect of the neutrality principle.[673] This correlates with the perception that laïcité is meant to be liberally applied without any distinction between religions or unnecessary confinement of religious freedom and its manifestation. The explanation delivered in this respect relies on the explicit words of the legislator that otherwise would have chosen a different formulation than that clearly used in Art. 1 of the 1905 Law, determining that religious freedom can only be confined insofar as it is prescribed by the interest of public order.[674] This entails logically that the aim of laïcité is not to decline religion; rather contrarily, it should respect all forms of religion and belief, reconcile the living together in French society albeit diversity in the religious domain, fortify religious pluralism, and provide different cultures with an adequate place to flourish.[675]

Naturally, this positive aspect of this notion intertwines the laïcité principle with other values, such as freedom of conscience, legal equality, and neutrality of the political power.[676]

This approach compels the state to provide its citizens all that is necessary so they can freely observe and practise their religion, i.e., facilitate worship places, qualify religious instructions that accord with their chosen religion, and enable undisturbed practice of religion including recognition of the right to celebrate religious holidays and the right to hold ceremonies. Further, it remains undisputable that religion plays a major role in the social dimension of its citizens

---

672 The guarantee of freedom of religion is inscribed in Art.1 of the 1905 Law.

673 *Palmer*, p. 31.

674 See Art. 1 of the 1905 Law.

675 *Decherf*, 'French Views of Religious Freedom' US-France Analysis Series (July 2001) at http://www.brookings.edu/fp/cusf/analysis/relfreedom.html.

676 *Rogoff*, pp. 347, 348; See also Conseil d'Etat ‚Réflexions sur la laïcité. Considérations générales. Un siècle de la laïcité'. (2004) to be found on the website of the Conseil d'Etat <www.conseil-etat.fr p.

and, therefore, demands that state authorities would not remain indifferent with respect to establishment of worship places or erection of places for collective gathering that will address the needs of different religious communities and faith groups.

Following this approach, the state has to guarantee and act positively in order to provide protection of religious freedom and not impose its ideas on the citizens.[677] This naturally obliges practical operation against impartial or detrimental acts of the state aimed to confine the free practice of religious freedom and the sphere of religious domain.[678] In this regard, the principle of neutrality is perceived as a right for citizens rather than a duty for public officials.

Respectively, it is only reasonable that the principle of neutrality cannot be absolute and prevail at all times. This naturally entails that several exceptions are legitimatized and recognized under different laws.[679]

cc) The Principle of Equality/Non-discrimination

The equality of citizens is a central part of French constitutional law and legal doctrine, evidently alluded in one of its most pre-eminent and famous constitutional provisions, namely Art. 2 of the 1958 constitution which is regarded as one of the republic's prominent fundamental pillars. This article determines that the maxim of the nation shall be 'Liberty, Equality, Fraternity'.[680]

---

677 *Bell/Boyron/Whittaker*, p. 171.

678 *Robert*, 2003, pp. 637, 643; In *Fetzer/Soper* examples are given to the French political approach towards religious practices, especially in the education context, and the way national policy on one of the most controversial issue in France, the headscarf, is claimed to impede the constitutional right to religious freedom rather than ensure its protection. See *Fetzer/Soper*, pp. 76, 78–90, 94–95; *McGoldrick* (2006), p. 39.

679 *Robert*, 2003, pp. 637, 641; For instance: The state owns Catholic places of worship built before 1905, so albeit the 1905 Law, it still finances the maintenance and restoration of many cathedrals – JO, 11 December 1905, Art. 3, at 7204; the state can even guarantee amounts borrowed by churches to construct new places of worship – Law no. 61 – 825 dated 29 July 1961, JO, 30 July 1961, at 7207; Religious associations enjoy an extremely favorable tax regime- C. Impots, Arts. 200–238 bis.; Government agencies are closed on Christian holidays and state employees who belong to Jewish, Muslim, or Armenian communities are granted leave for their religious holidays; Spirtual services are allowed also in hospitals and prisons, See in *Jeuffroy/Tricard*, Liberté Religieuse et régimes des Cultes en Droit Francais, 1996, p. 768.

680 Art. 2 of the 1958 Constitution.

Historically, elements of the principle of equality are to be found in the 1789 Declaration of the Rights of Man and the preamble to the 1946 constitution; however, it became an integral and formal part only in the 1958 constitution.[681]

(1) Legal Sources

(a) National law

The 1789 Declaration – only in the 1789 Declaration there are several provisions that relate to the right of equality and prescribe the abidance of the state to a general non-discrimination rule.

Art. 1 stipulates that: 'Men are born and remain free and equal in rights. Social distinctions may be based only on considerations of the common good'.

Art. 6 – prescribes general equality of all citizens before the law '… All citizens, being equal in its eyes, shall be equally eligible to all high offices, public positions and employments, according to their ability, and without other distinction than that of their virtues and talents'.

Art. 10 – declares the general prohibition of non-discrimination including discrimination based on religious grounds.[682]

The 1946 Constitution – the 1946 Constitution reaffirms already in its preamble its commitment to abide by the fundamental rights and freedoms of man and citizens as enshrined in the 1789 Declaration. Art. 3 goes further and specifies the right by ensuring gender equality. It sustains the equality rights of women to those of men in all spheres.

The 1958 Constitution – the 1958 Constitution proclaims through reference in its preamble its commitment to the rights attached and guaranteed in the 1789 Declaration and the 1946 Constitution. It then explicitly establishes the right to equality of all its citizens in its first article.

> …It shall ensure the equality of all citizens before the law, without distinction of origin, race or religion. It shall respect all beliefs. It shall be organised on a decentralised basis. [683]

Since the founding of the revolutionary First Republic, there exists a state norm entrenched by French politicians which settles the relation between the state and

681 Art. 1 of the 1958 Constitution guarantees the equality before the law of all citizens. *McGoldrick* (2006), p. 41.

682 Art. 10 of the 1789 Declaration states that: '*No one may be disturbed on account of his opinions, even religious ones, as long as the manifestation of such opinions does not interfere with the established Law and Order*'.

683 Art. 1 of the 1958 Constitution.

the citizen on an individualized base. However, France's obligation to respect the equality principle is settled both on a national and an international level, and its commitments to abide by this dual legislative framework will be outlined here briefly.

(b) International Law

The obligation of France not to discriminate against persons on grounds of religion and belief extends itself beyond domestic law to commitments it made under international law to adhere and respect as a signatory to several treaties the rights accorded in them. As mentioned before, some of France's obligations on the international level are of a legal binding nature, whereas others remain non-legally binding agreements which do not incur any positive action on its part.

(aa) ECHR

Art. 14 of the ECHR determines[684] a general prohibition of the non-discrimination principle with respect to enjoyment of human rights and fundamental freedoms. In addition, Art. 1 of Protocol 12 of the ECHR expressly states in its first paragraph that 'the enjoyment of any right set forth by law shall be secured without discrimination on any grounds such as, sex, race, colour, language, religion, political or other opinion, national or social origin…'.

The second paragraph of Art. 1 prohibits discrimination by any public authorities on any ground mentioned in its first paragraph.[685] Art. 9 para 2 ECHR is also a binding regulation that guarantees freedom of religion in France.[686]

(bb) ICCPR

The general declaration of equality of all people before the law and prohibition of non-discrimination on religious grounds lays down in Art. 26 ICCPR, which prescribes a general non-discrimination clause very similar in formulation to the provision stated in Art. 1 of Protocol 12 ECHR. It is a free-standing right that applies to all rights, even those not prescribed under the Covenant,[687] instructing

684 Art. 14 ECHR declares that: '*The enjoyments of rights and freedoms set forth in this Convention shall be secured without discrimination on any ground such as sex, race, colour, language, religion, political or other opinion, national or social origin, association with a national minority, property, birth or other status*'.

685 Art. 1 para 2 of Protocol 12 ECHR stipulates: '*No one shall be discriminated against by any public authority on any ground such as those mentioned in paragraph 1*'. See at http://www.echr.coe.int/Documents/Convention_ENG.pdf

686 *Riley*, CEPS Policy Brief no. 49, 2004, p. 5.

687 *Saxena*, pp. 765, 804.

states to enforce equal protection before the law without 'discrimination on any ground such as… religion, political or other opinion….'[688]

(cc) The Declaration on the Elimination of All Forms of Intolerance and of Discrimination Based on Religion and Belief

The Declaration on the Elimination of All Forms of Intolerance and of Discrimination Based on Religion and Belief (DEID on Religion or Belief) is regarded as a major international, standard-setting legal document drafted within the international legal framework for protection of minorities' right to religious freedom.[689] Notably, the document does not have a formal status of a legal binding argument upon the French government; hence, it is rendered to have solely a declaratory status. The prohibition of discrimination on grounds of religion or belief is stipulated in Art. 2 of DEID on Religion or Belief. Art. 2 para 1 of it forbids any discrimination by any state, institution, group, person, or persons on the grounds of religion or belief. In addition, it prescribes in Art. 2 para 2 not only discrimination, but also intolerance on grounds of religion or belief as being impermissible by way of distinction, exclusion, restriction, or preference and intolerance which has the effect or purpose of nullifying or impairing the recognition, enjoyment, or exercise of the right to religious freedom or any other fundamental human right on an equal basis.[690]

---

688 Art. 26 ICCPR declares: '*All persons are equal before the law and are entitled without any discrimination to the equal protection of the law. In this respect the law shall prohibit any discrimination and* guarantee *to all persons equal and effective protection against* discrimination *on any ground such as: race, colour, sex, language, religion, political or other opinion, national or social origin, property, birth or other status*'. See at https://treaties.un.org/doc/Publication/UNTS/Volume%20999/volume-999-I-14668-English.pdf.

689 The Declaration on the Elimination of All Forms of Intolerance and of Discrimination Based on Religion Belief was proclaimed by the General Assembly resolution from 25 November 1981. It is established based on principles laid down in another UN agreement, namely the International Convention on Elimination of All Forms of Racial Discrimination (ICERD). G.A. Res. 2106 (XX), U.N. Doc. A/RES/2106(XX) the ICERD has been opened for signature and ratification by resolution of the general assembly from 21 December 1965 and came into force on 4 January 1969. See at http://www.ohchr.org/EN/ProfessionalInterest/Pages/CERD.aspx.

690 Art. 2(2) DEID on religion or belief declares: '*For the purposes of the present Declaration, the expression "intolerance and discrimination based on religion or belief" means any distinction, exclusion, restriction or preference based on religion or belief and having as its purpose or as its effect nullification or impairment of the recognition, enjoyment or*

(2) The Notion of the Principle of Equality/Non-discrimination

The French model of citizenship is based on the republican values of individualism and equality.[691] It prescribes basically that neither region, nor race, nor religion, nor class, nor gender is to mediate relations between individuals and the state.[692]

Clearly, the motivation of France was to embrace citizens developing a strong individual sense of belonging to the French nation, rather than to a particular racial, ethnic, or religious community. This was meant naturally to ensure allegiance to the French nation.

Notably, the contention of French commentators that the principle of equality is interpreted in a way which guarantees its implementation in practice and not only in theory has raised criticism with relation to the strict and formal application of the principle, since it suggests that France in fact does not recognize the concept of minority rights or ethnic citizens.

> Since the basic principles of public law prohibit distinctions between citizens on grounds of origin, race or religion, France is a country in which there are no minorities…[693]

By doing so, France pretends to recognize no difference between its citizens and, as a consequence, no minorities. If all citizens are equal before the law, then the law must not recognize any differences between its citizens, simply because it cannot accept otherwise the concept of religious minority rights or of 'ethnic politics'.[694] That is, if a differentiation is not acknowledged there can be no discrimination.[695]

On the same token, there will be no acceptance of the 'right to be different' (*droit de difference*), for such an acknowledgement is foreign and contradictory to French legal and political traditions, namely the republican ideology which recognizes that only individuals and not groups have rights.[696] This provides an

---

exercise of human rights and fundamental freedoms on an equal basis'. See at http://www.un.org/documents/ga/res/36/a36r055.htm

691 *McGoldrick* (2006), p. 42; *Silverman*, in: Hargreaves/Leaman, Racism, Ethnicity, and Politics in Contemporary Europe, 1995, pp. 253 et seq.

692 *Poulter*, p. 50; *Auslander*, pp. 283, 294.

693 See 'Third periodic report of France' under the ICCPR (15 May 1997), UN Doc CCPR/C/76/Add 7, para 394; *McGoldrick* (2006), p. 43, 48.

694 *McGoldrick* (2006) pp. 43, 47–48; *Lochak*, in Fenet/Soulier, pp. 114–128.

695 *Scott*, p. 118.

696 *Vakulenko*, Islamic Veiling in Legal Discourse, 2012, p. 17; *McGoldrick* (2006), pp. 42–43; *Berthou*, International Journal of Comparative Law and Industrial Relations, 2005, pp. 281, 315. *Troper*, 1999, p. 93. The Conseil d'Etat has consistently held that group

explanation as to: first, insufficient development of anti-discrimination laws in France's legal system and, second, lack of case laws brought by complainants under French law invoking the right of non-discrimination founded on religious grounds.[697]

d) Neutrality in the Public Service

On a legal level, the principle of neutrality applies equally and uniformly to all offices in the public service, making them subject to the same policy.[698] The obligation for public officials to remain neutral while on duty had started initially in the field of public education and was later on extended to other sectors in the public service.[699] However, several particularities apply with respect to different offices in the public service. In the following, emphasis will be put on holders of a teaching post.

First, the public service recognizes four eminent principles to be adhered by office holders: neutrality, equality, continuity, and mutability.[700] A focus will be drawn to the applicability of the first two principles as the most relevant and significant for the purpose of this analysis.

Second, the neutrality principle establishes the duty of the state to remain neutral. This precludes the state from recruiting individuals on the basis of their religion or belief.[701]

Third, the principle of equality underlays the neutrality principle and prescribes the duty of public officials to treat the public identically in similar situations.[702]

Fourth, guarantee of equal access – if the state wishes to demonstrate equal access of all citizens to a post in the public service, it may only do so independently of adherence or non-adherence to a particular religion and by application of the neutrality principle. This approach was even affirmed by the French

---

or collective rights are incompatible with the French constitution and the notion of national unity.

697 *Curtit,* in: Hill, pp. 145, 154; *van Ooijen*, p. 167;

698 *Robbers* in: Staat und Religion, p. 253.

699 *Ziegler, in Kink/Ziegler,* pp. 326, 327.

700 *van Ooijen*, p. 179. These principles were laid down by the French legal scholar Louis Rolland. Continuity requires that public officials will respond in a continuous manner to citizens' claims or requests. Mutability requires that the public service will adapt according to changing circumstances and needs.

701 *van Ooijen*, p. 179.

702 *v. Ungern – Sternberg*, 2008, p. 119; *van Ooijen*, p. 179.

judicator upholding that within the exercise of a public function the right to practise a religion or belief should be excluded. It was held that this duty to neutrality must apply for all office holders in public education as well as to all other officials in the public service .[703]

Fifth, the French approach with respect to outer appearance of civil servants implies the essentiality of neutral appearance.[704] This mandates the prohibition on public officials to appear with conspicuous signs or garments while on duty as well as any form of religious expression or manifestation of belief. The prohibition extends to any form of religious manifestation exercised either by a conduct, verbal expression, or the donning of a garment or a sign.[705]

Sixth, public officials are assumed to take voluntarily upon themselves the duty to remain neutral, thence having their personal conviction neutralized. This will be applicable only when exercising their function. In their private sphere (i.e., when not on duty), public officials are not confined in their right to freely manifest their religion or belief. However, even outside their function they will be deemed responsible not to undermine the image of public service and, as a result, will be subject to a less strict obligation to act without prejudice to the proper function of the public service.[706]

Seventh, the obligation for neutral appearance in the public service makes no segregation as to the type and nature of religious expression. This means all signs or symbols are to be excluded from the public service. This all-inclusive ban applies regardless of the symbolic meaning of the sign, i.e. if the sign is interpreted in its religious or political context.[707] In addition, no relevance will be given as to the nature of public function. This means that whether the public official comes in contact with the public or obliged to abide by a uniform policy and by virtue of the function is not exposed to the public, will play no role, as the prohibition on religious symbols is general and applies equally to all public servants.[708]

Eighth, in principle, the underlying aim of the neutrality principle with respect to public officials is the demonstration of being impartial while on duty.

Ninth, adherence to the neutrality principle was meant to guarantee also the right of public officials to freedom of conscience. By that, the state is abstained

---

703 *v. Ungern-Sternberg*, 2008, p. 118.

704 *Ziegler*, in: *Kink/Ziegler*, p. 325.

705 Stasi Report (2003), para. 2.2; *McGoldrick* (2006), pp. 73–74; *van Ooijen*, p. 180.

706 *Ziegler*, in: *Kink/Ziegler*, p. 324.

707 *van Ooijen*, p. 180.

708 *McGoldrick* (2006), pp. 73; Stasi Report (2003), para 2.2.

from recruitment of individuals based on their religion or belief. This serves as a direct outcome of the guarantee of equal access to public services since no individual will be favoured or disfavoured due to his/her adherence, non-adherence to a particular religion. This rationale was even affirmed in 1954 by the Council of State in the Barel decision.[709]

e) The System of Judicial Review

Essentially, the task of enforcement and effective guarantee of fundamental rights in case of an abuse by organs of the state, i.e., local authorities, public agencies, and public services is left to a judicial review by the administrative courts, which are structured within the general jurisdiction of public law courts.[710]

The administrative courts are part of a three-tier system of rights protection which comprises of Administrative Courts of Appeal (*Cours Administrative d'appel*) and the Administrative Tribunals (*Tribunaux Administratifs*) supervised by the Conseil d'Etat.[711]

Since France has a dual system of courts, administrative on the one hand, and civil and criminal courts on the other, it is a general rule that violations of civil liberties conducted by public authorities will be challenged in the Administrative Courts.[712] The commitment of the Administrative Courts to serve as primary guardians of citizens' fundamental rights is even explicitly verified in Art. 66 of the 1958 Constitution.[713] This clearly indicates that the Administrative Courts in France play a significant role in the development and protection of fundamental rights, as they form an integral part of a mechanism available to aggrieved citizens. As a result, Administrative Courts exert full control over administrative actions or decisions affecting civil liberties or other rights of individuals.[714]

---

709 CE, Barel, 28 May 1954, Rec. Lebon, p. 308.

710 The structure of French court institutions makes a clear distinction between two structural branches of law: public law and private law courts and courts of substantive law with less rigid segregation between civil and criminal courts. See in *Bell/Boyron/Whittaker*, pp. 37, 39.

711 *Bell/Boyron/Whittaker*, p. 41.

712 *Bell/Boyron/Whittaker*, p. 119.

713 Art. 66 of the 1958 Constitution establishes that: 'The judicial authority, guardian of the freedom of the individual, shall ensure compliance with the principle in the conditions laid down by law'. http://www.assemblee-nationale.fr/english/8ab.asp#VIII

714 *Bell/Boyron/Whittaker*, p. 186; *Palmer*, p. 27.

On the other side of the token, the Cons. Const. operates mainly in order to review and assess the constitutionality of laws. Hence, in the constitutional hierarchy of judicial review it performs its control a priori rather than posteriori.[715] The task and authority of the Constitutional Council is elaborated extensively under the 1958 Constitution (Part VII). It carries an important task with respect to the constitutionality of laws and interpretation of the constitution as may be referred to it from the CE or revision courts. A reference for judicial review can be submitted also by individuals who wish to receive a decision on the constitutionality of statutory provisions claimed to infringe on their fundamental rights (Art. 61–1).[716]

Ultimately, the 1958 Constitution designates in Art. 62 the binding effect (*die Bindungswirkung*) of the Constitutional Council with respect to other state organs, and prescribes that all courts (private and public law courts), including administrative and public authorities will be bound by rulings of the constitutional council, and as a practical matter will have to respect and follow its decisions as an authoritative statement.[717] Strikingly, an identification of a 'binding effect', which formally compels lower courts in France to comply with the decisions of a higher or revision court, does not exist. Notwithstanding, a substantial obligation of the lower courts to comply with decisions of the highest judicial authority of the state is confirmed.[718]

f) Assessment of the Legal System

The distinctiveness of French law is featured and implicated in the historical development of its state-church relations, its constitutional organizational structure, the governmental system entrenched and shaped by the reverence of the

---

715 *Palmer*, p. 28.

716 Following to the revision performed in July 2008 to Art. 61 of the 1958 Constitution (now revised as Art. 61–1), the power to request a review of ordinary statutes from the Constitutional Council were granted only to high-ranking organs of the French government, as opposed to citizens of the republic which could not trigger a direct review and were able to do so only in the administrative courts. See the English version of Art. 61-1 of the 1958 Constitution. https://www.conseil-constitutionnel.fr/sites/default/files/as/root/bank_mm/anglais/constiution_anglais_oct2009.pdf

717 *Bell/Boyron/Whittaker*, pp. 147–156. Art. 62 of the 1958 Constitution: 'No appeal shall lie from the decisions of the Constitutional Council. They shall be binding on public authorities and on all administrative authorities and all courts'. http://www.assemblee-nationale.fr/english/8ab.asp#VII

718 *Hübner/Constantinesco*, Einführung in das französische Recht, 4th edn., 2001, p. 11.

French nation to the 'Republican Ideology', and the underlying perception of 'uniqueness' of the French nation. The probably most significant constitutional precept capturing the concept of French constitutional system is entrenched in Art. 1 of the 1958 Constitution. It establishes the three paramount pillars upon which the French nation is to be organized, namely: indivisible, secular, democratic, and social as foundational values of the French Republic.

Thence, salient features of France's legal system are inculcated in its adherence to its indivisible, secular nature and its state-organizational structure of a decentralized system. In addition, the Republican Ideology fortified the French conception of universalism, which suggests that relations of the state towards its citizens are established on the sameness of all individuals, also explicitly pronounced in the 1958 French Constitution (Art. 1). By that, the French nation declines any divisiveness based on origin, ethnic, religious, or social grounds and refuses to acknowledge the rights of religious groups, embracing rather the notion of individualism – offering its citizens equal protection before the law. The ideal of a unified and indivisible nation dates back to the French Revolution of 1789 which wished to replace the privileged monarchical regime with a republic whose citizens are all deemed equal and free. The underscored prominent constitutional pillars of: equality before the law of all its citizens, the respect of all beliefs without favouritism on part of the state constitute an integral element of its decentralized system as betoken in the second part of Art. 1 of the 1958 Constitution. These constitutional pillars prescribed in the second part of Art. 1 of the 1958 Constitution conjoined with those mentioned in the first part of Art. 1 of the 1958 Constitution, (indivisible, secular, democratic, and social), form the ideological fundament of French Republicanism.

The notion of French individualism will be achieved if all citizens are perceived to be the same. This universalist status was thought to be accomplished only through formal equality of all individuals before the law. In this respect, elimination of any distinctive characteristic between its citizens was meant to ensure allegiance to the French nation. It is for this reason that French society expects its immigrants to accept the unified approach and to assimilate to its norms, culture, language, and political ideology.

The historical events prior to the Revolution of 1789 were mostly characterized by basic conflict with the Catholic Church, and rejection of intolerance attributed to it. This contributed to the emergence of the French Enlightenment that opposed vehemently and radically any religious influence over the state, aiming especially to reduce the social influence of the Catholic Church. The long conflicts of France with the influential power of Catholicism throughout its history, linked with a hostile anti-clerical approach, provides an explanation to the core rejection of the French nation to accept the assimilationist approach of other Western European countries and accommodation to multi-culturalism and pluralism. In fact, France did not acknowledge nor wanted to accept an assimilationist approach towards its immigrants. The identity of being a French citizen, accepting the republican identity, took precedence over any individual characteristic interlinked with religious adherence or ethnicity. Especially during the Third Republic it was considered that aspects of religion or ethnicity must be consigned to the private sphere. In this regard, France also rejected the concept of ethnicity, as such classification contributes to societal division – a notion that in itself contradicts the Republican Ideology and its constitutional pillars of being an indivisible secular nation.

In this regard, the conceptual development of basic rights in France and in particular of religious freedom were induced by historical events, such as the period of French Enlightment (1715–1789), the French Revolution (1789), associated strongly with the French resentment to religious influence, in particular of the Catholic Church. The remarkable achievement of this period ended with declarations of rights being composed and drafted at the end of the eighteenth century, the 1789 Declaration.

In principle, the legal system in France did not perpetuate fundamental liberty rights under a single comprehensive document. They are rather scattered in several constitutions and legislation. The first legal document under which liberty rights were acknowledged and guaranteed was the 1789 Declaration. The 1789 Declaration is regarded to have an equivalent status to the current 1958 Constitution. In addition, civil liberty rights had been confirmed and recognized in ordinary laws as well as international human rights treaties to which France acceded authority and jurisprudence. However, the delineation of the scope of fundamental rights in France is not really drawn in its constitutional or legislative documents and, as a result, provides a very weak enforcement mechanism of fundamental rights, inter alia the right to religious freedom. As already mentioned, the fact that no legislative unity exists in France is mainly the outcome of the lack of federal and strong regional system. This naturally resulted in distinctiveness of the regions, reflecting demographical changes, religious control, and political priorities prevailing throughout their histories (as for instance in the Alsace-Moselle region).

The historical upheavals, the evolvement of the legal framework, and some paramount constitutional principles underlying the ideal of Republican Ideology cannot be discussed detached from the right to religious freedom.

The right to religious freedom is guaranteed in several constitutional documents (the 1789 Declaration and the 1946 and 1958 Constitutions), ordinary statues, and legislation of the republic. It is worth to note that though the statutory position of the right to religious freedom is imprinted in France's legislative hierarchy of norms, this does not really correspond with its separationist state-church model, nor does it reflect the guarantee one should have assumed should apply with respect to such a prominent fundamental human right. In addition, due to an integrated system of national law and international law, the commitment of France to international treaties prevails over domestic legislation. France adopted the ECHR and due to supremacy of international over national law, the enforcement of fundamental rights, including the right to religious freedom, achieves better protection in practice due to France's obligation on the international level.

In this context, the legal system in France does not share a uniform approach with reference to implementation of an extensive right of religious freedom (i.e., the forum externum). This is naturally to be attributed to several reasons: first, the right of an individual to manifest his/her religion is perceived by French society a matter that should be confined solely to the private sphere. This is mainly imprinted in the Republican Ideology that religion should be kept away from the public sphere, and a considerable constituent in promulgation of the 1905 law intending at its outset to perpetuate the separation between religion and the public sphere. Second, the vast terminology used for the definition of religious freedom: whereas a reference to the definition of liberty of conscience, as a general principle, will be interpreted by the judiciary so as to include religious manifestation as long as it is exerted out of a pure religious incentive, other terms such as *liberté de culte* will be regarded as not enfolding the right to manifest a religion. Hence, the inevitable outcome is a lack of consistency within the jurisprudence as to the scope and interpretation of religious freedom.

As seen, the French state perceives its task to ensure liberty of conscience; yet, this obligation is intertwined with its allegiance to the laïcité principle, obliging it to remain neutral and unbiased in order to refrain from any preferential treatment to a particular religion on the expense of others.

The attempt to delineate the scope of protection of the right to religious freedom is a difficult and complex task mainly due the constitutional structure of France's legal system. Underlying, some of the reasons identified for the absence of its clear confinement seem to correspond primarily to the fact that the right is scattered in several constitutional documents and statutory instruments. Second, simultaneous use of analogous definitions to the term 'religion'. Third, the allegiance of the French nation to its sacrosanct laïcité. This, in fact, was a crucial factor affecting the status of religious freedom, as it was never perceived constitutionally as an unconfined right.

Undoubtedly, this salient aspect of religious freedom had legal impact on the way the right could be upheld in legal actions and with respect to its interpretation: first, the right to freedom of religion finds explicit expression in the 1789 Declaration; at the same time it is identified as one of the three interconnected constitutional values establishing the principle of laïcité. These two pre-eminent principles upon which French society is established are constantly under tension, as it is presumed that any attempt to coincide them is deemed to be at odds. Religious freedom is mostly intertwined in the French jurisprudence with freedom of expression. However, this alignment between freedom of religion and freedom of expression was endorsed due to analogous use of the word freedom of conscience (*liberté de conscience*). The term 'freedom of conscience' includes not only religious freedom but also ideological, political, or philosophical creed. This, consequently, demonstrates that religious freedom and freedom of expression are fraught together in France's constitutional system; moreover, it reaffirms incontestably that freedom of religion is not granted a pronounced preference in comparison to other forms of manifestations. This entails naturally that while an individual may be denied the right to manifest his/her religion, the court may conclude that such a manifestation constitutes a forbidden exercise of freedom of opinion.[719] Second, the term 'religious freedom' is not used uniformly in the legal constitutional texts. In fact, there is an ample variety of analogous definitions to the term 'freedom of religion', which in part share an identical meaning, in part overlap, and in part are diverse. Thus, for instance, a prevalent phrase in the French jurisprudence and the 1905 law (Art. 1) relates to freedom of conscience (*liberté de conscience*),[720] while the 1789 Declaration (Art. 10) proclaims the right to freedom of religious opinion (*liberté d'opinion religieuse*).[721] Further references identified as synonyms for freedom of religion include: Art. 1 of the 1905 law refers to religious freedom (*liberté des cultes*),[722] Art. 1 of the 1958 Constitution uses the term freedom of belief (*de croyance),*[723] the preamble to the 1946 Constitution mentions religious liberty (*liberté religieuse*),[724] freedom of

719 See Counseil d'Etat decision on the headscarf-hijab in Avis no 346.893 du 27 novembre 1989; *McGoldrick* (2006), p. 69.

720 Art. 1 of the 1905 Law.

721 Art. 10 of the Declaration of Rights of Man from 1789.

722 The 1905 Law on state-church separation; *Morange*, p. 369;

723 Art. 1 of the 1958 Constitution and the 1905 Law on separation of state and church.

724 *Durand –Prinborgne*, La Laïcité, 1996, p. 91; *Ganz*, p. 64.

belief (*liberté de la foi*),[725] Art. 11 of the 1789 Declaration uses the word *de pensée* (freedom of thought).[726]

In principle, the legal system in France recognizes and guarantees *the forum internum* as well as the *forum externum* of the individual. Correspondingly, the forum internum enables an individual to freely choose a religion or belief (positive dimension), same as the right not to pertain to any religion or faith (negative dimension). An acknowledgement of the forum externum guarantees the right to practise and manifest a religion whether through acts of worship, performance of ceremonies, and/or the wearing of religious symbols or garments.

The limitation of the right of an individual to exercise his/her religious rights can be justified under French law only if it is made for the purpose of ensuring the 'public order'. Notably, the only restrictions permissible are those necessary in the interest of public order.

The recognition of public order as a legitimate justification for restrictions laid or violations made against the right to freedom of conscience appears in several constitutional documents dating back already to the first constitution of 1791 and even in the present 1789 Declaration (Art. 10).

Nonetheless, a discourse on religious liberty rights is intertwined with the principle of laïcité. The cornerstone inculcating the republican values and national identity is the constitutional principle of laïcité. The principle of laïcité depicts a system of public order that is meant to establish the proper relationship between religion and the state. The religious neutrality of the state is mostly intertwined and confused with the laïcité principle. However, while the neutrality principle connotes that the state adopts a non-recognition policy in the sense that it recognizes no official religion, places all religions on the same political level, and refrains from any favouritism or association with a particular religion, the principle of laïcité has a special meaning which cannot be easily translated into English or compared to other legal systems. The laïcité principle is a system of public order wishing to exclude religion from civil affairs in order to protect its citizens from any religious claims (i.e., indoctrination). The significance of the neutrality principle has a special meaning with respect to the public sphere and special duties incurred on public officials as representatives of

---

725 *Robert/Duffar*, Droits de l'homme et libertés fondamentales, 2009, p. 587; *Ganz*, p. 64.

726 Art. 11 of the Declaration of the right of Man 1789 prescribes: '*La libre communication des pensées et des opinions est un des droits les plus précieux de l'Homme: tout Citoyen peut donc parler, écrire, imprimer librement, sauf à répondre de l'abus de cette liberté dans les cas déterminés par la Loi*'.

the state, including state-school teachers, to refrain from religious manifestation. The sanctity of the neutrality principle is upheld especially in the public sphere due to the duty of state to neutrality of political power, and due to the perception that the public service should remain neutral. This requires that the state should abstain from display or manifestation of religious symbols, especially in the public school system, and forbear any religious influence in the educational realm. It is said that the principle of laïcité underlies the fundament of three judicial pillars: the freedom of conscience, the right to equality in religious and spiritual matters, and neutrality of the state.

Though the apprehension of the laïcité principle embodies the right to religious freedom, it should be emphasized that the notion did not arise historically as a unifying value shared by the French nation, nor was it minted by strong liberal approach on part of the state to its religious pluralistic society. On the contrary, the principle of laïcité originated in a period of time with harsh religious conflicts, antagonism, and hostility, aiming to eradicate the influence of the powerful Catholic Church.

Naturally, there is a need to reconcile between two pre-eminent principles: the principle of secularity of the state and the freedom of conscience. The French constitution does not anticipate the hierarchy between the principle of the secular nature of the state and freedom of conscience; nonetheless, guidance was delivered by decisions of the CE as to the adequate balance to be outweighed between these two allegedly contradicting rights.

The most salient characteristic of the French constitutional system is the model of strict separation between state and religion. The principle of neutrality of state imprinted by the term laïcité has a much more profound meaning than the one conferred to it in the German system. Laïcité, in its much stricter definition, promotes the notion of a society that is fundamentally and distinctively political in nature, loyal to the sacred republican values, and is independent of any religious authority.

On a legal level, disputes surrounding freedom of religion were subject to adjudication that established its ruling either on the right to religion or belief or state neutrality. The development of decisions on the basis of anti-discrimination norms were rather scarce.

The principle of equality is guaranteed through its stipulation in various norms scattered throughout different sources, such as several constitutional texts and enactments. As part of France's integrative dual system, it can be detected both under national and international law. The principle prescribes a general obligation for equal protection, and interdicts any form of discrimination taken on different grounds including religion, origin, race, language, etc.

The development of anti-discrimination laws has not been given such a strong emphasis by the legislator and the judiciary in preferential or disadvantageous acts of the state on account of a person's religion or belief. The reason for that lies in the fundamental principle of French national identity, its uniqueness of being French, and that all French are considered alike and equal before the state. This concept itself eliminates any claim of discrimination, since from a French perspective no discrimination exists if all citizens are equal. The principle of equality of citizens constitutes a fundamental part of the French constitution and its legal doctrine. However, it is for this uniqueness of equality, which declares that all French people must be alike in their Frenchness, taken together with the idea of unity and indivisibility that it becomes apparent why France declines recognition of differences among its citizens, at least in the public sphere. It is thence not surprising that in a land inscribing itself to be a protagonist of universalism and national unity, discrimination does not exist because differences of groups are not recognized. If the legal framework recognizes no differentiation and does not acknowledge it, there can be no discrimination.

The strong adhesion to secularism was meant to provide a solution in claims of discrimination elevated by religious minorities, since this notion was fraught with the concept of national cohesion or identity. In that sense, the denial of existence of differences between religious groups served an incontestable defence against discrimination claims. In practice, it seems that secularism in France tends to be rather more adaptive to Christianity than to other religions.

For this reason, the blatant refusal of France to ratify Protocol 12 of the ECHR, which establishes the prohibition of discrimination on account of different grounds (including religion) and its expansion to any legal right including obligation of public authorities to conform with the ban on discrimination, remains conceivable taking into consideration the historical development of its constitutional order, its uniqueness, and the reverence of the French towards founding principles of the republic.

In France, secularism or, to be more accurate, the entrenched principle of laïcité will serve almost always as the explicit justification for interferences in the individual religious freedom or discrimination on grounds of religion or belief.

To sum up, it should be emphasized that state-church relations in France and the remote, distant approach the French nation holds towards religion is deeply rooted in meaningful historical achievements in the eyes of French people, and the general sacred attitude to adhere to the Republican Ideology is held high as only through its strict application can the existence of their uniqueness as a unified, secular nation be guaranteed.

5. Comparative Assessment of the Legal Systems

a) Legislative Framework

The legal systems of the compared states Germany, England, and France differ substantially from each other in their classification. The Germanic law can be categorized into the larger group of the continental systems. English law is classically defined under the common law system, while French law is perceived as part of the civil law systems.

The distinctiveness of the legal systems can be characterized by the following: the legal framework which establishes its fundaments on entrenched constitutional values, developments of legal rules, jurisprudential evolvement, doctrinal theories, and legal procedures.

aa) Constitutional System

Germany – In contrast to England and France, Germany is the only state that endorsed and owns a fully fledged document of fundamental human rights which constitutes its comprehensive 'Bill of Rights'. In principle, Germany is a federation with a written constitution (*Grundgesetz*) and though each federal state has its own constitution regulating inner affairs of organizational structure (such as adherence to religion, administering state-church relations, the place of religion in education, etc.), it is also within the competency of the individual states to enact legislation within its jurisdiction. Nonetheless, the federal states still must conform to the Grundgesetz (including the preamble) and the values of a democratic republic which compel all of its 16 federal states. The importance of the Grundgesetz from a legal perspective and efficiency of the legal system is that it enables an easy and rapid access for individuals, who can invoke the constitutional rights prescribed in it directly before courts.

England – A distinctive characteristic of England's constitutional system is its lack of a written constitution. The absence of a codified document of liberty rights together with the constitutional principle of 'Parliament Supremacy' poses theoretically endangerment to the protection of fundamental rights, such as religious freedom, since the parliament has an exclusive power to change or amend legislation. This emanates that liberty rights may be subject to constant change and do not enjoy the highest constitutional rank in the hierarchy of norms, so potentially they can become infringed easily by ordinary laws or statutes.

France – The constitutional system of France, just like its legislative framework, is quite distinctive in nature as opposed to the other two systems. The different French constitutions (1946, 1958), including the 1789 Declaration had all underscored the special bond between the republic and its citizens. In addition, France, in comparison to Germany and England, has an ordained system of hierarchy of norms. Hence, fundamental liberty rights are ensured in France not only in several constitutional documents, but they also have a legal base in one of the following enumerated sources: international treaties, ordinary laws, customary practice, jurisprudence, and general principles of law. Apart from that, the French legal system underlies four momentous constitutional pillars which have their fundaments in the Republican Ideology: unity, laïcité (secularity), democracy, and equality are regarded sacred in French society. In fact, national unity, secularism, and the indivisibility of the French Republic are deeply entrenched in its history and are a source of reverence of the French people. These judicial pillars are of major significance in France's constitutional system, as they affect the legal status of fundamental human rights, such as religious freedom and the enjoyment of these liberty rights by individuals who feel confined or limited in their exercise.

bb) Domestic Law or Transformation of International Treaties

Germany – The constitutional order in Germany has its roots mainly in inner normative sources. On the highest legislative rank poses the German Constitution, i.e., Grundgesetz, which constitutes the foundation for protection of fundamental human rights as well as administering and regulating the organizational structure of the federation, prescribing the relationship between the federal states and the central state, and determining the structural relations between state and church, with most of the provisions incorporated from the WRV into the Grundgesetz. On the state-regional level, it is within the competency of each federal state to determine the character of its constitutional order, regulate inner state-church affairs, and govern fundamental rights as prescribed in the respective constitution of the land (*Landesverfassung*) and ordinary legislation generated by its legislators. The allocation of competences between the central political power and the federal states is stipulated in the Grundgesetz (Art. 30 and 70). As such, the competency to enact with respect to education and the governance of relations between religion and public state school is a matter assigned to the sole competency of the federal states. Finally, the German judicator, the BVerfG, is responsible for the development of fundamental human rights and for the interpretation of statutes through judicial review of their conformity to the Grundgesetz. This jurisprudential interpretation underlies case laws' development which has a binding force on lower judicial instances and state organizations and, by that, constitutes an eminent source of law. The obligation of Germany on the international level to accede to international human rights instruments such as the ECHR is not conferred a formal constitutional normative rank; thus, although outlined in the Grundgesetz (Art. 20 para 3, Art. 31), its legal position within the constitutional framework cannot be equivalent to that of a constitutional provision. Thence, the ECHR's provisions will allegedly not be eligible to the same constitutional protection as provided to fundamental human rights specified in the Grundgesetz.

England – In contrast to the constitutional order in Germany, not all fundamental human rights in Great Britain derive originally from the British legislator, development of common law doctrines, and jurisprudential decisions. The actual case in England is that fundamental human rights are incorporated into British Law from international treaties. Several international treaties have not been transformed into British law, but apply only for British authorities and courts as representatives of the British state, which accepted these treaties and regulations on the international level (e.g., UDHR); however, they remain declaratory in nature. Other international treaties, such as the ECHR, have been incorporated into domestic law and thus obtained its enforceable status as a binding legal document.

England as well as France have integrated the ECHR into their domestic laws. In the UK the ECHR does not obtain superior status over national law as this collides with the principle of parliament supremacy. Priority can be achieved only through the principle of statutory interpretation. Consequently, in both lands courts are bound to adhere to articles in the convention safeguarding religious freedom (as a matter of practice, mainly Art. 9 and Art. 10 were invoked by claimants who felt their religious freedom was infringed). This lowers the potential risk of domestic courts to disregard their international commitment especially due to the fact that they are bound by decisions of the ECtHR and are compelled to make necessary adaption of their inner laws so not to be found in breach of the ECHR.

France – As far as incorporation of international law into domestic law is concerned, the French approach differs substantially in comparison to the commitment of Germany and England to subordinate and abide by international human rights treaties to which they are signatories. The difference emanates from the dual system France has accepted upon itself, comprised of national and international law. International treaties to which France has acceded authority are ranked high in its constitutional hierarchy of norms and prevail over ordinary legislation. This in fact fortifies the commitment of France to abide by international human rights instruments so that their enforcement is stronger in comparison to the guarantee ascribed to these international treaties under German and English law. The reason for that is the guarantee of their self-executing right as stipulated in the 1958 Constitution, which bears importance on two significant levels: (i) direct applicability – the self- executing character of international instruments under the French legal system enables citizens to invoke infringements of their rights directly before national courts; (ii) supremacy of international treaties – in that sense international law is capable to override any legislation of the French Parliament, whether relating to previous or subsequent enacted legislation. This legal situation with respect to obligations taken on the international level will never become possible under UK's hierarchical system of norms. This is since an international treaty cannot obtain formal superior status over national law by virtue of the principle of Parliament Supremacy. Under German constitutional law international treaties obtain over a lower legal status in the rank of norms as they are equated with the status of federal legislation.

cc) The Role of Jurisprudence

Germany – The highest judicial instance in charge of interpretation of fundamental human rights and judicial review of infringements or violations accrued by public authorities, is the highest constitutional court, the BVerfG. This judicator is regarded as the guardian of the constitutional order and is empowered within construction of fundamental human rights to develop constitutional principles; however, even the BVerfG is bound by its guidelines and does not possess the authority to create new norms or values. Thence, within the task of construction of constitutional rights, it must keep its jurisprudential review of legal statutes as much as possible in conformity with the provisions of the Grundgesetz and within its spirit known as '*Pflicht zur verfassungskonformen Auslegung*'. Decisions delivered by the BVerfG have a binding effect on lower instances with the exception that rulings of the BVerfG will not apply with respect to itself.

England – The legal system in Britain, based on common law, establishes a different structural hierarchy for the protection of fundamental rights. As such, an action taken by a public authority may be regarded lawful under English law and simultaneously unlawful under international law. The reason for that is that international law does not have an immediate, direct effect under the English legal system. In principle, the rules that apply to the construction of statutes, given England's obligations on the international level prescribe that an interpretation of an ambiguous statute should support a construction which would not deem England to be under violation of its international obligation. Nonetheless, if the statute is unambiguous, the courts – by virtue of Parliament Supremacy – are bound to apply it as is, even if it runs the risk of standing in conflict with international law. Just like in Germany, complaints of violations of fundamental human rights may be submitted at first instance to lower civil courts, whereas submission of claims to discrimination on religious grounds in employment will be addressed before employment tribunals. In England, the lower instances are bound by decisions and judgements delivered by the House of Lords, the highest judicial instance, and are therefore less likely to deliver contradictory judgements or contribute to lack of consistency in the interpretation of religious related issues in the context of education as prescribed under domestic or European law.

France – The French jurisdictional hierarchical framework is characterized by a complex system of divergent judicial branches and strict division between the instances as to their fields of law. Judicial review of human rights violations conducted by public authorities or governmental authorities will be left to the supervision of the administrative courts and tribunals, which are considered to be part of the public law courts. Though the development of case laws and legal principles or rules are comprehended as an influential source of law, as a general practice, French jurisprudence is characterized by the non-binding effect of its higher instances. However, a formal binding effect is stipulated in the 1958 Constitution with respect to decisions delivered by the Cons. Const., which carries a valuable task of assessing the constitutionality of laws and reviews of aggrieved individuals. Consequently, in the absence of a formal obligation compelling lower instances to decisions of the higher jurisdictions, inconsistencies and vagueness with reference to interpretation of the law, especially in matters of religious manifestation in the education system, can be traced in their case laws.

dd) The Development of Social Pluralism and Its Impact on Domestic Legislation

Germany – The largest influx of Muslim immigrants to Germany occurred after the Second World War in a time when Germany was facing a shortage in workers it needed as labour power for reconstructing the state. In contrast with Britain and France, Germany had not recruited its work force from its former colonies, as decolonization ceased long before that time; thus, it was not exposed to a vast scale of immigration from different countries. In fact, Germany had faced mostly immigration of Turkish Muslims and envisaged them as a temporary work force. In stark contrast with Britain, Germany has never intended to enable citizenship for its migrants, as its policy was to return them back to their country of origin after a short-term period. This provides an explanation to the unaccepting and unwilling attitude of German society to integrate their foreign workers. The resentment, lack of recognition, and non-accommodative attitude characterized also German policy, which refused to recognise and did little to fulfil the cultural, religious, and educational needs of its migrants. For instance, the problem of state-funded private Islamic schools, the integration and consultation with the Muslim community as to contents of public school curriculum are not executed on the same scale as with Christian headship, not all federal states offer Muslim pupils the option of religious instructions as offered to most Christian students. In sum, as far as the accommodation of the religious needs of its immigrants goes, Germany is considered to represent the mid-position. Germany adopts an approach which is not as liberal and accommodating to the religious rights of its minorities as is the case in Britain. On the same token, it does not foster a strong reluctance to adapt to the religious needs of its Muslim population as practised by French policy-making.

Albeit some provisions in the Grundgesetz demonstrate adherence to religion, there is a decrease in the position of the church. This can be inferred from some of the WRV articles, from a general disentanglement of state-church relations, from a decrease of pupils' attendance in religious instructions, as well as from a remote relation to salient Christian symbols such as the display of crosses in classrooms.

England – The mass wave of migration to Britain ensued following the Second World War. However, in contrast to Germany, the largest percentage of immigrants came to Britain from its former colony, India. In addition, Britain had set liberal citizenship policy for residents of its former colonies. Acquiring the British citizenship was not detained from them as immigrants from commonwealth countries, enjoying by law all rights and privileges of a British citizenship. Notably, and similar to the situation in Germany, the expectation that the working force of migrants from India or Pakistan would return to their homelands did not prove to materialize. This welcoming and liberal approach of British policy towards its immigrants in the post-war period has subsequently changed to a more restrictive immigration policy and control introduced at the beginning of the early 1970s.

Nonetheless, on a general level, Britain adopted a remarkably accommodative approach towards the religious needs of its Muslim migrants. This benign approach was fostered by considerable flexibility of local authorities and school supervisory boards to adapt existing policies and introduce religious education also for minorities albeit their divergence from national curriculum, which prescribes public schools to be of mainly Christian character. In addition, the acceptance of education policy allows state funding of private religious schools. All this demonstrates that especially Britain ranks to a large extent as the most accommodating country to Muslim religious practice or needs in comparison to the adopted policy in France and Germany.

Though the Anglican Church is officially privileged by the status of the established church in England, there are several examples indicating the decline of the Church's influence in the public sphere and the wish to preserve its independent status so that no undue influence would take place within the state-church nexus. This was notable in the sphere of education, especially when permission was granted to religious minorities (such as Muslims) to establish their own faith schools. This privilege has been thus far preserved to the churches (Catholics and Protestants) and some ethnic minorities, such as Jews to erect their own faith schools. It thus suggests, more than anything, the decrease of the Church's position and the retrench of the exclusive status which it historically obtained with respect to the establishment of state schools. Further, in cases involving the display of religious symbols, e.g., wearing of a cross as a necklace by public officials, the judiciary adopted a clear line of non-favouritism towards specific religion or manifestation of religious symbols pertaining to the predominant religion (i.e., Christianity).[727]

France – The first migration waves of Muslims to France originated from its North-African colonies (e.g., Algeria) during the First World War. However, the flood of immigrants began, similarly to the situation in Germany and England, as a response to the severe shortage of labour force incurred in the aftermath of the Second World War. Similar to Britain, France also attempted to tighten and reduce immigration scales during the 1970s. However, similar government's attempts and legislative initiatives were proved unsuccessful, inter alia, due to citizenship rules based on place of birth. This for instance enabled North Africans born in France to obtain French nationality already with birth. Despite efforts to cut back the extent of immigration, France has become one of the most multi-ethnic societies on the European continent. France never wanted to accept this societal-cultural change incurred on it. Unlike the situation in Germany and Britain that was accepting and accommodating foreigners into their societies, France explained the hostility towards its Muslim population as induced by the French perception of assimilation. The unwillingness of Muslim migrants to assimilate to the French values and the Republican Ideology aggravated even

727 The ECtHR dealt with the conjoined applications of Ms Nadia Eweida and Ms Shirley Chaplin relating to restrictions imposed by their employers due to the wearing of a visible cross around their neck. The case of Eweida and Others v. The United Kingdom Application nos. 48420/10 and 59842/10 (ECtHR).

more the resentfulness of the French nation. As expected, a major clashing point was introduced with the question whether to permit the display of conspicuous religious signs (e.g., *hijab*) by Muslim female pupils in French public schools. Public opinion supports in its majority the view that religious signs should be eradicated from the public sphere in general and from public schooling in particular. The hostile French attitude to accommodation of the religious needs of its Muslim migrants can be ascribed above all to its dominant separationist approach comprised of institutional separation between state and church and its strong adherence to the principle of laïcité. Allegiance to this strict policy necessitates the state to refrain from endorsing religion or religious expression into its public education as well as inhibiting state funding for the erection of buildings of worship and publicly financed, private religious schools.

France is the only state which is less likely to accommodate the religious practices and needs of its Muslim immigrants.

In sum, the inevitable growth of religious pluralism in European societies underpins a consistent separation between state and church. This receives an ample and positive resonance especially with respect to public education and in the context of the importance conferred to schools in different societies. These views had been expressed and reasoned to a large extent in judgements delivered so far.[728]

b) Individual Rights

Germany is the only state with a written constitution which guarantees the protection of civil liberty rights in its constitution. England and France, on the other hand, own no overarching legislative document which safeguards fundamental human rights in the form of a constituted 'Bill of Rights'.[729]

Astonishing as it may seem, though England does not have a long tradition of a written profound constitutional right to religious freedom, it remains at odds whether its legal system offers in practice a consistent protection of religious

728 *Janz/Rademacher*, NVwZ 1999, pp. 706, 712, et seq.; BVerwG, JZ 2004, 1178, 1179, et seq.; BVerwG, ZBR 2003, 37, 38, et seq.: However, a different opinion was held in BVerwG, NJW 1999, 3063, 3064 determining that in legal literature and judgements of the Federal Constitutional Court it was acknowledged long ago that the obligation of the state to religious pluralism should not be matched against the strict separation of state and church.

729 *v. Ungern – Sternberg*, 2008, p. 219.

rights which by far transcends the guarantee conferred to it under the German and French legal systems.

aa) Liberty Rights

The guarantee of religious freedom in Germany is safeguarded without any reservation in Art. 4 GG. In France, however, religious freedom is not regarded as an unreserved right simply because the perception with reference to the state-church relation is completely different and accepts confinement with respect to religious freedom when the aim is to protect other fundamental interests of the nation.

England, on the other side of the token, though not having religious freedom or other fundamental rights entrenched in an overarching document safeguarding constitutional rights, incorporated the ECHR into its domestic law and attempts to follow the jurisdictions of the ECtHR, which regards religious freedom as a right subjected to confinements given that it fulfils several requirements (see in detail Chapter IV below).

Germany is the only state in comparison to France and England that has its liberty rights entrenched and guaranteed in its constitution, the Grundgesetz. As a consequence, liberty rights, which are protected under the German Grundgesetz, are ranked in the hierarchy of laws so high that a justification of their infringement will have to sustain several requirements before a prevalence is given to another protected interest or right. This will normally follow an implementation of doctrines and principles balancing competing rights like the '*praktische Konkordanz*' developed by the German High Constitutional Court in order to balance adequately between conflicting interests protected under its Grundgesetz.

Adversely, England has no written constitution and, as a result, liberty rights are not protected under an overarching document like a Bill of rights. This might increase the risk of abuse of liberty rights by the British Parliament, which can easily legislate contravening enactments thanks to the principle of Parliament Supremacy. Although this has been often raised as criticism outside and inside the British Parliament, it remains a fact that liberty rights in Britain, including religious freedom are by far less infringed compared to Germany and France even though they are not profoundly entrenched in a constitution.

The significance attributed to the French legislator during its history played a dominant role in the protection of liberty rights. So in fact, liberty rights were not only protected constitutionally but were also safeguarded by the French Parliament. This entails the commitment of the French nation to respect religious freedom and allow its practical operation. Nevertheless, the right to religious freedom, unlike its German parallel, can be confined in special circumstances (e.g., protection of public interests) and is not regarded originally as an unreserved constitutional freedom.

In practice, the situation in all three compared countries, namely Germany, the UK, and France is that interference in the right to religious freedom is often interlinked with members of minority faith groups who are mostly affected by the limitations which fall within Art. 9 para 2 ECHR.

Germany – The right to religious freedom enjoys the highest rank in the hierarchy of norms in the German legal order, as it is established and safeguarded in the constitution, i.e., Grundgesetz. Germany is the only state in this comparative analysis which has recognized the right to religious freedom as a positive right within its legislative system. Further, the right to religious freedom constitutes a pre-eminent right, establishing a high position in the constitutional hierarchy of norms as an unreserved right. From a legal perspective, that means that the right will be guaranteed without any reservations, it is absolute and safeguarded so that no ordinary laws can obtain prevalence over it, and its confinement can be outweighed only against other constitutional freedoms.

England – In the historical development of state-church relations in England and the evolvement of fundamental human rights and the liberal-accommodating political policy adopted towards its religious minorities, it might become apparent why the right to religious freedom was recognized as a tolerance-based right as opposed to an explicit, acknowledged fundamental right. In addition, until the introduction of the HRA 1998, religious freedom had not even been perceived as a positive right, but was rather acknowledged as a negative right. In practice, the legal situation until the mid-twentieth century left the protection of religious rights subject to development of common law doctrines, legislation, or regulations of British Parliament, and case laws of the judicator. It is therefore that in the absence of a written constitution religious liberty rights are neither inscribed nor safeguarded in a British 'Bill of Rights' or its equivalent. Due to lack of enforceable mechanism for the safeguarding of fundamental human rights, it is reasonable that their protection under English law was expected to be weaker than the constitutional protection offered in Germany and France. An infringement or confinement of fundamental human rights is more likely to occur under English law than under German or French law, as they are subject to amendments or changes by parliament due to the prevailing principle of Parliament Supremacy. Moreover, contradictory or vague judgements as to the interpretation of religious freedom may lead to more uncertainty for individuals who wish to invoke this right.

France – The right to religious freedom is recognized and safeguarded not only in the different French constitutions but also under regular statutes. However, it is rather astonishing that in a state like France, which has a long tradition of constitutions establishing the protection of fundamental rights, the right to religious freedom had been acknowledged only by the end of the nineteenth century and, until that time, had been recognized merely as a negative right.

bb) Equality Rights

Germany – Equality rights, just like fundamental liberty rights, are entrenched constitutional rights in Germany. In contrast to France, which maintains the legal frame of equality rights also in the form of regulations or ordinary legislation, the German nation embedded in its Grundgesetz, a mandatory obligation of the state towards its citizens for equal treatment, as well as an explicit ban prohibiting discrimination irrespective of a person's religion or belief.

Notably, in Germany a substantiation of a claim invoking an infringement of the right to religious freedom will not avail itself by sole reference to the equality provisions (Art. 3 and 33 GG); rather, the main path should support itself based on violation of the fundamental right to religious freedom (Art. 4 GG), while the equality provisions will be attached to the primary claim.

Adversely, until the endorsement of the HRA 1998 in England, the submission of a claim for infringement of an individual's fundamental liberty right to religious freedom would have invoked equality rights as the primary ground for the substantiation of the claim.

England – In contrast to the legal situation that characterizes the establishment of fundamental rights in absence of a legal basis in domestic law, the establishment of equality rights and anti-discrimination laws proved to have a long, profound stand in the evolvement of British law. In fact, the protection of religious rights has taken place through application of the different equality legislations which were subject to constant changes and amendments in the last two decades.

It is worth to note that even under previous anti-discrimination laws (e.g., the Race Relations Act 1976) the right to religious freedom *per se* was neither granted specific protection nor gained any statutory recognition. The only acknowledged discriminatory grounds under this legislation were race and ethnicity. The growing Muslim immigration into England required necessary legislative amendments to be made by the British Parliament, as they did not fit into the definition of race or ethnic group and, therefore, lacked protection of their religious rights. The evolvement of enactments in this field were taken in piecemeal measure as subject to constant change, and covered ample fields of discrimination (e.g., employment, education) as well as discriminatory grounds. The major legislative work of British Parliament to consolidate the ample array of equality legislations had been accomplished with the endorsement of the 2010 Act. It was meant to bring transparency through enforcement of positive duty of equality to larger groups of participants in the public sector and extension of the equality grounds entitled to protection.

The Equality Act 2010 is considered to make a significant contribution to the series of anti-discrimination laws as it aimed through codification of anti-discrimination laws to create an extensive scope of protection for various equality grounds and promote equality of opportunities in different public sectors. However, the 2010 Act may still raise complex problems, especially with respect to discrimination occurring in public education on grounds of religion and belief. The reason is that acceptance or rejection of a claim to accommodate to the religious needs of the majority may end with a breach of the duty to equality of the minority religious group or the right of non-believers to refrain from religious influence. In addition, a very liberal accommodating attitude, that endeavours to take into account the religious needs of each individual, not only is impossible but may even be counter-productive, as school administration should also preserve an atmosphere of religious neutrality within school realm. Finally, the 2010 Equality Act entails a list of exceptions to the general equality duty that is specified for each sector such that exceptions as to educational institutes exist as well (e.g., faith and denominational schools, school curriculum, religious practice, or acts of worship).

Germany and England recognize the rights of individuals to invoke legislation or constitutional provisions which prohibit discrimination on account of different grounds, including religion or belief. Since, traditionally, there was no overarching guarantee of fundamental rights in England it followed that acknowledgement of equality rights and anti-discrimination laws was peripheral in the British legal doctrine; thus, their rush development has been a contribution of the British legislature only in the previous two decades.

At first glimpse, it seems that the invocation of religious rights based on the HRA will be prima facia more enforceable than equality rights, since British courts are bound to keep compatibility with the ECHR and its provisions (Art. 9 and 10). However, the effect of the HRA is embracing and provides compliance of all domestic legislation with the Convention rights. In this context, the Equality Act 2010 must also be interpreted in light of the ECHR and its specific provisions relating to religious freedom, its manifestation, and the enjoyment of religious rights in the education. It is worth to note, though, that since the introduction of the Equality Act 2010, protection against religious discrimination may collide with the right to freedom of religion and accrue difficulties with the interpretation of the Equality Act 2010 in case employment practices discriminate disproportionately on religious grounds. In such a case, the right to manifest a religion is not regarded as absolute and may be legitimately restricted if it is necessary to protect the rights of others.

Taken a legal perspective, it seems that of all three compared states in this analysis Germany is the only state that offers an enforceable system of fundamental human rights' protection. This provides for the highest protection of fundamental rights as well as equality rights for they are entrenched in a single comprehensive document that forms its highest legislative hierarchy, the constitution (GG). The German Grundgesetz enables individuals to allege a breach of their constitutional rights to religious freedom based on Art. 4 as well as their right not to be discriminated on account of a person's religion or belief as constituted in Art. 3 para 3 and Art. 33 para 3, which prohibit discrimination in the public service based on religious grounds.

France – upholds seriously its republican ideology of individualism. This has triggered no incentive on part of the state to accommodate to the religious needs of its immigrants. On the contrary, the large waves of immigrants, especially Muslims of North-African origins, were expected to assimilate into the French society and adhere to its sacrosanct republican ideology and values. This was meant to fortify the perception that all French citizens are alike in their Frenchness and are equal before the law. France does not recognize minority groups simply because recognizing ethnic or religious groups will bring down its unique model of French citizenship. France aspired along its history to dissolve any allegiance of its individuals to a particular ethnic or religious community in order to foster a strong sense of national identity among its citizens. This was achieved during the French Revolution from 1789 and one of its salient goals to enforce civic and citizen's equality rights through the 1789 Declaration irrespective of religious adherence. Consequently, these civic equality rights were conveyed and codified in the Civil Code of 1804.[730] In that sense, 'the French model of integration is based upon equality, individual citizenship and resemblance'.[731] Accordingly, in the absence of any acceptance or recognition of the 'right to be different' (*droit de difference*), it is only conceivable that all citizens are equal and the law must not recognize any differences between citizens.

730 *v. Ungern-Sternberg*, 2008, p.31.

731 *Auslander*, pp. 283, 291; *Sole*, Le Monde, 1 December 1998.

c) Constitutional Principles

aa) Principle of Neutrality/Laïcité

Germany – The principle of neutrality constitutes a paramount constitutional precept in Germany's legal system. It establishes the notion of church separation from the state and prescribes institutional separation reflected by the duty of the state to religious neutrality in public affairs and segregation of religion from public institutions. Though it is not explicitly embedded in the constitution, there is no legal discourse as to its existence. The legal debate in the judiciary and legal literature concentrates mainly on its normative source and ways of interpretation. The reasons for divisiveness of opinions are due to the fact that Germany has not adopted a system of complete state-church separation. Thence, scholars promoting the strict application of the neutrality principle claim that its roots are to be found in Art. 137 para 1 WRV. The precept prohibits the founding of a 'state-church system'. This prohibition embraces two other rules: first, *non-identification* – the state should not identify itself with any religion. It must advert itself from recognition or favouritism of a particular religion. Second, *non-intervention* – the state should refrain from interference in the inner affairs of religious communities. Those in favour of a liberal application of neutrality support their view that its existence should be inferred from other constitutional provisions which indicate of the inseparable bond between state and religion (i.e. Art. 7 para 3 GG, Art. 173 para 5 WRV). Their assumption is that Art. 137 para 1 WRV refers only to the obligation of the state and church to act independently from each other; however, on the basis of mutual cooperation. Nonetheless, this by no means should insinuate a radical separation. The liberal approach accepts the notion that the state should not identify itself with a specific religion; at the same time it should not inhibit religion. It believes that the state should enable an adequate space for religion to flourish and perceives it as part of the state's obligation to accommodate to the religious needs of its individuals. This requires the state to respect all religions in order to maintain its unbiased position.

England – The notion of state neutrality is again a demonstrative segregation point for comparison between the states in this analysis. There is a general acceptance in England for the principle of neutrality; however, in the absence of a written constitution it lacks an expressed denotation in formal constitutional document or an explicit codification in ordinary legislation. Thence, though England has an established church and there is no formal separation between state and church, the prevailing notion is in favour of the state to remain neutral in religious issues, especially in the public sector and in particular in public education. Due to its lack of inscription in a legislative norm, the neutrality principle derives authority from other principles such as the rule of law and the principle of equality of treatment. The former confines state power to interfere with individual liberty rights and the latter prescribes the eligibility of all citizens to equality before the law. As far as application of the neutrality principle in the public service is concerned, there exists no all-inclusive obligation to refrain from appearance with conspicuous signs. Further, the strong prevailing notion in Germany and France that public servants should appear neutral due to their duty as state representatives is not strictly observed in England. However, since England has neither legal definition of the public service nor is it codified, the duty to religious neutrality can have its roots in the British public service ethos, which recognizes the duty of the state to impartiality in its actions.

France – The notion of state neutrality exists in the German as well as in the French legal system. However, the definition of state neutrality is attributed in the French legal system a different meaning due to its prominent laïcité principle. The principle of laïcité cannot be conferred the meaning of secularism according to its English translation, as it simply does not completely transmit its purport as ascribed to it in France's constitutional terminology. Laïcité denotes not only separation between state and religion, but also its non-identification with a particular religion which, as a result, prohibits any form of state support to religious groups or its involvement in their inner affairs. The idea behind it states that freedom of conscience and belief is a private and individual matter; hence, it should be kept from public interference. Yet, in both systems scholars are unanimous in their opinion as to the different approaches of interpretation existing with respect to the neutrality principle. However, the opinions remain divided as to whether a strict or liberal implementation of the neutrality principle is eligible.

The substantial differences in the constitutional systems of France and Germany, especially relating to the notion of separation and state, generate essentially divergent decrees of these states' jurisdictions. In principle, German jurisdiction will tend to balance the competing interests at stake and to favour observance of state neutrality only if its prevalence is justified in order to achieve a necessary aim (negative rights of other pupils, the educative parental right, or equality between men and women). French courts, adversely, would not even look into the question of competing rights and existence of justification for infringement of a liberty- or equality right that prohibits discrimination on religious grounds, as they would immediately raise the pre-eminent status of the principle of laïcité, which the French nation is committed to respect.

bb) Principle of Equality

The importance of the principle of equality gains significance on two levels: first, the fact that a state adopts the rule that all its citizens are equal before the law and no discriminatory grounds should be taken into account with respect to the application of the law; second, implementation of the equality principle in the public sector may pose difficulties, as public servants are in some countries subject to a different set of rules. In addition, public servants as public officials are perceived to be representatives of the state. In that sense, should the law apply equally to them as to any other citizen, or will it be reasonable to expect that equal application would not be possible under special circumstances? (Such circumstances could be health grounds requiring the removal of ostensible religious signs, the duty of the state to neutrality obliging in particular teachers and education staff to refrain from manifestation of ostentatious religious symbols so as to avoid any risk of indoctrination or proselytization of pupils in the public school system). Germany and France have integrated the equality principle into their constitutional systems, therefore its status as a pre-eminent value is strongly rooted in their legal frameworks and its violation would not be possible if other constitutional fundamental rights or values are not at stake. In contrast, since England has no constitution, the equality principle is not guaranteed in the highest constitutional rank of norms, but is rather inscribed in ordinary legislation and subject to constant changes or amendments by parliament.

Germany – The articles underpinning the equality principle in the Grundgesetz cover two aspects: first, the general all-inclusive right of equality before the law is prescribed in Art. 3 para 1 GG, whereas the absolute imperative prohibiting any discriminatory act on part of the state with respect to its citizens when established on different grounds is stipulated in Art. 3 para 3 GG. Second, the obligation to equality in application and admission for the public service is reserved to all citizens without any differentiation as stipulated in Art. 33 para 3 GG.

It is worth to underscore that as far as the right of public servants to equal treatment in application to the public service is concerned, there exists a significant segregation point between the legal systems. While the constructional imperatives of equality under German law mandate that the state should refrain from any detrimental treatment on account of a person's religion or belief, it will not prohibit outright the appearance of a public servant with religious garments while on duty given that it does not affect his/her qualification or professional aptitude. This is not true as far as French law is concerned. According to the tenets of equality derived from different legal sources in French law, everyone, including public officials, is under the duty to transfer their equality by demonstrating their impartiality and neutralizing their religious conviction. Since equality underlies the neutrality principle, it mandates that equal eligibility of all citizens to the public service requires their neutral appearance before the public as state representatives. It is due to this salient characteristic entrenched in French constitutional law, aiming to achieve sameness in all state-individual aspects, that public servants are subject to a different set of rules prohibiting them from manifestation or display of religious symbols while on duty.

England – The importance of the Equality Act 2010 should be evaluated with respect to the right of a teacher employed in state-supported schools to protection of his/her religious interest while on duty. Opposite to the situation in Germany, teachers in Great Britain are not defined as public servants (*Beamte*); therefore, duties attached to public servants do not apply to teachers.

France – The precept of equality is explicitly declared and entrenched in one of the most famous tenets of French constitutional law, establishing its paramount status as a constituent pillar founding the French Republic in the aftermath of the historical events inculcating the spirit of the period. The maxim is inscribed in Art. 2 of the 1958 Constitution featuring its three underlying interconnected values: liberty, equality, fraternity. The equality principle is prescribed also in other constitutional documents, and its high importance in the French legal doctrine can be traced back to the 1789 Declaration ensued by the French Revolution. The obligation of the nation to adhere to the equality principle is already expressed in its outset, which declares the eligibility of all French people to equality before the law.

It is very important to note that its significance as an elementary part of the Republican Ideal segregates this principle from the common notion ascribed to it under German and English law. The French perception of equality is distinctive in nature when compared with the plain legal definition of a general right to equality before the law, equality of treatment, and a prohibition of non-discrimination on different grounds, as acknowledged in German and English law. French law attaches to the equality principle the ideal of its republican doctrine. In fact, it does not recognize any differentiation between its citizens as they are all deemed to be equal. France refuses to accept recognition of religious groups and acknowledges only individuals in order to ensure their allegiance to the republic as part of its universalist approach. The French nation endeavoured throughout its historical conflicts to disentangle itself from any religious control, especially of the Catholic Church. Hence, it refuses to acknowledge any divisiveness and, in fact, made efforts to eradicate any grounds for segregation among its citizens, as this contradicts the notion of universalism. An acceptance of special treatment or accommodation to the religious needs of an ethnic or religious group would bring down the core essence of republicanism espoused strongly with individualism.

This explains also the reason for the insufficient development of anti-discrimination laws in France, since in the absence of grounds for discrimination the state cannot be held responsible for illegal, disadvantageous treatment.

III An Introspection of the Relations Between Religion and the Educational System in Germany, England, and France

1. Introduction

This chapter will provide an introspection of the church-state system and the different structural models adopted in the comparative legal order of Germany, England, and France. These structural differences constitute an essential key element for the comprehension of individual rights, like the right to religious freedom, as its effect on the development of religious rights and their enjoyment will mostly be subjected to the degree of separation between the church and the state.

An identification of the established model (strong entanglement or distant separation) will provide orientation as to the impact of the state on religious rights. The identification of the state-church model will assist in comprehending the following aspects: accommodation of religion and related aspects in public education, the extent to which religious freedom will be guaranteed in the education system, in addition, the guarantee of religious rights when colliding with other constitutional rights or obligations emanating from a public service duty.

The model of state-church relations is different in each of the compared states and is distinguishable in character as it reflects the struggle for dominance along the respective country's history between socio-political and clerical powers which, to a large extent, formed the base of the countries' organizational and constitutional structures persisting till this day.

The role of the Christian Church and its impact on the population was diverse; for instance, in Germany the church maintained a prominent position, whereas in France its position is rather marginal. This naturally affected the constitutional status of the church to the extent that the type and scope of cooperation with the state determined primarily the degree of its involvement in social activities in the public sphere. Since issues relating to organization and framework of public schools were recognized in the past as an integral task of the church, the impact on the educational content was largely dependent on the relevant state-church model. Respectively, cooperation, separation, or a combined relation (division and cooperation) between state and the church was able either to foster or to alienate state support in religion and establish the constitutional legitimacy for interference in the free exercise of religious rights.

The appropriateness of a suitable model is to be concluded from several elements: the organizational structure of each state, the constitutional law, or any other comprehensive document of fundamental rights, as well as judicial tests laid down by the courts. Since the prominent constitutional stipulations regulating state-church relations as well as individual religious rights were already depicted in detail (Chapter II), this chapter will provide an overview of the respective state-church model appropriated to each country, while underscoring the key elements advocating in its support. This will follow a chronological overview of the strife between the church and the state to gain control over public schools. Thereupon, the competency of the states with respect to formation of its public school system will be outlined. In this respect, the eligibility of the states to admit or ban religious rights in the education will be scrutinized based on the authority derived from the specific legal order unique to each country. Finally, the legitimacy of endorsement of religious symbols or elements into the school realm will be discussed at length referring thereby to the doctrinal jurisprudence and constitutional principles developed by the courts in underlying their judgements.

2. Germany

The German model of state-church relations does not comply fully with a model of a strict separation but rather fits a 'cooperationist' model that combines division and cooperation.[732] This means that there is no spatial separation between religion and the state but rather a partial cooperation based on mutual coordination that will be permissible in specific areas of the public sphere.[733]

The recognition of institutional links between the church and the state can be dated back already to the era of the 'Christian State' or 'Church State' known in German history.[734] In fact, the guarantee of special status granted to the church

---

732 Bloss, 2008, pp. 151–152; *Seifert*, Comp. Lab. L. & Pol'y J., Volume 30, (2009) p. 535; see also in that respect, Robbers, Staat und Kirche in der Europäischen Union, (1996), as cited in Brugger p. 38: *"The German approach to church-state relations is often considered as 'cooperationist'"*; *Heckel*, Tel-Aviv University Studies In Law, Volume 13, 1997, 187, 195: *"… Germany has developed a system of separation of Church and State that is moderate and pro-religious…"*

733 *Brugger/Karayanni*, Religion in the Public Sphere: A comparative Analysis of German, Israeli, American and International Law, 2007, p. 38.

734 See in that respect *Listl*, p. 287 et seq., 508 et seq. (FN. 5), the designation of agreements concluded between the Catholic Church and the federal states administering their right to conduct religious activities in the public sphere, known as 'paritätische Konkordate'.

and religious communities and the acknowledgement in forms of cooperation and support between the state and the church was sustained even later in the period of transition to a modern pluralistic state. The incorporation of various provisions from the WRV into the Grundgesetz substantiates an organizational entanglement between state and church, such as the right of religious communities to act as public law corporations,[735] as well as other sets of privileges laid down at the constitutional level.[736] Further, Art. 140 GG in connection with Art. 137 and 141 WRV allows various forms of cooperation to be introduced: by virtue of the constitution of the federal states, by statutes and public contracts (*Konkordate*) with religious communities (Art. 138 para 1 WRV).[737]

Regarding the fact that religious communities are recognized as statutory corporations and that the German state admits in its constitution their right to conduct religious services in the public sphere, this conceivably includes a co-operation in the educational sphere. Namely, the state recognizes the freedom of churches in the organization of religious instructions in public schools and naturally even their legitimacy to accept state subsidies for that matter.[738]

Simply put together, the privilege of the Christian churches with respect to formation of the content of religious instructions in state-supported schools is laid down in the constitution (Art. 7 para 3 GG). The stipulation goes even further, expounding that the content of religious instructions shall be determined in conjunction with the relevant religious community so to comply with its internal precepts.[739] This suggests, as a practical matter, that the Christian churches (Catholic or Protestants) are able solely to determine the structure and layout of the lessons and appoint respectively qualified teachers for the conveyance of religious instructions in compulsory schools. In addition, as will be demonstrated next, many of the federal states secure explicitly in the states' constitutions allegiance to Christian-occident values and tradition.

By no means, this sufficiently displays the significant place religion acquires in Germany's social-historical development,[740] its organizational as well as constitutional system (national and regional level). It is worth to note that this pronounced preference to Christianity engenders potential conflicts and

735 Art. 140 GG in connection with Art. 137 para 5 and 6 WRV.

736 *Von Campenhausen/de Wall*, Sec 31 VIII; *Seifert*, Comp. Lab. L. & Pol'y J., Volume 30, 2009, 529, 538.

737 *Jarass*, in: Jarass/Pieroth. Art. 138 WRV Recital 1; *Brugger/Karayanni*, p. 39.

738 *Seifert*, Comp. Lab. L. & Pol'y J., Volume 30, 2009, 529, 539.

739 Art. 7 para 3 sentence 3 GG.

740 *Eberle*, 78 Tul. L. Rev., 2004, 1023–1088; *McGoldrick*, p. 108.

implications arising on the background of formation and framework of the schooling system with the second largest religious community in the country, namely the Muslim population.

Alongside with the strong tradition of church-state entanglement enabling cooperation and admission of religion in state schools, several indications connote of the development of the German state towards a secularized nation.[741] Several argumentations recognizing the adaptation of secular characteristic are to be alluded here briefly: first, plurality of religions – Germany is no longer a homogenous society but rather evolved into a pluralistic state. Religious pluralism in a society necessitates compliance with the principles of neutrality, equality, and liberty to all religions and faiths so as to avoid any preference or identification with a specific religion that eventually will give rise to claims of discrimination and unequal treatment. Therefore, all religious communities are granted identical rights and must be treated equally (this includes the rights of philosophical creeds and non-believers). In that sense, subordination of all religious communities to the same legislation will guarantee compliance with the equality principle[742] (Art. 140 GG together with Art 137 para 1 and para 3 WRV). Second, references indicative of the secular character of the republic can be inferred from stipulations and the terminology used in the constitution (e.g., Art. 140 together with Art. 137 para 1 WRV determines the 'no established church' precept; whereas the rest of the provisions in Art. 137 WRV relate in general to 'religious communities' and do not designate solely the church).[743] Third, self-determination of religious communities – this principle emanates from the state's obligation to the neutrality principle and prescribes the right of religious communities to determine their inner affairs without any governmental interference[744] (Art. 140 t.w. Art. 137 para 3 WRV). In principle, this enfolds the right of all religious communities to provide religious instructions in schools without any state intervention.[745]

---

741 *McGoldrick*, p. 109.

742 *Heckel*, Tel-Aviv University Studies In Law, Volume 13, 1997, 187, 200.

743 *Heckel*, Tel-Aviv University Studies In Law, Volume 13, 1997, 187, 199.

744 This privilege granted to religious communities is subject to limitations prescribed in Art. 140 together with Art. 137 para 3 WRV; *Robbers*, BYU L. Rev. 2001, 643, 654.

745 Since there is no recognized representative that is accepted by the Islamic population as a legitimate entity or public corporation authorized to act for them before governmental officials, the outcome is that Islamic religious instructions deviate from the constitutional requirements (i.e., Art. 137 para 3 WRV); see also *Robbers*, BYU L. Rev. 2001, 643, 657, 658; *Avenarius*, 6 Yearbook of the European Association for Education Law and Policy, 2006, 143, 147.

In practice, the compliance of both Islamic and Christian tradition and values with the educational task of the state was often challenged in courts. Islam adherents claim the same religious rights either through conveyance of tenets of their religion (e.g., conducting religious instructions) or through practice (observance of religious dress code). However, since the German republic had undergone a secularization process which dissolves in several aspects the entanglement with religion, the legal challenge achieved a new dimension. The aforementioned grounds brought about new challenges and tensions in all fields of the public sphere. Nonetheless, most of the attention and focus were directed in particular to questions relating to the eligibility of the outwardly manifestation of religious belief in the school system taking place through wearing of religious symbols or garments.

The following illustration will outline the transitional development in the supervision of the schooling system. Then a review depicting the federal system in Germany and the impact it has in combination with its (state-church) cooperationist model on the competency of the federal states to determine inner affairs within their jurisdictions (including education) will be set out. Subsequently, a thorough introspection of the legal and constitutional background in four distinguishable federal states will be concluded. A discourse relating to the jurisprudential approach and its evolvement throughout the years underscoring the constitutional fundaments laid down in judgements of the courts will be considered at length. The discourse will present the shift from the conservative, constitutional approach practiced in the early judgements of the BVerfG and the Federal Administrative Court (hereinafter BVerwG) during the 1970s to the one encountered in the aftermath of the controversial *Crucifix* decision. Finally, the presentation of pronounced case laws delineating the path instructing the courts in their judgements when deliberating the eligibility of public display of religious references in the education will be concluded.

In particular, the following questions and aspects will be scrutinized:

- The role of religion in schools and its historical development
- The legislative relation and allocation of powers between the national and individual federal states
- The position of religious symbols in the particular federal states/different application of the state neutrality principle in the different states
- A ban of the headscarf by administration or legislator
- Admissibility of religious symbols in jurisprudence

a) The Accommodation of Religion in State Schools – a Historical Overview of Transferal from Church to State

The position religion acquires in public schools has always been and still remains a controversial issue. An intangible bond between the educational system and religion dates back to the history of the German state.[746] The notion of compulsory schooling in Germany had been gradually established in the eighteenth century; since then it has been the subject issue of a battle over control between the church and the state.[747] From the time of the reformation till 1918, German schools were run by the church and were mostly Catholic denominated.[748] The educational system was a sphere which was preserved to the Catholic Church and controlled by it. The traditional school form, founded by the churches already at the beginning of the nineteenth century, was the *Volksschule*, known also as *Bekenntnisschule* (hereinafter confessional schools) as they were predominantly visited by pupils and teachers of the same denomination (either Catholic or Protestant). Indeed, this type of school forms prevailed in most parts of West Germany till the 1970s.[749]

Efforts to disentangle the influence of the Catholic Church on the state were made already in the Kaiser era but remained unsuccessful. The first serious effort to break the church's monopoly on elementary education started with drafting the WRV in 1918, after Germany's collapse in the First World War. The national assembly formulated the Weimar school compromise (*Reichsvolksschulgesetz*), which aimed to establish non-confessional schools as the standard public school form in the federal school system.[750] This envisaged reform, embodied in Art. 146 WRV, recognized parents' rights and will concerning their children's education and prohibited in parallel the change of inter-confessional schools into confessional schools under Art. 147 WRV.

Nonetheless, in 1933, most of the common elementary schools in Germany were still constituted as confessional schools.[751]

---

746 Germann/Wiesner, Recht der Jugend und des Bildungswesens, 2013, p. 396.

747 *Avenarius*, 6 Yearbook of the European Association for Education Law and Policy, 2006, 143, 144; Germann/Wiesner, Rdjb, 2013, pp. 398–399.

748 *Spotts*, Journal of Church and State, Vol 18, (1976), p. 208.

749 *Avenarius*, 6 Yearbook of the European Association for Education Law and Policy, 2006, 143, 144.

750 *Czermak*, in FS Rüfner (2003), 79, 80.

751 BVerfGE 6, 309, 354 = NJW 1957, 705; *Currie*, The Constitution of the Federal Republic of Germany, 1994 p. 248.

After the Second World War, the Catholic Church regained its power and together with the Protestant Church struggled for the establishment of confessional schools. The struggle for control became more eminent especially in the post-war period due to large immigration of Turkish workers exposing the majority of Christian population to the growing strength of a new influential faith, Islam. This was followed by the Reunification in 1990 that affiliated a population of which only a minority adhered to Christianity (mostly were non-believers).[752]

Due to this cultural-political, social-demographical upheaval the state had been going through, during the 1970s many federal states began to change their constitutions and the respective provisions relating to the organization of their school system. The outcome was the endorsement by many of the states of a new form of schools known as *christliche Gemeinschaftsschule* (hereinafter Christian common schools or CGS) as a regular form of compulsory schools.[753] The notion behind the establishment of this type of schools was to maintain the bond to Christian tradition and values and, at the same time, as much as possible exclude any proselytizing effect on pupils who either pertain to a different faith or whose parents reject any religious influence (atheists).[754]

Parallel to the historical changes following the Second World War, efforts were made to draft the constitution for the new state whose result was the final adoption of the Grundgesetz in its current version.[755] The constitutional order of the Grundgesetz granted the states (*Länder*) an exclusive legislative authority with respect to the establishment of its educational system including the denominational organization thereof.

This exclusive authority is conferred in Art. 7 GG in tandem with Art. 141 WRV, which further prescribes the limits on the state's legislature regarding its

752 *Auslander*, Cultural Dynamics 12 (3), 2000, 283, 289.

753 *Avenarius*, 6 Yearbook of the European Association for Education Law and Policy, 2006, 143,144.

754 This idea of the establishment of the CGS was acknowledged in several famous decisions of the BVerfG; BVerfGE 41, 29; 41, 65, 41, 88.

755 The framers of the constitution were reluctant to grant the Grundgesetz the final term of a constitution (Verfassung) as the prevailing thought was to gap a transitional period until final reunification. Finally, when German unity was achieved on October 3, 1990, it was decided to retain the framework of the Grundgesetz; *Kommers/Miller*, p. 42.

educational mandate.[756] Art. 7 GG constitute an entire article relating to school education and it specifically provides in para 1 the responsibility of the state (regional parliament) to establish schools.[757]

The state possesses a comprehensive, autonomous educational task with reference to pupils within the public school system, as established in Art. 7 para 1 GG.[758] Accordingly, it was determined already in the German jurisprudence that this mandate to establish the educational system includes not only the competency to organize the school structure but also the power to determine the content of studied courses and to set up the educational goals of state schools.[759] Since the most popular form of schools in many of the federal states is the CGS, secular schools are rare and a matter of exception.[760] Thence, the inherent right of the federal states to establish Christian communal schools that foster the exercise of religious worship of any kind (whether in the form of religious prayer or instruction) of the predominant faith, Christianity, was recognized in the jurisprudence as legitimate and compatible with Grundgesetz.[761] Even to the extent that religious communities enjoy an extensive power to collaborate with the state in educational matters (e.g., Art. 7 para 3 GG).[762]

b) The Competency of the State with Respect to Its Public School System

Since Germany was unified as a nation state only in 1871,[763] it was merely intelligible whether the aforementioned disagreements between state and church

756 BVerfGE 6, 309, 354 = NJW 1957, 705; BVerfGE 53, 185, 196 = NJW 1980, 2403; BVerfGE 59, 360, 377 = NJW 1982, 1375; BVerfGE 75, 40, 66 et seq. = NJW 1987, 2359; BVerfGE 98, 218, 248 = NJW 1998, 2515.

757 Art. 7 para 1 GG.

758 Häberle, pp. 48, et seq., 66, et seq.; more restrictive *Schmitt-Kammler* in: Sachs, Grundgesetz, 3. Aufl. München 2003, Art. 7 recital 22, et seq.: *Lecheler* in Listl/Pirson: HdbStKirchR II, pp. 415, 420, et seq.

759 BVerfGE 52, 223, 236; BVerfGE 34, 165, 182; 47, 46, 71; BVerfGE 93, 1, 21.

760 Like in Berlin (See in detail under III. 2 c) cc) below).

761 BVerfGE 41, 29; 41, 65, 41, 88.

762 Art. 7 para 3 GG determines that religious instructions are to be conducted only in accordance with the precepts of the religious community concerned. Insofar as teachers are members of the church or its employees, the state has to reimburse the respective church. In addition, churches are entitled to co-operate with the state when appointing teachers for religious instructions. See further in *Avenarius*, 6 Yearbook of the European Association for Education Law and Policy, 2006, 143, 145.

763 *Auslander*, Cultural Dynamics 12 (3), 2000, 283, 288.

evolved to whether decisions concerning the character of a school (confessional[764] or denominational[765]), should be left to the *Reich* (realm) or to the land's (regional)[766] government to decide on such matters.[767]

The adoption of the Grundgesetz in 1949 introduced modern constitutionalism in Germany as known today. The Grundgesetz determines not only fundamental rights but also regulates the relations between the central and the individual states. Thence, the Grundgesetz divides authority between organs of the federation and organs of the states, whereby the state as a whole (*Gesamtstaat*) arises out of an alliance among the states in the form of a federation (*Bund).*[768]

Accordingly, members of the federation, the *Bundesländer* (federal states), are states with their own sovereign power. This power, though limited, is not derived from the federation but rather recognized by it.[769]

This is known in German constitutionalism as the fundamental principle of federalism as found in Art. 20, 30 GG. This chosen federal system, as determined in Art. 20 para 1 GG, serves as a limit for and weakening of a centralized political power.[770]

One of the direct consequences of the federal state principle is the distribution of competences between the central state and the federal states. When looking at the allocation of these competencies, one needs to differentiate between legislative and administrative competencies.

Inasmuch, Art. 30 GG determines allocation of rights and duties between the central state and the federal states; it states that exertion of state's competencies and compliance of tasks is a matter delegated to the federal state. This will be applicable as long as no other constitutional prescription comes into force. Art. 70 GG determines the assignment of legislative task between central and

---

764 A confessional school is usually Catholic or Protestant, *Kommers/Miller*, pp. 575, 576, p. 470.

765 "An interdenominational school is a Christian – oriented school designed to serve students of all denominations", cited in *Kommers/Miller*, p. 576.

766 *Alloway*, Dick.J.Int'l L. 15 (2), 1997, 361, 382;

767 *Alloway*, Dick.J.Int'l L. 15 (2), 1997, 361, 382; *Spotts*, Journal of Church and State, Vol 18, (1976), p. 208.

768 BVerfGE 12, 45 cited in *Kommers/Miller* p. 69.

769 *Kommers/Miller* p. 64.

770 The supposition of a new constitutional order for Germany was in accordance with the decision of the Allies after The Second World War to break up Prussia in order to disperse the power of a totalitarian state and establish a greater equality among the federal states. See *Kommers/Miller* p. 79; BVerfGE 55, 274, 318 et seq.

federal states. It declares that the federal states are competent to legislate and promulgate within their jurisdiction, unless the constitution assigns the central state an exclusive competency with respect to a particular legal matter. Consequently, the prerogative granted to the federal states with respect to their educative task derives authority from the principle of federalism.[771]

That means that the competency to regulate rights and obligations of civil servants accounts as a field of dual competency to which both the central state and the federal states (*Bundesstaat*)[772] share competing dual authority. Since the determination of dress code in the public service constitutes an obligation which the teacher (as a public servant) has to comply with, it then falls within this dual competency. Due to the fact that the federation did not exert its competency according to Art. 74 para 27 GG, the federal states were entitled to issue respective amendments. In principle, the competency the individual states obtain with respect to regulation of schoolteachers' dress codes yields from two constitutive precepts: first, the prescription of the rights and duties of civil servants (Art. 74 para 27 GG); second, the state's duty to organize its public school system (Art. 7 para 1 GG).[773]

Alongside the right conferred from the principle of federalism it should be underscored that the educative task of the state and its right to decide about formation of schools, their curricula, and their character is guaranteed and established in the Grundgesetz (Art. 7 para 1 GG).

The guarantee of fundamental rights like religious freedom and the prescription of a framework delineating the establishment and organization of the public school system as well as the role of religion in education are provided not only in the Grundgesetz but also in other constitutional documents. Since Germany is a federated nation, each federal state has an own constitution in which fundamental rights are guaranteed. This includes, in most cases, also the endorsement of religious freedom rights. The character of public schools and their general educational frame is determined in the lands' constitutions and statutory

---

771 BVerfGE 6, 309, 354 = NJW 1957, 705 *(para 215–216)*; *Kommers/Miller* p. 468; *Badura* in Maunz/Dürig, Art. 7 recital 2.

772 Art. 74 para 27 of the Grundgesetz confers both the central state and the federal states a parallel competency to regulate all aspects regarding the emanating rights and obligations of civil servants, apart from issues relating to remuneration, social security aspects which are conferred to the sole discretion of the federal states. See, *Pieroth,* in: Jarass/Pieroth, Art. 74, recital 76.

773 *Wiese*, p. 276.

enactments legislated in the respective land's parliament as will be demonstrated subsequently.

c) Endorsement of Religious Symbols into State's School System

Undoubtedly, schools carry a significant role and a special responsibility with respect to the education and cultivation of pupils. Therefore, one of the most important functions of schools is to encourage a cultural environment. In that sense, school is a place where the pupils should be able to develop their personality and build their identity.[774]

In this context, there exists a consensus in the legal literature as well as in the jurisprudence that schools are understood as the institution above all others, a mirror image of the citizens about their future, through which the nation is regenerated.[775] Consequently, the state is accountable for the free cultural-denominational development of pupils, parents, and teachers in the educational sphere.[776] In addition, according to the constitution itself, the state is obliged to give freedom of religion a reasonable and adequate consideration when implemented in compulsory public schools (Art. 7 para 3 and para 5 GG). It is also for this reason that critics have raised the issue that should religious contents or thereof related themes be factored out of the educational sphere, then the comprehensive educational task of the state would fail to achieve its purpose.[777]

As of the mid-twentieth century, questions relating to manifestation of religious symbols or garments – either through the display by the state or when worn by the teachers staff or pupils – raised the legal permissibility thereof in particular if standing in contrast to the guarantee of fundamental rights (e.g., religious freedom). This was and still is a topic that is fiercely debated in the public, especially due to the significance attributed to educational institutions and their pivotal influence on the population, as denoted earlier.

In general, national controversies encompassing aspects of state-church relations in German schools are predominately contested with: first, the eligibility of the state emanating from its mandate to establish the educational system (Art. 7 para 1 GG) to admit religious symbols (such as the Islamic headscarf, or the display of a cross) into state schools, and the circumstances under which

---

774 *Robbers*, ÖARR, 2003, 405, 409.

775 BVerfGE 93,1, 22=NJW 1995, 2477; *Auslander*, Cultural Dynamics 12 para 3, 2000, 283, 285; *McGoldrick*, p. 108; *Heckel*, DVBl 1996, 453, 468 recital 72.

776 *Robbers*, RdJB 51. Jahrgang, 1/2003, 11.

777 *Robbers*, ÖARR, 2003, 405, 417; *Robbers*, BYU L. Rev. 2001, 643, 653.

such religious references would be regarded as permissible so as not to contravene other constitutional rights (e.g., states' obligation to religious neutrality, minority's right to (negative) religious freedom, parental right to determine the education of their children).[778] Second, whether the state legislature should be confined in its educative mandatory task to the extent that the conveyance of religious values and precepts will be permitted only if delivered during religious instructions as guaranteed in Art. 7 para 3 GG. The answers to these questions may vary depending on the relevant federal state, as the outcome, to a large extent, would be a direct consequence of the state-church relations as rooted in the history, tradition, culture, and legal practice of each state.[779]

aa) The Legal Framework in the Federal States

The following examination will focus on a description of the legal situation and different approaches practiced in the federal states of Bavaria, Berlin, North Rhine-Westphalia, and Baden-Württemberg regarding the establishment and endorsement of religion in their common school system. These states took different approaches on that issue and serve as a suitable example for the bandwidth of legislative solutions. It will thence provide an overview of pre-eminent provisions ensuring the guarantee of religious rights as well as their interlink within the organization of the educational system as reflected in denotation made both in regular legislation as well as lands constitutions of the respective federal states.

Notably, the turning point in the German jurisprudence took place with the delivery of the famous *Ludin*'s judgement in 2003 as in its aftermath many federal states rushed to introduce amendments in their respective legislation prohibiting the outwardly manifestation of religious garments or symbols when worn by teachers.[780] Legal discussion made some further developments after a recent BVerfG judgement specified constitutional prerequisites for a ban of a

---

778 *Fogel*, N.Y.L.Sch.L.Rev, 51, 2006, 618, 645.

779 *Hennecke*, in: Ellwein/Grimm/Hesse/Schuppert, 1995, pp. 83, 86.

780 The first state, Baden-Wuerttemberg, came with the first proposal for modifications in its SchG BW (Amendment draft from 1.4.2004, GBl. p. 178). The rest of the seven federal states took similar steps as following: Niedersachsen (Amendment draft from 29.4.2004, GVBl. p. 140): Saarland (Enactment Nr. 1555 to the Amendment of the SchoGfrom 23.6.2004, Amtsbl. p. 1510): Hessen (Gesetz zur Sicherung der staatlichen Neutralität from 18.10.2004, GVBl. I p. 306): Bavaria (An amendment draft to the BayEUR from 23.11.2004, GVBl. p. 443): Berlin (Enactment to creation of a law relating to Art. 29 of the BlnVerf from 17.1.2005, GVBl. p. 92): Bremen (Amendment draft to the BremSchulG and School Administration Act from 28.6.2005, GVBl. p. 245): North

headscarf to be applied with respect to public schoolteachers.[781] Based on the background of the recent judgement from 2015, the analysis will attempt to provide an introspection of the legislative framework existing in the different federal states following delivery of the debatable *Ludin*'s decision and necessary legislative amendments taken to ensure their constitutional compliance in its aftermath. This legislative stand will be evaluated taking into account the recent judgement and its effect on the constitutionality of pre-existing legislation. Which measurements, if at all, are to be incurred by the lands' legislators so as to ensure their conformity to the new constitutional stand and legislative amendments already implemented will be assessed in retrospect to their former conceptualization prior to delivery of the recent judgement for determination of their compatibility with new constitutional safeguards. The implementation of the respective laws will be expounded next in detail.

bb) Bavaria

Bavaria is comparably highly influenced by Christian faith and culture in public life. The ruling party since the Second World War, the Christian Social Union (CSU), always emphasized the religious reference. Accordingly, legal regulations, acts, and guidelines[782] are often influenced by a Christian background. The dominating influence of the Catholic Church on the Bavarian inhabitants left a salient impact which was correspondingly noticeable in all fields of public life, but especially in the public school system.[783] This strong implementation of religion into public life persists until today; however, even in Bavaria secular influence is gaining ground.[784]

Rhine-Westphalia (Amendment draft to the SchulG NRW from 13.6.2006, GVBl. p. 270).

781 BVerfG 1 BvR 471/10, 1 BvR 1181/10.

782 For instance, the '*Guidelines for school lessons and education according to common principles of the Christian confession in elementary, secondary and schools of special pedagogical need*' known as '*Leitsätze für den Unterricht und die Erziehung nach gemeinsamen Grundsätzen der christlichen Bekenntnisse an Grund-, Haupt- und Sondervolksschulen*' edited by Cardinal Wetter and the Bavarian Bishop Hanselmann in 29 November 1988. These guidelines aimed to set forth the foundations for a social fabric in state schools that is based on Christian tradition and values such as fear of God, conduct of religious prayers, and the exercise of religious worship and celebration of holidays. See in *Czermak* in FS Rüfner (2003), 79, 98.

783 *Czermak* in FS Rüfner (2003), 79, 80, 81, 85, 88; *Auslander*, Cultural Dynamics 12 (3), 2000, 283, 284, 285, 292.

784 *Czermak* in FS Rüfner (2003), 79, 102.

(1) *Legal Framework*

The Bavarian legislator ascribes high significance to perpetuation of the Christian nature of the state and as such contributes a dignified amount of provisions in the land's constitution, the *Bayerische Landesverfassung* (BayVerf) to ensure allegiance of its population to Christianity through excessive entanglement of the church in all fields of public life.

In addition, the framework of establishment of state school system and its inimitable bond to Christianity are featured in two main legislative enactments: first, the Bavarian elementary School Ordinance,[785] and second, the Bavarian School Education Act.[786]

(a) Constitutional Law of Bavaria

The constitution in its original version from 1946 established key elements concluding the quintessence of the educative task in public schools and, in a like manner, regulated the employment of teaching staff in state schools. Several changes made throughout the years to the constitution of 1946 endorsed amendments in the provisions relating to the education and school system. A comparative reference with respect to the most pre-eminent provisions regulating the interplay of state-church relations in the education on the background of past and present versions will be outlined next.

At the outset, it is worth to note that the fundamental right of religious freedom, like other fundamental liberties, is comprehended in Art. 107 BayVerf. The wording of Art. 107 para 1 and para 2 BayVerf establishes in the precepts the freedom to have and cultivate a religion or faith as well as the right to manifest or practice a religion.

In principle, Bavaria recognized the obligation of the state to fulfil its educational mandate. This is conferred on the state by virtue of the authority granted to it in Art. 130 para 1 and 2 BayVerf.

In its original version of 1946, the constitution perceived not only monopoly over establishment of its school system but also a monopoly over teachers' training and education. For instance, the demand of religious training program for teachers in state schools was determined in Art. 135 para 2 BayVerf in its old version. The stipulation made explicitly clear that in confessional schools only

785 Schulordnung für die Grundschulen in Bayern (Grundschulordnung – GrSO) vom 11. September 2008, GVBl. S. 684, BayRS 2232-2-UK.

786 Bayerisches Gesetz über das Erziehungs- und Unterrichtswesen, BayEUG, vom 31. Mai 2000, GVBl. S. 414, ber. S. 632, BayRS 2230-1-1-K.

those teachers will be admitted who are willing to teach pupils in accordance with the fundaments of the relevant confession, namely, Christianity. Art. 135 in its current version provides explicitly that in state elementary schools children must be taught and educated according to the principles of the Christian creed and makes no denotation as to a teacher's professional freedom that is interlinked with his/her religious affinity. Art. 135 declares that 'state elementary schools shall be open to all children of school age. In them children shall be taught and educated according to the principles of the Christian creed. Details shall be the subject of the School Law'.

Notwithstanding, the Bavarian state recognizes alongside the educative mandate of the state the inherent right of parents to decide on the education of their children as prescribed in Art. 126 para 1 BayVerf. This demonstrates incontestably that the Bavarian state does not foster or adopt an all-inclusive, absolute prerogative with respect to its educational task but rather concludes an approach based on cooperation between the state, school authorities, parents, and children to determine on educational matters.

In addition to these provisions, a reference to the state-church relation in the Bavarian state relating to education and the school system is made explicit several times in various contexts inside the constitution. A brief reference to several stipulations underscoring this sacrosanct bond between state and religion in the context of education can be identified in the following: the state explicitly demands in the constitution that one of the declaratory, educational goals of the school system should include reference to God and respect for religious persuasion (Art. 131 para 2 BayVerf). Further, religious instructions will form a recognized subject in schools' curricula as well as the right to conduct religious instructions in all elementary schools, secondary schools, and high education institutions (Art. 136). The constitution acknowledges also the right of religious communities to exert influence on the education of the children (Art. 127 of the Bavarian constitution).

(b) Federal Law of Bavaria

(aa) The Bavarian School Regulations for Elementary Schools/Bavaria's Elementary School Ordinance (die Bayerische Volksschulordnung)

The Bavarian Elementary School Ordinance (BSR), known as Bayerische Volksschulordnung (VSO), is a legal regulation that takes effect with respect to public elementary schools, community, and secondary schools. The BSR was issued by the Bavarian ministry for Education and Cultural Affairs based on power delegated to the Bavarian legislator in two salient enactments: The

Bavarian Act on Education and Public Instruction (*Bayerisches Gesetz über das Erziehungs- und Unterrichtswesen*) and the already revoked Elementary School Act (*Volksschulgesetz*).

The BSR is an integral part of legislation promulgated in order to regulate the organizational design and framework of the school system in Bavaria.

Inevitably, the *Crucifix* decision affected relevant school legislation insofar as it declared an enactment of a federal legislator to be null and void as it was found to be incompatible with a guaranteed constitutional right, that is, the right of religious freedom (Art. 4 GG). In that sense, the BVerfG invalidated in its judgement from 1995 the third sentence of Sec. 13 BSR.[787] Notably, the repealed Sec. 13 para 1 BSR[788] ordered a cross to be affixed in every classroom in state elementary schools and stated the following:

> The school shall support those with parental rights in the religious upbringing of children. School prayers, school services, and school worship are made possible due this support. In every classroom a cross shall be affixed. Teacher and pupils are obliged to respect the religious feelings of all.

It is worth to note in this respect that the wording of the former Sec. 13 para 1 BSR is provided now under a new provision (Sec. 41 of the BSR); however, it excludes the precept relating to affixation of crosses in classrooms. Sec. 41 para 1 BSR prescribes the right of parents to decide on the religious education of children in cooperation with school authorities. In addition, the provision declares state support in organization of school prayers and other acts of religious ceremonies. As mentioned earlier, the Bavarian state does not only respect the inherent parental right but in fact it also fosters and supports a close interaction between parents and school authorities in educational matters as strongly affirmed in Sec. 16 para 1 BSR.

The BSR in its current version[789] still relates in significant parts to the Bavarian Act on Education and Public's instruction and therefore should be read in conjunction. It is therefore not surprising that further amendments following the *Crucifix* decision took effect also with respect to the latter. In response to the revocation of Sec. 13 of the BSR in the *Crucifix* decision, the Bavarian

---

787 BVerfGE 93, 1–1 BvR 1087/91; *Czermak*, in: FS Rüfner (2003), 79, 97.

788 The former Bavarian School Regulation for Elementary Schools from 21.6.1983 known as 'die Bayerische Volksschulordnung'Volksschulordnung (BayVSchO) (BayGVBl, p. 597).

789 The Bavarian School Regulations for Elementary Schools lastly amended on 2.9.2012 (BayGVBl p. 453).

legislator rushed following delivery of the judgement and introduced a new clause in the enactment, known as *das Bayerisches Gesetz über das Erziehungs und Unterrichtswesen*, the Bavarian School Education Act as of May 2000 (BayEUG). The amendment incurred in the BayEUG will be expounded in detail next.

(bb) The Bavarian School Education Act – Das Bayerisches Gesetz über das Erziehungs- und Unterrichtswesen (BayEUG)

Since the decision of the BVerfG in the Crucifix was not really accepted either by the Bavarian inhabitants or by politicians and members of clergy,[790] it was rather conceivable that the Bavarian legislator will not order the immediate removal of the cross from all state schools.

A direct consequence of the *Crucifix* decision was the introduction of amendments made to the BayEUG, which came into force in 1996.[791] The aim it sought to achieve was the conclusion of a compromise between all involved parties (i.e., school authorities, parents, and pupils) in case a conflict was raised due to affixation of crosses in state schools.

(aaa) Art. 7 BayEUG

Accordingly, the centrepiece of this legislation can be found in Art. 7 BayEUG, which established several stipulations that pronounced the educative task of elementary schools, the educational goals as well as the determination regarding affixation of crosses in classrooms, and the insertion of a compromise in case of a controversy.

Its most distinguishable part, however, was found in the amendment made in 1996 with respect to Art. 7 para 3 BayEUG. The clause is currently found in Art. 7 para 4 BayEUG and does not comprise any deviation from the original version of the clause. In its outset (first to third sentence) it declares unequivocally that the educational goal of the Bavarian legislator is to ensure orientation of state elementary schools in accordance with Christian denomination. This entails that in state schools pupils will be educated and taught according to the principles of Christian values.

The amendments made to the BayEUG, the second part of Sec. 7 para 4, included the 'objection principle', the so-called *Widerspruchsregelung*.[792] In

790 *Auslander*, Cultural Dynamics 12 (3), 2000, 283, 292, 300.

791 Das Bayerische Gesetz über das Erziehungs- und Unterrichtswesen from 31 May 2000 in BayGVBl. p. 414. The Act was lastly amended by Art. 9a para 18 Bayrisches E-Government Gesetz vom 22.12.2015.

792 The BayEUG (Bayerisches Erziehung und Unterrichtgesetz) in its version from 23. December 1995 came into force on 1 January, 1996 (BayGVBl p. 850).

principle, the provision suggests a compromise to be found between school authorities, parents, and pupils upon objection to the cross. It therefore appoints that in case an objection is raised by one of the parents' pupils, it will entail school authorities to achieve a compromise that will be acceptable for all involved parties.

Thereupon, the structure of Sec. 7 para 4 BayEUG is designed in two phases: whereas the first sentence of Sec. 7 para 4 BayEUG legitimizes the affixation of a cross in all Bavarian classrooms on grounds rooted in the historical and cultural evolvement of the state, the third and fourth sentences are anticipating a forthcoming conflict.[793] In other words, the intent of the legislator was prominently to preserve the salient Christian nature of the state. It was therefore of high importance to underscore that, albeit the endorsement of the objection principle, the ordering of a cross in every classroom remains incontestable. Its form, size, and location should be compatible with its value as a Christian symbol. Yet, it was concluded that there should be no provoking influence of the cross on non-Christians.[794]

The second phase of the clause anticipates rejection to the cross and suggests a solution to be achieved in the form of a compromise. Thence, Sec. 7 para 4 sentence 3 BayEUG guarantees parents the right, upon fulfilment of several requirements, to ask for a removal of the cross. Notably, this right is not conferred based on an objective perception; it is rather enough that parents will subjectively demonstrate that the cross is infringing their negative freedom of religion.

In addition, in order for an objection to be successful there are several conditions that need to be fulfilled. First, in case the exposure to the cross may raise a claim by the parents who will object to the cross, they will need to establish their objection on serious and foreseeable grounds. Second, if the grounds for objection lay within a different religion, or belief, or anti-religious ideology (atheism of the parents), it will be then the task of the principal to find a compromising settlement that will attempt to find an adequate balance between all competing interests so as to benefit all involved parties (Sec. 7 para 4 Sentence 3 BayEUG).

Third, insofar these efforts to achieve a compromising settlement should not be successful, then it is the task of the principal to find an adequate balance

793 BVerwG decision from 21 April 1999, NJW 1999, 3063.

794 At a later point, only the cross without the corpus was hanged in all classrooms.

which will take into consideration the (negative) freedom of religion of the objecting parents, on the one hand, and the (positive) freedom of religion of all other pupils in the class and their parents, on the other. Notwithstanding, the legislator emphasized the principal's task to take careful consideration of the majority's will when outweighing competing rights (Sec. 7 para 4 Sentence 4 BayEUG).

To conclude, the dissenting rule/objection principle will accord compliance with the constitution upon fulfilment of the following requirements: first, the claimant will be able to satisfy his/her claim based on reasonable and foreseeable grounds; second, no settlement could be reached with the school's management or school's principal; and third, no other reasonable, non-discriminating evading opportunities exist.

In order to fulfil the first requirement of 'serious and foreseeable grounds', it will be sufficient if the appellants clearly proved that due to the fact of their being atheists or because of their anti-religious view, they perceive the exposure of their child to the cross as unacceptable and as infringing on their negative right to religious freedom. Notably, mere differences of religious views will not be taken into account.

The second and third requirements of the dissenting rule were introduced for the same reasons, namely, in order to demonstrate conformity with the constitution. Therefore, in cases of predictable conflicts due to exposure to the cross, it will be the task of the school to prove either that preliminary efforts were made to avoid any further escalation, or that awareness with respect to a future conflict was already taken into consideration in assigning the homogeneity of the class.

(bbb) Art 59 BayEUG

The question relating to admissibility of religious symbols or garments worn by teachers was also taken into consideration by the Bavarian legislator. The incentive was a response ensued following delivery of the *Ludin*'s case.[795] It is worth to note in this context that a legislative ban did not take place but only after delivery of the *Ludin*'s judgement. In principle, prior to *Ludin*'s case the Bavarian legislator did not forbid Muslim pupils or teachers to appear in schools with a headscarf or veil.[796] Therefore, the reformation of existing school legislation was prompt especially among two federal states, Baden-Württemberg and Bavaria,

795 See in detail under III. d) dd) (1).

796 *Wiese*, p. 26.

which rushed to introduce new legislative instruction determining that donning of a headscarf-*hijab* in school would be regarded as illegal.[797]

The amended BayEUG sets out in Art. 59 para 2 several rules of conduct including dress codes with respect to teaching staff in public schools:

> … They must impart to their students the fundamental constitutional values. During lessons teachers are not allowed to wear outer symbols and garments that express a religious or ideological creed, in case students or parents may understand these symbols or garments as expression of an attitude that is not compatible with fundamental constitutional values and educational objectives of the constitution, including Christian-occidental educational and cultural values… For teachers in preparatory service exceptions from the rule in sentence 3 may be granted in individual cases.[798]

The purpose of introducing a new clause into the BayEUG, even though not explicitly mentioned in the explanatory notes of parliament or the wording of the clause itself, was to declare the headscarf and other head covering as impermissible. The justification for the ban was presented to be the defence of the Western-Christian tradition and values. This way, the provision was formulated in general terms so that any symbol or garment that might be interpreted as contravening constitutional or educational values will be deemed inadmissible.[799]

---

797 See The Amendement Act to the BayEUG (Gesetz zu Änderung des Bayerischen Gesetzes über das Erziehungs- und Unterrichtswesen) from 23.11.2004, GVBl. P. 443; *Langenfeld/Mohsen*, 3 International Journal of Constitutional Law, 2005, 86–94.

798 Amendement of Sec 59 Bayerisches Gesetz über das Erziehungs- und Unterrichtswesen (BayGVBl) 2000 p. 414. Art. 59 para 2 das BayEUG sets out: „Die Lehrkräfte haben den in Art. 1 und 2 niedergelegten Bildungs- und Erziehungsauftrag sowie die Lehrpläne und Richtlinien für den Unterricht und die Erziehung zu beachten. Sie müssen die verfassungsrechtlichen Grundwerte glaubhaft vermitteln. Äußere Symbole und Kleidungsstücke, die eine religiöse oder weltanschauliche Überzeugung ausdrücken, dürfen von Lehrkräften im Unterricht nicht getragen werden, sofern die Symbole oder Kleidungsstücke bei den Schülern oder Schülerinnen oder den Eltern auch als Ausdruck einer Haltung verstanden werden können, die mit den verfassungsrechtlichen Grundwerten und Bildungszielen der Verfassung einschließlich den christlich-abendländischen Bildungs- und Kulturwerten nicht vereinbar ist. Art. 84 Para 2 bleibt unberührt. Für Lehrkräfte im Vorbereitungsdienst können im Einzelfall Ausnahmen von der Bestimmung des Satzes 3 zugelassen werden."

799 See Amendment draft of the Bavarian government, Bay. LT-Drs.15/368 from 11.11.2004 http://www1.bayern.landtag.de/webangebot1/servlet/Vorgangsmappe?wp=15&typ=V&drsnr=368&intranet=false; *Langenfeld/Mohsen*, 3 International Journal of Constitutional Law, 2005, p. 91.

Remarkably, Bavaria as well as Baden-Württemberg provided an exemption for teachers in their training period.[800] It is overwhelming that the prohibition in Sec. 59 para 2 BayEUG on the Islamic headscarf is not applicable with respect to teachers in their training period.

This surprising step incurred by those two federal states served as incentive for initiation of draft laws espoused by other federal states which decided to follow the path and promulgate similar legislation interdicting indirectly the appearance of Muslim teachers or public servants to their workplace with a headscarf or a similar head covering.[801] Notably, the ban concluded in federal legislation of the states does not explicitly exclude the Muslim headscarf but is drafted in an all-inclusive way that allegedly intended to enfold all symbols or garments which carry a political or religious character.

Notably, following the recent BVerfG decision the constitutional compatibility of Art. 59 para 2 BayEUG stands in question in case its judicial scrutiny will be sought by the Bavarian judicator. Several aspects should be carefully considered in this regard:

First, *the advancement of or privilege to the Christian faith and tradition* – the BVerfG declared that any advancement of the Christian faith upon other religions such as Islam in the state school system is not only prohibited but also violates against pre-eminent constitutional precepts of equality. Since the Bavarian legislator intended to privilege the Christian faith and promote the endorsement of Christian-related themes and symbols into its state school system, it is very unlikely that Art. 59 para 2 BayEUG will be regarded to conform to the constitutional precepts of equality Art. 3 para 3 and 33 para 3 GG.

Second, *the interdiction of abstract endangerment* – the Bavarian lawmaker as well as other federal states legislators introduced the headscarf ban on grounds of the endangerment it poses to the Western-liberal tradition as well as prominent constitutional values, such as gender equality, the neutrality principle, the negative right of others to religious freedom, and the peaceful co-existence in school. As a result, it was upheld by the BVerfG that the threshold that existed so far and sufficed in order to curtail an individual's

800 Sec. 38 para 4 BWSchG.

801 The following federal states: Berlin (Sec. 2 of the law relating to Art. 29 of BlnLV), Bremen (Sec. 59 b IV of BremSchulG), Hessen (Sec. 68 para 2 and 3 of the Public Servants Act), Niedersachsen (Sec. 51 para 3 of the Niedersachsen NSchG), North Rhine-Westphalia (Sec. 57 para 4 to the SchulG NRW), Saarland (Sec.1 para 2 a SchoG).

right to religious freedom can no longer satisfy itself by demonstration of an abstract endangerment. The BVerfG determined that a teacher's right to appear with a religious garment in school can only be confined if a concrete endangerment can be demonstrated with respect to religious rights of pupils or parents, the obligation of the state to religious neutrality, and other constitutional rights and freedoms.

(2) Conclusion - Bavaria

The dominant influence of the Catholic Church on everyday lives of the Bavarian inhabitants was maintained in the course of history and was especially prominent in its efforts to preserve control over formation and organization of the educational system.

The allegiance to the Christian faith was set up as a pre-eminent aim of the Bavarian state as demonstrably pronounced in the Bavarian constitution (Art. 131 para 2 BayVerf). The Bavarian legislator recognized the inherent task of its public school system to foster proximity to the Christian faith and explicitly supported the positive right of the majority of pupils to practice Christianity through school prayers, religious instructions, as well as declaratory pronouncement in the constitution that the Christian values and tradition form an integral part of its educational aims (Art. 135 BayVerf). In addition, political power was interlinked with support of the dominant Christian faith and enabled a tight cooperation in all public areas, including education. This proximity between the Bavarian legislator and the Catholic Church enabled a free room for the religious headship to control the formation of the school system and influence its educational content. In that sense, Bavaria's political and religious headships were unanimous in their perception that the Catholic Church shares responsibility with respect to the educative task. This was held to foster the Christian social fabric, especially through the public school system, and strengthen the bond of the pupils with Christian tradition and values.

In addition, the influence of the church on education was so profound that in the past teachers were affected in admittance to the public school system if they could not establish personal conviction and professional knowledge in Christianity. This harsh intervention teachers had to incur with respect to their professional qualification was a requirement the Bavarian state practiced for many years. The former Art. 135 BayVerf stated that children should be educated in accordance with the principles of the Christian belief. Consequently, it was a common practice for years that teachers were requested by the Bavarian state to sign a declaration that they are willing and able to teach in accordance with the Christian fundaments and tenets of belief.[802] Teachers were not only confined in their freedom of profession as they were required to demonstrate knowledge in tenets of the Christian faith, but their right to religious freedom was also violated. Due to this strong religious piety of the Bavarian people and to the close entanglement between state and church, it was not surprising that the *Crucifix* case reached high resonance and large amount of criticism, especially in the Bavarian state. The severity in which Bavarians perceived the impact of the *Crucifix* decision was reflected in the harsh responses pronounced by the headship of the politics and the Catholic Church. Nonetheless, the significance of the *Crucifix* decision is also attributed to several amendments it induced in salient education enactments and public school regulations. These amendments attempted to introduce a milder approach towards endorsement of religious symbols like the cross in state school rooms, which is to be achieved through a compromising settlement agreed on by all parties in case an objection was raised (Art. 7 para 4 BayEUG).

In contrast to the display of the cross in public classrooms, the Bavarian legislator was more critical with respect to manifestation of political or religious symbols when worn by teachers as it allegedly attempted to insert an all-inclusive ban that will apply equally to all teachers (Art. 59 BayEUG). In fact, this amendment suffered criticism[803] as it was contended that the Bavarian legislator tacitly still favours the predominant faith, Christianity, while indirectly discriminates against other faiths such as Islam, and thereupon the right of Muslim teachers to appear in school premises with a headscarf.

To sum up, the legal situation in Bavaria raises the assumption that it is less plausible that constitutional complaints for removal of the cross in less religious states than Bavaria, as an extreme example of a highly Catholic state, are likely to occur. Should they occur at all, then the question remains whether the display of a cross in public schools would induce in other federal states the same impact it has reached in Bavaria. The answer cannot be conclusive, mainly due to divergence in constitutional and legislative layout which differs from one individual state to the other. Religious diversity, various composition of the population, and demographic dispersal which differs in each federal state are only partial factors that need to be taken into account when trying to assess how similar challenges are to be resolved on the regional level.

---

802 *Czermak*, in FS Rüfner (2003), 79, 98.

803 *Langenfeld/Mohsen*, p. 91; See also *Heinig*, Religionsfreiheit oder Neutralitätsgebot? in http://www.bpb.de/politik/innenpolitik/konfliktstoff-kopftuch/63259/einstieg-in-die-debatte

cc) Berlin

In this comparison, the state of Berlin is found at the other side of the scale with respect to its state-church affairs. It governs among all other federal states a rather laicist approach which underscores the obligation of the state to abide by the principle of neutrality. This approach of strict neutrality is a salient characteristic of Berlin and had embossed its legislative and political order.

The political order that was mostly prominent in the state of Berlin was influenced mainly by diverse conciliations made between social parliamentary parties (SPD, PDS, FDP, Bündnis 90 – Die Grünen). Their policy was mandated by a strong socialist influence characterized by religious alienation/antagonism. Thence, the political headship in Berlin attempted to banish any role of religiosity in the public sphere in fostering the strict apprehension of state neutrality as enshrined in various provisions of the Grundgesetz (e.g., no established church precept prescribed in Art. 137 para 1 WRV). Under this legal doctrine, the state of Berlin sought to entangle any institutional cooperation with religious communities and a denial of their influence or endorsement of any religious affairs into its state school system.

This political authoritative status in Berlin brought about educational reforms to fierce religious-political conflicts in public debate.[804] As will be demonstrated next, the legislative headship in Berlin endeavoured to temper the power of religious organizations or ideological groups, especially with regard to endorsement of religion-related themes into its school system. The doctrine to adopt a rather secular model in the public school system was explicitly pronounced in a resolution of the SPD in Berlin as was encountered in 2005 with respect to endorsement of Ethic instead of religious instructions as an obligatory ordinary subject in schools' curricula.[805] The strife over introduction of ethic lessons as a substitute for the common practice of religious instructions (Art. 7 para 3 GG) that prevail in most of the federal states demonstrates incontestably the strong will to

---

804 For instance, the amendment made to the SchulG-Berlin from 26 January, 2004 replaced the old Art. 12 para 6 through Art.V and introduced Ethic instruction as an obligatory regular subject in state schools curricula coming into force on 11 July, 2006.

805 Landesparteitag der Berliner SPD, Bildungschancen, 3. „Die schulische Aufgabe einer Wertevermittlung darf nicht an Weltanschauungs- und Religionsgemeinschaften delegiert werden. Ein bekenntnisgebundener Religions- oder Weltanschauungsunterricht kann ein allgemein bildendes Schulfach nicht ersetzen." See *Reuter/Kippenberg*, Religionskonflikte im Verfassungsstaat, 2010, p. 250.

preserve the secular character of its schools and segregates it from the latter.[806] The same approach guided the Berliner legislator when deciding to explicitly forbid the manifestation of religious symbols with respect to public servants (including teachers). Consequently, in the state of Berlin, secular state schools constitute the preferred form of school and, as a practical matter, follow a non-religious curriculum.[807]

(1) Legal Framework

The legal situation in the state of Berlin regarding the formation of the educational system and the nexus made between religion and schools differs considerably from that practiced in other federal states. The reason for that lies in the rather extensive scope of freedom it obtains with respect to its educative task which enabled it – as the first single federal state – to regulate all aspects of religion in state schools through enactment of regular laws, as these are not prescribed in the constitution of Berlin (BlnLV).[808]

This inimitable situation in Berlin can be further attributed to its rather liberal, open-minded approach towards religion that was mainly the outcome of a remote entanglement with the church, imprinted in the history of Berlin and the former GDR. It is due to this approach that the state of Berlin is viewed in many aspects as a pathfinder in contrast to other federal states. Whereas others encountered constitutional hurdles, the state of Berlin was able by virtue of its unique legislative situation, denoted earlier, to overcome through creative solutions conflicts relating to endorsement of religion in state schools.[809]

(a) Constitutional Law of Berlin (BlnLV)

The constitutional layout in Berlin is outstanding in its approach as the legislative method adopted for regulating its educational system differs considerably from that practiced in other federal states compared in this analysis. In comparison

---

806 These pronouncements released to the public by the prevailing political headship in Berlin impart the impression that the intention of the Berliner legislator was to gradually outcast any religious influence in state schools. See in that context pronouncements of Michael Müller, the chairman of SPD, and PDS parliament member, Carola Freundl, as cited in *Reuter/Kippenberg*, p. 238, 239. Frankfurter Allgemeine Zeitung, 19.3.2005; Berliner Zeitung 9.3.2005.

807 *Kommers/Miller*, p. 471.

808 *Reuter/Kippenberg*, p. 237.

809 *Reuter/Kippenberg*, pp. 235, 237.

to other federal states, the general prescription relating to issues of organization and formation of the school system, determination of the character and nature of state schools, and the competency of the state regarding religious influence in the education is simply not prescribed in the constitution.

The installation made in BlnLV is very interesting as aspects relating to the role of religion in the education remains outcast from the constitutional protection granted to educational institutions. This means that the scope of protection of emanating rights will be aligned with those of regular laws. The constitution makes this installation possible through a reference made in one of its stipulations (Art. 29 BlnLV) to the respective relevant legislation.

In that sense, the constitution only establishes and reaffirms the existence of eminent fundamental rights. The right to religious freedom is set out in Art. 29 para 1 BlnLV which declares that freedom of belief, conscience, as well as the freedom of confessional creeds remains unconfined. The practice of religious freedom will remain undisturbed. The second part prohibits any form of religious hatred or discrimination and makes it subject to a penalty in case of occurrence (Art. 29 para 2 BlnLV).

(b) Federal Law of Berlin

As mentioned earlier, Berlin is the single federal state that regulates its education system as well as aspects relating to integration of religion in state schools in regular state laws. Thus, the strong bond made between the constitutional percept (Art. 29 BlnLV) and the relevant school enactment confers the state more flexibility in formation of its schools and, consequently, makes designation of the essential provisions in the law almost indispensable.

The state of Berlin was among the eight federal states that deliberated on possible modifications to their school regulations in the aftermath of the decision delivered in *Ludin*'s case. It aimed to stipulate the prohibition of any religious expression made through outwardly appearance of teachers in the public service. However, even in a secular, liberal state like Berlin the promotion for such explicit enactment was not approved without implications in the land's parliament. The view in the parliament of Berlin was not unanimous as to creation of a legislation that would ban the wearing of a headscarf in the civil service. The major renouncement to the promulgation of the law was taken by the then governing (*beteiligt*) party, the PDS.[810] In contrast, the CDU party anticipated

810 Inner debate of the PDS party in the parliament of Berlin with respect to the 'headscarf ban in the civil service' Tagesspiegel, vom 26. September, 2004.

to bypass a law that would prohibit all officials in the public service of Berlin to refrain from wearing the headscarf while on duty.[811] A final approval of the Berliner lawmaker to the draft law was submitted on 27 January 2005.[812] So in practice, till *Ludin*'s case no legislative prohibition with respect to teachers or other public official to refrain from religious expression was at hand.[813]

The prohibition on civil servants to appear with religious symbols or garments while on duty is confined in the state of Berlin merely with respect to three fields: police, judiciary, and education, with some exceptions to be outlined next.

The reason for emphasizing the need to maintain the secular character of the state specifically with respect to those fields of public law were expounded already in the preamble of the law, known as the law relating to Art. 29 BlnLV (des Gesetzes zu Art. 29 BlnLV).

(aa) The Law Relating to Art. 29 BlnLV

The preamble underscores the significance of public officials to refrain from disclosure of religious affinity or pertinence to ideological creed. This emanates from their special duty and within the relations as representatives of the state that obliges them to adhere to the precept of religious neutrality.[814]

(aaa) The General Ban

The ban on public law servants to refrain from wearing ostentatious religious symbols when on duty is set out already in the first provision of the law. Thence, Sec. 1 to the law relating to Art. 29 BlnLV declares that:

Public servants on duty that work within the field of justice administration, penal law enforcement or police are not allowed to wear any visible religious or

811 Abgh. Bln, Drs. 15/2122 from 22.10.2003 and the planner protocol 15/37 from 30.10.2003.

812 A legislation for creation of enactment relating to Art. 29 of the Berlin constitution from 17.1.2005. Abgh. Berlin, Drs.15/3249; Bln GVBl. from 8.2.2005, p. 92.

813 The wearing of religious symbols through pupils was tolerated in the state of Berlin insofar they did not inflict the regular course of study. See in *Wiese*, p. 26.

814 „Alle Beschäftigten genießen Glaubens-und Gewissensfreiheit und die Freiheit des religiösen und weltanschaulichen Bekenntnisses. Keine Beschäftigte und kein Beschäftigter darf wegen ihres oder seines weltanschaulichen Bekenntnisses diskriminiert werden. Gleichzeitig ist das Land Berlin zu weltanschaulich-religiöser Neutralität verpflichtet. Deshalb müssen sich Beschäftigte des Landes Berlin in den Bereichen, in denen die Bürgerin oder der Bürger in besonderer Weise dem staatlichen Einfluss unterworfen ist, in ihrem religiösen oder weltanschaulichen Bekenntnis zurückhalten."

ideological symbols that signal to the spectator an affiliation to a specific religious or ideological group and any noticeably religious or ideologically imbued garments. In the area of justice administration this only applies to public servants that exercise governmental functions.[815] Noteworthy, the prohibition will apply also with respect to public servants within the field of justice administration, penal law enforcement or police that are in training or qualification period.[816]

The second provision stipulates explicitly the dress codes of teachers in public schools. In this context, it is worth to note that already in 1998 voices inside the land's parliament of Berlin held critical approach relating to the appearance of Muslim teachers with headscarf in schools.[817] Sec. 2 of the law relating to Art. 29 BlnLV determines that teachers in public schools are not allowed to appear with conspicuous symbols, signs, or garments that express a religious or ideological creed during school time; the demonstration of pertinence to a particular religion or ideological creed will also be forbidden. The provision reads as follows:

Teachers and other employees with pedagogical tasks on duty at public schools according to the public school act are not allowed to wear any visible religious or ideological symbols that signal to the spectator an affiliation to a specific religious or ideological community and any noticeably religious or ideologically imbued garments. This does not apply to religious or ideological instruction at school.[818]

---

815 Sec. 1 des Gesetzes zu Art. 29 BlnLV: „Beamtinnen und Beamte, die im Bereich der Rechtspflege, des Justizvollzugs oder der Polizei beschäftigt sind, dürfen innerhalb des Dienstes keine sichtbaren religiösen oder weltanschaulichen Symbole, die für die Betrachterin oder den Betrachter eine Zugehörigkeit zu einer bestimmten Religions- oder Weltanschauungsgemeinschaft demonstrieren, und keine auffallenden religiös oder weltanschaulich geprägten Kleidungsstücke tragen. Dies gilt im Bereich der Rechtspflege nur für Beamtinnen und Beamte, die hoheitlich tätig sind".

816 Sec. 5 Art. 29 BlnLV.

817 The then minister of education, Ingrid Stahmer, stated her resentment towards employment of teachers with a headscarf, see, *Wiese*, p. 26.

818 Sec. 2 of the Law concerning Article 29 BlnLV determines: „Lehrkräfte und andere Beschäftigte mit pädagogischem Auftrag in den öffentlichen Schulen nach dem Schulgesetz dürfen innerhalb des Dienstes keine sichtbaren religiösen oder weltanschaulichen Symbole, die für die Betrachterin oder den Betrachter eine Zugehörigkeit zu einer bestimmten Religions- oder Weltanschauungsgemeinschaft demonstrieren, und keine auffallenden religiös oder weltanschaulich geprägten

Intelligibly, the headscarf of the Muslim teacher may be conceived as an entrenched religious symbol and, as a result, fall within the scope of Sec. 2 of the law relating to Art. 29 BlnLV. The outcome will undoubtedly result in disadvantageous treatment of a Muslim teacher with a headscarf in comparison to the rest of the teaching staff. Nevertheless, it is more than certain that such a situation will not be regarded applicable as the wording of Art. 2 of the Act explicitly does not permit unequal treatment.

The wording of Art. 2 of the Berliner Act does not include prohibition of political/ideological symbols. In that sense, it differs from bans adopted in educational laws of other federal states[819] as it only applies to entrenched religious symbols and does not include prohibition with respect to political symbols. Under this aspect, it will be interesting to examine whether the constitutional legitimacy of a teacher to wear a headscarf in public state schools would be permitted according to the intention of the Berliner legislator as the headscarf may not be perceived solely under its religious context but can also fall within the category of a political symbol.

Finally, the Berliner Act applies equally to all religions and does not make any exception with respect to Christian religious symbols or garments, so in that sense there is no preferential treatment of Christianity over other religions or creeds.

(bbb) Exceptions to the General Ban

The general prohibition on teachers to wear ostentatious religious symbols during school time (Sec. 3 of the Act to Art. 29 BlnLV) includes several exceptions outlined as follows:

1. The prohibition will not apply with respect to professional schools and institutions of higher education. (Sec. 3 of the Act to Art. 29 BlnLV). Other school forms or schools of specific educational task may be granted an exception from the higher educational authority.
2. For teachers in preparatory service or training an exception with respect to the prohibition of appearance with religious garments or symbols made under Sec. 2 of the Act to Art. 29 BlnLV may also be admissible (Sec. 4 of the Act to Art. 29 BlnLV).

Kleidungsstücke tragen. Dies gilt nicht für die Erteilung von Religions- und Weltanschauungsunterricht."

819 Sec. 38 para 2 Baden-Württemberg SchG; Art. 57 para 4 NRW SchulG.

(bb) The School Act of Berlin (Schulgesetz für das Land Berlin -SchulG)[820]

In general, the content and spirit of the Schulgesetz-Berlin (SchulG-Berlin) are to a considerable extent formulated such as to preserve the secular nature of the state. This was demonstrated eminently already in Sec. 1 of the SchulG-Berlin which defines the educative mandate of the state. Although the provision specifically takes care to include Christianity (Sec. 1 para 9 SchulG-Berlin) as an integral part of the educational objectives aiming to form the personality of the pupils, it was not intended to emphasize the religious context. It rather aimed at a different context by implying the significance to convey pupils with cultural values rooted in the Christian faith, such as brotherly love, freedom, democracy, and humanism.[821]

Moreover, Sec. 3 SchulG-Berlin, which defines the educational goals, unlike other federal states does not specify that pupils are to be taught in accordance with the tenets of Christianity. It prescribes other objectives, such as gender equality, mutual tolerance towards other religions and cultures, human dignity, and peaceful co-existence of all mankind.

In addition, another attempt to preserve the secular nature of its school system is found in Sec. 12 para 6 SchulG-Berlin. Its endorsement followed political initiative in the land's parliament to substitute the common religious instructions mandated in compulsory schools and to provide an alternative to pupils and parents who wish to opt for a religiously neutral environment in public schools. This was to be achieved through implementation of ethic lessons comprising a more liberal content, such as general principles of morality, liberties and freedoms of individuals, and ideals of humanism rooted in the development of European enlightenment. Thence, even the constitutional privilege granted to religious communities to establish and administer religious instructions for their member pupils in state schools, prescribed in Art. 7 para 3 GG, does not apply with respect to the state of Berlin.[822] Instead, Art. 12 para 6 stipulates the

820 The SchulG-Berlin from 26.1.2004 was lastly amended on 26 June, 2013, GVBl. Berlin 2013, p. 199.

821 See Sec. 1 SchulG-Berlin Auftrag der Schule http://www.schulgesetz-berlin.de/berlin/schulgesetz/teil-i-auftrag-der-schule-und-recht-auf-bildung-und-erziehung-anwendungsbereich/sect-1-auftrag-der-schule.php

822 The states Berlin and Bremen are exempted from application of Art. 7 para 3 GG according to a provision contained in Art. 141 of the Grundgesetz; *Häußler*, European Journal of Migration and Law, 2001, Volume 3, ¾, 457, 464.

endorsement of ethic instruction as a mandatory subject in state schools curricula (from 7th to 10th grade).

(2) Conclusion - Berlin

There is no doubt that the state of Berlin is distinguishable in comparison to other federal states. This is not only due to the secular approach it administers in its state-church affairs but also due to the constitutional and legislative layout chosen for admission of religiosity and closely related themes into its public sphere. The wish to separate co-operation between state and religion is the result of strong alienation to churchly influences, which was not a rarity in the political history of Berlin. This approach of strict separation was dominating among the governing parties and shaped the distinctiveness of the state. It was even more unusual especially since Germany as a nation has never adopted a strict secularised approach.

This attempt to expel any religious influence whatsoever from the public sphere found its base in legislative enactment that was induced in Berlin as well as in other federal states following the delivery of *Ludin*'s judgement. The ban on manifestation of religious symbols incumbent on public servants is rather astonishing in its strictness and absoluteness since it enables the state to infringe outright upon a fundamental constitutional right, that is, the right of a teacher to observe her religion without the need to invoke legitimate grounds for such restriction. Indeed, the right to religious freedom is warranted in Art. 29 of the BlnLV. However, it is clear that an inclusive ban on religious expression in the state school system runs counter to the constitutional protection provided in the Grundgesetz. Given this background, it is overwhelming that implementation of religious related themes, especially in the context of the educational system where the task of the state to enable religion to play a certain role in public life is inherently assumed, are deemed to be completely banished. In addition, the reference made in Art. 29 BlnLV to the relevant enactment, stipulating a prohibition on teaching staff and employees with pedagogical task in compulsory schools indicates a lacking sufficient mechanism chosen for the safeguarding of religious rights.

In this context, the characteristics underlining the distinctiveness of Berlin can be summarized as follows: first, the exclusive legislative competence in education matters conferred upon the states in the Grundgesetz (Art. 70) enabled the state of Berlin to enjoy an extensive scope of freedom with respect to the formation of its public school system including the integration of religion-related themes. This way, a reference made in a specific provision in Art. 29 BlnLV legitimized the task of the state to ordain those matters in regular enactment and not in the land's constitution as mandated by other federal states. Second, the administration and organization of the relations between state and church and emanating religious rights, especially in such controversial and significant fields like education, are not supported in equivalent (analogous) constitutional safeguards but are merely confined within the framework of regular enactment. This means that the risk of state interference in protected fundamental rights of an individual such as religious freedom and or emanating rights is potentially higher. The reason provided is that the state can restrict fundamental liberties only if they clash against other pre-eminent constitutional rights. In the case of Berlin, the invoked grounds for limitation by the state may be ample as not prescribed in the constitution but rather in regular enactments. By that, the state is not required to substantiate a high proof of standard for restriction since the scope of protection is equated with those stipulated in regular law, thence conferring upon the state a wide margin of discretion. In fact, the state of Berlin substantiates a legitimate ground for restriction primarily in the preamble to the Law relating to Art. 29 BlnLV. Its perception that civil servants in the public sphere are deprived of the right to personal manifestation of their religion is made subject to their obligation to abide by the neutrality principle of the state. Third, in Berlin there is a general all-inclusive ban on all office holders in the public service to appear with religious symbols while on duty. In that sense, the prohibition will not contravene against the equality precepts stipulated in the Grundgesetz (Art. 3 para 3 and 33 para 3) as the state does not identify itself with a particular religion or act detrimental to other denominations or faith.

It is rather astonishing that a recent case of the Labour Court in Berlin[823] declared the dismissal of a schoolteacher for wearing the Islamic headscarf as admissible and will not amount to its violation of her right to religious freedom. In addition, the Labour Court determined that its decision does not run counter to the BVerfG's decision from 2015. The Labour Court emphasized its segregation points:

First, an all-inclusive ban on religious symbols – the Labour Court reasoned the dismissal of the teacher's claim on ground of the equality principle in Berlin which prescribes an equal treatment with respect to all civil servants in public office. Therefore, the prohibition on religious symbols applies equally and includes all religions and faiths without beneficial treatment to one particular religion like the NRW SchulG NRW that privileged Christian and Jewish

823 Az.58 Ca 13376/159.

symbols. The general prohibition on appearance with religious garments to school does not amount to a violation of the teacher's constitutional right to religious freedom.

Second, the neutrality principle has a special importance in the state of Berlin especially with respect to officials in the public service that are under the duty to appear neutral and unbiased. Therefore, the BlNLV does not even violate against the AGG since it applies its prohibition equally for all civil servants and forbids the wearing of all religious symbols equally whether it is a Jewish Kippa, an Islamic headscarf, or a cross. The duty to religious neutrality applies equally with respect to all office holders in the public sphere and therefore the BlnLV does not discriminate explicitly against the teacher wearing an Islamic headscarf. Unlike the NRW SchulG NRW, the Education Act of Berlin prescribes the duty to religious neutrality equally and does not confer any privilege to Christian-Western tradition and values.

Third, the teacher could alternatively apply for a teaching post in vocational schools where the order for teachers to refrain from religious garments does not apply, since the pupils are of full legal age and are less likely to be influenced by a religious symbol worn by their teacher.

dd) *North Rhine-Westphalia*

The state of North Rhine-Westphalia (NRW) has a relatively short history and tradition as it was officially recognized as a member state of the confederation only in 1949. Traditionally, the dominating political coalitions in the land's parliament were established mainly out of an alliance between the SPD and the green party. This explains prominently the hesitance of the NRW lawmaker to introduce corresponding amendments similar to those taken by other federal states following the judgement delivered in *Ludin*'s case, prohibiting the appearance of teachers with a headscarf in state schools. It was therefore that during the SPD governance only deliberations with respect to a reformation in the existing school legislation took place. However, those deliberations did not bring about the desired modifications into a final enactment of a law.[824] The main argument brought by the then governing SPD for not taking rush actions to pass the law was reasoned by the low number of teachers with headscarves in the state of NRW which makes such legislation redundant under these circumstances.[825]

824 LT NRW, Drs. 13/4564.
825 SZ 18.3.2005.

Unsurprisingly, as soon as the change of power accrued in 2006 and the CDU took over governance, the introduction of the new enactment was not late to come.[826]

(1) Legal Framework

The fundaments of the legal framework establishing the relations between the church and the state within the public school system can be found in the Constitution of NRW and legislation of regular enactments. From a constitutional point of view, framers of the NRW constitution draw the distinctive composition of the constitution as deriving a special duty from its obligation to comply with the Grundgesetz, and therefore explicitly declaring it in Art. 4 para 1 as an integral part of the NRW constitution (LVerfNRW). This strong allegiance to the Grundgesetz and pre-eminent constitutional principles served framers of the NRW constitution as a guiding line in designation of stipulations and formation of its spirit as reflected in many provisions including those relating to education.

Legislation in the field of education was a long-time anachronism mainly spread in different enactments dating back to the 1960s. These old enactments were abolished, and a new reform, which was initiated by the then minister of education Ute Schäfer (SPD), was enacted. This is regarded as the most relevant and significant legislation in view of formation of schools and the educational system in general that was ever accomplished in NRW. The School Education Act (SchulG NRW) was promulgated and took effect on 15 February 2005.[827]

(a) Constitutional Law of North Rhine-Westphalia

The LVerfNRW acknowledges the relations between the state and religion when referring already in its preamble to the affinity of the state and its citizens to God.

(aa) Art. 7 LVerfNRW

The wording of the preamble together with the wording prescribed in Art. 7 para 1 LVerfNRW, declaring that fear of God is perceived as a primary educational goal indicate that the state of NRW does not assume that religious affiliation is solely a matter of the individual. It rather concludes an extensive obligation of the state to incorporate and transfer religious values also in the educational system.

---

826 Heims, Hans-Jörg: NRW plant Kopftuchverbot, in: SZ 26.10.2005.

827 GV. NRW. p. 102.

The legislator of the land NRW had implemented in the third part of its constitution provisions that were meant to regulate and administer the endorsement of religion in the state school system. Apparently, framers of the NRW constitution considered an extensive formulation which sought to comply with its obligation to state neutrality as prescribed in the Grundgesetz (Art. 137 para 1), and at the same time introduce and foster a cultural-educational frame conveying fundamental values of the Christian faith to pupils in state-supported schools. This notion had been in fact realized in the final draft of Art. 12 para 6 LVerfNRW and reflects the compromise which was finally achieved in 1968 following long debates in the land's parliament.[828]

The suggested versions with respect to this momentous provision were changed constantly, and, as a matter of fact, demonstrate the difficulty to achieve reconciliation between these allegedly two contradicting perceptions. Finally, within the controversial debate surrounding the phrasing of Art. 12 para 6 LVerfNRW it was decided to diverge from the initial formulation. This formulation raised by the Committee of Culture suggested including a framework that will establish the cultural-religious fundaments in state schools solely based on the Christian faith.[829] This motion had undergone a long way till it finally achieved approval in the version accepted on 21 February 1968.

Notably, the conclusive version from 1968 which is valid to this day ensued a proposal to dispel any association between national socialism and the exclusivity guaranteed to the Christian religion over the state school system.[830] It was for this reason that the final version of Art. 12 para 6 LVerfNRW adopted a compromised approach intertwining between conferment of Christian values (*christliche Bildungs- und Kulturwerte*) and acceptance of other religious or ideological denominations that will be integrated together in the public school system of the state of North Rhine-Westphalia.[831]

---

828 Art. 12 LVerfNRW was amended in an act from 25 October 2011 taking effect as of 29 October 2011. The Act stipulated modifications in Art. 12 of LVerfNRW so that Art. 12 para 6 in its original version became Art. 12 para 3. See in GV. NRW p. 499. https://recht.nrw.de/lmi/owa/br_vbl_detail_text?anw_nr=6&vd_id=12916&ver=8&val=1291

829 A draft of amendments made to the constitution of NRW from 20.6.1967, LT-Drs. 6/320.

830 This was raised by a member of the NRW parliament, Dr. Dr. Josef Hoffmann, as documented in the discussions protocol for amendments to the constitution of NRW from 5.3.1968.

831 The final version of Art. 12 para 6 was approved in a conjoined meeting of the cultural committee and was compiled in the discussions protocol for amendments to the constitution of NRW from 5.3.1968.

(bb) Art. 12 LVerfNRW

In 2011, Art. 12 LVerfNRW was amended in a series of a modifications made to the constitution through special enactment.[832] Among the amendments, the old Art. 12 para 6 LVerfNRW, though it did not incur any modification in content, was changed to Art. 12 para 3 LVerfNRW (hereinafter Art. 12 para 3). Art. 12 LVerfNRW outlines eminently the school system and the different types of schools. It further administers in Art. 12 para 3 the relations between religion and the educational system, and prescribes that public schools carry the task of transferring to the pupils Christian education and values. Moreover, it goes further and explains that the Christian fundaments must be taught with openness towards other religions and ideological creed. The explicit wording in Art. 12 para 3 LVerfNRW prescribes that:

> Community (interdenominational) schools shall teach and educate children on the basis of Christian educational and cultural values and shall be open to Christian denominations and to other religions and ideological convictions. Denominational (confessional) schools shall teach and educate children of Catholic and Protestant faith or of any other religious community in accordance with the principles of the denominations concerned. Ideological schools, including non-denominational (secular) schools, shall teach and educate children in accordance with the principles of the ideology concerned.[833]

This defined characteristic of the state to decide on the formation of public schools enables the state of NRW to determine their establishment on the fundaments of Christianity. Yet, this freedom of the federal state with respect to its educational task does not necessarily contravene its obligation to religious neutrality as prescribed in the Grundgesetz.[834]

---

832 See in https://recht.nrw.de/lmi/owa/br_vbl_detail_text?anw_nr=6&vd_id=12916&ver=8&val=1291

833 „In Gemeinschaftsschulen werden Kinder auf der Grundlage christlicher Bildungs- und Kulturwerte in Offenheit für die christlichen Bekenntnisse und für andere religiösen und weltanschaulichen Überzeugungen gemeinsam unterrichtet und erzogen. In Bekenntnisschule werden Kinder des katholischen oder des evangelischen Glaubens oder einer anderen Religionsgemeinschaft nach den Grundsätzen des betreffenden Bekenntnisses unterrichtet und erzogen. In Weltanschauungsschulen, zu denen auch die bekenntnisfreien Schulen gehören, werden die Kinder nach den Grundsätzen der betreffenden Weltanschauung unterrichtet und erzogen". http://www.landtag.nrw.de/portal/WWW/GB_II/II.2/Gesetze/Verfassung_NRW.jsp

834 BVerfGE 41, 88, 108= NJW 1976, 952; *Dietlein,* in: FS Stern (1997), 443, 450.

The inherent right of parents to decide on the education of their children is depicted as an essential fundament for the organization and formation of the school system (Art. 8 para 1 and Art. 10 para 2 LVerfNRW).

(cc) Art. 14 LVerfNRW

Art. 14 para 1 LVerfNRW determines that, except for secular schools (*bekenntnisfreie Schulen*), religious instructions will constitute a mandatory subject in state schools' curricula. It further establishes the right of churches and religious communities to authorise the teacher personnel for religious instructions (Art. 14 para 1 LVerfNRW), decide on the course of instructions and the content of textbooks (Art. 14 para 2 LVerfNRW), as well as conferment of the right to conduct religious worship in state schools (Art. 20 LVerfNRW).

According to Art. 12 para 6 LVerfNRW, it is likely that affixation of the Crucifix in classrooms of public schools will not be regarded as an infringement of pupils' right to religious freedom. The display of a crucifix in a classroom may derive its eligibility from the stipulation in the NRW constitution, (Art. 12 para 6 LVerfNRW), prescribing that pupils should be conveyed with the values of the Christian tradition. In addition, it may support itself on the constitutional right of parents to decide on the education of their children (Art. 6 para 2 GG). In this respect, it will be advisable to recognize whether presentation of the cross is a state act, a form of social custom entrenched in the society, or rather an act of parental cooperation with school authorities as prescribed under Art. 10 para 2 LVerfNRW.

(b) Federal Law of North Rhine-Westphalia/The School Act of North Rhine-Westphalia

In practice, the situation in NRW until 2003 was that teachers were allowed to wear headscarf while on duty without the risk that any disciplinary measures or a general all-inclusive ban will be imposed on them by the land's legislator.[835]

However, the legal situation changed as the delivery of the *Ludin*'s judgement engendered the federal states to a reformation of their respective School Education Act or Civil Service Law. The state of NRW was among those states which rushed to introduce a reformation that aimed to ban teachers from wearing ostentatious religious garments or symbols while on school premises.[836]

---

835 *Wiese*, p. 27.

836 LT Drucks 14/569, pp. 7.

(aa) Enactment and Development of Schulordnungsgesetz NRW/The Ban of Individual Religious Symbols

The most important enactment in the sphere of public education is the comprehensive SchulG NRW of NRW known as *das Schulordnungsgesetz NRW* (SchulG NRW) from 15 February 2005.[837] The SchulG NRW was meant to conjoin all aspects surrounding the framework and establishment of the school system in NRW under a single comprehensive legislation, as those till its promulgation were dispersed in several different long-standing enactments.[838] In that sense, the SchulG NRW is the most cohesive legislative enactment ever delineated in NRW in the field of education. It is, therefore, not only confined to designate solely the school structure, that is, nature and school types to be established in NRW; it also ordains the task of schools, parents, pupils and teachers, administers the relations among all involved parties, sets out the general framework of its state schools and, not less important, it settles the endorsement of religion in schools and cooperation with religious communities for the purpose thereof. The SchulG NRW had undergone several changes since its original version so that new revisions were gradually implemented into it over the last years.[839] Still, the most notable amendment made to the SchulG NRW can be ascribed to the stipulation of the prohibition on teachers' outward appearance that can demonstrate in a public school their political, religious, or ideological affinity as it was initially prescribed in the former Art. 57 para 4 of the SchulG NRW.[840] However, the NRW legislator amended and modified the prohibition clause in order to reflect the prerequisites that have been specified by the BVerfG in its latest headscarf

837 GV. NRW. p. 102. See http://www.schulministerium.nrw.de/BP/Schulrecht/Gesetze/Schulgesetz.pdf

838 The main old enactments in the field of education were: The School Ordinance from 1952 (Das Schulordnungsgesetz), The Schulmitwirkungsgesetz 1977, and the Allgemeine Schulordnung Regulations 1978.

839 The latest revision made to the SchulG took effect as of 1 August 2015. See in GVBl. P. 499. https://recht.nrw.de/lmi/owa/br_vbl_detail_text?anw_nr=6&vd_id=15105&ver=8&val=15105&sg=0&menu=1&vd_back=NGV.

840 This was the first amendment made to the SchulG taking effect from 13 June 2006, GVBl. p. 270. See in https://recht.nrw.de/lmi/owa/br_vbl_detail_text?anw_nr=6&vd_id=1363&ver=8&val=1363&sg=0&menu=1&vd_back=N

decision in this regard.[841] The new clause is to be found in Art. 2 para 8 of the SchulG NRW.[842]

The SchulG NRW prescribes already in its outset that school authorities will need to take into consideration the right of the parents to decide on the education of their children, and that both school authorities and parents will cooperate with respect to the educative task (Art. 1 para 2 and Art. 2 para 3 SchulG NRW).[843]

In principle, the NRW legislator recognizes and respects to a large extent the parental right and, consequently, it has introduced in many provisions in the SchulG NRW the parents' right to be involved (*Mitwirkung*) and decide on the character and form of their elementary schools.[844] Notably, the right of pupils belonging to a religious minority was also taken into account in the sense that Art. 26 para 5 SchulG NRW enables them to attend another neighbouring school if the desired form of school is not available in their local community.

In addition, the SchulG NRW regulates the relations between religion and the educational system, and this actually finds expression in several provisions in the SchulG NRW. The inimitable bond between religion and the educative system is found in Art. 2 para 1 and 2 SchulG NRW, similar to its counterpart in the LVerfNRW (Art. 7 para 1) which declares the same educational goals (the conveyance of values like fear of God) to be fulfilled by school authorities. In addition, Art. 26 para 2 SchulG NRW stipulates that pupils in interdenominational schools in NRW will be taught in accordance with the principles of the Christian belief and with openness towards other religions.[845] A similar provision forming the entanglement between religion and education can be found in the NRW

841 Art. 57 para 4 SchulG NRW has been abolished with effect from 25 June 2015, following the decision of the BVerfG on 27 January 2015 that declared the respective prohibition to display and wear religious symbols as unconstitutional. GV. NRW. 2015. p. 479. https://recht.nrw.de/lmi/owa/br_vbl_detail_text?anw_nr=6&vd_id=15056&ver=8&val=15056&sg=0&menu=1&vd_back=N

842 https://www.schulministerium.nrw.de/docs/Recht/Schulrecht/Schulgesetz/Schulgesetz.pdf

843 The SchulG NRW 2012 provides in Sec. 2 para 3: „*Die Schule achtet das Erziehungsrecht der Eltern. Schule und Eltern wirken bei der Verwirklichung der Bildungs- und Erziehungsziele partnerschaftlich zusammen.*" *See* http://www.schulministerium.nrw.de/BP/Schulrecht/Gesetze/Schulgesetz.pdf

844 Art. 1 para 2, Art. 26 para 5, Art. 42 para 4, Art. 44 para 1 and 3, Art. 27 para 1 and X of the School Act (SGV. NRW. 223). Art. 28 para 1 prescribes the right of the majority of parents to apply for a secondary school (Hauptschule) to become of a confessional character.

845 The counterpart of Art. 26 para 2 of the SchulG NRW Act is Art. 12 para 3 of the LVerfNRW.

constitution, where a specific prescription orders the mandatory exercise of religious instructions in all state schools with the exception of non-denominational schools (Art. 31 para 1 LVerfNRW). The rest of Art. 31 LVerfNRW appoints the right of religious communities to decide jointly on the content and course of study conveyed in religious instructions, to authorise qualified teachers for this purpose, and to conduct inspection during the practice thereof (Art. 31 para 1, 3, and 5 LVerfNRW). The exemption from religious instruction is binding upon explicit request of the pupils or their parents (Art. 31 para 6 LVerfNRW).

The significance attached to the SchulG NRW with regard to the permissibility of teachers to appear with ostentatious religious symbols to school was the intention to introduce an ordinance imposing a duty on teachers to respect dress code in state schools in the retrospect of the *Ludin*'s judgement. The NRW legislator took action in the aftermath of the *Ludin*'s case and imposed a general prohibition on teachers in public schools to appear with religious symbols as was set out in the former Art. 57 para 4 SchulG NRW.[846] It should be noted that at that time the SchulG of NRW and similar acts introduced by the other eight federal states were generally drafted in such a way so as not to raise the impression that the real intention was specifically directed to deny the Islamic headscarf.[847]

(bb) Ban on Individual Religious Symbols Following the Headscarf Decision of the BVerfG (27.1.15)

Given the recent BVerfG judgement declaring the general ban on a headscarf to be unconstitutional, a comparison between the legislative stipulations is necessary in order to allocate whether the amendments incurred by the NRW legislator fully comply with the constitutional prerequisites set out by the BVerfG. In addition, it could serve as a yardstick for assessing Art. 2 para 8 SchulG NRW, especially in segregation with the abolished Art. 57 para 4 and the extent to which it created a significant effect on teachers' right to religious freedom. For this purpose, a comparison of the legislative phrasing will be set out. The former Sec. 57 para 4 NRW SchulG determines the following:

Teachers at public schools are not allowed to exercise political, religious, ideological or similar manifestations that may endanger or disturb the neutrality of the country towards pupils or parents or the political, religious or ideological peace of the school. Particularly illegitimate is a behaviour that can appear to pupils or parents to be a teacher's demonstration against human dignity, non-discrimination according to Article 3 [i.e., Grundgesetz], the rights of freedom

846 LT Drucks 14/569, pp. 8.
847 *McGoldrick*, p. 117.

and democratic order of the constitution. The exercise of the task of education according to Articles 7 para 6 and 12 para 6, LVerfNRW and the respective exhibition of Christian and occidental educational and cultural values or traditions does not contradict the duty of behaviour according to sentence 1. The duty of religious neutrality according to sentence 1 does not apply with respect to religious instructions taking place in faith and denominational schools.[848]

After this clause had been declared by the BVerfG as constitutionally invalid,[849] the NRW legislator phrased the respective prohibition in Sec. 2 para 8 SchulG NRW as follows:

The school enables and respects diverging opinions in the limits of the free democratic order of the constitution. Principals and teachers as well as employees pursuant to Sec. 58 execute their office impartially. At school they may not exercise political, religious, ideological, or similar manifestations that endanger or disturb the neutrality of the country towards pupils or parents or the political, religious, or ideological peace of the school. Particularly illegitimate is a behaviour of a principal, a teacher, or an employee pursuant to Sec. 58 that can appear to pupils or parents to be a demonstration against human dignity, non-discrimination according to Article 3, the rights of freedom, and democratic order of the constitution. Particularities of religious education and denominational schools remain unaffected.[850]

---

848 Sec. 57 para 4 Schulgesetz für das Land Nordrhein-Westfalen (SchulG NRW) determines:
„Lehrerinnen und Lehrer dürfen in der Schule keine politischen, religiösen, weltanschaulichen oder ähnliche äußere Bekundungen abgeben, die geeignet sind, die Neutralität des Landes gegenüber Schülerinnen und Schülern sowie Eltern oder den politischen, religiösen oder weltanschaulichen Schulfrieden zu gefährden oder zu stören. Insbesondere ist ein äußeres Verhalten unzulässig, welches bei Schülerinnen und Schülern oder den Eltern den Eindruck hervorrufen kann, das eine Lehrerin oder ein Lehrer gegen die Menschenwürde, die Gleichberechtigung nach Artikel 3 des Grundgesetzes, die Freiheitsgrundrechte oder die freiheitlich-demokratische Grundordnung auftritt. Die Wahrnehmung des Erziehungsauftrags nach Artikel 7 und 12 Absatz 6 der Verfassung des Landes Nordrhein-Westfalen und die entsprechende Darstellung christlicher und abendländlicher Bildungs- und Kulturwerte oder Traditionen widerspricht nicht dem Verhaltensgebot nach Satz 1. Das Neutralitätsgebot des Satzes 1 gilt nicht im Religionsunterricht und in den Bekenntnis- und Weltanschauungsschulen."

849 BVerfG 1 BvR 471/10, 1 BvR 1181/10 -; GV. NRW. 2015 S. 479.

850 Art. 2 para 8 SchulG NRW *stipulates: „Die Schule ermöglicht und respektiert im Rahmen der freiheitlich demokratischen Grundordnung unterschiedliche Auffassungen. Schulleiterinnen und Schulleiter, Lehrerinnen und Lehrer sowie Mitarbeiterinnen und Mitarbeiter gemäß § 58 nehmen ihre Aufgaben unparteilich wahr. Sie dürfen in der*

In sharp contrast to the general ban prescribed under the abolished Art. 57 para 4 SchulG NRW, the phrasing of Art. 2 para 8 NRW SchulG in its outset, declaring acknowledgement of and respect to all diverging opinions within the school realm, does not conflict with the wording of Art. 2 para 7 SchulG NRW which outlines the educational goals of schools. In the former, the prohibition on teachers to appear with ostentatious religious symbols in state classrooms created a potential tension point as it stood in conflict with the phrasing of Art. 2 para 7 SchulG NRW that set forth a general precept according to which schools should guarantee openness and tolerance towards different religions, ideological or political views. However, in the latter the initial guarantee of free exercise of religion and refrainment from insertion of a general ban on teachers to abstain from any religious manifestation creates a logical interlink in spirit and content to the general notion inscribed in Art. 2 para 7 SchulG NRW. In that sense, the NRW lawmaker wanted to ensure preference of tolerance and openness as leading guidelines to school authorities as opposed to creating tension and conflicts that are anyway more prevalent in state schools with diverging multicultural student body.

(cc) Limitation of Constitutional Provisions

The SchulG NRW determines that keeping conformity with the stipulations of this Act will necessitate the limitation of several constitutional provisions (Art. 125 SchulG NRW). The provision specifies that this may apply with respect to the right of a person to freedom and physical integrity as stipulated in Art. 2 para 2 GG. In that sense, there exists a presupposition that the personal right of a teacher to freely exercise her religious freedom should be set back if the negative right of pupils and parents to religious freedom is at stake.[851] The ground thereof is the perception that whereas the teacher entered her profession voluntarily, pupils are bound by the mandatory requirement of school attendance

Schule keine politischen, religiösen, weltanschaulichen oder ähnlichen Bekundungen abgeben, die die Neutralität des Landes gegenüber Schülerinnen und Schülern sowie Eltern oder den politischen, religiösen oder weltanschaulichen Schulfrieden gefährden oder stören. Insbesondere ist ein Verhalten unzulässig, welches bei Schülerinnen und Schü- lern oder den Eltern den Eindruck hervorruft, dass eine Schulleiterin oder ein Schulleiter, eine Lehrerin oder ein Lehrer oder eine Mitarbeiterin oder ein Mitarbeiter gemäß § 58 gegen die Menschenwürde, die Gleichberechtigung nach Artikel 3 des Grundgesetzes, die Freiheitsgrundrechte oder die freiheitlich-demokratische Grundordnung auftritt. Die Besonderheiten des Religionsunterrichts und der Bekenntnis- und Weltanschauungsschulen bleiben unberührt."

851 *Langenfeld/Mohsen*, 3 International Journal of Constitutional Law, 2005, 86, 92.

(Art. 34–41 SchulG NRW).[852] This leaves pupils no other alternative but to be confronted with the teacher's headscarf or religious donning and, as a result, will serve a legitimate aim for confinement of the teacher's right to religious freedom as declared in Art. 125 para 2 SchulG NRW. Furthermore, the inherent right of parents to decide on the education of their children as prescribed in Art. 6 para 2 GG may also constitute a legitimate ground for such limitation according to Art. 125 para 3 SchulG NRW.

(2) Conclusion - North Rhine-Westphalia

An overview of the constitutional and legislative layout designated in the state of NRW discloses that it is neither saliently religious in nature nor is it a supporter of the secular approach. Conceivably, framers of the NRW constitution did not consider the need to preserve the non-denominational character of the state in the sense that religious neutrality should be aligned with an absolute decline of any reference or conferment of religious or ideological values. This was reasoned by proponents of this approach asserting that the transfer of Christian values in state schools should enfold values of mutual respect and tolerance, acceptance of the other-minded, and promotion of gender equality. Taking this into account, the conveyance of Christian values in state schools should be legitimized even with respect to non-Christian participants in schools since it is to be perceived solely within its cultural-educative context. This view accentuates that Christianity founds the substantial elements for inter-relations between people of different origins, cultures, and faiths. Accordingly, the approach of the NRW lawmaker cannot be perceived as an identification of the state with a specific faith, that is, the Christian religion.

Therefore, the reference made in Art. 12 para 3 LVerfNRW to conferment of Christian values to pupils in compulsory state schools does not suggest a pure religious motive. The notion primarily dates back to the cultural-historical development of the European nations. The evolvement of the notion lies in the roots of the Christian religion and the perception that the foundations of human dignity and the respect of fundamental rights and religious liberties of others originate in Christianity.[853]

The precept in Art. 12 para 3 LVerfNRW, which ostensibly advances the Christian religion in mandatory community schools, does not connote an

---

852 *Heinig*, Beiträge zum ausländischen öffentlichen Recht und Völkerrecht 190, 181, 193.

853 BVerfGE 41, 29, 52 = NJW 1976, 947; BVerfG NJW 1995, 2477, 2480; *Dietlein* in FS Stern (1997), 443, 451.

identification or preference of Christianity over other religions. Rather, it rests on a two-fold notion: on the one hand, it obliges the state to fulfil its educative-pedagogical task as a matter subject to its sole competency (Art. 7 and 70 GG); this enables the state to introduce cultural-religious references into state schools. On the other hand, it obliges the state to comply with the neutrality principle as prescribed in the GG (Art. 170 para 1 WRV). Apparently, the inevitable tension between those two conflicting obligations of the state were overt to the framers of the NRW constitution; this consequently triggered long debates in NRW's parliament and eventually to the adoption of Art. 12 para 3 LVerfNRW in its final version. As a result, there is no exclusive guarantee of Christian values but rather a liberal approach advancing openness towards other religions and ideologies. However, this openness is founded on mutual respect and applies also with respect to the transfer of Christian values, tradition, and symbols.

In this context, the display of crosses in public school rooms is not compulsory in the state of NRW. If parents, pupils, and teachers reach consent and decide on affixation of a cross in the classroom, then the cross will not constitute a state act but will be regarded as derived from the free will of all involved parties as prescribed under Art. 10 para 2 LVerfNRW. This kind of cooperation between school authorities and parents endeavouring to achieve consensus with respect to presentation of religious symbols in classrooms provides parents with the opportunity to gain some influence on the nature of schools in which their children are taught (Art. 1 para 2 and Art. 2 para 3 SchulG NRW). Due to this rather midway approach chosen by the NRW legislator, it will be difficult to assess and clearly anticipate the respective decision of the BVerfG in case a constitutional challenge will be made by a pupil or a parent for the removal of the cross.

Notably, the BVerfG underscores that the display of a cross in public classroom walls poses an endangerment to the state's neutrality principle as this – as oppose to a Muslim teacher with a headscarf – is clearly an act made by the state which suggests that it advances a particular faith, Christianity, over other faiths or religions.[854] The teacher wearing a headscarf is to be perceived rather as an individual act that forms part of her personality and her freedom to express her religious identity; this act does not necessarily reflect an association of the state with a particular faith or religion and does not breach against the obligation of the state to religious neutrality.

The BVerfG acknowledges, however, that teachers bear a special duty emanating from their special status as civil servants; as such, their religious freedom

854 BVerfG 1 BvR 471/10 recital 94; BVerfGE 93, 1, 19.

should not prevail at all times. The right to religious freedom may be confined only in case an objection is raised by pupils or by parents, and if there is a concrete endangerment to either other constitutional fundamental freedoms or the principle of state neutrality.

Concerning the permissibility of a teacher to appear with a headscarf to school, there is a clear deviation from the old approach following *Ludin*'s case. Both cases demonstrate that the NRW legislator has attempted to implement necessary amendments in its inner educational law in the last years so as to ensure conformity with the constitution. Accordingly, the legislator's rapid initiatives to impose changes took place shortly after delivery of two significant judgements. The first phase, similarly to other federal states, which is the admissibility of public schoolteachers manifesting a religious behaviour by wearing ostentatious symbols was triggered by the NRW lawmaker as a response to the delivery of the *Ludin*'s judgement. The NRW legislator's following deliberations of necessary amendments introduced finally Art. 57 para 4 into its SchulG NRW. However, the second phase was induced following the recent NRW judgement delivered by the BVerfG, and was claimed to create a turnover in the judicial approach prevailing until that time. The following characteristics can be deduced from the decision of the BVerfG and were implemented accordingly by the NRW lawmaker in the new Art. 2 para 8 SchulG NRW:

No all-inclusive ban – at the outset, there is no all-inclusive ban on teachers appearing with a religious symbol or clothing while on duty. Following the recent judgement, this is no longer the case as a general prohibition on teachers to appear with a headscarf or other religious symbol will be regarded as unconstitutional.[855] Simply, such a clause is an expressed violation of the equality principle and the obligation to equal treatment in acceptance and admission in the public service (Art. 3 and 33 GG).

Abstract endangerment is not sufficient – the BVerfG deviates from the approach adopted in *Ludin*'s case accepting 'abstract' endangerment to the neutrality principle and other constitutional freedoms and values as sufficient for the confinement of a teacher's right to manifest her religious freedom. Teachers are allowed to appear with a religious symbol or clothing; however, the right to religious freedom of a teacher can be confined only when pupils or parents raise a claim that a concrete endangerment to state neutrality or other constitutional democratic values is given.[856] Nonetheless, the decision of the

855 BVerfG 1 BvR 471/10 recital 46.

856 BVerfG 1 BvR 471/10 recital 100 – 103, 112–115, 116, 117, 118.

BVerfG cannot withstand a critic point. The BVerfG did not provide sufficient guidelines as to what will be regarded as a religious symbol perceived to be contradictory to pre-eminent constitutional freedoms and values. In this respect, the interpretation of religious symbols and their effect on pupils remains a subjective matter that is left again to the sole discretion of school authorities. This runs the risk that school authorities may not act even-handedly, leaving an easy leeway for encroachment on teachers' right to religious freedom.

No privilege of the Christian faith – the BVerfG held that Art. 57 para 4 SchulG NRW in its formulation demonstrated a clear privilege of the Christian faith and tradition since Christian-related themes and content in the state school system were regarded as constitutional, permissible, and conforming with the educative mandate as explicitly declared in several provisions of the LVerfNRW (Art. 12 para 6). As a result, the BVerfG found that such an advancement of Christianity and Judaism due to their notional proximity to Western-occidental tradition and values is unconstitutional and breaches specifically against the equality provisions specified in the Grundgesetz that prohibit discrimination in access to the public office based on religious grounds (Art. 33 para 3 GG).[857] The BVerfG supports its decision by reference to its previous judgements and declares that the constitution comprehends "the state as a home place for all its citizens"[858] and must ensure equality to all that can be safeguarded through its duty to religious neutrality which obliges it to abstain from advancing or privileging a specific religion or faith and ostracism of other faiths and beliefs from its society. Therefore, the state should observe the precept of equality and treat all religions and faiths equally (Art. 3 GG).[859] The state is obliged to respect all religions and worldviews according to the equality precept and should refrain from identification with a particular religion.[860]

In addition, the ban on Islamic headscarf specifically infringes the religious right of Muslim women and is perceived as a constitutional breach of the right to gender equality as safeguarded in the constitution (Art. 3 para 2 GG).[861]

857 BVerfG 1BvR 471/10, recital 109.
858 BVerfG Urt. vom 14.12.1965 – 1 BvR 413, 416/60 = NJW 1966, 147.
859 BVerfGE 19, 206, 216; 24, 236, 246; 33, 23, 28; 93, 1, 17.
860 BVerfGE 30 415, 422; 93, 1, 17; 108, 282, 300.
861 BVerfG 1 BvR 471/10 recital 96.

Legitimate aim – the BVerfG explains that the limitation on the right to religious freedom can only be justified if that freedom is confined in order to safeguard another prominent constitutional right or values of a constitutional rank and prescribed in the constitution itself.[862] It recognizes the discretion of the NRW legislator to prescribe what will be regarded as a legitimate aim in its education enactment, and even regards the aims prescribed in the abolished Sec. 57 para 4 SchulG NRW to be legitimate. However, while the BVerfG regards the educational task of the state, the obligation of the state to religious neutrality, the parental educative right, and the negative right of pupils to religious freedom as legitimate aims for the purpose of avoiding conflicts in public schools, it refuses to accept the peaceful co-existence in school as a legitimate aim.[863] It provides that peaceful co-existence in itself is not an aim mentioned in the constitution but it may be achieved through the safeguarding of the aims explicitly outlined by the NRW lawmaker in order to prevent conflicts that may occur in the school realm from the outset.[864] It is only through safeguarding of the aims mentioned earlier and the tolerance precept that the state is able to ensure available and accessible public education to all of its citizens.[865]

The problematics raised when examining whether the interdiction on teachers to appear with religious symbols during school lessons is justified on a case-by-case basis runs the risk of an ease of encroachment upon highly ranked constitutional freedoms and values. Evaluation on a case-by-case basis may enable a marginal interference in the scope of the teacher's right to religious freedom. At the same time this means that the legal position of other, equally ranked constitutional freedoms like the negative right of pupils to religious freedom, the inherent right of parents to decide on the education of their children, and the precept of state neutrality is placed on a lower rank if one presuppose the ultimate right of the teacher to religious freedom. As a result, these highly ranked constitutional rights are placed at a disadvantage, as interference in the enjoyment of these rights will be always subject to an examination placing the burden of proof on the complainant. This in comparison to a definite order inscribed by

862 BVerfG 1 BvR 471/10 recital 98; BVerfGE 28, 243, 260; 41, 29, 50; 41, 88, 107; 44, 37, 49, 53; 52, 223 247; 93, 1, 21; 108, 282, 297.

863 BVerfG 1 BvR 471/10, recital.7.

864 BVerfG 1 BvR 471/10, recital 99.

865 LT Drucks 14/569, pp. 7.

law placing a prohibition on teachers to refrain at ouset from religious manifestation while on duty.

ee) Baden-Württemberg

The population in the state of Baden-Württemberg (BW) is divided between two pre-eminent religious communities: Protestant and Catholic. Unlike Bavaria, it is not a state which is predominantly Catholic; nevertheless, in most parts, it adheres to the Christian faith and keeps strong allegiance to its traditions and values.

Although there are similarities in the proximity of state-church relations between those two federal states, the differences are notable in the legislative and constitutional layout.

The endorsement of religious symbols in the educational system in BW became eminent due to the famous *Ludin*'s case.[866] This case constitutes a milestone in the German jurisprudence, as it was the first one to challenge a confrontation between the German state and Islam. Till *Ludin*'s case, the focus in judicial review of the courts was restricted to the permissibility of religious symbols, like the Islamic headscarf, when manifested in school realm by pupils. However, the legitimacy of a Muslim teacher to express her belief through wearing a headscarf was raised for the first time in *Ludin*'s case.[867] This case demonstrates to a considerable extent the reluctance of the BW legislator to endorse into its common school system religious symbols or garments that do not coincide with the Christian faith and Western-liberal traditions and values. In addition, it reflected the hardship, even in a salient Christian state like BW, to achieve unanimity in a land's parliament with respect to the headscarf ban. The political opinion diverged massively: whereas members of the governing party, CDU, welcomed the introduction of the ban, others, like the FDP or the Greens, were rather reluctant. The opposing parties suggested a case-by-case decision-making that would leave school authorities the sole discretion as a preferable solution to that of comprehensive ban.[868] The then minister of education, Annette Schavan, expounded in public that the decision of school authorities to expel a teacher from her duty due to a refusal to remove the headscarf was based on the plausibility

866 BVerfGE 108, 282. See in detail under III. 2 d) dd) (1) below.
867 *Mahrenholz* in FS Badura (2004), 749, 750.
868 *Wiese*, p. 28.

that her behaviour may influence members of her own religion or other faiths or creeds.[869]

(1) Legal Framework

The prevailing common practice regarding the permissibility of teachers and pupils in common public schools and higher educational institutions to manifest their religious adherence through wearing of religious garments, such as the headscarf and *chador,* was principally permitted till 2003. Nevertheless, school authorities were entitled to ban a Muslim teacher from appearing with a headscarf or *chador* in school premises if it was found to be necessary following due regard.[870]

In principle, the legislative layout administering the framework of public school system, regulating their educative task, and prescribing tasks and responsibilities that coincide with this educative mandate is embodied in the land's constitution. A detailed designation of dress code rules to teaching staff and admission of religious influence into state schools found legal anchorage in amendments made to federal legislation following the delivery of *Ludin*'s judgement.

(a) Constitutional Law of Baden-Württemberg

The state of Baden-Württemberg regulates the relations between the educational system and religion in detail in Chapter 3 of the constitution (BWVerf).[871] Reference is made to educational themes, such as designation of different types of school (Art. 15), the obligatory school participation (Art. 14 para 1), the parental right to determine the education of their children (Art. 15 para 3 and 17 para 4), and the character assigned to public schools.

The most significant constitutional provisions that regulate the nature and type of schooling and the nexus made between state schools to religious and spiritual influences are designated in Art. 12, 15, and 16 BWVerf.

Art. 12 para 1 BWVerf declares that the educative mandate of the state is to convey to pupils social and moral values including Christian brotherly love, respect of the other, brotherhood and peace, also with religious content such as the fear of God. Art. 12 para 2 BWVerf stipulates that the responsibility for the upbringing of the children is granted to parents, the state, and religious

---

869 See http;//www.bpb.de/themen/NNAABC,0,Konfliktstoff_Kopftuch.html. (20/9/2005); *Reuter/Kippenberg*, p. 379.

870 *Wiese*, p. 26.

871 http://www.lpb-bw.de/bwverf/bwverf.htm

communities. This provision clearly demonstrates that the state of BW did intend to incorporate religious influence in its state school system and, further, that it perceived the inimitable bond of parental educational right to decide with respect to the upbringing of their children.

Principally, Art. 15 para 1 BWVerf establishes that Christian interdenominational schools (elementary and secondary schools) will constitute the uniform type of public schools within the state.[872] Art. 16 para 1 BWVerf declares explicitly that the character of public schools is to be Christian in principle and that pupils will be taught and educated on the basis of Christian values and culture.[873] In addition, Art. 16 para 2 BWVerf prescribes that the appointment of teachers in public schools, if possible, will take into consideration the religion of the majority of pupils. Nevertheless, it is established under this clause that teachers of no faith will not be discriminated during an application process.[874]

Consequently, a significant contribution of the constitution is made in Art. 16 para 3 BWVerf suggesting the achievement of peaceful solutions to conflicts on a consensus base. The framers of the constitution anticipated an increase of conflicts that may arise against the background of an establishment of the Christian character in public schools. For this reason, they proposed a mechanism seeking a general consensus to be accepted by all involved parties: the state, relevant religious communities, parents, and teachers.

---

872 It was contended in the jurisprudence and in the legal literature that interdenominational schools are not to be regarded as missionary schools with the intent to enforce acceptance of Christianity as the only true faith and commitment to its tenets. It is rather the perception that this type of schools affirms Christianity in its formative cultural and educational influence on the German population and Western tradition. The reference is made to generally accepted values conferred by Christianity and prescribed in Art. 12 para 1 of the BWVerf, such as love and help to the poor, brotherhood of all mankind, fear of God, etc. See in this context: BVerfGE 41, 29, 31, 59= NJW 1976, 947; *Böckenförde*, NJW 2001, 723, 726; *Kommers/Miller*, p. 470; *Brugger/Karayanni*, pp. 61–62.

873 See http://www.lpb-bw.de/bwverf/bwverf.htm#Erziehung Art. 16 para 1 das BWVerf states that: „*In christlichen Gemeinschaftsschulen werden die Kinder auf der Grundlage christlicher und abendländischer Bildungs- und Kulturwerte erzogen. Der Unterricht wird mit Ausnahme des Religionsunterrichts gemeinsam erteilt.*"

874 Art. 16 para 2 das BWVerf states that: „*Bei der Bestellung der Lehrer an den Volksschulen ist auf das religiöse und weltanschauliche Bekenntnis der Schüler nach Möglichkeit Rücksicht zu nehmen. Bekenntnismäßig nicht gebundene Lehrer dürfen jedoch nicht benachteiligt werden.*"

(b) Federal Law of Baden-Württemberg/Baden-Württemberg School Education Act (SchG BW)

The school-related federal law in BW is comprehensively codified in the School Education Act (BW SchG).

In respect to admissibility of religious symbols, the legislator in BW implemented a ban following quickly after the delivery of the *Ludin*'s judgement. Obviously, the BW legislator identified the necessity to take immediate action in order to comply with the prerequisites that have been set up by the BVerwG and the BVerfG.

(aa) The Ban on Individual Religious Symbols

The motion to establish an explicit ban on symbols was triggered by the absence of a specific stipulation in the BW Civil Service Law (*Landesbeamtengesetz*) prescribing a dress code that prohibits the wearing of a headscarf for public schoolteachers. Since the BVerwG had found no legitimate ground to ban a Muslim teacher from appearing with a headscarf in compulsory state schools, it decided that in the absence of legislative prohibition the public administration lacks competency to enforce the ban. Under these circumstances it forwarded the issue back to the legislator of Baden-Württemberg to pass a suitable enactment.

Albeit the rapid steps initiated by the BW lawmaker to introduce the necessary amendment in present legislation, the final approval has not been delivered prior to controversial debate in the parliament. This accrued despite an initial rejection of a general ban by the FDP and resulted in a decline of their proposal that impermissibility of the garment in question should be considered only on a case-by-case basis.[875] Finally, the law known as the School Education Act of the state of Baden-Württemberg (das 'SchG BW') was passed in April 2004[876] and has been approved later by a decision of the BVerwG. Sec. 38 para 2 of the SchG BWSchG BW determines the following:

> Teachers at public schools are not allowed to exercise political, religious, ideological or similar manifestations that may endanger or disturb the neutrality of the country towards pupils or parents or the political, religious, or ideological peace of the school. Particularly illegitimate is a behaviour that can appear to pupils or parents to be a teacher's demonstration against human dignity, non-discrimination according to Article

---

875 Amendment draft from 27.1.2004 –LT BW, Drs. 13/2837.

876 The final version of the SchG BW from 1.4.2004 was published in GBl. Bad-Württ. p. 178, Nr.6; LT BW, Drs. 13/3091; The amendment draft of the land's parliament from 14.1.2004 can be traced in LT BW, Drs. 13/2793, 3: The plenary protocol in LT BW, PlenProt 13/67 from 1.4.2004.

> 3 [i.e., Grundgesetz], the rights of freedom and democratic order of the constitution. The exercise of the task of education according to Art. 12 Sec. 1, Article 15 Sec. 1, and Article 16 Sec. 1 of the constitution of the land of Baden-Württemberg and the respective exhibition of Christian and occidental educational and cultural values or traditions does not contradict the duty of behaviour according to sentence 1. The duty of religious neutrality according to sentence 1 does not apply within religious instruction according to Article 18 Sentence 1 of the constitution of the land of Baden-Württemberg.[877]

It is worth to note that the SchG BW extends its scope of application and prescribes implementation of the requirement specified in Art. 38 para 2 also with respect to applicants for teaching posts in the state of Baden-Württemberg (Sec. 38 para 3 SchG BW).[878]

The inclusion of a reservation clause – albeit the endorsement of a ban on public schoolteachers to appear with religious symbols while on duty, the BW lawmaker decided to implement a reservation clause in Sec. 38 para 2 SchG BW. The exception with respect to the ban on religious symbols as prescribed in the

---

877 The amendment to Sec. 38 of the Baden-Württemberg School Education took effect on 9.4.2004 through enactment from 1.4.2004. GBl. 2004, p. 178. Sec. 38 para 2 das Baden-Württemberg Schulgesetz sets out: „Lehrkräfte dürfen in der Schule keine politischen, religiösen, weltanschaulichen oder ähnliche äußeren Bekundungen abgeben, die geeignet sind, die Neutralität des Landes gegenüber Schülern und Eltern oder den politischen, religiösen oder weltanschaulichen Schulfrieden zu gefährden oder zu stören. Insbesondere ist ein äußeres Verhalten unzulässig, welches bei Schülern oder Eltern den Eindruck hervorrufen kann, dassdas eine Lehrkraft gegen Menschenwürde, Gleichberechtigung der Menschen nach Artikel 3 GG, Freiheitsgrundrechte oder die freiheitlich-demokratische Grundordnung auftritt. Die Wahrnehmung des Erziehungsauftrages gem. Artikel 12 para 1, 15 para 1para1 und 16 para 1para1 der Verfassung des Landes Baden-Württemberg und die entsprechende Darstellung christlicher und abendländlicher Bildungs- und Kulturwerte oder Traditionen widerspricht nicht dem Verhaltensgebot nach Satz 1. Das religiöse Neutralitätsgebot des Satz 1 gilt nicht im Religionsunterricht nach Art. 18 para 1para1 der Verfassung des Landes Baden-Württemberg." GBl. 1983, 397; http://www.landesrecht-bw.de/jportal/?quelle=jlink&docid=jlr-SchulGBW1983V33P38&psml=bsbawueprod.psml&max=true

878 Sec. 38 para 3 BWSchG determines: „Die Ernennung eines Bewerbers nach Sec. 8 des Landesbeamtengesetzes für eine Tätigkeit an öffentlichen Schulen nach Sec. 2 para 1 setzt als persönliches Eignungsmerkmal voraus, dass er die Gewähr für die Einhaltung des Absatzes 2 in seiner gesamten voraussichtlichen Dienstzeit bietet. Für die Versetzung einer Lehrkraft eines anderen Dienstherrn in den baden-württembergischen Schuldienst gilt S. 1 entsprechend".

first part of Sec. 38 para 2 of the SchG BW could apply in two situations (as stipulated in the second part of Sec. 38 para 2 SchG BW):

First, it determines the exclusion of the ban with respect to Christian symbols and other symbols that are closely related to Western values. The justification provided for this reservation, which indicates religious discrimination, was given on the grounds that the latter type of symbols are not conceived as contradicting the duty of behaviour and the constitutional precepts laid down in the Grundgesetz. Second, the ban will not apply with respect to manifestation or display of religious symbols taking place during religious instructions.

On the face of it, the amendments to the SchG BW endorsed a provision (Sec. 38 para 2) that carries a pronounced discriminatory character. In the second *Ludin*'s case, when the applicant sought a declaration of the regulation's incompatibility with the Grundgesetz, it was rather surprising that the BVerwG decided not only to the contrary but also pursued to establish its conformity with the constitution.

The second judgement in *Ludin*'s case triggered criticism among commentators and in the legal literature, especially due to difficulties to establish its conformity with several constitutional precepts. The constitutional inconsistencies arising under Sec. 38 para 2 SchG BW and the difficulty to establish their conformity with the Grundgesetz will be demonstrated in the following.

First, indefiniteness of the law with respect to the symbols encompassed by the prohibition – critics claim that the words of the provision are drafted in a broad and general manner.[879] For instance, it does not convey certainty as to what will be regarded as a 'political' or 'religious' symbol that may be encompassed under the ban. Thus, the provision is left open to interpretation since it is not specified enough to confer certainty to the citizen of how to comply with the law. Especially the phrases on outwardly 'manifestation' or 'behaviour' are left ambiguous. In particular, there is no specification as to what will be considered as a 'behaviour' that is capable to endanger the peaceful co-existence in school, or the obligation of the state towards parents and pupils to adhere to the principle of religious neutrality, or the impression that a teacher's 'behaviour' infringes against other constitutional provisions. The BW legislator does not designate specifically that the law relates to the Islamic headscarf, although this can be read explicitly in the explanatory notes of the land's parliament. Since the explanatory notes do not constitute an integral part of the law, they are not visible to the citizens; therefore, they are not foreseeable and cannot satisfy the rule of certainty of the law.[880] The

879 *Langenfeld/Mohsen*, p. 90.

880 *Wiese*, p. 277; BVerfGE 80, 103, 107; 62, 169, 183: 59, 104, 114.

BW lawmaker thus simplifies its task and prefers rather to leave the final discretion to school authorities to decide upon exertion of self-interpretation and discretion on a case-by-case basis. This broad and vague formulation of Sec. 38 para 2 was said to confer uncertainty and equivocal formulation which qualifies its inadmissibility.[881]

Second, no equal application of the prohibition with respect to all religions – the provision explicitly privileges the 'Christian-occidental tradition' in its second part and, thus, confirms the advancement of the Christian religion and its symbols over other faiths. Importantly, the incorporation of Jewish symbols into school realm can be comprehended from the text to be closely related to occidental-Western culture and values. Likewise, Jewish symbols are regarded as in line with the values prescribed in the constitution and the obligation of the state to neutrality. This clear prevalence granted to specific faiths or denominations run counter to the constitutional imperative of equality which prohibits discrimination on religious grounds in access to public office (Art. 3 para 3 and 33 para 3 GG).[882]

Eminently, the second part of Sec. 38 para 2 SchG BW, prescribing a reservation to the ban on religious symbols, establishes an inimitable bond to the duty of behaviour incumbent on the teacher (prescribed in the first part of Sec. 38 para 2 SchG BW). It determines that the educative mandate according to the precepts as laid in the land's constitution (Art. 12 para 1, 15 para 1 and 16 para 1 BWVerf), namely to convey to the pupils 'Christian-occidental tradition and values' and the display of Christian symbols, conforms to the alleged duty of behaviour. In BW, therefore, the exhibition of Christian or occidental-related symbols, likewise the transferal of values thereof, will be approved as they are considered to comply with the duty of behaviour prescribed in the BW constitution. In this respect, the right of a teacher to manifest her religion will be confined if it does not conform to this duty of behaviour. The duty of behaviour enfolds the rights and obligations incumbent on the teacher emanating from her special position as a civil servant. This special status allows a moderate limitation on her fundamental right and compels her to comply with certain requirements. The headscarf of a teacher was claimed by the public administrator in BW to

881 *Wiese*, p. 277: *Böckenförde*, JZ 2004, 1178, 1183.

882 *Heinig* raises doubts as to the conformity of the privilege granted to Christian Symbols with the Equality principle pursuant Art. 3 GG. See in http://www.bpb.de/politik/innenpolitik/konfliktstoff-kopftuch/63259/einstieg-in-die-debatte. The FCC explicitly invalidated a prevalence to Christian faith in its latest decision BVerfG 1 BvR 471/10, 1 BvR 1181/10.

infringe on this duty of behaviour drawn from the constitution since this symbol is objectively suited to impede school operation or pose an infringement against state neutrality or other constitutional precepts.[883]

It is worth to note that some doubt was raised by legal commentators as to whether the interpretation of Sec. 38 para 2 SchG BW in respect of its discriminatory character is adequate and reasonable.[884] The reason for this lies in the controversial opinion held in the legal literature and the jurisprudence as to the proper interpretation of the phrases 'exhibition' or 'display' (*Darstellung*) designated in Sec. 38 para 2 SchG BW as opposed to 'manifestation' (*Bekundung*). It was expounded that the legislator must have intended to ban also teachers who are adherents of the Christian or Jewish faith from an outward manifestation of their religious insignias while on duty. The reason provided was that the BW lawmaker must have intended to include the phrases 'display' or 'exhibition' as they will be used in the context of symbols displayed in a classroom and accordingly permitted. In contrast, the phrase 'manifestation' is adequate in the context of garments or insignias worn by an individual such as a teacher, and as such subject to moderate limitations.

The same view was held by the BVerwG as it concluded that the wording in Sec. 38 para 2 SchG BW was not intended to advance Christian teachers as opposed to their Muslim counterparts. The reason for that is that the provision denotes specifically the word 'exhibition' and not 'manifestation' and, as a result, could not have intended to exempt teachers wearing Christian-motivated garments or symbols from the ban. The BVerwG explains accordingly that the provision intended to permit solely the 'exhibition' or 'display' of Christian motivated objects within the context of educational-cultural knowledge transferred to pupils and not the illegibility in the individual sphere.[885] The BVerwG justifies its view with the explicit wording in the provision which pronounces that the prohibition will not apply with respect to the display of Christian-occidental tradition and values. This applies as long as the display accords with the educative goals to convey the tenets of the Christian faith (Art. 15 para 1 and 16 para 1 BWVerf) and values rooted in Christianity which marked and shaped the

883 BVerfGE 108, 282, 314–340.

884 *Wiese*, p. 281; *Bergmann*, ZAR – 2004, 135, 141; *Böckenförde*, JZ 2004, p. 1183; Häussler, ZAR 2004, 6, 13; *Kühling*, p. 132.

885 *Wiese*, p. 279; BVerwG, JZ, 2004, 1178, 1181. The criticism in the legal literature with respect to this interpretation in *Baer/Wrase*, DÖV 2005, 243, 249.

Western world, such as tolerance for the other-minded, and the grace of charity (*Nächstenliebe*) (Art. 12 para 1 BWVerf).

In this respect, it was contended that a segregation ought to be made between the presentation of Christian values and traditions taking form through conveyance of a general educational knowledge, and the outwardly manifestation of a religious garment worn by a teacher. The two situations differ substantially: the latter implies an identification with a specific religion, for example, the teacher's individual commitment to the tenets of the Muslim faith that demonstrates to the viewer her personal religious adherence; the former, on the other hand, makes no interlink with the inner personal belief of an individual.[886]

Nevertheless, the reasoning provided by the legislator as pronounced in parliamentary notes contradicts this rather mild interpretation provided by the judiciary. According to the explanatory notes, the BW legislator intended to exclude the application of the ban with respect to teachers that manifest symbols or insignias that correspond with the values and tradition of the Christian faith.[887] This wish of the legislator to privilege the Christian and Jewish religions was not hidden from the jurisprudence sight that affirmed this intent based on references made to the legislative history of the law.[888]

For instance, the question whether to endorse an exemption with respect to religious garments, such as the traditional habit of nuns teaching in state elementary schools was discussed extensively during debates in the land's parliament. Overt pronouncements taken on part of the political leadership, such as the state representative and the then minister of education, Annette Schavan, were one-sided and partial when argued that it will be inconceivable to request nuns following long tradition in state schools to stop wearing their habit.[889] The then minister of education, who was responsible for passing the law, claimed rigorously that the habit of a nun does not constitute a manifestation that falls within the prohibition of the law; rather, it should be comprehended as a professional clothing carrying a religious context.[890]

---

886 *Wiese*, p. 279; BVerwG, JZ 2004, 1178, 1180; VG Stuttgart, ZBR 2007, 135, 137.

887 LT BW, Drs. 13/2793,7.

888 VG Stuttgart, ZBR 2007, 135, 137.

889 The recommendation and report of the Committee for Education, Youth and Sport from 14 April 2004 in LT BW, Drs. 13/3071, 3; and also plenary protocol from the same date in LT BW 13/67, 4719.

890 FAZ 2.10.2003; Tagesspiegel 26.6.2004. Similar statements were made by the advocate of the BW state, Ferdinand Kirchhof, before the BVerwG alleging that it would be most probable that a nun appearing with the habit in a state school in the Black Forest

Consequently, the comprehensible conclusion with respect to Sec. 38 para 2 SchG BW suggests that it cannot be reconciled with the Grundgesetz as it clearly contravenes against its equality precepts, namely the constitutional precept of equality (Art. 3 para 3 GG) and the equality treatment (Art. 33 para 3 GG). It thereby advances Christian and Jewish symbols to the detriment of Muslim symbols such as the headscarf or *chador* and may be regarded unconstitutional.[891]

Third, appropriateness of legislative-executive powers – there is a contention in the legal literature as well as in the jurisprudence that the stipulation in Sec. 38 para 2 SchG BW is difficult to reconcile with the constitution since a fundamental right like religious freedom can be easily curtailed.[892] This holds true inasmuch as the ban on a teacher to appear with a religious or political symbol can take place even in an abstract situation without the need to demonstrate concrete violation of other protected constitutional rights. Sec. 38 para 2 SchG BW uses the phrases 'manifestation' that 'may' or 'be capable of' endangering state neutrality or school peace. Likewise, that 'can appear' to pupils and parents as a behaviour that may run counter to the constitutional precepts and values. This designation in the provision actually enables the executive branch (school authorities) to forbid religious symbols like the headscarf at any situation, whether a threat is assumed abstract or concrete.

Insofar, the delegation of the executive with such extensive power and scope of discretion that enables it to ban a teacher from appearance with a headscarf even on occurrence of abstract, non-viable threat to other constitutional values cannot be reconciled with the confinement of liberty rights that can be regulated solely by the legislator. In the *Ludin*'s case, the BVerfG affirmed that outweighing competing constitutional values, if examined in an abstract situation, is a matter that should be left exclusively to the legislator. It made clear that the duty under the rule of law and the principle of democracy prescribe that redefining the balance between state neutrality and religious freedom is not to be decided by public administrators; otherwise it will risk improper balance between the executive and legislative powers.[893] In its decision from 27 January 2015 the BVerfG even clarified that an abstract endangerment does not constitute a sufficient

---

(Schwarzwald) will not be held accountable for infringement of the state neutrality precept nor for the peaceful co-existence in school.

891 This view was affirmed in the legal literature, see in *Wiese*, p. 281; *Traulsen*, RdJB 2006, 116, 130.

892 *Wiese*, p. 278; *Baer/Wrase*, DÖV 2005, 243, 248; BVerfGE 90, 263, 275;85, 36, 69.

893 BVerwG, JZ 2004, 1178, 1179,1181.

justification for the ban and actually violates the right of religious freedom of a teacher who intends to wear a headscarf.

Accordingly, Sec. 38 para 2 SchG BW could have been found compatible with the constitution if the discretion of the executive to declare the ban of a religious insignia would have been exerted on a case-by-case basis, following fulfilment of specific requirements established by the legislator and only after all possible solutions to achieve compromise have been exhausted. This method of interpretation, known as *verfassungskonforme Auslegung*, is used by the courts in order to keep dubious provisions compatible with elementary principles of the Grundgesetz.

Nevertheless, the incompatibility with the constitution does not emanate merely from the allegedly extensive discretion delegated to the executive. In fact, pursuant to Sec. 38 para 2 SchG BW, the ban on religious insignias is inclusive/conclusive and does not enable a discretion on a case-by-case basis. This meant to say that the BW legislator, at the outset, leaves the executive no room for discretion, as it declares a priori that symbols like the headscarf will be regarded inadmissible. The explicit intent of the BW legislator to establish in principal a ban on the headscarf with respect to all teachers in the public school system can be inferred from the explanatory notes. These justified the inclusion of the ban on the headscarf on the grounds that even proponents of this symbol claim it to represent the inferiority of women in society and to be a salient feature of fundamentalist Islamic groups and a theocratic state-church model.[894]

Consequently, critics claim that Sec. 38 para 2 is incompatible with the constitution since it empowers the executive to an outright cut of protected fundamental rights of individuals to religious freedom.[895]

Albeit the listing of several controversial points that may deem Sec. 38 SchG BW to be incompatible with the constitution, there are some exceptions to the general ban which prohibits teachers to manifest religious symbols while on duty made by the BW legislator. These are stipulated in Sec. 38 para 2 SchG BW and will be set forth next.

(bb) Exceptions to the Ban

(aaa) Exception upon Application

Trainee teachers and applicants for a teaching post – Sec. 38 para 4 SchG BW prescribes that an exception will exist with respect to trainee teachers and

894 BW LT-Drs. 13/2793, 7.

895 *Gerstenberg*, International Journal of Constitutional law 3(1) (2005), p. 94, 100.

applicants for a teaching post. In case teachers in practice or applicants wish to appear at school with a religious garb, they can apply with a request that school authorities will exempt them from the duty of behaviour established in Sec. 38 para 2 and para 3 SchG BW. The right of the applicant to religious freedom will then be given precedent given that this practice of religion is claimed to be necessary in order to comply with the tenets of his/her faith. In addition, no other competing interests, such as negative right to religious freedom of pupils and parents, adherence to religious neutrality, or the maintenance of the peaceful co-existence at school conflict with the teacher's right to religious freedom.

Therefore, the provision relating to internship and applicants for a teaching post does not raise any concerns with respect to its constitutional compatibility, as no general ban prohibiting the wearing of a headscarf or other ostentatious religious garment applies in their case. The right to wear religious symbols is not denied at the first place and cannot even be ignored to the extent that the teachers' appearance may give rise to conflicts. It can only be prohibited following fulfilment of several requirements.

In this respect, the legislator delegates school authorities with a discretion that will enable it to decide on a case-by-case basis whether a religious symbol or garment worn by an intern or applicant falls within the prohibition stipulated in Sec. 38 para 2 and para 3 SchG BW or not. It further confines the extensive discretion given to school authorities in the sense that a ban can be imposed only if conflicts arise at school and if they cannot be resolved by any other reconciling means, such as a compromising settlement agreed on by all parties, or the dislocation of the intern or applicant to a substitutive school.

(bbb) Equal Application to Civil Servants and Privately Employed Teachers

Equality of treatment – Sec. 38 para 3 SchG BW declares that salaried teachers will be equated with the position of teachers who are regarded as civil servants (*verbeamtete*). Consequently, the duty of behaviour prescribed in Art. 38 para 2, para 3, and para 4 SchG BW will apply equally both to salaried teachers and to civil servants (*verbeamtete*), who either manifest their religious or political adherence outwardly through insignias, or imply with their behaviour a defiance against the constitutional precepts and values which safeguard the democratic, liberal Western state. This equalization ensures compliance with the constitution.

(2) Conclusion - Baden-Württemberg

Among the four compared federal states, the state of BW fosters and maintains close nexus to the Christian religion and its cultural heritage that is very similar in notion to that established in Bavaria. Though both states support the endorsement of religiosity into their state schools system, including the pronouncement of it among their educational objectives, they demonstrate disparities in their legislative layout. In context of the admissibility of teaching staff to manifest religious symbols in the public school system, the state of BW contextualized a different perception as to the exclusion of religious expression or behaviour from its state school system. It is very important to designate that until the delivery of the judgement in *Ludin*'s case, the endorsement of religious symbols in state schools and the eligibility of teachers as civil servants to express religious behaviour through abidance to a religious dress code was neither regulated by law nor contested in state courts. It was only following the delivery of the first *Ludin*'s judgement that the legislator of Baden-Württemberg, in the absence of any prescription in its Civil Service Law, rushed to take action and promulgated the necessary amendments in its regional school legislation.

Naturally, a reconciliation of this judgement with the strong allegiance of the state of Baden-Württemberg to Christian faith and tradition could not be aligned. Therefore, the BW lawmaker was induced to find a legislative response. Since state-church relations are saliently overt, as explicitly conveyed in BWVerf, this facilitated the task of the lawmakers in drafting the new amendments to its existing educational law. In fact, this immutable entanglement between state and church served as an incentive for the legislator of Baden-Württemberg to act for amendments which will banish any religious manifestation from the public sphere. However, the prohibition on teachers to appear with ostentatious religious symbols while on duty, as outlined in Sec. 38 para 2 SchG BW, did not intend to include all religious symbols equally. Though not explicitly stated in the provision itself, the BW lawmaker introduced the ban so as to exclude the headscarf. By that, the legislator in BW intended to continue legitimizing the admission of Christian and occidental symbols in state schools. The justification given was that a teacher's freedom of religion must be set back if it does not conform to pre-eminent constitutional precepts like the principle of neutrality, or if it collides with other fundamental constitutional rights and freedoms, the negative right of pupils to religious freedom, or the parental educative right. In support of its right to permit the endorsement of Christian and Western-related symbols into state schools, the legislator has made references to provisions in the constitution which prescribe its educational objectives to observe and foster Christian tradition and values (Art. 12 para 1, 15, para 1 and 16, para 1 of the BWVerf). A part of the educative task of the BW state is to protect the interest of the religious majority, which is Christian in nature. As a result, the admission of Christian and Jewish symbols, as opposed to the headscarf, may be permitted since they are regarded to comply with the educational aims and the duty of behaviour prescribed in its constitution. It is worth to note the BW legislator's approach conforms to the request laid down by the BVerfG in its recent decision, namely that a curtailment of a teacher's right to religious freedom can be outweighed only against a legitimate aim.[896] Though the BVerfG referred to the NRW SA, it recognized the religious neutrality of the state and peaceful co-existence in school as well as the negative religious rights of pupils and parents, specified in the abolished Sec. 57 para 4 NRW SA as a legitimate aim. It is therefore only reasonable that a similar phrasing, as initially chosen by the BW legislator, will also be considered to be a legitimate aim; however, it will have to fulfil other prerequisites set out by the BVerfG in order to prove compatibility with the constitution. In this regard, the preference granted to Christian and Jewish symbols, reasoned by their proximity to the Western-Christian tradition and heritage, would be regarded as unconstitutional since they infringe upon the constitutional precepts of equality (Sec. 3 para and 33 para 3 GG).

In principle, the former phrasing chosen by the NRW legislator (Art. 57 para 4 NRWSA) is identical to its counterpart provision introduced by the BW lawmaker (Sec 38 para 2 BWSA). Thereby, criticism raised as to the conformity of the wording in this stipulation with the German Grundgesetz. Art. 57 para 4 NRWSA is similar in nature and as a result it will be interesting to observe whether necessary amendments will be taken by the BW lawmaker to ensure conformity of its educational law to the constitution.

This dubious formulation of Sec. 38 para 2 BWSA, which indicates indirect discrimination aimed towards Islamic symbols like the headscarf, raises difficulties as to its adequacy, appropriateness, and conformity with the Grundgesetz.

Taking into consideration the judgement delivered by the BVerfG in the recent NRW headscarf case – which declared the NRW SchulG to be unconstitutional and void – and due to similar phrasing of its school education act, the BW lawmaker is obliged to make necessary amendments in order to keep the conformity of its BWSA with the constitution.

Art. 38 BWSA may well be declared to be non-compatible with the constitution, based on the same grounds specified by the BVerfG in its judgement relating to the NRWSA: first, it violates the prohibition of imposing an all-inclusive ban on all religious symbols, as such a comprehensive ban infringes the safeguarded right of a teacher to religious freedom; second, it breaches the precepts of equality (Art. 3 para 3 and 33 para 3 GG), as it explicitly privileges the Christian faith and tradition and further extends its discriminatory character

896 BVerfG 1 BvR 471/10, 1 BvR 1181/10.

also with respect to salaried teachers and not only to teachers employed as civil servants (*verbeamtete*). Third, the BVerfG's pronouncement that abstract endangerment will not suffice in order to curtail the fundamental, unreserved right of a teacher to outwardly manifest his/her religion obliges the BW lawmaker to amend its phrasing, similar to the NRW legislator, since only concrete endangerment posed to the religious neutrality of the state or other constitutional rights and freedoms can justify a violation of a teacher's right to religious freedom.

ff) Assessment

In retrospect of Germany's history of state-church relations, it is rather salient that Christian influences generated by the predominant Catholic Church left a pronounced impact on the German population. Since the attempt to retrench the extensive power of the Catholic Church during the 'Kaiserreich' had not been successful, the Catholic Church was able then to establish its position during the Weimar Republic through attainment of its legal status as public corporation, thereby maintaining those fundamental structures up to this day.[897]

It is due to this fact that the nexus between state and church was not administered on the national, federal level; rather, the integration of religion and churchly influences on the life of the German population was reinforced and fostered on a regional level. This contributed to the development of a varying religious character of the individual states, which was correspondingly strong or remote, depending on the degree of religious accommodation entrenched in their different historical traditions. Consequently, aspects emanating from state-church relations would not be determined on a uniform basis at the national level. Apart from the historical-traditional development of state-church relations, the constitutional framework plays a major role with respect to the state's competency to legislate at the regional level.

Constitutional aspects challenging the admissibility of an individual to wear religious attire or garment or of the state to display a symbol in public classrooms reflect the inevitable tension existing in Germany between the federal states and the central state with respect to their legislative competency.

The most distinguishable cases that had reached the BVerfG and brought for judicial review the question of permissibility of the regional legislator to admit or prohibit the exhibition of religious symbols in primary school education were the cases of Ludin (individually displayed symbol) and the Crucifix (state-imposed symbol).

---

897 *Auslander*, Cultural Dynamics 12 (3), 2000, 283, 288.

Following legal issues were addressed by the German jurisprudence in this discourse and provide an overview of the challenges both judiciary and legislator have encountered by virtue of this intrigued controversy. Distinctive features sketching out key elements of the German legal system and analogous comparison of the legal measures infused by the individual states within this legal discourse will be accordingly highlighted.

(1) Legislative Competency of the State's Legislator to Regulate Inner Affairs

As mentioned earlier, the German educational system differs from one federal state to another, as it is the task of the lands' parliaments to determine the rules and set regulations with respect to matters of their inner affairs (Art. 70 GG).

It is due to the historical development and to the federal structure of Germany that the responsibility of the federal states to resolve their inner affairs, including proximity to religion and embodiment of religious insignias in state schools remained subject to the sole competency of the federal states (Art. 7 GG).

Accordingly, within the process of legislation each federal state is entitled to take different factors into account when establishing its school system. Legislative enactments and regulations are naturally imprinted by the individual character of each state, and notably diverge from one to the other based on different components specific to each region. These may include the individual historical development of state-church relations, traditions of schooling, customs, denominational composition of the population, namely, the mixture of religious groups within its realm and their composition, religious identification and closeness to religious habits, as well as the affinity towards entrenched religious rituals.[898] These factors consequently affect the lawmaker's discretion with respect to endorsement of religious insignias into the respective school system and result henceforth in varying resolutions by the individual states.

(2) Confirmation of Federal States' Competency by BVerfG

The sovereignty of the states with respect to their inner affairs was affirmed by the BVerfG as it acknowledged the right of the states to take account of those specific customs, heritage, traditions, and the extent of piety of the citizens as an adequate course which is conferred to them by virtue of their prerogative to

898 This view concerning state's neutrality and the specificity of each federal state, which is finally accountable to legislative and constitutional differences in each of the federal states was not stated in the Crucifix case (16.5.1995, BVerfGE 93,1, et seq.), and it seems like the court wished to depart from it.

supervise their school system at own discretion. This, according to the BVerfG, would be regarded as appropriate and constitutional even to the extent of divergent outcomes and regulations among the states, as long as conducted within the framework of constitutionally permissible prescriptions.[899]

These components characterize distinctively each of the federal states, given that they had formed eventually their reputable nature as well as established the fundaments for their constitutional and legislative order. In that sense, various outcomes with respect to endorsement of religious insignias in state schools are inevitable and, as a result, an alignment of the legislative educational order in all of the federal states is deemed impossible.

(3) Criteria Deliberated by Federal States for a Ban on Religious Insignias

Identifying legal criteria is of an important relevance for the purpose of finding a common lineament among the legislative amendments initiated by the compared federal states and the judicial review following their implementation.

Consequently, as far as the permissibility to display religious symbols or attire in the public school system is concerned, it is crucial to make a distinction with respect to two different scenarios deliberated by the federal states prior and during to the endorsement of the proposed modifications into prevailing legislation. In parliamentary debates, segregation was made as to: (i) type of symbols the prohibition meant to enfold, coupled with (ii) the identity of the symbol-displayer.

In the context of case laws involving the permissibility to display religious insignias in public education, judicial review focused on how the display of religious insignias will affect the symbol-viewers, in other words, pupils. It was rather due to the fact that the BVerfG tends to rule in favour of the protection of pupils' rights to be free from any religious influence (e.g., the most famous are the *Crucifix* and *Ludin*'s case) in the majority of its judgements, and due to the legislative competency of the states with respect to their educative mandate that the recent decision of the BVerfG from 2015 appears astonishing to some extent.

(a) Type of Symbol

As was demonstrated earlier, the states purported to distinguish between different religions; however, they refrained from explicit mention of the Islamic headscarf in their text laws. Instead, they sought to discern between the various symbols, laying the focus in part on non-religious grounds (e.g., a symbol

---

899 BVerfGE 108, 282, 303, 310.

which expresses a political significance or the disturbance of a peaceful co-existence in school realm), and in part emphasized the contravention of constitutional and educational goals, including those prescribed in the individual lands' constitutions (violation against the constitutional precepts of equality, infringement of gender equality, negative right to religious freedom of pupils and their parents). By doing so, the states attempted to avoid any annulment of the proposed amendments based on incompatibility with the constitution.

In particular, the following considerations were taken into account by the federal lawmaker with respect to the type of the symbol:

- The manner of the display or manifestation (i.e., nature, scope, and frequency);
- The type of observance or confrontation;
- The interpretation given to the symbol (objective or subjective).

(b) Identity of the Right Holder

The second legal criterion for segregation in case a display of a religious attire or symbol in public schools has taken place was recognized with respect to the identity of the right holder, that is, the person who enjoys the right to manifest a religion. In that sense, the legal entitlement to display a symbol was distinguished between, first, a state-imposed symbol (e.g., the cross) or, second, an individually displayed symbol (e.g., a teacher with a headscarf).

In contrast to the latter scenario, the legal challenge with respect to the legitimacy of a state-imposed symbol in state schools did not involve an infringement of fundamental personal right (Art. 2 para 1 GG) or infringed the teacher's right to profession (Art. 12 GG). In the BVerfG's jurisprudence it was upheld more than once that the display of the crucifix in public schools is regarded more as an identification of the state with a particular faith, prohibited by the principle of neutrality, as oppose to a teacher wearing a religious symbol. It was explained that the religious garment of a teacher will be regarded as a personal, individual act which should be segregated distinguishably from a state act, since the state does not necessarily have to identify itself through the act of its individuals.[900] This fact, for instance, eased the BVerfG's ruling in the *Crucifix* decision in favour of its removal from state classrooms. It was reasoned on the grounds of being a state-displayed symbol which contradicts

900 BVerfGE 108, 282, 305.

the obligation of the state to religious neutrality and which violates the duty of the state to protect the right of its religious minority not to be exposed to religious influence, as it poses an identification of the state with a specific religion. Moreover, it was underscored by the BVerfG that pupils are confronted with the crucifix and do not have any possibility to escape from its presence when displayed in state classrooms.[901] The outweigh of rights in case of a state-displayed symbol is hard to align from a constitutional point of view as opposed to the outweigh of rights in case of an individually displayed symbol. The reason is that in a state-displayed symbol the violation of the guarantee of the state towards its religious minority to negative right of religious freedom is difficult to justify or balance constitutionally, as the state has no legal entitlement itself and is, in fact, under a double-obligation: a positive duty to ensure that public school education is accessible, and also guarantee negative religious freedoms of its individuals in a religiously neutral educational environment. In contrast, a restriction on an individual's freedom to wear a religious attire or garment (i.e., a teacher with a headscarf) is difficult to align against the rights of other individuals, the symbol-viewers (i.e., the pupils), since both obtain a guaranteed legal entitlement to religious freedom. The teacher's positive right to observe her religion as well as the pupils' negative religious liberty to an education free of religious coercion – both are regarded as primary right holders.

Further, the special position of the teacher as a civil servant and a representative of the state constitutes a pivotal factor which needs to be taken into account when balancing interests.

In particular, following criteria were taken into account by the legislator with respect to the identity of the right holder:

- The identification of the legal 'right holder' who is entitled to invoke constitutional protection;
- Assessment and outweigh of the clashing fundamental rights;
- Evaluation of the threshold (high or low) for the degree of symbol interference (*Eingriff*) with other liberty rights;
- The underlying justifications for limitation on the scope of the right to religious manifestation (i.e., educative mandate of the state, peaceful co-existence in school, religious neutrality of the state, the right to negative religious freedom of others).

901 BVerfGE 93, 1, 15.

(4) *The Legislative Prohibition of the Federal States*

The legal approach of the federal states with respect to the manifestation of religious symbols or garments when exercised by teachers was not regulated in text laws prior to *Ludin*'s judgement, so in practice this behaviour was mostly tolerated.[902] In the aftermath of *Ludin*'s case, the state of BW was the first one to promulgate a corresponding legislation. This step was consequently followed by other federal states.[903] The legislator in BW, NRW, Bavaria, and Berlin implemented provisions in the respective school education acts prohibiting the endorsement of religious or political symbols that may have the effect of infringement of the state's obligation to religious neutrality, or that may endanger the peaceful co-existence or atmosphere in the domain of state schools.

Henceforth, the legal challenge that arises with respect to the modifications deliberated by the federal states is the difficulty to establish their permissibility within the framework of the constitution.[904]

Since this question stood in the centre of the legal debate and was subject of judicial review, it is then necessary to identify the aspects which were considered by the lawmakers to legitimize the ban of the headscarf. The recent judgement of the BVerfG[905] questioned the constitutionality of the ban imposed by NRW and decided that it is incompatible with the Grundgesetz. The NRW lawmaker, shortly after the publication of the ruling, implemented modifications in its SchulG NRW. The following aspects constitute the basis for an assessment of the relevant amendments that may be initiated by the federal states. It will thence aim to establish:

---

902 *Wiese*, p. 26; *McGoldrick*, p. 110: *Fetzer/Soper*, p. 129; *Häußler*, 3 European Journal of Migration Law 2001, 457.

903 *Vakulenko*, Islamic Veiling In Legal Discourse, 2012, p. 35.

904 BVerwG, NJW 2004, 3581; VG Stuttgart, NVwZ 2006, 1444; Other federal states that were confronted with the constitutionality of their school statutes are: the state of Bavaria, which was alleged to have infringed the constitutional by virtue of Art. 59 para 2 of the BayEUG. In this respect the Bavarian constitutional court declared compatibility of Art. 59 para 2 with the Bavarian constitution BayVerfGH, BayVBl. 2007, 235. In the state of NRW the following decisions VG Düsseldorf 5.6.2007, 2 K 6225/06; VG Düsseldorf 14.8.2007, Az. 2 K 1752/07; VG Aachen, 9.11.2007, Az 1 K 323/07; VG Gelsenkirchen, 27.2.2008; ArbG Herne,7.3.2007, Az 4 Ca 3415/06; ArbG Wuppertal 29.7.2008, Az 4 Ca 1077/08.

905 BVerfGE 138, 296 = NJW 2015, 359.

First, whether the states intended to ban exclusively the headscarf from the domain of the public school system and by that confer preferential treatment to symbols associated with Christian-occidental culture and tradition and;
Second, if the states did intend to create differentiation between various religious groups so as to inhibit specifically the admission of a headscarf from public education or, adversely, privilege Christian symbols. In that case, their (in)consistency with regard to fundamental constitutional precepts, such as state obligation to religious neutrality, the guarantee of religious freedom, the obligation of the state to ensure equality among all religious groups and denominations will need to be contested in order to reason their constitutional legitimization.

Finally, the manner in which different justifications in the federal states argued to impact on the scope of individuals' rights to manifest their religion or belief as opposed to a symbol imposed by the state, acting for the interest of the religious majority will provide an observation as to how limitation of religious manifestation in the public school system has been legitimized in the German debate.

The following points will serve as a yardstick for a proper examination of convergence and discrepancies of the earlier-mentioned questions:

- Subject of the ban
- Abstract or concrete endangerment
- Equal application
- Legislative aim/justification

(a) Subject of the Ban (type of symbol)

In principle, there was a broad support of the political majority in the respective federal states to pass correspondent legislation that will ban Muslim teachers from wearing the headscarf. Nonetheless, as clearly inferred from deliberation in the lands' parliaments, the intention was to strike at 'oriental' religious symbols;[906] however, the lands' lawmakers refrained from a blatant segregation thereof. As a result, no explicit prohibition of the headscarf exists in any of the relevant text laws.

---

906 See in that reference the pronouncement made in favor of the headscarf ban by the Bavarian minister of education, Monika Hohlmeier, as well as by the government representative, Ingeborg Berggreen-Merkel, in NRW, in BW and in Berlin; *McGoldrick*, p. 115.

It is, therefore, indispensable to make a delineation of the type of symbol the text laws intended to include under the ban. A reference to the various text laws[907] will disclose the spectrum of the scope of the ban (i.e., type of symbol: oriental insignias like the headscarf as opposed to Christian or Jewish symbols; or nature of the symbol: merely religious or political symbols).

The wording of the text in the state BW relates in Art. 38 para 2 ShulG to an exclusion of all symbols that constitute the '...exercise of political, religious, ideological or similar manifestations'. The NRW legislator in its Art. 2 para 8 SchulG did not deviate from this formulation and actually prohibits the exercise of religious, political, or ideological manifestation by teachers. The only difference is that the NRW lawmaker excluded the general ban on all religious symbols and eliminated the privilege granted to Christian-occidental tradition. Thence, BW and NRW are explicitly combining religious, political, and ideological insignias. Following the recent BVerfG decision relating to the headscarf in NRW, it is very likely that the BW lawmaker will have to make necessary amendments and adapt its SchulG in similar manner to the NRW legislator, since the all-inclusive prescription at the outset, which allegedly attempts to capture all religious insignias and prohibit their endorsement in school, is regarded as unconstitutional. The ruling of the BVerfG dictates that the legislator should initially admit all religious symbols into its state school system without any segregation of nature or type of symbol (i.e., religious, political, or ideological).

In Bavaria, teachers are not allowed to wear 'outer symbols and garments that express a religious or ideological creed'. In this context, one should note that Art. 59 para 2 BayEUG makes a reference to Art. 84 para 2 BayEUG, which prohibits any political indoctrination (*politische Werbung*) within school premises. It remains, therefore, to see how a legal challenge to the headscarf, invoking its prohibition on grounds of its perception as a symbol of political indoctrination will be resolved within the German legal discourse. According to the Act in Berlin, 'teachers are not allowed to wear any visible religious or ideological symbols and any conspicuous religious or ideological insignia that signals to the spectator an affiliation to a specific religious or ideological community'.[908]

907 Sec. 59 Bayerisches Gesetz über das Erziehungs- und Unterrichtswesen; Sec. 2 des Gesetzes zu Art. 29 BlnLV; Sec. 57 para 4 Schulgesetz für das Land Nordrhein-Westfalen (NRW-SchulG); Sec. 38 of the SchG BW.

908 § 2 des Gesetzes zu Art. 29 der Verfassung von Berlin, in: http://www.lexsoft.de/cgi-bin/lexsoft/justizportal_nrw.cgi?t=152828906418446493&sessionID

Respectively, the Acts in Berlin and Bavaria apply only to entrenched religious symbols and do not include prohibition with respect to political symbols.

(b) Abstract Endangerment

In common to all the amended text laws (with the exception of the state of Berlin) is that the legislator in each of the respective federal states legitimized the prohibition of religious insignias on grounds of an abstract endangerment that their display may pose to other protected constitutional values. This accords with the declaratory aim of the state's legislators in parliamentary deliberations on the suggested modifications. Lands' parliaments explicitly pronounced the intention to prohibit religious insignias (i.e., the headscarf) that may be comprehended as 'capable' or 'suitable' predominantly to contravene fundamental constitutional values (e.g., negative right of pupils to religious freedom, state neutrality, the precept of equality or peaceful school order). By setting a low standard of proof (no necessity to demonstrate a concrete danger), the states aimed with the modified laws to forestall any possible negative influence which is conceivably perceived or associated with the display of the headscarf in state schools.

There is, however, an issue that arises with respect to demonstration of an abstract danger which the display of the headscarf may allegedly pose to protected constitutional values and rights. This relates to the shift in the burden of proof in the process of outweighing rights (from the state to the legal right holder). This enables the state to interfere with a protected right of an individual to practice a religion or belief without the need to demonstrate a concrete threat to other competing rights or interests. The abstract danger test enables a subjective, coercive interpretation by the state, which will ease the standard and burden of proofs so as to substantiate a legitimate ground for interference with fundamental religious rights. This minimal substantiation on part of the state risks an engraved curtailment of individuals' right to freedom of religion. In this context, it was even held that in case of a doubt, prevalence will always be given to the right of pupils and parents not to have their children exposed to religions and faiths they consider as harmful or negative for their education.[909]

Moreover, the abstract danger test exempts these federal states from a review taken on a case-by-case basis, which would need to establish a concrete threat in a particular case of a teacher with a headscarf. Nonetheless, this right of the

---

909 *Langenfeld/Mohsen*, 3 International Journal of Constitutional Law, 2005, 86, 92.

state's legislator to act at own discretion when setting a threshold during the exercise of balancing rights in symbols cases was confirmed by the BVerwG.[910]

Nonetheless, against the background of the recent BVerfG judgement from 2015, the state of NRW enacted a new regulation Sec. 2 para 8 in its NRW SA, as the former Sec. 57 para 4 was declared to be null and void. The BVerfG held that an abstract endangerment will not suffice any longer for the curtailment of a fundamental right to religious freedom. In order to justify a harsh infringement in a teacher's right to exercise her undisturbed right to religious freedom, it is incumbent on school authorities to prove that the exposure to a religious insignia like the headscarf poses indeed a concrete endangerment to the neutrality of the state, peaceful co-existence in school, or fundamental democratic liberties and freedoms set out in the constitution. This adjudication of the BVerfG retrenches the scope of discretion granted to the individual federal states in designation and establishment of their public school system and prevents the states from conferring the administrative excessive power to infringe upon a teacher's fundamental right to religious freedom.

It is worth to note that the BW legislator has not yet taken measures to change its regulation prescribed in Sec. 38 para 2 SchulG BW, although the regulation relates specifically to a potential endangerment and thence is forbidden as an abstract endangerment. An abstract endangerment will be regarded un-proportional and cannot justify such a harsh infringement in a fundamental constitutional right as the right to religious freedom.[911]

(c) Equal Application

Foremost among the problems to reconcile federative school legislation with the constitution is the difficulty to establish the legitimacy of the amended provisions due to their incompatibility with the principles of equality and equal treatment (Art. 3 para 3 in tandem with 33 para 3 GG). The formulation of the respective School statutes or Education Acts in different federal states presume preference with respect to Christian symbols or traditions, as they are conceived not to contravene the duty of behaviour prescribed in their lands' constitutions; likewise, they conform with the educational mandate conferred on the state by their lands' constitution.[912]

---

910 BVerwG, 24.06.2004 – 2 C 45.03.

911 BVerfG 1 BvR 471/10 recital. 90, 110.

912 FAZ, 24 June, 2004.

The expressed preference to display Christian tradition and symbols is especially notable in the legislative text of the federal states NRW and BW. In this respect, the jurisprudence already acknowledged that the lawmaker is entitled to lay down official duties that may bar access to the public service; however, it also emphasized that these must be imposed only when strict equality between all religious groups is observed.[913]

However, the state of Baden-Württemberg as well as NRW introduced an exception according to which the ban will not apply with respect to '…exhibition of Christian and occidental educational and cultural values or traditions'.[914]

Nonetheless, even with respect to the inequality exceptions, there is a clear demand delivered by the BVerfG in its judgement of 2015 which requires the NRW legislator to take necessary amendments, as the prevalence given to Christian and Western tradition and values is regarded to be unconstitutional since it does not conform with the equality precepts prescribed in it (Sec. 3 para 3 and 33 para 3 GG).[915] The disadvantage posed to other religions (i.e., Islam) as opposed to Christianity and Judaism cannot be constitutionally justified. The BVerfG explains that Sec. 33 para 3 GG forbids direct discrimination in admission and job application to the public service that is based on religious grounds. This does not contradict the fact that civil servants are subject to a special duty emanating from their position as state representatives and obliges them to adhere to their obligation and appear neutral while applying for or within office. However, this special obligation requires sufficient and genuine reasons for justification in order to enable curtailment of the unreserved right to religious freedom, as prescribed in Sec. 4 para 1 and 2 GG.[916] Given the case that unequal treatment can be justified on other constitutional grounds, it then has to apply equally to all religions or faiths without any segregation. Naturally, similar requirement will apply with respect to the BW legislator to modify the BWSA to refrain from advancement of a particular religion, that is, influence of the Christian faith, and apply its dress code regulations equally for teachers to all religions.[917]

Similarly, amendment drafts were deliberated by Bavaria, among other federal states,[918] with the intention to privilege Christianity and Judaism, but those

913 BVerfGE 108, 282, 313.

914 Sec. 38 para 2 s.3 of the SchG BW.

915 BVerfG 1 BvR 471/10 recital 123–129.

916 BVerfG 1 BvR 471/10 recital 126.

917 BVerfG 1 BvR 471/10 recital 128.

918 Such as Hesse (Sec. 86 para 3 Hessisches Schulgesetz, 18.10.2004, GVBl. p 306); Lower Saxony (Sec. 51 para 3,4, Niedersächsiches SchulG, 29.4.2004, GVBl. P. 140).

were finally not implemented. Though the Bavarian legislator did not include an explicit privilege of Christian-displayed symbols, it rather took care to establish the advancement of Christianity over other religions or faiths simply by eliminating all symbols or garments which presumably may run counter to its constitutional objectives or the tenets of Christianity.[919] Thence, the Bavarian lawmaker introduces an indirect privilege of Christian references in state schools, as can be inferred by reference to the educational objectives prescribed in the Bavarian constitution. This explicitly mentions that 'state elementary schools shall be open to all children… In them children shall be taught and educated according to the principles of the Christian creed'.[920] This exception aimed to introduce from the backdoor Christian and Jewish symbols such as the habit of a nun or the Jewish Kippa.[921]

On the face of it, this ban runs counter to the principle of equality (Art. 3 and Art. 33 para 3 GG), as the legislators in those federal states allow explicitly the advancement of Christian or Jewish symbols on the ground that they are closely related to the Western-liberal tradition and values.[922]

The state of Berlin adopted the same prohibition on endorsement of religious symbols. The only exception of the Berliner ban on religious symbols displayed by teaching staff in segregation to the ban imposed by the federal states BW and NRW relates to its equal application. The wording in Sec. 2 of the law relating to Art. 29 BlnLV (Berlin) differs from the formulation introduced by the lawmakers of NRW and BW insofar as it applies equally to all religions and does not make any exception with respect to Christian religious symbols or garments.[923] In that sense, there is no preferential treatment of Christianity over other religions, creeds, and denominations.

---

919 The second part of Art. 59 para 2 BayEUG outlines "…*During lessons teachers are not allowed to wear outer symbols and garments that express a religious or ideological creed, in case students or parents may understand these symbols or garments as expression of an attitude that is not compatible with fundamental constitutional values and educational objectives of the constitution, including Christian-occidental educational and cultural values…*"

920 Art. 135 of the Bavarian Constitution.

921 See in that reference the parliamentary discussions: Baden-Württemberg – BW LT-Drs 13/2793, 7: Bavaria – Bay. LT-Drs 15/368, 4; NRW LT-Drs 14/569, 8 f. As well as other federal states such as Saarland – Saarl. LT-Drs 12/1072,4; Hessen- Hess. LT-Drs 16/1897, 4.

922 *Ganz*, p. 245; *Wiese*, p. 279.

923 Sec. 38 para 2 of the SchG BW and Sec. 57 para 4 of the SchulG NRW.

Conceivably, the headscarf of the Muslim teacher is likely to be prohibited in the state of Berlin, as it is to be apprehended within the meaning of 'entrenched religious symbols' that falls within the scope of a ban on religious symbols encompassed in Sec. 2 of the law relating to Art. 29 BlnLV. The outcome will undoubtedly result in disadvantageous treatment of a Muslim teacher with a headscarf in comparison to the rest of the teaching staff. Nevertheless, such a scenario is unlikely to be substantiated by the state of Berlin, or even regarded as applicable, simply as Sec. 2 of the law relating to Art. 29 BlnLV does not permit unequal treatment.

To conclude, the outcome in *Ludin*'s case generated direct response in the lands' parliaments that aimed to regulate the introduction of religious symbols into the public school system. The genuine trigger for the proposed amendments in some of the federal states was interlinked with the wish to outcast the Islamic headscarf from public school premises and fortify the position of the dominant faith (Christianity). In other federal states, motivated by the same incentive, this objective remained within the framework of parliamentary deliberations which did not materialize in practice.

The legislative solution adopted by the federal states can be divided, thence, into three categories:

First, *explicit segregation in text law* – the wording prescribed by the lawmakers in NRW and BW is rather similar in formulation. Their respective school legislation clearly stipulates that the incorporation of symbols which coincide with the Christian-occidental tradition will comply with the duty of behaviour that is prescribed by the law. This formulation legitimates the inclusion of Christian and Jewish symbols in elementary and secondary schools, whereas Islamic insignias are to be excluded by the lawmaker simply on the ground that they do not accord with the duty of behaviour and the educative constitutional task.

Second, *indirect segregation in text law but advertent in constitution* – the state of Bavaria underscores in its constitution that a declaratory educational aim of the state is the transferral of Christian-occidental tradition and values to pupils in public elementary schools. Thence, though not explicitly advancing Christian religion over various faiths and denominations in Art. 59 para 2 of the BayEUG, the prohibition on teachers in the School Education Act to abstain from religious insignias may still be regarded as incompatible with the German Grundgesetz. The reason is that the headscarf as a symbol and its meaning are more likely to run counter to the Christian educational objectives prescribed in the Bavarian constitution. As a result, the Bavarian legislator may be held to stand in breach to its obligation to conformity with the equality precept prescribed in the German constitution.

Third, *explicit exclusion in text law without any exception* – the only distinguishable legal situation applies with respect to the federal state of Berlin, which makes no exception with respect to the ban on public servants to appear with religious insignias while on duty. The prohibition thence operates equally with respect to all religions and faiths.[924]

Thus, it seems that the exception clauses adopted by the three federal states (BW, NRW, and Bavaria) with the specific intent to prefer Christian symbols upon those of other denominations would contradict the judicial guidelines mentioned earlier as well as the constitutional imperative of equality. Accordingly, it remains doubtful whether the legislative ban on teachers to abstain from demonstrating religious adherence as imposed by the federal states would be held compatible with the constitutional precepts of equality and equal treatment according to Art. 3 para 3 and 33 para 3 GG. This is the case mainly because these norms explicitly prohibit discrimination in access to public service which is conducted based on affiliation or non-affiliation to a particular religion.

It is worth to note in this respect that the permissibility of wearing Christian or Jewish symbols by a public schoolteacher was not brought for legal challenge before German courts so far. It therefore remains interesting to see how German courts will review similar cases involving the display of religious symbols other than the headscarf. Undoubtedly, judicial revision examining the constitutionality of the respective legislation is still essential and would probably continue to engage German jurisprudence in future case laws.

(d) Legislative Aim/Justification

During parliamentary consultations on proposed amendments to their respective school or education acts following the *Ludin*'s case, some federal states refrained from an explicit indication of the ban on Islamic headscarf or any differentiation that is based on religious grounds (like the case in NRW and BW). Instead, they sought to endorse a ban on symbol or garments that might – in the eyes of the symbol-viewers – be perceived objectively as an expression of belief, which is repulsive to the constitution and its values or contradicts sharply Christian-Western tradition (like the case in NRW, BW, and Bavaria). The aim was to capture those cases where a symbol would not be regarded forbidden merely due

924 Art. 1 and 2 of the law relating to Art.29 BlnLV.

to its religious statement or the doctrine it aims to propagate, but rather due to its potential outward effect that intrigues conflict or tension at school.[925] In its recent ruling, the BVerfG scrutinized the grounds for justification imposed by the NRW lawmaker in order to prohibit the headscarf, as was inscribed in the abolished Art. 57 para 4 SchulG. The land's lawmaker referred to several possible justifications that may be divided as follows: first, when a symbol endangers or disturbs the duty of the state to neutrality or the religious or ideological peaceful order in school; second, the symbol seems to stand in contrast to the constitution and its protected legal values, and repudiates the educational goals prescribed in it. Constitutional protected legal values encompass the educative task of the state, human dignity, gender equality, educative goals adhering to the Christian tradition and its values as inscribed in the individual lands' constitutions, and other fundamental principles inscribed in the Grundgesetz.

Bavaria, for instance, prescribes in Art. 59 para 2 BayEUG that teachers are prohibited from wearing religious symbols which may confer the impression that they contravene pre-eminent constitutional principles and educational objectives, which are prescribed in the constitution, including the conveyance of Christian values and Western cultural tradition. Accordingly, the Bavarian state cannot forbid the headscarf purely due to its religious symbolism. Nonetheless, the headscarf may be prohibited if its symbolic meaning can be understood as a manifestation that is repugnant to the constitution and to educational goals. In that sense, Art. 59 para 2 BayEUG, though it does not explicitly legitimize the advancement of Christian symbols, may still be regarded discriminatory since it is probable that symbols of different ideological creeds or worldviews are more likely to fall within this constitutional reservation. From a perspective of Bavarian school authorities, it will suffice then to prohibit a teacher's head-scarf if parents and pupils may perceive the garment or symbol of the teacher as contradictory to the tenets of the Christian faith, Western cultural tradition, or fundamental constitutional values.

Other federal states, alongside an explicit exception granted to Christian-Western symbols, opted to emphasize the possible abstract endangerment of the state's duty to neutrality of religion and worldview. This is the case in the states of BW and NRW that made a reference in their respective School Acts to several constitutional protected values that are supposed to justify the ban on religious symbols in state schools. The state of BW in Art. 38 para 2 SchulG BW and even

925 *Heinig* in Brugger/Karayanni (eds.), Religion in the Public Sphere: A Comparative Analysis of German, Israeli, American and International Law, 181 (195).

NRW in Art. 2 para 8 SchulG NRW allude pre-eminent constitutional values, such as human dignity, fundamental freedom rights, the rights of freedom, and democratic rights rooted in the constitutional order of the state.[926]

The state of Berlin prescribes no differentiation between symbols or garments that are not explicitly based on religious grounds. The prohibition, therefore, will apply only with respect to entrenched religious symbols. In that sense, all public servants – whether in the judiciary, police force or teaching staff – are all equal before the law, and affiliation or non-affiliation to a specific religion or denomination is irrelevant; this is because the ban to appear with a religious symbol while on public duty is absolute and applicable to all religions.[927]

Finally, the constitutional legitimacy of confinement of teachers in their behaviour and dress code which is not based on religious grounds was left open by the jurisprudence.[928] Thence, constitutional safeguards for a prohibition on a teacher's dress code may – dependent on the situation – be admissible. The reason is that non-religious differentiation is not directed against a specific religion; it is rather the negative outward and the objectively determinable impact[929]

926 This alignment of the principle of religious neutrality with other pre-eminent constitutional rights in the same paragraph which postulates prohibition of religious symbols drew criticism, especially among proponents of the headscarf. The critics stood against the alleged presupposition that the headscarf poses a threat to any of the prescribed protected values. It claimed that the state not only acted unilaterally when interpreting the symbolic meaning of the headscarf, setting aside the motivation of the wearer (i.e., the teacher). Moreover, it actually distinguished between the headscarf and symbols of other faiths, disregarding its religious symbolism whilst attaching to it different meanings that denote its incompatibility with fundamental constitutional values and the state's educational mandate. Consequently, it was presumed that states' legislators intended to discriminate against the headscarf from the start. This mainly since they attempted to establish the ground for differentiation on arbitrary interpretation, suggesting that the headscarf – in contrast to symbols of Christianity or other western beliefs – would automatically be considered as a symbol hostile to these fundamental protected values and, as such, should be kept away from school premises.

927 The criticism raised with respect to this strict approach in the state of Berlin is the difficulty to justify such a general ban in an open pluralistic society which is supposed to embrace a more religion-friendly attitude, especially given the fact that the adopted state-church model in Germany is not one of a strict separation. See also *Heinig* in Brugger/Karayanni (eds.), Religion in the Public Sphere: A Comparative Analysis of German, Israeli, American and International Law, 181 (196).

928 *Heinig* in Brugger/Karayanni (eds.), ibid., 181 (196).

929 *Heinig* in Brugger/Karayanni (eds.), ibid., 181, (194, 196).

that such a religious symbol may have on the surrounding (symbol-viewers, e.g., pupils, parents, teachers, or schools' principal).

Nonetheless, a restriction on teachers' dress code that creates a differentiation based on non-religious grounds raises some problems. This is since the myriad of interpretations given to a specific symbol may be indefinite and result in various judicial resolutions that would only contribute further to the uncertainty and vagueness already existing with respect to the permissibility of religious symbols in public education. It is due to the difficulty to confer religious symbols, like the headscarf, a monolithic meaning that multiple of interpretations are possible and could be taken into account. Accordingly, the lawmakers in each federal state may feel free to accord the headscarf a subjective, arbitrary interpretation (i.e., a political symbol associated with Islamic extremism). This enables the states to introduce the ban on the headscarf through the back door, claiming it to be a sign of extremism and women's oppression that is hostile to the fundaments of Western tradition. Thereto, it was also criticised that the state arrogates itself a unilateral right to define the meaning of a religious symbol without paying any regard to the real motivation of the wearer (the teacher).[930]

d) Relationship of Educational System and Religion in the Jurisprudence of BVerfG und BVerwG

Notably, since Germany had never adopted a strict separation between state and religion,[931] it was not surprising that from a socio-historical perspective religion had accommodated a prominent place in the educational system of many of the federal states.[932] The following analysis will examine whether the earlier jurisprudence delivered by the high instances (Federal Constitutional Court and

930 *Langenfeld/Mohsen*, 3 International Journal of Constitutional Law, 2005 86, 91.

931 This was mentioned by the High Administrative Court, VGH Mannheim, NJW 2001, 2899, 2902. „*In der Rechtsprechung des BVerfG ist anerkannt, dass dieses Gebot (gemeint – weltanschaulich – religiöse neutralität) nicht gleichzusetzen ist mit einer strikten Trennung von Staat und Kirche bzw. Religion .... Schon dem Wortlaut des Grundgesetzes lässt sich eindeutig entnehmen, dass die Bundesrepublik Deutschland nicht als ein laizistischer Staat verfasst ist.*"

932 For instance: Art. 7 para 3 of the Grundgesetz permits religious instruction in state schools, in many of the federal states' constitutions there is an acknowledgement of the predominant status of the Christian faith among the population; likewise, the importance of conveyance of Christian traditions and values is an aspect of high importance in many of the federal states and as such integrated also in their constitutions and legislative acts.

Federal Administrative Court) was rather lenient and supportive in their approach towards manifestation of Christian references in state schools – either outwardly expressed, like in the case of a religious symbol such as the crucifix,[933] or taking the inner form of transmission of religious values, like the practice of religious prayers in schools (*Schulgebetentscheidung*).[934] In this context, emphasis will be put on the role that the principle of state's obligation to religious neutrality played as a constitutive element of German constitutionalism, and to its impact on the development of German jurisprudence dealing with admissibility of religious influence made either through conveyance of religious values and tradition or through the manifestation of religious attire or the display of insignias in states' school system.[935] Yet, the criticism raised with respect to the nexus made between the principle of neutrality and the expression of religious symbols that are perceived as 'secular', 'liberal', and 'Western' was contended to be overestimated, especially by the jurisprudence delivered following the *Crucifix* decision. It was asserted that the neutrality principle was often invoked to the extent that its usage was made in order to curb the right of minorities to religious freedom.[936]

Albeit the special significance attributed to religious neutrality on part of the state, in particular with regard to the educational sphere, the BVerfG has characterized the school system in Germany as an institution, the place where the cultural heritage, including the religious heritage, of the German society is transmitted to the young generation and renewed.[937]

In the face of this pronouncement, it is interesting to detect that the constitutional legal debate raised two sets of conflicts, as far as the conveyance of

---

933 BVerfGE 93, 1.

934 BVerfGE 52, 223.

935 *Mancini*, 30 Cardozo Law Review 2009, 2629, 2630.

936 *Heinig* in Brugger Karayanni (eds.), Religion in the Public Sphere: A Comparative Analysis of German, Israeli, American and International Law, 181 (182); *von Campenhausen*, BYU L. Rev. 2004, 665; *Sydow*, ZG 2004, 313; *Huster*, in: FS für Tsatsos (2003), 215; *Triebel*, Kopftuch und staatliche Neutrlität, BayVBl. 2002, 624; *Janz/Rademacher*, JuS 2001, 440; *Rademacher*, Das Kreuz mit dem Kopftuch, 2005, p. 30; *Mann*, Das Kopftuch der muslimischen Lehrerin als Eignungsmangel im Beamtenrecht, 2004 p.; *Lanzerath*, p.; Religiöse Kleidung und öffentlicher Dienst – Zur Zulässigkeit dienstrechtlicher Bekleidungsverbote in Schule, Gerichtsbarkeit und Polizei, 2003 p.; *Mager*, Der Kopftuchstreit vor dem Bundesverfassungsgericht, Religion – Staat – Gesellschaft 2004, p. 275.

937 See BVerfGE 93,1, 22=NJW 1995, 2477; *Heckel*, DVBl 1996, 453, 468; *McGoldrick*, p. 108; *Häußler*, 3 European Journal of Migration Law 2001, 457, 465.

religious values and tradition as well as the expression of religious convictions made through manifestation of religious symbols in the public school system are concerned. The sets of conflicts are as follows:

First, *the institutional level of church-state relations* – emphasis was deliberated with respect to the permissibility of organizational entanglement between state and church, in particular in view of the constitutional demand barring the establishment of a state-church (Art. 140 GG together with Art. 137 para 1 WRV). In this respect, the legitimacy of the state to substantially support a particular religion had been sharply contested, especially with regard to the exclusive prerogative of the federal states to structure their educational systems (Art. 7 para 1 GG). For instance, in the *Crucifix* decision the legitimacy of the Bavarian state to order affixation of a symbol of religious identification carrying a cultural significance had been subject to judicial review.[938]

Second, *fundamental liberty rights of the individual* – the juridical instances analysed the influence of structural, constitutional interplay between state and church on personal liberty right to religious freedom and the constitutional right to equality (of other religions and non-religions). Controversial was the establishment of a threshold (high or low) which determines whether encroachment on fundamental rights occurred. The threshold would vary depending on (i) the state-church model (accommodative/separationist) and (ii) the court's corresponding interpretation (restrictive or lenient) of constitutional structural precepts (i.e., neutrality, equal treatment, separation, and non-identification). The accommodative state-church approach upheld by the BVerfG in the cases of Ludin and the recent headscarf in NRW was more accepting towards the teacher wearing a headscarf due to a lenient interpretation of the neutrality principle. This favouritism of the teacher's right to religious freedom as opposed to the obligation of the state to religious neutrality was made possible due to a different balance of the competing rights. The emphasis was placed on the fundamental right of an individual to religious freedom requiring a higher threshold for its confinement by other constitutional precepts or rights. This enabled the court to sustain a less restrictive approach of the neutrality precept, while implementing the principle of 'practical concordance' tilting the scale finally in favour of the teacher.

---

938 BVerfGE 93, 1, 19, 20, 21; = NJW 1995, 2477, 2481; BVerfGE 16.10.79, 52, 223, 236 – 1 BvR 647/70; BVerfGE 26.3.1957, 6, 309, 356 2 BvG 1/55; BVerfGE 17.12.1975 41, 29, 45–1 BvR 63/68.

Given reference to the historical development of state-church relations in Germany, the constitution that still relies on provisions provided for in the WRV of 1919 and its federal structure, which enables each federal state to decide on the educational system within its realm, it is not surprising that in the earlier jurisprudence reviewing state-church controversies, especially in the context of school, development of case laws under Art. 4 GG were relatively rare. The reason for that was the reluctance of the German jurisprudence to decide on issues relating to the endorsement of religious influence in state schools, as it preferred to leave it to the discretion of the state's legislators as a matter subject to their exclusive competency. It is also due to this tendency of the BVerfG that many controversies arising with respect to the endorsement of religious symbols in state schools have remained open and blur simply as they were addressed to the competent authority to decide on the matter.[939] This naturally contributed further to the uncertainty and lack of coherence, especially in the judgements delivered following the *Crucifix* decision, as will be exemplified subsequently. The following illustration will thence outline in general the positions of the BVerwG and BVerfG before and after the delivery of the *Crucifix* decision. It will attempt to identify the prevailing approaches of the courts in their development of judicial tests, delineating the tests under which an organizational entanglement between state and church would qualify the unconstitutionality of its institutional structure (structural unconstitutionality). In addition, the guidelines proposed by the courts for determining whether a state's endorsement or disapproval of religion would amount to impermissible encroachment of an individual's right to religious liberty will be contrasted. The assessment of the guidelines prescribed by the German judicator remained relevant in many aspects, also in the recent decision of the BVerfG relating to the headscarf ban in NRW and will be evaluated respectively in the relevant legal requirements.

aa) Leading Position of the BVerfG and BVerwG until the Mid-1970s[940]

The first cases that demonstrated the tendency of the German courts regarding church-state interaction in the field of education revealed, as mentioned before,

939 BVerfGE 108, 282 for instance the decision of the BVerfG with respect to a teacher with a headscarf was reversed back to the state's legislator of Baden-Württemberg, so that it will enact regulations regulating the wearing of religious insignia in the civil service.

940 BVerfGE 52, 223; BVerfGE 41, 29; BVerfGE 41, 65; BVerfGE 41, 88; BVerfGE 35, 366; BVerfGE 6, 309.

a jurisprudence characterized by an accepting and integrating approach towards incorporation of religious references.

An expression for this salient approach was noticeable in several cases delivered during the 1970s and was mostly predominant until the decade's mid-half. The most significant case laws, such as school prayer and inter-confessional schools set a line of constitutional criteria that provide some indication as to when an excessive organizational entanglement between the state and church in the field of education will be regarded as impermissible. The school prayer decision reached the BVerfG as a conjoined constitutional complaint following a similar factual situation debated in two federal states (NRW and Hesse) and raised the same legal question. Surprisingly, the decisions yielded a different outcome and, as a result, the question regarding the permissibility of school prayers when conducted outside the frame of religious lessons in state compulsory schools, given that an objection was raised by parents of a pupil was referred to the BVerfG for judicial review.[941] The first case brought before the Administrative Court of Hesse dealt with the permissibility of a school prayer conducted voluntarily by a schoolteacher outside the frame of religious instruction.[942] This raised objection by the pupil's parents who claimed an infringement of his negative religious freedom, since he was compelled by the exercise of the prayer even if he was not forced to participate in it. The Administrative Court found that the school prayer was impermissible if it was to inflict against the negative religious freedom of the objecting pupil. It was underscored that the negative freedom of minority pupils cannot be inferior to that of the majority of pupils in the sense that the only way to avoid the exercise of religious worship would be to leave the classroom. Vice versa, in the second case a pupil asserted against the state of NRW that his positive right to exercise his religion was breached due to the ban of prayer in his school.[943] The BVerwG held that the right of religious minorities to keep silent or leave the class during a school prayer cannot gain precedence over the majority's positive right to express their belief so as to prohibit religious prayers. Apart from that, the BVerwG explained that the exclusive prerogative to organize its school system confers upon each of the federal states the right to establish public schools of inter-denominational character and the educational aim thereof.

941 BVerfGE 52, 223 = DÖV 1980, *Böckenförde*, DÖV 1980, 323.

942 HessVGRspr. 16,1=DÖV 1966, 51; BvR 647/70.

943 BVerwGE 44, 196 =DÖV 1974, 278; BvR 7/74.

Eminently, the jurisdiction of the BVerfG in this regard dealt mainly with two different aspects: first, the competency of the states (*Bundesländer*) with respect to religious education and Christian references and, second, the constitutionality/permissibility of religious references made either through conveyance of religious values or the outward manifestation of religious symbols in state schools.

(1) *The Competency of the State with Respect to Religious Education and Christian References*

The jurisdictions during the 1970s followed a consistent path acknowledging the immutable bond between the church and the state in Germany, and the inevitability to disentangle any ecclesiastical influence on the school system. Thence, the leading approach of the jurisprudence with respect to the role and place of religion in German state schools was rather of accommodating the needs of the Christian churches.

The competency of the federal states to legislate and regulate the framework and structure of their school system alluded to a large extent to the respective constitutions and legislation of each of the federal states. Consequently, questions relating to the competency of the states were interlinked with the constitutionality of state's legislation prohibiting or permitting religious practice in schools and, as a result, had been subject to judicial review of the courts.

An affirmative recognition of the educative mandate of the state was explicitly demonstrated in the Konkordat decision (*Konkordatsurteil*) in which the BVerfG affirmed the extensive competency and freedom of the federal states to establish and design their school system.[944] The Court upheld its affirmation based on the specific wording of the Grundgesetz (Art. 7 para 1) as it guarantees the educational mandate of the state requiring that the 'entire school system shall be under the supervision of the state'. It further guaranteed the exclusive right of the Catholic Church to conduct religious education lessons in public schools and state-supported confessional schools given that it met the wish of Catholic parents.

The jurisprudence recognized the need to respect the exclusive discretion granted to the state's legislator in educational matters. This rather ample competency empowers the state to decide on the character and nature of its school system. In deciding to admit, for instance, voluntary religious prayers in

944 BVerfGE 6, 309, 355 = NJW 1957, 705.

compulsory state schools the state is permitted to take into consideration the will of the religious majority and by that fulfils its legitimate task.[945]

The school prayer case determined that the parental right to control the education and upbringing of their children (Art. 6 para 2 GG) includes the right that the children will be conveyed with religious precepts that accord with the parents' belief as encompassed in Art. 4 para 1 and para 2 GG. However, this parental right to decide on the education of the children does not stand on its own but is rather subject to the limitations prescribed in Art. 7 GG. Since Art. 7 para 1 GG accords the state a constitutional mandate to organize school structure; this power includes naturally all inherited tasks emanating from it (e.g., determination of the curriculum, setting up educational goals, recruitment of teaching staff, and delineation the courses of study).[946] Intelligibly, discrepancies relating to the perceived educational goals may take place and lead to collision between the parental right to free exercise of religion and the state's commitment to the non-establishment principle. Hence, the parental right accorded in Art. 6 para 2 does not override the educative mandate of the state established in Art. 7 para 1 GG; instead, it needs to be balanced against the latter as both rights are autonomous and stand equally without one gaining priority over the other.

In addition, the conveying values of Christianity in compulsory state schools was claimed to mark Western culture and, hence, was often interwoven with it. It was therefore argued that incorporation of Christian references or the establishment of Christian community schools was not to be comprehended in a confessional sense, but rather as non-denominational form of conveying ethical norms and Western values, such as tolerance and respect for the other-minded.[947] These general accepted values which symbolize the Western tradition are also deeply rooted in Christian ideas and, consequently, cannot amount to affirmation of a formal confession in its theological sense. The state's legislator is, hence, permitted to incorporate those values if it considers them to be accepted by all parts of the society.[948] The defence of the Christian faith and its religious practices was often argued as a protection of the fundamental values of Western culture. It was underscored by the dissenting judges BVerfG that manifestation of religious symbols (e.g., the cross) should not be perceived under its pure religious meaning

945 See Landsverfassung Bayern, Landesverfassung NRW, Landesverfassung Beden-Würrtemberg.

946 BVerfGE 52, 223, 236; BVerfGE 34, 165, 182; 47, 46, 71; BVerfGE 93, 1, 21.

947 BVerfGE 41, 29 = NJW 1976, 947; BVerfGE 41, 65.

948 BVerfGE 93, 1, 28.

affirming the Christian faith, but rather in connection with its historical-cultural rooted tradition in the German society.

The question relating to the legitimacy of the state to endorse within its educative task religious references in interdenominational schools was not confined solely to their general permissibility but was subject to judicial review examining whether religious or ideological references should be permissible only when conducted within religious classes which are guaranteed under Art. 7 para 3 GG, as will be explained subsequently.

(2) *The Permissibility of Conveyance of Religious Values and Manifestation of Religious Symbols*

The earlier decisions of the BVerfG and BVerwG during the 1970s followed a very clear path that recognized endorsement of Christian symbols in public education as legitimate, and that was reluctant to accept their admission as unconstitutional. In one of its former decisions, the *Christliche Gemeinschaftsschule*, the so-called 'Interdenominational School Case' from 1975, the non-denominational Christian school paradigm was established to be compatible with the Grundgesetz, and the Federal Constitutional Court coined the principle that 'the incorporation of Christian references is not absolutely forbidden when establishing public schools.'[949]

Albeit this explicit pronouncement, the admissibility of religious practices was subject to fulfilment of the prerequisites, namely, that any religious practice would have to take place on a voluntary basis[950] and without coercion.[951]

For instance, in the school prayer decision (*Schulgebetentscheidung*) the BVerfG held that the conflicting interests of pupils who wish not to participate in prayers are adequately taken into consideration and counterweighed against the majority's will, as they were left with an option to leave classes for the duration of the prayers or stay in the class and remain silent.[952]

The BVerfG indeed recognized that a voluntary prayer led by a teacher while at school may result in tension between the free exercise of religion and the non-establishment part of the clause (the right not to have or practice a religion safeguarded as well under Art. 4 GG). However, the Court attributed this tension to the inherent nature of the rights safeguarded in the Grundgesetz, necessitating

949 BVerfGE 41, 29 = NJW 1976, 947; *Kommers/Miller*, p. 477.
950 BVerfGE 52, 223, 239.
951 BVerfGE 52, 223, 248.
952 *Brugger/Karayanni*, p. 174, 175.

that they will eventually be counterweighed against each other.[953] Accordingly, it was sustained that minority pupils do not have an irrevocable right to have their negative religious freedom prevail over the right of the majority Christian students to conduct a school prayer. This notion maintained its support when the BVerfG determined that parents and pupils do not have a constitutional right that the state should accommodate the needs of all religions and faiths when establishing school forms.[954]

Moreover, the impact resulting from an exposure to a religious symbol or practice on pupils of no denomination or of other religious adherence was highlighted so as to guarantee that no exertion of concerted influence on part of the school and teachers takes place. It was, therefore, decided that coercive elements must be reduced to the absolute required minimum.[955] In this respect, the majority's opinion in the earlier courts holding in church and state issues underscored mainly that religious themes in non-denominational schools must be conducted in a non-discriminatory and non-compulsory manner, so that no exertion of concerted influence would be deployed on pupils by school authorities and teachers.[956]

Being confronted with points of view which admit the formative force of Christian thinking does not lead to a discriminatory perspective on minorities not attached to Christianity if no absolute truths are conveyed, but the building of the autonomous personality in the area of religion is the focus.[957]

Surprisingly, despite the establishment of the earlier-mentioned pre-requirements, participation in religious school events like a school prayers was regarded as admissible. In the German school prayer case from 1979, the BVerfG, by acknowledging this form of school prayer[958] as a state action necessitating the observance of basic constitutional rights (e.g., pupils, school authorities, parents, and teachers), implicitly made clear that a pupil was neither exposed

953 BVerfGE 52, 223; *Kommers/Miller*, p. 461.

954 BVerfGE 41, 29, 46, 48; BVerfGE 52, 223, 242; BVerfGE 93, 1, 22.

955 *McGoldrick*, p. 108.

956 BVerfGE 41, 29; BVerfGE 41, 65.

957 BVerfGE 41, 29; BVerfGE 41, 65.

958 Notably, the case dealt with a special situation as the prayer was neither conducted during religious lessons, where it would have been permitted anyway according to the precept of Art. 7 para 3 of the Grundgesetz, nor was it recited during other lessons of the school's curriculum. The issue was raised since the state ordered the prayers recital at the beginning of the school day.

to inadmissible coercion nor unequal treatment by virtue of the right to remain silent or leave the classroom.[959]

In that sense, it is interesting to notice that the Court's view with respect to the disentanglement of church and state is not supportive of a strict separation, as religious influences even on minorities would be regarded as admissible as long as they are conducted within permissible limits (i.e., minimum elements of coercion, voluntariness, and non-discriminatory manner).

It was overwhelming that a shift in the approach held by the Court was noticeable already in the mid-1970s as the BVerfG departed from its traditional position, pronouncing that the affixation of crosses in classrooms cannot be divested from the religious meaning attached to the symbol. Accordingly, it held that the strong reliance to its symbolic meaning as a sign of Western culture may definitely run counter to the different beliefs of other individual pupils and their fundamental (negative) right not to be effected by the sight of the cross as safeguarded in Art. 4 para 1 GG.[960]

bb) Leading Position of the BVerfG and BVerwG after the Crucifix

The aspects of, first, the competency of the state with respect to religious education and Christian references and, second, the permissibility of religious references made either by conveyance of religious values or manifestation of ostentatious garments/the display of religious symbols in classrooms remained relevant even after the *Crucifix* decision.

However, it has become questionable whether the BVerfG de facto followed the line set up in its earlier decisions, or whether it has marked a breakup from that former set of requirements established already in the 1970s.

(1) The Competency of the State with Respect to Religious Education and Christian References

The interference of the BVerfG in the educative mandate of the state accrued for the first time in the *Crucifix* decision. From a German constitutional point of view, it is not surprising that the judgement encountered major criticism, as the competence of the state regarding formation and structuring of the school system is not only guaranteed in the Grundgesetz (Art. 7 para 1, Art. 70 GG) but was also reaffirmed many times in the history of the Court's jurisprudence.[961]

---

959 BVerfGE 52, 223, 248 =NJW 1974, 574.

960 BVerfGE 93,1; *Brugger/Karayanni*, p. 178.

961 BVerfGE 41, 29 = NJW 1976, 947; BVerfGE 6, 309, 355= NJW 1957, 705.

Additionally, the German constitution imposes on the state a duty of adherence to religious neutrality in the public sphere in the sense that the state should not support or prohibit any religion, creed, or ideological worldview, known also as the no state-church precept prescribed in Art. 137 para 1 WRV. This entails that schools, as public institutions in charge of the education of future generation, should maintain openness and tolerance towards other religions, faiths, or philosophical/ideological creeds and should not demonstrate favouritism towards a specific dominant religion.

In this context, schools should not exert any proselytizing effect on the pupils, given that the reference to Christianity as a dominant religion may only be conducted in its historical-cultural aspect so as to act as an integrative force. The implication to Christianity as a religious doctrine will be regarded as unconstitutional and hence inadmissible.[962]

Finally, it was alleged that religious pluralism in the German society necessitates that the term 'religious neutrality of the state' should be given a liberal interpretation that tilts towards a more 'religion-friendly' understanding of neutrality. This view supports the establishment of a reciprocal-oriented relation which is based on open, friendly, tolerating, and accepting interaction between religious groups and the state that will support all faiths equally.[963] Remarkably, regarding the lapse of almost two decades since the delivery of the *Crucifix* decision, the same legal aspects have been considered in the recent BVerfG decision relating to the headscarf in NRW. The BVerfG intervened in the educative mandate of the state granted to all federal state pursuant to Art. 7 para 1 GG when it decided to overrule the NRW discretion with respect to the privilege it granted to Christian-occidental tradition and values. This raises heavy doubts, especially as it may be regarded as judicial activism of the BVerfG as the *Länder*-prescribed educational goals within their lands' constitution and should be respected accordingly. In addition, it can be claimed to be a sharp interference in the discretion of the federal states to regulate their inner affairs at own discretion. Another aspect relates to the extensive scope of protection granted in favour of the teacher's right to religious freedom, however, retrenching at the same time possible interferences that the scope of protection may pose to other constitutionally protected values, such as the negative right of pupils to religious freedom, the duty of state to religious neutrality, and the principle of equality. In the jurisprudence of the BVerfG, special consideration and due attention were granted in particular with respect to

962 BVerfGE 93, 1, 19; BVerfGE 41, 29, 52; *McGoldrick*, pp. 108, 109.
963 BVerfGE 108, 202.

these prominent constitutional values. The counter-weight given to those highly ranked values, degrading their constitutional position as opposed to the right of a teacher to manifestation of her religion, may indicate the very accommodative approach of the BVerfG towards endorsement of religion in public education. Regarding this legal aspect, it is worth to note that multi-culturalism in a society imposes a difficult task on the state, as it entails a reappraisal of the extent to which religious symbols should be permitted at school. The difficulties to set up the boundaries with respect to the permissibility of religious symbols in state schools will be exemplified next.

(2) *The Permissibility of Religious References Made Through Conveyance of Religious Values and Manifestation of Religious Symbols*

The shift in the argumentation underlying the Court's jurisprudence in the aftermath of the *Crucifix* decision and regarding the legitimacy of religious insignias in schools can be identified substantially through the following determinations:

The BVerfG delivered in the Crucifix a precedent with respect to admissibility of religious symbols in state schools.[964]

First, *protection of minorities (religious) rights* – for the first time, the aspect of protection of the rights of individuals belonging to a minority group prevailed over the majority's right to express their religious freedom. Thus, in the *Crucifix* case the mandated display of crosses in classrooms, though entrenched in a legislative act and accorded with the majority's will since it presented their adherence to Christianity, would have to retreat if a minority found the cross offensive such that it infringes their negative right to religious freedom.

On the same token, the recognition of a minority's right to realize its religious interests was affirmed in the case of a teacher wearing the headscarf during school instructions (*Ludin*'s case), thereby admitting the comprehensive constitutional protection of the teacher (Art. 4, Art. 3 para 3 and Art. 33 para 3 GG) to gain preference over the negative right of the majority of pupils, their parents, and school authorities.[965]

---

964 The BVerfG in the Crucifix decision actually followed one of its earlier precedents, delivered, however, not with respect to the legitimacy of religious insignia in schools, but rather in courtrooms. The precedent, dated from 17.7. 1973, accepted an application of a Jewish lawyer claiming that his court hearings under the cross amount to an act of coercion that infringes his right to religious freedom; therefore, he pleaded to refrain from its confrontation. See BVerfGE 35, 366, 375 = NJW 1973, 2196.

965 BVerfGE 108, 282.

The right of a public official like the teacher to invoke her right to religious freedom (Art. 4, para 1, 2 GG) was recognized by the BVerfG as a fundamental freedom worth protection, albeit the special status deriving from compliance with duties and obligations in the civil service. Therefore, the interests of a public servant cannot be a priori excluded but, rather, deliberate separately with respect to each sector in the civil service. Accordingly, the BVerfG found that, as a practical matter, there should be no restriction on a teacher to exercise her religious freedom if this represents a fulfilment of her religious obligation.[966] In wearing the headscarf, the teacher exercises her fundamental right to have and cultivate a faith, to manifest it outwardly, and to live according to it – to orient her entire life towards specific religious doctrine as accorded to her in the Grundgesetz (Art. 4 para 1)[967] This position has been explicitly confirmed by the BVerfG in its latest judgement from 27 January 2015.

Second, *mandatory school attendance* – the mandatory participation of pupils in schools does not enable them to escape from the influence of an expressed belief they do not share. This was the majority's opinion held in the *Crucifix* decision that refused to overlook the rights of minority pupils not to 'study under the cross'. A similar view was held in *Ludin*'s case, however, by the dissenting judges determining that the teacher's right to practice her religion by wearing a conspicuous garment should retreat when weighed against the negative right of pupils. This is simply because the teacher entered voluntarily the pedagogical sector, whereas the pupils are subject to a mandatory attendance with no alternatives.[968] Nonetheless, similarly to the majority's view in *Ludin*'s case, the same was held by a majority's opinion in the recent BVerfG decision of the headscarf in NRW. The BVerfG recognized the right of a teacher as a public servant to manifest her religion even while on duty, and act and orientate her whole life in accordance with the precepts of her religion as safeguarded to her in the constitution (Art. 4 para 1 and 2).[969]

Third, *the extensive interpretive method of the BVerfG* – the eligibility of admission or prohibition of religious symbols will be dependent on their specification in legal regulation. The courts, therefore, will enjoy an extensive flexibility in their decisions, as the interpretation of the norms would be resolved based on the German *verfassungskonforme Auslegung* in order to keep their conformity

966 BVerfGE 108, 282.

967 BVerfGE 108, 282, 197.

968 BVerfGE 108, 282; *Brugger/Karayanni*, p. 193.

969 BVerfGE 138, 296, 297 = NJW 2015, 1359, 1360–1361.

with the constitution. This technique of interpretation enables German courts to interpret a provision explicitly permitting the affixation of religious symbols so as to keep in conformity with the constitution.

(3) Rating of Jurisdictional Development

(a) The Early Decisions

The guidelines set forth by the early jurisprudence relating to the competency of the federal states to regulate religious affairs, including endorsement of religious insignias in state schools can be summarized as follows:

First, the comprehensive authority of the state to introduce religious references in state compulsory schools must arise from its educative mandate prescribed in Art. 7 para 1 GG.[970]

Second, the permissibility of incorporation of religious references in interdenominational schools will be permitted as long as no violation of the negative right of individuals to religious freedom or other prominent constitutional values occurs.

Third, the school prayer case demonstrated incontestably that the incorporation of Christian references in compulsory state schools is not strictly forbidden, and will not trigger immediately the infringement of minority rights. This will be regarded permissible as long as the requirement of voluntariness and absence of coercion are fulfilled.[971]

Fourth, the introduction of Christian references in non-denominational state schools should not be comprehended within the pure religious context, but rather under its cultural-educational aspect rooted in the historical development of Western countries.[972] If the educational goal is to permit solely Christian references, then these must be conveyed within the context of religion classes.

Fifth, in the interdenominational school case, the BVerfG decided that the parental right pursuant to Art. 6 para 2 GG does not grant parents an exclusive right on the education and upbringing of their children. Given that this is the case, it will be impossible to satisfy the rights of religious minorities in

---

970 BVerfGE 52, 223, 236; BVerfGE 93, 1, 21; BVerfGE 34, 165, 181; BVerfGE 41, 29 = NJW 1976, 947; BVerfGE 6, 309, 355= NJW 1957, 705.

971 *Kommers/Miller*, p. 575.

972 BVerfGE 41, 29, 52.

a multi-cultural society if each group is to demand from the state to establish a school of a particular religion or ideology.[973]

Since it is only conceivable that the state cannot take the religious interests of all parents and all pupils into consideration when structuring its state school system, the Court recognizes a possibility that a minority of parents will be compelled to send their children to a school that conveys different religious views than their own. Such a situation will not trigger immediately the impingement of the negative freedom of religious minorities, as it was acknowledged that the state is allowed to introduce a variety of ideologies, creeds, and beliefs as long as no proselytization or a commitment to the precepts of the prevailing faith, that is, Christianity, takes place. Notably, although parents cannot derive from their right by virtue of Art. 6 para 2 and 4 para 1 and para 2 GG a claim against the state that their children will be educated with the religion or ideology they determine, they can still object to governmental actions which adversely affect their constitutional right.

Sixth, in that sense, the BVerfG confirmed that the competency of the federal states to decide independently on the organization of the denominational character of their school system was meant to be extensive, so as to enable the states' legislature to decide freely on matters within their realm (i.e., the exclusive right on educational matters), by virtue of the powers conferred in the principle of federalism.[974]

Seventh, the state mandated by its educative task must find the balance between the affirmative right of the majority (parents and pupils) to allow the establishment of interdenominational state schools within its region or introduce religious reference, such as the school prayer, into compulsory state school, and the negative freedom of other parents and pupils objecting to the school prayer. This method of harmonization between two countervailing rights is made through a method known as 'practical concordance', as it will try to coincide between the protected legal values insofar as both will attain maximum effect but neither will gain precedence over the other.

Eighth, given that the state encroaches upon the negative freedom of pupils and parents in the sense that they are compelled to send their children to a state school which contradicts their ideological conviction and no other school of the parents' denomination is available within their local community, then the result must be balanced within the interpretive boundaries of the practical

973 BVerfGE 93, 1, 22.

974 *Kommers/Miller*, pp. 462, 468.

concordance. The competing rights based on the practical concordance will tilt towards the protection of the negative right of minority pupils not to be adversely affected by the specific religious orientation of the school in the sense that only the minimum elements of coercion will take place.

Ninth, notwithstanding, the obligation of the state to religious neutrality and the principle of non-establishment (no affirmative support of religion) must on its part endeavour to provide for its citizens an adequate room in order to develop and flourish their religious belief, including in public. This must be achieved on the basis of mutual commitment for tolerance and acceptance, so that it will be possible for religious individuals in that way to practice their religion on the one hand, and refrain on the other hand from any coercive element ascertaining religion that may adversely affect the negative right of minorities not to believe or even disclose their belief.

(b) The Recent Judgements

The guidelines to be inferred from judgements delivered following the *Crucifix* decisions are as follows:

First, *school as an institute worth special protection* – in both judgements, namely, interdenominational schools and the Crucifix, the BVerfG confirmed the negative aspect of religious freedom conferred to individuals by virtue of Art. 4 para 1 GG. The right of an individual based on Art. 4 para 1 GG was said to include the freedom to uphold a belief, act in accordance with its precepts and participate in cultish activities, as well as the right to refrain from holding a religion and participation. It was determined that Art. 4 GG applies also to symbols of a religious character and, as such, may be acknowledged and respected by some, whereas rejected by others who do not share the same religion.

Second, *place and nature of the display* – the BVerfG affirms that albeit the obligation of the state to refrain from imposing a religion, it cannot ensure the banishment of all religious symbols which an individual may encounter or become exposed to in all areas of life. It, thence, segregates between religious symbols or activities presented or conducted in public places to which an individual has no claim towards the state to ban their presence, and other areas of life which enjoy the special protection of the state.[975] This was based on the grounds that while a state cannot interfere in the organization and

975 BVerfGE 1, 18.

activities of religious communities and ban, for example, the presentation of a religious symbol on the street due to its commitment to secure an adequate room for all religions to flourish, their displacement in elementary schools can grant a claim to minorities who venerate them since they are compelled by their presence. Underpinning its reasoning, the BVerfG refers to specific provisions in the constitution, Art. 140 GG in tandem with Art. 136 para 4 WRV, recognizing those special areas in life worth safeguarding by the state.

Third, *an affirmative state favouritism* – the BVerfG expounds further that encounters with religious symbols in daily life are not induced by the state and, consequently, will not be regarded as a state action. At least, the degree of compulsion endured by the sight of religious manifestation in public is absent, as these encounters are transitional and will not accrue sanctions on part of the state.

Fourth, *equality of religions* – in the *Crucifix* case the, BVerfG acknowledged the equal right of all parents to sustain their positive religious freedom and not only the right of the majority of (Christian) parents and pupils. If these are to collide with each other, then prevalence has to be given to the negative right of religious minorities, as the BVerfG perceived the main aim of Art. 4 para 1 GG to guarantee primarily the protection of religious minorities. This argument has been confirmed by the BVerfG when limiting the prevalence of Christian influence in public schools in its latest judgement.[976] The same approach of equality of religions was upheld by the BVerfG in its recent decision of the headscarf in NRW,[977] and actually constitutes a key element in the general discussion over admissibility of religious symbols in the state school system.

(c) Concluding Evaluation – The Alignment of the Crucifix with Earlier Decisions of the BVerfG

From a constitutional perspective, the BVerfG found a way to reconcile its prima facia contradicting judgement delivered in the Crucifix on the one hand with the decisions relating to the interdenominational and school prayer, on the other hand. The determination upheld by the BVerfG that the display of the cross violates Art. 4 para 1 GG was justified based on the following grounds:

First, the *Crucifix* decision dealt with the affixation of a symbol in classrooms that is associated predominantly with the faith it represents, hence affirming Christianity as the only faith acknowledged by the state. In this respect, it was

976 BVerfG 1 BvR 471/10, 1 BvR 1181/10.

977 BVerfGE 138, 296 = NJW 2015, 1359, 1363–1364.

uncontroversial that the Crucifix, in particular, is an impressionable symbol whose effect on the mind of young pupils in elementary schools when subject to its constant confrontation cannot be denied. In contrast, the BVerfG held that establishment of inter-denominational (Christian) public schools will be constitutionally permissible given that they incorporate cultural-historical values (i.e., tolerance, mutual respect), and as long they do not actively impose the tenets of the Christian faith. Consequently, this will not amount to a discrimination or deferment of a non-Christian ideology that runs counter to the constitutional guidelines set by the BVerfG in its previous decisions.

Second, the conduct of school prayers, religious instructions, or any other religious events permits pupils of religious minorities to abstain from participation in school activities of a religious character. The reason is that they must be conducted on a voluntary basis, unlike an exposure to the display of the cross that does not give any possibility of evasion.

Third, in the Crucifix it was determined that in light of the rather open approach in public elementary schools towards religion, as expressed in the previous judgements of the BVerfG as well as guaranteed in the Grundgesetz (Art. 7 para 3 and para 5), a determination in favour of the right of the religious majority of parents will amount to an excessive suppression of the rights of religious minorities (other-minded). The BVerfG explains that since the reality in practice is very Christian accommodative in the sense that religious instructions and voluntary prayers are permissible, then constant exposure of religious minorities to a display of the cross during all school instructions will be incompatible with a proper, adequate application of the principle of practical concordance.

Fourth, to sum up, the *Crucifix* decision does not appear to stand in sharp contrast to the view held in the earlier decisions, especially since it coincided with the doctrinal structures set up in the 1975 decisions.[978] The cross was often accorded by the courts a twofold context: first, significance as a pure religious symbol, and second, a historical-cultural significance which embodies the origin of constitutional values of tolerance, human dignity, and reciprocal respect.[979] The latter was often used by the earlier decision of the Court as a method of interpretation meant to neutralize its religious significance so as to ensure its compatibility with the fundamental rights prescribed in the constitution.[980]

978 *Brugger/Karayanni*, p. 178.

979 *Mancini*, 30 Cardozo Law Review 2009, 2629, 2637.

980 This view was held by the minority in the Crucifix decision, see BVerfGE 93,1; *Mancini*, 30 Cardozo Law Review 2009, 2629, 2633.

cc) Crosses in Classrooms

(1) The Crucifix *Decision*

The most prominent jurisprudential decision relating to admission of religious symbols in German elementary (non-denominational) schools is the *Crucifix* decision. Through its extraordinary verdict, the case provoked overwhelming resonance in all parts of German society and numerous critical voices from legal commentators and politicians. Thence, the following will outline the factual background as well as the leading legal aspects setting up the line in this controversial case:

(a) Factual Background

In that case the claim was brought by parents, followers of the Rudolf Steiner's philosophical movement, who tried to convince the elementary school in which their daughters attended that they reject the exposure of their daughters to the cross due to their atheist conviction; as a consequence, they asked for a removal of the cross from all classrooms their daughters attended. Their main allegation was that the command in proviso 13 para 1 BSR (VSO) to hang a cross in every classroom in Bavaria violates the basic right of religious freedom as guaranteed in the constitution (Art. 4 GG)[981] taken together with Art. 6 para 2 and Art. 2 para 1 GG.[982] The exposure to the crucifix (the cross with a portrayal of a dying male body) and even to the cross,[983] according to their perception, has a Christian influence on their daughters that runs counter to their philosophical conviction. Thereupon, the complainants challenged the legitimacy of the affixation of crosses in Bavarian state schools and brought an action against the state of Bavaria.

It is worth to note that because the complainants did not achieve an acceptable compromise with the school administration, they abstained from sending their children to school. By their allegation they aimed to have all crosses removed from classrooms frequented or yet-to-be frequented in public schools by their children.

---

981 BVerfGE, 16 May 1995, 93, 1.

982 Art. 2 para 1 GG.

983 In order to solve the conflict, it was offered to the parents by the school administration to achieve a compromise to exchange the crucifix with a smaller cross (not including the corpus). Nonetheless, the BVerfG decided to review the constitutionality of both, crucifixes as well as cross when affixed in public schools. BVerfGE 93,1, 17.

The complaint was unsuccessful in the Bavarian High Administrative Court[984] and was consequently brought for revision before the BVerfG.

(b) Leading Legal Aspects

The *Crucifix* decision established several pronounced guidelines which delineated the path for the future development of constitutional law in Germany, where the legitimacy of religious symbols in state schools was put into question. Due to its exceptional importance in the German jurisprudence, the key elements of the judgement will be laid down as follows.

(aa) Religious Neutrality of the State

The Court expresses three major aspects with regard to the principle of neutrality.

First, the obligation of the state to avert from any expression or favouring of ideological position is the direct outcome emanating from its obligation to religious neutrality. The BVerfG underscores the due reference to be given to the duty of the state to keep its neutrality in aspects of religion. The Court states that the right to religious freedom guaranteed in Art. 4 para 1 GG enables the individual to adopt a faith and act in accordance with the religious convictions prescribed to him by his faith.[985] However, the state, unlike a citizen who has the basic right to express his/her religious and ideological belief, should refrain from any identification favouring or detracting religious denominations or ideological creeds. The reason for this is that the state is not considered as the legal right holder and addressee of Art. 4 para 1 GG.

This obligation was said by the Court to be infringed by the state when deciding to equip all public school classrooms with crucifixes or crosses.[986] By doing so, the state has demonstrated an enhanced profession of the Christian faith.

Second, the BVerfG finds it necessary to distinguish the case when the right of an individual to profess a religion is impinged due to a state action exposing him to the influence of a particular faith without any possibility of evasion, as opposed to a daily encounter with religious manifestation, not bound with compulsion.

---

984 VG Regensburg BayVBl 1991, 345; BayVGH, NVwZ 1991, 1099.

985 BVerfGE 93, 1, 15; BVerfGE 32, 98, 106.

986 In the Crucifix case, the court reviewed justification of both crucifix and the cross since during the first negotiations round of the objecting parents with school authorities a settlement to remove the crucifix was achieved. After a while, school authorities exchanged the crucifix with a small cross, thereby triggering the objecting parents to invoke their rights according to Art. 4 para 1 in tandem with Art. 6 para 2 of the Grundgesetz.

It makes thereby reference to Art. 140 GG taken together with Art. 136 para 4 WRV that explicitly prohibit any compulsion on an individual to participate in religious practices.[987]

Third and finally, it was determined that the peaceful co-existence of various religions and confessions in a pluralistic society can be maintained only through adherence of the state to the principle of neutrality.[988] This necessitates that the state should ensure equality of treatment while supporting and promoting the mutual acceptance and tolerance of various religious communities. In view of this pronouncement, the Court clarified that a general and remote cooperation of the state or support to a religious community may not amount to identification of the state with a particular religion.[989] Nonetheless, the Court in the *Crucifix* case found that the display of the cross is a clear state act advancing Christianity over other faiths or non-religions and consequently amounts to an impermissible identification of the state with a particular religion, namely Christianity. In this respect, the Court had already upheld in its previous decision that a state support of a specific tenet of Christianity would undermine freedom of religion and devalue the religious rights of minority pupils.[990] Moreover, this favouritism of the Christian faith discriminates against all other religious minorities and in fact encroaches upon constitutional protected rights (i.e., Art. 4 para 1, Art. 3 para 3, Art. 33 para 1, Art. 140 para 1 GG incorporated with Art. 136 para 1 and para 4 and 137 para 1 WRV).[991] Consequently, the Court found no justification for the interference with the religious freedom of the minority parents and pupil.

(bb) The Symbolism of the Cross

In principle, the majority's opinion can be discerned from that of the dissenting judges given different interpretation attached to the symbolism of the cross.

Remarkably, the legal challenge to the state's obligation to religious neutrality was interwoven with techniques of interpretation deliberated with respect to the meaning of the cross. Such interpretive method established a test meant to determine the objective meaning of a symbol.[992] This means that the affixation of

987 BVerfGE 93,1, 16=EuGRZ 1995, 363.

988 BVerfGE 93, 1, 16,17; The BVerfG declares that the obligation of the state to religious neutrality finds its fundaments not only in Art. 4 para 1 GG but also in Art. 3 para 3, 33 para 1 and Art. 140 GG combined with Art. 136 para 1 and 4, Art. 137 para 1 WRV.

989 BVerfGE 30 415, 422.

990 BVerfGE, 41, 29, 52.

991 BVerfGE 93, 1, 16, 17.

992 *Walter* in *Brugger/Karayanni*, p. 171.

crosses could be justified or negated depending on the viewer, as only the person who is concerned or affected by the symbol is suitable for determining whether according to his/her plausible perception the symbol in question infringes on their religious right. The majority in the Crucifix were criticised as they have tried to find an interpretation that took into consideration merely the negative right of a minority pupil to religious freedom.[993]

The majority argued that the Crucifix cannot be perceived remotely from its pure religious meaning as a salient tenet of the Christian faith, and that its Christian theological message[994] and its effects on other religious minorities are applied without having regard to other possible messages the cross may induce on minorities. Consequently, the majority declared the affixation of the cross in classrooms as a provocative act that due to its place of display in the classroom without any possibility to evade it amounts to an illegitimate coercion on religious minorities.[995] The minority, by contrast, attached the symbolic meaning of the cross a milder message interlinked with its imprint and contribution of general protected values (such as respect and dignity for the other, advocacy for the poor) in the Western culture and its impact on German folklore and tradition.[996] It argued that the Court's majority were mistaken in their disregard of the majority of Christian parents' and pupils' wish to profess the Christian faith and tradition through this 'weak' and remote symbol.[997]

The majority in the BVerfG rejected the view held by the dissenting opinion in this judgement that the cross is to be apprehended solely in its context as a symbol of an expression of the Western-cultural values and tradition. Opposite to this view, the majority upheld that the cross is a specific faith symbol of Christianity. It even proclaimed that the denial of its salient character as a religious symbol

---

993 *Muckel* in Muckel, Schriften zum Öffentlichen Recht, 2010, 234 (244–245); *v. Ungern-Sternberg*, 2008, 251–252; Other opinion negating infringement in the negative right to religious freedom was expressed by *v. Campenhausen*, in Archiv des Öffentlichen Rechts 121 (1996), 448 (450).

994 BVerfGE 93, 1 (19) = BVerfG 1 BvR 1087/91 para.44; "The cross continues to be one of the specific faith symbols of Christianity. It is, indeed, its symbol of faith as such. It symbolizes the salvation of man from original sin brought about through Christ's sacrificial death, but at the same time also Christ's victory over Satan and death and his lordship over the world."

995 BVerfG decision from 16.5.1995 – 1 BvR 1087/91 para. 57.

996 BVerfG 1 BvR 1087/91 para. 71; BVerfGE 41, 65, 84.

997 BVerfG 1 BvR 1087/91 para. 86.

would be regarded as a profanation to the cross which runs counter to the perception of Christianity.[998]

(cc) Negative Right of Pupils to Religious Freedom – Art. 4 GG

At first, the BVerfG referred to the perception of the cross as viewed by religious minorities and declared that a constant presence of the cross could sufficiently amount to contravene the fundamental right of parents as well as pupils wishing not to be exposed to the cross, as it stands for a religious symbol that contravenes their conviction as atheists. Accordingly, it announced the incompatibility of Art. 13 of the VSO with Art. 4 para 1 GG.

As a second step, the judges attributed a significant relevance to the context in which a religious symbol is displayed. It was explained that a direct exposure to the cross amounts to an inescapable compulsion due to the fact that the pupils were confronted constantly with presentation of the cross without any opportunity to evade because attendance at state schools is compulsory.[999] Insofar, since compulsory attendance in schools is prescribed by the state and given the compulsory affixation of crosses in public elementary schools prescribed in the VSO, it is then the obligation of the state to protect minority pupils from the influence of a specific religion or belief which is perceived by their parents to be harmful.

In this context, the BVerfG made clear that since all federal states mandate compulsory schooling, the pupils are left with no choice or preference as to attendance in a school of their choice; rather, the attendance in schools is determined according to the child's residence. This means that the pupils are compelled by view of the cross and cannot opt for non-attendance if no denominational school of their choice is available within their residential area.

Though the BVerfG states that the affixation of crosses per se does not compel minority pupils to associate or identify with the Christian religion, it cannot decline that it amounts to a factual coercion (*faktischer Grundrechtseingriff*), as in fact they are coerced to 'learn under the cross'.[1000] Further, the effect it may have on minds of elementary school pupils had also been taken into account.

---

998 BVerfGE 93,1, 20 = BVerfG 1 BvR 1087/91 para.44; "It would be a profanation of the cross running counter to the self-perception of Christianity and the Christian churches to regard it, as the decisions challenged do, as a mere expression of Western tradition or cult token without a specific reference to faith."

999 BVerfGE 93,1, 18= EuGRZ 1995, 364.

1000 German constitutional law distinguishes between normative or classic intrusion on liberty rights of individuals (klassicher Grundrechtseingriff) and factual intrusion (faktischer Grundrechtseingriff). The courts will identify a state's act as a factual intrusion on the liberty rights of an individual only if it intended to intrude on the

The possible influence on the children, even if subtle, could not be denied, especially when referring to children of a younger age.[1001] The Court affirms that children can be easily influenced by outwardly impressions and are less capable than adults to defend themselves from negative or harmful influences.[1002]

(dd) Parental Educative Right (Art. 6 para 2 GG)

The Court emphasized that the right conferred in Art. 4 para 1 in conjunction with Art. 6 para 2 GG enables parents to convey their children the principles of belief or philosophy of life as they find suitable.[1003] This suggests also the right to keep their children away from any convictions they perceive to be wrong or harmful.

(ee) The Educative Mandate of the State (Art. 7 para 1 GG)

The BVerfG ascertained the educational mandate conferred upon the state in the constitution.[1004] This freedom granted to the state in forming and setting up the educational goals in its schooling system enables it to be independent from parental influence.[1005] Nonetheless, the state of Bavaria captured an interesting form of appropriating the educative task between the state on the one hand (Art. 7 para 1 GG), and parents' right on the other hand (Art. 6 para 2 GG) comprised in its constitution (Art. 135 BayVerf).[1006] In fact, the Bavarian state was conferred the mandate to accommodate non-denominational state schools with the tradition and values of the Christian faith by a referendum through the majority of its population.

It was determined that the principle of neutrality does not oblige the state to be completely secular. The state simply cannot ignore traditions and values rooted in its history and conceivably may allow an adequate conveyance of the foundations of the Christian faith, in particular, when this right was even recognized in its constitutional precepts.[1007]

---

right or if its infringement will be regarded as substantial. A marginal infringement on religious rights will not fall within the scope of the latter, *Brugger/Karayanni*, p. 75.

1001 BVerfGE 93, 1, 20.

1002 BVerfGE 52, 223, 249.

1003 BVerfGE 41, 29, 44, 47, et seq.

1004 BVerfGE 93, 1, 21; BVerfGE 34, 165, 181.

1005 BVerfGE 93, 1, 21; BVerfGE 34, 165 182; 47, 46 71 et seq.

1006 *Campenhausen v.*, in FS Maier, 1996, p. 670.

1007 BVerfGE 93, 1, 21- The reference is made to Art. 7 para 3 and 5 GG as well as jurisprudential affirmation in case laws: BVerfGE 41, 29, 49; 52, 223, 240 et seq.

The BVerfG does not negate the right of the state, as a practical matter, to introduce Christian references in its school system, even if such endorsement may be rejected by minorities since it contravenes their right to religious freedom. Nonetheless, the confrontation with a Christian-marked symbol or with tenets of the Christian belief need to be retrenched to the indispensable, minimal elements of coercion imposed on non-Christians or atheists. In that sense, the Court also acknowledged that in a pluralistic society the state cannot take account of all denominational or philosophical conceptions in fulfilling its educational task. This point suffered criticism, as it was contended that the majority's opinion in the Crucifix demonstrated the ability of the state in its monopoly over education to frustration of individual religious freedom rather than its advancement. It was argued that the state secured the right of the atheist parents only at the cost of negating the majority's right to have the Crucifix as a symbol of the majority's confession and a reflection of their strong piety. This was contended to be 'a net loss in practical freedom of religion'.[1008]

(ff) Colliding Constitutional Rights

The BVerfG establishes the lack of constitutional grounds justifying intervention in the unreserved right to religious freedom. It explains that the affixation of crosses in state schools, even if claimed to protect other constitutional rights, transcends the requirement for minimum element of compulsion since the element of voluntariness is eliminated.[1009] Consequently, it found no legitimacy for the interference in the negative right to religious freedom of minorities. This was neither justified by the educative task of the state pursuant to Art. 7 para 1 GG, nor by the positive right of the majority pupils and parents to practice their religion as protected under Art. 4 para 1 GG.[1010]

The BVerfG concludes that the objective of Art. 4 para 1, aiming at protecting the fundamental right of religious freedom of minorities, was nullified given that the administrative courts conferred primacy to the positive confessional freedom of the majority (parents and pupils) over the negative confessional right of minorities to refrain from any religious influence. In that sense, the state confirmed its unobjectionable support of the majority's right to exert their positive religious freedom through affixation of crosses in classrooms.

1008 *Coon*, in: *Burmeister Joachim* (ed.), Verfassungsstaatlichkeit Festschrift für Klaus Stern, 1997, p. 927, 931.

1009 BVerfGE 93,24 = EuGRZ 1995, 363.

1010 BVerfGE 93, 1, 29.

It is, therefore, concluded by the Court that the positive right of the majority of pupils and parents to exercise their religious freedom cannot be upheld unrestricted permanently. Since the tension arising between pupils and parents of divergent beliefs and convictions in schools is inevitable, it is only the task of the state's legislature to avoid confrontations through a compromise acceptable by all. Resolving the tension between negative and positive religious freedom should be accomplished through application of the principle of 'practical concordance', which demands reconciliation of the competing rights when both are maximally protected and asserted.[1011]

(c) Position of Dissenting Judges

The dissenting judges were reluctant to accept that the mandated display of crosses in all elementary school classes according to Sec. 13 of the BES Ordinance stood in breach to the negative right of the minority pupils according to Art. 4 para 1 of the GG.

(aa) No Transcendence of Constitutional Legitimacy in Educational Matters

It was contended mainly that the intention of Art. 7 para 1 GG in the retrospect of its legislative history was to confer an exclusive, extensive authority on the individual federal states in the field of education. This includes the legislative authority to determine the nature, operation, and educational aims of public elementary schools.[1012] Art. 7 para 5 GG assigns an extensive discretion with respect to the type of schools.

Taking account of the provisions in the Bavarian constitution of 2 December 1946 (Art. 131 para 2 and 135 para 2 BayVerf) setting forth the educational objectives and bearing in mind that these were approved in a referendum by the majority of the Bavarian people (affixations of crosses in all public buildings and keeping the Christian nature of the state),[1013] the Bavarian legislature was not erred in its discretion to mandate the display of the cross in compulsory elementary education.[1014] The reason is that such discretion lies within its authority to establish community schools with an ideological or religious

1011 BVerfGE 93, 1, 21; BVerfGE 28, 243, 260 et seq.; BVerfGE 41, 29, 50; BVerfGE 52, 223, 247, 251.

1012 BVerfGE 93, 1, 25; BVerfGE 52, 223, 236.

1013 BVerfGE 93, 1, 28; BVerfGE 41, 65, 67.

1014 BVerfGE 93, 1, 26, 27.

character and by virtue of this empowerment the Bavarian state had fulfilled its task towards its people and affixed crosses as expected in all of its public schools.

(bb) Lack of Coercive Elements Rules Out Violation of Religious Freedom

Sec. 13 para 1 of the Bavarian Ordinance complies with the guidelines set out by the BVerfG in its previous decision,[1015] namely: first, the mere display of the cross does neither amount to a missionary practice nor does it incur on pupils of religious minority any participation in religious practice or mode of conduct.[1016] Second, taking account of the state's obligation to religious neutrality, especially in areas given to its exclusive responsibility such as education, it must exercise minimal influence of coercive element on pupils. It was underscored that if an act of a voluntary prayer in non-denominational schools will not be regarded as an infringement of the negative right to religious freedom, then under no circumstances can the view of the cross constitute an unacceptable burden.[1017] Third, non-discrimination – the display of the cross did not negate in practice the presentation of other religious symbols, nor did it segregate the introduction of other faiths and creeds.[1018] It actually remained open to other ideological or religious ideas and values. Fourth, non-identification – the affixation of the cross in classrooms demonstrates the acknowledgement of a symbol that characterizes the type of school, a Christian community school.[1019] However, this fact by itself does not suffice to establish that the school on its part transferred precepts of the Christian faith.

(cc) The Interpretive Symbolism of the Cross

The dissenting judges refused to attribute the cross a pure religious character as the main tenet of the Christian faith, but rather attempted to confer a mild interpretation associating the cross with Western-liberal tradition and values.[1020]

(d) Conclusion

The Crucifix has established its position as a momentous milestone in the constitutional jurisprudence of Germany insofar as that for the first time the BVerfG had changed the emphasis when outweighing the constitutional interplay

---

1015 BVerfGE 41, 29, 51.
1016 BVerfGE 93, 1, 29.
1017 BVerfGE 93, 1, 31; BVerfGE 52, 223.
1018 BVerfGE 93, 1, 29.
1019 BVerfGE 93, 1, 29.
1020 BVerfGE 93, 1, 32,33.

between the organizational state-church structure and liberty-oriented rights such as religious freedom.

The Crucifix suffered extensive amount of criticism from all parts of society, especially due to the importance attached to the cross in German history.[1021] The cross was rendered as a symbol whose significance goes beyond its folkloristic nature; thus, it was rendered more a pronouncement of the Christian-occidental tradition entrenched in German history due to the strong proximity between the people and the Christian faith.[1022]

The central learnings of the *Crucifix* decision can be summarized as follows:

First, *the constitutional principle of Federalism* – the *Crucifix* decision demonstrates to a large extent the level of conflict that may accrue between the federal states and the central state by virtue of the principle of federalism. The federal states enjoy sovereignty of power with respect to formation of their constitutional order and organs. This competency extends over to their administrative and legislative authority in all areas of life (including education) which fall within their jurisdiction. The Crucifix scrutinized the extensive power of the federal states to determine over the ideological and religious character of public schools as conferred to it in Art. 7 GG.

Both the majority[1023] and dissenting[1024] judges in the Crucifix attempted to trace the consideration delivered by framers of the GG with respect to the intention of Art. 7. This was meant to find out whether framers of the constitution had in mind to confer upon the federal states an exclusive legislative authority with respect to establishment and operation of their school system. As a general rule, there exists a consensus in the German jurisprudence that the responsibility for the educational system falls within the exclusive jurisdiction of the federal states[1025] as it is prescribed within the constitutional provisions Art. 7, Art. 30

1021 It is therefore no wonder that the Crucifix case reached high resonance, especially in Bavaria. The severity in which Bavarians perceived the impact of the Crucifix decision was reflected in the harsh responses pronounced by the leadership of politics and the Catholic Church. For instance, the Prime Minister of Bavaria, Edmund Stoiber, argued that the very soul of Bavaria was in danger. The then Chancellor, Helmut Kohl, argued not only that the decision is 'unintelligible' but also that "the values of western culture are in danger … the free social order is based on Christian principles".

1022 BVerfGE 93, 1, the dissenting opinion of the judgement.

1023 BVerfGE 93, 1, 21, 22.

1024 BVerfGE 93, 1, 26.

1025 BVerfGE 93, 1, 21, 22: BVerfGE 34, 165, 182; 47, 46, 71.

and Art. 70 GG. However, in the *Crucifix* case the BVerfG, for the first time, restricted the legal legitimacy of the federal states to establish and form their school systems and respectively granted the protection of fundamental liberty rights and minority protection prevalence over the historical will to establish a cooperationist state-church model.[1026]

In this respect, legal commentators raise the claim that although the educative mandate remains a domain inclusively within the jurisdiction of the federal states, the influence incurred by judicial activism of the BVerfG enfolds the risk of weakening the legislative and judicative authority of the individual states, as they will feel restrained in their accommodative state-church approach.[1027] This view finds support in the pre-Crucifix judgements which, as mentioned earlier, were more supportive in their approach towards cooperative elements of religion when introduced by the federal states in context of formation of their educational system.[1028] Accordingly, the criticism raised with respect to the manifestation of the principle of federalism is directed to the post-*Crucifix* decision, as in its aftermath it purported to restrain the discretion of the legislator and judicator in the different federal states with respect to formation of the educational system in their territory, though this authority is unlimitedly prescribed to them in the GG.

Second, *no resolution at the national level* – at the same time, it is interesting to note that although the BVerfG voted against affixation of the cross in Bavarian classrooms, it refrained from dictating the federal states an absolute prohibition with respect to endorsement of religious references when accomplishing its educative task.[1029] In fact, the majority's view attempted to reconcile the inevitable tension arising from the prerogative of the federal states to introduce religious and ideological influence in their educational system on the one hand (Art. 7 para 1 GG), and the rights of religious minorities that religious pressure will be kept away from school premises on the other hand (Art. 4 para 1 GG). This was done through a method of interpretation known as the principle of 'practical concordance'. The majority, when invoking it, endeavoured to achieve a compromise that will attempt as much as possible to respect and preserve both of the

---

1026 *Manterfeld*, Die Grenzen der Verfassung. Möglichkeiten limitierender Verfassungstheorie des Grundgesetzes am Beispiel E.-W. Boeckenfoerdes, 2000, Parts B. and C.

1027 *Dietlein*, in: FS Stern (1997), 443, 444.

1028 BVerfGE 41, 29 = NJW 1976, 947; BVerfGE 41, 65 = NJW 1976, 950; BVerfGE 41, 89 = NJW 1976, 952; BVerfGE 52, 223 = NJW 1980, 575.

1029 BVerfGE 93, 1, 22.

corresponding values that were sought to be achieved through Art. 4 and 7 GG. Thence, it seems in this sense that the *Crucifix* case did not provide a remedy at the national level but rather decided to leave this task of accomplishing an acceptable settlement to the discretion of the federal states.

Third, *unlimited prevalence of liberty rights may affect the structural state-church model* – in constitutional complaints (*Verfassungsbeschwerde*), like in the *Crucifix* case, brought by an individual claiming that the state had infringed his/her constitutional right to religious freedom according to the GG, it is the task of the BVerfG to review whether a substantial violation of a constitutional right occurred. The criticism raised with respect to Crucifix was directed to the judicial activism of the BVerfG, as it took upon itself an active function that attempted to change the constitutional order of the federation (from a moderate co-operative to a strict model of state-church).[1030] Judges should not apply jurisprudential activism if it is to change the structure of state-church relations.

Fourth, *a distinguishable emphasis in favour of minority rights to religious freedom* – given that state-institutional perspective and liberty rights are intertwined, this necessitate the judges to be more careful in judicial activism and in the balance of competing rights. In fact, most of the criticism regarding the *Crucifix* decision contended that it was at odds with the earlier jurisprudence delivered by the BVerfG. In this context, it was criticized that the *Crucifix* decision failed to provide sufficient reference to the educative mandate of the federal states. Instead, a pronounced emphasis was deliberated to outweighing of individual rights in the public school system. This pronounced discussion of the BVerfG, seeking to retrench the scope of debate solely with respect to outbalancing minorities right to negative religious freedom over the majority's right to exercise their positive right, had nullified in practice the federative mandate of the states to form their educational systems.[1031]

Fifth, *the type of observance or confrontation* – in a cooperationist model like in Germany, slightest cases of inequality must be taken into account and will not be immediately defined as unconstitutional. In this context, another factor recognized in the jurisprudence as crucial for the achievement of an adequate solution relates to the type of school in which a Crucifix is displayed. The character and type of school (whether public schools, private schools, faith or denominational school or non-denominational schools) may affect the decision with respect to

1030 *Brugger/Karayanni*, pp. 82, 83.
1031 *Dietlein,* in: FS Stern (1997), 443, 448.

affirmation of the Crucifix or refusal of its presentation in classrooms.[1032] This emanates naturally that the extent of interference in the fundamental right to religious freedom is variable and may accrue different outcomes depending on the character of the school. It is only reasonable that such a degree of interference will be set high when manifestation of religious symbols are introduced in public inter-denominational schools and, accordingly, may be low if these are to be presented in confessional schools.

Application of the objective meaning test – the risk raised by critics with respect to alignment of the requirements for presentation of religious symbols in all school forms (public denominational as well as inter-denominational) is that the educative task of the federal states would become redundant and of no significance.[1033]

Sixth, *no coercion test* – the Crucifix gained significance especially due to the imprint of the 'coercion test'. Inasmuch pupils are not able to escape the view of the cross; they are bound by the influence of its presence (this coined the phrase 'learning under the cross'). The BVerfG extends the scope that will identify infractions against constitutional principles such as neutrality and equality treatment and non-identification, so even a marginalized support of the state in the context of incorporating religious references into state schools will suffice as 'unavoidable coercive element'.[1034] Due to a stricter concept of the constitutional principles mentioned earlier, even the slightest amount of coercion or discrimination will suffice to spill over into unconstitutionality.

Seventh and finally, *assessment based on the respective state's constitution* – it was ascertained by the dissenting judges in the Crucifix that the scope of protection of individuals according to Art. 4 para 1 and Art. 6 para 2 GG can only be defined and determined in combination with the constitution of the respective federal state, in that case Bavaria.[1035] This approach maintains that outweigh of colliding interests detached from the context of the lands' constitutions will not reflect a genuine guarantee of rights protection.[1036] The majority's opinion in the Crucifix and proponents of the decision disclaim the assumption by the dissenting view that Art. 4 para 1 GG confers an absolute claim to respect only

1032 BVerfGE 41,88, 108 = NJW 1976, 952; BVerfG NJW 1995, 2477, 2480; OVG NRWNW, NVwZ 1994, 597.
1033 *Dietlein*, in FS Stern (1997), 443, 449.
1034 *Brugger/Karayanni*, pp. 80, 81.
1035 BVerfGE 93,1, 26.
1036 BVerwGE 44, 196, 199 = NJW 1974, 574; *Herzog*, in: Maunz/Dürig, Art. 4 recitals. 61 and 121.

the majority's will to keep presentation of the cross in public schools merely as it conforms with the values of the predominant religion, namely, Christianity.[1037]

(2) The Bruckmühl Decision

The circumstances in this case were very similar to those discussed in the *Crucifix* decision, with the only difference that the allegation against affixation of crosses in public state schools faced a new legal situation accrued in the aftermath of the *Crucifix* decision. The endorsement of amendment to the BayEUG following delivery of the Crucifix was rushed, as it sought to hinder an all-inclusive order to remove the cross from all state schools. It is therefore interesting to observe under the perspective of the amendment made in Art. 7 para 3 BayEUG[1038] how despite its determination to display crosses in public school classrooms, the BVerwG [1039] acknowledged its conformity with the constitution.

(a) Factual Background

In this case, the daughter of the claimant attended an elementary school in Bruckmühl during the years 1995–1996. She shared no religious denomination and visited regularly ethic lessons.[1040] The claimant then approached school administration with a letter demanding removal of the Crucifix from all classes his daughter attended due to their atheist belief. He supported his demand based on Art.7(4) BayEUG which introduced the 'objection principle' (the so-called *Widerspruchsregelung*) for parents objecting to the presence of the cross in their child's classroom. His challenge was established on the grounds that the Crucifix cannot be appropriated values of tolerance and humanism, as in his view this symbol stands contrary to these notions. He also asserted that the posing of a human body through such a symbol does not promote gender equality but rather the opposite. Moreover, his philosophical belief collides with the tenets

---

1037 BVerfGE 93,1, 16 = NJW 1995, 2477, 2478; *Muckel* in Muckel (ed.), Schriften zum Öffentlichen Recht 2010, 234, 244; *Kästner*, JZ 1998, 974, 981.

1038 Currently, Sec. 7 para 3 is to be found in Sec. 7 para 4 BayEUG. The original amendment to Art. 7 para 3 BayEUG came into force on 1 January 1996, shortly after the claimant brought an action against school administration before the administrative court of Munich in November 1995. The amendment was incorporated through an enactment from 23 December 1995. See in BayGVBl, p. 850.

1039 BVerwG decision from 21 April 1999, NJW 1999, 3063.

1040 The state of Berlin does not prescribe mandatory attendance in religious lessons and school prayers. As an alternative to the customary religious lessons, the state of Berlin offers pupils participation in ethic lessons.

of the Catholic Church. The claimant supported his allegation on grounds that Art. 7 para 4 BayEUG, by prescribing a general rule of affixation of crucifixes in state schools does not conform to the constitution and violates his rights as guaranteed in Art. 4 para 1 and 6 para 2 GG.

The claimant then submitted his allegations to the Administrative Court following failure to achieve a compromise with the school administration.[1041] As the Administrative Court declined his claim, the claimant decided to appeal to the High Administrative Court requesting an injunction order that will oblige the elementary school to remove all crosses from the classrooms his daughter visited or yet to visit in Bavarian elementary schools. The High Administrative Court declined his appeal, stating that there exists no sufficient claim justifying removal of the cross from classrooms in which his daughter attending nor from other classes in school premises.[1042] Finally, the charges remained unsuccessful in both instances (Bavarian Administrative Court and the High Administrative Court of Bavaria).[1043]

1041 VG München vom 21.10.1996 – Az.: VG M 3 K 95.5323; The claimant prior to the application in the administrative court sought a compromise with the school's principal pursuant to Art. 7 para 3 BayEUG. A settlement was then achieved to remove the crucifix from classrooms his daughter attended. However, a short while after the agreement crucifixes were affixed again in all school's classrooms, thereby triggering the claimant to bring a suit against the school administration.

1042 The decision from 22.10.1997 in VGH München, NJW 1999, 1045; BayVerfGH NJW 1997, 3157= NVwZ 1998, 57L=BayVBl 1997, 686, 689.

1043 VGH München vom 22.10.1997 – Az.: VGH 7 B 97.601 – 5; NJW 1999, 104; The claimant's request was deferred by both instances upholding that the presence of the cross (Sec. 7 para 3 BayEUG) does not constitute an infringement of the claimant's fundamental rights, neither with respect to his negative right to religious freedom nor his parental right to education safeguarded under Art. 4 para 1 and 6 para 2 Grundgesetz. Further, it was underscored that the 'objection principle' may be invoked only when the claimant can prove his claim is based on 'serious and foreseeable' grounds. However, the High Administrative Court declared that no objective detriment arising from the sight of the crucifix was sufficiently laid down by the claimant. It was further set out that the privilege of an individual not to disclose his belief (the right to remain silent), pursuant to Art. 4 para 1 and 2 GG as well as Art. 140 WRV together with Art. 136 para 3 WRV does not apply with respect to parents invoking the 'objection principle' (in contrast to soldiers in the army or other obligatory duties in the public service). Simply because an objection not genuinely motivated may tilt the balance of competing rights (ausgleichende praktische Konkordanz) privileging the objecting parents on the one hand, and encroaching on the majority's right who desire a religiously cast upbringing for their children, on

The claimant appealed then to the BVerwG and applied for a revision on the following grounds: first, the judgements of the lower instances are in breach of the constitutional stipulations safeguarding the fundamental right of religious freedom.[1044] Second, the decisions disregard the guidelines laid down by the High Constitutional Court in the *Crucifix* case, which has a binding effect on decisions of first instance, the so-called *Bindungswirkung*[1045] (Sec. 31 para 1 BVerfGG).

Respectively, the claimant sought on appeal the following remedies to be ordered by the court: first, the judgements of the Bavarian Administrative Court (21 October 1996), of the High Administrative Court of Bavaria (22 October 1997), as well as the decision of the elementary school principal (1996) to be null and void. Second, additionally, oblige the school administration to remove crosses from all teaching rooms his daughter visits regularly.

It was finally decided that the claimant had established his claim on solid grounds. The judgements of first instance in effect infringed explicit stipulations of constitutional law and, as a result, should be declared null and void.

Ultimately, the claimant had successfully substantiated the legal action against the principal of the public school in Bruckmühl and was entitled to request the removal of all crosses from teaching rooms his daughter regularly attended.

(b) Leading Legal Aspects

At the outset, the BVerwG established that the right pursuant Sec. 7 para 4 BayEUG to order the display of the crucifix in Bavarian state schools subject to the demand of its removal with the 'objection principle' is valid and accords with the constitution (*verfassungskonforme Auslegung*). It was explained that the amendment made to the BayEUG, in Sec. 7 para 4, prescribing a general rule of affixation of crucifixes in all public school rooms constitute by no means a violation of the fundamentals rights guaranteed in the German constitution.[1046] The BVerwG upheld that the educational mandate bestowed by Sec. 7 para 1 GG does not require a state to abandon all religious references only due to its duty to

---

the other. See VGH München NJW 1999, 1045, 1047; BayVerfGH NJW 1997, 3157, 3160; BVerfGE 41, 29, 49, et seq.= NJW 1976, 947.

1044 A specific reference was made with respect to infringement of the following provisions: Art. 4 para 1, 2 and Art. 140 GG together with Art. 136 para 3 WRV.

1045 The provision determines that in cases of collision between federal and state law, federal law will prevail.

1046 The BVerwG declared that the 'objection principle' does not infringe against the constitutional precepts laid down in: Art. 3 para 3, 4 para 1 and 2, 33 para 3 and 140 GG. See BVerwG, NJW 1999, 3063 3064; BayVerfGH NJW 1997, 3157 3158.

accord with the neutrality principle in a pluralistic society.[1047] Therefore, there is no general ban on the display of the cross in mandatory schools and its affixation in classrooms will not amount immediately to infringement of the state obligation to neutrality. The notion of religious neutrality of the state does not suggest a strict separation between the state and church to the extent adopted in a laicist country.[1048] It was therefore decided that Art. 7 para 4 BayEUG infringes neither on the obligatory duty of the state to observe religious neutrality nor on the negative right of religious freedom.[1049] However, the BVerwG underscores that observance of the neutrality principle with the objective to maintain a peaceful co-existence in state schools cannot be concluded solely with respect to religious rights of the majority.[1050]

Further, the 'objection principle' prescribed in Sec. 7 para 4 BayEUG does not infringe upon the 'binding effect', simply as the legal prescription upon which the Crucifix was delivered was distinguishable. It was explained that in the *Crucifix* case the element of voluntariness of the pupils in mandatory schools without any alternative to escape the presence of the cross was absent.[1051] In this case, no infringement of the 'binding effect' with respect to affixation of crosses in public schools was established by the claimant, as the elements of enforceable compulsion were excluded due to the 'objection principle'. The 'objection principle' does not infringe on Art. 4 para 1 GG since it accords with the demand of voluntariness expressed by the BVerfG in the Crucifix in the sense that it offers pupils of other faiths or convictions a non-discriminatory way to draw aside.[1052]

The BVerwG then analyses the 'objection principle' so to prescribe its conformity with the precepts of the constitution. Insofar, only if the objecting parents

---

1047 BVerwG NJW 1999, 3063, 3064; BVerfGE 93, 1,22 = NJW 1995, 2477; *Böckenförde*, in: FS Forsthoff (1967), 75, 93; *Heckel*, DVBl 1996, 453 468.

1048 BVerwG NJW 1999, 3063, 3064 The BVerwG finds support for its approach in the legal literature: *Böckenförde*, ZevKR 1975, 119, 128, et seq.; Heckel, DVBl 1996, 453, 472, et seq.; as well as in other jurisprudential decisions: BVerfGE 41, 29, 46 et seq., 49= NJW 1976, 947; BVerfGE 52, 223, 238, et seq, 240, et seq. = NJW 1980, 575.

1049 In this respect, it is interesting to view the similar approach held by the High Administrative Court declaring conformity of Sec. 7 para 3 BayEUG with Art. 107 para 1 BayVerf (right to religious freedom), see in BayVerfGH NJW 1997, 3157, 3158 u. 2, 3159, 3160 u. 3B.1. Despite similar determinations, the final outcome reached by the BVerwG with respect to the right of the claimant to invoke his negative right to religious freedom was essentially different; Merten, in FS Stern, 1997, p. 987, 993.

1050 BVerwG NJW 1999, 3063, 3065; BVerfGE 93, 1, 24 = NJW 1995, 2477.

1051 BVerwG NJW 1999, 3063, 3064.

1052 BVerwG NJW 1999, 3063, 3066.

following establishment of their claim on 'serious and foreseeable' grounds did not achieve a settlement with school authorities and, in addition, all efforts to achieve a non-discriminatory alternative were excluded, then the parents will be entitled to have the cross removed from teaching classrooms of their child.[1053] This rule should be enforced even against the wish of the majority of parents.[1054]

It explains that the words of the stipulation demand explicitly that in case that no settlement can be achieved, then it is the task of the school principal to pay due regard to religious rights of the objecting parents. This obliges at the same time his endeavour to achieve an adequate balance with other competing rights, like the majority's rights of parents and pupils to exert their religious freedom, so both rights will be maximally attained ('practical concordance').[1055] The Bavarian legislator recognized the obligation to balance competing rights in order to achieve an adequate compromise, and consequently prescribed in the last sentence of Sec. 7 para 4 BayEUG the duty towards the majority of parents that their right to religious upbringing of their children should be taken 'as possible into consideration'.

The general ordering of the crucifixes in state schools rooms was made subject to dissenting rule enabling minorities the right to invoke the 'objection principle', only insofar as they can establish their claim on 'serious and foreseeable' grounds. It will be therefore sufficient if the objecting parents can demonstrate that their objection to the crucifix accrues due to their atheist belief and their wish to keep any religious influence away from their children. The BVerwG underscored that a subjective, genuine anti-religious view will fulfil the requirement of 'serious and foreseeable' grounds, so a demand from objecting parents to establish their claim objectively was rendered by the BVerwG as overstrained.[1056]

1053 BVerwG NJW 1999, 3063; BayVerfGH, NJW 1997, 3157=BayVBl 1997, 686.

1054 BVerwG NJW 1999, 3063; VGH München, NJW 1999, 1045, 1047 = BayVBl.1998, 305, 306 II 3a.;BayVerfGH NJW 1997, 3157 = NVwZ 1998, 57L = BayVBl. 1997, 686, 689 B 1c =EuGRZ 1997, 455.

1055 BVerfGE 28, 243, 260, et seq. = NJW 1970, 1729; = BVerfGE 41,29, 50 = NJW 1976, 947; BVerfGE 52, 223, 247, 251 = NJW 1980, 575; BVerfGE 93,1, 21, et seq. = NJW 1995, 2477.

1056 BVerwG NJW 1999, 3063 (3066, 3067 para 4) This view held by the BVerwG stood in contrast to the opinion shared both by the High Administrative Court and the Bavarian Constitutional court, as their dismissal of the claimants allegation was founded on lack of objective grounds to support the objection. See VGH München NJW 1999, 1045, 1047 in 3b); BayVerfGH NJW 1997, 3157 = BayVBl 1997, 686, 690.

Finally, the BVerwG suggests a different model for avoidance of future conflicts that may accrue due to precedence granted to parents when invoking the 'objection principle'. It was proposed to avoid in advance disputes arising due to the display of the cross in a manner of disclosure of approval or denial of the cross affixation by pupils (the disclosure will take place in written form).[1057] By that, a school administration will take into consideration the results of the disclosure and will be able to evaluate a proper assignment of the pupils already before allocating them into classrooms. It was further mentioned that the obligation of the principal to keep strict discreteness with respect to the identity of those invoking objection to the cross must be observed so as not to provoke further conflicts.[1058]

(c) Conclusion

The conflict raised with the formulation of Art. 7 para 4 BayEUG relates to the 'objection principle' and the decision of the school principal in case an objection to the crucifix had been raised by one of the minority parents. In case the principal of a school receives a demand for removal of the crucifix then he must consider and take into account the wish of all parties including the majority of parents in order to achieve a settlement that is acceptable on all parties.

The words of Art. 7 para 4 BayEUG demosntrate clearly the aim of the Bavarian legislator to accord with the spirit of the German constitution (GG) and the fundamental rights prescribed in it. Therefore, it prescribes explicitly in Art.7 para 4 S.4 BayEuG that the constitutional rights of the parents (i.e., Art. 4 para 1 GG and Art. 6 para 2 GG) should be taken into account, while the principal is trying to find a suitable balance of rights so as to accommodate the wish of all involved parties.

Art. 7 para 4 BayEUG includes in its fourth sentence the obligation of the state at first step to find a settlement that will be accepted on all parties and respect the religion of the objecting parents. In addition, it states that the school principal should take the wish of the majority of parents as much as possible into account when dealing with the presentation of the crucifix in state schools.[1059]

1057 BVerwG NJW 1999, 3063, 3065; BVerfGE 41, 65, L 2 = NJW 1976, 950.

1058 BVerwG NJW 1999, 3063, 3065; The BVerwG declares that the obligation to keep discreteness emanates also from the following constitutional precepts: Art. 2 para 1 together with Art. 1 para 1, Art. 4 para 1, Art. 140 GG and Art. 136 para 3 WRV; BVerfGE 1965,1, 49 = NJW 1984, 419.

1059 „Gelingt eine Einigung nicht, hat sie bzw. er (die Schulleiter/in)… für den Einzelfall eine Regelung zu treffen, welche die Glaubensfreiheit des Widersprechenden achtet und die religiösen und weltanschaulichen Überzeugungen aller in der Klasse

Consequently, the legal controversy surrounded the interpretation of Art.7 para 4 BayEUG and its conformity with the Bavarian constitution (Art. 107 para 1) and the precept of religious neutrality.

The high constitutional court of Bavaria decided that there was no clear evidence that the lower instances (Bavarian Administrative court and High Administrative court of Bavaria) exceeded legal interpretation norms. They rather sought to take the wish of the majority of parents as much as possible into consideration. As a result the emphasis was put on accommodating the religious needs of the majority of parents when balancing between the competing rights (the second half of the fourth sentence of Art. 7 para 4 S. 4 BayEUG).

It was held further that the words of Art.7 para 4 BayEUG suggest that the wish of the majority 'is also to be taken into consideration' only 'insofar it is possible'.[1060]

However, the BVerwG reversed the decisions of the lower instances. It approved the prevalence of the constitutional right of the claimant over the majority's right to have the crucifix displayed in the classroom. By doing so, the BVerwG affirmed that the words of Art. 7 para 4 BayEUG provide a clear balance in favour of the first half of its fourth sentence as opposed to its second half. Eventually, the court underscored that the rights of the objecting parents should not be withdrawn to satisfy the wish of the majority of parents as they have an equal legal standing that their constitutional rights should be equally guaranteed.

(3) Crucifix in NRW

The legal debate surrounding the constitutional legitimacy of the attachment of crosses in instructions rooms of public schools reached even the state of NRW and was brought for a judicial review before the High Administrative Court (HAC) of Münster.[1061]

(a) Factual Background

The facts of the decision may be summarized as follows: the claim rested on a request of a mother that all religious symbols, in particular a pronounced emphasis on the cross, should be removed from each teaching room in the elementary school her daughter attended.

Betroffenen zu einem gerechten Ausgleich bringt; dabei ist auch der Willer der Mehrheit, soweit möglich, zu berücksichtigen."

1060 BayVBl. 1997, 686, 689 zu B1.c=EuGRZ 1997, 455.

1061 OVG Münster NVwZ 1994, 597, 19 B 1934/93.

The complainant established her claim based on the right conferred to her under Art. 6 para 2 GG that defines the care and upbringing of children as a natural right of parents and consequently enables them to convey their children with convictions in matters of religion and belief they perceive fit. She argued that the display of the cross presents an educational influence on the children that stands in contradiction to the educational right of the parents. The complaint remained unsuccessful.

(b) Leading Legal Aspects

The HAC ruled against the complainant's claim though it reaffirmed the guarantee of parental natural right to take care for and foster their children according to Art. 6 para 2 GG. Likewise, it acknowledged that Art. 4 para 1 and 2 GG convey parents the right to educate their children in a way that conforms to their perception of religion or conviction. In that sense, the right of education includes the religious shaping of the child's education. By virtue of the same constitutional guarantees it assumes the inherent right of parents to alienate from their child anything they believe has a damaging religious influence. Yet, the Court underscored that these fundamental freedoms do not confer upon parents an exclusive right on the education of their children. In this regard, the Court emphasized the supervisory task of the state prescribed in Art. 7 para 1 GG with respect to its public school system, thereby confirming the state's mandate over education. It was explained by the Court that if the natural right of parents with respect to the religious education of their child in compulsory state schools is not completely satisfied due to lack of accordance with their confessional view, it is likely to infringe on their fundamental rights as safeguarded in the GG. Notwithstanding, it was pointed out that an increasing religious plurality bears on the state no obligation to take into account all religions and confessions when exercising its educational mandate (with the only exception relating to school prayers as prescribed in Art. 7 para 3 GG).

Finally, it was concluded by the Court that the issue of religious elements in public school endorses a tension field between various groups of religions and faiths that try to realize their religious interests both in their positive and negative aspect. The state cannot simply eliminate any religious reference from its school system, as this will not nullify the existence of tension; rather, it will violate the positive right to religious freedom of parents who wish their children to be conveyed with the values and tradition of the Christian religion. Insofar, reconciliation can only be achieved through a careful consideration of the adequate balance between the colliding legal interests and liberty rights that are constitutionally protected. Freedom of religion is a fundamental freedom that is guaranteed without any reservations; as such, this is a matter left to the sole competency of the legislature.

The Court held that the weighing of the triangle set of conflicting constitutional rights, namely the parents' right to education (also religious education), the pupils' right to religious freedom, and the authority of the state to form and organize the education in state schools is a task incumbent on the lawmaker. Accordingly, the HAC permits expressly the federal states to reach divergent outcomes, since the states are able to incorporate school traditions, the denominational composition of the state, and the extent of piety of its citizens into the formation of their educative system.[1062]

The HAC determines that the wording of Art. 12 para 6 NRWC, prescribing the 'general conveyance of Christian values with openness towards other faiths and confessions in universal mandatory schools', satisfies the requirements of an adequate balance, since none of the involved parties would have their religious freedom repressed.[1063] In this respect, the HAC strengthens its view by reference to a decision of the BVerfG holding that a neutral educative system does not connote of public schools that are free from display of any religious insignia and that includes no disposal of Christian symbols as the cross.[1064] Openness towards other religions and confessions requires, on the same token, acceptance of the cross as a symbol that transfers the tradition and values of the Christian faith. As a practical matter, it should be taken into account that pupils in compulsory state schools cannot avoid the possible influence of other faiths or confessions that are overt.

(c) Conclusion

To sum up, the decision of the HAC Münster from 1993 demonstrates clearly that there is no obligation in the state of NRW to order the display of crosses in classrooms and, as a result, there is no obligation to remove them as their existence in the first place is not prescribed by the state.[1065]

In this respect, the HAC held that the NRW lawmaker did not violate by the constitutional percept prescribed in Art. 12 para 6 NRWC the negative right

---

1062 OVG Münster NVwZ 1994, 597, 19 B 1934/93; BVerfGE 41, 29, 50, et seq. = NJW 1976, 947; BVerfGE 108, 282, 303; *Brugger/Karayanni*, p. 192.

1063 OVG Münster NVwZ 1994, 597 19 B 1934/93; BVerfGE 41, 88, 108 = NJW 1976, 952.

1064 OVG Münster NVwZ 1994, 597 19 B 1934/93; BVerfGE 41, 88, 110 = NJW 1976, 952.

1065 OVG NW NVwZ 1994, 597.

of non-Christian pupils to religious freedom, as the display of the cross in state schools did not impart any elements of coercion on them. Further, it was explained that the state did not infringe on its obligation to religious neutrality, as there is nothing to suggest that the state identified itself with a particular religion.

The HAC opined that, at its strongest, the religious endorsement of the cross in state schools is safeguarded by virtue of the constitutional precept prescribed in Art. 7 para 1 GG granting the state the sole authority to exercise its educational mandate in accordance with the precept of Art. 7 para 1 GG[1066] at own discretion. Nonetheless, it emphasizes the obligation of the state as supervisory of the public school system to take into account the fundamental right of others and ensure the safeguard thereof through evaluation of the competing rights ('practical concordance').[1067] It is therefore of major significance to accord the state a wide margin of appreciation so as to enable it to accomplish its educational mandate conferred to it by the constitution. It may be realized as long as it gives due attention to the protection of other fundamental freedoms (e.g., the right to religious freedom pursuant to Art. 4 GG). The exclusive competency of the state with respect to its educational task in state schools enables it to provide a framework that ensures free practice of religion. The HAC reaffirms thereby the admissibility of the Christian character of non-denominational school as pronounced in Art. 12 para 6 NRWC as well as its compatibility with the Grundgesetz, and by that pronounced the non-identification of the state with a specific religion by virtue of the display of the cross in state classrooms.[1068]

dd) Headscarves Worn by Teachers

A further controversial debate is the permissibility of a teacher to manifest her religious affiliation in public schools. The legal challenge posed by a prohibition on teachers to abstain from manifesting religious affiliation of any kind by their outer appearance is problematic since, on the first level, it contravenes on her fundamental right to religious freedom as guaranteed under Art. 4 GG, and, on a second level, impinges her professional right to equal eligibility in

---

1066 OVG Münster NVwZ 1994, 597 19 B 1934/93; BVerfGE 52, 223, 240 = NJW 1980, 575; *Böckenförde*, DÖV 1980, 323, 324.

1067 OVG Münster NVwZ 1994, 597; BVerfGE 52, 223, 240 = NJW 1980, 575; *Böckenförde*, DÖV 1980, 323, 324.

1068 OVG Münster NVwZ 1994, 597; BVerfGE 41, 29, 49 = NJW 1976, 947; BVerfGE 52, 223, 241 = NJW 1980, 575.

admission to the civil service according to Art. 33 para 2 and para 3 GG and the guarantee to occupational freedom pursuant to Art. 12 GG. There are several courts' decisions discussing these aspects, while applying constitutional principles such as 'practical concordance' in order to evaluate the adequate balance to be conferred to competing rights at stake. The balance will change according to the circumstances particular to each case (i.e., having due regard to inner lands' constitutions (*Landesverfassung*) and specifications in their education acts (*Schulgesetz*)). The judicial rulings in this respect reflect two sides of the spectrum. On the one hand, it demonstrated in the case of Ludin and the following cases a restrictive approach towards the teacher's right to manifest her religious freedom. The common practice was that in any case of a doubt the teacher's right to appear with a headscarf had to be set back so as to avoid possible negative influence on pupils exerted by the exposure to ostentatious religious insignia like the headscarf. This was especially underscored since pupils, by virtue of compulsory schooling, are left with no option to avoid its view. On the other hand, this prevailing approach of the judicator had been reversed in a recent judgement of the BVerfG[1069] delivered with respect to a ban imposed on Muslim teachers in the state of NRW to appear with a headscarf in school lessons. In this outstanding decision, the BVerfG overruled its previous statements, thus tilting the balance in favour of the teacher and emphasizing her constitutional rights to manifestation of religion and equality of treatment.

The holdings of the jurisprudence and the judicial path followed in this controversy will be highlighted having due regard to divergent case laws considering the impermissibility of religious garments displayed by teaching staff in public schooling. Eminently, these findings will be contested against the background of the recent BVerfG decision.[1070]

(1) Ludin's Case

The case of Ludin is an important milestone in the jurisprudential development over admissibility of religious symbols in the school system. It observed the legal conflict that accrues when a teacher appears with a headscarf to school and challenged it against the duty of the state to religious neutrality.

The case reached the BVerfG following unsuccessful challenge of the plaintiff at the various levels of the administrative jurisdictions.[1071] In principle, the case

1069 BVerfGE 138, 296 = NJW 2015, 359.

1070 BVerfGE 138, 296 = NJW 2015, 359.

1071 BVerfG, NJW 2003, 3111=BVerfGE 108, 282; BVerwG, NJW 2002, 3344 = BVerwGE 116, 359; VGH Mannheim, NJW 2001, 2899; VG Stuttgart, NVwZ 2000, 959.

of Ludin was deferred by the BVerwG on the ground that her wearing of the headscarf during school times amounts to identification with a specific religion that runs counter to the neutrality principle. It was expounded in the decision that the constitutional obligation of the state to religious neutrality justifies the state's denial to hire her as a teacher. Further, the judges supporting their argument on former decisions of the BVerfG held the view that a constant confrontation of the pupils with the headscarf could have a detrimental religious influence on the pupils especially those of minor age.[1072]

(a) Factual Background

The plaintiff, a teacher of Afghan origin, applied to the state preparatory service for grade schoolteachers in Baden-Württemberg following her teacher-training period and was accepted. Nonetheless, following her second state exams she was refused the job as a permanent teacher in that public school. The school board (*Oberschulamt Stuttgart*) justified the refusal on grounds of the plaintiff's failure to take off the headscarf during instructions; as a result, so the argumentation, the plaintiff lacked the necessary 'personal aptitude'. The plaintiff sued before the Administrative Court, Higher Administrative Court, and the Federal Administrative Court; however, her claim was rejected in all instances. Finally, the teacher appealed before the BVerfG. The BVerfG ruled against the decision of the school board to exempt the plaintiff from her teaching post and in the aftermath, quashed the decision of the BVerwG and remanded it for further review. The key guidelines highlighted by the BVerfG relating to admission of the Muslim headscarf worn by a teacher in state compulsory schools will be summarized next.[1073]

(b) Leading Legal Aspects

At the outset, the BVerfG upheld that in the relevant legislation of Baden-Württemberg, the Civil Service Law (Art. 11 para 1 *Landesbeamtengesetz*), there is no sufficient, statutory basis that could prohibit schoolteachers from wearing the headscarf.

1072 BVerwG, NJW 2002, 3344, 3345; BVerfGE 52, 223, 249 = NJW1980, 575, 578; BVerfGE 93,1, 20 = NJW 1995, 2477, 2478.

1073 BVerfGE 108, 282 decision from 24.9.2003 – 2 BvR 1436/02; An English translation of the decision can be found at http://www.utexas.edu/law/academics/centers/transnational/work_new/german/case.php?id=613.

It goes further and explains the constitutional guarantee of equality in admission to the civil service. First, the BVerfG makes a reference to the guarantee in the constitution prescribing equal eligibility of all German citizens in application to the civil service (Art. 33 para 2 and para 3 GG) regardless of religious adherence.[1074] Second, the Court acknowledges that the federal states have a broad discretion (*Gestaltungsfreiheit*, i.e., 'a wide margin of appreciation') with respect to formation of their school system pursuant to Art.7 GG. This includes the right of the individual states to decide on the endorsement of religious themes, *inter alia*, develop 'aptitude criteria' for their public servants.[1075] Nonetheless, these criteria will be admissible as long as due regard is given to other fundamental rights and constitutional norms. Since hiring criteria is a matter left to the legislator, the prohibition of the Islamic headscarf should be first prescribed in a relevant legislation or regulations. Third, the Court underscores the right of the plaintiff to religious freedom according to Art. 4 para 1 and para 2 GG and determines that the two provisions constitute a single comprehensive fundamental right.[1076] It was explained that this right includes not only the right to have a religion but also the right of an individual to manifest his/her religion outwardly, and in fact enables the individual to design his/her life so as to conform with the tenets of his belief and to act in accordance to his/her inner beliefs.[1077]

In this context, the BVerfG asserts that freedom of religion is an unreserved right. This does not mean, however, that the legislator may not lay down official duties that restrain the religious freedom of applicants in the public service. A constraint of the right of religious freedom, thereby baring access to public office must be strictly justified. Accordingly, this necessitates not only that its limitation must be based on a specific statutory provision, but it should also purport to protect other fundamental rights or values of constitutional rank. As a result, the BVerfG found that the doubt raised by the school board, claiming that the teacher is unfit for duty or breached the duty of office by reason of her refusal to abandon the headscarf while at school lacks legal foundation that could justify the infringement of her right to wear the headscarf. By this, the school board actually infringed the plaintiff's right to have an equal opportunity

---

1074 BVerfG, NJW 2003, 3111, 3112.

1075 BVerfG, NJW 2003, 3111, 3113; BVerfGE 52, 223, 242 =NJW 1980, 575.

1076 BVerfG, NJW 2003, 3111, 3112.

1077 BVerfG, NJW 2003, 3111, 3112; BVerfGE 32, 98, 106 = NJW 1972, 327; BVerfGE 33, 23, 28 = NJW 1972, 1183; BVerfGE 41, 29, 49 = NJW 1976, 947; BVerwG Nov. 23, 2000, 3 C 40/99 = NJW 2001, 1225 (Schlachten Urteil).

while applying for a post in the public service (Art. 33 para 2 und para 3 GG)[1078] and her fundamental right to freedom of religion (Art. 4 para 1 and 2 GG).[1079]

In addition, the BVerfG stated clearly that the constitution imposes on the state the duty to behave neutrally with respect to religious issues. It emphasizes therefore that the form of neutrality should not be of a strict separation of church and state but should rather take an open-minded, liberal approach which would treat all faiths equally.[1080] It even determined that as long as Christian symbols are not forbidden in public schools, the same should be applicable with respect to other religions and creeds.

Remarkably, albeit the pronouncement of the BVerfG that the school board infringed on the plaintiff's right to religious freedom, it still confirmed that manifestation of religion on part of a teacher expressed by wearing a religious symbol or garment can contravene fundamental rights of others and, eventually, may result in the ex-communication of religious symbols by teachers as long as on duty. It was asserted that the wearing of a religious symbol or garment by a teacher is indicative of the teacher's pertinence to a specific religion. This may affect not only the state's duty to remain neutral in its educative task but may also collide with parents' right to educate their children in accordance with the religion they perceive fit. In a like manner, this may collide with the negative right of the pupils not to be influenced in their right to believe or not to believe.

In the end, it was held that there is an unavoidable tension between the teacher's positive freedom of religion on the one hand, and, on the other hand, the state's educational function that must be exercised in accordance with the principle of neutrality in matters of religion as well as the educational right of parents towards their children (Art. 6 para 2 GG) and the negative right of the pupils not be exposed to such a symbolic garment (Art. 4 para 1 GG).[1081] It remains the task of the legislator of the state of Baden-Württemberg to solve this inevitable tension through the right balance to be achieved in the tolerant spirit of the requisite even-handedness.

Notably, the dissenting opinion declined the majority's verdict, determining mainly the following:

1078 BVerfG, NJW 2003, 3111, 3112, 3116.

1079 BVerfG, NJW 2003, 3111, 3112, 3116; BVerfGE 83, 341, 353 = NJW 1991, 2623.

1080 BVerfG, NJW 2003, 3111, 3113; BVerfGE 19, 1, 8 = NJW 1995, 1427; BVerfGE 19, 206, 216 =NJW 1966, 147; BVerfGE 24, 236, 246 =NJW 1969, 31; BVerfGE 93, 1, 17= NJW 1995, 2427.

1081 BVerfG, NJW 2003, 3111, 3116; *Robbers*, ÖARR 2003, 405, 408.

The dissenting opinion held the view that a teacher breaches the law and her official duties when she decides to appear in classes of elementary and secondary schools with her headscarf. It was ascertained that the teacher chose her profession of her free will voluntarily, whereas the children attend state schools due to a compulsory prescription made by law. Thence, since the teacher took upon herself intentionally a duty in the public service, she was aware that she cannot invoke the protection of her basic rights as those will be constrained by virtue of the functions and obligations incumbent on her due to her profession.[1082]

The objective behind this perception is the avoidance of any hurdles in a school's daily organization and the retrenchment of further tension and conflicts within a school's realm. As a reasonable ground for their determination, it was asserted by the minority judges that the uncompromising and unwilling attitude of the teacher with relation to the wearing of the headscarf during school lessons suggested not only that her motives were not balanced with regard to the principle of neutrality but rather contradict it.[1083]

Finally, the second senate of the BVerfG found the complaint admissible and sufficiently founded. It was held that the plaintiff suffered an infringement of her fundamental rights according to Art. 33 para 2 together with Art. 4 para 1 and para 2 and Art. 33 para 3 GG. Consequently, it quashed the ruling of the BVerwG and remitted the case back there since the BVerfG declared that there is no legal basis for the expulsion of a teacher on grounds of religious manifestation by her outer appearance. The BW legislator rushed then to amend its education act to regulate teachers' dress code in public education.[1084] The deliberation in BW parliament to the statutory ban were made parallel to the procedure in this case.[1085]However, even following amendments to the BW education act, the teacher was not successful and her complaint was rejected again by the BVerwG.[1086]

1082 BVerfG, NJW 2003, 3111, 3117, 3118; BVerfGE 39, 334, 366 = NJW 1975, 1641.

1083 BVerfG NJW, 3111, 3119, 3121; *Robbers*, ÖARR 2003, 405, 407.

1084 The amendment to the School Education Act from 1.4.2004 (GBl. P. 178) Sec. 38 para. 2.

1085 The amendment to Sec. 38 of the SchulG BW took effect on 9.4.04 GBl. 2004, p. 178; http://www.landesrecht-bw.de/jportal/?quelle=jlink&docid=jlr-SchulGBW1983V33P38&psml=bsbawueprod.psml&max=true

1086 BVerwG NJW 2004, 3581 = DVBL 2004, 1424; The amendment to the SchG BW from 1.4.2004 (GBl. P. 178).

(c) Conclusion

It is interesting to note that until the judgement delivered in *Ludin*'s case, most of the judgements were focusing on Art. 4 para 1 GG and rather emphasized the negative interest of the children not to be exposed to the headscarf. However, throughout this case the Court was finally willing to challenge the problematic core of relationship between Muslim culture and the German state.[1087]

Though the BVerfG made no clear pronouncement as to how the lawmaker in BW is supposed to solve the admissibility of teachers to overtly manifest their religious affiliation by display of religious symbols in public schools, it had laid down several significant holdings: first, the controversy must not be left solely to the decision of public administrators or school authorities but should rather remain the task of the legislator. This judgement actually plays a significant role, as it triggered the federal states to take initiative and modify their education enactment, while redefining the balance between state neutrality and the constitutional right of teachers to religious freedom. Second, it held the obligation of the state's legislator to prescribe the commitment of a teacher in the public school system to adhere to the principle of neutrality by law. The endorsement of religious symbols in public schools must be considered by the regional parliament of each state in order to ensure the safeguarding of fundamental constitutional freedoms and rights. The BVerfG declared it the task of the lawmaker to amend vague legal regulations in their school enactments. The legislation in BW relating to its civil servants lacked legal clarity with respect to permissibility of a teacher to display overtly religious insignias in public education. As a result, any resolution – whether prohibiting or admitting religious symbols in state schools – must be explicitly authorized by law so as to avoid insufficiency and uncertainty.

Following the recent ruling of the BVerfG on the headscarf in NRW, the lawmaker in BW is yet to take legislative steps to make necessary amendments in the Education Act in order to ensure conformity with the constitution. The BW legislator is left with two legal options: either to maintain the ban on religious insignias in public school, in which case it should be applied evenly and equally to all religions and faiths without any segregation, or admit the endorsement of religious symbols with reservation of their exclusion in case proselytizing effect on pupils is substantiated.

To sum up, it is not an easy task to conclude whether these legislative solutions meet the declaratory aim the BW legislator had in mind when it initially introduced the interdiction of conspicuous signs into its public school system

1087 *Mahrenholz* in FS Badura (2004), 749, 750.

following *Ludin*'s case. In this respect, the intent to keep the status quo while preventing Muslim teachers from applying for a teaching vacancy as long as they refuse to remove the headscarf or any other head covering while being on duty is difficult to justify. As a result, it is not certain what kind of measure the legislator should adopt in order to achieve conformity of state law with the constitution as redefined by the BVerfG in its recent ruling.[1088]

(2) The Revision of the Headscarf Decision (Ludin II)

The following will take account of the revision brought for a judicial review before the ACS in the aftermath of the BVerfG ruling in *Ludin*'s appeal, referred to in the legal literature as *Ludin II*. It is rather surprising that after the case was remitted from the BVerfG to the BVerwG[1089] the final result did not turn out different than the first hearing by the same instance. Nonetheless, the teacher submitted her claim again before the ACS on grounds that the BVerwG erred in its decision for the second time due to the way it constructed Art. 38 para 2 BW SchG.[1090] She claimed that her head covering cannot indicate of her religious affiliation. One should bear in mind though that the different ruling provided by the ACS on this occasion followed the legislative amendment taken by the BW lawmaker to its education act (i.e., BW SchG). The statutory ban on public schoolteachers in the state of BW to refrain from exercise of any political, religious, or ideological manifestation that is likely to endanger the state's neutrality towards students and their parents or disturb the peaceful co-existence in school was endorsed in Sec. 38 SchG BW. Despite the introduction of the amendment (Sec. 38 SchG BW) made to the already existing BW SchG, the ACS declared finally by its ruling from 7 July 2006 that a teacher who converted to Islam is allowed to keep her headscarf while on duty.[1091] In sum, the factual background ensued the endorsement of amendment to the BW SchG and the grounds for justification provided by the ACS will be provided hereupon.

(a) Factual Background

The teacher has been in service since 1973 and converted to Islam in 1984. From 1995 on, the teacher started wearing a headscarf while on duty. In July 2000, the High Education Office (*Oberschulamt*) in Stuttgart asked the teacher to carry

1088 *Robbers*, ÖARR 2003, 405, 408.
1089 BVerwG NJW 2004, 3581 = DVBL 2004, 1424
1090 NVwZ 2006, 1444, 1445.
1091 VG Stuttgart decision from 7.7.06, NVwZ 2006, 1444, 1445.

out her duties bareheaded while she is in contact with students. The teacher objected to the instruction prohibiting her to wear a headscarf in the classroom. Her appeal against the decision of the High Education Office was rejected by the ACS ruling from 24.3.2000, as well as by HAC and the BVerwG.[1092] The High Education Office proclaimed that by wearing her head covering the teacher violates school peace and endangers the neutrality obligation of the state towards pupils and parents. In support of their assertion, the High Education Office relied on the BVerfG's decision delivered in *Ludin*'s case and the legislative steps taken thereinafter by the lawmaker in amendment of Sec. 38 SchG BW. In fact, the amendment to the SchG BW came into force on 9 April 2004 and established the ground for the later decision of the High Education Office from 18 December 2004 to insist on the removal of the headscarf. The High Education Office contended further that the headscarf is a symbol that stands for gender inequality and inferiority of women. In addition, it underscored that the headscarf is perceived as a political symbol of Islamic fundamentalism and was even recognised as such in the appeal of Ludin before the BVerfG.[1093]

The teacher asserted in adverse that her head covering does not amount to an exercise of ideological, political, or religious manifestation. She declined the motivation for wearing the headscarf as being founded on religious grounds. Her head covering was not carrying a religious character unlike other garments, such as the Jewish Kippa or the habit, the traditional dress of nuns. Thence, the decision of the High Education Office infringes upon the ban of unequal treatment in application and access to the public service. She explained that throughout her teaching career she has never encountered resistance or negative feedbacks with respect to her headscarf neither from pupils, their parents, nor from work colleagues. Further, her head covering was not immediately recognized as a salient religious headscarf, as she herself was not originally a Muslim. She underscored her active role in fostering peaceful atmosphere in school by encouraging mutual tolerance and respect between pupils of different beliefs and faiths. She also contributed to the integration of Muslim pupils who found her accessible to seek for advice.[1094]

1092 VG Stuttgart, NVwZ 2000, 959; VGH Mannheim, NJW 2001, 2899; BVerwG, NJW 2002, 3344 = BVerwGE 116, 359.

1093 NVwZ 2006, 1444; NJW 2003, 3111, 3114.

1094 NVwZ 2006, 1444, 1445. The teacher submitted therefore that the decision of the BVerwG (BVerwG 24.6.04 NJW 2004, 3581=DVBL 2004, 1424) is not applicable in her case due to differing circumstances.

Finally, it was argued that even if the headscarf is to be perceived in its religious context, it cannot endanger the obligation of the state to religious neutrality nor disturb the peace in school.

(b) Leading Legal Aspects

The ACS annulled the contested decision of the school authority. It was held that the stipulation made in Sec. 38 para 2 SchG BW infringes upon the constitutional obligation for equal treatment in the public service (Art. 3 para 1 and 3 GG) as well as its correlating provision (Art. 14 ECHR) prohibiting discrimination on religious grounds in application to a post or working conditions in the public service.

In principle, the ACS accepted the contention that by wearing the headscarf in the classroom the teacher violates against the ban prescribed in Sec. 38 para 2 SchG BW prohibiting teachers in state schools any outwardly form of religious, political, or ideological manifestation if it violates other fundamental constitutional freedoms or rights. These can be one of the following: endangering the duty of the state to religious neutrality, disturbing the peaceful atmosphere in school, violating against human dignity, the equality principle (Art. 3 GG), and other prominent democratic values.

The ACS made clear that no doubt was left as to the adherence of the teacher to Islam, and her conscious outer appearance was a clear evidence to her observance of the religious precept. However, the ACS decided that it will not seek to establish whether the appearance of a teacher with the headscarf in this particular case raised the impression by pupils and parents to contradict any of the earlier-mentioned protected values. Nor is it to be questioned whether the motive for wearing the headscarf was voluntary or coerced. In fact, the constitutional questions to be reviewed were set out as follows: first, how the expression of outwardly religious symbols are to affect third parties, that is, an objective observer. Second, whether the inclusion of an abstract danger suffice in order to legitimize the negation of the teacher's fundamental right to undisturbed exertion of her religion. Third, whether an abstract danger to the neutrality obligation of the state or disturbance of school peace is predictable under the given circumstances.[1095]

The ACS declared that the establishment of influence on pupils due to exposure to the headscarf cannot be decided on a case-by-case basis but is rather

1095 NVwZ 2006, 1444, 1445, 1446.

a general objective one. It asserts that more detrimental is the impression the headscarf raises in a significant part of the population, inter alia school pupils.[1096]

The abstract danger aspect had been explained to be part of a risk every citizen may encounter on a daily confrontation with the display of religious insignias in the public sphere. However, there exists no absolute right that spares a person from this encounter. Religious pluralism in state schools increases the probability for religiously motivated tensions and disputes, so the jeopardy of encroachment upon prominent protected values can be easily evoked. The lawmaker relates in Sec. 38 BW SchG to an abstract danger in order to prevent in advance situations that may enfold a concrete danger to prominent protected values. Therefore, the headscarf worn by a teacher is capable of endangering the state's obligation to religious neutrality or disturbance of the peaceful co-existence in school or fundamental rights of others. The headscarf is a symbol that bears an abstract danger, as the constant confrontation of school children with no ability to escape its view may contradict with the negative freedom of pupils as well as of their parents wishing no exposure to an unwanted religious influence on their children.[1097] Given that, Sec. 38 para 2 SchG BW is legitimate, as the lawmaker gave due reference to competing rights through an adequate application of the principle of practical concordance.[1098]

However, the strong entanglement between the obligation on civil servants to comply with dress codes rules in order to avoid an abstract danger requires strict application of the equality treatment. If the state does not apply and implement the ban on manifestation of religious garments or symbols also with respect to other faiths or creeds (dress of nuns or Jewish Kippa) in an equally strict manner, it simply violates the obligation of equal treatment (Art. 3 para 1 and 3 GG, Art. 14 ECHR).

In addition, it was held that a determination that the educative task of the state to convey Christian values – as prescribed in the state's constitution (Art. 12 para 1, 15 para 1 and Art. 16 para 1 BWLVerf) – legitimizes in fact the garments of nuns as it corresponds with the duty of behaviour (the first sentence of Sec. 38 para 2 SchG BW). It was stated that such determination cannot be constitutionally justified. By that, the state of BW admitted an intention to explicitly

1096 NVwZ 2006, 1444, 1446; BVerwG, NJW 2004, 3581= DVBl 2004, 1424; BVerfGE 108, 282, 304 = NJW 2003, 3111.

1097 NVwZ 2006, 1444, 1446; BVerfGE 108, 282, 303, 307 = NJW 2003, 3111; BVerwG, NJW 2004, 3581= DVBl 2004, 1424.

1098 NVwZ 2006, 1444, 1446; BVerfGE 108, 282, 309 = NJW 2003, 3111; BVerwG, NJW 2004, 3581 = DVBl 2004, 1424.

exclude Christian and Jewish symbols from the ban prescribed in Sec. 38 para 2 SchG BW and privilege them over the Muslim religion. The fact that nuns are not required to remove their religious garments when teaching in public schools, whereas the Muslim teacher is obliged to do so constitutes an indirect unlawful discrimination against the latter.[1099]

(c) Conclusion

Eminently, a significant ground for segregation between the different rulings of the VG Stuttgart (prior to the amendments made to the BW SchG and in the aftermath) can be attributed to the explicit prevalence granted by the BW lawmaker to Christian and Jewish symbols, which infringes upon the constitutional principle of equality pursuant to Art. 3 para 3 GG. In addition, the ban inhibited harshly on the teacher's right to equal eligibility in the public service and constitutes an indirect discrimination on religious grounds that is forbidden according to Art. 33 para 3 GG.

(3) A Teacher with Headscarf in NRW

The legal debate surrounding a teacher with a headscarf was prominent also in the state of NRW. The following cases[1100] depict the complaints of Muslims teachers who challenged the constitutional legitimacy of Art. 57 para 4 NRW SchulG inscribing the headscarf ban, following the amendment initiated by the NRW lawmaker in the aftermath of *Ludin*'s case. The complainants were unsuccessful in the lower instances and by their appeal to the BAG (Federal Labour Court) finally submitted a conjoined appeal to the BVerfG (Federal Constitutional Court).[1101] The final ruling was delivered on 27 January 2015[1102] and remarkably turned the Federal Labour Court's (BAG) decisions upside down.[1103] Hereby, the Muslim teacher, following dismissal of her claim in the Labour Court in Herne (*Arbeitsgericht Herne*),[1104] appealed to the High Labour Court in Hamm (*Landesarbeitsgericht Hamm*)[1105] and, at a final stage, to the BAG. The grounds

1099 NVwZ 2006, 1444, 1447; NJW 2004, 3581 = DVBl 2004, 1424.
1100 See the cases in Chapter III 2 d) dd) (3) & (5).
1101 To be discussed thoroughly in Chapter III 2 d) dd) (7).
1102 BVerfGE 138, 296 = NJW 2015, 359.
1103 BAG 10.12.2009 -2 AZR 55/09; BAG 20.8.2009 2 AZR 499/08.
1104 Urt. 21.2.2008 – 6 Ca 649/07 and 7.3.2007 – 4 Ca 3415/06.
1105 Urt. 16.10.2008 – 11 Sa 572/08 and 11 Sa 280/08.

for application and the jurisdictional ruling specifying the legislative layout will be set forth.

(a) Factual Background

The legal conflict over the teacher's headscarf was addressed even by the BAG following the allegations of the claimant, a Muslim teacher in a compulsory school in the state of NRW to sustain her claim for recognition of her right to appear with headscarf during school instructions were discharged by the Higher Labour Court. Quite similar to *Ludin*'s case, the claimant here also alleged before the BAG[1106] that her expulsion from school due to her donning of a headscarf infringed on her right to religious freedom. The teacher argued that:

First, wearing of a headscarf does not amount to an expression of a political or religious manifestation but rather forms a part of her personality. Hence, it neither presents a concrete endangerment to a peaceful school operation, nor to the state's religious-worldview neutrality; accordingly, it cannot contravene the precept of Art. 57 para 4 of NRW SchulG. Second, the ban on the headscarf amounts to an unjustified discrimination since the state explicitly contravenes against its constitutional duty to respect the imperative of equal protection for all religions and beliefs established in Art. 3 para 3 GG. Third, Art. 57 para 4 of the NRW SchulG infringes on her right to cultivate and practice religion as guaranteed in Art. 9 ECHR. Fourth, the practice of schools prohibiting Muslim women to appear with headscarf defies the ban of unequal treatment in working places and in fact introduces and supports discrimination against women. It should be noted, however, that the teacher wore a headscarf during language lessons which were optional and in which mostly Muslim children had participated.

(b) Leading Legal Aspects

The BAG rejected the complainant's claim based on the amended Art. 57 para 4 of the NRW SchulG prescribing that teachers will not be allowed to exercise any form of religious manifestation which may disturb the peaceful school operation or infringe upon the state's duty to neutrality.[1107]

The Court thereby upheld its decision to decline the teacher's claim based on the reasons set forth: first, the Court found that the claimant had infringed

1106 BAG (Bundesarbeitsgericht): decision from 10.12.09 – 2 AZR 55/09 = BeckRS 2010, 68518.

1107 The amendment to Sec. 57 para 4 of the SchulG NRW came into force on 1 August 2006.

the neutrality principle prescribed in Art. 57 para 4 of the NRW SchulG and consequently violated her duty as a representative of the state to remain neutral and refrain from any religious or political manifestation that may challenge the obligation of the state towards parents and pupils; she thus disturbed the amicable atmosphere at school. The Court explained that a conscious wearing of a religious garment or symbol is an outwardly manifestation of the teacher's religious belief which is forbidden by Art. 57 para 4 of the NRW SchulG.[1108] It underscored further that it was the pronounced intent of the NRW legislator to exclude any religious or political influence from the realm of public schools, as they pose fertile ground for potential conflicts. This prohibition was interpreted by the Court to include even a situation where merely an 'abstract danger' exists with respect to religious freedom of pupils and parents, the religious neutrality of the state and the peaceful operation of school.[1109] The appearance of a teacher with an ostentatious religious symbol is a conscious act of religious manifestation and as such may establish a potential ground for a conflict that parents will likely wish to avert as unwanted influence on their children.[1110] Ultimately, the Court reaffirmed that confinement of religious freedom for the benefit of a peaceful school operation would be regarded as admissible since it serves a legitimate aim.[1111] Notably, the Court does not make any segregation with respect to the fact that the majority of pupils are Muslim and participate willingly in the claimant's lessons.

In addition, the state did not infringe upon constitutional rights as it acted within its competency, and by virtue of this authority it is able to enact legislation for public education that will take into consideration the competing interests of all involved parties: teachers, parents, pupils, and the state as the competent authority for supervision of the school system.[1112] Thence, a provision prohibiting teachers the donning of religious garments or symbols, as they indicate their

---

1108 BAG 10.12.09 – 2 AZR 55/09 NZA – RR 2010, 383; BVerwG (16.12.08), NJW 2009, 1289 = ZTR 2009, 167; BVerwG (24.6.2004),], BVerwGE 121, 140 = NJW 2004, 3581.

1109 BAG 10.12.09 – 2 AZR 55/09 NZA – RR 2010, 383: BVerwG (24.6.2004), BVerwGE 121,140 = NJW 2004, 3581.

1110 BAG 10.12.09 – 2 AZR 55/09 NZA – RR 2010, 383; Senat, NZA 2010, 227; BVerwGE 121, 140 = NJW 2004, 3581.

1111 BAG 10.12.09 – 2 AZR 55/09 NZA – RR 2010, 383; BVerfGE 108, 282 = NJW 2003, 3111: BVerwG (26.6.2008), BVerwGE 131, 242 =NJW 2008, 3654; BVerwG, NJW 2009, 1289 =ZTR 2009, 167; BVerwGE 121, 140 = NJW 2004, 3581.

1112 BAG 10.12.09 – 2 AZR 55/09 NZA – RR 2010, 383; BVerfG (24.9.2003), BVerfGE 108, 282 = NJW 2003, 3111; BVerwGE 121, 140 = NJW 2004, 3581.

religious affiliation, conform to the state's freedom of action and, as a result, will be regarded eligible. The Court explained that the constitutional solution offered by Art. 57 para 4 NRW SchulG for potential controversies and tension points does not infringe upon the principle of 'practical concordance' and the fundamental rights of the involved parties. In that case, the Court acknowledges an explicit prevalence of the parental right to take care of the education of their children, the negative right of the pupils, and the duty of the state to maintain its religious neutrality as opposed to the positive right of the teacher to exercise her religious freedom and practice her profession without discrimination.

Second, her assertion of unequal treatment was rejected by the Court as insufficiently established. It was held that Art. 57 para 4 does not infringe upon Art. 3 para 1 GG since the ban on manifestation of ostensible symbols was objectively suited to all religions and faiths without distinction,[1113] and the claimant could not prove that she was treated differently than other teachers (either Muslim men wearing religious garment or female teachers of other religious or ideological pertinence).

Third, the claim of infringement against Art. 9 of the ECHR was declined as well on grounds that the ECtHR recognized the right of pupils and parents not to be impaired in the public school system by virtue of the necessity to guarantee undisturbed operation of state schools that will be achieved through observance of the right to state neutrality as a legitimate aim.[1114] Fourth, Art. 57 para 4 NRW SchulG makes no gender differentiation, so the restrictive dress code precept applies equally to all teachers irrespective of their gender.[1115] The second point in this regard relates to the discriminatory character of the ban in access to public service that is based on religious affiliation. The Court declined the teacher's claim that display of Christian symbols or garments of Christian teaching staff are given preference as opposed to schoolteachers of a different religious adherence since neither the wording of the ban prescribed in Art. 57 para 4 nor the administrative school practice permit unjustified religious discrimination.

In the end, the Court decided that such a legislative confinement of the right to religious freedom is admissible.

1113 BAG 10.12.09 – 2 AZR 55/09 NZA – RR 2010, 383: Senat, NZA 2010, 227; BVerwGE 121, 140 = NJW 2004, 3581.

1114 BAG 10.12.09 – 2 AZR 55/09 NZA – RR 2010, 383; ECtHR (10.11.2005), NvWZ 2006, 1389; EctHR (15.2.2001)), NJW 2001, 2871.

1115 BAG 10.12.09 – 2 AZR 55/09 NZA – RR 2010, 383; NZA 2010, 227.

(c) Conclusion

The BAG declared that the complainant infringed on her duty to abide by the neutrality principle and the prohibition prescribed in the now abolished Art. 57 para 4 of the NRW SchulG to refrain from any manifestation – religious, political, or philosophical – that expresses outwardly the religious affiliation of a teacher. It refused to accept the complainant's request to remove the remark made in the personnel records of the teacher and decided to give prevalence to the duty of the teacher to abide by the neutrality principle upon her fundamental right to manifestation of her religion. Furthermore, the assertion of the teacher that she did not infringe on the negative right of the pupils to religious freedom since the majority of pupils were Muslim themselves did not avail her. The BAG emphasized that the obligation of a teacher to appear neutral in her teaching profession gains further significance, in particular as the teacher must appear unbiased within her role as state representative so that pupils would not feel pressured to act in a similar way. In addition, the peaceful operation of school lessons had been underscored by the Court as a protected value that must be guaranteed and even prevail over the teacher's right to religious manifestation. The teacher's claim for unequal treatment and violation based on gender equality were rejected based on the fact that legislative ban applied allegedly with respect to all religions equally.

(4) The Bhagwan Case

This case presents the challenge made with respect to the legitimacy of a teacher to wear the Bhagwan typical clothing. The complaint was rejected by the High Administrative Court in Hamburg[1116] and, as a result, was appealed to the Bavarian Administrative Court.

(a) Factual Background

The complainant was occupied as a teacher in a Bavarian public school (*Hauptschule*: secondary school) during the years 1984 and 1985. As a member of the Rajneesh-Bhagwan sect (also known as 'Mala'), he conformed to the traditional religious garment worn by followers of the sect and appeared at school with the traditional red-coloured garb and a wooden necklace carrying a Bhagwan print.[1117] In a decision from 3 January 1985, the state of Bavaria

1116 The decision from 26.11.1984 OVG Hamburg, NVwZ 1986, 406.
1117 The decision from 9.9.1985 VGH München BayVGH NVwZ 1986, 405.

ordered a ban on wearing the traditional Bhagwan garb (a conclusive ban on all colour varieties of their red shades clothing) within public school premises. The complainant then sought a revision of the decision after his claim was already rejected by the High Administrative Court.

The conclusions laid down by the Bavarian Administrative Court will be summarized here as follows:[1118]

(b) Leading Legal Aspects

At the outset, the Court established the duty of the teacher pursuant to Sec. 62 para 1 of the BBG to comply and act in accordance with the laws and the democratic values as stipulated in the Grundgesetz and take due reference for maintenance of a peaceful atmosphere while on duty.[1119] Further, it was declared that the teacher carries a special educative task towards the pupils, which is prescribed to him/her by law, Sec. 38 para 1 BayEUG.

The Court explained that the teacher violated his educative task incumbent upon him in the provisions of the constitution (i.e., Art. 7 GG as well as Art. 130 para BayVerf). It was underscored that the educative task comprehends the religious neutrality of the state and, as a result, obliges the teacher in his duty to remain neutral in aspects of religion and belief.

In addition, it was declared that the neutrality principle maintains an adequate balance to other constitutional rights standing along the educative task of the state, like parental right to education of their children prescribed in Art. 6 para 2 GG and Sec. 126 para 1 of the Bavarian constitution. In a like manner, it guarantees the (negative) religious freedom as recognized and established in several constitutional provisions (Art. 4 GG and Sec. 107 para 6 of the Bavarian constitution, Art. 140 together with Art. 136 para 3 WRV) and in case laws.[1120]

At the same time, the BCC acknowledges the undisturbed right of a teacher to practice his/her religious freedom (Art. 4 para 1 GG and Art. 107 para 1 BayVerf). However, it declines the assertion that Art. 135 of the Bavarian constitution in its second sentence, prescribing the conveyance of Christian tenets to pupils in Bavarian state schools impinges in any way the undisturbed right of

---

1118 BVerwG, NVwZ 1988, 937, 938; BayVerfGH, BayVBl. 1985, 721, 722.

1119 Sec. 62 para 1 of the BeamtStG is now endorsed in Sec. 33 para 1 of the BeamtStG, lastly amended on 5.2.2009 (BGBl. I p. 160). See also http://www.gesetze-im-internet.de/beamtstg/BJNR101000008.html.

1120 BayVGH NVwZ 1986, 405; BVerfGE 52, 223, 246 = NJW 1980, 575.

the teacher to practice his religious freedom. In that sense, it was stated that the complainant suffers no restrictions on his right to religious freedom.

The BCC explains the legitimacy to restrain the scope of unreserved right to religious freedom[1121] if this is prescribed either in the Grundgesetz or the Bavarian constitution and the pursued aim is the protection of colliding pre-eminent rights of third parties.[1122] Hence, if tension arises, especially in the state school system, it is crucial to attain the right balance between competing rights. An adequate balance is to be achieved through application of the obligation to act tolerantly towards other-minded.[1123]

It was concluded that by the constant confrontation with the colourful garment of the teacher (colours range from red to pink, orange, and purple) the (negative) right of pupils is endangered, as they are compelled by the view of their teachers without any ability to escape. Further, the influence on the pupils accrues due to confrontation with the unique garment of their teacher and the interest it triggers cannot be excluded.[1124] With an appearance of the Bhagwan traditional dress the teacher, therefore, ostentatiously manifests his religion to the extent that his behaviour violates his obligation to religious neutrality and maintenance of peaceful co-existence.[1125]

(c) Conclusion

This case demonstrates that there is no general ban of the headscarf per se; rather, the prohibition on manifestation of religious garments or garbs worn by teachers during school times would be regarded in general as unconstitutional as such an action explicitly defies the school's obligation to religious neutrality.

1121 BayVGH NVwZ 1986, 405; OVG Hamburg, NVwZ 1986, 406; BVerfGE 33, 23, 29.

1122 BayVGH NVwZ 1986, 405. Notably, the High Administrative Court justified interference in the teacher's right to religious freedom not only if it contravenes fundamental rights of third parties. A confinement of the teacher's right to religious freedom emanates of his duty as a civil servant and the special obligation of allegiance towards prominent constitutional values, and commitment not to endanger the peaceful co-existence prescribed in Art. 33 para 4 GG. See in OVG Hamburg, NVwZ 1986, 406, 407; BVerfGE 41, 88, 107 = NJW 1976, 952.

1123 BayVGH NVwZ 1986, 405; BVerfGE 52, 223, 246, et. Seq. = NJW 1980, 575.

1124 BayVGH NVwZ 1986, 405, 406; OVG Hamburg, NVwZ 1986, 406, 407 = DVBl 1985, 456.

1125 BayVGH NVwZ 1986, 405, 406; OVG Hamburg, NVwZ 1986, 406, 407; BVerwGE 14, 21, 24, et seq.= NJW 1962, 1532.

(5) *Inclusion of a Cap or a Basque Hat*

The BAG (Federal Labour Court) was required to determine in another case which occurred in a state school in the land NRW whether wearing a head covering in form of a wool cap by a teacher would be regarded as eligible when used as a substitute for the headscarf.[1126]

(a) Factual Background

The complainant, a Muslim teacher, has worked in a mandatory state school as a social education teacher in the state of NRW since 1997. Since the introduction of the NRWSchulG in 2006, stipulating the prohibition of religious manifestation with respect to all teachers in state schools, it was incumbent on the complainant to refrain from wearing the headscarf during class lessons. In the aftermath of a requirement addressed by the school authority the complainant decided to rid of the headscarf, substituting it with a different head covering, a wool cap that covers the whole hairline including her ears. The complainant then received a disciplinary warning establishing that the wool cap constitutes a head covering that is headscarf-like and worn as a substitute for the Islamic headscarf; therefore, it infringes upon the legislative ban stipulated in Art. 57 para 4 NRWSchulG. The claimant charged the withdrawal of the warning from her personnel records since this violates her fundamental right to religious freedom and eligibility for equal treatment (Art. 4 para 1 and para 2, Art. 3 para 3 GG). She asserted that the wool cap does not constitute a religious symbol and so does not infringe upon the prohibition on religious manifestation stipulated in Art. 57 para 4 NRWSchulG.

(b) Leading Legal Aspects

Similar to the former ruling delivered by the BAG,[1127] it was interesting to recognize that the Court made no deviation from its outlined argumentation and the final verdict to reject the claim. Hence, the quintessence of the judgement will be provided as follows:

It was determined that the claimant had infringed her obligation as a state official to observe the neutrality principle. By choosing to wear a specific garment that may amount to an expression of a religious manifestation the teacher consciously infringed the ban prescribed in Art. 57 para 4 of the NRWSchulG.

1126 BAG decision from 20.8.2009 – 2 AZR 499/08 – NZA 2010, 227 = BeckRS 2010, 65571.
1127 BAG decision from 10.12.09 – 2 AZR 55/09.

In that case, the constant appearance with a wool cap amounts to an outwardly manifestation of the teacher's religious adherence.[1128]

The Court held that the decision of the school authority was constitutionally legitimate and justified, for the state has a monopoly on school education that enables it to take account of other constitutional values when fulfilling its educational mandate. Values with which religious freedom of teachers has to be balanced are religious freedom of pupils and parents, the principle of religious neutrality of the state, the supervision of the state over the public school system, and the maintenance of peaceful school operation that will be accomplished through fostering of tolerance and acceptance between different religions and ideological convictions at school.

Foremost, the Court maintained that the character of a symbol does not have to ensue from the garment itself. More important is the way an insignia is perceived from an objective perspective of third parties (pupils and their parents).[1129] A religious manifestation may occur when the garment or the symbol convey the wearer a special significance that is recognized as extrinsic to the educational framework and worn at all times without any exception. In this particular case, the claimant allegedly wore a plain wool cap; however, the impression perceived by pupils and their parents is that the teacher identifies herself through this religious garment denoting she is a professed Muslim. The religious character of the wool cap was concluded from the following facts: the rigorous donning of the teacher was especially accentuated as she took care to cover her head and ears including the neck, she appeared with the wool cap in school at all times without any exception of year seasoning or daytime, and the substitute of the wool cap ensued immediately following the ban of the headscarf. The Court stated that this strengthened the impression of an objective viewer that the purport behind wearing the wool cap was the plain substitute of a religious symbol that closely resembles a headscarf.

It was further underscored that the possibility of an abstract danger to (negative) religious freedom and the impairment of peaceful operation resulting from the teacher's appearance with a headscarf may justify in itself a prohibition of religious insignia. The BAG explained that the NRW legislature intended to prevent the possible occurrence of an abstract danger in the first place and not

---

1128 BAG decision from 20.8.2009 – NZA 2010, 227; BVerwG (16.12.2008), NJW 2009, 1289 = ZTR 2009, 167; BVerfG (24.6.2004), BVerwGE 121, 140 = NJW 2004, 3581.

1129 BAG decision from 20.8.2009 – NZA 2010, 227; BVerfG (24.9.2003), BVerfGE 108, 282 = NJW 2003, 3111.

subject to the application of the ban till an indication of a concrete threat to school peace should emerge. Likewise, the forbearance in compulsory schools from any conflicts motivated by religion or ideological view was recognized as a weight-worthy protected value.[1130] The achievement of this goal, thence, permits the confinement of the teacher's religious freedom to wear the headscarf.[1131] Respectively, a concrete danger does not have to exist, as the mere possibility that the teacher with a headscarf or a similar head covering may pose an abstract threat to the fundamental rights of children and their parents or to school peace will suffice for its prohibition.[1132] The Court concluded that the appearance of a teacher with head covering constitutes a violation of the state's obligation to religious neutrality that can definitely trigger the application of Art. 57 para 4 NRW SchulG.[1133] In addition, the claim of a violation of her right to equal treatment according to Art. 7 para 1 AGG (the general equal treatment regulations) was also declined by the Court. The Court refers to Art. 8 para 1 AGG[1134] establishing that the ban on religious symbols fulfilled a legitimate aim (religious neutrality of the state) and the restraint on teaching staff was regarded as adequate.

(c) Conclusion

The jurisdictional ruling in this case took place following the amendment to NRWSchulG (Sec. 57 para 4) inserting the ban on teaching staff to manifestation of their religious affiliation through display of ostensible religious insignias in state schools. Remarkably, the BAG considered even a plain wool cap or Basque to form a prohibited manifestation of religion since it imparted on the teacher a special significance as worn by her at all times without any exception. The BAG refrained from going into the teacher's real intention by wearing such a head covering. It rather focused on the question what impression the view of

1130 BAG decision from 20.8.2009 – NZA 2010, 227; BVerfGE 108, 282 = NJW 2003, 3111; BVerwG (26.6.2008), BVerwGE 131, 242 = NJW 2008, 3654.

1131 BAG decision from 20.8.2009 – NZA 2010, 227; BVerwG, NJW 2009, 1289 = ZTR 2009, 167; BVerwGE 121, 140 = NJW 2004, 3581.

1132 BAG decision from 20.8.2009 – NZA 2010, 227; BVerwGE 131, 242 = NJW 2008, 3654; BVerwG, NJW 2009, 1289.

1133 BAG decision from 20.8.2009 – NZA 2010, 227; BVerwGE 121, 140 = NJW 2004, 3581.

1134 Art. 8 para 1 AGG prescribes an exception to the general ban of unequal treatment set forth in Art. 1 and Art. 7 para 1 AGG. An unequal treatment will be regarded as eligible given that it serves a legitimate aim and is adequate to the aim sought to be achieved.

a religious symbol inspires by an objective observer, that is, the pupils or their parents. In this case, it was alleged that the pupils as well as their parents associated with the wool cap an expression of a religious symbol which served as substitute for the forbidden headscarf. In addition, the BAG rejected the need to substantiate a concrete danger to another protected value when outweighed against the teacher's right to religious freedom. It was reasoned that a state action in the aftermath will fail to forbear religiously motivated conflicts within school realm from the beginning.

(6) Religious Garment Worn by a Teacher – Bavarian Case

It is remarkable in this case that the allegation before the Bavarian Constitutional Court (BCC) requesting to revise the eligibility of Art. 59 para 2 BSEA with the Bavarian constitution was not brought by a Muslim teacher, but rather by an Islamic community associated with an Islamic roof organization in Bavaria, known as the Islamic Centre of Munich (Islamisches Zentrum in München, IZM).[1135]

(a) Factual Background

The constitutional question challenged by the claimant before the Bavarian Constitutional Court aimed to seek a declaration that a Bavarian state's legislation was incompatible with the enunciation in the state's constitution. It was alleged before the BayVerfGH that Art. 59 para 2 of the BayEuG prescribes a general ban prohibiting teachers from wearing ostensible signs or garbs if they constitute an expression of religion or ideological creed. The claimants, therefore, established their claim on grounds that Art. 59 para 2 infringes the right of all Muslims living in Bavaria to religious freedom as bestowed by Art. 107 BayVerf. It was asserted that it is only comprehensible that Art. 107 BayVerf enfolds also the right of a Muslim teacher to wear a headscarf as it pertains an integral part of her Muslim belief. Further, Art. 59 para 2 BayEuG stands in contradiction to the wording of several stipulations pronounced in the Bavarian constitution.[1136] The allegation was declined by the BayVerfGH for lack of substantial grounds to support the claim. The main aspects are to be specified next:

1135 BayVerfGH decision from 15.1.2007 NVwZ 2008, 420 = DÖV 2007, 980 L. Since religious communities in Germany are recognized as a statutory public law corporations, they are entitled under this status to bring a claim against the state, as in this matter.

1136 BayVefGH NVwZ 2008, 420 = DÖV 2007, 980.

(b) Leading Legal Aspects

First, the BayVerfGH held that the Bavarian lawmaker is entitled by virtue of the authority granted to it in Art. 130 para 1 BayVerf to enact legal regulations administering the establishment and organization of its educational system. This competency of the state to supervise the school system stretches itself conceivably also with respect to shaping of dress code regulations for schoolteachers.[1137] The Bavarian state therefore did not transcend its supervisory task by designating criteria for aptitude of teachers in the public service. In fact, the Bavarian legislator, by regulating the dress code of civil servants in a proper legislation demonstrated conformity with previous decisions of the BVerfG in a similar matter (i.e., *Ludin*'s case).[1138] Given this is the case, the legislative obligatory ban on ostensible symbols or garments worn by teachers in school was declared by the Court to be valid and permissible.

Second, Art. 59 para 2 BayEUG does not infringe upon the principle of law pursuant to Art. 3 para 1 BayVerf. This was justified on the following grounds: first, Art. 59 para 2 BayEUG bears no exceptional cases – the BayVerfG found no constitutional ground for the endorsement of exceptional cases since according to the BayVerf they would only be permissible if an impingement took place with respect to the structural principles of the Grundgesetz (the principle of equality or other constitutional legitimate aims).[1139] In this view, it made clear that Art. 59 para 2 of the BayEuG is abstractly and generally formulated so that it applies equally with respect to all symbols or garments whose religious or ideological manifestation seem to be repugnant to the fundaments and the educational goals of the Bavarian constitution. Accordingly, the grounds for exception do not apply in this case and, as a result, the court declined to provide a case-by-case solution (objection or preventive ban with permitted exceptions). Nonetheless, it determined that under the rule of law and the principle of democracy, even if the Bavarian legislator was to order an exception with respect to a specific type of garments or symbols, it would be permitted to do so as it accords with the competency granted to it in the constitution.[1140]

1137 BayVefGH NVwZ 2008, 420; *BayVerfGHE* 50, 156, 166; *BayVerfGH*, BayVBl 2006, 530. It was expounded that the competency of the state can take form either through legislation, administrative regulation, or a strict supervision, *Meder*, Art. 130, recital 2.

1138 BayVefGH NVwZ 2008, 420: BVerfGE 108, 282=NJW 2003, 3111.

1139 BayVefGH NVwZ 2008, 420.

1140 BayVefGH NVwZ 2008, 420; BayVerfGHE 31, 17, 32; 37, 148, 162; 48, 99, 108.

Third, the BayVerf refuses to state explicitly which signs or symbols will be regarded as permissible or not. It establishes that even the Bavarian lawmaker was under no obligation to designate precisely in the BayEuG itself what symbols or garments will be regarded ostensible so as to constitute an expression of a religion (as long as an adequate and reliable construction of the regulation can be inferred).[1141]

Fourth, Art. 59 para 2 BayEUG fulfils the requirement of certainty of the law. It refused in this respect to acknowledge that an inherent task of the Constitutional Court is to provide legislative construction with respect to a state's legislation. It was decided that a specific designation of symbols or garments and determination to which extent they may constitute a manifestation of religion is not a matter for the Constitutional Court to solve but rather for the state's legislator.[1142] The BayVerfGH acknowledged that the alignment of the first prong of Art. 59 para 2 BayEUG (ban on manifestation of religious symbols or garments) with its second prong (if to contravene with the Christian values, culture, and tradition) can be achieved through a simple construction. The BayVerfG, however, refused again to deliver its interpretation on the matter.

In this respect, the Court provides an interpretation aiming to reconcile between the allegedly contradicting parts of Art. 59 para 2 BayEuG. It established that conveyance of values that accord with the Christian belief cannot be perceived in its strict religious meaning of Christianity as a faith. As a result, it reasoned that the explicit reference to the Christian faith does not connote of its religious orientation but rather of its social-philosophical perception.[1143] Therefore, an impact on pupils should not be evaluated from a subjective perspective (how it affects the pupils in a particular case), but rather objectively (how a manifestation of a religious symbol can be understood).

Fifth, it was established that the right to religious freedom bestowed by Art. 107 para 1 and para 2 of the BayVerf is not infringed due to the stipulation in Art. 59 para 2 BayEuG. The BayVerfG held the view that the freedom of the teacher to practice her religion is unreserved according to the Bavarian constitution. Nevertheless, her personal right does not relieve her from her duty to act in accordance with the special obligation incumbent on her as a schoolteacher. It was explained that though her right to freedom of religion is protected as a

1141 BayVefGH NVwZ 2008, 420, 421; BayVerfGHE 56, 28, 45: 57, 113, 127.

1142 BayVefGH NVwZ 2008, 420 [421];BayVerfGHE 41, 17, 26.

1143 BayVerfGH, NVwZ 2008, 420, 421; BayVerfGH 55, 189, 196, et seq 196 f., BVerfGE 41, 65, 84 et seq. = NJW 1976, 950.

fundamental right, it can only be taken into a limited consideration in the context of her role as a public official,[1144] which obliges her to observe the duty of the state to religious neutrality.[1145]

Sixth, the BCC distinguishes the necessity to weigh the teacher's right to religious freedom against the conflicting fundamental rights of parents and pupils (Art. 107 BayVerf). It eventually opines that the inherent rights of parents (Art. 126 para 1 BayVerf) to establish the religious education of their children includes the (negative) right to protect their children from any religious or ideological influence they consider not to be suitable.[1146]

Finally, the BCC concluded that Art. 59 para 2 BayEuG did not breach the equality principle established in Art. 118 para 1 of the Bavarian constitution since the ban applies equally to all teachers and makes no segregation with respect to gender and religious adherence. It further prescribes that the equality principle does not demand its strict application without segregation, but rather will permit different treatment in special cases in order to achieve equality.[1147]

(c) Conclusion

At the outset, this ruling reaffirmed the educative mandate conferred to the state with respect to organization of educational matters and formation of its public school system pursuant to Art. 130 para 1 BayVerf. In addition, it underscored the enjoyment of the federal states (*Länder*) to a wide margin of appreciation with respect to their inner affairs,[1148] inter alia the supervision of education and regulation of teachers' dress code that will take place following careful outweigh of the competing interests. The BayVerfG thereby defers its competency to intervene in the discretion granted to a democratically legitimate legislator to decide on the permissibility of religious symbols into its state school system. It thence refuses to examine on a case-by-case basis which ostentatious religious symbols are envisaged to be banned from school premises by the Bavarian legislator, be it the Islamic headscarf, the traditional red garment and necklace (*Mala*) worn by Bhagwan followers, the *burqa* – a traditional garment worn by women of the Taliban –, or the *chador*. Accordingly, the state of Bavaria is entitled to lay

---

1144 BayVerfGH NVwZ 2008, 420, 421; BayVerfGHE 43, 148, 156.

1145 BayVerfGH NVwZ 2008, 420, 422; BayVerfGHE 50, 156, 167.

1146 BayVerfGH NVwZ 2008, 420, 421, 422; BayVerfGHE 55, 189, 196.

1147 BayVerfGH NVwZ 2008, 420, 423, 3; BayVerfGHE 56, 178, 191.

1148 BayVerfGH NVwZ 2008, 420, 422, 2c); BVerfGE 50, 290, 332 = NJW 1979, 699; BVerfGE 99, 367, 389 f.= NJW 1999, 1535.

down prerequisites for the manifestation of religious symbols. The Court further accentuates that the constitutional demand in Art. 130 para 1 BayVerfG for conformity of religious symbols with the Christian belief does not overextend the educational mandate conveyed on the Bavarian state, as it merely constitutes an integral part of the discretion granted to it in the constitution.[1149] Finally, the right of a teacher to religious freedom and its exertion by outer appearance according to Art. 107 para 1 and 2 BayVerfG is not violated, as the obligation of the teacher to appear neutral and unbiased emanates from her duty as a public servant.

(7) The NRW Headscarf Ban (decision from 27 January 2015)[1150]

(a) Factual Background

In this revision, two appellants brought a conjoined constitutional complaint against the decisions of the BAG (Federal Labour Court) to discharge their claims based on their unlawful dismissal from teaching posts. The complaints were substantiated on grounds of unconstitutionality of Art. 57 para 4 of the SchulG NRW which imposes a general ban on teaching staff from appearance with ostentatious religious or political symbols while on duty.

In both proceedings brought before the BAG, the complainants were female Muslim teachers of German citizenship who were dismissed by school authorities due to their refusal to remove their head-coverings. In the first proceeding, the teacher who has been wearing the headscarf for many years was summoned by school authorities and was asked to remove the headscarf; she decided to appear with a beret, a wool hat, with a matching polo-neck sweater, received a warning and rejected the request for its removal.[1151] In the second proceeding, the schoolteacher for the Turkish language who was wearing a headscarf during lessons was subject to dismissal by school authorities for her refusal to abandon her head covering.[1152] Both complaints remained unsuccessful and were dismissed by the BAG.

The two appellants submitted a conjoined claim which is the subject matter of the revision before the BVerfG.

1149 BayVerfGH NVwZ 2008, 420, 423.

1150 BVerfGE 138, 296 = NJW 2015, 1359.

1151 1BvR 471/10.

1152 1BvR 1181/10.

(b) Leading Legal Aspects

No all-inclusive prohibition – in principle, the BVerfG upheld the right of teachers, just like any other individuals, to freely exercise their religious freedom according to Art. 4 para 1 and para 2 GG, even if this is motivated by prescription of the tenets of their religion. The confinement of the right to manifest a religion through wearing of external ostentatious symbols would be admissible only following a narrow interpretation of constitutional rights and a case-by-case review. Accordingly, the all-inclusive ban imposed on teaching staff to refrain from manifestation of religious symbols through their outer appearance for the mere purpose of abstract endangerment to religious neutrality or peaceful co-existence in school is disproportionate.[1153]

The subjective perception of the right holder – the BVerfG accepts the fact that for many Muslim teachers wearing the headscarf goes beyond the mere religious imperative to which they must abide, but it also enfolds part of their personal identity as protected in the constitution (Art. 2 para 1 and Art. 1 para 1 GG). The fact that the headscarf forms a part of a teacher's identity hinders her access to employment in the public service as a qualified teacher (Art. 12 para 1 GG) since a refusal will be justified on the ground that the headscarf runs counter to the principle of gender equality (Art. 3 para 2 GG).

The abstract endangerment – it was determined that the curtailment in the teacher's right to religious freedom is too severe and disproportionate to the pursued aim as laid down in the first sentence of Art. 57 para 4 SchulG NRW.[1154] The BVerfG contended that its former corresponding interpretation accepted a justification for interference in the fundamental right of the teacher that was based merely on an abstract endangerment to the neutrality principle, fundamental constitutional liberties and values, or the peaceful co-existence in school. However, it upheld that the right to religious freedom is so prominent that it cannot be outweighed against an abstract, non-concrete endangerment which can be proved substantially.

A different outweigh of competing rights – the prohibition *a priori* of ostentatious garments or symbols due to the potential impairment of the negative right to religious freedom of pupils and parents (Art. 4 para 1 and para 2 and Art. 6 para 2 GG) does not have legal justification if no evidence for proselytization on part of the teacher was provided.[1155] In that sense, the BVerfG deviates from

---

1153 BVerfG 1 BvR 471/10.

1154 BVerfG 1 BvR 471/10 recital 100.

1155 BVerfG 1 BvR 471/10 recital 105.

its former general approach as upheld in *Ludin*'s case and attempts to adopt a milder approach towards the negative right of pupils not to be exposed to distracting religious symbols worn by a public schoolteacher. This judgement can be characterised by its appeasing attitude towards the teacher's (positive) right to practice her religious freedom as oppose to the emphasis put so far on the (negative) right of pupils not to be exposed to any harmful or indoctrinating influence.

In principle, while in *Ludin*'s case the teacher's right to religious freedom had to set back when outweighed against other constitutional freedoms and values (e.g., the negative religious right of pupils, the educative mandate of parents or the precept of state neutrality); in this case, the BVerfG rejects the notion that the teachers' right should be withdrawn at outset only for the possibility that pupils may feel harmed due to their daily confrontation with the teachers' headscarf. As a comparison, the main argument provided in *Ludin*'s case advocating the confinement of a teacher's right to religious freedom was supported on grounds of her duty to appear unbiased and neutral as a public servant. It was underscored that the teacher had voluntarily chosen her profession which imposes on her, especially by virtue of her special duty as state representative, to abide by the principle of religious neutrality of the state. The act of voluntariness cannot be attributed to the pupils since they are subject to statutory compulsory education and cannot escape the outer appearance of a teacher and are presumed to be influenced by this view.

In the recent headscarf case, the BVerfG held that the exposure to multiculturalism, plurality of religions and faiths, especially in public community schools, is an inevitable part of the daily school scenery and, thus, even an interaction with a teacher wearing a headscarf would be relativized due to the presence of teachers of other faiths. The BVerfG holds that the scenery in community schools should not only reflect the religious plurality existing in a society but also convey pupils with values such as tolerance and mutual respect towards other religions.

The same outweigh should apply with respect to the educative task of the state pursuant to Art. 7 para 1 GG. The educative task enfolds the guarantee of the state's obligation to religious neutrality. It was reasoned by the BVerfG that, in general, wearing an Islamic headscarf by a teacher while on duty would not contradict the notion of religious neutrality.

No strict apprehension of religious neutrality – the BVerfG explains that religious neutrality of the state does not suggest a strict separation between state and church. It must rather be apprehended in an open, liberal comprehensive form that provides all faiths and religions an equal position even within compulsory public education. The strict prohibition on a teacher to appear with a headscarf poses a disproportionate encroachment on her fundamental right to religious freedom.

It further segregates between two situations: an institutional symbol like the crucifix when displayed on a classroom wall, as opposed to the individual wearing of a religious symbol. In the former case, the BVerfG acknowledges by far a stark identification of the state with a specific religion, contrary to religious manifestation by an individual, which cannot be ascribed to the state.

The BVerfG prescribes the duty of the legislator to outline in regulations distinguishing rules for the purpose of determining the existence of a concrete, as opposed to abstract, endangerment. Given that the legislator refrains from prescribing such segregation by law, then the presumption at the outset should not be detrimental to the (positive) right of a teacher to exercise her religious freedom. It was explained that the visibility of a religious symbol like the headscarf and the exposure of others to it cannot amount by itself to an act of indoctrination. In the absence of evidence to prove the contrary, there exists no entitlement of others in a society to remain untroubled by its presence.

Such an interpretation should be valid also with respect to Art. 57 para 4 s. 2 of SchulG NRW. The BVerfG refuses to accept a comprehensive ban of all religious symbols that may evoke with pupils or their parents the impression they contradict pre-eminent constitutional values such as the duty of the state to religious neutrality, human dignity, the equality principle according to Art. 3 GG, other constitutional liberty rights, and the basic order of a democratic state.

No privilege to Christian and Western tradition – the BVerfG establishes that the privileged status granted by the NRW legislator to the display of Christian and occidental Western tradition (Art. 57 para 4 s. 3 SchulG NRW) is contradictory to the equality principle. The advancement of the Christian and Jewish religion is disadvantageous to members of other faiths and constitutes in itself discrimination on religious grounds that violates the constitutional precepts laid down in Art. 3 para 3 and 33 para 3 GG.

It was held that there is no constitutional justification to a direct discrimination established on religious grounds. Should a ban be imposed on manifestation of ostentatious religious symbols, then it should apply equally with respect to all teaching staff without any exception.

Finally, the BVerfG determines that factors other than religion cannot substantiate a justification for different application of the ban either. As such, the explanation given that the headscarf is perceived as a sign for women's oppression that runs counter to the Western ideology of gender equality cannot be used as a justification ground for a comprehensive ban of the headscarf. The Court therefore declared Art. 57 para 4 s. 3 SchulG NRW as incompatible with the constitution (Art. 3 para 3 s. 1 and 33 para 3 GG) and, as a result, null and void.

The dissenting opinion upheld in adverse that the majority's restrictive interpretation of Sec. 57 para 4 NRW SchulG is not dictated by the constitution. It was reasoned that such an interpretation risks an imbalance of the competing rights (i.e., the educative task of the state, the duty of the state to religious neutrality, the educative right of parents, and the negative rights of pupils to religious freedom), as the teacher who is obliged by her function as a state representative to respect the neutrality precept will be favoured in her position and will not incur any limitations. Such a restrictive interpretation of Sec. 57 para 4 NRW SchulG enables the right of one individual, the teacher, to override other fundamental rights which are equivalent in constitutional rank.[1156] Therefore, it was concluded that the right of a teacher to manifest her religion should be limited by virtue of her function and not prevail at outset other equal-ranked constitutional fundamental rights. In addition, it was asserted that the majority's decision contradicts and cuts sharply into the freedom of discretion conferred to the federal states to decide on the organization of their educational system. They opined that the majority's approach contrasts with a previous decision of the BVerfG (i.e., *Ludin*'s judgement), where it conferred upon the states the privilege to promulgate regulations relating to establishment of their school system; within the process of designation they may, at sole discretion, take into account the different religions and cultural variety of their citizens. Accordingly, the states using the wide margin of appreciation can either generally opt for an extensive admissibility of religious symbols into their public state schools[1157] or interdict religious symbols on basis of a strict abidance of the neutrality precept on condition that no proselytization on part of the teacher takes place with respect to the pupils.[1158] This constitutional right enables the NRW legislator as well as lawmakers of other states to decide on the educational framework of public schools, and this prerogative includes the state's discretion to promulgate teachers' dress code regulations.[1159] The measurements taken by the NRW legislator to introduce a prohibition on the manifestation of ostentatious religious insignias worn by teachers in order to prevent possible conflicts between pupils,

1156 BVerfG 1 BvR 471/10 recital 2 dissenting opinion of Judges: Schluckebier and Hermanns.

1157 BVerfG 1 BvR 471/10 recital 6; BVerfGE 52, 223 the 'school prayer' case (Schulgebetentscheidung).

1158 BVerfG 1 BvR 471/10 recital 2; BVerfGE 108, 282.

1159 BVerfG 1 BvR 471/10 recital 2, 6, 7.

parents, and other teaching staff in the first place are adequate and admissible.[1160] The NRW legislator had stable grounds to decide that even abstract endangerment to peaceful co-existence in school and the duty of the state to abide by the religious neutrality precept should suffice as legitimate aims that will justify an all-inclusive ban on manifestation of religious symbols through the outer appearance of teaching staff.[1161]

Further, the dissenting opinion disagreed with the majority's view that a teacher with a headscarf does not infringe on the negative right of pupils and their parents to religious freedom. It held that a teacher holds special dependence relations with respect to pupils in primary schools as well as to their parents. Her pedagogical-educational duty and the constant confrontation with her presence in state classrooms does not enable the pupils any leeway to escape. The teacher constitutes a role model for the pupils and the influence of her behaviour, including her wearing of religious garments especially with respect to pupils of tender age, cannot be denied.[1162]

Although they held the opinion that a teacher owns a right to religious freedom, the dissenting opinion explained that the state is represented through its public servants; therefore, the duty of the state to religious neutrality extends itself to its public officials who should remain neutral in their appearance while on duty.[1163] The general ban on manifestation of ostentatious religious symbols imposed on pedagogics in public education should raise no constitutional claim, even to the extent that an interdiction would be triggered following abstract endangerment. The decision whether an abstract or concrete endangerment to other constitutional fundamental freedoms and values should trigger a prohibition on a teacher's right to manifest her religion is left eminently to the sole discretion of the states. The dissenting judges supported their decision by reference to the general approach delivered by previous judgements of the ECtHR in similar cases.[1164] They proclaimed that a state may accept an extensive endorsement of religious insignias into its public education system in order to promote understanding and tolerance in its society; however, it is under no constitutional obligation to do so.

1160 BVerfG 1 BvR, 471/19 recital 6; BVerfGE 108, 282, 307, 309, 310.
1161 BVerfG 1 BvR recital 6, 7.
1162 BVerfG 1 BvR 471/10 recital 11, 12.
1163 BVerfG 1 BvR 471/10 recital 14.
1164 BVerfG 1 BvR 471/10 recital 18.

(c) Conclusion

A distinguishable segregation point between the recent BVerfG decision relating to the headscarf in NRW as opposed to its ruling in the *Ludin*'s case can be summarized as follows:

First, *the margin of appreciation* – conferred constitutionally to the states and confirmed by the BVerfG itself to change their education laws at sole discretion had been retrenched extensively in the recent headscarf case, as judicial intervention in the competency of a state's legislator, NRW, especially with respect to formation of the public education system, is deemed harsh and shifts finally competency to the administrative level to decide on a case-by-case basis.

Second, *proper implementation of the 'practical concordance'* – the major shift in the BVerfG's approach can be attributed to the balance of competing rights and the considerable weight accorded to the teacher's right to appear with religious donning even while on duty. This is in sharp contrast to previous decisions upholding the special responsibility of the teacher which emanates from her duty, in particular with respect to primary school pupils that can be easily influenced by her view. The main incentive of the majority of the federal states to introduce an all-inclusive general ban on teachers' right to appear with religious insignias to school was motivated by their will to exclude the headscarf from the public education sector. This was considered by the BVerfG in its recent decision as disproportionate measure to the aim sought to be achieved by the NRW legislator.[1165] In addition, the BVerfG emphasized

---

1165 This recent decision of the BVerfG found it's support in the legal literature that strengthens the constitutional approach expressed in it. See in *Muckel* Juristiche Arbeitsblätter 6 (2015), 476 (478). Muckel justifies this quintessential decicion and holds the view that the BVerfG underscored rightfully the legal precept of proportionality in order to assess whether an infringement of a constitutional fundamental right is justified. He also confirmed the view expressed by the court that statutes formulated in a strict, sweeping (*pauschal*) manner and do not leave any room for consideration on a case-by-case basis whether to ban a religious symbol or not, are not in conformity with the constitution. Further, he argued in favour of the position of the BVerfG that a careful balance between the competing rights in order to achieve an adequate settlement is necessary so to ensure such a harsh encroachment in the teachers' right to freely practice her religion will not occur. Nonetheless, Muckel raised the critic that the BVerfG did not determine what will be regarded as a concrete endangerment for the peaceful co-existence in school or the state neutrality precept and under which circumstances can it be identified. In that sense, the highest constitutional court was criticsed for delivery of a dubious judgement th right of a

the right of a teacher to religious freedom as safeguarded in Art. 4 para 1 and para 2. GG, which includes the right of a teacher to act in accordance with the precept of her religious belief. This freedom is guaranteed even if the teacher was not directed by a religious imperative but by her subjective feeling. The BVerfG established that the negative right of pupils and their parents to religious freedom and other pre-eminent goals declared by the NRW lawmaker cannot overrule the teacher's personal right (Art. 2 para 1 GG) as well as her right to free access for a teaching post (Art. 12 para 1 GG).

Third, *substantiation of a concrete endangerment* – as a consequence of the improper implementation of the 'practical concordance', a harsh interference in a fundamental human right like the teacher's right to undisturbed manifestation of her religious freedom can only be justified if a concrete endangerment with respect to one of the declared goals is at stake and will not be triggered in the case of a mere abstract endangerment.

Fourth, *the privilege to 'Christian-occidental tradition or values'* that includes the preference granted to symbols and even educational content deliberated in a land's parliament to disguise the real incentive of keeping the Islamic headscarf out of school premises had been held to be unconstitutional and void (Art. 3 para 3 and 33 para 3 GG). In that sense, a prohibition on religious insignias in public education can be regarded as admissible and legitimate if it applies to all symbols equally.

ee) Necessary Legislative Amendments by the Federal States

Following the recent headscarf decision, the NRW legislator was obliged to introduce amendments in its NRW SA as the BVerfG had declared Sec. 57 para 4 to be null and void. The NRW lawmaker swiftly rushed to adapt its education act so as to conform to legal principles outlined by the BVerfG. Other federal states need yet to take measures to integrate necessary amendments.

(1) Bavaria

Bavaria – The High Constitutional Court of Bavaria (BCC) declared already that Art. 59 para 2 BayEuG does not infringe upon the constitutional right of a teacher as safeguarded in Art. 4 GG.[1166] This ruling of the BCC was delivered

Muslim teacher to wear a headscarf subject to demands raised by third parties and as a result exposed to potential violations.

1166 *BV*, decision from 15.1.2007 – Vf. 11-VII-05 (F.R.G.).

prior to the recent BVerfG judgement of the headscarf in NRW and concluded the constitutionality of Art. 59 para 2 BayEuG even with respect to the advancement of Christian-occidental tradition, as it found it in no violation to the equality precepts prescribed in the constitution. The BCC reasoned its ruling by explaining that Art. 59 para 2 BayEUG declares religious symbols worn by teachers to be inadmissible if they can be perceived by pupils or their parents to contradict the constitutional order and the values of Christian-occidental culture. Since adherence to the Christian faith is a pronounced declaration outlined in Art. 135 BC then the general prohibition on schoolteachers to abstain from wearing ostentatious religious symbols,(Art. 59 para 2 BayEuG), did not violate the constitutional rights of Muslim teachers to religious manifestation. This as long as the exclusion was justified by a legitimate aim (i.e., negative right of pupils and parents to religious freedom, natural right of parents to nurture their children in accordance with their religious views, neutrality of the state or peaceful school operation). The outlawing of the Islamic headscarf worn by Muslim teachers was proved to be appropriate and necessary due to the majority's wish of Christian population in Bavaria to foster the Christian tradition in schools and a concrete endangerment to other protected constitutional values was demonstrated. Nonetheless, Art. 59 para 2 BayEUG may encounter difficulty to establish conformity with the constitutional precepts of equality (Art. 3 para 3 and 33 para 3 GG), as it clearly places Muslim teachers at a particular disadvantage compared with Christian teachers or colleagues of other faiths. This was explicitly pronounced by the latest BVerfG ruling as impermissible discrimination which infringes upon the equality principle prescribed in the constitution. It also remains doubtful whether the demand for a concrete endangerment will be adhered by the Bavarian legislator or correspondingly school authorities as the likelihood of peaceful school operation in a Catholic state like Bavaria remains at odds if the position of the Islamic headscarf will prevail over that of a Crucifix merely due to its being a state-displayed symbol which cannot be equated with an individually displayed symbol.

(2) Berlin

Berlin is the only state that would probably not have to incur any legislative amendments with respect to its education act following the recent BVerfG decision with respect to admissibility of the headscarf ban in NRW. Although Art. 29 BLnlV prescribes a ban on teaching staff to appear with religious symbols during school lessons, it may be regarded as complying with the criteria established by the BVerfG in the NRW headscarf case, as the ban is all-inclusive in form and applies to all religious symbols without any segregation. In addition, it does not advance a specific religion as opposed to other faiths and religions, that is, no preferential treatment of Christian-occidental religious symbols so no violation of the constitutional precepts of equality. The special duty of civil servants in Berlin to abide by the constitutional demand to religious neutrality of the state dictates their obligation to appear unbiased in their role as representatives of the state. This approach has been affirmed recently by the Federal Labour Court of Berlin (not yet published)[1167] that declared the ban on Islamic headscarf in public schools to conform to the constitution. Consequently, it is due to the aspect of religious neutrality and the importance attributed to it in the state of Berlin that if Art. 29 BlnlV was to be brought to judicial review by the BVerfG, it would be regarded as conforming to the constitution (*Grundgesetz*).

(3) North Rhine-Westphalia

The state of NRW took initiative and amended its SchulG shortly after the BVerfG scrutinized Art. 57 para 4 of it and declared it to be unconstitutional. The NRW lawmaker adopted the legal criteria laid down by the BVerfG and subsequently implemented the following: first, *no all-inclusive ban* – instead of a general ban on religious symbols worn by teachers it declares the permissibility and acceptance of all religions in school realm. This will be achieved by teaching pupils the fostering of tolerance towards different faiths and religions and by fortifying a peaceful school operation that will consequently eliminate the possibility of school conflicts triggered by religious pluralism. Second, the use of an *abstract endangerment* indicated by the words 'capable of', 'can appear', or 'may endanger' had been set back and the legislative provision prescribed in Art. 2 para 8 SchulG NRW will justify a ban on religious symbol worn by teaching staff only if a concrete endangerment to other fundamental constitutional freedoms and values had been substantiated. Third, the former abolished provision enabled the *prevalence conferred to Christian and Jewish tradition* and values by reference to the NRW constitution and protected goals prescribed in it (Art. 12 LVerfNRW) in order to capture the ban on the Islamic headscarf. This privilege no longer exists under the amended legislation so no violation of the constitutional principle of equality takes place.

1167 See in FAZ from 16 April 2016 http://www.faz.net/aktuell/feuilleton/debatten/grundsatzfragen-im-berliner-kopftuch-streit-14180746.html and in DW from 14 April 2016 http://www.dw.com/de/berliner-arbeitsgericht-weist-kopftuch-klage-ab/a-19189326

(4) *Baden-Württemberg*

The provision in Sec. 38 para 2 SchulG BW is similarly formulated to that of the abolished Sec. 57 para 4 SchulG NRW. It is therefore very likely that in case of a judicial review the legal outcome will have to be identical, namely, the declaration of its unconstitutionality and nullification of Sec. 38 para 2 SchulG BW. Taking into consideration the BVerfG's ruling in *Ludin*'s case as well as the last decision of the Federal Labour Court in Berlin, a limitation on a teacher's fundamental right to religious freedom can be legitimized in order to safeguard the religious neutrality of the state and its educative task according to Art. 7 para 1 GG to maintain a peaceful school operation. In parallel, the negative right of pupils to religious freedom pursuant to Art. 4 para 1 and 2 GG and the educative right of parents according to Art. 6 para 2 and Art. 4 para 1 GG had been acknowledged and considered in the jurisprudence as prominent constitutional freedoms that are equal in rank to the neutrality precept and are capable to retrench the teachers' scope of freedom to religious manifestation.[1168] Nonetheless, the difficulty to substantiate the conformity of Sec. 38 para 2 SchulG BW with the constitution will concentrate mainly on: first, *privilege of Christian symbols* will be regarded as indirect discrimination in favour of Christian and Jewish symbols that is detrimental to other religious symbols and runs counter to the equality precept. Second, the *abstract endangerment* posed by the display of the headscarf worn by a teacher to other fundamental constitutional freedoms and values will not suffice to curtail on the fundamental right of a teacher to religious freedom. An encroachment on the teacher's right to appear with a religious garment will be possible only in case a concrete endangerment should be established. The mere possibility of a negative influence on the pupils will not suffice any longer.

e) Conclusion – Germany

aa) *The State-Church Relation and Its Impact on the Educational System*

The German constitutional system favours an institutional structure of state-church which combines separation and coordination. This model neither embraces a system of strict separation[1169] nor one that advances religion but is rather situated in the middle as it combines elements of both. Albeit the constitutional obligation of the German state according to the non-establishment clause provided in Art. 140 in tandem with Art. 137 para 1 WRV not to establish

1168 BVerwG, NJW 2004, 3581, 3583.

1169 *Brugger/Karayanni*, p. 61.

a state-church, it was not considered to be the binding standard. Thence, in the earlier decisions of the German jurisprudence it was keen to accommodate religion especially in the educational sphere and, as a result, constitutional criteria were developed that subject to interpretation (strict or accommodative) will assist it in keeping the line of a very accommodating, religion-friendly approach. The structural constitutional requirements developed in order to distinguish between un/permissible entanglement of state and church in the separation-division model are independence, neutrality, non-identification, and non-discrimination (equal treatment).

Since Germany advocates a rather moderate model of separation and cooperation, the close proximity between state and church taking place especially in the context of an institutional support of the Christian religion in public schools will not be regarded as constitutionally impermissible provided it fulfils several requirements. These requirements were identified by the BVerfG in its earlier decisions and encompassed the following: first, the endorsement of religion in its positive aspect supporting religious rights of Christian parents and pupils will be made solely within the context of its historical influence marked in the German society and not in its affirmative context perceiving Christianity as the absolute true religion. Second, no inadmissible coercion to remain present, participate, or perform a cultish activity should be imposed on religious minorities. Third, any exercise of religious worship and ceremony taking place in the school realm must be conducted on complete voluntariness of the pupils. The freedom of choice to refrain from participation or taking active part in religious ceremony or events organised by the school is a highly important factor for determining the impermissibility of a state's act that otherwise may appear as unlawful advancement of religion. Fourth, no serious pressure on part of the school towards religious minorities to accept or exercise a religion should take place; otherwise, it will be considered as a forbidden substantial discrimination. And fifth, no attempt on part of the school authorities to proselytize the children should occur, insofar the pupils will feel obliged to accept the precepts of Christianity as the only true religion.

This line of threshold depicted earlier will yield a different outcome with respect to a state's endorsement or disapproval of religious references in its school system. The reason for that is that a declaration of unconstitutional entanglement of state and church will depend on the adopted state-church model of the state. That is to say, the co-operative organizational bond between state and church in Germany will serve as an indicative of the threshold level that will be placed prior to a declaration of unconstitutionality of a state's act. An observation of the German jurisprudence suggests that this strong institutional proximity between state and church in educational matters placed a higher threshold as general courts were reluctant to declare the entanglement of religious affairs in compulsory public schools as unconstitutional.[1170]

Finally, in Germany a mild support of religion in the educational sector should be permissible as the relation between religion and state is drawn back to the special bond of its society rooted in the cultural heritage of Christianity. The incorporation of religious references in public elementary schools will be subject to a judicial review of the courts based on an interpretative method and fulfilment of constitutional requirements developed in order to negate any excessive entanglement between state and church. In general, inclusion of Christian references even if seemingly may advance a particular religion (Christianity) over other religions will be permitted and not result in unconstitutionality as long as their effect remains indirect, remote, and incidental. Therefore, the adoption of a moderate state-church model in Germany that accepts and recognizes the display of religious symbols so to accommodate to the religious needs of its majority will not immediately trigger the illegitimacy of a state's act.

bb) Legislative Diversity Emanating from the Federal System

The characteristic of the German state as a federation presents the inability of the central state to provide an all-inclusive solution which will be applicable to all the federal states.[1171] In addition, the individual states are delegated with power and discretion in the constitution itself to regulate their inner affairs at own discretion (Art. 70 GG).

In Bavaria, a state which is mostly pre-dominated by the Catholic Church, the significance to convey Christian values and traditions through state schools is already prescribed in several of its constitutional provisions.[1172] Integration of Christian precepts and references is regarded as an integral part of the daily school life and a pre-eminent educative task of the state.

Baden-Württemberg demonstrates a similar affinity to the Christian religion. The significance attributed to endorsement of Christian tradition and values into its compulsory school system can be found in several provisions of BW's Constitution.[1173] Unlike Bavaria, in Baden-Württemberg there is no constitutional or legislative enactment obliging school authorities to endorse the Crucifix

---

1170 *Brugger/Karayanni*, p. 59.
1171 Auslander, Cultural Dynamics 12 (3), 2000, 283, 301.
1172 Art. 130, 131 para 2 and 135 to the Bavarian Constitution.
1173 Art. 12 para 1, 15 para 1 and 16 para 1 to the BW Constitution.

into state schools.[1174] However, the endorsement of crosses into state schools is permitted in those states[1175] and will be regarded as conforming to the educative mandate to convey pupils with Christian tradition and values as prescribed in their lands' constitutions.

Following delivery of the *Crucifix* judgement, many federal states that ordered presentation of the cross as a general rule did not haste to order removal of the cross from public classrooms. This case was not different in the state of Baden-Württemberg that wished to preserve the Christian nature of its public schools. Consequently, a significant contribution of the BW constitution is made in Art. 16 para 3 suggesting the achievement of peaceful solutions to conflicts on a consensus base. The constitution anticipated an increase of conflicts that may be raised on the background of establishment of the Christian character of public schools and proposed a mechanism seeking a general consensus accepted by all involved parties, such as the state, relevant religious communities, parents, and teachers.[1176]

The state of NRW adopted in its constitution a rather compromised approach intertwining the Christian religion and its tradition to be introduced together with acceptance and mutual respect towards other faiths and denominations into its state school system.[1177] Nonetheless, the amendment that had been integrated into its SchulG NRW following *Ludin*'s case in the former Art. 57 para 4 privileging the Christian faith and symbols in primary education indicated the difficulties to establish its alignment with its constitutional obligation to foster openness and mutual respect towards other faiths and creeds. The latest decision of the BVerfG,[1178] however, that declared Art. 57 para 4 SChulG NRW as unconstitutional urged the NRW legislator again to amend the SchulG and finally further reduce any privilege to the Christian tradition and heritage. Albeit the amendment endorsed in its school education act, the legislator refrained from any prevalence to the Christian faith still preserved in Art. 2 para 8 SchulG NRW and the adherence to Christian-occidental tradition and values.

1174 *Dietlein*, in FS Stern (1997), 443, 447.

1175 Baden-Württemberg and North Rhine-Westphalia
Also in NRW.

1176 Art. 16 para 3 das BWVerf sets out the following: *„Ergeben sich bei der Auslegung des christlichen Charakters der Volksschule Zweifelsfragen, so sind sie in gemeinsamer Beratung zwischen dem Staat, den Religionsgemeinschaften, den Lehrern und den Eltern zu beheben."*

1177 Art. 12 para 3 LVerfNRW.

1178 BVerfGE 138, 296 = NJW 2015, 359.

According to Art. 12 para 3 of the LVerfNRW, one can assume that affixation of the Crucifix in classrooms of public schools will not be regarded as an infringement on pupils' right to religious freedom insofar its eligibility accords the stipulation in the constitution that pupils should be transferred with the values of the Christian tradition and with parents' right to decide on the education of their children (Art. 6 para 2 GG). In this respect, it will be advisable to recognize whether presentation of the cross is a state act or an act of parental cooperation with school authorities as prescribed under Art. 10 para 2 of the LVerfNRW.[1179] The answer for that will provide a filter mechanism relevant for the determination whether an infringement of the fundamental right to religious freedom of minority pupils has taken place or not. Further, this kind of cooperation between school authorities and parents endeavouring to achieve consensus with respect to presentation of religious symbols in classrooms provides parents with the opportunity to gain some influence on the nature of schools in which their children are to be taught.

The legal situation in the federal states NRW and BW before delivery of the recent BVerfG judgement with respect to the NRW headscarf, demonstrated an attempt to achieve a compromise or a consensus with respect to the display of the cross in public classrooms. Initially, a similar approach was adopted by the Bavarian legislator following delivery of the Crucifix judgement.[1180] The balancing of rights in case the display of the cross will be regarded as a state act as opposed to a situation where the majority of parents agree on its presentation on a classroom wall is not altered. The reason is that the right of minorities to (negative) religious freedom will at any case be subject to interference. Even in a situation where a compromise among all involved parties should be achieved, there is a risk that religious minorities would feel coerced to accept the display of the cross and would keep quiet so as not to be outcast or expelled from school; or they would be left with no other nearest educational alternative.

The state of Berlin adopts a rather liberal, multi-cultural approach and as a result prescribes no adhesion to a particular religion in its constitution. Consequently, infringement of an individual right to manifest a religion (i.e., a

1179 Art. 10 para 2 of the NRW Verfassung establishes: „*Die Erziehungsberechtigten wirken durch Elternvertretungen an der Gestaltung des Schulwesens mit.*“

1180 The amendment made to the BayEUG introduced Art. 7 para 4 in an attempt to bypass the removal of the cross from public classrooms. Instead, the provision underlies several requirements to be fulfilled in case a claim to remove the cross is made by parents or pupils of a religious minority in an attempt to achieve an agreed compromise.

teacher with a headscarf) is not likely to infringe solely on minorities' rights to religious freedom, as restriction on display of religious symbol or attire in public schools is equally applicable to all religions. In Berlin, there is no emphasis on part of the state to deliver any religious content into its educational sphere or prescribe a religious nature in the orderly running of its public schools. Notably, though Berlin may remain indifferent to Christian symbols or the transfer of religious values within the educational system, they do not mandate a complete denial or prohibition of religious-cultural themes from school premises.[1181]

To sum up, the competency of the individual states to decide on their inner educational matters is prescribed in the German constitution, however, it will be subject to judicial scrutiny. It was demonstrated in the Crucifix and Ludin that efforts to defuse such a controversial issue of religious symbols in public schools can not be referred to administrative solutions at the local level but require regulations on part of the lands' legislators. It is also due to this reason that creating a judicial coherence on the national level remains very complex.

cc) *The Educative Task of the States*

The question of how this legal situation squares with the protection of minorities' rights to religious freedom (those sharing a different religion or those opting for a religiously neutral educational environment for their children) demonstrates that in Germany's federal structure this is a matter that should be left solely for the discretion of the regional lawmakers. There is no clear-cut solution that implies prevalence of a state-imposed symbol (acting for the interest of the religious majority) upon negative religious liberties of minorities. Likewise, there exists no unlimited entitlement of minorities (a teacher with a headscarf) as legal right holders to overrule at all times the rights of the majority of parents and pupils to keep education of their children in conformity with their own religion (e.g., a majority wish that teacher dispose of the headscarf). This will need to be resolved within the process of balancing competing rights when other constitutional legitimate grounds are at stake and therefore should not be left within the competency of the public administrator to decide.

Insofar, taking into account the exclusive educational competence of the *Länder* to establish the framework of their school system at own discretion in case of restrictions religious symbolism in the education (Art. 7 para 1 & Art. 70 GG), the standard of proof or threshold to be imposed in the states which are religious in nature (i.e., Bavaria, BW) should not be higher than in those which

1181 Art. 1 of the SchulG Berlin.

are more neutral or accommodative to religious pluralism as long as legitimate grounds for restriction are at hand.

The obligation of the state to remain neutral in the context of its state-church relations falls within the ambit of Art. 140 GG read together with Art. 137 para 1 WRV. This constitutional principle was incorporated following amendments introduced by the individual states[1182] into their regional educational laws as a justified ground for limitation on public schoolteachers to manifest religious symbols or garments while on duty. The real incentive of the lands' legislators, even though not explicitly stated in the text law, was to prevent Muslim teachers from wearing the Islamic headscarf in compulsory schools. The main argument for the ban was expounded by the relevant lawmakers, namely that especially pupils in primary schools, due to their young age, are likely to be influenced by the dress code of a teacher and its indoctrinating effect. The states interpreted the headscarf as an expression of religiosity, which may have a missionary or indoctrinating effect on the pupils. In addition, the obligation of a teacher to accord with her professional duties as a civil servant (Art. 33 para 5 GG) permits a limitation on the exercise of her fundamental right due to this special status. These arguments conjoined with the assertion that a teacher, in contrast to pupils, enters her profession voluntarily were held sufficient in the German jurisprudence to legitimate the permissibility of the ban on a headscarf.[1183] Even the degree of a threat (abstract or danger) to state neutrality or the endangerment of school operation was held by the German judicator to be a task of the lawmaker to consider until the recent decision of the BVerfG. In any case of a doubt, it was established that prevalence should be given to the negative right of pupils to religious freedom over placement or further occupation of a teacher.[1184]

In this respect, one should note that the constitutional obligation of the federal states to adhere to the neutrality principle as prescribed in the Grundgesetz (Art. 140 GG in tandem with Art. 137 para 1 WRV) will generally not negate their inherent right to form and organize the school system within their territory as a prerogative conferred to them by virtue of the principle of federalism.[1185]

1182 Art. 59 para 2 of the BayEUG; Art. 57 para 4 NRW SA; Art.38 para 2 BWSChG.

1183 BVerfGE 108, 282, 303.

1184 BVerfGE 108, 282, 303.

1185 BVerfGE 93, 1, 21 16.5.95 – 1 BvR 1087/91 dissenting opinion; BVerfGE 41, 29, 45 = NJW 1976, 947, 949; BVerfGE decision from 26.3.1957, 2 BvG 1/55, Juris Fn. 196, 197, 199, 204, 222= BVerfGE 6, 309, 356;. *Kommers/Miller*, pp. 467–468. It was explained that in contrast to the legal situation during the Weimar Constitution, which allocated legislative authority in educational matters to the Reich, the legislative history of Art. 7 demonstrated the exclusive right of the individual states

To sum up, since Germany has no centralized body responsible for the administration and organization of the public school system on the national level, matters within the context of its nexus to cultural-religious affairs are left to the local-regional control of the individual states (*Länder*).

Against the background of the federal structure of the German Republic and the constitutional provision conferring on the individual states' competence to organize school system at own discretion (Art. 70 GG), one can determine that the presence and importance of religious themes, especially within the educational context, varies extensively depending on the religious demographic dispersal, tradition, and affinity to religiosity in each of the individual states.[1186] The nexus between state and religion and its influence on the everyday lives of the inhabitants is largely resolved on the federal state-, rather than national, level.[1187]

Naturally, the discretion of the federal states will be subject to inner political-churchly powers and the entrenched traditions specific to each region, so that these will be reflected in the formation of legislation and enactments promulgated by each of the individual states. For this reason, one cannot prescribe an equal formula that will conform to the situation in all of the federal states. Consequently, no uniformity exists with respect to endorsement and permissibility of religious symbols in the public school system on the national level.

dd) The Guarantee of Religious Freedom

Indeed, in compulsory public schools there is an inevitable tension between negative and positive right of religious freedom. This is inherent from the specific provisions of the Grundgesetz. Pupils' right to positively exercise their religion and parents' right to have their children educated in accordance with the belief or confession they perceive to be true (Art. 6 para 2 and 4 para 1 GG) should be respected and balanced against other competing rights when the court invokes the principle of 'practical concordance'. Nonetheless, the BVerfG recognized that parents cannot claim to have an exclusive right under Art. 4 para 1 GG that the

---

emanating from the principle of federalism to enjoy an extensive discretion over the nature, character, and organization of its public schools. This prerogative of the individual states may be confined solely within the limits established in Art. 7 and 141 of the Grundgesetz. Art. 7 para 1 in tandem with Art. 20, 30 and 70 GG.

1186 *Lock,* in: Hunter-Henin, Law Religious Freedom and Education in Europe, 1998, 347, 348.

1187 *Auslander,* Cultural Dynamics 12 para 3, 2000, 283, 288.

state must not accommodate the interests of all religions and beliefs existing in a society and accept the establishment of a community school of their chosen faith.

The fundamental right to religious freedom is a constitutional protected right under the German Grundgesetz (Art. 4 para 1). Thence, any attempt to infringe or retrench its scope of protection should be executed with due regard and outweighed only against other protected constitutional rights. This means that a state act against the inherent right of an individual to manifest a religion will need to substantiate its limitation if challenged in court, demonstrating the existence of legitimate grounds (it contravenes against other pre-eminent constitutional rights), the necessity of interference, and showing that the restriction is proportionate to the aim it sought to achieve. A confinement of the right to religious freedom imposed by a legislator and which cannot be justified based on the need to protect other constitutional protected rights, will be invalid.[1188]

ee) Institutional Symbols

Strikingly, the delivery of the *Crucifix* decision triggered criticism by legal scholars and constitutional commentators since the outcome was perceived to be harsher and not proportional to the aim sought to be achieved when placed in comparison to the court's previous decisions (e.g., school prayer, Inter-denominational schools). This decision was comprehended as unintelligible especially due to the moderate constitutional model common in Germany towards incorporation of religion in the educational sphere. Moreover, it was contended that the display of the cross in classrooms deemed to exercise no more 'illegal coercion' on religious minorities than would a non-voluntary school prayer. In that respect, it seems that the BVerfG applied a different threshold when implementing its standard constitutional requirements, as otherwise the necessary outcome ought to be a declaration of the Crucifix constitutionality. It seems that the difference of outcome between the Crucifix and previous decisions can only be aligned based on the implementation of a different threshold. In the aftermath of the *Crucifix* decision, a shift in the jurisprudence of the BVerfG was noticeable as in fact it changed the balance of counter-weighing interests when applying the 'practical concordance'. This interpretative method, aiming to achieve harmonization between conflicting interests, tilted crucially in favour of the non-establishment principle (i.e., state's obligation to religious neutrality Art. 7 para 1 GG) upon the free exercise clause (i.e., the majority's right to freely exercise their religion in accordance with Art. 4 para 1 and 2 GG).

1188 BVerfGE 93, 1= NJW 1995, 2477, 2479.

At first glance, it seems that the BVerfG not only departed from its guidelines set forth in its previous decisions, but also converted the standard of threshold, placing a low burden for establishment of 'coercive' and 'discriminatory' elements in order to suffice the unconstitutionality of what will be regarded as an excessive state-religion entanglement within the field of education. It was noticeable that Germany's educational system, which had originally begun as function of the church, was undergoing a transformation reflected in the decisions delivered by the BVerfG in the Crucifix and *Ludin*'s case.

Remarkably, this salient change of positions reached resonance already in 1967 by a decision of the Bavarian Constitutional Court, in which the right of religious minorities to rely on Art. 4 GG had been acknowledged.[1189] This judgement symbolized not only the birth of inter-confessional schools as conforming an integral part of the educational system, but rather established them as the common elementary public schools.

Virtually, the Court's decision in the *Schulgebetentscheidung* and the *Crucifix* case were paving the road for religious minorities not only while relying on Art. 4 GG but also when challenging it in the context of infringement on their negative right not to accord to the majority's educational principles in public elementary schools. Moreover, the *Crucifix* case gained significance as it symbolized the pronouncement of the BVerfG in disputes between the church and the state over control of common elementary schools.

Legal scholars did not hesitate to criticize the decisions concerning endorsement of prayers into school, in respect that neither of the involved jurisdictions (HessStGH, BVerwG und BVerfG) scrutinized the incompetence of the state towards events of religion practice.[1190] It was explained that performing a school prayer under supervision of a teacher is a state act of its own besides 'administrative legal act' (*Verwaltungsakt*) and 'ordinary, simple administrative act' (*faktisch hoheitliches Handeln*), which cannot be assigned to the school authorities. The Constitutional Court was not even raising the problem of state's competency any further. This method of the BVerfG of repressing the problem, keeping reluctant to interfere with the educative task of the state, and refraining from scrutinizing its legitimacy to factor out religious rights from the education was not by accidently repeating itself years later in the *Crucifix* decision. This was accepted in legal literature with unease and was perceived to be rather stringent, especially since the question of competency of the state with respect to a teacher with a

1189 BV, decision from 17.10.1967 – VerfGH 20, 171/181.

1190 Böckenförde, DÖV 1974, 253, 255; DÖV 1980, 323.

headscarf was all of a sudden subject to a judicial review of the courts, whereas the same question with respect to Christian references or their conveyance at school remained ignored and undebated.

As far as segregation made between the Crucifix and the headscarf as prominent symbols responsible for fierce public debates, the following indicators can be inferred from the German judicator. First, *the meaning of the symbol* – the Crucifix is not only a religious symbol; the cross is distinguishable as it is not perceived only as a religious symbol but also as a sign associated with the Western-occidental, liberal tradition and values. In sharp contrast, the headscarf is understood merely within its pure religious meaning.

Second, *state neutrality* – if the state should remain neutral in its acts that necessitate that a ban on the Crucifix will initially demand a ban on the headscarf when worn by teachers. In contrast to the headscarf, the Crucifix is not understood as a political symbol, in particular, as it is not interlinked with ideas of fundamentalism and extremism. Third, *conformity with fundamental constitutional principles* – in the jurisprudence, the Crucifix was not given the interpretation that it carries a potential of endangerment to democratic values, such as gender equality, human dignity, neutrality of the state, and peaceful school co-operation as in fact it was alleged to enfold them. Apart from that, the Crucifix was presumed to accord with the majority's will adhering the Christian faith. The claim of a potential endangerment to the peaceful co-existence in public schools as well as for gender equality, religious neutrality of the state, other democratic values, and non-discrimination principle may be more successful with respect to the headscarf as opposed to the Crucifix. The reason lies in the fact that the headscarf is associated with religious extremism as it negates human dignity and is perceived as a sign of women oppression; it symbolizes the inequality between men and women and collides with the democratic constitutional order of the German state. In addition, it collides with the negative religious freedom of the majority of Christian pupils and their parents. Fourth, *the raising of an objection* – by pupils or parents is a significant factor that had been taken into account in the recent NRW headscarf judgement as well as the *Crucifix* decision for evaluation of whether a request for removal of religious insignia was objectively and genuinely raised. Insofar, the permissibility to display or manifest a religious symbol will be subject to judicial scrutiny following indication that an objection was raised by pupils or their parents, and their ability to demonstrate that a violation with respect to one of the following has taken place: other fundamental constitutional freedoms and values [e.g., the duty of the state to religious neutrality (Art. 137 para 1 WRV), the negative religious freedom of pupils or their parents (Art. 4 GG), the equal treatment principle including. gender equality (Art. 3 para

3 and 33 para 3 GG), other democratic values, and the free democratic order as inscribed by the constitution].

ff) Individual Symbols Worn by a Teacher

The BVerfG developed in the case of Ludin prerequisites to be considered when imposing a ban on the display of religious symbols by an individual. The first determination was the necessity to imprint the ban in legislation, since otherwise the state could not challenge the legitimacy of the wearer (i.e., the teacher) to wear a religious symbol like the headscarf unless it is explicitly prohibited by law. Second, the right of the teacher to religious freedom is unreserved and is constitutionally conferred to her in tandem with the right to self-development and freedom of profession (Art. 2 para 1 and Art. 12 para 1 GG). This entails that restrictions on the teacher's freedom of religion as a pre-eminent constitutional right will be admitted only if it demonstrated an endangerment to protected fundamental freedoms, such as state neutrality, the negative right of pupils to religious freedom, the right of parents to rear their children in accordance with their religious precept, and peaceful school operation. Third, the authority to determine the adequate threshold (high or low) for rethinking the balance between religious display in public school as opposed to the state's duty to religious neutrality. Fourth, the state is banned from denial of equal access to the public service and must ensure equal treatment of teachers in the public service as constitutionally guaranteed in Art. 33 para 3 and Art. 3 para 3 GG.

Several federal legislators amended their School Education Acts (SchulG) and implemented explicit bans on manifestation of religious symbols by teaching staff as it would obviously be regarded as unlawful under the rule of law and the constitutional democratic order. The political pressure within lands' parliaments aimed to ban in particular the Islamic headscarf, as it was no longer able to infringe upon the fundamental right of a teacher to religious freedom without specification in law.

Each legislator chose a neutral phrasing, not mentioning the Islamic headscarf; however, at the same time it was trying to preclude Christian symbols from a ban by referring to Christian values and traditions or the manifestations thereof as conforming to the educative mandate of the state as inscribed in the constitutions of the individual states.

The legislative amendments incurred by the individual states reveal the intention of the lawmaker to segregate between different religions and confer preference to Christian symbols as opposed to symbols of other denominations as was clearly demonstrated in the amendments incurred in the education acts of the states of BW and NRW.

This by no means suggests that symbols of various faiths or creeds may well be held as impermissible or irreconcilable under all given circumstances. In order for a ban to be regarded as justifiable, the state would have to prove that protected fundamental rights (e.g., peaceful school order, negative religious freedom of others, the educative mandate of the state, or state neutrality) exist. As a result, possible endangerment to constitutional-protected rights would need to be outweighed adequately in order to justify a blatant interference with the personal right to manifest a religion (the so-called 'forum externum').

The recent decision of the BVerfG relating to the headscarf in NRW raised by no means the controversy relating to endorsement of religious symbols, specifically the Islamic headscarf worn by a public schoolteacher, to the focus of public debate by imparting a new constitutional interpretation to former criteria established by the Court. The BVerfG, so far criticized for lack of specification and guidance to the administrative in respect to the interpretation of religious symbols and their meaning, the determination of threshold for evaluation of the constitutional conformity of states' education, and in general its restrictive attitude towards interference in the legislative competency of the individual states, could no longer be attached with these allegations. In fact, the BVerfG specified and increased the threshold for infringement on individuals' right to free exercise of religion and has developed new interpretation to the prerequisites established in its former jurisprudence. The BVerfG turned former determinations upside down and introduced new binding precedent with respect to the following: first, *concrete endangerment* – the need to establish a 'concrete' as opposed to a mere 'abstract' endangerment or disturbance posed to prominent constitutional principles and values by virtue of a teacher's display of religious attire. The lands' legislators stipulated so far a ban on manifestation of religious symbols satisfying the demand for an abstract endangerment to religious neutrality of the state, non-discrimination, or peaceful operation of the school. This naturally imposed a low threshold on school authorities for infringement on a protected constitutional right of the teacher to religious freedom as accorded to her in the constitution (Art. 4 GG). Second, *no privilege to Christian-occidental tradition* – this means that the special privilege for Christian symbols, as endorsed by the states of BW and NRW and in indirect manner even by Bavaria, is no longer recognized by the BVerfG. This was declared by the BVerfG to constitute an unlawful discrimination based on religious grounds. Third, *no all-inclusive ban on religious symbols* – the intention of the BVerfG was to override the general ban on the headscarf and advance assessment of the contradicting protected rights and values ('practical concordance') on a case-by-case basis.

Consequently, the lands' legislators were obliged to take action and bring again necessary suggestions for modifications in their respective education acts in order to conform to the Grundgesetz based on the criteria established by the BVerfG. Taking recourse to the amendment incurred by lands' parliaments of the individual states in their respective school enactments in the aftermath of *Ludin*'s case and having due regard to the recent BVerfG decision with respect to the headscarf in NRW turning upside down its previous determinations, the lands' legislators were left basically with two options: first, providing an extensive formulation accepting in general the endorsement of all religious symbols including the Islamic headscarf into its state school system, leaving no room for exceptions. This provision would signify moving towards adoption of the multi-cultural pluralistic, liberal approach as prevalent in the British system. The second option is to adopt a more restrictive approach excluding religion from school realm and running closer towards a secularized educational system. The states would enforce the weakening of the role of religion and endorsement of religious symbolism in public education, thus taking a further step towards a stricter understanding of neutrality and banning any kind of religious influence from statutory schooling. This step would indicate the development towards a more secularized, neutral, or laicist educational system exhibited on the other side of the spectrum in the French legal system.

3. England

The model of church-state relations adopted in England is one of formal unification.[1191] This means that albeit the state identifies itself with a particular religion, it will distinguish itself from the national, recognized religion in several distinctive features. The prominent characteristic of this conceptual model can be discerned through the following: first, institutional/organizational structure – in general, a distinction on the institutional level suggests that both entities are independent from each other and maintain a separated organizational structure.[1192] Second, toleration of religious freedom of other denominations – the right of other religious groups to practice their religion and obey by the tenets of their faith, including their right to religious education and the establishment of

1191 Brugger/Karayanni, pp. 41,42; *Van Ooijen*, pp. 250, 251

1192 *Brugger/Karayanni,* p. 40; *Liederman-Molokotos*, pp. 105, 114.

own faith schools[1193] are tolerated and respected.[1194] This suggests that while the dominant faith is naturally Christian, its identification with the state will be constitutionally permissible to a large extent as long as the right to religious freedom or ideological views of other individuals or religious communities are respected.

England has an established church, the Church of England, whose head is the monarch.[1195] The Anglican Church upholding protestant Christianity is the dominating faith in England. It maintained its strong position until the sixteenth century,[1196] whereas from that time onward Britain politics was characterized by an open and accepting approach towards other religious groups and faiths.

Since mid-seventeenth until the end of the nineteenth (early twentieth) century, rivalry was known between different streams of Christianity (i.e., Anglicans, Roman Catholics, and Protestant non-conformists) which in the following was directed against non-religious groups and religious minorities (Protestant non-conformists, Jews).[1197]

The major influx of immigrants to England took place during the 1950s and 1960s and constituted mostly a composition of various nationalities and religions.[1198] The most predominant minority groups emerged from Islam, Hinduism, and Sikhism.[1199] This initially open and welcoming immigration policy has changed and was followed by stricter, restraining steps from the 1960s onwards.[1200]

In this respect, England became confronted with two main areas of controversy relating to its religious minorities: first, when they started to claim for protection of their religious rights, which included among others their right to establish state-funded faith schools for Muslims and other minority faiths.[1201] Nonetheless, this right to establishment of religious faith schools is not recognized

---

1193 Muslims enjoy the right to establish their own faith schools since 1997, House of Commons Briefing Number 06972, 14 October 2015.

1194 *Brugger/Karayanni*, p. 40.

1195 *Van Ooijen*, p. 218; *Vakulenko*, p. 23; *Vickers*, 4 Religion and Human Rights, 2009, 137, 146.

1196 *Fetzer/Soper*, p. 33.

1197 *Fetzer/Soper*, p. 33; *Van Ooijen*, p. 218.

1198 *Fetzer/Soper*, p. 26; *van Ooijen*, p. 213.

1199 *van Ooijen*, p. 213; *Fetzer/Soper*, p. 26; *Poulter*, p. 281.

1200 *Van Ooijen*, p. 214.

1201 The right of the following minority groups (Muslim, Sikh, Adventist and Greek Orthodox) was expanded in amended provision since 1997 so to increase their involvement in education and establishment of own faith schools. See *Vickers*, 4 Religion and Human Rights (2009), 137, 141.

on the international level.[1202] Second, in the absence of a guarantee of religious freedom in a constitutional document delineating its scope of protection, there was a need to find a suitable enforceable mechanism that would resolve conflicts arising with respect to religious practice in state-supported schools.[1203]

Even in a state like England, known for its relatively liberal multi-culturalism, it had taken some time until the British government acknowledged that its religious minorities are entitled to have their religious freedom protected and respected by the state.

Yet, the lapse of time until political-legislative initiative for protection of immigrants' religious rights has taken place can be attributed to the following factors: first, the British government's indifference with respect to its minority of ethnic and religious groups and the lack of motivation to enforce legal protection that would offer the immigrants freedom to manifest and exercise their religion openly in public.[1204] Second, the fact that in England's legislative tradition religious rights were not protected in a constitutional document confronted its religious minorities with religious discrimination in comparison to the mainstream of the British population, which is Christian in its majority and nature.

Third, the failure on part of its religious minorities to enforce claims against the state in order to advance protection of their right to religious manifestation was regarded as a contributing factor to stagnation and lack of success in recognition of their religious rights.[1205]

Fourth, England holds a very proud tradition of accommodating religious diversity in its society, which is founded on reciprocal respect, acceptance, and tolerance towards multi-culturalism.[1206] It was thence advocated in the legal literature that the English policy, characterized by its lack of incentive to safeguard

---

1202 Since Art. 18 para 4 of the Covenant does not require states to subsidize private schools, and due to the fact that even the European Court of Human Rights decided that there is no obligation on the state to establish at their own expense or subsidize education of any particular type (Belgian Linguistic Case, Series A No 6 (1968), 33), it is unlikely the claimants invoking the principle of parental choice to assign their children to schools of their own choice under the ECHR and ICCPR are likely to succeed; *Harris/Joseph*, 62.8 (42) p. 382.

1203 *Harris/Joseph*, 62.8 (42) p. 380.

1204 *Fetzer/Soper*, pp. 27 and 30; van Ooijen, p. 214.

1205 *Fetzer/Soper*, pp. 27 and 31; *Poulter*, p. 284; *van Ooijen*, p. 214.

1206 *Vakulenko*, p. 22.

minorities' religious rights can be attributed to its long and stable multi-culturalist tradition that eventually made the formation of special guarantees surplus.[1207]

Fifth, the legal system in England is characterised by the rule of parliament supremacy that enables parliament to declare any legislation void. Since enactments are made by parliament and can only be abolished by parliament, this system runs the risk that encroachment on individual rights are easy to incur.

This risk is even fortified by the fact that England had never adopted a constitution in the form of a legal written document that provides the foundation for the exercise of state power; instead, it comprised of constitutional framework which is established on a variety of legal rules and practices. These legal rules obtain no special status in the English legal system, as they are regarded more as expectations of a proper conduct.[1208]

The integration of the European Convention of Human Rights (ECHR or Convention) into domestic legislation, the HRA 1998, embarked upon a new period in the legislative history of England with respect to protection of fundamental human rights, inter alia the right to religious freedom. The protection mechanism adopted from the ECHR prescribes English courts the obligation to take due account of the rulings and decisions delivered by the European jurisdictional organs in Strasbourg. In that case, similar examination to detect whether infringement of the right to religious freedom in public schools has taken place or not will be applied by English courts. This made England accountable to infringement of fundamental rights and, thence, enforcement of religious rights is likely to achieve better observance and protection under inclusion of the ECHR into domestic law.

Since the formal entanglement of church and state is not excessive in England, it enables a substantive division in several areas. Nonetheless, the field of education still remains a privileged sphere of the Anglican Church.[1209]

In the following, an overview will be provided with respect to the nexus of religion and endorsement of religious themes into the British educative system, having regard to historical retrospect and development up to date. A focus on the legislative educative framework designating the establishment of state schools, their supervision, their erection, appointment of teaching staff, and

---

1207 *Poulter*, p. 73; *van Ooijen*, p. 214.

1208 The expectation of proper conduct is directed towards parliamentary institutions or bodies or those capable to exercise their legal power so as to regulate their conduct when exercising their legal power. *Edge* p. 76.

1209 *Vickers, 4 Religion and Human Rights, 2009*, 137, 144.

their qualification and regulation of religious-churchly affairs in the education will assist in drawing a line regarding religious freedom and its entanglement in the educative context. The legitimacy of religious manifestation through outer appearance by display of symbols or wearing garments will be outlined both with respect to teachers and pupils. This sub-division will cover in fraction the legal legitimacy of pupils to display religious symbols and examination of their scope of protection. However, there were so far hardly jurisprudential determinations regarding teachers and this is due to lack of controversies brought on the background of objections made by pupils or parents with respect to a teacher's conspicuous outer appearance. Given the emphasis in my analysis on the permissibility of teaching staff to manifest their religious affinity, the discussion will concentrate also on anti-discrimination aspects in employment relations; eventually, it will try to demonstrate whether complainants can better succeed in their claim if established on anti-discrimination laws – as the case would be if they were to claim for violation of their fundamental human right to freedom of religion.

In particular, the following aspects will be underscored and evaluated: the impact that the state-church model adopted in England has on the protection of minority rights to religious freedom; the meaning and perception attributed in the English context to the principle of neutrality – in particular the obligation of the state to neutrality will be considered as possible ground for curtailment on the teachers' right to religious freedom; the ability of the legislative framework established in England to provide an adequate protection of the fundamental right to religious freedom, in particular in the fields of employment and education.

a) The Accommodation of Religion in State Schools

Historically, the educational sector was a sphere dominated by the church.[1210] The Anglican Church established most of the schools and provided education, naturally enjoying the privilege of deciding on employment criteria for teaching staff and prescribing admission requirements for pupils. This was the prevalent situation until 1870 when the state decided to introduce public education. Insofar, the turning point with respect to education control took place with the occurrence of the following:

1210 *Vickers*, in Hunter-Henin, Law, Religious Freedoms and Education in Europe, 2011, 87, 88.

First, introduction of public schooling into state system – the need to provide for public education substituted the so far only available education controlled by the church and offered public education for all based on shared control between the state and religious bodies.[1211]

Second, the promulgation of the Education Act 1944 altered not only the allocation of financial funding by the state, as it included church schools which could benefit from governmental support that till this point was offered only to public schooling. In addition, it introduced a new type of state schooling into its state system, the establishment of voluntary schools.[1212] It enabled church schools to opt between two types of schools: the opportunity to be fully funded and administered by the state (voluntary controlled) or have mere financial support by the state leaving the rest of control to the church (voluntary aided).[1213]

In fact, the distinction between the types of school existing in England's educational system is of great significance, especially due to the fact that a designation of their legal status will trigger the application of a different set of rules. This means that as far as administration governance, employment requirements for state schoolteachers, and controlling admissions are concerned, different legislation will apply according to the type of school concerned. The law then makes segregation between different types of schools: those which carry a religious character (faith schools), and those without a religious character (non-faith schools).[1214]

Therefore, a brief description of the types of school existing in England and Wales will be provided henceforth:

Religious or faith schools – are mainly Christian in nature (either Anglican or Roman Catholic) and constitute the majority of maintained schools. Faith schools in general account for over a third of the total number of schools in

1211 *Vickers*, 4 Religion and Human Rights, 2009, 137, 139.

1212 *Vickers*, in: Hunter-Henin, Law, Religious Freedoms and Education in Europe, 2011, 87, 88.

1213 *Vickers*, 4 Religion and Human Rights, 2009, 137, 139.

1214 Currently, there are 19,783 maintained schools in England and Wales. Out of which 6,750 are schools with a religious character. 4,600 are Anglican schools and the remaining 2,000 are Roman Catholic schools. *Oliva/Cranmer*, European Public Law, 2013, 19(3), 552, 566.

England.[1215] The category of faith schools also includes schools of faiths or religions other than Christianity such as Muslim schools. A large number of faith schools are primary schools, followed with a considerable share by secondary faith schools.[1216]

Faith schools with a religious foundation can be either *voluntary controlled* or *voluntary aided.*

Voluntary controlled schools – are predominantly schools whose land and buildings are churchly controlled, whereas administration, employment of teaching staff, organizational framework, controlling admissions, and financial support remain within control of the Local Education Authority (LEA).[1217]

Voluntary aided schools – schools where the whole building, premises, and land are kept within control of the church whereas financial funding is made through the LEA; the responsibility of controlling admissions and employment of teaching staff is obtained by the governing body.[1218]

Non-faith schools can be basically divided in *community schools* and *foundation schools.*

Community schools are state schools which are funded by the central government through the LEA. In addition, the LEA owns the buildings and bears responsibility for the administration and employments of teaching staff. This type of schools is not influenced by religious groups.

Foundation schools are also state-funded schools, which means that they are funded by the central government via the LEA with the only difference that the governing body owns the building as well as carries the administration and organization of school and employment of teachers. This means that the governing body enjoys an ample scope of freedom in determination of schools employment requirements, admission control of pupils, and the

1215 *Van Ooijen*, p. 230; *Vickers*, in Hunter-Henin, Law, Religious Freedoms and Education in Europe, 2011, 87. See at: http://findoutmore.dfes.gov.uk/2006/02/religious_educa.html.

1216 *Vickers*, 4 Religion and Human Rights, 2009, 137, 138, 150.

1217 *Vickers*, 4 Religion and Human Rights, 2009, 137, 138, 150.

1218 *Vickers*, 4 Religion and Human Rights, 2009, 137, 138, 150. In 2008 there was an initiative of a coalition of organizations aiming to end the special treatment of the Anglican Church in schools as far as employment terms, teachers- and admission controls are concerned. Available at: http://www.accordcoaliation.org.uk/

general running of the school.[1219] This type of schools may or may not be faith-based, depending on the governing body.[1220]

Despite the fact that many of the schools carry a religious character they still achieve primarily financial funding from the state,[1221] while some funding may occasionally be granted by the church.[1222]

In fact, many of the maintained schools,[1223] which were originally established as church-supported schools, have kept this distinctive religious character until today.[1224] They are recognized (inaccurately) as 'faith schools' and protected by law.[1225] This religious ethos of maintained schools is preserved through mandatory requirement in legislation, the Education Reform Act 1988, prescribing endorsement of religious education as part of a school's basic curriculum and commencement of a daily act of worship.[1226] The wish to reflect the Christian nature of the state was achieved within this legislative framework through implementation of a guarantee that religious education in schools should 'reflect the fact that religious traditions in Great Britain are in the main Christian'.[1227] Though the number of faith schools has retrenched since 1944, the majority of maintained schools remain Christian in nature and are predominantly Church of England schools.[1228] In addition, in most schools there must be an act of

1219 Foundation schools were set up under the School Standards and Framework Act 1998 and were meant to replace the former Grant-Maintained Schools.

1220 *Vickers*, 4 Religion and Human Rights, 2009, 137, 138, 150.

1221 The grants to faith schools amount to up to 90 percent of their total costs. This includes capital costs of property and teachers' salaries. See in *Vickers*, 4 Religion and Human Rights, 2009, 137, 139; *van Ooijen*, p. 230; *Vickers*, in Hunter-Henin, Law, Religious Freedoms and Education in Europe, 2011, 87. See at: www.atl.org.uk/atl_en/education/position_statements/faith_schools.asp.

1222 *Vickers*, 4 Religion and Human Rights, 2009, 137, 139.

1223 Maintained schools are funded by the central government through the local authority.

1224 *Blair/Aps*, 17(1–2) Education and the Law, p. 1; *Vickers*, 4 Religion and Human Rights, 2009, 137, 138, 140.

1225 School Standards and Framework Act 1998 Schedule 19 para 3 and 4.

1226 The Education Act 1944 requires the performance of a daily act of collective worship including the conveyance of religious instructions regardless the nature and type of schooling. *Blair/Aps*17(1–2) Education and the Law; *Brugger/Karayanni*, p. 41 quoting *Doe*, National Identity, the Constitutional Tradition and the Structures of Law in the United Kingdom, in: European Consortium for Church- State Research, eds., Religions in European Union Law, 1998, 93 (Note 56), 114.

1227 *Blair/Aps*, 17(1–2) Education and the Law 2005, 1, 2 (Recital 403).

1228 *Vickers*, 4 Religion and Human Rights, 2009, 137, 138, 140; *van Ooijen*, p. 230; *Vickers*, in Hunter-Henin, Law, Religious Freedoms and Education in Europe, 2011, 87.

collective worship that is wholly or mainly Christian in character. Collective worship in state schools is governed by Sec. 70 and Schedule 20 of the School Standards and Framework Act 1998. However, parents may opt their children out of religious education or collective worship or both.[1229]

Subject to parents' right of withdrawal,[1230] all registered pupils are required to take part in an act of collective worship each day. In community schools and foundation schools without a religious character, the collective worship is required to be 'wholly or mainly of broadly Christian character',[1231] unless this requirement is expressly misapplied by the LEA's Standing Advisory Council on Religious Education.

The fact that the Church of England still has prevalence over education, including determination of the basic curricula in all maintained schools and the expansion of faith schools[1232] indicates that although the British society has undergone social changes and has become a multi-cultural society, it still perceives the significant role religion plays in its education system.[1233]

According to the European Court of Human Rights (ECtHR or Court) in *Cosans v UK* ECtHR 25 February 1982: 'the education of children is the whole process whereby in any society adults endeavour to transmit their beliefs, culture and other values to the young' and the fundamental nature of this task means that education is inevitably a source of both political and legal controversy. It was also noted in Baroness Hale in *Begum v Denbigh High School* (2006) UKHL 15, para 97:

> …schools are different. Their task is to educate the young from all the many and diverse families and communities in this country in accordance with the national curriculum. Their task is to help all of their pupils achieve their full potential. This includes growing up to play whatever part they choose in the society in which they are living. The school's task is also to promote the ability of people of diverse races, religions, and cultures to live together in harmony.[1234] However, this responsibility for developing a unified school system may find itself in conflict with the desire of individual pupils or parents to

1229 *McGoldrick*, p. 174.

1230 School Standards and Framework Act 1998, sec. 71.

1231 Schedule 20, para 3 para 2.

1232 *Vickers*, in Hunter-Henin, Law, Religious Freedoms and Education in Europe, 2011, 87., *Vickers, 4 Religion and Human Rights 2009*, 137, 138, 140; *van Ooijen*, p. 230; *Vickers*, in *Hunter-Henin*, Law, Religious Freedoms and Education in Europe, 2011, 87.

1233 *Vickers*, 4 Religion and Human Rights 2009, 137, 140.

1234 *Addison*, p. 92.

manifest their religion or follow specific patterns of religious belief, which may conflict with general school policies and priorities.

Nonetheless, the main evident trends demonstrating the undergoing change in state schools all over the country relate to collective religious prayers and religious education which has become more secular in nature.[1235]

In fact, this shift in the late 1970s marked the beginning of radicalization over educational methods, departing from traditional teaching methods to a sphere of secular education.[1236]

b) The Competency of the State with Respect to Its Public School System

In England, the supervision of the educational system, including the establishment and organization of its state schools, is a task of the local authorities.[1237] State schools receive financial support allocated through national taxation.[1238] The practice of state funding does not apply equally to all types of schools but rather alternates depending on the nature and type of school. While the funding of denominational schools is granted by local authorities, 'grant-maintained' schools, which are discerned by the degree of public control, normally receive central government financial support.[1239]

The state supports financially the high costs of public religious schools. Apart from that, religious instruction is taught as part of the basic curriculum with an emphasis on the Christian nature of the state. However, an adequate consideration is given to the teaching and practices of the other principal religions represented in Great Britain (e.g., Muslims, Hindus, Sikhs, and Jews).[1240]

The attempt of the British parliament to disempower LEAs from vast discretion rights with respect to school curriculum occurred with the intent of the British government when it introduced the Education Reform Act 1988. It was

1235 *Meredith*, Religious Education in Public Schools: Study of Comparative Law, Yearbook of the European Association for Education Law and Policy Volume 6, 2006, 155, 158; at *Lopez-Muniz/De Groof/Lauwers*, "Religious Education in Public Schools: Study of Comparative Law", Kluwer Law Int'l, 2006 Vol. 6.

1236 William Tyndale, Junior and Infants School Public Inquiry: a Report to the Inner London Education Authority, ILEA (1976).

1237 This applies only to England and Wales, as Scotland and North Ireland have their own educational system. *Molokotos/Liederman*, p. 106; *van Ooijen*, p. 230.

1238 *Molokotos/Liederman*, p. 107; *van Ooijen*, p. 230.

1239 *Molokotos/Liederman*, p. 107

1240 *Vakulenko*, p. 23; *Mc Goldrick*, pp. 173, 174.

meant to compensate for the lack of a national curriculum which was applicable across England and Wales, leaving vast discretion enjoyed by LEAs in respect to curriculum's content. The fear of the British government was growing especially by virtue of radicalization of the contents of the curriculum and the teaching methods in some LEAs, permitted by this wide curriculum discretion.[1241]

aa) Privileged Constitutional Position of the Anglican Church

The special position of the Church of England, especially in the context of its involvement in educational matters,[1242] raises heavy doubts as to the ability of the English state to conform with its obligation to equality treatment on the national level, as well as respective fundamental human rights according to commitment to international human rights agreements. This close involvement of the church, enabling it to determine a school's curriculum and admission of teaching staff is regarded in the legal literature as most problematic.[1243] A very notable example for the privileged position of the Anglican Church or other religious organizations can be also viewed with respect to the waiver granted to religious organizations to comply with the provisions of the ECHR.

In effect, the need to maintain compliance of religious organizations with the conventions precept regarding religious rights accorded the insertion of section 13 to the HRA.

Section 13 requires domestic courts, given that their determination in issues prescribed by the HRA may affect the exercise of religious freedom by religious organization or their members, to give a particular regard to the religious interests of religious organizations ('must have particular regard to the importance of that right').[1244] Since the COE (Church of England) enjoys a special status and certain notable privileges under English law, the aim of section 13 was to ensure that special protections granted to religious organizations (especially churches) relating to the administration of ecclesiastical issues (such as the ban on marriage of same-gender couples) will be consistent with the Convention.[1245]

1241 *Meredith*, Study of Comparative Law, Yearbook of the European Association for Education Law and Policy Volume 6, 2006, 155, 159.

1242 *Van Ooijen*, pp. 251, 252.

1243 *Vickers*, 4 Religion and Human Rights 2009, 137, 146.

1244 Human Rights Act 1998, p. 13; cf. http://www.hmso.gov.uk/acts/acts1998/19980042.htm

1245 *Palmer*, Religious Liberty: The Legal Framework In Selected OSCE Countries, 2000, p. 167.

The criticism raised with relation to the insertion of section 13 asserted that it suggests to be beneficial for the churches, as there is no legal or logical justification for directing the courts in the process of judicial review.

bb) The Role of the State as an Employer – Duty for Equal Participation in the Public Service

The obligation of the state in its role as employer to remain neutral in the context of religious issues acquires significance especially in the public service. The state then has a commitment to religious pluralism. The encouragement of equal participation/opportunities of religious groups encompassing its society will, first, improve integration of religious minorities into society; and second, fulfil the state's commitment to equality in access to employment and demonstrate to society that all of its citizens are equal and valued.[1246]

cc) The Monopoly of the State as an Employer

Especially in the public service the state acts as a monopoly employer. Should the state apply religious discrimination in sectors of the public service, it will bar a significant part of its religious minorities from employment opportunities and by that apply religious discrimination.[1247]

c) The Endorsement of Religious Symbols into the State's School System

In principle, the wearing of religious symbols by state schoolteachers is not prohibited by law. Since hardly any cases challenging religious donning of a teacher were brought before English courts, there existed no urgent necessity to implement relevant regulations. Further, limitations on teachers' dress code were not induced by local authorities in their capacity as the responsible authority for implementation of school education policy.[1248] In this respect, the wearing of religious symbols by pupils, as opposed to teachers, had been often subject to judicial review, mainly due to school uniform policies regulated on a local level.

There are, however, several grounds advocating in favour of the state's duty to remain religiously neutral in public sector employment:

1246 *Vickers*, 4 Religion and Human Rights 2009, 137, 145.
1247 *Vickers*, 4 Religion and Human Rights 2009, 137, 145.
1248 *Van Ooijen*, p. 231.

First, *equality treatment principle* – the state will ensure equal participation of all religious groups in the society.
Second, *social integration* – by applying similar employment requirements that apply equally to all religious groups and faiths, the state transfers the message that it treats all its citizens on the same level and thus encourages and promotes social cohesion.
Third, *the state as an employer* – if the state acts as an employer, it can ensure neutrality by enabling several sectors to remain free for entrance and by ensuring that they will not be barred to teaching staff on religion-related grounds.

aa) The Legal Framework

The ban on the wearing of religious symbols in England's school system may constitute a ground for a claim based on two different legislative heads: first, a violation of the fundamental human right to freedom of religion. Second, a breach of anti-discrimination law.

School governors or principals are not only obliged to adopt dress code policies prescribed by their local authorities but also under obligation to conform to national anti-discrimination legislation.[1249]

(1) Equality Act 2010

In Britain, religions are heavily involved in education and for that reason the Equality Act 2010 provides a list with special exemptions that have been granted to public schools; in particular, faith schools or schools which carry a religious ethos were exempted from the legislative scope of the Equality Act 2010.[1250]

In *Begum v Denbigh High School* (2006) UKHL, Baroness Hale said:

> Like it or not, this is a society committed in principle and in law to equal freedom for men and women to choose how they will lead their lives within the law. Young girls from ethnic, cultural or religious minorities growing up here face particularly difficult choices: how far to adopt or to distance themselves from the dominant culture. A good school will enable and support them.[1251]

Private schools as well as state-supported schools are governed by the Equality Act 2010 and will be subject to a claim of unlawful discriminatory act if a school discriminates against a teacher on religious grounds. A school authority may

1249 *Van Ooijen*, p. 232; *McGoldrick*, 2006, p. 178.
1250 See in Sub-section 5 part 2 of Schedule 11 of the 2010 Equality Act.
1251 *Addison*, p. 95.

be exempted from its general duty to non-discrimination as outlined in Sec. 149 para 1 of the Equality Act 2010 if it is listed under Schedule 22 of the 2010 Equality Act which excludes its scope of application with respect to institutes pursuing a religious ethos or agenda.

Subsection 5 of Schedule 11 to the 2010 Equality Act prescribes that the obligation of non-discrimination in admission of pupils to state schools outlined in Sec. 85 para 1 and 2 (a) to (d) 2010 Equality Act will not apply with respect to a school designated under Sec. 69 para 3 of the School Standards and Framework Act 1998, nor will they apply to a school carrying a religious character as listed in the register records.[1252]

In case a school is designated under Schedule 11 of the Equality Act 2010, then the law provides school authorities a complete defence against any claim of discrimination founded on religious grounds.

Nonetheless, a discrimination claim brought by a pupil or his/her parents under Sec. 85 para 1 and para 2 (a) to (d) 2010 Equality Act may have a chance to succeed and does not provide any defence to school authorities in case of a substantial discriminatory act or event which occurs with respect to a public school not designated under the exempted list of Schedule 11 to the Equality Act 2010. These sub-provisions specified in Schedule 11 to the 2010 Equality Act exclude their application and will not provide a defence to acts of discrimination conducted by school authorities founded on religious grounds.[1253]

The reason for that provides that denominational schools can discriminate against a child on religious grounds and decline his/her admittance to school; however, an exclusion of the pupil following a change or loss of his/her faith will not avail school authorities and they will not be able to argue for the defence provided for them in Schedule 11 of the 2010 Equality act.

(2) The Education Act 1944

The education Act 1944 was seen as a landmark enactment fundamentally reshaping the structure of school education in England and Wales. It provided for compulsory primary and secondary education for all pupils between the ages of five and sixteen.[1254] The Education Act 1944 was repealed by the Education Act

1252 The register itself is being authorised by Sec. 158 of the Education Act 2002.

1253 The various exemptions to the general prohibition of discrimination as established under Art. 85 para 1 and 2 (a) to (d) of the 2010 Equality Act are listed in Schedule 11 of it.

1254 *Meredith*, Study of Comparative Law, Yearbook of the European Association for Education Law and Policy Volume 6 2006, 155, 156; *Lopez-Muniz/Groof/Lauwers*,

1996. Nonetheless, due to the significance it accrued in the educative system of England, the following will be outlined.

The vast majority of schools were county schools controlled by the LEA and were non-denominational in nature. Voluntary schools, on the other hand, were almost entirely controlled and supported by church authorities.[1255] The extent to which school authorities maintain adherence to religion depended on their categorization (voluntary controlled, voluntary aided, and special agreement schools).

The law mainly provided for the compulsory primary and secondary education for all children (between the ages of five and sixteen).[1256] In addition, the Act provided for a variety of forms of religious instruction in state-supported schools, depending on the nature of the school concerned.[1257] In fact, the inclusion of statutory requirements for religious education or collective worship was a distinguished feature of education law in 1944.

Surprisingly, though religious education and collective worship had been widely provided and practised in state schools they never possessed the position of a statutory requirement.

The relevant provision is Sec. 25 of the Education Act 1944 which provided that a school day in all maintained schools (whether faith-based or not) will begin with an act of collective worship and that religious education shall be delivered in these school forms.[1258] An exemption from school prayers and religious education will be allowed on the basis of parental objection to their child's participation in these school events. Nonetheless, not all faith schools explicitly promote their religious identity in way of conveyance of the religious ethos of schools. At the same time, other faith schools may emphasize their religious

---

"Religious Education in Public Schools: Study of Comparative Law", Kluwer Law Int'l, 2006 Vol. 6.

1255 Voluntary schools were sub-divided to three categories: voluntary controlled schools, voluntary aided schools and 'special agreement schools'schools; *Meredith*, Study of Comparative Law, Yearbook of the European Association for Education Law and Policy Volume 6, 2006, 155, 157.

1256 *Meredith*, Study of Comparative Law, Yearbook of the European Association for Education Law and Policy Volume 6, 2006, 155, 156.

1257 *Meredith*, Study of Comparative Law, Yearbook of the European Association for Education Law and Policy Volume 6, 2006. 155, 157.

1258 *Meredith*, Study of Comparative Law, Yearbook of the European Association for Education Law and Policy Volume 6, 2006, 155, 157.

character, in particular through expansion of acts of worships and compliance with other religious duties.[1259]

(3) The Education Reform Act 1988

The Education Reform Bill 1988 (1988 Act) is considered as the most comprehensive reform of the school education system in England and Wales since the Education Act 1944.

It is worth to note that though the 1988 Act had established provision for a national curriculum for secular education for the first time, there had been no reform with relation to the content of religious education and collective worship as originally planned.

There were many proposals, especially on part of religious peers within the British parliament to emphasize the centrality of Christianity in religious education.[1260] These proposals, however, remained unfulfilled and provoked fermentation inside and outside the British parliament.

Strikingly, a series of amendments proposed and initiated by the Bishop of London at that time, Dr Graham Leonard, were subsequently introduced to the Bill.[1261] These amendments sought to establish a compromising solution with relation to school curriculum which would still accentuate the Christian nature of the state but, at the same time, would allow enough room for other, non-Christian religions to flourish, especially with respect to schools which pertain mainly religious minorities.[1262]

Finally, the 1988 Act attempted to establish a more compromised attitude with relation to school syllabus, and provided therefore that:

> ...reflect the fact that the religious traditions of Great Britain are in the main Christian whilst taking account of the teaching and practices of the other principal religions represented in Great Britain.[1263]

1259 *Vickers*, in Hunter-Henin, Law, Religious Freedoms and Education in Europe, 2011, 87.

1260 House of Lords Debates, Vol 498, col. 641 (21 June 1988).

1261 *Meredith*, Study of Comparative Law, Yearbook of the European Association for Education Law and Policy Volume 6, 2006, 155, 159.

1262 *Meredith*, 52 Modern law Review, 1989, 215, 220–1; *Meredith*, Study of Comparative Law, Yearbook of the European Association for Education Law and Policy Volume 6 2006, 155, 158, 160.

1263 Education reform Act 1988, s. 8 para 3; *Meredith*, Study of Comparative Law, Yearbook of the European Association for Education Law and Policy Volume 6, 2006, 155, 160.

In practice, these compromise provisions remain a central feature of the current law applicable in England and Wales, though the actual provisions of the 1998 Act have been replaced by the School Standards and Framework Act 1988 and the Education Act 2002.[1264]

(4) *The School Standards and Framework Act 1998*

Implementation of the provisions in the School Standard and Framework Act 1998 (SSFA) varies according to the type of school involved (voluntary aided, voluntary controlled, community schools, and foundation schools).[1265] The SSFA was meant to govern the employment of teachers in faith schools. Its objective was to provide faith schools with an ample scope of freedom when imposing religious requirements on teaching staff even if discriminatory in nature. Thence, given that teachers may encounter a discriminatory occupational requirement, founded on religious grounds, in their application for a vacancy in faith schools, this will not be subject to the provisions set under the Religion and Belief Regulations 2003 (now consolidated under the Equality Act 2010).

In principle, the SSFA aimed at the protection of teachers on two different levels. On the one hand, under some circumstances it enabled faith schools to impose employment requirements on teaching and non-teaching staff regarding religion and belief, which are discriminatory in nature. It thence permits such schools (foundation or voluntary aided schools), under certain circumstances, to deploy religious occupational requirements and rules of conduct to which teaching and non-teaching staff must conform.[1266] This exception for schools with a religious character was made possible through the Education and Inspections Act 2006, which amended the SSFA so as to enable faith schools to discriminate in favour of teaching applicants who share the same religious ethos of the school without being subject to application of anti-discrimination laws.[1267] This will be regarded permissible, especially due to the denominational character of schools. On the other hand, it aimed at the protection of teaching staff from religious discrimination in non-faith schools.[1268]

1264 *Meredith*, Study of Comparative Law, Yearbook of the European Association for Education Law and Policy Volume 6, 2006, 155, 160.

1265 See depiction of the different school types as outlined in 3(a) above; *Vickers*, 4 Religion and Human Rights, 2009, 137, 150.

1266 Section 37 para 2 Education and Inspection Act 2006.

1267 Section 37 para 2 Education and Inspection Act 2006; *Vickers*, 4 Religion and Human Rights, 2009, 137, 149.

1268 Section 59 SSFA; *Vickers*, 4 Religion and Human Rights 2009, 137, 149.

It also imposes a duty on state schools in England to endeavour for achievement of a social cohesion and tolerance among all religious communities.

Sections 58 to 60 and 124A of the SSFA govern the appointment and dismissal of teachers in schools with a religious character.

The permission of preference in employment or promotion is allowed in Sec. 60 to the SSFA to be granted to teachers:

(i) whose religious opinions are in accordance with the tenets of the religion or religious denomination specified in relation to the school under section 69 (4), or
(ii) who attend religious worship in accordance with those tenets, or
(iii) who give, or are willing to give, religious education at the school in accordance with those tenets; and…[1269]

Additionally, provisions 124A and 124B were added to the SSFA as a response to the endorsement of Employment Equality (Religion or Belief) Regulations 2003.[1270] The idea behind those provisions was to allow independent schools with religious character to give teachers with the required background preference in employment, promotion, or remuneration.

Eventually, the 2010 Act imposing an active duty to implement equality of treatment in the public sector will be relatively easy to apply in cases relating to discrimination of teachers in public schools if established on religious grounds. This is simply because schools which do not fall within the exemption list prescribed in Schedule 11 of the 2010 Act will encounter difficulties to dismiss their liability for unlawful act given that a dismissal of a teacher due to his/her display of religious symbol has taken place.

Finally, each case will be reviewed independently and may vary in result depending on the status of school in question (denominational or public common school) and the exact role and duties of the teacher.[1271]

(5) The Education Act 2002

The Education Act 2002 determines with relation to curriculum in both secular and religious state-maintained schools in England and Wales to promote:

1269 *Addison*, p. 100.

1270 The wording of section 124A of the School Standards and Framework Act 1998 are identical in their formulation to those stated in Sec. 60 of the Employment Equality Regulations 2003.

1271 *Addison*, p. 100.

> ...the spiritual, moral, cultural, mental and physical development of pupils at the school and of society...[1272]

In addition, the statutory framework requires that the curriculum for every state-supported school shall compromise a basic curriculum which includes religious education for all registered pupils at school.

It is worth to note, religious education is part of the 'basic curriculum' and not the national curriculum, which is of a considerable significance. The reason is that religious education syllabus is left to decide on the local rather than the national level. As a result, it may vary between regions as the content of the religious syllabus will take into account the cultural-ethnical complexion which is particular to the area concerned.

(6) The Education Act 2011

The Education Act 2011 became an Act of Parliament on 15 November 2011. The 2011 Act did not alter the formation of its school system and the types and forms of schools remained the same in configuration. However, the only relevancy of the Education Act 2011 can be observed in Section 55 of Part 6 enabling the Secretary of State with consultation of the appropriate religious body to convert a foundation school, voluntary aided schools, or voluntary controlled schools to an academy. According to the Academies Act 2010, it is made possible for all publicly funded schools subsequent to the transfer to a status of an academy to achieve an increased degree of autonomy with respect to setting of teaching staff and diverging from the content of the national curriculum. In this respect, it is yet to be seen how the new acts will be, if at all, significant with respect to teachers' right to religious manifestation or their access to employment. This is because the legal situation remains in principle to be determined at the level of the LEAs, subject to their competency, and within their discretion.

bb) Religious Symbols in Schools

(1) 'Institutional' Symbols – Religious Symbols in Schools

In principle, there is no general mandatory requirement in England to affix the cross in state classrooms. The display or affixation of religious symbols in state schools in England is determined on a regional level rather than on a nation-wide basis. The reason for that is that while all types of schools are controlled

---

1272 Education Act 2002, Sec. 78 para 1; *Meredith*, Study of Comparative Law, Yearbook of the European Association for Education Law and Policy Volume 6, 2006, 155, 161.

by school governors, the distinction between the different types of schools and their nature depends to a large extent on who funds the school and who employs teaching staff.[1273] The respective entity responsible for school funding or the employment of teaching staff will determine the religious character of school. It is therefore not unusual in England that different entities will get a hold of the same school. For instance, while premises (buildings and land) may be owned by the church, financial funding may be provided by the state via the LEA, and employment of teaching staff may be determined by the governing body. Accordingly, not only that a different set of rules will apply, depending on the type and nature of schools but also the religious ethos of schools will vary depending on the entity responsible for their funding, admission controls, or employment of teaching staff. This will affect the level of religious ethos promoted by the school, leaving religion-related themes to be decided on a regional level.

Accordingly, the responsible entity for determination of a school curriculum or other religion-related themes, including affixation of crosses in classrooms will be subject to determination made either by the LEA or school governors.

Although the vast majority of maintained schools carries a religious character, the level of religious adherence and promotion of religion as part of the school ethos can vary within these schools.

In general, the display of religious symbols in higher education has been more common.[1274] The strong nexus between religion and higher education has been imprinted in England's history and tradition. This strong allegiance is demonstrated by display of religious symbols in higher education buildings to this day and bears significance especially on the background of its transferal from a homogenous to a multi-cultural, multi-religious society. Based on this close bond and the fact that many of the higher education buildings are listed, a removal or an attempt to remove religious symbols displayed in higher education buildings would raise difficulties considering the long tradition and heritage.[1275]

1273 *Vickers*, 4 Religion and Human Rights 2009, 137, 150.

1274 For instance, Oxford and Cambridge colleges were established as religious foundations with own chapels. Even the University College London, which was established in 1826 as a secular institute, did not deny incorporation of religion. The chapel of King's College was founded in 1829 as an Anglican establishment and is considered in itself as an 'institutional religious symbol'. See in *Garcia/Cranmer*, European Public Law, 2013, 555, 567.

1275 *Garcia/Cranmer*, European Public Law 2013, 555, 567.

(a) Religious Faith Schools

In religious faith schools or schools that carry a salient religious ethos, like voluntary controlled or voluntary aided schools, there is no general mandatory requirement to display the cross in classrooms. However, customary practices vary within different types of faith schools and distinguish the nature of their religious character.

For instance, in most of the Roman Catholic schools a crucifix is affixed in each classroom.[1276] Other religious items such as ikons may be displayed as well. It is also common in Roman Catholic primary schools to have a 'prayer corner' with a display of religious symbols.[1277] This situation differs from the situation in the Church of England schools.

The display of crucifixes or other religious symbols is less common in Church of England schools. The absence of Christian symbols in Anglican schools is unclear. It is presumed to relate to the fact that the majority of Anglican primary schools had been established in rural areas where the exhibit of overt religious symbolism was perceived as inappropriate.[1278] Anglican schools will be, thence, inspected for their religiousness by the Church's Education Officer. The recommendations made by the inspectors refer to the absence of Christian symbols in Anglican schools and suggest increasing instalment of Christian emblems into these schools. The idea was to increase the presence of Christian symbols in state school buildings in general and not specifically in each classroom.[1279]

Albeit the recent tendency to integrate Christian symbols into the design of buildings, chapels, and 'faith rooms' in Church of England's academies, it has been claimed by the Chief Education Officer that it was the absence of religious symbols in schools, rather than their presence, that was the subject of the debated inspections.[1280]

However, the only obligatory religious requirement exists with respect to participation in daily acts of worship, such as school prayers at the beginning and end of the day and religious instructions.

1276 *Garcia/Cranmer*, European Public Law 2013, 555, 566.
1277 *Garcia/Cranmer*, European Public Law 2013, 555, 566.
1278 *Garcia/Cranmer*, European Public Law 2013, 555, 567.
1279 *Garcia/Cranmer*, European Public Law 2013, 555, 567.
1280 This information was received through personal communication from Janina Ainsworth, Chief Education Officer for the Church of England. See in Oliva, *Garcia/Cranmer*, European Public Law, 2013, 555, 567.

(aa) Voluntary Controlled Faith Schools

In practice, voluntary controlled school is a state-funded school where a charitable foundation, mostly a Christian denomination, owns the land and buildings. This means that voluntary controlled schools are funded by the central government whereas, the local authority employs the school's stuff and the charitable foundation will have the right to appoint a quarter of the school governors and as a result will have some influence in the running of the school. These schools may carry a Christian-religious ethos due to their voluntary controlled status. However, this does not necessarily suggest that religion-related themes will focus mainly on Christianity as a privileged religion. This means that although being maintained by the state voluntary controlled schools are allowed to have acts of worship 'in accordance with the beliefs of the religion or denomination specified for the school'. The religious ethos of a controlled school with respect to issues such as affixation of religious symbols in school premises, participation in acts of worship like religious ceremonies or assemblies as well as religious prayers that usually takes place at the beginning and end of each day will be in accordance with the denomination specified for the school. Faith schools enjoy some exemption from the general duty to equality according to sec. 85 of the Equality Act 2010. This section enables voluntary controlled schools which in their majority are associated with the Church of England to prioritise pupils of Christian faith in application and admission to school.

Since the legal question relating to display of religious symbols in state schools depends on the identity of the funding entity or the governing or controlling body, these aspects will be governed on the local or regional level. Therefore, there is no legislative obligation in England to display the cross in classrooms on a nation-wide basis.

(bb) Voluntary Aided Faith Schools

The legal position with respect to voluntary aided schools is not different than the one which applies with respect to voluntary controlled schools. This type of state-maintained school constitutes a faith-based school and as such shares a religious ethos. Albeit carrying a religious ethos, the legal position is dependent more on the identity of funding and admission entity rather than on aspects of religious advancement and extent of its input within the school. Since most of the costs will be covered by the state and a contribution of the building costs will be met by the foundation or a charitable trust, the foundation will gain more influence on aspects like school curriculum, admission, and appointment of teaching staff.

Therefore, schools with a voluntary aided status may still carry a multicultural ethos even if in practice the buildings and premises are controlled by a foundation (usually a religious organization). In that case, the display or affixation of religious symbols like the cross in classrooms will be subject to the legal obligations prescribed by the LEA or school governors (their majority are appointed by the foundation). The conveyance of religious ethos within these schools is Christian in nature. In fact, Christianity as a privileged religion is advanced within these types of schools. According to Sec. 85 of the Equality Act 2010, voluntary aided faith schools are allowed to privilege pupils applying faith criteria in admission to school.

(b) Community and Foundation Schools

Normally, community or foundation schools are secular in nature. Therefore, the display of 'institutional' religious symbols in secular schools is not a common sight in these types of schools. However, due to historical reasons, the exhibit of Christian symbols in a small number of schools, most of which are chapels of state boarding schools, remains inevitable.[1281]

(2) Religious Symbols Worn by an Individual

In principle, the legal right of an individual to exert or manifest his/her religion outwardly by wearing religious conspicuous signs in public state schools is recognized to fall within the scope of protection of the right to religious freedom. This has been acknowledged for both pupils and teachers by the British jurisdiction.[1282] Legally, the subjective intention of the wearer will suffice in order to extend the protection of religious symbols within the religious freedom's scope of protection. That means that the British jurisprudence will neither accord high importance to the religious meaning of a symbol nor consider the fact that the majority of this practiced religion comply with the religious precept.[1283] In other words, the permissibility of an ostentatious religious symbol will not be subject to a judicial determination that it is considered an obligatory precept by the majority of the specific religious community in order to legitimize

---

1281 *Garcia/Cranmer*, European Public Law, 2013, 555, 567.

1282 R (Begum) v Headteacher and Governors of Denbigh High School (2006) UKHL 15, (2006) 2 All ER 487, para 21; Azmi v Kirklees Metropolitan BC (2007) All ER (D) 528 (Mar) (EAT).

1283 As was demonstrated in the case of Shabina Begum. See in detail in this Chapter 3 C) bb) (b) (bb).

its protection. So far, however, LEAs in England were not keen to impose limitations on teachers' dress. This can be attributed to the fact that complaints lodged by teachers on grounds of a breach of their right to religious freedom were not that prominent as was the case regarding pupils.[1284]

(a) Religious Symbols Worn by Teachers

(aa) Teachers' Position in Employment

The display of religious symbols by a state schoolteacher belongs to the public service sphere. However, public service is not legally defined in English law.[1285] Teachers are not regarded as civil servants in the UK.[1286] The public employment sphere is not identified as a secular one nor as neutral to religion and non-religion.[1287] As a result, there is no general rule with respect to all public officials prescribing their permissibility to display religious symbols while officially fulfilling a public function.[1288] It is due to this fact that each sector in the public service can prescribe its own rules and no uniform distinctiveness applies equally with respect to all capacities in the public service.[1289] The absence of clear specifications as to the capacity a public official has to qualify with, or fulfil, while on duty makes it difficult to impose any obligations as to his neutral appearance. Further, if there is no segregation between civil servants' public and private function there is no real personification of public officials with the state and as a result no demand to appear neutral within their function.[1290] Simply put, the state does not identify itself with the public service.

Finally, if a state decides to confine teachers' access to its school system while imposing faith requirements, there are several factors that need to be taken into account: the nature of the job, the extent to which religious belief is a defining element, and the extent to which other employment opportunities are available to potential applicants.

(aaa) Scope of Protection

As already mentioned earlier, state schoolteachers are not banned from display or manifestation of religious symbols. Since educational matters are left solely

---

1284 *Van Ooijen*, p. 231.
1285 *Van Oojien*, p. 220, 246, 248.
1286 *Vickers*, 4 Religion and Human Rights (2009), 137, 145.
1287 *Freedland/Vickers*, 30 Comp. Lab. L. & Pol'y J. 2009, 597, 599, 600; *van Oojien*, p. 220.
1288 *Van Oojien*, p. 221.
1289 *Van Oojien*, pp. 246, 248.
1290 *Van Oojien*, pp. 246, 247, 251, 252.

to the discretion and determination of the LEA or school governors, there is no general, nation-wide legislative prohibition on teachers to appear with religious symbols. Thence, absence or existence of dress policies will be made, if at all, only at the regional-local level.

The admissibility of a teacher to exercise her religious freedom by appearing with a headscarf or another religious garment while on duty will need to be reviewed within the context of several significant legislations: first, the Equality Act 2010, which enfolds the criteria governing employment relations within the public sector, inter alia, teaching staff in public schools. These criteria were formerly covered by the Religion or Belief Regulations 2003 and the 2006 Equality Act; second, the Schools Standards and Framework Act 1998. These legislative acts are of an important relevance in the English discourse since each of them aimed to enclose different types of state schools and, consequently, affected the protection offered to teaching and non-teaching staff in exercising their right to religious freedom. The distinction is made between faith or non-faith schools, as they will be entitled to apply different set of rules with respect to employment and admission criteria of teachers.[1291] Third, the HRA 1998 – following classification of teaching staff in the respective schools, an examination will take place with respect to the fundamental right of a teacher to manifestation of his/ her right to religious freedom. A substantiation of infringement will follow the same scheme of proof established by the ECtHR.

The permissibility of a teacher to appear with a headscarf has not been challenged yet in British courts; however, the stricter form of Islamic veiling, for example, the *niqab*, had been called into question and was found on professional-technical grounds that would justify its removal from school premises to be an impermissible symbol.[1292]

Finally, teachers in England do not enjoy the status of public servants and, as a result, are be eligible to the special protection offered to those working as civil servants. Given that, the infringement of their professional right within their capacity as teachers would not be called into question.

(bbb) Infringement

The ban on a teacher not to appear with a headscarf or other head covering to school will not be regarded as an infringement on her right to exertion of her religion. The reason is that teachers are considered to enter the teaching profession

1291 *Vickers*, 4 Religion and Human Rights 2009, 137, 150, 151; *Vickers*, in *Hunter-Henin*, Law, Religious Freedoms and Education in Europe, 2011, 87, 90.

1292 Azmi v Kirklees Metropolitan BC (2007) All ER (D) 528 (Mar) (EAT).

willingly and without any coercion, whereas pupils have no option to escape the view of a teacher due to compulsory schooling. In case it was demonstrated that a teachers' religious dress hindered communication with the pupils she may opt either, to take off the head covering, or alternatively, the teacher can exchange to a private faith school where she can freely manifest her religion.

In principle, British jurisprudence follow the line provided by the Strasbourg institutions and will not recognize an infringement in the right of an individual to manifest his or her religion according to Art. 9 HRA, if there are other means open to the person to observe his/her religion without undue hardship or inconvenience. Therefore, if an individual is permitted to wear the disputed religious garment in another available suitable alternative school, the courts will not acknowledge an interference in Art. 9 rights as often the offer of an alternative place will satisfy the requirements of the proportionality test.[1293]

(ccc) Justification

An infringement in a teacher's right to wear religious symbols to school should be substantiated on justified grounds. Applicable justification grounds are specified in Art. 9 para 2 HRA 1998. This means that the same criteria applied by the ECtHR will also be carefully considered by the British judicator in similar circumstances. It is worth to note that English law does not confer special obligations applicable to teachers with respect to their duty to appear neutral and unbiased and, as a result, it will not serve as a ground for justification as practiced under the German and French legal systems.

- *Prescribed by law* – in practice relevant school regulations even if published by LEAs will suffice for this purpose as applicable law.
- *The protection of fundamental freedoms of others* – this will be often used as a justification ground for banning the wearing of a *niqab* by teaching staff in England as often confirmed by the ECtHR jurisprudence.[1294] Within this justification ground following aspects will be taken into account:
- *Ostracism between religious groups* – the teacher is a representative figure and a role model for the pupils. The teacher exerts some degree of influence on pupils with her outer appearance; thus, by wearing a conspicuous symbol like the *niqab* or *jilbab* she may contribute to division and social exclusion

---

1293 R (Begum) v Headteacher and Governors of Denbigh High School (2006) UKHL 15, (2006) 2 All ER 487, paras. 23–24; *R (X) v The Headteacher and Governors of Y School* (2007) EWHC 298 (Admin), (2007) All ER (D) 267 (Feb) (QB), para 30.

1294 *Taylor*, Freedom of Religion- UN and European Human Rights Law and Practice, 2005, p. 163.

between religious groups in school. This will amplify and underscore differences between religious- and faith groups[1295] that will damage school uniformity and its peaceful co-existence. Also, it may encourage female pupils who abstained from appearing with religious head covering to school to do so. Similarly, it may have an adverse effect on female pupils who wish to escape from the social pressure in their environment obliging them to act in accordance with a religious precept ordering the wearing of a head covering simply as they will feel coerced acting in the same manner viewing their teacher.[1296]

- *Impinging teachers' performance – the wearing* of a *niqab* in *Azmi*'s case was asserted to hinder the ordinary course of a lesson since pupils could not understand the teacher and grasp her mimics due to the veiling of her head and mouth. As an English teacher there was no doubt that this art of veiling negatively affects her performance at school.[1297] Under these circumstances, the ordinary course of a lesson could not be safeguarded such that prohibiting the teacher from appearance with a *niqab* while on duty was justified.
- *Negative right of pupils to religious freedom* – the exposure of pupils to a veiled female teacher (whether *niqab* or *jilbab*) could not be denied to have an adverse effect on pupils as it symbolizes a rejection of the norms, values, and culture of Western society.[1298] The negative effect on the right of pupils to be free from any religious coercion applies equally to all pupils. However, it cannot be negated that especially female Muslim pupils who wish to refrain from any religious coercion are more likely to be affected by the teacher's outer appearance, in particular as she is a role model from which they cannot escape due to daily confrontation.
- *Gender equality* – the Islamic veiling is regarded and perceived to be a symbol which underscores the inferiority of women to men and thus infringes the principle of equality. The wearing of the Islamic dress, like the *niqab* or *jilbab* especially by pupils, has demonstrated in many cases that legitimization of their ban from school has triggered the right to gender equality as a justifcation ground.[1299]

1295 *Howard*, Law and the Wearing of Religious Symbols, 2012, p. 33–34. The argument had been used with respect to the importance of keeping uniform dress policies with respect to pupils.

1296 *Howard*, Law and the Wearing of Religious Symbols, 2012, p. 37. The author cites the decision of Begum and the concerns raised as to the increasing pressure on women to conform to the dress code of the *jilbab*.

1297 *Sandberg*, Law and Religion 2011, p. 110–111.

1298 *Howard*, Law and the Wearing of Religious Symbols, 2012, p. 33.

1299 *Vakulenko*, 2007, pp. 717, 727.

- *Margin of appreciation* – the British judicator had acknowledged the right of LEAs and school governors to include within their capacity to formation of their school system any other justification for the ban of a religious symbol as they see fit and within the boundaries of their discretion to accomplish their educative task.[1300]

(bb) Teachers in Faith Schools

The fact that the majority of maintained schools in England carries a religious character, in general Christian in nature, and that a considerable amount of these schools operates as primary schools affects the freedom of teachers in access and employment to the education sector.[1301] In addition, since the vast majority of maintained schools obtain an inherent religious Christian nature, this confines teachers who are members of other faiths or religions not only in employment opportunities but also regarding the right to freely practice or exercise the precepts of their own religion.[1302] This enables faith schools which are state-supported to adopt discriminatory measures based on religious grounds against state schoolteachers. The school board may justify its discriminatory act on grounds of insufficient professional aptitude to carry his/her task properly in that type of schools, given that a teacher's lack of qualification falls within this ambit. This may affect the career prospects of a significant number of teaching staff that would be prevented from work opportunities in an ample scope of maintained schools.[1303]

(aaa) Human Rights Aspects

Though complaints brought by teachers claiming an infringement of their fundamental right to religious freedom are scarce, an establishment of infringement will need to prove a breach in accordance with Art. 9 of the ECtHR as incorporated in Schedule 1 of the HRA 1998.

One of the famous cases with respect to an assistant teacher submitting a claim to an English Employment Tribunal (*Azmi v Kirkelees*) on grounds of violation of her right to religious freedom was proved to be unsuccessful. The case

---

1300 See *Azmi v Kirklees Metropolitan Borough Council* UKEAT/0009/07 (30 March 2007) (EAT) para 79 with respect to the 'apparent neutral policy'policy applied by school authority with respect to dress code of teachers.

1301 *Vickers*, 4 Religion and Human Rights 2009, 137 at; *Vickers*, in Hunter-Henin, Law, Religious Freedoms and Education in Europe 2011, 87.

1302 *Vickers*, 4 Religion and Human Rights 2009, 137, 138.

1303 *Vickers*, 4 Religion and Human Rights 2009, 137, 138.

to be alluded here briefly concentrated on the breach of her religious right under anti-discrimination laws rather than on violation of her fundamental human right to religious freedom under the HRA 1998.

(bbb) Anti-Discrimination Aspects

Employment of teachers in schools with a religious ethos will differ in their legal position than in non-faith schools as they permit these schools an ample scope of freedom to impose religious requirements on staff. In practice, the discriminatory effect on pupils by view of the teacher was not used to curb her right to religious manifestation since such a negative influence on the pupils or the right not be discriminated by her view would not be easily held against her fundamental right to manifest her religion.[1304]

Teachers in faith schools will be subject to a different set of rules in questions relating to admission, employment, and dismissal requirements. This will be governed by the SSFA, which distinguishes between different types of faith schools: (i) voluntary controlled or foundation schools and (ii) voluntary aided schools.

(ccc) Voluntary Controlled or Foundation Schools

The SSFA permits voluntary controlled or foundation schools to discriminate in the appointment of teaching staff and head teacher if they lack fitness or competency to develop the religious character of the school.[1305] On the same token, failure to comply with the religious tenets of the school will provide a ground for dismissal of teaching staff. Further, schools will be entitled to reserve up to fifth of their teaching staff for teachers with a religious background.[1306] The regulations also protect (non-reserved teacher) and support staff from discrimination on religious grounds (either due to religious opinion, failure to attend religious ceremonies, or conveyance of religious education at school). Eminently, the Act enables discrimination in the appointment of teaching staff and head teacher ('reserved staff'), which can be justified based on failure to comply with religious requirement or lifestyle prescribed by school authorities.[1307]

Accordingly, the SSFA permits voluntary or foundation schools to discriminate against 'reserved' teachers even if the religious requirement is not detrimental to his/her ability to teach.

1304 *Van Ooijen*, pp. 248, 250 and 252.

1305 SSFA, p. 60 as amended by the Education and Inspections Act 2006, p. 37.

1306 SSFA, p. 58.

1307 *Vickers*, in: Hunter-Henin, Law, Religious Freedoms and Education in Europe, 2011, 87, 92.

(ddd) Voluntary Aided Schools

The legal situation in voluntary aided schools permits discrimination of teaching staff on the basis of religious grounds. However, in contrast to the situation in voluntary controlled schools where discrimination of teaching staff on religious grounds can occur only with respect to 'reserved teachers' (one-fifth of the teaching staff), in voluntary aided schools discriminatory religious requirements can be imposed on all teaching staff.[1308] Since the employer in voluntary aided schools is normally the church, then the risk of power abuse in which advancement or promotion of Christian teachers may take place raises significantly. In this type of school, there is a clear preference to discriminate in favour of Christian teachers with respect to issues of dismissal, appointment, remuneration, and promotion of teaching staff.

On a practical level, a voluntary aided school reflects merely the legal constitution of the school and does not necessarily connote of its salient religious ethos. Those schools are also not to be regarded as more religious than other schools. Nevertheless, they are given a wider discretion for discrimination on religious grounds even when teachers are not engaged in religious instructions. This stands in contrast to the precept of the Equality Act 2010 as well as the EU Employment Equality Directive 2000/78. The same problem exists also with respect to voluntary controlled schools where the employer is the local authority. In such a case, it was already determined that the state cannot be regarded as a religious organization which maintains a religious ethos.[1309] Thus far, the state could not comply with the requirement in Art. 4 of the EU Directive which allows for religious organizations a broader exception to the non-discrimination principle.[1310]

Therefore, the SSFA provisions cannot comply with the EU Employment Directive. The reason for that is that the limits to the non-discrimination principle provided under the SSFA are so broadly formulated that they are unlikely to fulfil the requirements under the Directive.[1311]

1308 *Vickers*, in: Hunter-Henin, Law, Religious Freedoms and Education in Europe, 2011, 87, 92.

1309 Glasgow City Council v McNab (2007) IRLR 476.

1310 Art. 4 para 2 of the Employment Equality Directive 2000/78.

1311 An exception to the non-discrimination principle may comply with Art. 4 para 1 of the EU Directive 2000/78 insofar: 1. There is a genuine occupational requirement. 2. It serves a legitimate aim. 3. The discriminatory act or practice is proportionate to that aim. *Vickers*, in: Hunter-Henin, Law, Religious Freedoms and Education in Europe, 2011, 87, 93, 94.

Application of the SSFA will not regard any religious requirement for teaching staff as unlawful, as it fails to impose the proportionality test. By that, the school is neither obliged to consider whether a religious requirement is proportionate with regard to the ethos of school nor whether other less discriminatory means to achieve the school's aim could be found.[1312]

Thence, a voluntary aided school obtains competency to dismiss a teacher insofar his/her duty of conduct stands in contrast to the precepts of religion, or with the upholding of its tenets.[1313] In other words, a teacher can be dismissed from work if he/she fails to share the religion of the respective school regardless of whether the religious employment requirement is detrimental for the job in question.

(cc) Teachers in Community Schools

(aaa) Human Rights Aspects

For teaching applicants or employed teachers in non-faith schools, protection will be provided under the SSFA. The protection offered is similar to that established under the Equality Act 2010, which covers all employment sectors and protects against most forms of discrimination subject to the 'genuine occupational requirement'.[1314]

(bbb) Anti-Discrimination Aspects

Teachers applying for a vacancy or facing a dismissal in community schools, which are in nature non-faith schools, cannot discriminate at all on grounds of religion or non-religion.[1315]

To sum up, exceptions for discriminatory employment requirements for teachers in state schools are generally restricted in comparison to those imposed on teaching staff in faith schools since they are being subject to a different set of rules. It would be very difficult to establish that a discriminatory employment requirement that is based on religion or belief of a teacher will be regarded as permissible since the employer, in that case the state, would have to prove that

---

1312 *Vickers*, in: Hunter-Henin, Law, Religious Freedoms and Education in Europe, 2011, 87, 92.

1313 SSFA, p. 60.

1314 In the past protection against forms of discrimination in employment were covered under the Religion and Belief Regulations 2003. The legal situation has changed as of April 2010 when the Equality Act came into force.

1315 *Vickers*, in Hunter-Henin, Law, Religious Freedoms and Education in Europe, 2011, 87, 93.

it was a genuine and determining occupational requirement. Moreover, if the state acts as a monopoly employer, then it cannot operate as an organization with a religious ethos since the state is regarded as neutral and cannot have a religious ethos.

(dd) Conclusion – The Protection of the Fundamental Right of Teachers to Religious Freedom under English Law

Teachers lack adequate protection under both legislative heads: anti-discrimination laws as well as fundamental right aspect. The provisions of the SSFA which permit discrimination on religious grounds coincide with the requirements that apply to other employment sectors under the Equality Act 2010. The provisions of the SSFA permit discrimination on religious grounds when applied in certain circumstances to teachers in faith schools. All other aspects relating to employment requirements of teaching staff other than in faith schools are subject to the Equality Act 2010.

As a result, the legal position of teachers to exercise their fundamental right to religious freedom is retrenched extensively compared to other employment sectors.[1316]

The Equality Act 2010 permits discrimination in the public sector given that the discriminatory religious requirement are (i) a 'genuinely occupational requirement' that is detriment for the performance of the job (ii) proportionate – the school must prove that the imposed religious requirement was proportionate under the particular circumstances and in order to achieve a legitimate aim. The SSFA in contrast to the Equality Act 2010 offers a significant lower level of protection for teachers, as it applies no proportionality test that will need to satisfy that, first, the religious requirement is necessary for the performance of the job or, second, that no other, less discriminatory mean was available.

Thence, the protection against the 'non-discrimination' principle is much broader under the Equality Act 2010 than under the SSFA.

The Equality Act 2010 imposes a new public sector equality duties which added newer equality grounds (religion and belief, age, sexual orientation, maternity, and pregnancy) to those which were already available (race, gender, and disability). The duty designated in s. 149 of the Act is imposed on public authorities, including governing bodies of maintained schools.[1317]

1316 *Vickers*, in *Hunter-Henin*, Law, Religious Freedoms and Education in Europe, 2011, 87, 93.

1317 Equality Act 2010, Schedule 19.

The new equality duty imposed on public authorities was meant to harmonize the protection available to the newer equality grounds and impose them on governing bodies of maintained schools. In addition, the new equality duty can be seen as complementing the duty to promote equality in schools and foster community cohesion as set up by section 38 of the Education and Inspections Act 2006.[1318] In that sense, the extension of equality duties is considered as a motive for the elimination of discrimination and promotion of equality in schools. However, even strict adherence to the new equality duties on grounds of religion and belief may hinder community cohesion unless implemented thoroughly.

Decreased job opportunities are also problematic for teachers who apply for vacancies in urban areas where the type and character of schools is retrenched in the first place to faith schools, which are church schools (Anglican or Catholic). Therefore, if a teacher is unwilling or unable to teach in such a school, then his/her career progression would be limited.[1319]

The Education and Inspections Act 2006 imposes a duty on school governors in England to promote community cohesion in their conduct of the school.[1320] Nonetheless, since the duty is established by a different legislation it may be that the addition of a new ground, religion and belief, is likely to cause some difficulties at schools as opposed to other offices in the public sector.[1321]

Thence, the additional equality duty on grounds of religion and belief imposed on the public sector with the aim to hinder discrimination and promote equality also in public schools will probably not extend the protection it offers to teaching personal. The reason is that this is already protected under the Education and Inspections Act 2006 and is recognised in most schools as part of the well-established duty to foster community cohesion.

An exception to the general duty to promote community cohesion in the public sector is the right of faith schools to discriminate against teaching staff in employment and admission requirements based on grounds of religion and belief as prescribed in the SSFA.[1322]

1318 http://www.legislation.gov.uk/ukpga/2006/40/section/38.

1319 *Vickers*, 4 Religion and Human Rights 2009, 137, 147; *Vickers*, in *Hunter-Henin*, Law, Religious Freedoms and Education in Europe, 2011, 87, 89.

1320 *Vickers*, 4 Religion and Human Rights 2009, 137, 139; *Vickers*, in *Hunter-Henin*, Law, Religious Freedoms and Education in Europe, 2011, 87, 97.
Vickers, 4 Religion and Human Rights 2009, 137, 138.

1321 *Vickers*, 4 Religion and Human Rights 2009, 137, 139; *Vickers*, in *Hunter-Henin*, Law, Religious Freedoms and Education in Europe, 2011, 87, 97.

1322 The duty to promote community cohesion stipulated in s. 38 of the Education and Inspections Act 2006 was meant to foster good relations between different religious

(b) Religious Symbols Worn by Pupils

(aa) Scope of Protection

In principle, there exists no primary legislation regulating the visibility of religious dress or symbols in public places in any UK jurisdiction.[1323] Accordingly, public schools are not subject to any rules regulating religious dress code when forming their uniform dress policy. The increase of conflicts in schools has been registered especially with respect to pupils as the display of religious symbols or garments will be subject to the uniform dress code prescribed by their local school authorities. This is also the reason why manifestation of religious symbols worn by pupils as opposed to those involving teachers have found much resonance in the British jurisprudence.

The reason relates mainly to the fact that pupils are subject to school uniform policies; thence, when pupils' religious dress does not conform to school uniform policy, this will inevitably trigger the increase of tension and conflicts in schools, which will result in submission of complaints.

School uniform policies are regulated on a local level. Therefore, as an integral characteristic of the decentralized nature of the English school system, the responsible authority for determination of school uniform policies is either the local authority or the respective school board.[1324]

The general tendency of school authorities in England is very pluralistic and favours to accommodate uniform policies to the rights of religious minorities that feel obliged to conform to the dress code prescribed by the tenets of their religion.[1325] This has been demonstrated to a large extent in several cases involving the permissibility of pupils to appear with religious symbols to school. For instance, in the *Begum* case, school authorities banned the female pupils

---

groups in a society, affirm their community identity, and promote equal dignity in a society. Abidance by this duty will encourage the integration of minority groups into a society, strengthen their sense of belonging in a community, and improve positive relationships and continuation in the workplace, in schools and in the wider community. See in *Vickers*, in *Hunter-Henin*, Law, Religious Freedoms and Education in Europe, 2011 87, 103.

1323 *Garcia/Cranmer*, European Public Law 2013, 555, 572; Sherlock/Williams, Wales Journal of Law and Policy 2005, 4, 214, 215.

1324 *Van Ooijen*, 232; *McGoldrick*, 178; See also Department for Education, 'School Uniform. A Guide for Head Teachers, Governing Bodies, Academy Trusts, Free Schools and Local Authorities', 2012, p. 1, to be found on www.education.gov.uk/schools/leadership/schoolethos/b0014144/schooluniform.

1325 *Van Ooijen*, 232; *Fetzer/Soper*, p. 42.

from appearing in a *jilbab* following that it had already permitted the donning of a headscarf and *shalwar kameeze* into school (a long garb that covers completely the arms and goes over the knees). Similarly, in the case of *X v Y school,*[1326] the school head teacher permitted girls to cover their hair with a scarf, however, they refused to admit the claimant, a twelve-year-old female pupil, to appear in a *niqab* ordering it to collide with their school uniform policy.

(bb) Infringement

The British jurisprudence does not deliver a clear submission as to the legal occurrence of infringement and remains dubious as to the question whether a ban on pupils' right to appear with religious symbols to school will be classified at all times as an infringement. The reason can be explained due to lack of coherence and uniformity in British schools relating to admission of religious symbols into their premises. Two tests were developed by the judicator in order to decline an infringement in a pupil's right to freely exert his/her religion by display of religious symbols. First, voluntariness – if a pupil entered a school voluntarily, knowing and accepting that the school follows a strict policy of its uniform dress code and bans the visibility of conspicuous religious symbols within its premises, then this would normally be sufficient not to be classified as infringement. Second, alternative school – if a pupil had an alternative to register to another school in his/her surrounding and the alternative school offered a lenient approach with respect to its dress code, then this would suffice to decline the existence of an infringement.[1327] The HL underscores that compulsory schooling obliges the state to offer lessons, but the right of an individual does not exist with respect to a school of his own choice.[1328]

This approach had been reflected by the ruling of the HL in the *Begum* case, as it reiterated the decision of the ECtHR prescribing that Art. 9 ECHR does not protect every act motivated by a religion or belief.[1329]

1326 *R (X) v The Headteacher and Governors of Y School* (2007) EWHC 298 (Admin), (2007) All ER (D) 267 (Feb) (QB).

1327 R (Begum) v Headteacher and Governors of Denbigh High School (2006) UKHL 15, (2006) 2 All ER 487, para 23, 87; R (X) v The Headteacher and Governors of Y School (2007) EWHC 298 (Admin), (2007) All ER (D) 267 (Feb) (QB) para. 25 decision of Justice Silber J.

1328 R (Begum) v Headteacher and Governors of Denbigh High School (2006) UKHL 15, (2006) 2 All ER 487, para. 57.

1329 Kalac v Turkei as cited in R (Begum) v Headteacher and Governors of Denbigh High School (2006) UKHL 15, (2006) 2 All ER 487, para 50.

(cc) Justification

Since British courts are obliged to bring their decisions into alignment with the ECtHR decisions as much as possible, they will follow the same method of analysis with respect to application of the limiting criteria recognized by Art. 9 para 2 ECHR, given that restrictions are imposed on pupils to refrain from display of religious symbols during school attendance.

In general, grounds for justification of a ban should fulfil the following requirements: first, the prescription by law; second, necessity in a democratic society; and, third, legitimate aim – the mean that was adopted in order to achieve one of the legitimate aims prescribed in Art. 9 para 2 ECHR. The first requirement will be met usually by reference to School regulations or Guidance Notes. In the case of *R (X) v. the headteacher* and governors of Y school, the court declared that even a clear communication in a school assembly would satisfy the requirement of 'prescribed by law'.[1330] The second requirement should establish that there is a pressing need for the restriction imposed on an individual and it is necessary for the protection of the rights of others. Normally, this requirement will be met considering the head justifications provided by the school.[1331] As possible justifications heads for 'legitimate aim', the following had been acknowledged by British jurisprudence to satisfy this requirement: (i) the maintenance of school order had been argued so as to achieve an ordinary school operation,[1332] (ii) the peaceful co-existence and social balance so that pupils will feel comfortable in school, (iii) encourage a sense of equality and cohesion within school, (iv) ensure gender equality, (v) the public security aspect would argue to prevent social pressure and to protect children of the same faith to dress in a particular way.[1333] As can be viewed, the tendency of the British judicator is to grant school authorities an extensive margin of appreciation.

1330 R (X) v The Headteacher and Governors of Y School (2007) EWHC 298 (Admin), (2007) All ER (D) 267 (Feb) (QB) para. 43–45 decision of Justice Silber J.

1331 R (X) v The Headteacher and Governors of Y School (2007) EWHC 298 (Admin), (2007) All ER (D) 267 (Feb) (QB) para 69.

1332 Azmi v Kirklees Metropolitan Borough Council UKEAT/0009/07 (30 March 2007) (EAT) para 66–69.

1333 R (X) v The Headteacher and Governors of Y School (2007) EWHC 298 (Admin), (2007) All ER (D) 267 (Feb) (QB) para 70.

In both of the discussed case laws, albeit final conclusion that no infringement has taken place the judicator went to examine whether an infringement would have been justified had the claimant substantiated its complaint successfully.[1334]

The Guidance to Schools on School Uniform and Related Policies adopted by the Department for Children, Schools and Families (2007) made several recommendations in this regard:

A decision of a school with respect to its uniform policy must be fair and reasonable.[1335]

Local school governors should co-operate and consult with all involved parties including religious community leaders in order to achieve an agreement with respect to the proposed school uniform policy.[1336] In addition, when and if possible a careful consideration would be taken into account when a specific request is made by an individual pupil to vary school uniform policy so as to accommodate his/her religious needs.[1337]

The governing body of a school will consider the religious needs and requirement of all religious groups involved.[1338] This will provide a justification insofar religious rights of minorities cannot be accommodated and suggest that even fundamental rights are not unconfined and will be subject to limitations.[1339]

1334 R (Begum) v Headteacher and Governors of Denbigh High School (2006) UKHL 15, (2006) 2 All ER 487, para 27; R (X) v The Headteacher and Governors of Y School (2007) EWHC 298 (Admin), (2007) All ER (D) 267 (Feb) (QB) para 43.

1335 School Uniform Guidance for governing bodies, school leaders, school staff and local authorities, September 2013; Department for Education https://www.gov.uk/government/uploads/system/uploads/attachment_data/file/514978/School_Uniform_Guidance.pdf, Para 4.

1336 School Uniform Guidance for governing bodies, school leaders, school staff and local authorities, September 2013; Department for Education, para 4; In 2009 a survey regarding Scottish religious education revealed that in a primary school with a majority of Muslim children an agreement was achieved between parents, pupils and school governors as to the colour of the headscarf Muslim girls will be allowed to wear as part of their school uniform. See in *Riddell/Ahlgren/McCluskey/Weedon*, Religious Education in a Multicultural society: Scotland National report, 2009; *Garcia/Cranmer*, European Public Law, 2013, 555, 573.

1337 School Uniform Guidance for governing bodies, school leaders, school staff and local authorities, September 2013; Department for Education, para 4.

1338 School Uniform Guidance for governing bodies, school leaders, school staff and local authorities, September 2013; Department for Education, para 4.

1339 School Uniform Guidance for governing bodies, school leaders, school staff and local authorities, September 2013; Department for Education, para 20.

Notably, compliance with school uniform policy is perceived less with the duty of the state to abide by the neutrality principle.[1340] The rationale behind school uniform policies is triggered more by discipline and the need to preserve internal cohesion of the school community and harmony among pupils.[1341] In adopting school uniform policies, local school governors are bound to comply with national anti-discrimination legislation.[1342]

(dd) Pupils' Fundamental Right to Religious Freedom

Similar to the case of a teacher that would apply for a violation of her fundamental right to manifest or practice her right to religious freedom based on the established Articles of the ECHR, so is the case with respect to pupils. The breach of a pupil's right to manifest a religion by wearing a religious garment will be subject to proof that a violation of Art. 9 ECtHR took place. Pupils will normally invoke their main claim to free practice of their religion established on Art. 9 ECHR conjoined with Art. 2 of the first protocol ECHR establishing the right to education.

cc) Conclusion

To sum up, there is no general prohibition on teachers to refrain from appearing with religious symbols or garments while on duty.[1343] In addition, teachers are not regarded as public civil servants and, as a result, there exists no duty on their part to identify with the state. On the same token, if teachers are not expected to identify with the state or presume to represent the state, then there exists no legal justification for curtailment of their right to religious freedom prohibiting their appearance with religious attire or symbol.

Additionally, due to the fact that the majority of primary schools are faith schools, job opportunities for atheists or teachers of a religious minority who do not share the faith of the prevailing religion in these types of schools is considerably reduced.

However, the school system in England is governed by a different set of rules respective employment of teaching staff.

1340 Guidance, paras. 1 and 22. See also *Blair/Aps*, Education and the Law, Volume 17, Issue 1–2, 2005; *Liederman-Molokotos*, p. 110.

1341 *Blair/Aps*, Education and the Law, Volume 17, Issue 1–2, 2005, 1, 16; *van Ooijen*, p. 233.

1342 *McGoldrick*, p. 178.

1343 *V. Ungern-Sternberg*, 2008, pp. 178–179.

This means that the extent of a school to impose religious requirement on a teacher, which is discriminatory in nature, may result in different outcomes depending on the type of school concerned.

In principle, the employment of teachers in non-faith schools will be governed by the Equality Act 2010, which protects all workers in the public sector against direct and indirect discrimination. Further, a religious employment requirement will have to comply with the 'genuine occupational qualifications' exception.

Nonetheless, the genuine occupational requirements will not apply with respect to teachers in non-faith schools. The applicable relevant law in such a case will be the provision of the Equality Act 2010, which protects against most forms of discrimination.

A salient case in this regard which can demonstrate discrimination against a teacher employed in a non-faith school can be seen in the *Azmi v Kirklees Metropolitan Council.*[1344] The claim was brought by an assisting teacher who was dismissed from a non-faith school due to her wearing of a religious dress (*niqab*) and was finally declined before the employment tribunal. The teacher claimed for indirect religious discrimination on ground of the demand of school authorities to remove her religious dress which covered her face during lessons. The Court reasoned the decision determining that the request of school authorities to remove the veil was proportionate and served a legitimate aim, as it fostered better communication between pupils and the teacher. This was of considerable significance, especially since the teacher had to communicate with immigrant pupils who had to improve the English language. Thence, offering the pupils the best possible education was regarded as an aim justifying the potential discrimination.

The legal position regulating employment, admission, or dismissal of teachers in faith schools will be subject to the set of rules contained in the SSFA. Nonetheless, even within the faith schools category the SSFA permits voluntary aided schools an extensive scope of freedom to discriminate on religious grounds.[1345]

As demonstrated earlier, if a teacher refused employment, was dismissed, or deprived promotion by reason based on religion or belief in schools where the state acts as an employer, then the ample exception that exists with respect to

---

1344 Azmi v Kirklees Metropolitan Council, (2007) ET, Case no. 1801450/06 (Eng.), (.), (2007).

1345 *Vickers*, in Hunter-Henin, Law, Religious Freedoms and Education in Europe, 2011, 87, 91.

schools which carry a religious ethos would not be applicable. As a result, any discriminatory occupational religious requirement imposed on teaching staff in such a school would be significantly restricted according to the protection provided under the Equality Act 2010.

The protection provided for teachers under the Equality Act 2010 is much more extensive than the protection offered under the SSFA. A discriminatory occupational requirement imposed on teachers will only be justified if the requirement is genuine and a defining element of the job. Additionally, it needs to be proportionate and serve a legitimate aim.

These elements are not necessary to proof under the SSFA. Therefore, the scope of protection offered for teachers under the SSFA is more retrenched in comparison to the protection under the Equality Act 2010.

The duty of the state to promote social cohesion – as long as the state is funding schools, then it lies within the state's responsibility, irrespective of whether the employer is the local authorities or school governors to accept wider exceptions for the non-discrimination principle. The Education and Inspections Act 2006 imposes a duty on state school governors in England to promote social cohesion in their running of schools.[1346]

In a sense, this requirement contradicts itself since the freedom of state schools to discriminate teaching staff on religious grounds cannot coincide with the obligation to promote community cohesion.

Since the term 'religion and belief' is not clearly defined in the Equality Act 2010, then schools may be unclear about the scope of the new duty and become uncertain as to the question of how far they should accommodate any religious request, whether of individuals or of religious groups.

Since most of the schools in England are maintained schools which are state-funded either through the LEAs or school governors, this implies a special status because the state acts as a monopoly employer.

Considering the fact that the state acts as a monopoly employer, there are a few facts to be taken into account when arguing against endorsement of wider exceptions to the non-discrimination principle. This emanates from the considerable significance given to education – and schools in particular – in their duty of reshaping society, which makes it distinguishable to other employment sectors. Along with the proportionality test, following facts need to be taken into account:

1346 Education and Inspections Act 2006, Sec. 38.

First, since the vast majority of state schools in England carry a religious character, this will often have a negative effect on teaching applicants and their career aspects, as they will be confined to work within this sector even to the extent that their right to religious freedom would be restricted. Consequently, their employment opportunities will be significantly reduced if they are to be excluded from a large part of the education sector on grounds related to religion.[1347]

Secondly, as long as the state adheres to the neutrality principle respective employment in the public sector, it will foster equal participation from various religious groups. Such imposition of equal employment rights will, in turn, mirror the varied social groups who encompass society. This will signalize to the citizens that all are equal and valued and encourage community cohesion by fostering access to employment and integration among the different religious groups in a society.[1348]

Thirdly, religious discrimination is of special significance in the public sector, as employment requirement would be considered as endorsement of religion by the state. The endorsement of a specific religion into schools is regarded as contradicting the notion of equality in access to employment. In addition, in the absence of equal participation of various religious groups in state schools the legislative duty incumbent on schools to promote community cohesion would be nullified.[1349]

d) Relationship of Educational System and Religion in the Jurisprudence

The intention of the British parliament for incorporation of the Convention rights into domestic law was that it would no longer be the state but rather the individual who becomes the centre of the framework of the HRA. This notion was to be achieved through direct application of citizens before British courts, who on their part will give further effect to the rights enshrined in the ECHR. The HRA even determines further that when British courts come to evaluate or

---

1347 *Vickers,* 4 Religion and Human Rights, 2009, 137, 139; *Vickers*, in Hunter-Henin, Law, Religious Freedoms and Education in Europe, 2011, 87, 95.

1348 *Vickers*, in Hunter-Henin, Law, Religious Freedoms and Education in Europe, 2011, 87, 95.

1349 *Vickers*, in Hunter-Henin, Law, Religious Freedoms and Education in Europe, 2011, 87, 95, 96.

decide on a matter or any question that arises in connection with the Convention, they must take into account the jurisprudence of the ECtHR in this respect.[1350]

Thence, the British judicator acknowledged according to Art. 9 para 1 ECHR many religious symbols or garments as manifestation of religious belief that is included within its scope of protection. This is true also with respect to stricter forms of religious symbols like the *shalwar kameeze* or the *jilbab* that were not negated by virtue of their religiosity when worn by female Muslim pupils. The British judicator does not capture its task to inquire whether a claimant's belief conforms with the majority professing the same religion. The reason is that a religious belief may vary from individual to another. The courts will ensure only that the asserted religious belief is made in good faith and that the claim to hold on one's own religious belief is the individual's honest subjective belief and not one that will be measured according to objective standards. The British judicator acknowledges the right of Muslim female pupil to wear headscarves and even admits its protection under Art. 9 para 1 ECHR. Thus, for instance, in the famous case of the pupil Shabina Begum, the HL accepted the *jilbab* as a religious symbol which is encompassed within the protection of Art. 9 para 1 ECHR. The court did not investigate whether the *jilbab*, a stricter form of clothing that covers the whole body conforms with the belief of the majority of practicing Muslims. However, the HL refused to acknowledge that there was an infringement in the pupils right to religious freedom since she had an alternative, moving to a nearby school which allowed the wearing of the *jilbab*. In addition, the incorporation of the HRA into domestic law affected individuals, especially, pupils since it enabled submission of a claim on grounds of religion. As a result making it possible for other religious minorities (e.g., Muslim pupils) who would find it difficult to establish an anti-discrimination claim based on the former legislation to invoke their right to profess their religion pursuant to Art. 9 para 1 ECHR. Previously, the right to wear special religious clothing or head coverings was recognised under the Race Relations Act 1976 but only with respect to specific racial or ethnic groups.

Consequently, due to the significance the case acquired in the British jurisprudence, it would be impossible to overlook the importance this judgement had on the interpretation of Art. 9 of the ECHR. This is true in particular with respect to religious apparel of pupils and their ability to challenge directly before

1350 Human Rights Act 1988, Sec. 2 para 1 declares: "taking into account any judgement, decision, declaration or advisory opinion of the European Court of Human Rights". In other words, violations of the ECHR can be remedied in UK Courts.

British courts based on Art. 9 para 1 ECHR as their legal base was much more retrenched in comparison to teachers. Teachers were still able to support a claim based on employment or anti-discrimination laws (e.g., the former Religion or Belief Regulations 2003 or the Euquality Act 2006).

The right of civil servants to wear head coverings like the turban of Sikhs or headscarf of Muslim women was recognised in the jurisprudence. This right to religious manifestation by outer appearance will be allowed even with respect to functions where the state is presumed to appear unbiased, as, for instance, in the justice system and police force. The reason is that the public service does not prescribe a general duty to state neutrality. As a result, teachers are able within their duty to wear religious symbols and it can be recognised as their legal right to religious practice of their faith. The legal right of teachers to religious manifetstaion can be acknowledged either according to the HRA or anti-discriminations laws, namely, the Equality Act 2010 which practically offers teachers a better protection than the one offered under Art. 9 para 1 ECHR.

It should be noted that due to the rather liberal-secular approach of the state and since religious themes are within the compatibility of the local authorities and depend on the types of faith schools involved, there were no cases discussing the admissibility of religious symbols like the cross when presented in state-maintained schools.

The following case law will attempt to assess whether the legislative framework in England offers public schoolteachers an adequate legal protection to profess their religion within fulfilling their function as public office holders.

The case involved a school teaching assistant who insisted on wearing the *niqab* (a face-covering garment) while on duty. She applied before the Employment Tribunal (ET) and subsequently appealed to the Employment Appeal Tribunal (EAT) on grounds of religious discrimination. The claimant did not succeed and her case was dismissed in both instances.[1351]

aa) Factual Background Aishah Azmi

In this case, a teaching assistant informed her school authorities that for religious reasons she could not teach without using a veil that completely covers her face.[1352]

1351 *Aishah Azmi v Headfield School and Kirklees Metropolitan Council* (2006)

1352 Azmi v Kirklees Metropolitan Council, (2007) ET, Case no. 1801450/06 (Eng.), (.),(2007).

The local authorities denied her request on the ground that it will impinge her teaching performance, as such a face cover would hinder the communication between the pupils and the teacher because the pupils could not look into the teacher's eyes.[1353] The motivation of the teaching assistant to wear a face-veiling garment appeared dubious and was heavily questioned, especially due to the fact that she intentionally refrained from wearing the veil when she had attended her job interview.

As a result, the teaching assistant decided to hand a claim against the school authorities on grounds of religious discrimination in the work place.[1354] She applied several complaints: first, direct discrimination (compared to a Muslim teacher who would be allowed to appear with head covering) and, second, indirect discrimination (school authorities intended to target the veil). Third, her suspension and the following dismissal amounted to harassment and victimization which run counter to the precept prescribed in the Employment Equality (Religion and Belief) Regulations 2003.

bb) Leading Legal Aspects Aishah Azmi

The Employment Tribunal decided to reject her claim based on the following:

No direct or indirect discrimination – no direct discrimination was established on part of the teacher as she could not prove that she was treated less favourably than other non-Muslim teachers.[1355]

Further, the assisting teacher could not base an indirect discrimination claim, as it was not established that the practice of school authorities placed her at a distinguishable disadvantage in comparison to others.

In order for such a practice to be regarded as illegal it needs to comply with the proportionality test.

Proportionality – the Tribunal determined that the actions of school authorities constitute a proportionate mean for achieving a legitimate aim. It was proved that the prohibition on the assisting teacher not to appear with a face cover was sufficiently proportional, as it served a highly public interest supporting uniform rules in public schools for the purpose of a better learning environment.[1356]

1353 Azmi v Kirklees Metropolitan Council, (2007) ET, Case no. 1801450/06 (Eng.), para 17.

1354 Azmi v Kirklees Metropolitan Council, (2007) ET, Case no. 1801450/06 (Eng.),.) para. 25.

1355 Azmi v Kirklees Metropolitan Council, (2007) ET, Case no. 1801450/06 (Eng.).

1356 Azmi v Kirklees Metropolitan Council, (2007) ET, Case no. 1801450/06 (Eng.) para. 45.

The case was also withdrawn by the Employment Appeal Tribunal on similar grounds to those delivered by the lower instance.

It was therefore reaffirmed that no direct religious discrimination had occurred since non-Muslim women would have been treated in the same way according to school practice and would have found themselves in an identical situation regardless of their religious convictions.[1357] So, in fact, the claimant could not prove that the school's uniform rules had worked to her detriment in comparison to teachers of others faiths nor had they intended to single out Muslim practices.

Likewise, it was determined by the Appeal Tribunal that the school did not even indirectly discriminated against the assisting teacher, as the practice according to the uniform rules was proportional to the public interest it meant to serve, that is, providing the children with a good learning environment.[1358]

To sum up, *Azmi*'s case demonstrates incontestably the English outlook on the nexus perceived between public officials and the citizens in the context of their duty to abide by the neutrality principle. The school board was able to provide evidence that dismissal of the assistant teacher did not occur light-heartedly, but following careful deliberations and observations of her work with pupils. It was only after concluding that the *niqab*, as a face-covering garment, hinders her communication with pupils and affects her teaching performance that an initial decision ordering its removal was issued by the school.

In this context, *Azmi*'s case illustrates that emphasis was placed on professional aptitude of the claimant due to the face covering rather than on the religious meaning of the *niqab*.[1359]

e) Conclusion – England

aa) The State-Church Relation and Its Impact on the Educational System

The conceptual church-state model that exists in England reveals the impact and extent of religious influences on the state. Especially, in the context of education the formation of faith schools was headed by two main entities: the Anglican and Catholic Church. The historical importance of the Anglican as well as the Catholic Church can be upheld with respect to establishment of

1357 Azmi v Kirklees Metropolitan Council, (2007) ET, Case no. 1801450/06 (Eng.), para 56.

1358 *Garcia*, BYU L. Rev. 2008, 877, 893.

1359 *Van Ooijen*, p. 249.

primary and secondary schools and the availability of basic education also to weaker parts of the society. At the beginning of the nineteenth century, the state began to provide grants to elementary schools and as such even faith schools were practically maintained by the state. The influence of religious organizations on school admission, curriculum, and appointment of teaching staff will depend on the way they choose to fund their costs. As a result, two types of faith schools were developed: voluntary aided schools and voluntary controlled schools.

This model, however, recognizing the formal position of the Protestant Church as the only powerful faith within the monarch had changed. Social changes incurred due to massive immigration waves, loss of power of the Anglican Church, and the tolerant-accommodative policy administered by the British government during the 1950s and 1960s towards its religious minorities enabled within time adequate space also for other religious communities to flourish.

In the long tradition of England and Wales, religious education and collective worship have been regarded as a central, legitimate element within the curricula of state-supported schools.

The prevailing notion in England and Wales up to 1944 perceived that the nature and content of the curriculum should comply with the Christian character of the state. However, since 1944 the British society has encountered upheaval which was led by the teaching profession in state schools calling to amend the 1944 Act due to its lack of reference to rights of other faiths to participate in religious education and collective prayers and thus being out of date.

The fact that the British society was undergoing a significant social change – from a homogenous society to a distinctive multi-faith society – had strengthened the notion among state schools during the 1970s that an alteration with respect to the 1944 Act needs to take place in order to accommodate the shift in the nature of the British population.

This positioning of the state schools took place due to a realization that the aim of the 1944 Act, namely, supporting Christian orientation in schools not only did no longer exist but also failed to adapt to the situation of modern times by not comprehending the changes which occurred in British society. Hence, schools acknowledged and anticipated the need to facilitate amendments to the 1944 Act.

This call for a change brought about an education reform which was largely debated and criticized in the British parliament, mostly by conservative Christian traditionalists who were troubled by the trends towards multi-faith approaches to religious education and secularization of collective worship. The criticism raised the concern that the multi-faith approach did not reflect the view that Christianity still remained the predominant faith underpinning British society.

Eventually, the Education Reform Act 1988 was introduced, seeking to establish a compromise while naturally reflecting an element of centrality for Christian education; at the same time it recognized and respected the needs of non-Christian faiths. The notion behind the education reform represents a compromise which reflects, to a large extent, the multi-faith approach towards curricula and educational syllabuses adopted for non-denominational schools. Proponents of the multi-faith approach and its intertwining into school curricula regarded these steps as inevitable in non-denominational schools, especially due to the change in the social-cultural structure of British society.

The current applicable provisions are to be found in the School Standards and Framework Act 1998 and the Equality Act 2010, which replaced the former provisions of the Education Reform Act 1988.

It is due to the fact that Britain has transferred from a homogenous to a multicultural pluralistic society that the gap between the different religious groups and their demand for accommodation of their religious needs is becoming more difficult to overcome.

A compromise endeavouring to satisfy the religious demands of all cults, faiths, and denominations in England and Wales is unlikely to be achieved, mainly because these aspects are governed on the regional level and conflicts arising due to religious divisiveness are inevitable and may spring very often in the educational sphere. Therefore, it remains unlikely that a consolidation of a uniform approach with respect to religious education and collective prayers in non-denominational schools would take place.

There exists, however, a strong pressure for the increase in establishment of faiths schools representing other prominent religions; this pressure was strikingly responded to positively by government policy. Nonetheless, a worrisome probable outcome that may yield from such demand would urge the increase of denominational schools and inevitably lead to greater disparities and tension between different religious and cultural groups in British society.

bb) Origin of Rights and the Guarantee of Religious Freedom

The constitutional framework in England prescribes that due to a lack of written constitution there exists no legal document that regulates state power and that sets the fundaments for its state-church relations.

In addition, the fact that England had never adopted a written catalogue that guarantees fundamental liberties and rights or equivalently an adequate bill of rights contributes to the ease with which the state may encroach upon internationally recognized fundamental human rights, such as the right to religious freedom. The risk of infringement upon individuals' fundamental rights is even fortified when taking into consideration the rule of parliament supremacy. In fact, it is rather surprising that for a country characterised by a policy of multiculturalism, the right to religious freedom was never recognized in the legal history of England as a positive right. In fact, religious rights of ethnic minorities had been ensured through different legislation on grounds of race or ethnicity. The right had been acknowledged for a long time as a negative right and took a turn only towards the end of the twentieth century, with promulgation of the HRA 1998.

The commitment of England to respect and abide by international fundamental human rights treaties to which it is a signatory had made England more accountable on the international level to state's encroachment on minorities religious rights than one would have assumed on the domestic level. Albeit the fact that England was the first country to ratify the ECHR, it has never become a part of the domestic law. The inclusion of the protection offered in the ECHR to fundamental human rights and liberties, inter alia, the right to freedom of religion, conscience, and belief and their guarantee took form only at a later stage through its incorporation into domestic law in the HRA 1998.

These facts, conjoined with the rule of parliament supremacy which enables the British parliament to disregard any law, treaty, or convention which did not become an Act of Parliament circumvents prima facie, any possibility to legally challenge British parliament at court even to the extent that fundamental rights or constitutional values are safeguarded in them.

All these factors indicate that the British tradition, as far as recognition and protection of fundamental rights such as the right to religious freedom is concerned, constituted a system that had been more tolerance-based than rights-based. It had also been demonstrated that in earlier times, until the abolition of the Race Relations Act 1976, cases involving claims of minorities against the state to accommodate their religious needs focused primarily on questions of ethnicity and race as recognizedprotected grounds against discrimination. However, religious discrimination was not recognised nor encompassed by this legislation.[1360]

1360 As for instance in *Mandla and another v Dowell Lee* (1983) 2 AC 548; (1983) 1 All ER 1062.

Thence, the infraction on the fundamental right of individuals to religious freedom and possible limitations that may be imposed on its scope of protection are more likely to be subject to judicial scrutiny due to the existing, special constitutional framework.

cc) Religious Symbols Worn by a Teacher

Since there is no uniformity and clear definition of the public sphere and the denotation of specific obligations incumbent upon different officials in the public sphere in England, it is very difficult to conclude a general guiding concept applicable to all duty holders in the public sphere.

In England, there is no explicit limitation on public officials to appear with religious symbols while acting within their public capacity. In fact, there exists no distinction between the public and the private sector according to the rule of employment law. The public and personal capacity of a public official will not be regarded as two spheres which need to be separated from each other. An overview of the case laws that were challenged before English courts demonstrates that, in practice, the visibility of religious symbols will not be regarded in general as incompatible with the neutrality of the state but will be examined on a case-by-case basis. Consequently, there is neither an all-inclusive prohibition on public officials to refrain from appearance with religious symbols during fulfilment of their public capacity nor will it be regarded from the legal perspective as contradicting the duty of the state to abide by the neutrality principle.

Salient characteristics in the British jurisprudence and in the legal debate concerning the permissibility of public servants, such as state schoolteachers, to manifest their religious adherence by wearing ostentatious religious garb or insignia while on duty concentrated less on their obligation to remain neutral and impartial as state representatives but rather highlighted the importance of professional capacity and the equality of education offered to pupils. In case the effective communication with a teacher is impinged due to her religious apparel, then it will constitute a justified ground for infringement of her right to religious freedom.

In practice, there are hardly case laws brought by schoolteachers against school authorities by reason of visibility of religious insignias and the prohibition of their overt manifestation while on duty. In the English jurisprudence, the perception with respect to admissibility of teachers as public officials to appear with religious symbols did not call into question their ability to remain neutral. National controversies surrounding the permissibility of a teacher to appear with face veiling did not include the headscarf but rather the *niqab*, a less revealing garment which is associated with religious extremism and political radicalism. In the case of *Azmi*, the school underscored as a ground for justification that the wearing of a face covering, a *niqab*, by a schoolteacher hinders or impedes the interpersonal communication with pupils, as they could not understand her properly. This paramount factor had been upheld by all jurisprudential instances and served as a sufficient ground for encroachment on her right to religious manifestation. It was explained that in particular the position of a teacher necessitates effective communication with the pupils. In addition, British law takes into consideration the aspect of voluntariness in employment as a sufficient ground for infringement on a teacher's right to exert her religious freedom. Although teachers are not regarded as civil servants under English public law – and in that sense in contrast to the legal situation in France and Germany are not under a special duty to appear and act neutrally as state representatives – the approach held by the British jurisprudence was that a teacher choses her profession voluntarily and normally enters a contractual relationship with school authorities accepting school regulations. Further, the aspect of alternative schooling for a teacher will be taken into consideration, as school regulations apply also with respect to permissible dress code in school premises, and the knowledge of the teacher and her acceptance substantiated the defence of the school authorities that in case the teacher was not satisfied with the terms she could opt for an alternative school, as was pronounced in the case of Azmi.

In the English discourse, the perception with respect to admissibility of teachers as public officials to appear with religious symbols did not call into question their ability to remain neutral.

Taking into account the only case brought so far before English courts with respect to visibility of religious symbols by a public schoolteacher, it can be concluded that, first, in the British jurisprudence the ban on the wearing of religious symbols – whether by teachers or pupils – would not be necessarily classified as a breach of an individual's fundamental right to manifest his/her religion pursuant to Art. 9 ECHR. The common practice of LEAs or school governors in England is known to be very liberal and accommodative as far as the display of religious symbols by its religious minorities was concerned. However, if school authorities imposed on a teacher a prohibition to refrain from appearance with religious clothing to school they may be successful if it will be established that the teachers' religious garment hindered her performance and that other convenient alternatives to practice her religion were still available to her. Second, so far the permissibility to display a headscarf – whether by teachers or pupils – has not been called into question. Instead, the Islamic veiling which was challenged before British courts was more restrictive and less revealing in form than the ordinary headscarf. The *niqab* worn by a Muslim teacher in the case of Azmi was argued to be justified not by reason that the view of the teacher may influence the pupils or their right to religious freedom negatively. Actually, in both instances, where the complainant lodged her claim, it was the educational performance of the pupils and their provision with a good learning environment which were underscored by the British judicators to play a significant role in justifying the restriction on the fundamental right of the teacher to wear the *niqab* during school lessons. Third, the likelihood of success based on grounds of the claim plays a significant role when British courts were addressed with the ban on religious apparel in public schools. The special legislative framework in England enables an individual to substantiate a claim based on two different legal heads. It can be founded either on the fundamental human right to religious freedom as recognized in Art. 9 ECHR, or as a religious discrimination claim pursuant to anti-discrimination/ equality laws. Legal practice had demonstrated that insofar an individual wish to invoke his/her right to religious freedom based on an interference incurred by the state prohibiting his/her religious manifestation, the claim is likely to be more successful if it supported itself based on anti-discrimination laws rather than on fundamental human rights.

The reason for this prevalence can be explained as follows: first, Art. 9 ECHR does not impose a duty on public authorities to impose/consider the proportionality test when carrying out their actions. The 2010 Act imposes an active and positive duty on public authorities to refrain from any discriminatory act; as a result, the threshold of the proportionality test would be much higher than the one imposed by a fundamental human rights claim. Second, a teacher banned from display of religious garment while on duty is more likely to fall within the confines of Art. 9 para 2 ECHR as opposed to possible justifications for restrictions alluded to her/him based on the equality acts. The right of a state schoolteacher to manifest outwardly his/her religion in public schools lacks sufficient protection in the existing legislative framework. This is demonstrated in British case laws, as the ban on a teacher to manifest his/her religion by appearance with a religious symbol would not necessarily be regarded as violation of his/her fundamental human rights. Moreover, this fact by itself is indicative of a lack of compliance with the EU Anti-Discrimination Directives prohibiting discrimination in employment on religious grounds.

The fact that state schoolteachers may be discriminated on religious grounds will only contribute to further alienation albeit the fact that the Education and Inspections Act 2006 imposes a duty on state schools in England to promote social cohesion within their realm.

Essentially, despite the clear provisions of the HRA the Court encountered difficulties in deciding how to enforce this right and, consequently, contributed more uncertainty with respect to the controversy relating to the permissibility to display religious symbols in the education. This was contended in the legal literature to constitute a reasonable explanation for why cases involving manifestation of religious symbols by public schoolteachers, brought under Art. 9 of the ECHR, were less successful than those brought under anti-discrimination laws.[1361]

It is due to supremacy of jurisdiction of the ECtHR that the major impulses for jurisdictional developments, especially in the context of religious symbols and their display by teaching staff did not come from the HL but in fact from the ECtHR.

To conclude, the interaction of the protection against religious discrimination and the right to religious freedom may give rise to some tensions and conflicts and generate difficulties in the state school system. Such a conflict can arise when the religious rights of individuals working as teachers in state schools and manifesting their religion would collide with the right of others (i.e., pupils, parents, or other teaching staff) who do not pertain to this religious group and prefer to keep away from school premises any religious influence they take to be negative or harmful. For instance, taking the fundamental human right approach, the right to manifest a religion or belief is not absolute, and as a result it may be restricted and be justified in case such manifestation interferes with other legitimate aims prescribed in Art. 9 para 2 ECHR and the measure is proportionate to the aim sought to be achieved.

Taking the anti-discrimination aspect, the 2010 Act applies equally to believers as well as to non-believers (atheists). Accordingly, any protection given to a specific religious group in a workplace has the potential to infringe on religious rights of other groups or the interests of those who share no religion or faith and wish to have confessional neutrality in public education. The extensive duty to protection of equality in the public sector enfolds the field of education and applies to different grounds, including religion. As a result, a justification of infringement on a teacher's right to manifestation of religious affinity by virtue of her religious apparel may not be easy to justify on the part of school authorities.

The contention in the legal literature is that the state, in particular in the public sector, owes a special duty to abide by: first, the neutrality principle by refrainment from demonstration of any favouritism towards a specific religion as it may

---

1361 *Howard*, Religion and Human Rights 6 (2011), p. 127, 144; *Van Ooijen*, p. 212.

be liable for religious discrimination. This entails that the state should provide equal representation of all religious communities in employment and admission to the public service, for it will thus promote the integration of religious minorities into society as well as encourage social cohesion, which will truly mirror the cultural-religious diversity of the society.[1362] Second, the equality principle in order to enable public officials in general and teaching staff in particular free access to public sector employment. Since the majority of maintained schools in England is of a Christian nature and due to the reminiscent power which the Anglican Church still holds in education, permitting faith schools to discriminate teachers of other faiths in admission requirements on religious grounds has the potential effect of circumventing to a large extent enhanced employment prospects of religious minorities.[1363]

In this respect, as far as the ability of school authorities goes to impose restrictions on teaching staff to comply with religious requirements, the expansion of denominational schools will be confined having due regard to the extensive equality duty imposed by the 2010 Equality Act.

dd) Religious Symbols Worn by Pupils

The endorsement of religious insignias by pupils into state school has proved that the British approach is much more accepting and accommodative to the special religious needs of its minority pupils. Although England adopts uniform dress code for its pupils, it will accept wearing of special garments in addition to school uniform and will not regard it as a violation of school regulations (e.g., the acceptance of turban for Sikh boys, the Islamic headscarf had not been perceived as problematic so far, and the *shalwar kameeze* worn also by adherents of Islam).

In the *Begum* case, the HL reasoned its decision to dismiss the applicant's claim as it was satisfied with the school's handling and approach. It was demonstrated that the school authorities acted with respect and sensitivity to ensure that the religious needs of minority pupils are met. They showed flexibility by allowing female Muslim pupils to wear the headscarves; however, wearing a *jilbab* did not accord with the school's uniform dress code – the pupil knew it and accepted the conditions prior to her registration to school. Similarly, as in the case of teachers, the fact that a pupil has an alternative, namely to register to another nearby school where uniform regulations are more lenient, will serve as a sufficient ground to repudiate the claim of infringement on the pupil's right

1362 *Vickers*, 4 Religion and Human Rights, 2009, 137, 138.
1363 *Vickers*, 4 Religion and Human Rights 2009, 137, 138; *van Ooijen*, p. 250.

to religious freedom. It can be summed up that, in general, wearing religious symbols by pupils in public education would not be quite restrictive and the jurisprudential dogma delivered so far has been careful of keeping in line with its non-interventionist approach.

4. France

The conceptual church-state model in France is of total separation. In that sense, France maintains remote relations to churchly affairs and thus adopts a position of strict separation that places its governmental policy – in contrast to the other states compared in this analysis – at the other end of the spectrum.[1364]

The distant relations of the state to churchly ecclesiastic influence can be explained against the background of the historical upheaval France had undergone in its attempt to disempower the church from state affairs. An overview of the historical retrospect will demonstrate the efforts taken by the French nation to reduce the power of the Catholic Church in the course of centuries. Prior to the French Revolution, the state and the church had known bitter conflicts and struggles over the church's role and involvement in state affairs.[1365] The revolution prompted to bring to an end the privileges, including legal arrangements granted to the Catholic Church during past centuries (*ancien régime*).[1366]

Eventually, since the notion of Enlightenment was more radical in France than in other European states, it accomplished to thrust aside from the public domain any religious influence by the end of the nineteenth century.[1367] The outcome of this development is the retrenched position religion had acquired in the public sphere that, in turn, put in focus the conveyance of its Republican values.

The sacrosanct allegiance among French people to the novel notion of Republicanism required immigrants to adhere to these republican ideals and assimilate into French culture. Therefore, the French approach had been much characterised by its demand from its religious minorities to adapt to the rules and integrate into the French society and were less forgiving or accommodative to the religious needs of those minorities. For instance, the right of religious

1364 As Fetzer and Soper proclaimed: 'Even in the largely "post-Christian"Christian Western Europe, France stands out in the extent to which it has become throroughly secularized'. Fetzer/Soper, p. 77

1365 *Van Ooijen*, p. 172;

1366 *McGoldrick*, p. 34; *Baubérot* in Lindholm/Cole Durham Jr./Tahzib –Lie, p. 442; *Fetzer/Soper*, p. 77.

1367 *Van Ooijen*, p. 173; *McGoldrick*, p. 35.

minorities not to attend school during religious holidays would be admitted as long as the general duty of attendance and the guarantee of public order are preserved.[1368]

There are several religious groups present in France today, whereas Muslims have developed into the second most widely practiced religion. The reason for which the 'Islamic question' attracted fierce criticism, not only in France but also in other European and non-European countries, is related to the strong Islamic presence of this community (in France it is considered the second largest religious group and by that amounts to the largest Muslim population living in Europe),[1369] the unwillingness of its majority to assimilate in the integrating countries, and the association with religious fundamentalism and resulted in sincere concerns about loss of national identity and culture of the French nation. The large immigration of North-Africans to France had only intensified this fear among French people as it was not a marginal group to be ignored.

The reluctance of Muslim immigrants to assimilate into French society and accept the republican ideals may be explained by several factors:

First, *combat against past colonialism* – the contention in legal literature is that Franco-Arab women had been making use of their religious practice in order to show solidarity with their community against French people. It was explained that the need to demonstrate adherence to Islamic custom was set forth by wearing headscarves and other practices expressing religious manifestation as a means of fighting back against what was recognized by them as the 'imperial culture'.[1370]

Second, *segregation* – the ideal notion of French Republicanism gives strong preference to assimilation and integration as opposed to liberal multi-culturalism. Especially with respect to its immigrants, who to a large part come from Muslim countries, this leads to a difficult situation due to their reluctance to separate from their religious identity and cultural values and tradition that cannot be aligned with Christian-Western morals and concepts of citizenship and national identity enshrined in France's history. In the absence of adaption to French society and the constitutional order of the Republic on part of Muslim communities, they were encouraged to social closure, tightening

1368 *Poggeschi*, European Yearbook of Minority Issues, Vol. 3, 2003–2004, 263, 268.

1369 *Fetzer/Soper*, p. 65; *Britton*, 34 Boston College Int'l and Comp. L. Rev. 2011, 117.

1370 *Hamdan*, Muslim World Journal of Human Rights, 4 (2) (2007), p. 1,3; *Auslander*, Cultural Dynamics 12 (3) (2000), p. 283, 298; *Achour*, in: Hargreaves/Heffernan, p. 203, 216.

their sense of belonging by underlying their ethnicity and religion as an intangible bond. This resulted in exacerbated feelings of exclusion, alienation, and perception of disadvantaged, oppressed communities.[1371]

Third, *preservation of identity* – wearing religious garments like the veil, *hijab* or *jilbab* by Muslim women suggests not only their unwillingness to assimilate into the society they chose to live in but also of their wish to remain distinct in their culture, tradition, and religious pertinence.

Fourth, *inability to accommodate to Christian-democratic values* – the clash of religious and cultural values underscores the disparity between the Muslim community and the French people. However, these distinctions are not confined merely to the religious aspect but rather, reflect the fear of a loss of the nation's Christian identity. The recent development of the French debate on the secular nature of the state demonstrates clearly that clashes do not occur only due to religious and cultural differences but also as a result of the inability to accord with the norms and values of the state.[1372]In fact, French people seriously consider that the immigration from the Maghreb countries (Arabs of North African origin) are culturally incompatible with the values and norms of a Christian democratic Western state.[1373]

In the face of Islamic expansion and the refusal of the Franco-Arab population to adapt or conform to French cultural norms, it was only a matter of time until French people felt threatened from intrusion of Islam. This sense of a threat increased the need to defend the French nation from Muslim invasion, as this religion was anyway associated with foreign origin and extremism seemed to bring down the foundation of the French nation.

In this respect, President Nicolas Sarkozy sparked a controversy when he took the opportunity to express his distaste for the *burqa*, describing it as unwelcome on French soil and a violation of 'the French Republic's idea of women's dignity.'[1374]

The headscarf as a symbol of religious fundamentalism remains a crucial factor which plays a significant role in the distinctiveness of the veil and its perception by the people as an intolerable insignia, especially when coming to analyse why

1371 *Baker*, 13 Cardozo J.L. & Gender 2007, 341, 346.

1372 *Poggeschi*, European Yearbook of Minority Issues, Vol. 3, 2003/2004, 263, 265.

1373 *Danchin*, Yale G. Int'l. L. 33 (2008) p. 1, 20, 23.

1374 *Kirby*, Sarkozy Stirs French Burka Debate, BBC NEWS (June 22, 2009), http://news.bbc.co.uk/2/hi/europe/8113778.stm; *Britton*, 34 Boston College Int'l and Comp. L. Rev. 2011, 117, 118.

the veil detracted extensive public attention. The veil became the focus of this controversy simply as it is perceived by politicians, scholars, citizens, and even the feminist movements as an emblem of radical Islamist politics.[1375]

The reasons for which the controversy over the Islamic headscarf attracted attention, especially in the context of the French dispute in the educational system are diverse, but they are mainly interlinked with the pre-eminent position that schools hold in public life. State-maintained schools have always been perceived by society to be a sacred space. Since schools serve the entire population, it is clear that the controversies regarding the task public school obtain as an instrument for constructing the nation from the republican perspective on the one hand, may collide and not coincide with the private ideology of the individual, on the other hand.

The purpose of this chapter is, first, to provide an overview of the historical development of the French school system and its relationship to religion, especially in view of the Catholic Church's attempt to gain power over education. This will be followed then by an embodiment of the entrenched republican and secular ideas, which are unique to French history and character, and their impact on the role of schools. In addition, the analysis will underscore the differentiation made in the legal discourse with respect to apparel of teachers with a headscarf or other face veiling as opposed to pupils within the public school system. Due to scarcity of case laws relating to the manifestation of conspicuous religious symbols by teachers, the emphasis throughout the work will be given to teaching staff; however, reference to the legal position of pupils and their legitimacy to freely practice their religion in the context of public education becomes inevitable. In this respect, the nexus made between the Islamic headscarf as an ostentatious religious symbol and the social dissidence and deferment demonstrated by French society, especially with respect to teaching staff, will be examined. The examination will focus on the position of teachers as public servants and the exacerbated development towards their right to religious manifestation taken a historical-political and constitutional perspective.

Finally, a general reference will be made to decisions of the CE and its dominating approach with respect to the headscarf dispute in general and display of ostentatious religious symbols, such as the *niqab* or *burqa* as a more restrictive donning of the Islamic faith in particular. Lastly, a brief observation over other challenges the French Republic encounters given the tension arising between

1375 *Scott*, p. 4.

religion-related issues and the fundamental principles of neutrality and laïcité will be delivered.

a) The Accommodation of Religion in State Schools

Historically, the French monarchy had supported the establishment of a primary education system, which was dominated by the Catholic faith.[1376] The educational system in France is one of a centralized system. The majority of confessional schools are Catholic. Faith schools of other confessions such as Muslims are private schools, which are entitled to receive state financial support.[1377]

In general, the organization of state education is under the responsibility of the state that obtains extensive control over its state school system. In practice, the authority of the government is comprehensive and stretches from determination of schools' curricula to recruitment, qualification, training, and remuneration of teaching staff. Since education is a field controlled by governmental ministries, only certain tasks are delegated to the local level.[1378]

The most common form of schools in the education system of France is the compulsory public schools, which constitutes the majority of schooling and is almost free of charge.[1379]

As mentioned already in the previous chapter,[1380] it was the objective of the French Revolution to eliminate any social and cultural influence the Roman Catholic Church had on the French nation. As a result, France adopted several repressive steps against the Church, its clergy, and its property in order to ensure alienation from state affairs.

These occurrences reflected the wish articulated by the French society and its leadership to depart from any clerical domination over the state and was followed later on by the adoption of the 1795 Constitution. This constitution introduced a partial separation between state and church in the spheres of marriage, health, and education.[1381]

During the nineteenth century, French education was marked by two distinct and segregated educational systems: first, in 1833 a law (*loi Guizot*) established

---

1376 *McGoldrick*, pp. 77–78.

1377 Though Muslim state schools are entitled to financial funding by the state in practice only few of them are afforded with state funding. See *Fetzer/Soper*, p. 85.

1378 *Van Ooijen*, p. 186.

1379 *Van Ooijen*, p. 186.

1380 Chapter II4b).

1381 *McGoldrick*, p. 35.

state primary education, and in 1850 another law (*loi Falloux*) extended it to secondary schools.[1382] However, the Catholic Church provided an alternative for secular schooling.

Second, the secularization of the educational system initiated in the 1880s by the then education minister, Jules Ferry. The notion was embodiment of the laïcité principle in state schools and is dated to what is known as the Third Republic's Ferry laws (1881–82). The Jules Ferry laws[1383] are a set of French laws which established two significant changes in primary education in France. On the first level, the set of Ferry laws passed in 1881 declared free education for boys and girls in primary schools. On the second level, the law of 28 March 1882 introduced these schools as mandatory and endorsed laicist education in them.[1384] It is due to this development of the laicist educational system that religious instruction as a compulsory subject was banished from schools' curricula.[1385] In addition, deferment of priests and nuns from their jobs as teachers took place.[1386] The dual system of state- and church schools that were largely staffed by religious officials was replaced by state schools and lay schoolteachers. The educational reforms enacted by Jules Ferry are often attributed to a broader anti-clerical campaign in France.

The actual situation, however, was that the Catholic Church had still possessed enormous state powers in 1905 by its control of the schools.[1387] This situation changed with the introduction of the 1905 Law. It was the first legislation to set officially a complete separation between state affairs and religion, imprinting the principle of laïcité. This encompassed in literal interpretation the meaning of, first, an obligation of the state to secularism, and second, religious neutrality.

1382 *Van Ooijen*, p. 173; *Saunders* in: *Levey/Modood*, Tariq, Secularism, Religion and Multicultural Citizenship, 2008, p. 61.

1383 Jules Ferry was a French lawyer who held the office of Minister of Public Instruction during the 1980s and is accountable for the creation of the modern Republic school system (l'école républicaine), http://en.wikipedia.org/wiki/Jules_Ferry_laws.

1384 *Wick* in von Campenhausen/Frisch/Heckel ua (eds.), Beiträge zum evangelischen Kirchenrecht und zum Staatskirchenrecht, 2007, 29 (33).

1385 Albeit the intention to secularize education and the ban on religious instructions as prescribed under the Ferry laws, a reservation was integrated for parents who wish to provide their children with religious education. Accordingly, Article L 141–3 enables pupils who attend primary education to be granted, on parental request, a leave one day a week for attendance of religious instruction.

1386 *Wick* in von Campenhausen/Frisch/Heckel ua (eds.), Beiträge zum evangelischen Kirchenrecht und zum Staatskirchenrecht, 2007, 29 (33). *Scott*, pp. 99, 107.

1387 *McGoldrick*, p. 35.

b) The Competency of the State with Respect to Religion in Its Public School System

The gradual efforts to eradicate any churchly influence from the public sphere were accomplished by the end of the nineteenth century. The sphere of education was the first to be affected by religious alienation in its domain.

It was under the regime of the Third Republic that schools were considered the key to disseminating and stabilizing republicanism, to creating France as a unified and indivisible nation ('one and indivisible').[1388]

The reasons for which the educational field stood in the focus of state-church disentanglement can be attributed to the following: Firstly, the significance given to the role and function of schools in our society. Since historically both the church and the state perceived schools as institutions through which they can form the young generation, they became a central battleground for the conflict.[1389] It is also due to the social importance of schools that they served as an ultimate channel for conveyance of republican values, such as individualism, equality, and citizenship.[1390] Teaching staff as well as pupils played an important role in the transferal of the laicist and secular values of the French Republic aiming to achieve national integration.[1391] Therefore, the headscarf ban was perceived necessary in order to prevent a foreign Islamic takeover of French schools and that will attempt to disintegrate the republican ideology.

Secondly, the French constitutional perception under the principle of laïcité regards matters of individual conscience as a private matter which should consequently be free from public interference. Hence, according to this perspective, it is the task of the state to protect this privacy.

c) The Evolvement of Laicist Education in State Schools

The events following the French Revolution (1789) marked a steady transition of the French nation and its institutions towards a laicistic society, endeavouring to disentangle state-church relations in the public sphere and in particular in the educational system.

1388 *Scott*, p. 107.

1389 Rémond, Cahiers d'histoire 3, pp. 71–89; *Auslander*, Cultural Dynamics 12 (3), 2000, 283, 287; *McGoldrick*, p. 77.

1390 *McGoldrick*, pp. 77, 78.

1391 *Von Ooijen*, p. 173.

The period of the nineteenth century was characterised especially by the evolvement of educational laws which aimed towards accomplishing this transfer of educational laws and public school system to a secularized system disempowering churchly powers and influence over education.

aa) Legal Framework

(1) Ferry Laws 1881–1882

The Ferry laws, named after Jules Ferry, the Minister of Education at that period of time, was responsible for fostering promulgation of the law and imparted a momentous event in the history of France following the French Revolution since he established mandatory, free, and secular (*laïque*) education for all French pupils under the age of fifteen.

Jules Ferry introduced in the 1880s several laws implementing the principle of laïcité in education. Conceivably, schools are considered to be institutes through which a nation can form its future generations and convey values and principles that are aligned with its constitutional system. From a French perspective, the aim was to cultivate a common republican identity in children with different backgrounds; France endeavoured to imbue pupils with the quintessence of the republican values since the founding of the Third Republic. Hence, schools were perceived as a tool to distribute and stabilize republicanism in order to foster and maintain French *unicité* (uniqueness) as an indivisible and unified nation.[1392]

The main achievements to be accredited to the establishment of the Ferry laws were marked by an anti-clerical approach designated to disentangle the power of the Catholic Church which prevailed in primary education at that time as it was regarded to be an enemy of the republic. The significance of the law of 28 March 1882 was attained in two aspects: first, the laicization of education through formation of a free secular education system. This was fraught by replacement of a religious staff by lay schoolteachers and the abolishment of religious education in state schools to be substituted by moral and civic instruction. Second, the displacement of the role of school as an instrument for constructing the nation through identical savours such as language, national culture, national identity, and ideology was meant to accomplish national cohesion and indivisibility of the French Republic.[1393]

1392 *Scott*, pp. 99 and 107.

1393 *Scott*, p. 99.

(2) *Goblet Law 1885–1886*

The Goblet law, named after the then presiding minister of education, René Goblet, was meant to endorse the process of laicizing education. As a successor of its former in the ministry of education, the Goblet is considered an integral part in a row of enactments. Goblet law was introduced in 1886 as a follow-up to Ferry's legislative project.[1394] The declaratory aim of the law intended at laicizing teachers in state schools in order to avoid the danger perceived by having religious teachers in laique schools.

(3) *Loi Debré of 31 December 1959*

This law was the initiative of Michel Debré, the then presiding prime minister and interim Minister of National Education. The act was meant to regulate the relations between the state and private schools in France since 31 December 1959. The idea was to regulate the subventions provided to private schools, including private faith schools, out of a state fund established for that purpose.[1395] In 1942, there was a proposal for a general reform in education with the intention of the law to shape further the principle of neutrality in order to enable schools to integrate various levels of laicism with the state.[1396]

(4) *Law no. 2004–228 of 15 March 2004 on the Wearing of Religious Symbols in State Schools*[1397]

(a) Introduction

Though legislative uniformity is not a salient feature of the legal system in France, it was the French idea of the *loi* (general law) that served as a guideline to the adoption of the law of 15 March 2004 on the Islamic headscarf (2004 Law).[1398]

The need for a general law regulating the wearing of religious symbols in the public sector, and especially in the education, has been underlined by many

---

1394 See the website of the French Sénat www.senat.fr/evenement/archives/D42/loi1886.html

1395 *Healey/De Gaulle*, Journal of Church and State 12(2) (1970), p. 213.

1396 *Van Ooijen*, p. 186.

1397 See Law no. 2004–228 of March 15, 2004 (Loi no 2004–228 du 15 mars 2004), J.O. March 17, 2004, p. 5190, J.C.P. 2004, III p. 640. The text is also available at http://www.legifrance.gouv.fr.

1398 *Langenfeld, Mohsen*, 3 International Journal of Constitutional Law, 2005, 86, 93; *Poggeschi*, European Yearbook of Minority Issues, Vol. 3, 2003/2004, 263, 266.

of the parliamentary, judiciary, and social discussions around this topic.[1399] The growing concern was even expressed and emphasized by the report of the Parliamentary Commission (*Commission des lois constitutionnelles, de la législation et de l'administration générale de la République*).[1400]

Further, the necessity to endorse some uniformity has been increasing mainly due to a series of cases brought to French courts during the 1980s and 1990s, incited by a wave of exclusion of Muslim schoolgirls wearing the headscarf from state schools, known as the headscarf affair, *affaire du foulard*. The cases were further intrigued due to the refusal of Muslim pupils to take it off and resulted in disparate outcomes.[1401] This seems to add more vagueness and disconcertment as opposed to clarity with respect to this matter. It was the inability of the judiciary to deliver uniform prescription to school headmasters directing them to prohibit pupils from religious manifestation by wearing religious garments or signs within school premises when encountering similar problems.[1402]

Notably, the Advice issued by the CE in 1989 and the ensued Circular of the same year intended to provide a guideline for school administrators and headmasters, developing criteria that would justify limitations with respect to prohibition of religious symbols in state schools. Though these two documents from 1989 conferred considerable discretion to headmasters, they have been applied in different ways resulting in diverging outcomes.

This has naturally led to a situation where in some schools the Islamic veil was allowed, in others it was prohibited only during break-time, while in others it was strictly prohibited.[1403]

Surprisingly, this legal uncertainty served the judiciary while continuing to deliver inconsequent decisions since they were incapable to set a clear line during this period of time. However, most of the decisions at that time ruled in favour of the appellant.[1404]

1399 It was argued that the protection of French secularism as the essence of French identity served as one of the reasons to ban the *hijab* in the Law of 2004, see in *Hamdan*, Muslim World Journal of Human Rights 4 (2) (2007), p. 1, 8. Citing the following: "It is hard for foreigners to grasp just how strongly the French feel about the separation of church from state. Their stand is: worship as you will, but keep it off public places. The French world of keeping religion at bay is laïcité, which I won't try to translate: secularism is much too tame.".

1400 See at http://www.assemblee-nationale.fr/12/rapports/r1381.asp.

1401 See in III. 4) d).

1402 *Poggeschi*, European Yearbook of Minority Issues, Vol. 3, 2003/2004, 263, 268.

1403 *Poggeschi*, European Yearbook of Minority Issues, Vol. 3, 2003–2004, 263, 268.

1404 *McGoldrick* (2006), p. 71; *Fetzer and Soper* (2005), p. 81.

Eventually, the promulgation of the Law of 2004 was followed by a publication of two different reports (the Stasi report and the Debré report).[1405] They served as a base for its composition since they contained hearings of the most relevant institutions for this topic, such as trade unions, teachers' representatives, the associations and representations of the various religions, as well as individuals.[1406]

(b) Leading Legal Aspects

The law of 15 March 2004 passed by the French government bans pupils from wearing 'conspicuous signs' in public primary and secondary schools that connote their religious affiliation. It is notable that the law regards merely state school pupils and does not relate to teachers, who must conform to similar norms, however, yielding from a different perception (the general duty of public servants to strict neutrality, and former legislation the law laicizing education from 1886).

The regulation, which prohibits the wearing of 'ostentatious religious symbols' in academic institutions funded by the state is included in Art. 1, which is a key provision of the new law. It is revised in Art. 141–51 of the Code of Education and pronounces that:

> In the public elementary schools, in the secondary and high schools, it is forbidden to wear symbols or dresses through which the pupils show in a conspicuous way a religious belonging.[1407]

In order to mitigate the rigidity of the provision, it is provided in its second paragraph that disciplinary procedures to implement this rule will be preceded by a discussion with the student, as set forth:

> The regulations of those institutions must specify that the fulfilment of a procedure of discipline must be preceded by an attempt at a settlement through a dialogue with the pupil.[1408]

1405 The Stasi report, commissioned by the President of the Republic and chaired by Bernard Stasi, published its findings on 11 December 2003, while the other was commissioned by the National Assembly, chaired by President Jean-Louis Debré.

1406 *Poggeschi*, European Yearbook of Minority Issues, Vol. 3, 2003/2004, 263, 269.

1407 Law no. 2004–228 of 15 March 2004, Journal Officiel de la Republique Francaise (J.O.) (Official Gazette of France), March 17, 2004, P. 5190, available at http://www.legifrance.gouv.fr/affichTexte.do?cidTexte=JORFTEXT000000417977&dateTexte=(hereinafter law no. 2004–228).

1408 Law no. 2004–228.

Although the law applied to Jewish boys in skullcaps and Sikh boys in turbans, as well as to anyone with a large cross around his or her neck, it was aimed primarily at Muslim girls wearing headscarves (*hijab* in Arabic; *foulard* in French).[1409]

In fact, the intent behind the inclusion of other religious groups under the law was to prevent accusation of discrimination against Muslims and to comply with a requirement that such laws apply universally.

However, the new law was commonly understood by many commentators and politicians[1410] to have a main purpose which was to eradicate Islamic headscarves from educational institutions and control the spread of Islam.

This new provision favours the practice of supporting an equal, open, tolerant, and integrative dialogue between all involved parties (school institutions, the pupil, and his/her family). Nevertheless, if a settlement had not been achieved and the pupil had refused to remove the veil, then she had to face the obvious disciplinary sanctions that are consequent to the spirit of the law.

Nonetheless, the promulgation of the Law of 2004 which bans pupils in general from wearing or displaying conspicuous signs that form religious, political, or philosophical manifestation raises in the legal literature heavy doubts as to its constitutionality and as to the availability of possible justification grounds for its permissibility.[1411]

(c) Ostentatious Symbols

The ban explicitly differentiates between conspicuous and discrete religious symbols, providing explanation of what will be regarded as 'conspicuous'. The law specifies that:

The clothing and religious signs prohibited are conspicuous signs, such as a large cross, a veil, or a skullcap. Not regarded as signs indicating religious affiliation are discreet signs, which can be, for example, medallions, small crosses, stars of David, hands of Fatima, or small Korans.[1412]

1409 *Wiles*, Law & Soc'y Rev. 41 (2007), p. 699, 701; *Danchin*, Yale J. Int'l L. 33 (2008), p. 1, 2.

1410 For instance, the President at that time, Jacques Chirac, was expressing directly his aversion to the notion of the veil, asserting in 2003 that "wearing a veil is a kind of a Basic Law": *Richburg*, French President Urges Ban on Headscarves in Schools; Chirac Confronts Spread of Islam, Wash. Post, Dec. 18, 2003, at A1; *Barbibay*, Cardozo J. Int'l & Comp. L. 2010, 159, 174.

1411 *Gunn*, BYU L. Rev. (2004), 419, 479.

1412 *Scott*, p. 1.

Following the Law of 2004, the Minister for Education decided to publish in the same year an order defining the following as ostentatious symbols: the Islamic veil, the Jewish Kippa and also the Christian cross of large dimension.[1413]

In fact, the adjective 'ostentatious' was inserted in order to replace the proposal in the draft using the adjective 'visible', as it would have the effect of inclusion of too many symbols. In order to leave no room for speculations, the order quotes specifically what symbols are allowed: small crosses, Fatima's hands, and Stars of David.

(5) The French Ban on Face Covering – Law of 2010 – 1192 (LOI n° 2010–1192)[1414]

In a subsequent follow-up to the Law of 2004 that ordered the prohibition of conspicuous religious symbols worn by pupils, the French government introduced legislation banning the wearing of face veils in public. The act came into force in April 2011 and attracted a lot of criticism mainly due to the fact that the prohibition on the face veil comprised two significant aspects: first, the prohibition does not apply only in public institutions but extended the ban to the public space in general;[1415] second, its wider scope of application was confirmed according to a Ministerial Circular[1416] to be addressed exclusively to citizens.

France was amongst the first European states to initiate legislation that would completely prohibit the face veils in public.[1417] The French confrontation with the donning of face veils by Muslim women can be traced back to an application request brought in 2008 for referral before the CE.[1418] Its decision for rejecting the applicant's request was justified on the basis of its incompatibility with

---

1413 Seeathttp://www.laic.info/Members/webmestre/Droits_et_devoirs..2004-05-24.3305.

1414 LOI n° 2010-1192 du 11 octobre 2010 interdisant la dissimulation du visage dans l'espace public. See in, https://www.legifrance.gouv.fr/affichTexte.do?cidTexte=JORFTEXT000022911670

1415 *Davis*, B.C. Int'l and Comp. L. Rev. 34, 2011, 117, 118; *Van Ooijen*, p. 199.

1416 The Ministerial Circulars was issued in March 2011 prior to the coming into force of the 2011 Act. Circulaire d'application du 2 mars 2011 (JORF no. 0052, 3 March 2011), p. 4128.

1417 *Van Ooijen*, p. 198.

1418 The application was submitted by a Moroccan woman wearing a face veil for recognition of the French nationality. The Council of State rejected the applicant's request on grounds of the face veil's incompatibility with essential republican values, such as gender equality. See CE, 27 June 2008, Madame M., décision no. 286798; *van Ooijen*, p. 198.

paramount pillars of France's Constitution and the republican values, such as gender equality.

Shortly after this incident, the French government had accepted the resolution of a parliamentary report submitted by the Gerin Committee, which was established specifically for investigating the common practice of wearing the face veil by Muslim women. The Gerin Report recommended the prohibition of the face veil to be introduced by parliamentary resolution. The French government adopted accordingly the committee's conclusions and passed in 2011 an act ordering the banning of all forms of face covering in the public space (2011 Act).

However, since the ban addresses its application exclusively to citizens, then its justification on grounds of adherence to the principle of neutrality and laïcité is unlikely to become successful. The reason for its inapplicability lies in the explicit distinction made by French law between public officials and citizens. Thence, the ban on face veils according to the 2011 Act is of minor relevance with respect to state schoolteachers. Since public officials are subject to a different set of rules and are obliged by virtue of their special duty to abide by the laïcité and neutrality principle, it is less expected that they would attempt to wear even extrinsic form of garments such as a face veil.

On the face of it, the enactment constitutes a deviation from France's Republican values and ideology that makes it difficult to find a justification for such a general prohibition even under French constitutionalism.[1419]

Though the 2011 Act appears to carry a strict character which adamantly encroaches upon an individual's right to religious freedom, it was not passed easily by the French government. As already mentioned prior to the promulgation of the act, it received a recommendation from the Gerin Committee that was in favour of a prohibition of the veil.[1420] The Gerin Committee saw it to be necessary – in the absence of an adequate legal basis for a prohibition – that the parliament should adapt an applicable resolution. The French government accepted the Gerin Report and drafted several parliamentary and governmental bills. The last bill on that matter was submitted to the CE, which finally gave

1419 See Gaelle Le Roux, Anti-Veil Law Risks Being Shot Down by Constitutional Council, France 24 (July 8, 2010), http://www.france24.com/en/20100708-anti-veil-law-risks-being-shot-down-france-constitutional-council-burqa-ump-party-government.

1420 The Gerin Committee headed by André Gerin (La mission d'information sur la pratique du port du voile intégral sur le territoire national) was established by the French Parliament in June 2009 to investigate the practice of face veils worn by immigrant females, mostly of Muslim countries. The Gerin Committee published its findings in a report from January 2010.

its requested Advice in March 2010 (hereinafter 2010 Advice) against a general prohibition. Though the CE explicitly condemned the face veil as a religious symbol, which contradicts gender equality, it found no legal justification that would establish a ground for its wide scope of application. In addition, the lack of established ground for the ban could not be justified on the principle of laïcité since its application would only be valid with respect to public officials and could not be imposed also on citizens.[1421]

Finally, the French government managed to overcome the constitutional problem questioning the eligibility of such a general prohibition and, as a result, passed the test of the Cons. Const.[1422] for an affirmation of the respective legislation.

bb) *Religious Symbols in Schools*

France did not insert the obligation of neutrality in a specific codified legislation so as to apply for the public service as a whole. As a result, there have been initiatives to introduce a consolidated act, which were promoted through recommendations published in several governmental reports.[1423] Subsequent

1421 Several approaches are attested with respect to the permissibility of a citizen in contrast to a public official to wear religious symbols. On the one hand, the French approach to the principle of laïcité asserts its application only with respect to public officials since, unlike a citizen, they owe a special duty emanating from their function. They do not act as 'outsiders'„outsiders making use of the public service. Consequently, a citizen is under no obligation to abide by the laïcité principle and is not bound to preserve the proper functioning of the public service or the public order in case he/she decides to wear a religious symbol. On the other hand, citizens appear to form part of the collective that should endeavour to convey an impartial image rooted with strong allegiance to republican ideals and values. *Van Ooijen*, p. 199.

1422 The Constitutional Council did not conclude that an unfair balance of competing rights (public order against constitutional protected rights) may occur as a result of the proposed act. See Conseil Constitutionnel, 7 October 2010, Décision Loi interdisant la dissimulation du visage dance l'espace public, no. 2010–613 DC, to be found on www.conseil-constitutionnel.fr

1423 The two most important reports are: 1. The Rossinot Report 2007, which was concluded for the purpose of application of the principle of laïcité in the public service and which raised two significant aspects: a. the necessity to adopt legislation that will guarantee the principle of laïcité more effectively. b. the need to codify the duty of neutrality incumbent on public officials. 2. The 2007 Recommendations on the Project of a Charter of laïcité in public service (charter recommendations) by the High Council of Integration (Haut Conseil à l'Intégration).

to those recommendations, in 2008, the government submitted a draft bill that recommended public officials to refrain from any manifestation of conspicuous religious garments or symbols. The Bill of 2008 aimed at achieving two significant aspects: first, it affirmed the importance of the laïcité principle with respect to public officials and emphasized their obligation to refrain from the display of any symbol or wearing of a garment which constitutes a manifestation of religion or belief. Second, it demonstrated explicitly the endeavour to prohibit the display of religious or political symbols.

(1) Institutional Religious Symbols

Historically, there was no formal ban on the presence of crucifixes in state classrooms. The laicization process that the public school system had undergone with the introduction of the Ferry laws from 1882 to 1883 aimed at extending further dismantling of any entanglement between compulsory education and religion. Apart from the abolishment of religious education and its replacement with moral instruction (Art. 1 of the 1882 Law) and the removal of Ministers of Religion (Art. 3 of the 1882 Law), the government's objective towards secularization of the French Republic did not officially interdict the presence of crucifixes in public state school.[1424]

In fact, even the introduction of new school programs such as moral education did not pursue a complete elimination of any spiritual level to the extent of the removal of all crucifixes from state classrooms. Crucifixes were to be taken off only if hostilities should take place. If no hostilities took place, crucifixes remained in place. This demonstrates that even within such a strong governmental policy to secularization of the state it was not so rigorously implemented, since a majority of parents' wish that public education would preserve some element of religious nature was responded positively.[1425] So in practice, public schools continued to display crucifixes on classroom walls until the end of 1906.[1426]

It is due to the fact that the 1905 Law prohibited discrimination on grounds of religion and faith that it was possible for the state to eliminate any entanglement between religion and its educational system. As a result, crucifixes were taken down from classrooms.[1427]

1424 *Idriss*, 25 (2) Legal Studies, 2005, 260, 264.

1425 *Idriss*, 25 (2) Legal Studies, 2005, 260, 264.

1426 *Curtis*, Educating the Faithful: Religion, Schooling and Society in Nineteenth Century France, 2000, p. 142.

1427 McGoldrick, p. 37.

(2) *Religious Symbols Worn by Individuals*

In principle, public officials in France are regarded like every other citizen with regard to the entitlement of individual rights and freedoms and cannot be deprived of them by virtue of their duty as public servants.[1428] The view envisaged by legal scholars with respect to the right of public officials to freedom of conscience is considered as preserved to them through the strict application of the neutrality principle. This means that the safeguarding of public officials' freedom of conscience will be regarded effective only insofar as the state, in its duty to remain neutral will foreclose any outward manifestation of religion or belief on part of its civil servants.[1429] This, in turn, would guarantee equal access to admission and employment in the public service, as no affinity to a particular religion would be demonstrated by the state or impart such impression and eventually preserve the right of civil servants to freedom of conscience.

In other words, the duty incumbent on public officials to refrain from any external expression of religion or belief was meant to foster equal access to the public service.[1430] However, within their function, their right to express or exercise freedom of religion collides with the duty of neutrality and, as a result, demands their right to be set aside while preference should be given to the neutrality principle in order to ensure proper functioning of the public service.

It should be noted that due to the uncontested status of the principles of laïcité and state neutrality within the public service no efforts have been made to establish their validity in a codified legislation.

1428 See Loi Le Pors, Chaptire 1, Article 6: "La Liberté d'opinion est garantie aux functionnaires." This implies in principle that the eligibility of public officials to individual rights such as freedom of conscience accords with the principle of citizenship; *Van Ooijen*, p. 181.

1429 *Gunn*, Journal of Church and State, 2004, 1, 7; *Birnbaum*, 30 Cardozo L. Rev. 2008/2009, 2431, 2443.

1430 Art. 6 of the 1789 Declaration which guarantees equal access to public functions as well as its confirmation in the general law on the status of public officials. In reality, since the principle of equal access to public functions is not guaranteed properly there had been a governmental initiative in cooperation with HALDE, a body established to fight all forms of discrimination, (*Haute Autorité de Lutte contre les Discriminations et pour l'Égalité*) to promote equality in the public service. See on the website of the Ministère de la Réforme de l'Etat, de la décentralisation et de la Fonction Publique www.fonction-publique.gouv.fr

(a) Religious Symbols Worn by Teachers

(aa) Scope of Protection

Teachers in primary and secondary schools are compelled to abide by the strict application of state neutrality, which means their duty to appear unbiased and impartial emanating from their special position as public officials.

In fact, the duty incumbent on public officials to religious neutrality applies equally with respect to all public officials in the civil service and, as a result, can provide an explanation as to scarcity of case laws brought by teachers for judicial review. The courts will bestow due regard to the subjective understanding of the teacher with respect to the symbol and whether the motivation for wearing it is religious in nature.

Though the French jurisprudence insinuates indirectly that the display of a headscarf will be regarded as exertion of religion, it still refuses to accept it as falling within its confines and to be worth its protection. This approach is upheld especially with respect to teachers on duty as public servants. So in principle, the display of religious symbols or garments by teachers, though it may be regarded as an individual right to exert or practice one's religion in public, would not fall within the confines of the right to religious freedom. This is mainly due to the strong adherence and allegiance imposed in the public service to the principle of laïcité.

The same obligation prescribed in the Education Code applies with respect to teaching personnel at universities, who are bound as well to comply with the principle of laïcité.[1431]

The most significant provision with respect to the duty of schoolteachers to observe the laïcité principle is laid down in Article 141–5 of the Education Code (*Code de l'Education*).[1432] The rule states that public education, including its teaching personnel, should be laic.

Moreover, the Charter of laïcité in the public service from 13 April 2007 declared the duty of every public official to strictly abide by the neutrality principle. This results in a further demand stating that every public official is

---

1431 The principle of laïcité as prescribed in the Code de l'Education applies also for teaching personnel in higher education. In fact, the Council of State acknowledged the importance of guaranteeing the freedom of expression of teaching staff in universities; *van Ooijen*, p. 186.

1432 Article L 141–5 reads: "Dans les établissements du premier degrè publics, l'enseignement est exclusivement confié à un personnel laÏque.".

under obligation to treat all individuals equally and respect their freedom of conscience.[1433]

(bb) Infringement

The infringement on a teacher's right to appear to school with a religious insignia like a headscarf is presumed immediately without any need to legally substantiate its existence. The reason for that is attributed to the fact that in the constitutional framework of France, there exists no clear apprehension of fundamental human rights and their interpretation; thus, the division of scope of protection, infringement, and grounds for justification are not as clear cut as in other legal systems (e.g., Germany).

(cc) Justification

As possible grounds for justification on the teachers' right to wear symbols or attire that conspicuously exhibit religious affiliation, the following will be considered:

(aaa) The Principle of Neutrality

The principle of neutrality prescribes the duty of state schoolteachers to abstain from any manifestation of religion or belief while exercising their public function.[1434] The religion or belief of a public civil servant alone cannot prevent him/her from submitting employment application for a specific duty, but rather the manifestation of religious freedom is a factor to be taken into account.[1435] This approach with respect to the duty of state schoolteachers to abide by the neutrality principle has been consistent and straightforward both in lower and in high instances.

In the decision of the CE from 1989 it was held that the obligation to adhere by the principle of laïcité obliges not only educational content and curriculum within the public school system to remain neutral but also underscores the duty of teaching staff to their neutral appearance.

In addition, another decision of the CE from 2000[1436] had been composed in order to assist the Administrative Court in Chalons-en-Champagne in deciding whether the dismissal of a teacher assistant wearing a headscarf to school can be justified.

1433 *Van Ooijen*, p. 191; ‚Charte de la laïcité dans les services publics', no. 52009/SG (13 April 2007).

1434 *Van Ooijen*, p. 187.

1435 *Van Ooijen*, p. 187.

1436 CE, Mlle Marteaux (3.5.2000) numéro 217017.

The CE concluded the following: first, public servants, by virtue of their duty in the public service, are obliged to keep their neutrality and impartial appearance and consequently should refrain from any manifestation of religious affinity by display of religious attire. In this context, the fact that a teacher does not perform her educative task or practice her teaching profession would not avail her as long as she acts within the framework of the public service. The CE denies outright public servants' right to freely practice their religion by display of religious symbols as it presumes the immediate infringement of their obligation to appear neutral within their capacity as public officials.

(bbb) The Negative Right of Pupils to Religious Freedom

The obligation of a teacher as a public official to appear neutral and unbiased gains significance, as especially in the public service the close and exposed work of civil servants with the public obliges them to maintain impartiality so as not to raise any claim of discriminatory behaviour by virtue of affinity towards a specific religion or faith disclosed through the outer appearance of a civil servant.[1437] In a case involving the refusal of an external observer in examination to remove the headscarf, the Court in Versailles upheld the protection of the negative right of pupils to religious freedom and the educational right of parents to decide on the religious education of their children.[1438] Thence, the dismissal of the teacher was justified on grounds of the pupils' right not to be subject to the view of a teacher's religious apparel as they are entitled to protection of their negative right to religious freedom as well as the teacher's obligation to self-restraint. The mere possibility that pupils feel infringed in their right to religious freedom or discriminated by view of the teacher's appearance will suffice to justify the setting back of the teacher's right to religious manifestation.

(dd) The Right of a Teacher to Non-Discrimination

Since the demand on teachers as public officials to refrain from any religious affinity by outward manifestation of symbols or garments applies equally to all civil servants and with no segregation relating to religious adherence or non-adherence, then the filing of a complaint of direct discrimination on religious grounds will fail. However, the path of a Muslim teacher to submit a complaint of indirect discrimination established on religious grounds is more likely to have a founded base, as application of specific dress code rules may be detrimental to specific ethnic or religious minorities. This enables a Muslim teacher who had

1437 *Ganz*, 2010, p. 202.

1438 TA Versailles, 14 avril 1992, Mlle Braza.

been suspended by school authorities for wearing a head covering to submit a claim for indirect discrimination on religious grounds in accordance with Art. 6 para 2 of the law from 13 July 1983.[1439] The teacher will have to substantiate the specific dress code rules act to her detriment since she is adherent of a religious minority group, i.e, Islam, thereby indirectly discriminating her as opposed to believers of the Christian faith who may be minimally confined by their right to manifestation of religious symbols.

(b) Religious Symbols Worn by Pupils

Since the display of religious symbols by pupils does not constitute a key element in this analysis, the examination whether a constitutional infringement of a fundamental right to religious freedom has taken place or not will be shortly reviewed, underscoring core elements that will be considered within judicial scrutiny.

(aa) Scope of Protection

In large contrast to the legal position of teachers, the prohibition on pupils is prescribed in legislation, regulating the ban on pupils to display conspicuous garments or insignias that connote their religious affinity.

Similar to the ban on teaching personnel, an equal prohibition precluding pupils from appearance with ostentatious religious symbols was introduced in the law of 15 March 2004.[1440] In the Law of 2004, the ban was introduced with respect to pupils in all compulsory state schools to refrain from manifestation of ostentatious religious symbols insinuating of their religious affinity.

The wearing of religious symbols, in particular the headscarf, falls within the confines of the protection of the right to religious freedom. In addition, the subjective intention of the wearer will be estimated by the courts when coming to decide whether manifestation was religiously motivated or not.[1441]

The scope of protection offered to pupils for the manifestation of their religion by wearing ostentatious symbols or garments will not be retrenched due to the

---

1439 The law of 13 July 1983 and Art. 6 specified in it had been promulgated so as to comply with the EU Equality directive 2000/78.

1440 The prohibition is established in Article L141-5-1 of the Law no. 2004–228 from 15 March 2004 encadrant, en application du principe de laïcité, dans les écoles, les collèges et les lycées publics, le port de signes ou de tenues par lesquels les élèves manifestant ostensiblement une appartenance religieuse est interdit (Journal Officiel, no. 118, 22 May 2004) p. 5190 texte no. 1.

1441 Ganz, 2010, p. 98.

principle of laïcité and the obligation to religious neutrality applied in the state school system.

Contrasted on the background of the importance known to the principles of laïcité and state neutrality, the role of religion in public took a rather surprising development when claims of the right to wear religious symbols were brought by pupils. The conflicts surrounding pupils' right to wear religious symbols gained alertness and were more controversial than those surrounding teachers since the former are citizens unlike the latter who are subject to special duties inherent to their function as public officials.[1442] Similarly to case law development in England, claims brought by pupils, especially schoolgirls with a headscarf, outnumbered by far those regarding teachers. In addition, these case laws pertain an integral and indispensable part of the legal discourse and served as an incentive for legislative development in the public service promulgated subsequently. It is for that reason that a brief overview of the legal position relating to religious symbols worn by pupils is indispensable for the purpose of this analysis.

The public debate in French society with respect to the headscarves worn by Muslim girls when attending public schools emerged following a series of incidents, known as the 'headscarf-*hijab* affairs' (hereinafter l'affaire du foulard).[1443] The French expression *l'affaire du foulard* had been strongly entrenched in the political-cultural debate as it designates a historical event which had occupied the French nation for more than two centuries. Apart from that, the headscarf was and still is considered as the most controversial symbol in the public discourse surrounding manifestation of conspicuous religious symbols in the education context.[1444]

(bb) Infringement

An infringement of the right to religious manifestation will take place only in case the symbol in question is ostentatious, in other words, distinctively visible (*ostensiblement*). The clear visibility of a sign will be given extensive interpretation in courts so to enfold as many symbols as possible within the ambit of the law of 2004.[1445]

1442 *Fetzer/Soper*, p. 78.

1443 D Le Tourneau, 'La Laïcité à l'épreuve de l'Islam: le cas du port du "foulard islamique" dans l'école publique en France' 28 para 2 Revue générale de droit (1997) 275–306; *Idriss*, 25 para 2 Legal studies 2005, 260–95.

1444 *Fetzer/Soper*, pp. 78, et seq.; *McGoldrick*, pp. 65 et seq.; *Liederman-Molokotos*, pp. 109, 111.

1445 *Ganz*, 2010, p. 117–118.

As was mentioned before, the Stasi Commission was requested to deliver its opinion whether the wearing of religious symbols in the education poses a violation of the neutrality precept. Before the introduction of the Law of 2004, the legality of inner school regulations banning religious symbols from their premises was left open by the jurisprudence and it refrained from providing a clear-cut answer whether such a ban constitutes an infringement on a pupils' right to religious manifestation.[1446]

According to the Law of 2004, religious symbols will be prohibited if worn with the intention to demonstrate manifestation of religious affinity. However, if the sign worn can be objectively recognized by way of its wearing as a religious symbol, then the intention of the wearer will not be considered. This comes to explain that the French legislator wanted to capture all forms of conspicuous signs within the ambit of the 2004 law.[1447] So in principal, if the wearer displayed a symbol which is not purely religious in nature, but the objective indications support the conclusion that it was religiously motivated then the symbol will be banned. Objective indications may include the constant wearing of a head covering at all times and without any exception during school lessons, the wearing of a head covering regardless of yearly seasons (e.g., wearing a wool hat even in the summer) or the refusal of its removal, all these may raise doubts as to the true motivation of the wearer. In such a case, the French jurisprudence will not take into account the subjective intention of the wearer whether the symbol in question was worn due to religious reasons or not, but rather how it is objectively perceived by its surrounding.[1448] The objective circumstances under which the garment has been worn will suffice in the French jurisprudence to extend the scope of ban prescribed under the 2004 law.

(cc) Justification

As grounds for possible justification in pupils' right to wear headscarf to school there is a differentiation between two periods: The report of the council from 1989, and the period following the 2004 prohibition on religious symbols.

First, *no all-inclusive ban on religious symbols* – in its opinion from 1989, the CE declined to accept an extensive interpretation of the neutrality principle that prescribes a complete ban of all religious symbols from state classrooms. The

1446 *Ganz*, p. 106.

1447 *v. Ooijen*, Religious Symbols in Public Functions, 2012, p. 197.

1448 CAA Paris, 19 juillet 2005, *Ranjit X*, req. no. 05PA01831, AJDA 2005, 2012; CAA Paris, 19 juillet 2005, Bikramjit X, req. no. 05PA01833; TA Melun, 19 avril 2005, *M. Gurdial Singh*, req. no 05-0766/5, AJDA 2005, 917.

neutrality principle should be reflected through educational content, teaching personnel, and the observance of the pupils' right to religious freedom. It was underscored that the principle of neutrality enables pupils in the public school system to manifest their religious freedom. This approach presumes the manifestation of all religions in public education which should be achieved through tolerance and acceptance. Albeit this general pronouncement, the right to religious manifestation of pupils can be limited under certain circumstances.

The interpretation of the headscarf as ostentatious, suppressive, and indoctrinating symbol was not challenged under French jurisprudence but was rather accepted and perceived as such in order to fortify it as a legitimate justification. In contrast to small, discrete symbols, the headscarf was distinguishable by virtue of its visibility and the ability to recognize the wearer and his/her affiliation to a particular religious group. Manifestation by way of wearing religious garments that indicate an affiliation to a specific religion may have an indoctrinating effect on the viewers (i.e., other pupils of the same religion, other religious minorities or atheists). On grounds of this constellation it was easy, albeit the Council's opinion, to ban headscarves in general. The CE refused to take position with respect to proper interpretation of the headscarf and its symbolic meaning. It refrained from delivering its explicit opinion in order to enable the ban of the headscarf based on its retrenched evaluation, and by that has found itself in future prospective controversies surrounding the headscarf.

Second, *public order* – French constitutional law considers it necessary to ensure the maintenance of proper function in the public service. Thence, in case the display of religious symbols (i.e., wearing of a headscarf) should disturb the ordinary school operation, this will be often used as a justification ground derived from the general protection of public order. However, in the decisions of the CE it was not acknowledged as a justification ground with respect to a general headscarf ban imposed on pupils.[1449] The curtailment on pupils' right to manifestation of religious freedom will not be justified on grounds of need to maintain the ordinary school operation if an alternative (e.g., an exemption from a lesson or a suitable accommodation in school curriculum) exists and no concrete endangerment to peaceful operation of school lessons was demonstrated. However, albeit the fact that the CE did not release general pronouncement of admittance of maintenance of ordinary school operation as a justification ground for the general headscarf ban, this was especially recognized with respect to sport lessons

1449 CE, 20 mai 1996, *Outamghart*; CE, 9 octobre 1996, *Unal*; CE, 27 novembre 1996, *Akkaba*.

and will justify the encroachment upon pupils' right to religious manifestation even if only abstract endangerment exists.[1450]

The abstract endangerment posed to fundamental protected rights such as public order will suffice in practice and there will no need to demonstrate a visible concrete endangerment, thereby placing the right to religious freedom under constitutional deficit and lack of sufficient protection under the French legal system.

The approach held by French jurisprudence is to refrain from any attempt of outweighing the competing rights at stake insofar as a hindrance to school operation exists even potentially.[1451]

The test of proportionality will also not be conducted in order to substantiate that the measure taken by school authorities was proportionate for achieving the declared protected aim, for instance, public order (i.e., the ordinary undisturbed school operation), or public health. That means that school authorities are under no obligation to find an alternative to a female Muslim student wearing the headscarf such as an exemption from participation in sport lessons, as the judicator will accept the interference in the running of school operation as a justified ground for limitation on the pupil's right to religious manifestation.[1452]

Third, *the protection and safeguard of the right and freedoms of others* – in any case demonstrating that the religious apparel of a pupil may encroach upon the fundamental freedoms of other pupils or other persons in school, it will be justified to allow the ban. This may occur, for example, by way of pressure imposed on other female pupils of the same religion who wish to refrain from wearing the headscarf, face veil, or any other headcoverings, the indoctrinating nature of the symbol, and any form of proselytization that may endanger the fundamental freedoms of others.

Taking the perspective of the Law of 2004, it was argued in the legal literature that the principle of laïcité played a significant role in the introduction of the enactment; however, it was claimed to be a new constitutional interpretation of the laïcité deduced from the right to religious freedom,[1453] thus creating two different constitutional perceptions of the principle of laïcité. As possible

---

1450 Conseil d'Etat, 10 March 1995, *M. et Mme Aoukili*, No 159981, AJDA 1995, 335; CE, 20 octobre 1999, *M. et Mme Ait Ahmad*, AJDA 2000, 165.

1451 *Ganz*, (2010), p. 127.

1452 *Ganz*, (2010), p. 127.

1453 *Idriss*, 25(2) LS, (2005), 260, 285.

considerations for justification grounds of the ban, the following factors were taken into account: first, the principle of laïcité as an educational mandate of the state – the laïcité is starkly intertwined with the republican goals featured with respect to its educational system, namely, emancipation, citizenship, equality of opportunities for its pupils, universalism, and assimilation.[1454] This requires from its citizens elimination of any identification by ethnicity or religion that is to be achieved through state schools as institutions responsible for the formation of the future society and responsible citizens. Second, till the promulgation of the Law of 2004, the principle of laïcité had not been perceived as an own standing justification ground for interdicting the headscarf. The incentive for its implementation in the enactment was explained to yield from the changes incurred in the religious-cultural structure in public schools that contributed to classification of religious groups, and creation of pressure and oppression on other female pupils to comply with the wearing of a headscarf. The outcome was disturbances in classrooms. Third, other justification grounds derived from the principle of laïcité considered the violation against the right of other minority religious groups to negative religious freedom, the infringement of public order in statutory state schools, and contravention of gender equality.

The protection of public order has been fortified as justification ground for imposing the ban since it was demonstrated that manifestation of religious symbols, in particular the headscarf, contributed to conflicts in the school realm. This endangered the peaceful co-existence in school due to segregation between different religious groups and emphasis given to divisiveness based on ethnic and religion which constitutes disturbance to the public order in school.

Fourth, *gender equality* – this had been explained as the right of female Muslim pupils not to be exposed to pressure practiced by their surrounding religious communities to wear the headscarf so as to comply with a religious precept.[1455] The argumentation provided with regard to the controversial interpretation of the Islamic headscarf suggests that it discriminates against the position of women as a sign of her invisibility and subordination to men who, unlike women, are not obliged to wear a head covering. The principle of laïcité has been used as an argumentation to safeguard the right of female Muslim pupils who do not wear the headscarf to (negative) religious freedom.

1454 *McGoldrick*, 2006, p. 79.

1455 *Danchin*, Yale J. Int'l L. 33, 2008, 1, 4.

d) Relationship of Educational System and Religion in the Jurisprudence

aa) Decisions of the Conseil d'Etat

Towards the end of the 1980s and the beginning of the 1990s, there was a series of cases filed by Muslim girls on the background of their refusal to remove the headscarf after they were explicitly authorised by school management to abstain from appearance with their veils within school premises.

The conflict over scarves started in 1989 when the headmaster of a college in Criel, a suburb of Paris, decided to expel three Muslim girls appearing with the Muslim *hijab* (headscarves) to school.[1456] It should be noted in this respect that the actions of these schoolgirls marked the beginning of religious and political conflicts brought into school environment. It started with a petition to construct a mosque in the city of Criel and developed later on to a demand to appear with a headscarf during classes. Eventually, a compromise was reached declaring the demand to appear with a headscarf in school acceptable, however, requiring its removal while in the classroom.

The compromise was violated when the girls decided after a while to wear the headscarves even when attending classrooms. The principal justified his decision for their exclusion by reference to the principle of religious neutrality, declaring the need to ban any form of religious or political insignia from schools.

Following the initial suspensions, there was an attempt to negotiate the return of the girls to school. The result of the negotiations conducted between school officials, the girls' parents, Islamic religious leaders and organizations yielded a partial success as one of the girls was persuaded to concede her previous practice (removal of the headscarf in classes) while the other two had refused to do so.[1457]

The decision on these matters was referred to the CE which ruled in principle that the mere attendance of pupils in state schools with religious symbols or garments will not amount to infringement of the precept of secularism, as long as the wearer exercises his/her right due to pure religious motives.[1458]

Accordingly, it seems like the CE preferred to adopt a more flexible approach with respect to pupils, tending to accept the endorsement of religious

---

1456 *Poulter*, OJLS 17 (1) 1997, 43, 57.

1457 *McGoldrick*, p. 67.

1458 Conseil d'Etat, Avis 'Port du foulard islamique', 27 November 1989, no.346893; *Poulter*, OJLS 17 (1), 1997, p. 43, 58; *Wick* in von Campenhausen/Frisch/Heckel ua (eds.), Beiträge zum evangelischen Kirchenrecht und zum Staatskirchenrecht, 2007, 29 (60).

symbols into state schools as a general rule, while sustaining its prohibition as an exception.

Shortly after delivery of the significant CE ruling from 27 November 1989, the Ministry of Education published two Ministerial Circulars: the first, from 12 December 1989 (hereinafter 1989 Circular)[1459] and the second, from 20 September 1994 (hereinafter 1994 Circular).[1460] The Circulars were issued in spirit of the CE's opinion with respect to manifestation of religious belief through donning of religious garments in state schools.

In detail, the 1989 Circular was meant to serve as a guideline for teachers and schools in providing them guidance as to the interpretation of 'conspicuous religious symbols'. It also introduced criteria that would serve as justifying limitations on religious symbols (e.g., public order, security, and health). It also introduced in the foreground the possibility of a confinement of religious right of the pupils and established they should refrain from wearing any conspicuous symbols which aimed at promoting a religious belief.[1461]

The unease resulted from the decision of the CE delivered in 1989, followed by another ministerial circular that was issued by the Minister of Education at that time, Francois Bayrou. Published in 1994, the circular, known as the Bayrou circular, regarded the wearing of ostentatious signs in public schools.[1462] This 1994 Circular gained its importance as it proposed to make a distinction between conspicuous and discreet symbols. In principle, it allowed the wearing of religious or discreet signs, while prohibiting signs which in 'themselves are elements of proselytism or discrimination'.[1463]

The earlier decisions relating to pupils wearing headscarves emphasized as a ground for justification of a ban the endangerment such a conspicuous symbol

---

1459 Circulaire du 12 décembre 1989, (Education national, Jeunesse et Sports) found on the website of the National Assembly www.assemblee-nationale.fr; *van Ooijen*, p. 194.

1460 Circulaire du 20 septembre 1994, known as Circulaire Bayrou.

1461 *Wick* in von Campenhausen/Frisch/Heckel ua (eds.), Beiträge zum evangelischen Kirchenrecht und zum Staatskirchenrecht, 2007, 29 (61).

1462 Circulaire du 20 septembre 1994 (Circulaire Bayrou).

1463 *Saxena*, University of Detroit Mercy Law Report 2007, 765, 780; *Van Ooijen*, p. 195. The prohibition would take effect by inserting the following text into internal regulations of school: "The wearing of discreet signs by pupils, manifesting their personal belonging to particularly religious convictions is permitted at school. But conspicuous signs which in themselves constitute elements of proselytism or discrimination, are prohibited". *Saxena*, University of Detroit Mercy Law Report 2007, 765, 780.

may pose to public order. In fact, the 1994 Circular leaves the final decision to the headmasters of schools to decide on the character of signs and their categorization. Since the Circular was issued, the CE, affirming its earlier decisions, has struck down several decisions expelling Muslim girls from schools, on the grounds that no evidence was introduced that they were wearing their scarves 'as an act of pressure or proselytism'.[1464]

The CE, however, declared in a later judgement (1995) that those Circulars have no normative value and can, therefore, serve only as guidelines for the interpreter.[1465]

It should be underscored in this context that the tendency of the CE, as expressed in their judgements with respect to the wearing of Islamic headscarves in state schools, is not conclusive and irrevocable. In fact, the assumption that female Muslim pupils were given a general permission to appear at all times with headscarves in school premises was misleading since in practice it did not avail female pupils at all times.

Eventually, this decision from 1989 caused a turmoil in French society; on the one hand, Muslim leaders were furious due to the fact that crucifixes and skullcaps are allowed in schools, whereas on the other hand, overwhelming voices of politicians in society called for the necessity to keep conformity with the principle of laïcité.

Accordingly, when the question was referred to the CE, France's highest Administrative Court, to decide whether Muslim schoolgirls may appear with headscarves in public schools, the CE took a milder approach. The CE held the position that the wearing of religious symbols per se will not be regarded as contradicting the principle of laïcité if the act constitutes religious manifestation.[1466] The criteria or requirements that will preclude manifestation of religious symbols by pupils were provided by the CE in its determination.

1464 CE, No 172721, Nov 5, 1997; CE, No 169539, Mar 10, 1997; CE, no. 172721, Nov 27, 1996; Nexis/lexis.

1465 *Poggeschi*, European Yearbook of Minority Issues, Vol. 3, 2003–2004, 263, 267.

1466 Conseil d'Etat, Avis 'Port du foulard islamique', 27 November 1989, no. 346893, retrieved from the website of Revue de l'Actualité Juridique Francaise www.rajf.org. Section 1 last paragraph sets forth: "Il résulte de ce qui vient d'etre dit que, dans les établissements scolaires, le port par les élèves de signes par lesquels il entendent manifester leur appartenance à une religion n'est pas par lui-meme incompatible avec le principe de laïcité, dans la mesure où il constitue l'exercice de la liberté d'expression et de manifestation de croyances religieuses".; *McGoldrick*, p. 69. The same approach was held by the Minister of National Education, see *McGoldrick*, p. 68.

bb) The Determination of the Conseil d'Etat from 1989

As already explained, the significance imparted on the decision of the Council of State from 27 November 1989[1467] relates to it determination that a religious symbol or a garment worn by a pupil and which connotes of her/his religious affinity will not amount in itself to an infringement of the principle of laicism.

It established that 'in the buildings of the schools, the wearing by the pupils of symbols through which they intend to express their belonging to a religion is not on its own incompatible with the principle of secularity if it is related to the exercise of the freedom of expression and the manifestation of religious beliefs'.[1468]

Nevertheless, the CE held that there are limits to freedom of religion and established three sets of criteria that will forbid pupils from wearing religious symbols which individually or collectively may constitute:

First, signs or symbols that 'due to their nature', or 'due to the conditions in which they are worn', or 'due to their conspicuous or calming nature' as campaigning or protesting;

Second, an act of oppression, provocation, proselytism, or propaganda;

Third, a threat to the dignity or to the freedom of the pupils or of other members of the education community, as well as to liberty, health, or safety and the normal functioning of the public service.[1469]

Essentially, it is of high importance to review the motive behind the wear of a religious symbol. This task was appropriated for the headmasters of schools to decide on an individual case basis especially whether the wearing of a headscarf is considered an 'act of pressure, provocation, proselytism, or propaganda, which would violate the dignity of freedom of other students and members of the educational community, disturb school activities and disturb public order, in which case it was legitimate to ban the student from the school'.[1470]

Apart from identifying the core of discipline that will be permitted with respect to the wearing of religious symbols in state schools, the CE transferred a wider scope of discretion to the headmasters themselves, ruling that conflicts

---

1467 Circulaire du 12 décembre 1989, (Education nationale, Jeunesse et Sports) as found on the website of the National Assembley, www.assemble-nationale.fr.

1468 *Poggeschi*, European Yearbook of Minority Issues, Vol. 3, 2003–2004, 263, 267; *Weil*, 30 Cardozo L. Rev. 2009, 2699, 2700 (quoting *Benhabib/Post*, pp. 54–55.).

1469 *Poggeschi*, European Yearbook of Minority Issues, Vol. 3, 2003–2004, 263, 267.

1470 Religious Liberty: The Legal Framework in Selected OSCE Countries, 2000, p. 38.

should be resolved based on the unique and individual circumstances particular to each case.[1471]

A similar decision was delivered at a later stage by the CE when it decided to strike down school regulation, prohibiting the wearing of any political, religious, or philosophic signs in school, on ground that it was too broad and general. The CE reiterated and reaffirmed its former decision, emphasizing the importance of classification of such an act as provocation, propaganda or an act that may disturb public order.[1472]

In 1999, a decision by the local school board to allow two Turkish girls to wear headscarves during school time triggered major protest and strikes organized by the majority of the teaching staff in that junior high school.

The efforts of the Education Ministry through a mediator[1473] sent to accomplish an agreement between the girls' parents and the school authorities did not prove to be successful. On the one hand, the parents rejected a compromise requiring the girls to remove their headscarves during certain classes for reasons of safety and health. The teachers, on the other hand, refused to accept symbols of religious fundamentalism that deny women the equality which is their due in France.

Finally, the girls were banned from school and, as a result, appealed the decision in front of the administrative tribunal.[1474] However, the tribunal eventually decided to support the school authorities in their decision to ban the girls from school.[1475]

In another case law, two French girls who converted to Islam were authorized to attend school again and study together in their regular class. They were prohibited from sitting in the same class for several months, due to a teacher's refusal to teach them as long as they insist on wearing headscarves during their lessons.

1471 It determined that disciplinary matters should be administered on the local level by local school rules. *Palmer*, OSCE, p. 38.

1472 *Robert*, La Liberté Religieuse, 46 R.I.D.C. 630 (2–1994).

1473 This method of meditation prompted in 1994 was an initiative of the French Education ministry aimed to solve conflicts over headscarves in public schools and conclude a compromised agreement which would be suitable for all parties.

1474 Le Monde, Jan 9 and 11, 1999 and Feb. 13, 1999; Nexis/Lexis, Presse, Le Monde.

1475 Le Monde, "Flers: confirmation de l'exclusion des collégiennes portant le foulard" October 11, 1999, Nexis/lexis, Presse, Le Monde. The idea was that religious clothing or symbols should not be used as a ground for hindering the regular course of physical instruction or other practical instructions conducted at school.

A directive issued by the local school authority, permitting their return to the same classroom induced a strike on part of the teaching staff. The teachers decided to strike as long as the school authority maintain their directive permitting their return to their regular classrooms. Despite this objection, it was decided by school authorities to admit the girls back to school and approve their joint resumption to the former classroom.

In its decision from 1999, the CE ruled that school principals have a justified right to request that school uniform should be appropriate according to the circumstances. The CE emphasized the importance of school uniform policy and the obligation of the pupils to abide by its dress code rules, in particular with respect to lessons such as gymnastics. An infringement of the obligation to conform with the schools' uniform may result not only in endangering the safety and health of the pupils that are found to be in breach but also of other pupils in school.[1476]

Additionally, it is also due to the fact that freedom of expression and/or freedom of religion are not absolute rights that they cannot always prevail and serve as a permanent obstacle to the right of the headmaster, school authorities, pupils, or parents.

cc) *The Admissibility of Teachers to Religious Manifestation*

The case of Mademoiselle Marteaux – this case was brought before the CE in 2000[1477] and contested the preclusion that applies with respect to teachers from wearing religious symbols. Miss Marteaux was a teacher who had been dismissed from school for wearing a headscarf. The teacher submitted a claim to revoke her dismissal. The ruling of the CE affirmed the following: first, the duty of public officials to refrain from any expression or manifestation of belief or religion. By that, the CE confirmed the strict application of the neutrality principle regarding the right of teaching personnel to wear conspicuous religious symbols. Second, it was further established by the CE that the strict application of the neutrality principle will apply without any differentiation as to the type of public service or type of function. Third, in addition, the CE confirmed that the wearing of a headscarf or any other conspicuous religious symbol by teachers would be regarded as a breach of their obligation to remain neutral while on duty. Any conduct to the

---

1476 Le Monde, "Port du foulard: arrêt restrictif du Conseil d'Etat" October 23, 1999, Nexis/lexis, Presse, Le Monde.

1477 Conseil d'Etat, Avis 3 May 2000, Melle Marteaux no. 217017.

contrary will be doomed to sanctions. The severity of the sanction will depend on the circumstances, including the conspicuous nature of the symbol.[1478]

It is worth to note that, following this decision, disputes questioning the admissibility of public servants to wear the headscarf were referred for the CE's determination. Nonetheless, the judicial approach remained unaltered.[1479]

A similar outcome was reached in a subsequent case involving the dismissal of a state schoolteacher due to the wearing of a headscarf. In that case a PhD student, who also served as a teaching assistant at the University of Toulouse, was wearing the headscarf while on duty. The student wore a headscarf while providing tutorials and refused to accept the university's demand for its removal. Her refusal to remove the headscarf brought to her dismissal in 2009. The legal proceeding submitted to the administrative tribunal of Toulouse against the university was unsuccessful.[1480]

It was held in the judgement that was delivered in 2010 that when public officials manifest their religion or belief during the exercise of their function, they commit a severe violation of their obligation.[1481]

dd) Decisions Following the 2004 Act

The prohibition on pupils to wear conspicuous religious symbols was introduced in Article L-141-5-l of the Law of 2004.[1482]

The promulgation of the 2004 Law gave rise to many complaints and protests held by a wide range of legal entities. Therefore, whether it involved national bodies such as the League of Muslim Women in France or international bodies such as human rights organizations, all claimed mainly that the Law of 2004 constitutes an illegal infringement of an international recognized right, that is, the right to profess a religion freely and in accordance with the religious precepts dictated by one's own faith or belief.[1483]

1478 *Van Ooijen*, p. 187.

1479 *Van Ooijen*, p. 187.

1480 http://www.liberation.fr/societe/2010/11/25/une-institutrice-voilee-bientot-mise-au-ban-de-l-ecole_696136; *Van Ooijen*, p. 189.

1481 *Van Ooijen*, p. 191.

1482 Loi no. 2004–228 du 15 mars 2004 encadrant, en application du principe de laicite, le port de signes ou de tenues manifestant une appartenance religieuse dans les ecoles, colleges et lycees publics.

1483 http://en.wilipedia.org/wiki/Freedom _of _religion_in_France, http://en.wilipedia.org/wiki/Freedom _of _religion_in_France

Naturally, allegations were also raised by many Muslim pupils claiming against the French government the illegality of the Law of 2004, as it serves an unlawful infringement on their freedom of religion.

It is worth to note that following the adoption of the Law of 2004, a new Ministerial Circular was issued in order to provide clear interpretation with respect to the application of the Law of 2004, thus replacing former Circulars.[1484] The 2004 Circular endeavoured to capture an appropriate interpretation of the definition 'conspicuous signs'. It was decided that conspicuous religious symbols mean symbols 'which can immediately be recognized as denoting the belonging to a religion'.[1485] The Circular mentioned some symbols to be included within the definition, such as headscarves, *yarmulkes*, or excessive large crosses. The CE declared the compatibility of the Circular with the ECtHR.

(1) The Kehrouaa et al. Decision

In this judgement, the CE had straightened a line with its former rulings declaring as void a provision in the internal school regulation prohibiting the wearing of religious symbols without any exception.[1486] The decision confirmed that laïcité in itself is not sufficient in order to declare its incompatibility with the wearing of religious symbols by pupils.[1487]

(2) The Case of Alma and Lila Lèvy

In 2003, another incident occurred in a Parisian high school where two of its students, Alma and Lyla Lévy, were expelled as they refused to remove their headscarves, claiming that they wish to conform to modesty rules prescribed by their religion.[1488] Moreover, the girls even refused to wear an alternative head covering which was accepted by school administrators and referred to as 'un foulard léger'.[1489]

1484 Circulaire du 18 mai 2004 relative à la mise en oeuvre de la loi no. 2004–228 du 15 mars 2004 (Journal Officiel, no.118, 22 May 2004), p. 9033, texte no. 10; *van Ooijen*, p. 196.

1485 Article 2.1 of the Law of 2004; *McGoldrick*, p. 92; *van Ooijen*, p. 196.

1486 See Conseil d'Etat, 2 November 1992, no. 130.394 (Kehrouaa, Kachour, Balo, Kizic) available in Lexis, CONSET file; R Errera Public Law (1993) 198; *Poggeschi*, European Yearbook of Minority Issues, Vol. 3, 2003-/2004, pp. 263, 267.

1487 CE, K., 2 November 1992, no.130394; CE, époux A., 20 October 1999, no. 181486; McGoldrick, p. 71; *Wick* in von Campenhausen/Frisch/Heckel ua (eds.), Beiträge zum evangelischen Kirchenrecht und zum Staatskirchenrecht, 2007, 29 (61–62).

1488 *Winter, Unveiling the French Headscarf Debate, 2008, 253–254.*

1489 *Scott*, p. 30.

It is worth to note that the case gained its uniqueness especially since the girls were willingly converting to Islam. In other words, the girls were not coerced by the family or the surroundings to wear the *hijab* (as both parents were atheists) nor were they pertaining to an Islamic group. This fact may appear troublesome, in particular, as it demonstrates the power of Islam to proselytize even a secular upbringing.[1490]

In the face of no evidence that the girls were exposed to external pressure to wear the headscarf, it becomes lucid that the general contention of those who sought to ban the *foulard* under the justification of liberating Muslim women from control of Islamist patriarchal practice becomes surplus under these circumstances.[1491]

This proves demonstratively that a general ban on the headscarf, justified on grounds of its recognition as a sign of women's subordination to men will not avail, as each case needs to be reviewed and analysed on an individual basis.

e) Conclusion – France

aa) The State-Church Relation and Its Impact on the Educational System

Naturally, the conceptual model of state-church in France, which adopts a strict, formal application of a separationist approach, finds its roots in French history and the tedious struggle between the church and the state. The need of the French nation to dissociate itself from any religious influence, especially alienation of the Catholic Church from state affairs, imprinted the secular character of the state underpinning a prominent principle in French constitutional law.

The uniqueness of the principle of laïcité in France's constitutional system derives its existence from the constitutional principle of state neutrality. Both principles are used interchangeably in legal literature. Thence, the principle of laïcité can be inferred as the French conception of neutrality and the right to freedom of religion. As explained earlier, the specificity of the term and its interpretation, which are imparted from tradition and historical development, does not have an equivalent in the constitutional systems of other states.

The notion of laïcité, together with republican principles of equality and fraternity constitute the three fundamental pillars of the French Republic and preeminent constitutional fundaments of the French state.

1490 *Scott*, p. 31.

1491 *Scott*, pp. 30, 31.

In the history of France, the principle of laïcité accords its political-historical importance to the modern perception of citizenship invigorated in the French Revolution, and the notion to be separated from any distinctiveness based on ethnic identities, racial, or religious differences. The safeguarding of state neutrality was to be achieved only through a process of laicizing the state. This neutralization process was to be fulfilled through the implementation of the state's duty to remain neutral in its actions and policies in the course of governing its state affairs. Thence, the secular nature of the state was to be achieved only through a complete disentanglement of religion or its visibility from any state function. The educational field and its institutes were expressed to be included first within the neutralization process, and the dissociation of any churchly influence on public education was highly underscored.

The disempowering of the Catholic Church influence over education was a gradual process initiated in the course of the nineteenth century with a series of educational enactments purported to assist public schools in the transition to a secular system. This process was initiated with the promulgation of the Ferry laws during the 1880s. It was ensued with a series of enactments which aimed to bring religious education to an end and foster the laic process of education.

For this reason, the legislation regulating the relationship between the educational system and religion-related issues prescribes that state-supported schools should remain secular in form. Hence, state-maintained schools are strictly lay schools, they employ only lay personnel and do not have religious education in their curricula.[1492]

In addition, France has a centralised organizational structure of schooling, which means that all aspects relating to schools' curricula, regulations governing school uniform policy with respect to pupils, and appointment of teachers is administered and determined on the governmental level. Albeit decentralization of specific areas in secondary schools' administration, which delegates limited powers to local authorities, on a general level education remains within the centralized ambit of the state.

Nonetheless, problems arose towards the end of the 1980s and the beginning of the 1990s when the first generation of Muslims who were born in France entered the French school system and encountered hardships of integration into the educational system, including adjusting to the secular nature of the state.[1493] This

---

1492 *Palmer*, Religious Liberty: The Legal Framework In Selected OSCE Countries, 2000, p. 38.

1493 *Poggeschi*, European Yearbook of Minority Issues, Vol. 3, 2003/2004, 263, 267.

brought about conflicts and tension in public education, which were intrigued with the wearing of the headscarf by Muslim women. That, in turn, increased the fear in France of the loss of national identity and threatened the cornerstone of the French Republic of being one and indivisible.

Another aspect regards the duty of teaching staff since the formal application of the principle of neutrality excludes the display of religious symbols with respect to all functions of public officials. The obligation on public officials to refrain from manifestation of religious symbols is incumbent on them by virtue of their function as state representatives and demands their absolute abidance by the neutrality of state.

bb) Laïcité as an Instrument to Enable Religious Freedom

The significance of the laïcité principle has been emphasized following the French Revolution and constitutes until today one of the most paramount pillars of the Republic. The laïcité underlays the ideology and values of the French Republic and requires strict adherence, especially in public functions. The first field affected by the laicizing process was education. The notion of laïcité enfolds in several aspects: it is laid down as a constitutional pillar in the 1958 Constitution, the rigorous adherence to the principle of laïcité is especially observed in posts for the public service, it symbolizes the commitment of the French State to dissolve from any influences of the church, and it reflects the wish of the Republic to keep a strict separation between state and religious affairs emanating from its historical development.

The principle of laïcité can be perceived as a double-edged sword, as, on the one hand, the state is under a duty to keep its neutrality by enabling religion an adequate place in its public sphere and by guaranteeing adherents of different religions and faiths the free exercise of religion, and, on the other hand, it is used as a justification ground for limitation of the right to religious freedom that curtails its scope of protection.

The un/successful attempt to codify the principle of laïcité with respect to persons vested with public authority will not alter the unambiguous application of the principles of laïcité and neutrality to the public service.

cc) The Cursory Definition of Religion and Absent Specification in Law

It is worth to note that many conflicts arising in the French educational system with relation to endorsement of religious garbs or any religious interference in state schools are tightly bound with the fact that the French government refuses to legally define what is religion and what is not and does not delimit its boundaries.

Indeed, the preamble of the Constitution of 1946, which is part of the *bloc de constitutionnalite* in force today, determines that 'it shall be the duty of the state to organise free, public, secular education at all levels'.[1494]

However, it is the allegiance of the French nation to secularity of the educational system, on the one hand, and the lack of clarity and specificity with respect to the definition of religion on the other, that significantly increased the number of claims around this issue.

The Law of 2004 prohibiting manifestation of conspicuous religious symbols or garments with respect to pupils seem to run counter to French constitutionalism, as it makes a clear distinction between the rights and obligations of public officials and the citizens.

The Law of 2004 provided the courts some guidelines of interpretation relating to the term 'conspicuous' religious symbols. Nevertheless, the legislator left some uncertainties when coming to decide what would be considered 'conspicuous' or not. In any case, the Law of 2004 set new rules between the relationship of religious freedom and the secularity of state and determined that Islamic garments, regardless of their degree of coverage can no longer be found in France's public classrooms.[1495] To conclude, the earlier headscarf affairs put their focus on endangerment to the public order, health, and security as justified limitations for religious freedom. Later on, cases that were brought around the twenty-first century affirmed that the increasing number of cases dealing with expulsion of Muslim schoolgirls from school due to wearing of the headscarf emphasized contestably the need to protect the principle of laïcité.

Following issuance of the 1989 Circular, claims that were brought before the CE were still decided in favour of claimants.

The interpretation of conspicuous religious symbols remained distracting even following the promulgation of the Law of 2004 since in distinctive cases where a symbol would not qualify as a conspicuous religious symbol, for example, kerchief, bandanas, or bonnets, it was declared as a prohibited religious symbol.[1496] The ground for justification attested that these symbols were clearly worn for

1494 *Poggeschi*, European Yearbook of Minority Issues, Vol. 3, 2003/2004, 263.

1495 *Barbibay*, Cardozo J. Int'l & Comp. L. 2010, 159, 174; Cumper/Lewis, J. L. & Religion 24, 2008–2009, pp. 599, 603.

1496 CE, 5 December 2007, Mdlle G., décision no. 295671; *van Ooijen*, p. 197.

religious reasons and as a result justify their ban (i.e., by virtue of the behaviour of the wearer that indicates the symbol is worn for a religious motivation).

On a general level, the tendency is to exclude conspicuous religious symbols or garments from state schools based on the principle of laïcité gained support. In this respect, even determination of the CE had changed as it adopts a negative, stricter application of the principle of laïcité.

As a general rule, the right of teachers in public schools to religious manifestation has to set back by virtue of the sanctity attributed in France to impartiality and unbiased appearance of public officials. Their obligation towards the public prescribes the duty to remain neutral so as not to confer the impression of discrimination or unequal treatment due to demonstration of religious affiliation through outer appearance. This rule has even special significance with respect to teachers who work in proximity with children, and the risk that they may be influenced by the teachers' religious view or subject to an indoctrinating influence on their part.

The adherence to the neutrality principle is strict in the public service and applies to all religions equally. As a result, the courts will not attempt to rule on a case-by-case basis. Rather, due to rigidity of the abidance to the neutrality principle the substantiation of an abstract endangerment will suffice in order to justify an infringement on a teacher's right to manifestation of his/her religion by display of religious attire.

In addition, the size, form, and display of religious symbols will not be considered when examining the proportionality of the request of removal of a headscarf or the dismissal of a teacher refusing to remove the headscarf. There is no application of the proportionality test under French constitutional law. The reason is that a strict application of the neutrality principle would make any attempt to delineation of the right to exercise a religion by virtue of religious manifestation, surplus. The French judicator will not examine whether other, less intrusive means for the protection of the Muslim women's right to religious manifestation, are at hand. If the headscarf poses even an abstract endangerment to other protected constitutional freedoms and rights, it will normally suffice for demand of its removal from state school system. The ban imposed on the manifestation of religious symbols under the Law of 2004 does not apply with respect to all religious symbols, otherwise it would be regarded as disproportionate. Given that the prohibition declared in the Law of 2004 applies in general to all visible religious signs equally, it should still offer some adequate place for the free exercise of religion by pupils. The wearing of religious symbols in the individual's private sphere poses an alternative to female pupils who do not wish to remove the headscarf during school and decline the assertion that the ban is inclusive and absolute so it infringes on the proportionality test. The tender age of pupils will also not act as a determining factor when a judicial review regarding dismissal of a teacher assesses the harshness of the imposed measure, simply as the obligation to self-restraint of public officials is highly evaluated in the public service.

dd) Religious Symbols Worn by a Teacher

The way the principle of laïcité plays out in the discourse relating to the right of public officials to wear religious symbols, and the extent to which it can be used as a ground justifying encroachment on their fundamental right to religious freedom is effectuated by several factors. Some of these factors are peculiar to French constitutionalism as imprinted in its Republican ideology and will be underscored as follows:

First, *personification with the state* – the public servant in his/her duty is perceived as personifying the state. Consequently, public servants will assume the duty incumbent on the state as being their own duty, subjecting it to assimilation with the state's ideology and republican values. The public official equates his/her actions with actions of the state and, as a result, needs to forfeit any manifestation of religious expression, as this in turn may be attached or associated with the state. Nonetheless, public officials are not expected to give up completely on their individuality. Their right to freedom of conscience remains – in comparison to the right of religious freedom – absolutely warranted. The reason for this segregation emanates from the clear distinction the French law upholds these rights with respect to public officials.

Second, *recognition of freedom of conscience* – albeit the duty of public officials to identify with the state, they are not expected to lose their individuality and their right to freely practice their religion in their private sphere. However, the right to freedom of conscience is segregated from the freedom of religious manifestation. The reason for such distinction is attributed to the fact that a public official (*publics agent*) is obliged to retreat his/her individual right to display a religious symbol as subject to the duty of neutral appearance in the public service. This special duty of a public official emanating from his/her function as a representative of the state on the one hand, and his/her duty towards the citizen to remain impartial in his/her task, on the other hand, justifies the neutrality principle to gain priority over the official's freedom to manifest his/her religion. While the freedom of conscience does not incur any collision with duties as a public official, the right to religious freedom may pose threat with respect to the public official's obligation to neutrality while on duty. This obligation to remain neutral in the public service gains further significance, especially since the official voluntarily took upon himself/herself to abide by the neutrality principle by virtue of his/her public function. It is only conceivable that any manifestation of religion or belief through wearing of religious symbols may run the risk of impairing the duty of a public official to impartiality.

Third, *citizen-public official relation* – within the context of public official-citizen relations there is a perception that the obligation of the former to abide by the neutrality principle was intended primarily to safeguard the interests of citizens upon those of public officials. Therefore, limitations placed on the freedom of public officials, barring their right to wear religious symbols will be regarded as justified even if only to the extent of eliminating the mere risk of proselytizing or the feeling of different treatment perceived by the citizen. In other words, citizens' rights and interests are regarded paramount.

Fourth, *distinctiveness of public officials* – the 2011 Act prohibiting face veils explicitly with respect to citizens demonstrated the exceedance in the perception of the French legislator which assumes absolute duty of neutrality only with respect to the public service. Imposing such a limitation on a fundamental freedom of citizenship to religious freedom revoked any segregation known so far between public officials and citizens/users of public services (*usagers*). In principle, citizens are not subject to any limitation on their right to manifest their religious freedom. The endorsement of this legislation poses legal difficulties as to its application under French constitutionalism that thus far proclaimed high importance regarding its ability to draw a strict division between public officials and citizens. The same can be said as to the extension of the laïcité principle also with respect to the right of pupils to appear with conspicuous religious symbols, as established in the Law of 2004. The problem arising under this legislation is the difficulty to determine what would qualify as a conspicuous symbol and what would not. On a legal level, this demonstrates the problematic of delimiting the definition of conspicuous symbols. A broader interpretation of what would be regarded as a conspicuous religious symbol may extend the scope of application not only with respect to symbols of a salient religious character but also to those which are suspected of being worn for religious motives (such as caps, hats, bandanas).

This clearly demonstrates the difficulty, even in a state like France that adopts a strict state-church conceptual model, to delineate the boundaries with respect to conspicuous symbols. Inter alia, manifestation of symbols which are not recognised per se as religious signs.

As previously explained, due to the obligation of state neutrality which applies uniformly in the public sphere, the French conception of neutrality dictates its uniform, all-inclusive application in an identical manner with respect to all types and functions of public officials. Eventually, the visibility of religious symbols will be a detrimental factor irrespective of the type of symbol displayed and the function exercised by a public official.

This explains that the principle of laïcité, emanating from the principle of neutrality and the strong allegiance in the public service to appear impartial and unbiased demonstrates the sanctity imparted to it as a constitutional pillar of the French Republic.

ee) Religious Symbols Worn by Pupils

Many claims were brought by Muslim students wishing to challenge this secular nature of the state and oblige the state to acknowledge and accept the wear of traditional Islamic scarves in state-maintained schools.

As far as a prohibition on manifestation of religious symbols in public schools is concerned, there is a need to segregate between the display of religious insignias which by virtue of their religious affiliation are ostensibly manifested, and signs which, in contrast, by manner of their display or manifestation transfer to the viewer their religious connotation.

The right of pupils to religious manifestation has been retrenched extensively with the promulgation of the Law of 2004, as the ban does not apply with respect to garments or insignias that indicate clearly the manifestation of religious affinity, but rather applies to display of symbols or garments that by way of their wearing suggest the adherence of pupils to religious manifestation. This naturally makes it difficult to decide what religious signs are regarded as conspicuous signs. For instance, the wearing of a wool cap or bandana as a head covering may be interpreted objectively as a religious symbol by way of the usage made by the wearer. That means that the court will infer the objective meaning. To sum up, the Law of 2004 applies extensively and captures also religious symbols demonstrating religious affinity and not only cultural symbols that fall within the meaning of 'religious affinity'.

The jurisprudence acknowledged that the right of pupils to manifestation of religion will set back if endangerment to one of the following as possible justification grounds takes place: public order, peaceful co-existence in school, and the rights and freedoms of others. This indicates even further that the Law of 2004 demonstrates an extensive scope of application.

5. Conclusion

The purpose of this chapter was to identify how state-church relations and the model adopted in each of the countries in this analysis influence their educational system. It then examined what input religion carries in the respective education acts of the states, and how this translates into the legal discourse evaluating the exertion of individuals' fundamental right to religious freedom, in particular in public education which reflects the pluralism of modern society. Finally, the assessment provided an overview of how the countries legitimize interference in the fundamental right to religious freedom making use of the state-church interplay practiced in those countries. All three countries had encountered cultural diversity that affected the religious right of minorities to exercise their freedom of expression and religion and, in parallel, raised claims of equality and non-discrimination as an added aspect of the legal controversy.

Due to the federative constitutional system of Germany, the legal debate surrounding the admissibility of religious symbols in its state school system bestowed considerable significance to affixation of the crucifix on state schools walls and addressed the constitutionality of the 'privilege granted to Christian-occidental tradition' in the German context. The national public controversy surrounding the Crucifix was not shared in the compared states, England and France, due to reasons underpinned by their socio-political structure, legal framework, and history. The reasons for which especially the headscarf, as a religious symbol of Islam has become the focus of this public controversy are commonly shared in the European countries and will be briefly mentioned.

A prevailing problem shared with respect to Muslim communities in Europe relates to the fact they are identified as a closed society which prefers to distinguish itself from other religious or faith groups. As was already explained in legal literature, it was not only France but also other European countries, like Germany and Great Britain, which perceive Western civilization to be threatened by the permanent settlement of large numbers of non-Christian, non-white immigrants in their homelands.[1497] The wish of the Muslim community to segregate itself from the new society it became part of resulted in failure of their integration and a stronger will to preserve their original identity. A major role in keeping their identity is played by closeness to religion and compliance with religious precepts such as wearing of religious attire or head covering, applying especially with respect to women. Thence, a common challenge encountered in

1497 *Auslander*, Cultural Dynamics 12 (3), 2000, 283, 294.

many of the European countries in relation to their Muslim immigrants was the need to accommodate to their religious needs. In particular, the Islamic headscarf or stricter forms of head coverings (i.e., *niqab*, *jilbab*, or *burqa*) have triggered heated national debates, in particular when their permissibility in the education context was put into question as defying Christian-Western tradition and values; as a result, several European countries, inter alia France and Germany induced their ban from public schools.

The headscarf ban had been justified based on several possible grounds that vary in each of the compared countries due to different emphasis conferred in the legal systems to the following factors: constitutional principles and values, tradition, cultural practices, social structure, history, and policy making. For instance, Germany justifies a ban on the headscarf based on the duty of the state to religious neutrality, an unwanted influence on the pupils' right to negative religious freedom, the right to gender equality, and other pre-eminent constitutional rights. England justifies the ban based on technical reasons (i.e., the inability of pupils to understand the teacher, undue social pressure, peaceful co-existence in school), nonetheless, it enables the teacher in principle to wear the head covering after school hours. France establishes the legitimacy of the ban on teachers founded on the sacrosanct principle of laïcité. This demonstrates that the policy of state education and the formation of a framework for public schools, which regulates among others the endorsement of religious insignias in the educational sphere, taking into perspective the compared states in this analysis, is influenced by divisive factors. These factors combined with the following features: the constitutional order of a state, the adopted state-church model, the religious interplay in the public sphere, cultural diversity, and historical evolvement of religion reflect the difficulty and complexity of providing a legal solution that would be equally legitimized and applicable in the legal framework of all compared countries in this analysis.

The following points of convergence and divergence will be summarized as follows:

a) State-Church Model

Germany – adopts the co-operationist model of state-church, which is in a sense a midway approach since it does not administer a strict separation of religion from state and does not fit a strict theocratic model. The German Republic incorporates religious themes in several areas of life, as it is obliged by its constitution to provide its citizens with an adequate space for religious worship and the freedom to undisturbed practice of their religion (e.g., Art. 4 para 1 and 2 GG, Art. 6 para 2 GG, Art. 7 GG, Art. 140 GG in tandem with Art. 136 WRV).

Though there is no strong allegiance on the national level to the dominating faith, Christianity, the importance of the role of religion and transferral of Christian tradition and its values in several individual states indicates the tension that may accrue between religious majority and minority, especially in public education.

England – the adopted state-church model is of a formal unification which accepts and recognizes the position of the Anglican Church, but the state is neither bound in institutional relations to the Church nor does it provide it with financial support. On the same token, the Church does not interfere in state affairs. Nonetheless, in the historical evolvement of religion, the Anglican Church has held power over public education either with respect to formation of schools, determination of curriculum content on a national level, and even regarding the execution of daily prayers and collective worships taking place in several school forms until today.

France – the French model is distinguishable as it illustrates a salient concept of strict separation of state and church. That means that the two institutions act separately, and the state does not feature or display any religious symbols in the public sphere so as not to be attached with promotion or advancement of religion. The strict adherence to laïcité is held in sanctity, in particular with respect to the public sphere including the state school system. In fact, the French and the English models are considered as representing two extreme opposites on the scale, whereas the German model is regarded to represent a mid-position that can be located somewhere between both poles as it incorporates characteristics of co-operation and separation.

b) The Prevailing Legal Order for Protection of Fundamental Rights

Germany has an established federal constitutional system. Fundamental rights and protected constitutional values are entrenched in the German Grundgesetz. Even though international conventions apply in Germany, the domestic level of freedom and equality rights reflects or even transcends the standards that are included in international conventions. Accordingly, the right-holder in Germany usually tends to base his/her claims or grievances on domestic regulations. The constitution grants merely a defence position of an individual against the state, at first instance in form of liberty rights that are meant to keep the state away from any influence on private life. These liberty rights are accompanied by equality rights that are to be considered as vital, strong, and effective; however, they are not as dominant as in England.

England – the common law system in England does not include a written constitution, no written catalogue or established Bill of Rights. This explains the perception in the English discourse regarding the right to religious freedom in general and manifestation of religious right by display or wearing of ostentatious symbols or garments in particular. The English system hardly imposes restrictions on the rights of individuals to manifest outwardly their religion (forum externum). Therefore, prior to promulgation of the HRA 1998 it was regarded a system where fundamental rights are safeguarded more due to its being a tolerance-based approach rather than a right-based approach. In the development of its legislative system, anti-discrimination and equality rights acquired a salient position, in particular with respect to claims established on religious grounds. A complaint will always be founded on the equality heads as the golden way for substantiation of infringement of religious rights and will be preferable on part of the claimant as opposed to their establishment on fundamental human rights claim based on the HRA 1998. This may be attributed to the fact that the evolvement of equality rights is rooted in the legislative system of Britain and dates back to an earlier period in history in contrast to fundamental human rights which have received final formal recognition towards the end of the twentieth century, taking place with the incorporation of the ECHR into domestic law with the HRA 1998. Therefore, on a general level, anti-discrimination rights possess an extraordinary relevance and form a substantial part of a complaint for a breach on an individual's right to manifestation of religious freedom.

France has a constitutional established system with an emphasis and expectation for assimilation and acceptance of the three pre-eminent constitutional French pillars: equality, liberty, and fraternity. There is no comprehensive constitution in place, but rather a number of different constitutional sources that had developed during the centuries and still apply in parallel. Due to France's unique structure of courts, the division between courts within their jurisdictional power to adjudicate in public and administrative law in issues relating to violation of fundamental human rights, and with the CE as the Supreme Administrative Court in France whose referral is sought by the lower courts, it can be said that the mechanism offered for protection of human rights in general is one that is truly safeguarded and entrenched in France's legal system. The legal position of fundamental human rights does not achieve its prominent status only in domestic law but also by virtue of France's acceptance of its obligations on the international level and conferment of precedence over domestic legislation. In theory, fundamental human rights are expected to achieve outmost protection in France due to their constitutional fundaments in domestic law which are even fortified by precedence conferred to its obligation on the international level. Though France demonstrates that, in theory, religious rights are supposed to achieve outmost protection by law, in practice it suffers the most of insufficient and adequate protection granted to religious rights and that in comparison to the systems adopted in England and Germany.

c) Organizational Structure of Education

Germany – The federal structure in Germany privileges the individual states to exclusive administration of their inner affairs including education (Art. 70 GG), and the educative mandate conferred on the state which is based on sole discretion without any interference on the national level (Art. 7 para 1 GG).

England shares a similar de-centralized structure of its educational system. This is a salient constituent of its school system since historically the establishment and funding of state schools were left an issue within the responsibility of the local authorities. The local authorities, thence, bear responsibility for the administration of the state educational system. In both Germany and England, there exists a non-centralised educational system.

France – though the constitution carries a unitary character, Art. 1 of the 1958 Constitution provides that the organization of the Republic is decentralised. Nonetheless, educational matters are not carried out on the regional level but rather are left to the supervision of the state. Therefore, the educational system in France is characterised by its highly centralized and organised system.

d) The Cultural and Religious Interplay in Education

Germany – since the state-church model is not of a strict separation, and the endorsement of religion or religious themes in public education is determined to a large extent on the regional level, it can be said that in principle churchly affairs and Christian content in state schools are not remote and extrinsic to society. In fact, many federal states (e.g., Bavaria, BW, and NRW) still preserve this inimitable bond to Christian tradition and values to be transferred as educational goals in their state schools. Likewise, the German interplay with its religious minorities accepts the change of the German nation into a pluralistic society. The general state-church relations advocate in favour of the accommodative-integrative approach of religion into public education. The perception in the legal literature as well as of the jurisprudence is that German society is no longer a homogenous one but has rather evolved to be a multi-cultural, multi-pluralistic society and as such must mould and form its future citizens towards tolerance and integration that will be achieved only through their implementation into the public school system. One can sum up the German paradigm with respect to accommodation of religion and in particular the needs of its religious minorities with the support of a famous pronouncement of the BVerfG that the 'state is the home-place for all its citizens'.

England manages pluralism with tolerance towards other religions, faiths, and denominations. However, a major role, especially in the educational sector, plays the established status of the Church of England, the Anglican Church.

A significant change the school system had undergone since the outdated Education Act 1944 until recent times demonstrates that there was a noticeable shift in state schools which drifted from the ultimate Christian nature characterizing religious education to a multi-faith approach. On the one hand, the multi-faith approach enjoyed popularity among those who perceived it as fostering respect, tolerance, integration, and harmonious co-existence between the different ethnic and religious groups in Britain. On the other hand, the multi-faith approach suffered massive criticism especially on the part of conservative Christian groups who strongly comprehended this shift as detrimental to the transfer of the Christian faith and its values through education in state schools. Finally, even religious education was becoming increasingly multi-cultural in nature (with the exception of daily prayers and collective worship).

France – a state that by its nature adheres to the principle of laïcité as one of its salient constitutional fundaments negates religious references in the public sphere. Due to the historical importance of this principle in the politics of the French nation, there was and still exists an expectation from its religious minorities to assimilate in society and accord with its constitutional precepts. Therefore, France perceives the French 'assimilationist' model as one that requires integration from its religious minorities that is to be achieved through internalization of the French Republican values. This demonstrates a clear preference for conformity and assimilation to be taken on part of its immigrants and even more so in public education.

As such, France and England are to be found at two opposite sides of the spectrum. Whereas England demonstrates a more inclusive approach towards religious pluralism as well as acceptance and inclusion of religious symbols into its public sphere, France demonstrates an approach of decline towards its religious minorities and a repugnance from anything that may run counter to fundamental elements upon which the Republic is established. This includes exclusion of religious symbols from its public sphere since they underscore differentiation and emphasize segregation made on religious, ethnical, or racial grounds as oppose to identification with the French ideology of one unified nation. In addition, the identification of individuals through religious apparel rejects the definition of individualism and focuses rather on the association with a specific religious group and the adherence to its precepts. This notion in itself contradicts the fundaments of the Republican ideals that accepts and expects the allegiance of all its citizens with the French nation.

The significant role of school as a melting point for all religions, ethnics, and faiths in society has been underscored in all countries in this analysis. Schools as educational institutions are perceived by society as a place responsible for the formation of future society, where pupils acquire not only education but also values and morals (e.g., self-restraint, responsibility). The legal approach in Germany and England supports the notion that in multi-cultural, pluralistic societies the significance of educational institutions has raised and thence emphasized the necessity for education towards integration and tolerance. In France, the jurisprudential approach relating to admissibility of pupils to wear religious symbols in public education indicates acceptance and willingness towards religious manifestation of female Muslim pupils. This is, however, will be tolerated only to the extent the manifestation of a religious symbols will not endanger the peaceful co-existence in school and pose excessive pressure on other Muslim pupils to conform with the wearing of this religious attire or garment. This opinion that find its support in decisions of the CE demonstrates the alienation from the notion of integration in favour of assimilation.

e) Nature and Form of Display of Religious Symbols

Germany – in practice, the German jurisprudence attributes high importance to the interpretation of religious symbols and their perception by the symbol-viewers as a means to downplay the legitimacy of right-holders to display religious symbols. This has been and still is a considerable factor which the courts consider as far as the permissibility of a teacher to manifestation of her religion by her external appearance (e.g., the wearing of the headscarf) needs to be outweighed. Especially, within its retrenched scope of confrontation with elementary school pupils. The prevailing approach in the German jurisprudence up to the recent decision of the BVerfG reviewing the constitutionality of the headscarf ban in the state of NRW was very restrictive towards the teacher's freedom to practice her religion by virtue of her religious apparel, in particular, if there is danger of a proselytizing or indoctrinating effect on the minds of pupils. In this respect, the jurisprudence underscored many times that the possibility of an indoctrinating effect on pupils of tender age, even if it cannot be substantiated de facto, cannot be negated completely and only by that reason should tilt the balance when outweighing competing rights in favour of the pupils (the 'practical concordance'). The permissibility of a teacher to display religious attire other than the headscarf, even if it does not carry a religious meaning as, for instance, with a teacher wearing a Basque-style beret, had been dismissed by the BVerfG. The argumentation of the Court upheld that though the nature of the sign may not be religious, it is the way it is worn and the context within which it is displayed (e.g., at all times and without exception) which suggest that the intention or the motivation of the wearer was religious and thus may impart on the viewer its religious connotation.

The indoctrinating effect had also been argued by the BVerfG in the *Crucifix* decision. However, this was argued with respect to a state-imposed symbol (i.e., the affixation of a cross in state school classrooms) and the right of religious minorities (non-believers) to abstain from unwanted religious influence. The verdict ruled in favour of the minority pupils since the proselytizing effect of the cross or its negative influence which does not conform with the educative parental right to religious education of their children (Art. 4 para 1 and para 2 in tandem with Art. 6 para 2 GG) cannot be denied. This argumentation was fortified by the lack of opportunity to evade the Crucifix since pupils are obliged by compulsory schooling to constant confrontation with its view, as it is displayed on every classroom wall in all Bavarian public schools.

England – in the English discourse the religious meaning attributed to religious symbols is not regarded as problematic. In fact, the headscarf specifically is known for its rarity in the English discourse and has never been subject to public debates or has initiated controversies in public school system. The headscarf was not precieved as a threat whether, by virtue of its religious connotation as a sign of women's oppression and subordination to men nor, by its political association with Islamic extremist-fundamentalist groups. Similarly, the shalwars, loose-fitting trousers, worn mostly by Asian women in order to pursue their cultural tradition did not pose any objection by reason of its religious meaning. Consequently, religious insignias, such as the *turban* worn by Sikha men or *jilbab* worn by Muslim women can be regarded inadmissible by reference to other grounds and not necessarily by virtue of their religiosity. These grounds may include health, safety concerns, equality, the need to keep away other pupils from undue pressure, racism, and disturbance of the harmonious order in schools. For instance, the more restrictive form of head covering like the *niqab* worn by a teaching-assistant was regarded impermissible due to the fact that her communication with pupils was disrupted, and it was for this reason the teacher could not fulfil her educative function properly.

France – in decisions of the CE with respect to visibility of religious symbols worn by teachers in public education, it was pronounced that, as a general rule, religious symbols are interdicted especially for teachers, as they are perceived as officials of the public service employed in the public school system. The significance attributed to the nature and form of the symbol in question does not play a role under French law, as the prohibition is inclusive and applies to all religious symbols equally. The nature and form of religious insignias will be relevant only relating to the appropriateness of sanctions and the gravity that will be deployed on a teacher who was found in violation of the ban. The size of religious symbols is also a factor that was taken into account since under French law the ban on manifestation of religious symbols relates mainly to ostentatious insignias which, in contrast to discreet signs, are capable of disturbing the peaceful co-existence in school and thus infringe upon the interest of public order and the principle of laïcité.

f) The Perception of Religion in Education

Germany – from a constitutional point of view, the legal status of religious freedom under Art. 4 GG is unreserved and its scope of protection is considered as very extensive. Art. 4 GG is the pivotal element in controversies arising in the public school system: on the one hand, a teacher's right to exercise her right to religious manifestation by reference to the positive dimension, and, on the other hand, the pupils by reference to the negative dimension when being unwillingly exposed and confronted with a teacher wearing a headscarf as a powerful, extrinsic symbol to which they cannot associate. Another aspect of the negative dimension includes parents' right to decide on the education of their children and ensure that they conform to their religious ethos pursuant to Art. 6 para 2 GG. The discussion is therefore centred around the construction of the liberty to religious freedom that needs to be contrasted with the majority's wish for Christian education and perpetuation of its tradition and values on the background of its endorsement as an educational goal in the constitutions of several individual states (e.g., Bavaria, NRW, and BW). An interpretation of constitutional religious references as in the form of privilege to the Christian faith and tradition that has been appreciated so far by the federal legislators is no longer admissible since the recent ruling of the BVerfG which explicitly declared such prevalence as unconstitutional and invalid. In order to comply with constitutional demands of denominational and religious equality, the educative task of the state to transfer Christian values should be confined only by reference to its humanistic and moral context. Churchly influence on school curriculum should be moderate and not demonstrate a strong allegiance and preference to the Christian faith. Religious emphasis on Christian values as part of the educational framework that takes form whether by conferment of Christian content or the display of Christian symbols has to retreat in favour of a retrenched form.

England – in principle, the general approach in England is very open and liberal towards religion, and accommodation of religious needs of minorities is normally accepting and welcoming. However, the state no longer sets up a religious imperative with regard to the school curriculum, with the exception of faith schools. In principle, the admissibility of teachers or pupils to display religious insignias in state schools, is not denied outright. For instance, the practice of daily prayers and collective worship is still upheld in several school forms. Nonetheless, the powerful position of the Anglican Church with respect to education has been substantially decreased, as the religious character of schools became more a historic reminiscent instead of a vivid part of state schools' practice. England does not actively order a religiously influenced educational goal, but it rather provides a space that is to a certain extent open to religious activity of individuals. Consequently, tension points in England are not focussed on the limits of religious freedom itself, but rather on equal treatment of all religions and the ability of an individual to practice his/her religion in terms of strict compliance of the state with the general duty of non-discrimination. The duty of the state with respect to teachers' right to religious practice had been extended in the last centuries under the obligation of non-discrimination in employment and included other discriminatory heads as unlawful. In the past, prior to the HRA 1998, lack of state willingness to comply or accord with demands of its minorities to religious practice was given emphasis based on discrimination on grounds of race or ethnic. This allows, even today, for conflicts to be resolved within the boundaries of racial or religious discrimination.

France – the disentanglement of state-church relations and disempowering the Catholic Church from its educative control and supervision of state schools is entrenched in France's history and dates back to the pre-revolution period. The general approach underestimates and rejects religious differentiation and prefers to underscore the importance of the principle of laïcité and its adhesion especially in the public sphere, inter alia in compulsory state schools. The French nation does not allow any form of religious reference in its public sphere that may indicate of any religious favouritism on part of the state. The manifestation of religion as such is excluded from public education, as it constitutes a part of the public sphere in which the state must not confer any religious affiliation. Therefore, the affixation of crucifixes in state school classrooms is banned from the educational scene. The visibility of religious symbols per se is excluded from public education when displayed by teachers due to their function as public servants. Following promulgation of the 2011 law, the prohibition to appear with ostentatious religious symbols applies also with respect to pupils.

g) The Admissibility of Religious Symbols in the Education

Germany – the legal status of teachers as public servants and their right to manifestation of religious symbols while on duty was not regulated by law up to *Ludin*'s case. The general pronouncement of the BVerfG refrained from an explicit guidance to the federal states as to which symbols should be permitted, and further interpretation rules in order to determine their admissibility in state school system remained undiscussed. In the aftermath of *Ludin*'s case, many federal states took initiative and implemented modification into their education laws with the explicit intention to outlaw in particular the Islamic headscarf. The recent decision of the BVerfG reviewed two conjoined appeals relating to the headscarf ban in NRW, declaring it to be unconstitutional and invalid. The decision has triggered amendments to the education act on part of the NRW legislator, which ensued shortly after delivery of the judgement.

The BVerfG recognized the incontestable right of a teacher to religious manifestation and underscored her right to live according to the precept dictated by her religion and as safeguarded to her in the constitution without reservation. It declared that the right to religious manifestation of a teacher will be confined only when a concrete danger exists to other fundamental or constitutional protected rights that are safeguarded in another constitutional provision. The classic German perception of infringement of a fundamental right is very extensive in form. As such, it will not be problematic under German constitutional law to establish an interference on an individual's right (i.e., a teacher) to practice his/her religion (e.g., by wearing a headscarf).

Thence, as possible grounds for justification on a teacher's right to exertion of her right to religious freedom, the lands legislators' can take the following factors into consideration: the negative right of pupils to religious freedom, the educative task of parents to rear their children as they consider fit, the educative mandate of the state, the duty of the state to religious neutrality, and the non-discrimination precept. Notably, the BverfG held in its recent judgement of the headscarf ban in NRW that the endangering of peaceful school operation as well as the interpretation of the headscarf as a symbol contradictory to the gender equality precept do not raise a sufficient justification for the ban of the headscarf and a harsh infringement on the teacher's right to religious freedom.

It should be noted that in this decision of the BVerfG it accorded high importance to the teachers right to religious manifestation when outweighing it against other competing rights (implementing the principle of 'practical concordance'). The BverfG in a very exceptional manner decided that the negative right of pupils not to be exposed or influenced by the teachers' view should not be given prevalence over the teachers' right to religious freedom. In previous case laws, the aspects of a teachers' willingness and voluntariness were also considered, when evaluating the competing rights at stake. The fact that the teacher entered her job willingly, as well as the existence of an alternative for her to work in a private faith school or alternative schooling in which her headscarf may be permitted, had been emphasized by the courts in order to downplay the encroachment on the teachers' right to practice her religion.

The admissibility of state-imposed symbols like the Crucifix in a Christian state like Bavaria was negated by the BVerfG. The German jurisprudence endeavoured to delineate the boundaries between the legitimacy of the state to display symbols as opposed to an individual-displayed symbol, for instance, by using the justification that the Crucifix affixed on a classroom wall demonstrates incontestably an unlawful state's recognition with a specific religion, thus contradicting the obligation of the state to religious neutrality. In the legal literature as well as in the jurisprudence, criticism has been raised that the teacher acts as a role model for pupils who may be affected by her view. In addition, the duty of the teacher as a state representative does not disclose any religious affinity emanating from her function as public servant. It was argued that the legitimacy of a teacher to wear the Islamic headscarf raises the question of the state identification with a particular religion no less than is posed by virtue of the affixation of the Crucifix.

England – there is no general prohibition on teachers or pupils under English law to refrain from display of religious symbols. The scope of protection of the right to religious freedom is remarkably extensive. An infringement of the right of a teacher is not defined by law or by the jurisprudence (i.e., HL) whether with respect to teachers or pupils. As possible justification for interference in a teacher's right to religious freedom, the judicator will take into account hindrance of the teacher that makes her unable to fulfil her educative task properly, as was demonstrated in the case of *Azmi*. In addition, the preferable path for a teacher to hand in a complaint of a breach of her right to religious manifestation is normally the substantiation of her claim based on equality rights as opposed to fundamental human rights. The reason is imprinted by the fact that in Britain's legal history anti-discrimination laws were much developed under English law as opposed to fundamental human rights which have perceived legal recognition only at a later stage (i.e., the enactment of the HRA 1998). In addition, equality rights offer a claimant an extensive scope of protection since employers are subject to a comprehensive duty of equality under employment law. In particular, taking the perspective of the proportionality test that claimant will be likely more successful to prove that less intrusive measures could have been deployed by the employer for achieving the aim (i.e., the teacher could wear the head covering only during her work with men as teaching staff).

Nonetheless, the right of a teacher to manifest her religious freedom is not guaranteed at all times and may also be confined, as was substantially proved in the case of Azmi. The teacher could not fulfil her function properly, and although other alternatives were offered to her, she refused to accept them.

The duty of teachers to abide by the neutrality principle as a possible justification ground for encroachment on their fundamental right to religious freedom has not been underscored under English law. Unlike the legal situation in France and Germany where the adherence to the neutrality principle is much observed and evaluated due to its strong roots in the constitutional systems of these countries, this is not the case in the constitutional history of England. The obligation of the state to religious neutrality, inter alia of teachers as state representatives, did not hold water in British jurisprudence. The duty of teachers to remain neutral, emanating from their position as public officials had been not considered in British jurisprudence, especially since teachers are not considered civil servants and accordingly are not subject to special rule of conduct.

To sum up, in England, great significance is attributed to the conduct of a public official rather than to his/her outer appearance that qualifies as a standard for complying with the neutrality principle.

As possible grounds for justification on encroachment of pupils' right to religious manifestation the following will be given due regard by the English jurisprudence: (i) undue pressure on other pupils, whether Muslims or members of other faiths, to accord with a religious precept, (ii) the proselytizing or indoctrinating effect of the symbol on other pupils to conform with strict religious dress rules, (iii) the formation of groups inside school realm that will aggravate inner conflicts and harm peaceful co-existence in school, (iv) ostracism and alienation of pupils as an outcome of segregation based on religious apparel that indicates of the pupils' pertinence or non-pertinence to a religious group, (v) the necessity to demonstrate equality of all pupils in school.

France – The right of a teacher to undisturbed manifestation of her right to religious freedom is confined and that has merely taken the perspective of its strict separationist state-church model and the importance known to the principle of laïcité in the public sphere. Due to lack of legal criteria setting the boundaries of an infringement and the lack of its delineation in French jurisprudence, there is no clear-cut understanding of what will be regarded as infringement on teachers' or pupils' right to religious manifestation.

Nonetheless, as possible grounds for justification the French law differentiates between those applicable to teachers and those relevant to pupils. As justified encroachment on teachers' right to display a religious attire or symbol when executing their public function and under their duty as a teacher, the legal literature as well as the jurisprudence confer high significance to abide by the laïcité principle and the duty of public servants to adhere by it, as ascribed under French public law. The French perception of its public service and the special duty that applies with respect to all public officials (*agents public*) to appear unprejudiced stipulates their obligation to refrain from display of any sign that may indicate their religious or ideological affinity. This perception is entrenched in French law and applies equally, in particular, with respect to public servants by virtue of their close daily work with the public, without any reservation. This duty is imposed also on teachers as public servants and obliges them to appear impartial and unbiased.

It should be noted that the French law, unlike the German and English legal systems does no tend to separate the duty of public officials within their professional capacity from their private lives.

The right of pupils to manifestation of religious freedom had been perceived in the past (i.e., prior to the introduction of the Laws of 2004 and 2011) as more extensive in its scope of protection, as its retrenchment would have been more difficult to align constitutionally. Following the coming into force of the legislative acts of 2004 and 2011, the right of pupils to display religious symbols could become extensively limited. The risk these enactments may unveil is an excessive encroachment on fundamental human rights disguising the real intention of a complete forbearance of ostentatious oriental symbols like the headscarf or other head coverings from the school realm.

Astonishing as it may sound, the recent enactments of 2004 and 2011 highlighted the duty of the state to religious neutrality as a justification ground for the guarantee of pupils to religious freedom. As far as the visibility of religious signs with respect to pupils is concerned, there has been an extensive interpretation of the neutrality principle which was meant to offer protection for pupils by upholding the obligation to keep religious neutrality of the state in public education. The state has a very active duty to promote and enforce adherence to the neutrality principle. It was explained that compliance with the neutrality precept with respect to pupils would eliminate conflicts, discrimination, and racism between pupils that are founded on religious or racial grounds, and would help to downplay segregation made by formation of religious or ethnical groups that will only contribute to aggravation of conflicts in the school realm.

It is necessary to underscore that in contrast to the German approach the French apprehension with respect to religious neutrality of the state will not fulfil its task to neutrality if it enables the endorsement of every religious practice into its school system. On the contrary, the strict adherence to neutrality will guarantee the freedoms and rights of others and thus avoid unnecessary pressure, discrimination, and conflicts between various religious groups in schools and ensure the negative right of other pupils to religious freedom. In particular, it was argued to safeguard the negative right to religious freedom of the wearer himself by offering him a neutral sphere to flourish which is distant from any community pressure to which he may be exposed to in his private sphere.

Nonetheless, the 2011 Act interdicting the manifestation of conspicuous religious symbols in the public sphere raises heavy doubts as to its constitutionality on the domestic as well as on the international level. On the domestic level, the fact that the prohibition applies also to private people and by that extends its scope also with respect to pupils and their permissibility to manifest religious symbols in state schools cannot be justified constitutionally. So far, the legal framework in France was able to justify the prohibition on teachers to religious manifestation due to their duty as public servants; however, this justification cannot apply with respect to pupils as they are regarded under French public law as *usagers* of the public service. On the international level, France's obligation under international law to respect and incorporate international treaties to which it is a signatory, and the precedence it gives to its obligation on the international level (e.g., ECHR or ICCPR) leaves the conformity of the 2011 Law with these international standards with heavy doubts.

To sum up, the dogmatic structure of scope of protection, infringement, and justification are not really deployed under the French and English legal systems. This dogmatic examination exists extensively solely in the legal framework of Germany.

In addition, the focus given under the German and French legal systems with respect to infringement of an individual's right to free practice of religion concentrated on the fundamental human rights aspect, whereas under the English system claims of complainants were supported mainly by anti-discrimination laws.

In Germany, just like in England, the aspects of voluntariness and availability of an alternative form of schooling had been considered with due regard by the jurisprudence as a supportive factor justifying the encroachment upon teachers' right to manifestation of religious affiliation when implementing the proportionality test. In this context, it was reasoned by the judicator that a teacher, unlike pupils who are subject to compulsory schooling, entered his/her profession willingly and voluntarily so that in case he/she is not willing to accord with school regulations, he/she always has the opportunity to opt out. In addition, in the German as well as in British jurisprudence the fact that a teacher could find an alternative in a private (Islamic) school or professional school was not negated in order to dismiss a complainant's claim that the measure adopted by the state was not proportionate. In fact, it seems that in both judicial systems the aspect of alternative schooling for a teacher would suffice to negate the lack of proportionality to the pursued aim, that is, maintenance of peaceful school operation; in Germany, it is the guarantee of the negative right of pupils to religious freedom, as it was often substantiated that the respective teacher had known and agreed to school regulations prior to her job application.

Finally, the jurisprudence in all three countries (England, France, and Germany) had taken due account of the following factors: formation of religious groups, classification made on grounds of ethnic and religion, undue pressure and oppression against other female Muslim pupils to comply with the wearing of head coverings such as *jilbab* or *niqab* as possible justification grounds when assessing the decision of school authorities to impose a ban on a pupil from attendance in school realm due to his/her religious apparel.

h) Development Towards Secularized Nation

Germany – the process the German nation had undergone till adoption of its midway secularized nature was adduced along several factors mainly due to societal changes and recognition that it had to accept and integrate the plurality of religions which for many years have settled and have become an integral part of the country. On the legal level this acknowledgement was reflective in case laws adjudicated by the courts as well as changes and amendments initiated by the federal states in order to adapt their legislative framework with contemporary challenges induced by this social-demographical transformation. On the social level the German society, with the exception of several federal states carrying a salient Christian character (e.g., Bavaria, Baden-Württemberg) has become more secular. It is worth to note that following the recent decision of the BVerfG relating to the headscarf ban in NRW the possibilities the lands' legislators are left with from the legal perspective are either to adopt a more accommodative-liberal approach towards religious pluralism, as common in England, or to undertake a separationist model eliminating any religious references from the public sphere, and supporting the transformation to a secularist-laicist system in public education as envisaged in France. The former approach can be achieved through an extensive construction of the right to religious freedom and its manifestation in the respective education act of the individual state so that they would fit the modern concept of religion and a multi-cultural, pluralistic society. The latter can be achieved through a stricter implementation of the neutrality principle, which prescribes a complete elimination of religious references, including the display of religious symbols from state schools like the strict laicist approach practiced in France.

England – similarly to the case in Germany, the secularization process did not leave the English nation unaffected. Albeit the relative liberal, accommodative-friendly approach towards immigrants that Britain's long tradition is associated with, it was demonstrated that the situation in theory and practice is often diverged to a large extent. The fact that England also had to struggle to maintain its liberal-secular approach was noticeable in two aspects. On the legal level, by the long way undergone till legislative recognition was granted to the fundamental human right of religious freedom. Likewise, the achievement of a minimal legal protection to freedom of religion and protection of religious minority rights also through equality laws have proved to develop in a piecemeal manner in England. These factors indicate that the British legislator had realized the need to find a written legal basis for the protection of human rights. On a social level, there is the decrease in the importance of the church and religion in general within British society. This was shown by a decline of church membership and attendance at churchly acts of worship and ceremonies.[1498]

France – is already situated at the other side of the scale characterised by its strict state-church separation. This is reflected through strict application of the principle of laïcité, in the non-intervention and non-identification principles of state with churchly affairs, and vice versa. Nonetheless, the promulgation of the 2011 Act raised criticism in the legal literature whether this legislative step was adequate and necessary at all. The 2011 Act demonstrates a gradual escalation towards further laicization of society and thus poses great difficulty to justify its constitutional existence even in a laic state like France.

i) The Neutrality Concept and Its Impact on Manifestation of Religious Symbols in the Education

Germany – the obligation of the state to adhere to the neutrality principle is considered in Germany as a constitutional principle prescribed in the German Grundgesetz (Art. 137 para 1 WRV). On a conceptual level, it remains arguable in the German literature and jurisprudence whether the state's duty to remain neutral, especially within the context of religion and its interplay with the public sphere should adopt a strict or rather a liberal approach. Considering the ample jurisprudence delivered in Germany with respect to the permissibility of schoolteachers to manifest their religion given that they do not disturb or

1498 *Fetzer/Soper*, pp. 35, 36; *van Ooijen*, p. 213.

endanger the obligation of the state to religious neutrality by wearing ostentatious symbols or garments while on duty, it seems that following the last NRW headscarf ruling the BVerfG had provided a clear legal criterion that only concrete endangerment to neutrality would justify a violation of a teacher's right to manifestation of her religious freedom. The legal criteria that were established by the BVerfG were meant to provide the lands' legislators more certainty and predictability as to the constitutionality of their education acts. Nonetheless, the latest decision of the Federal Labour Court in Berlin from April 2016 (yet to be published),[1499] declaring the interdiction of the headscarf on teaching staff in the state of Berlin to be constitutional based on the significance ascribed to the duty of its public servants to appear neutral and unbiased had emphasized again the considerable weight of the neutrality principle in German constitutional law. The neutrality principle is recognized in the jurisprudence as a pre-eminent constitutional principle which can be used as an own standing justification for limitation of the fundamental right to religious freedom.

The obligation of the state to religious neutrality had been emphasized in the German jurisprudence also with respect to state-imposed symbols like the Crucifix. The prevailing approach of the BVerfG would favour a strict apprehension of the neutrality principle as far as the permissibility of a state to impose symbols in public education is concerned and would advocate the rights of religious minorities not to be confronted with the view of the Crucifix without an opportunity of evasion. Following the recent decision of the BVerfG relating to the headscarf ban in NRW, it remains questionable whether pupils of religious minorities will be required to demonstrate a concrete endangerment to their negative religious right not to be exposed to the view of a Crucifix in order to justify a breach of the state's duty to neutrality and to uphold their right for removal of the cross.

England – there exists no formal obligation to neutrality in the public sphere. The principle is not explicitly recognized under English law, but it is acknowledged as a substantive neutrality deriving its recognition when inferred from other constitutional principles: the rule of law, and equality before the law. The principle is not used by itself as a ground for curbing fundamental rights of individuals, but it is rather used to pursue aims other than the neutrality

1499 See in FAZ from 16 April 2016 http://www.faz.net/aktuell/feuilleton/debatten/grundsatzfragen-im-berliner-kopftuch-streit-14180746.html and in DW from 14 April 2016 http://www.dw.com/de/berliner-arbeitsgericht-weist-kopftuch-klage-ab/a-19189326

principle. For instance, in the case of Azmi the arguments adduced in favour of the teacher's dismissal from school emphasized rather her lack of professional aptitude or performance-related capabilities other than the importance to adhere to the neutrality principle. Under this aspect the following can be concluded: first, the insignificance known to the neutrality principle in England's legal framework; second, the display of religious symbols by public officials such as teachers will not be regarded as contravening state neutrality as this will be examined on a case-by-case basis; third, since the display of religious symbols in the public service, according to English law, may trigger the question of having a possible discriminatory effect against the citizen, the policy in practice demonstrates that the use/display of religious symbols in public state schools will not be regarded per se as discriminatory against the negative right of pupils to refrain from the view of a teacher with a head covering. This was explained to be a direct outcome of the non-secular nature of the state and the fact that no strict separation between state and church has ever existed in England due to the influence of the Anglican Church. The fact that the established Church of England played a major role in the sphere of education helped to preserve the endorsement of religious elements in the public sphere and prevented the disentanglement of religion and its notable influence in public education.

France – the French system adopts a formal version of the neutrality principle. There is a general principle to abide by the neutrality principle in the public service. This principle is one of the fundamental pillars of the French Republic and as such it is strictly adhered in French politics in general, and in the jurisprudence in particular. The obligation of public officials to adhere to the neutrality principle in the public sphere cannot be undermined due to the importance the French attribute to the principle, as it derives authority from its sacrosanct principle of laïcité. In France, the abstract endangerment to the principle of neutrality or to the equality percept will suffice in order to justify the infringement on a teacher's right to manifestation of his/her religious freedom by way of display of religious donning. The ban imposed on pupils to refrain from manifestation of religious symbols that by virtue of their outer appearance indicate religious affiliation received statutory legitimization by promulgation of the Law of March 2004. Following the introduction of the Law of 2004, the perception of the laïcité principle has gained an extensive construction, interlinking the precept of neutrality with the republican ideals of equality and its educational goals of emancipation, sovereignty, and responsibility of the citizens to respect the Republic and the liberties enshrined in its constitution. The incentive of the drafters of this legislation was inclusion of the laïcité principle as a justification ground for the interdiction of the Islamic headscarf from school realm.

The neutrality principle is perceived fundamentally differently in France and Germany. However, due to the introduction of the law in 2004 aiming specifically at the Muslim headscarf, it remains doubtful whether the situation in most of the federal states in Germany – with the exclusion of NRW following its recent amendment to its school act (Art. 2 para 8 SchulG NRW) – differs substantially from that existing in France.

j) Neutrality and Its Impact on the Conception of Public Officials

Germany – neutrality was recognized in the German jurisprudence as a constitutional principle and had been used as a justifying ground for imposing obligations on part of its public officials to identify with the state. This does not apply with respect to all public officials but bears emphasis with respect to several duty holders, especially in education, judiciary, and the police force. Until the recent ruling of the BVerfG relating to the dismissal of a teacher with a headscarf in NRW, the prevailing opinion in the German jurisprudence accepted that abstract endangerment posed to the precept of neutrality, may confer it prevalence not only over the teacher's right to manifestation of her religion but also against other fundamental rights that are at stake. The possibility of endangerment to another competing constitutional right would have sufficed to interfere in the teacher's right to demonstrate her religious affinity by virtue of her overt appearance. However, following the recent decision it will be necessary to prove a concrete endangerment to the principle of neutrality or other constitutional rights in order to justify an encroachment on a teacher's right to religious freedom.

England – the reason why the neutrality principle is not clearly conceptualized in the English context is interlinked with several notable characteristics underlying its legislative system. The first dates to the fact that England does not attribute a significant meaning to the state's concept within the context of the public sphere. In other words, the English state does not perceive its role as a distinct entity which, taken on with the public service, would generate a uniform entity. The uniqueness and conception of the state as an entity was not emphasized and recognized as in France (e.g., the notion that all French people share the identity of their Frenchness). The second emanates from the first one and prescribes no obligation of an individual as a public official to identify with the state. There is no legislative obligation of public service holders to identify or personalize with the state within duty. This naturally stems from the absence of a defined notion of the public service in English law. In the absence of clear, uniform rules imposing on public officials' abidance by the state's conception of neutrality, there exists no obligation on part of its public officials to identify with the state. Hence, public officials in general will not be required to concede their individual right to exercise their religious freedom due to the fact that it may entail their 'personification' with the state. This suggests that no limitations would be imposed on public officials' right to display religious symbols. Nonetheless, a confinement would not be introduced based merely on a general principle like neutrality, but rather based on specific circumstances of each case and application of the proportionality test. In other words, neutrality does not play a role on its own. The justifications on public officials to refrain from appearance with conspicuous symbols while on duty will be founded, as case laws showed, on other grounds than the principle of neutrality (e.g., the duty to equality).

France – adopts a clear obligation of public officials to refrain from manifestation of affinity towards religion. The obligation emanates from the strict adherence to the neutrality principle in the public service. The neutrality principle obliges teachers as civil servants (*agents publics*) to obey to special duties of self-restraint and impartiality, in particular, as they work with the public and their outer appearance should transfer the impression of being unbiased. In the French jurisprudence, the abstract endangerment to the neutrality principle plays a significant role in justifying the infringement of a teacher's right as a public servant to exertion of religious freedom. A segregation point to be underscored with respect to abidance by the laïcité principle of teachers as opposed to pupils is that the duty of teachers under French law emanates from their duty as civil servants (*agents publics*) to appear unbiased and unprejudiced due to their work with the public as opposed to pupils as *usagers* of the public service. However, even pupils were ascribed to adhere by the neutrality principle, as within public education the state is obliged to fulfil its educational task, namely the conveyance of republican goals and ideals to its future citizens. The school, as a laicist place should preserve its neutrality. This can be achieved through elimination of any form of divisiveness and classification based on origin, ethnic, or religion.

IV The European Framework for Protection of Human Rights

The safeguarding of fundamental human rights on the European level is guaranteed in the ECHR,[1500] which functions as a 'Bill of Rights' for all the European states that are members in the Council of Europe.[1501] The uniqueness of the ECHR on the international sphere can be attributed to its function as an instrument aimed at reinforcement and advancement of fundamental rights.

1. Relevant Provisions of the ECHR

The Convention safeguards fundamental human rights such as freedom of religion and freedom of expression. The main paramount article that guarantees the freedom of conscience, religion, and belief is prescribed in Art. 9 ECHR. The right to have or own a religion, established in Art. 9 para 1 ECHR, is conferred to everyone and includes the right not to have a religion or belief or the right to change one's belief or faith.[1502] The right to profess a religion or its manifestation in public is safeguarded under Art. 9 para 2 ECHR. It is rendered that public officials are included within the definition of 'everyone' and that they are therefore entitled to the protection granted under Art. 9 ECHR, as this approach has been confirmed by the European instances.[1503] This entails, first, that public officials are subject to conditions that apply to individuals as long as they comply with limitations justified under the Convention. Second, though Art. 9 does not explicitly attach a special position for public officials, inherent limitations were

---

1500 The ECHR was signed in Rome on 4 November 1950 and came into force on 3 September 1953.

1501 The Council of Europe was founded on 5 May 1949 by ten member states. It has currently 47 member states. For a list of the member states see: www.unhcr.org/pages/4a2cffc86.html.

1502 Art. 9 para 1 ECHR: 'Everyone has the right to freedom of thought, conscience and religion; this right includes freedom to change his religion or belief and freedom, either alone or in community with others and in public or private, to manifest his religion or belief, in worship, teaching, practice and observance'.

1503 *Van Ooijen*, p. 120; *Konttinen v Finland*, (Appl. no. 24949/94 ECHR, 3 December 1996), *Tepeli and others v Turkey* (Appl. no. 31876/96 ECtHR, 11 September 2001), *Ahmed and others v United Kingdom* (Appl. no. 65/1997/849/1056 ECtHR, 2 September 1998), *Vogt v Germany* (Appl. no. 7/1994/454/535 ECtHR, 2 September 1995).

recognized with respect to persons of a special legal status.[1504] Other significant provisions that are relevant in the context of education and related case laws are: the freedom of expression guaranteed in Art. 10 ECHR, the equality/non-discrimination provision prescribed in Art. 14 ECHR, and the right to education prescribed in Art. 2 of the First Protocol 1 ECHR. The importance of the latter provision in the context of enabling a framework for religion in schools is known in the perspective of human rights not only as a guarantee of the right to education but also the right of parents to ordain the ideological orientation of their children's education.[1505]

On a practical level, a submitted claim based on violation of the anti-discrimination provision that is established on religious grounds (Art. 14 ECHR) cannot stand by its own, as it needs to be supported in conjunction with another substantive article. In other words, complaints made on the discriminatory nature of a ban on religious symbols can only be challenged in relation to other substantial fundamental rights prescribed under the ECHR, in which case they will be generally intertwined with Art. 9 ECHR.[1506] Nonetheless, an establishment that a discriminatory act of the state (whether direct or indirect) took place will not amount immediately to a violation of Art. 14 ECHR given that the discriminatory ban can be objectively justified.[1507]

There is no general equality stipulation in the ECHR itself, as this is mentioned in Art. 1 of the 12 Protocol ECHR. The only form in which it is conceptualized in the ECHR is through a non-discrimination prescription established in Art. 14. Art. 14's scope of protection is confined with respect to the fundamental human rights that are prescribed in the Convention itself.[1508] In addition, Art. 14 cannot be invoked as an own standing claim but is attached in general to the main claim challenging the breach of another fundamental human right prescribed in the ECHR.[1509]

1504 This is known as the doctrine of inherent limitations identified by legal scholars; see *van Dijk/van Hoof/van Rijn/Zwaak*, Theory and Practice of the European Convention on Human Rights, 2006, p. 345.

1505 Article 2 of Protocol 1 states the following: 'No person shall be denied the right to education. In the exercise of any functions which it assumes in relation to education and to teaching, the state shall respect the right of parents to ensure such education and teaching in conformity with their own religious and philosophical convictions'.

1506 *Van Oojien*, p. 132; *Howard*, Law and the Wearing of Religious Symbols, 2012, p. 80.

1507 *Howard*, p. 94.

1508 *Hambler*, Religious Expression in the Workplace and the Contestetd Rule of Law, 2015, p. 76; *Grabenwarter/ Pabel*, Art. 26 recital 1, p. 627.

1509 *Grabenwarter/Pabel*, Art. 26 recital 4, p. 629.

As a general practice, the ECtHR does not examine further a claim based on a violation of Art. 14 ECHR if the main claim founded on the violation of fundamental human rights prescribed under the Convention had been substantiated. The reason is that a declaration of the ECtHR that a violation existed as to the main claim, which established itself on one of the fundamental rights (e.g., Art. 9 ECHR), will not avail the main claim by demonstrating in addition that a violation of Art. 14 ECHR took place. In other words, the substantiation of discrimination on grounds of religion pursuant to Art. 14 ECHR will not add to the unlawfulness of an act.[1510]

The examination scheme based on Art. 14 ECHR will have to substantiate the following: first, the occurrence of direct or indirect discrimination; and second, justification which will have to prove the existence of (i) a legitimate aim and (ii) satisfaction of the proportionality test.

Legitimate aim – Art. 14 ECHR, unlike other provisions of the ECHR, is not restricted to a closed list of legitimate aims. In that sense, the ECtHR enables the member states an extensive margin of appreciation to substantiate that a discrimination was justified.

Proportionality test – finally, the assessment of a legitimate aim will be considered within the fulfilment of the proportionality test (the measure is adequate and proportionate to the aim the state pursued to achieve).[1511]

Third, in the context of individuals' right to visibility of religious insignias in the state school system, it is possible to include two discrimination grounds: (i) discrimination on religious grounds and (ii) discrimination on grounds of equality of men and women.

Discrimination on religious grounds – the ECtHR acknowledged the duty of member states to appear neutral and unprejudiced when enabling the right to religious freedom in its public sphere; consequently, it will implement the strict application test.[1512]

Discrimination on grounds of equality between men and women (gender equality) – the ECtHR confers the obligation of member states to promote and foster the right to gender equality as a legitimate, high significant aim. The inability, however, to determine a general European standard applicable to all MS, equating the rights of men and women is not possible due to the divisiveness

1510 *Grabenwarter/Pabel,* Art. 26 recital 2, p. 628.
1511 *Grabenwarter/Pabel,* Art. 26 recital 15, p. 636–637.
1512 *Grabenwarter/Pabel,* Art. 26 recital 22, p. 643.

> of their legal framework and their inner hierarchy of norms. In the absence of a general standard, the ECtHR will have to accept an extensive margin of appreciation of the member states in this respect. Nonetheless, social changes that take place over time and evolvement towards a modernized society may raise the threshold applied by the ECtHR.[1513]

In addition to the ECHR, fundamental human rights are prescribed within the framework of the EU legislation also in the Charter of Fundamental Rights of the European Union (Charter) whose authority is binding. The Charter includes the right to freedom of thought, conscience, and religion (Art. 10) and the right to education (Art. 14).

Since the ECHR functions as an international treaty, it binds the member states that are its signatories. In order to ensure effective enforcement of the rights protected under the ECHR on the European level a specific judicial body was purported for this aim. An efficient protection of the rights and freedoms guaranteed under the ECHR is thence subject to jurisdiction of the ECtHR.[1514] This enables submission by way of direct application of any individual or non-governmental organization to the ECtHR. All decisions of the Court have a binding force on the member states. In fact, the decisions of the ECtHR have an indirect effect with respect to all other member states even if not acting officially as direct applicants (inter parts).[1515] This means that interpretation of the ECHR provisions by the European judicial instances (ECtHR and ECJ) will not only have an indirect binding effect, which extends beyond the inner scope of the involved member states, but also exercise an affirmative impact (*Bekräftigungswirkung*) with respect to all member states and their judicial organs when requested to deliver solutions in national conflicts.[1516]

However, the question whether in practice national courts explicitly bind themselves to decisions of the ECtHR even if not directly affected by it as involved parties is subject to review since the position of the ECHR in the inner legislative system is different in each of the compared states.

1513 *Grabenwarter/Pabel*, Art. 26 recital 17–18, p. 639–640.

1514 *Martinez-Torronin*, in: Hill, Religious Liberty and Human Rights, 2002, 99, 100.

1515 *Grabenwarter/Pabel*, Europäische Menschenrechtskonvention, 6th ed., 2016, Sec. 16 recital. 2.

1516 The indirect effect binding national courts of the member states to comply as much as possible with the ECHR and jurisprudence delivered by the Strasbourg instances when requested to a decision in inner conflicts also help them to support their decisions by an explicit reference to judgements of the ECtHR, *Grabenwarter/Pabel*, Sec. 16 recital 8.

The ECtHR specifies under Art. 1 that 'the High Contracting Parties (i.e., member states) undertake to secure to everyone within their jurisdiction the rights and freedoms defined in Section 1 of this Convention'. However, the article does not require the member states to incorporate the Convention into their national laws[1517] and does not specify in which manner they are expected to secure those rights and freedoms. Since the Convention does not specify in which way Convention rights should be integrated respectively into the national law of its member states, then its conveyance and application into domestic law was a matter left to their own discretion. It was upheld in this respect that a party may satisfy Art. 1 in whatever manner it choses[1518] as long as it ensures that its national law and practice guarantee Convention rights. This naturally resulted in a different form of the Convention's incorporation in each of the member states.

Notably, the question of transporting Convention rights into the respective national law of the individual states is not by itself crucial for the effectiveness of the enforcement of fundamental human rights. It is also the position the Convention features in the hierarchy of norms and legislative system of the member states. Each of the countries in the compared analysis made necessary accommodations in domestic law so as to ensure conveyance of the Convention rights. These, however, vary in way and form of incorporation and position it maintains in the hierarchical normative structure in each of the compared states. Consequently, there is a difficulty to establish uniform application of the Convention rights. The ECtHR, when required to prove compliance of national laws with the rights safeguarded under the Convention had therefore developed through judicial interpretation a scheme of identical requirements that the involved member states need to meet.

Given the case that the European instances are approached with a complaint of an individual for interference of the state in his/her right to manifest a religion or belief by virtue of the public character of the function, an assessment whether the individual merits protection under the Convention would be taken. Thence, the admissibility of a claim will be examined in the following steps: first, whether a personal conviction falls within the ambit of Art. 9 and is identified as religion or belief. As a second step it will question the act claimed to be a 'religious manifestation' and whether it falls within the scope of Art. 9. Third, in case an interference with the right to religious manifestation was found, then

1517 See *Observer and Guardian v UK* A 216, (1991); 14 EHRR 153 PC; *Harris/O'Boyle/Bates/Buckley*, Law of the European Convention on Human Rights, 3rd ed, 2014, p. 26.

1518 *Swedish Engine Drivers v Union* Case A 20 (1976); 1 EHRR 617.

compliance with the justification requirements prescribed under Art. 9 should be established. The interference needs to be prescribed by law, pursue a legitimate aim, and redeemed necessary in a democratic society.

In this respect, the following aspects will be reviewed and analysed in consideration of the framework established under the ECHR in cases involving manifestation of religious symbols in the context of state education.

First, the transposition of the ECHR into national law will be illustrated. The divergence in form of transposition made into domestic law and the position it retains in the legislative hierarchical structure in each of the compared states affect the compatibility of the member states with Convention rights. As a result, the different compliance with the Convention regimes will be depicted with respect to each of the compared states individually and provide details as to its manner of incorporation in the respective national laws and the statutory position it obtained in the hierarchy of their legal norms.

Second, in order to ensure observance of the member states to their commitment undertaken under the Convention, it ordered the setup of the ECtHR (Art. 19 ECHR). It therefore established rules as to the application of the judicial process and the safeguarding of several fundamental human rights, and assured through establishment of the ECtHR that state parties will apply the substantive provisions of the ECHR.[1519]

Since it is the task of the ECtHR to interpret the freedom and rights guaranteed in the Convention, a detailed overview will be provided with respect to two types of cases involving primarily infringement of the right to religious freedom (Art. 9 ECHR) taking place in public education. On the one hand, the Court was challenged with questions relating to infringement of religious and educational rights in the context of state-imposed symbol (e.g., the display of a cross in public school classrooms). On the other hand, the legal entitlement to manifest a religion or belief in a public school as a fundamental human right when this is practiced by an individual (e.g., a teacher with a headscarf) had also reached the Strasbourg instances for judicial review.

Though the cases analysed do not involve directly any of the compared states in this analysis (Switzerland, Italy, and Turkey), they are still very significant, for the Court's judgements can influence all other national jurisdictions even if not direct parties to a case. The introspection into judgements of the Court in similar cases will help to assess subsequently whether the compared states comply with the ECHR.

1519 *Rogoff*, p. 424.

Third, the obligation of the individual member states to incorporate the Convention into their national legal system will be analysed. This will entail an individual examination of each of the compared states to find compliance of their domestic law and national jurisdiction with the ECHR. In that sense, the extent to which member states give effect to convention rights will be evaluated on the basis of their conformity with specific requirements as to legitimate interference in the right to manifest a religion or belief as prescribed in Art. 9 para 2 ECHR (i.e., the interference needs to be prescribed by law, pursue a legitimate aim, and necessary in a democratic society).

In addition, the following aspects will be considered when assessing the protection offered to individuals by the ECtHR in religious liberty claims involving the manifestation of religious symbols in Europe's public education system.

The margin of appreciation – the compatibility of the compared states with protected fundamental rights under the Convention (i.e., religious freedom, equality/non-discrimination provisions) should be assessed subsequent to the doctrine known as 'margin of appreciation'. This prescribes a certain discretion premised to member states in implementing measures that intend to keep observance of their obligations under the ECHR.[1520] The aspect of the margin of appreciation granted to member states has been largely debated in the legal literature.[1521] The most controversial aspect evolved around the wide 'margin of appreciation' offered to member states in respect of regulating their state-church relations (including manifestation of religious symbols in public education) and whether it provides a real and satisfactory guarantee to the right of religious freedom enshrined in the Convention.[1522] This question becomes even more complex given the diversity of approaches taken by national authorities in relation to endorsement and influence of religious symbols in their secular education system.

The principle of neutrality – the illustration of restraints imposed on the freedom to manifest a religious sign whether worn by individuals, like, a schoolteacher or displayed by institutions poses a challenge to the legitimacy of a state's duty to neutrality and impartiality as a possible ground for justification. This is mainly due to the fact that it has not been explicitly mentioned in the text of Art. 9 of the Convention.

1520 *Van Oojien*, p. 123.

1521 Radacic, Religion and Human Rights, 7 (2012), 133, 149.

1522 *Selbmann*, European Yearbook of Minority Issues, 2003/4, 199, 213.

The equality treatment principle and right to gender equality – the aspect of a teacher's right to protection of religious expression in the workplace may involve questions specific to employment in the public service. This is because a special account has to be given to the right of equal treatment in the application- and hiring process. The protection offered under the Convention is not confined solely to an individual's fundamental right to religious expression. Therefore, a breach of a teacher's right to manifest her religion may trigger application of several rights enshrined in the Convention; for instance, the right to freely wear a religious symbol (Art. 9) conjoined with the right to equality (Art. 14). This would necessitate a new evaluation of an anti-discrimination law as an independently qualified right for violation of individuals' rights to religious expression. As up till now, public servants claims have been established on the fundamental human right aspect (i.e., religious freedom) coupled with anti-discrimination rights (i.e., equality of treatment, gender equality); it remains questionable whether emphasis on equality rights would result in a more comprehensive European approach than addressed so far.

This question poses a problem in light of the new headscarf case delivered by the German BVerfG. It will be especially challenging to reconcile the German judgement with former decisions of the ECtHR determining the difficulty to bring the wearing of a headscarf by Muslim women in line with the principle of gender equality. This view of the ECtHR was exemplified in the Dahlab case, as the ECtHR held the assumption that wearing the headscarf is an oppressive patriarchal practice which suggests women's submission to men. This patriarchal practice ignores the personal autonomy of the teacher and by reason of this apprehension and other connotation associated with the headscarf the ECtHR found it very difficult to align this symbol with the principle of gender equality.

2. The Transposition of ECHR in Different Countries

In general, all European states that are members of the Council of Europe are subject to the provisions prescribed in the ECHR and are obliged to implement them into their judicial system.[1523] However, the form and nature of its implementation in the various member states differ, as the ECHR remains silent with respect to the way Convention rights are to be transposed into the respective

1523 *Arthur/ Holdsworth*, British Journal of Educational Studies, Vol. 60 (2), 2012, 129, 135.

domestic law[1524]. The way the compared states in this analysis implemented the ECHR into domestic legislation varies and depends on the judicial system and the way the lands' legislators decided to transcribe Conventions' rights into its already existing legislative system. This intelligibly will lead to different outcomes between the compared states as the effect of the Convention terms on domestic law will vary according to the legal status it acquired in the hierarchy of norms.

a) Germany

According to German law, as all other international treaty or obligation the ECHR is considered equivalent in rank to national federal law pursuant to Art. 59 para 2 GG.[1525] Germany had ratified the Treaty on European Union (TEU) on 7 December 1992.[1526] In order to dispel any constitutional vagueness as to its legal stand, the German parliament endorsed several amendments into the Grundgesetz.[1527]

The transposition of the ECHR into the legal system – the reference to the ECHR in the Grundgesetz is made in the so-called European Article, whose centrepiece is outlined in Art. 23 GG. The article supports the goal of the European Union and accepts transfer of the national government's sovereign power to the European Union as long as this shift of power guarantees that the German parliament will act within democratic lines. This notion is strongly upheld by the courts and the predominating opinion in the legal literature, which at large interpreted and developed the ECHR to have an equal rank to that of an ordinary federal legislation.[1528] National legislation, thence, is to be interpreted in conformity with provisions of the ECHR. According to Art. 31 GG, the constitutional position of the ECHR as an international treaty will even superpose legislation of the individual states.[1529]

1524 ECtHR Swedish Engine Drivers Union, 6.2.1976, no. 5614/72; ECtHR James and Others v. the United Kingdom, 21.2.1986, no. 8793/39.

1525 *V. Ungern- Sternberg*, 2008, p. 219; *Grabenwarter/Pabel*, Sec. 3, recital 8, p. 19; *Traub* in Muckel (ed.), Schriften zum Öffentlichen Recht, 2010, 273 (280).

1526 BT Drs. 12/3334, 12/3895.

1527 *Kommers/Miller*, p. 107.

1528 BVerfGE 74, 358, 370; 82, 106, 120; 111, 307, 317 (Görgülü); *Frowein*, in: Frowein/ Peukert, EMRK- Kommentar, Einführung, recital 67; *Papier*, EuGRZ 2006, 1; *Grabenwarter/Pabel*, Sec 3 recital 610.

1529 *Papier*, EuGRZ 2006, 1.

The significance of the ECHR provisions and jurisprudence laid down by the ECtHR with respect to development and interpretation of the Grundgesetz was even recognized by the BVerfG, which guided the judicator to take into account their extensive validity as indispensable for the comprehension of fundamental human rights prescribed in the Grundgesetz.[1530] The development of case laws delivered by the BVerfG with respect to interpretation of the EMRK and the binding effect of the ECtHR decisions demonstrate the importance German courts confer to conformity of its domestic law and constitutional guarantees with provisions of the Convention. Since delivery of the Görgülu judgement in 2004, the BVerfG held that decisions of the ECtHR have a binding force which extends all over state organs and obliges them within their exclusive competency and having due regard to the rule of law (Art. 20 para 3 GG) to eliminate any violation of the Conventions' rights and to establish a legal basis that corresponds with the rights prescribed in it, the so-called *Berücksichtigungspflicht*. This approach had been recently approved by the decision of the BVerfG, which explicitly stated that it is guided by the requirements laid down by the ECtHR deriving from its construction of the Conventions' rights.[1531] The BVerfG perceives itself bound by this method of construction for determination of the compatibility of constitutional freedoms with the rights prescribed in the Convention.[1532]

It had been affirmed in the legal literature that a general tendency since 1975 demonstrates an increased influence of the ECHR in the constitutional framework of Germany and other European states. This had been strengthened with the view of the BVerfG in the Görgülü decision that foresaw a fortification of the ECHR and its legal position as an effective mechanism for protection of fundamental rights.[1533] Albeit the fact that the ECHR does not attain a constitutional stand in Germany's inner constitutional hierarchy, it is still possible for appellants to submit a constitutional complaint, which admonishes indirectly an infringement of the ECHR provisions as well as failure to comply (*Nichtberücksichtigung*) with jurisprudence of the ECtHR. Such a constitutional complaint may be substantiated on the basis of violation of constitutional provisions prescribed in the

1530 BVerfGE 74, 358, 370; 111, 307, 317; *Fielder*, VVDStRL 59 (2000), 200, 206–207; *Papier*, EuGRZ 2006, 1; *v. Ungern-Sternberg*, 2008, p. 290.

1531 BVerfGE 2 BvB 1/13, decision from 17.1.17, para 607 (decision on the ban of NPD, right wing political party); BVerfGE 128, 326, 366 (*Sicherungsverwahrung*).

1532 BVerfGE 2 BvB 1/13, decision from 17.1.17, para 276–277, 510, 607–610, 617–620, 624–626.

1533 *Fielder*, VVDStRL 59 (2000), 200, 207; v. Ungern-Sternberg, 2008, p. 219–220.

Grundgesetz itself in tandem with infringement of the rule of law (outlined in Art. 20 para 3 GG).[1534]

Nonetheless, there is an approach upheld in the legal literature that the position of the ECHR in the national hierarchy of norms in German law should be equal in rank to that of a constitution. Proponents of this approach proclaim that without conferment of a formal position equivalent to a constitution, the provisions in the ECHR could not qualify otherwise for the same legal protection.[1535]

Direct effect with respect to third parties – therefore, the admissibility of a constitutional complaint submitted by an individual against German public institutions on grounds of non-compliance with the jurisprudence of the ECtHR even if no legal right holder is directly affected by it remains unspecified. The enforceability of German governmental organs by virtue of the indirect effect of the ECtHR jurisprudence is still a controversial issue which has not been attested so far.[1536] The horizontal effect of the ECHR on an individual against another private person, which is common under German law and known as *Drittwirkung*, does not exist with relation to the Convention as it affects merely complaints of individuals against states.[1537]

b) England

England is the only state that directly incorporated the terms of the ECHR into its legal system. Prior to incorporation of the HRA into domestic law, it had the status of a treaty obligation under international law.[1538] Following the introduction of the HRA 1998 into its system, it obtained the status of a parliamentary statute. However, from a constitutional law perspective it enjoys the privilege of legislation that is superior to that of some ordinary parliament legislation and is considered as a constitutional statute. This affects naturally the interpretation of Convention rights.

The significance of the incorporation of the fundamental rights guaranteed in the ECHR into domestic law has the advantage that complaints of applicants

---

1534 BVerfGE 111, 307, 329 (Görgülü); *Breuer*, NVwZ 2005, 412.

1535 *Grabenwarter/Pabel*, Sec 3 recital 710; *Borowski*, Die Glaubens- und Gewissensfreiheit des Grundgesetzes, 2006, pp. 139, et seq.

1536 *Breuer*, NVwZ 2005, 412.

1537 *Harris/O'Boyle/Bates/Buckley*, p. 23.

1538 *Hill*, in Hunter – Henin, Religious Freedoms and Education in Europe, 2011, 307, 309.

who feel aggrieved can invoke the rights prescribed in the ECHR through a direct submission before British courts.[1539]

British courts are obliged under the 1998 Act to interpret UK legislation as far as possible in a manner compatible with the rights guaranteed in the ECHR.[1540]

The obligation of British courts to interpret domestic statutes or judicially review administrative decisions in order to guarantee consistency with the ECHR is prescribed in Section 2 para 1 of the HRA. The section establishes a rule of interpretation that domestic courts need to observe in encounter with queries arising from the Convention. It prescribes the statutory duty of UK domestic courts to take decisions of the ECtHR into account in interpretation of Convention rights as follows: a UK 'court or tribunal determining a question which has arisen in connection with a convention right must take any judgement, decision, declaration or advisory opinion of the European Court of Human Rights into account'.

Thence, the provision established in Art. 2 para 1 HRA 1998 requires British courts to take into account, where possible, the provisions of the ECHR when coming to interpret British legislation so as to ensure its compliance with the rights protected under the Convention. This emanates that violations of the ECHR can be remedied in UK courts.

Given the case that domestic legislation encounters irreconcilable inconsistency with ECHR rights, then the British executive will be able to introduce the necessary amendments through rush action (fast track) so that English law will keep compatibility with the ECHR.[1541] In fact, prior to entry into force national legislation must follow a verification test to ensure compliance with the ECHR.

This applies as well to jurisprudence delivered by the ECtHR.[1542] In case a judicial declaration of non-conformity with the ECHR provisions is issued with respect to national legislation, there exists a special rapid process to amend the law to ensure its compliance with the Convention.[1543]

Principally, British courts are not committed to follow the decision delivered by the ECtHR; however, they at least must take it into consideration.[1544]

1539 *Howard*, p. 55.

1540 Section 3 (para 1) HRA 1998.

1541 *Hill*, A new Dawn for Freedom of Religion: Grounding the Debate in Religious Liberty and Human Rights, pp. 1, 6.

1542 *Arthur/Holdsworth*, British Journal of Educational Studies Vol. 60 (2), 2012, 129, 135.

1543 *Grabenwarter/Pabel*, Sec 3 recital 13.

1544 Section 2 HRA 1998.

The fact that the British legislature merely recommends the judiciary to take the decisions of the ECtHR into consideration (Sec. 2 para 1 (a) HRA), while not necessarily declaring them to be legally binding, casts uncertainty and vagueness as to the definition and limitations set on guaranteed rights under the Convention, such as the right to religious freedom, as they are open to different interpretation.[1545]

British courts are required to interpret UK legislation as far as possible in compatibility with the rights outlined in the ECHR (Sec. 3 para 1 HRA). By doing so, they must take into account and not necessarily follow the decisions of the ECtHR.[1546] This consequently makes them less bound by the Strasbourg jurisdiction when interpreting domestic legislation.[1547] Nonetheless, as a result, it makes the task of British courts more difficult as they are obliged to pay considerable respect to decisions of the ECtHR on the one hand, but, on the other hand, given they decide not to acquiesce they are under a constitutional obligation to explain their decision. This requirement on British courts to solely 'take account' as opposed to be 'bound by' the Strasbourg decisions was debated intensively in the United Kingdom.[1548] The vocal debate in politics[1549] and legal literature opined the common approach suggesting that domestic courts are subject to the duty prescribed in Sec. 2 HRA to be bound by the Strasbourg jurisprudence. It was raised that lack of consensus would make British courts strive continuously to bring their decisions into alignment with the decision of the ECtHR.[1550]

Courts in the United Kingdom have addressed controversial issues with respect to religious freedom under the HRA, especially those relating to religious symbols worn by pupils or teachers in state-maintained schools.

1545 This was a clear intention of British Parliament in order to allow British courts flexibility and discretion as far as the interpretative authority of the Strasbourg Case law is concerned. See *Donald/Gordon/Leach*, pp. 116–119.

1546 *Sandberg* in Hunter-Henin, Religious Freedoms and Education in Europe, 2011, 327, 331–332.

1547 This approach was even fortified by the Supreme Court itself. See the words of Lord Neuberger, in: *Pinnock v Manchester City Council* (2010) 3 WLR 1441, para. 48.

1548 See in this respect the wording of *Lord Irvine of Lairg* (The Labour Lord Chancellor at the time the HRA was introduced) in Donald/Gordon/Leach, The UK and the European Court of Human Rights, Equality and Human Rights Commission Research report 83, 2012, p. 119.p. 119.

1549 See the words of *MP Dominic Raab* in: Donald/Gordon/Leach, p. 118.

1550 *Oliva*, BYU L. Rev., 2008, 877, 882.

On a practical level, the number of claims brought in front of British court by pupils dissenting of racial or religious minority groups was by far higher compared to claims brought by teaching staff against school authorities due to a ban or prohibition on appearance with a religious garment.

c) France

France, as a member of the EU, took upon itself to respect and obey by the obligations prescribed in the ECHR.[1551] The ECHR was entered into force in France in 1974 and obtains the position of an international treaty obligation, which is considered in the inner constitutional hierarchy of France's system equal in rank to any other international treaty. Nonetheless, albeit strong significance in France's constitutional system the ECHR has not attained a constitutional status yet.[1552]

On a general level, application of international law including European human rights law and their relationship to the French legal system are governed by provisions of the French Constitution.[1553] The French Constitution of 1958 is the present legal document which governs the application of international treaties and agreements into domestic law.

In France, the relationship between the ECHR and domestic law confers priority to international law over domestic law.[1554] Thus, the fundamental rights prescribed in the ECHR have the highest legislative rank and superimpose ordinary national legislation as prescribed in Art. 55 of the 1958 Constitution. It is due to this dualist approach of respect and acceptance of international legislation into France's legislative system that France considers itself subject to decisions and jurisdictions delivered by the ECtHR and ECJ even without explicit legislation ordering its compliance thereof.[1555] Although they have delivered inconsistent judgements with respect to the legal stand of the ECHR for a long time, the French courts acknowledged finally their obligation to interpret domestic law so as to conform as much as possible to fundamental rights safeguarded under the Convention.[1556] As a result, French courts are authorized to declare

---

1551 *Rogoff*, p. 406.
1552 Const., 16 janvier 1975, Interruption volontaire de grossesse, 74–75 DC.
1553 *Rogoff*, p. 424. *Reference to legal framework Chapter.*
1554 *Rogoff*, p. 406.
1555 *Rogoff*, p. 407; *Grabenwarter/Pabel*, Sec 3 recital 154.
1556 *Grabenwarter/Pabel*, Sec 3 recital 154.

domestic legislation illegal and inapplicable given that it violates provisions in the ECHR.[1557]

For instance, the Constitutional Council. in its decision from 8 October 2004 upheld that the Law of 2004 prohibiting the display of a headscarf in public places does not violate Art. 9, 10 ECHR.[1558] The Law of 2004 complies with the requirements prescribed in Art. 9 para 2 ECHR, as an infringement can be justified on grounds that it pursued a legitimate aim (the right to equality of all French people and the principle of *laïcité*). In addition, it was held that the means pursued is proportionate to the aim sought to be achieved (i.e., compliance with paramount pillars underlying French constitutional law).

3. ECtHR Case Laws Involving Religious Symbols in Education

The cases brought so far before the ECtHR that relate to the display of religious symbols in state education do not involve directly the countries in this analysis (Italy and Switzerland). However, the case laws represent the divergent ways in which the ECtHR explained its rulings when addressed with questions relating to the compatibility of religious dress and symbols in the state school system with Convention rights.

The significance of the case laws can be attributed to the examination provided by the ECtHR and the scheme of arguments it established with reference to prohibition of religious symbols in education-related cases and their compatibility within the ECHR context. Notably, the ECtHR did not establish a rule for the prohibition of specific symbols, but rather laid down basic arguments to assist in the verification of the justification criteria of Art. 9 para 2 ECHR.[1559] According to these justification arguments, the domestic practice of the individual member states in religious symbols cases would need to be evaluated in order to establish their conformity to the Convention.[1560]

1557 Cour de Cassation, 24 mai 1975, *Jacques Vabre*; CE, 20 octobre 1989, *Nicolo*; *Fromont*, in: Stern/Tettinger, Europäische Grundrechte -Charta, 99, 103.

1558 *Rogoff*, p. 350.

1559 *Van Dijk/van Hoof/van Rijn/Zwaak*, p. 340 the criteria of Art. 9 (para 2).

1560 The cases of the European Court of Human Rights are available at www.echr.coe.int.

a) Institutional Symbols/*Lautsi v Italy*

The only case that dealt with the display of a crucifix in public school classrooms was decided in the famous case of *Lautsi v Italy* by the Grand Chamber of the ECtHR on 18 March 2011.[1561]

aa) Factual Background

The case known as 'the Italian Crucifix Case' was brought by the applicant, Mrs Lautsi who challenged the display of a crucifix, which was mandatory in Italy in classrooms since the 1920s. Mrs Lautsi claimed the right for her children to obtain education without the presence of a crucifix in the classrooms they attended. The case was significantly in focus, especially due to a strong nexus between church and state in Italy that demands the obligatory presence of crucifixes in governmental offices and in the public sphere in general. Albeit this mandatory requirement to display the crucifix in public buildings, the claimant, Mrs Lautsi, decided to establish her claim on grounds that the crucifix stands in contrast to the Italian constitutional principle of secularism and thus infringes on the duty of neutrality imposed on public authorities.

The claim was rejected by the Veneto Regional Administrative Court on the ground that the crucifix cannot be attributed solely a religious character. It was further determined that the crucifix cannot be contextualized within its meaning purely as a religious symbol. The claim was even dismissed following appeal to the Italian Supreme Administrative Court that determined the crucifix constitutes one of the 'secular' values of the Italian Constitution and a symbol of the Italian state and its identity. In 2006, the claim was redressed to the ECtHR.

The ECtHR decided against Italy and claimed for violation of Article 2 Protocol 1 as well as Article 9 of the ECtHR.[1562] While the Second Chamber decided against affixation of the crucifix in classrooms, the Grand Chamber reversed its decision and upheld the contrary.

1561 *Lautsi and others v Italy*, Appl. no. 30814/06, 18 March 2011 (ECtHR).

1562 The ECtHR established its arguments on guidelines designated in *Kjeldsen v Denmark*, App No 5095/71 (A/23), 7 December 1976, (ECtHR) and in *Folgerø and others v Norway*, App No 15472/02 Judgement 29 June 2007 (ECtHR).

bb) *Leading Legal Aspects*

The Second Chamber established its decision on the following grounds:

(1) *Endangerment of Proselytism or Indoctrination*

First, the ECtHR emphasized the duty of the state to refrain from acts of proselytism or any attempt to impose a religion. This duty of the state to remain neutral should be sacrosanct, especially in places where the encounter of people with a display of religious symbols becomes vulnerable. The ECtHR encompasses schools as such places due to the significance attached to them by the society. The ECtHR underscores the powerful effect which the display of a religious symbol may have on minds of young children, as they are unable to distance themselves from a religious message freely expressed by the state[1563] (the negative effect or vulnerability of pupils may change based on the age and level of maturity of the child). The affixation of a crucifix in public schools may easily transfer the impression to pupils that the state tends to favour a specific religion.[1564]

(2) *Negative Right of Religious Minorities*

Second, the right to freedom of religion guaranteed in the ECHR enfolds also the negative right of other pupils (non-believers and religious minorities) not only with respect to participation in acts of religious worship or religious education but also the exposure to practices which express a belief. It explains that the display of a symbol like the crucifix, which is associated with Christian-Catholicism, serves the majority of Italians who are Catholics themselves, as it fails to transfer the values of a 'democratic society' comprised by the ECtHR.[1565]

(3) *Parental Right to Education of Their Children*

Third, the ECtHR perceived Mrs Lautsi's parental liberty to ensure the education of her children to be in conformity with the dictates of her conscience[1566] as a right that must not prevail at all times so it will impede an equal right of the majority of pupils and parents to positively exercise their religious freedom (i.e., the display of a crucifix in a classroom).[1567] The Grand Chamber refers specifically

---

1563 *Lautsi and others v Italy*, Appl. no. 30814/06, 18 March 2011 (ECtHR) para. 48.
1564 *Lautsi and others v Italy*, Appl. no. 30814/06, 18 March 2011 (ECtHR), para. 55.
1565 *Lautsi and others v Italy*, Appl. no. 30814/06, 18 March 2011 (ECtHR), para. 56.
1566 Second sentence of Article 2 of Protocol 1 of the ECHR.
1567 See concurring opinion of Judge Bonello in *Lautsi and others v Italy*, Appl. no. 30814/06, 18 March 2011 (ECtHR), para. 3.6: 'If the parents of one pupil claim

to the right of parents to decide that the education of their children conforms to their religious conviction, ignoring the general right to education *per se*[1568] in order to substantiate the claim of the religious majority of parents in the education context. Thus, the Grand Chamber ignores the religious and educational rights of pupils as an own standing right. In fact, it identifies parental liberties as the *lex specialis* in religious freedom claims which involve children in order to intertwine the parental education right and the right to public school education of children.[1569] It finally upheld that the Italian state should leave parents a free choice regarding the education they wish to have for their children, including accordance with the religious precept they follow or the refrainment from any religious influence.[1570]

The decision of the Second Chamber was accompanied with fierce and heated criticism in Italy and other European states, and following the matter was referred in 2010 to the Grand Chamber for final resolution.

(4) Resolution of the Grand Chamber

The Grand Chamber outlined the following in its decision:

(a) The 'Passiveness' of a Symbol

The majority of judges in the *Lautsi* case held that the presence of the crucifix connotes of its passivity as it was in no way coercive or could be regarded wrong for its indoctrinating manner. In fact, Italy was able to provide evidence for the liberal, diverse, and multi-cultural representation in schools' environment. Moreover, no evidence was provided for any signs of intolerance towards other non-believers or religious groups in school realm.[1571]

---

the right to have their child raised in the absence of a crucifix, the parents of the other twenty nine should well be able to claim an equal right to its presence'.

1568 First sentence of Article 2 of Protocol 1 of the ECHR.

1569 See *Lautsi and Others v Italy*, para. 59 and 60. This opinion of the Grand Chamber was criticized as first the ECHR perception of pupil's autonomous right to education contravenedcontravene the international perception. By that it contravened the provision in the ICCPR. Second, merging the parental right of Mrs Lautsi with the educational right of her children could not be aligned at the same legislative level so to determine that they did not suffer a breach of their fundamental right to public schooling.

1570 *Lautsi and others v Italy*, Appl. no. 30814/06, 18 March 2011 (ECtHR), para. 62.

1571 *Lautsi and others v Italy*, Appl. no. 30814/06, 18 March 2011 (ECtHR), para. 2.11.

(b) Meaning of the Symbol

It was asserted by one of the majority judges that one cannot ignore the fact that symbols, whether religious, cultural, or otherwise are perceived as 'carriers of meanings'.[1572] On the other hand, the dissenting opinion conceded that the crucifix may enfold multiple meanings. However, its religious meaning remains the predominant one.[1573]

(c) No Delimitation of the Principle of Secularism

It was explained that in the ECtHR exists no consensus by the member states as to the appropriate interpretation of the principle of secularism, as each state adopts a different model of state-church separation.[1574] The ECtHR determined that it is due to the cultural-historical diversity existing among the European nations that it is obliged to respect the discretion of the member states, including the place they accord to religion in state-school classrooms. It underscored that the member states enjoy a margin of appreciation with respect to the exercise of the function they assume in relation to the educational framework. The ECtHR perceives its task as ascertaining that the decisions or acts of the member states do not exceed the limit of protection offered under the Convention. It refers to its previous judgements relating to the visibility of religious symbols in the school environment[1575] and compulsory religious lessons prescribed in schools' curricula[1576] in which it decided that no violation of the pupils' right to religious freedom (Art. 9) or the right of their parents regarding the education of their children (Protocol 2 of Art. 1) takes place as long as alleged acts did not amount to any form of indoctrination or a teaching practice with a proselytizing tendency.[1577] The concurring opinion of the majority underscored the importance of religious freedom as a fundamental human right with value; however, it refused to comprehend other constitutional principles and values such as secularism, state neutrality, the notion of state-church separation, religious pluralism, and

---

1572 Supra n 85, for the concurring opinion of Judge Power p. 45.

1573 Supra n 85, Dissenting opinion of Judge Malinverni and Judge Kalaydjieva at para 5.

1574 *Lautsi and others v Italy*, Appl. no. 30814/06, 18 March 2011 (ECtHR) para 26–28; 70.

1575 *Dahlab v Switzerland*, Appl. no. 42393/98, 15 February 2001 (ECtHR).

1576 *Kjeldsen, Busk Madsen and Pedersen v Denmark*, Appl. nos. 5095/71, 5920/72, 5926/72,
7 December 1976 (ECtHR), para 50–53 Series A no. 23; *Folgerø and others v Norway*, Appl. no. 15472/02, 29 June 2007 (ECtHR) para 84 and *Hasan and Eylem Zengin v Turkey* 1448/04 para 51–52 ECHR 2007-XI.

1577 *Lautsi and others v Italy*, Appl. no. 30814/06, 18 March 2011 (ECtHR) para 69.

religious tolerance as interchangeable to freedom of religion.[1578] Thence, the ECtHR asserts its obligation to protect religious freedom as a fundamental right, yet it demonstrates reluctance to safeguard other constitutional values which it perceives facultative and not equivalent in rank to fundamental rights and liberties. It was further asserted that no European consensus was achieved as to the permissibility of displaying religious symbols in public state schools.[1579] As a result, the ECtHR refused to provide a comprehensive statement that will extend the admissibility of religious symbols in public buildings or institutions in general.[1580]

(d) Secularism and Neutrality

The Grand Chamber (GC) confirmed that in the field of education Art. 2 of P. 1 was regarded as the *lex specialis* in relation to Art. 9 ECHR.[1581] The provision imposed on member states (MS) the duty to ensure neutrality and impartiality when resolving disputes between various religious groups and faiths. This duty of neutrality towards religion has rapidly evolved to favouritism of an absolute secularism in the context of education. This strict duty of neutrality imposed on the MS, especially in the educational establishments to guarantee a secular educational environment could not be found in the ECHR. The main difficulty the GC encountered was to align this duty of neutrality in cases where the exclusion of religious symbols/garments from public schooling was required by the state as opposed to a similar demand argued by an individual like in Lautsi's application. The difference in approach can be attributed to the fact that member states enjoy the privilege conferred to them by the doctrine of the margin of appreciation. This can explain the tendency of the ECtHR to uphold in favour of the party arguing for a secular approach in the context of state education, even if the 'right holder' was alleged to be the state arguing for infringement of its domestic principles of secularism.

The main criticism with respect to the state neutrality principle is its usage as a justification ground for interference with Art. 9 ECHR. The reason is that the neutrality principle is not explicitly mentioned in the Convention's text. This

---

1578 *Lautsi and others v Italy*, Appl. no. 30814/06, 18 March 2011 (ECtHR) see concurring opinion of Judge Bonello para 2.2–2.3, 2.5.

1579 *Lautsi and others v Italy*, Appl. no. 30814/06, 18 March 2011 (ECtHR) para 26–28; 70.

1580 *Lautsi and others v Italy*, Appl. no. 30814/06, 18 March 2011 (ECtHR) para 57.

1581 *Lautsi and others v Italy*, Appl. no. 30814/06, 18 March 2011 (ECtHR) Supra n 85 para 59 citing *Folgerø and others v Norway*, Appl. no. 15472/02, 29 June 2007 (ECtHR) Supra n 158 at para 84.

was also a point of divergence between the concurring and dissenting judgement in the *Lautsi* case. The state neutrality evolved to play a special role, especially in cases examining the limitations on public officials' freedom to manifest their religion or belief by displaying religious symbols. Criticism was directed first not only to the fact of the growing importance of the neutrality principle that evolved to form part of the general principles.[1582] This was questioned especially in examining whether the state neutrality principle has any relevance to the Convention given that it is only read into it. The second criticizing point relates to the understanding of state neutrality, as it was gradually developed and shaped by the ECtHR to be a concept which imparts a positive obligation on the state that transcends its duty to be neutral and impartial. This positive obligation employed a concept of neutrality that forbids the state from endorsing religion on a general level in the public sphere or recognition and advancement of a specific religious community at the expense of another. It was harshly noted by the Grand Chamber that the Second Chamber was mistaken in the interpretation of the state neutrality principle to pursue a secularist rather than a pluralist approach. It upheld that a preference of a secularist agenda risks venturing of intolerance – a concept which is in itself contrary to the values of the Convention. It was, therefore, often the case that the concept of state neutrality was intertwined with high values such as pluralism, tolerance, and broadmindedness.[1583]

The dissenting opinion upheld that even if the display of the crucifix safeguarded universal values such as tolerance and mutual respect, its religious meaning remained the predominant one. Especially in state education where children are exposed to a symbol without any possibility to extract themselves, the crucifix as an integral part of school environment is considered a powerful external symbol.[1584]

(e) Indoctrination

The endorsement of religious aspects or teaching into schools' curricula has been already determined by the GC in previous case laws to be a matter that falls

1582 *Van Oojien*, p. 126; *Evans*, Manual on the Wearing of Religious Symbols in Public Areas, p. 43.

1583 See *Lautsi and others v Italy*, Appl. no. 30814/06, 18 March 2011 (ECtHR) par. Concurring opinion of Judge Power and Judge Bonello.

1584 *Lautsi and others v Italy*, Appl. no. 30814/06, 18 March 2011 (ECtHR). Dissenting opinion of Judge Malinverni and Judge Kalaydjieva.

outside the scope of the ECtHR and is conferred upon the member states to decide within the margin of appreciation. The solution as to the place of religion in school curriculum, thence, may vary among the countries and area.[1585] Accordingly, the obligation on the member states to respect other religions and beliefs within the education context as established in Art. 2 Protocol 1 did neither impose on the states an obligation to refrain from imparting directly or indirectly religious education of any kind, nor did it confer parents the right to object to this kind of teaching of the state or privilege parents with the right to demand from the state a particular form of teaching.[1586]

The competency of the member states will not be subject to scrutiny of the ECtHR as long as it fulfils several requirements: first, compliance with the ECHR provisions of fundamental rights and liberties; second, religious knowledge or education that takes place within the school's curriculum must be conveyed in an objective, pluralistic manner that is free from any proselytizing atmosphere. The notion underlies this approach percieves the task of education to foster self-thinking and promote the ability of pupils to decide independently, without extrinsic indoctrinating influence on them.[1587]

Eminently, the GC accepted that the member states enjoy a certain margin of appreciation that enables them to impose limitations in matters of education. A member state will not exceed the discretion granted to it regarding its obligation to respect parents' rights in the education (Art.2 of Protocol 1 ECHR), if the limitation serves a legitimate aim, such as: hindering the indoctrinating effect of a religious symbol. In order to ensure that restrictions that are imposed do not curtail the right to education, the ECtHR must be satisfied that a limitation will only be compatible with Art. 2 of Protocol 1, if it pursues a legitimate aim and that limitation is proportionate to the aim sought to be achieved.

1585 *Lautsi and others v Italy*, Appl. no. 30814/06, 18 March 2011 (ECtHR) para. 62 citing *Kjeldsen, Busk Madsen and Pedersen v Denmark*, Appl. nos. 5095/71, 5920/72, 5926/72,

7 December 1976 (ECtHR) para. 50–53; *Folgerø and others v Norway*, Appl. no. 15472/02, 29 June 2007 (ECtHR) para 84 and *Hasan and Eylem Zengin v Turkey* 1448/04 para 51–52.

1586 *Lautsi and others v Italy*, Appl. no. 30814/06, 18 March 2011 (ECtHR) para. 61 citing *Bulski v Poland* no. 46254/99 and 31888/02.

1587 *Lautsi and others v Italy*, Appl. no. 30814/06, 18 March 2011 (ECtHR) para 62. The GC refers again to its previous judgements citing *Kjeldsen, Busk Madsen and Pedersen v Denmark*, Appl. nos. 5095/71, 5920/72, 5926/72, 7 December 1976 (ECtHR) para 50–53; *Folgero* para 84 and *Hasan and Eylem Zengin v Turkey* 1448/04 para 51–52.

(f) No Infringement of Minorities' Right to Religious Freedom

No evidence was provided as to the negative influence on religious minorities or atheist pupils by their exposure to the display of the crucifix. In the absence of clear evidence that the display of the cross in state school classrooms may pose some endangerment of indoctrination of the minority pupils, no breach of Art. 2 of the first protocol of the ECtHR was established.[1588]

(g) Margin of Appreciation

The ECHR upheld that due to lack of sufficient evidence that the display of the crucifix affects religious rights of minority pupils, the Italian government did not fail to accord with the discretion conferred to member states. The Italian state, as a domestic authority, exercised rightfully its discretion based on the 'margin of appreciation'[1589] and imposed no influence or indoctrination that constitute a breach of the requirement prescribed in Article 2 of the first protocol.

(h) Outweigh of Contrasting Interests

In outweighing the interests of the religious rights of minority pupils as opposed to the majority of pupils, the GC reached the conclusion that school authorities did not overrule the duty of impartiality by the mere presence of the crucifixes. In the concurring judgement of Judge Bonello, he explicitly outweighs the religious liberties of the majority of Catholic Italians against the right of minority believers.[1590] It explained that the affixation of the cross in a classroom did not amount to illegal indoctrination of the minority pupils since it was not accompanied by conveyance of the Christian religion and its precepts in adamant manner as the only absolute faith. On the contrary, the school demonstrated openness towards other religions and beliefs and form of their expression within its realm. The Grand Chamber decided that under these circumstances the religious right of the majority of pupils should be given precedence over those of the minority

---

1588 *Lautsi and others v Italy*, Appl. no. 30814/06, 18 March 2011 (ECtHR) para 71.

1589 The margin of appreciation was held by the ECtHR as the scope of discretion delegated to member states or their national authorities when a confinement of fundamental rights which fall within the protection of the ECHR takes place. See in *Evans*, Manual on the Wearing of Religious Symbols in Public Areas, p. 125.

1590 See concurring opinion of Judge Bonello in *Lautsi and others v Italy*, Appl. no. 30814/06, 18 March 2011 (ECtHR) para. 3.6: 'If the parents of one pupil claim the right to have their child raised in the absence of a crucifix, the parents of the other twenty nine should well be able to claim an equal right to its presence'.

pupils. In this context, it was argued that the legal question to be settled did not really orientate the aspect of contrasting fundamental rights, which would have necessitated the balance of the majority of Catholic Italians against the right of religious minorities. It rather posed the difficulty to align the rights of the majority of the Italian society to have the crucifix affixed in classrooms against the recognized right of all parents to educate their children in conformity with their religious convictions.[1591]

The parental right to supervise that the education of their children conforms to their own religious conviction or at least does not contradict their religious life philosophy has been also considered by the GC. It was held that Mrs Lautsi's negative religious right not to have her children exposed to religious symbols was not infringed. Moreover, she could not claim for interference in the negative right to religious freedom as she did not account as a legal right holder and thence no direct breach of her religious right took place. Although the Chamber found that no infringement of the negative religious right of Mrs Lautsi's children had occurred, it was nevertheless striking that the Grand Chamber decided to underscore its understanding towards pupils who adhere to the neutrality principle and perceive by display of the crucifix a breach of their fundamental right to religious freedom.[1592]

In the end, the Grand Chamber refrained from delivering its ruling regarding the compatibility of affixation of crucifixes in public school classrooms. It determined that it is not within its competency to intervene in the margin of appreciation conferred upon the member states to decide what would be regarded an appropriate entanglement between state and church, how religious neutrality and secularism should be discerned,[1593] and to what extent secularism in

1591 *Temperman*, Lautsi Papers 2012 Volume 11, 143, pp. 146–147.

1592 *Lautsi and others v Italy*, Appl. no. 30814/06, 18 March 2011 (ECtHR) para. 78.

1593 It is worth to note that the Grand Chamber remained silent with respect to the appropriate definition of the principle of 'secularism'. The arguments for proper interpretation of secularism were rather put forward by the Italian Government and Mrs Lautsi. On the one hand, the Italian government claimed that secularism, as enshrined in various provisions of the Italian constitution (Articles 2, 3, 7, 8, 19 and 20), substantiates the affixation of crucifixes in state school classrooms as it underpins the Italian perception of fundamental norms and values. In other words, the compulsory display of a crucifix encompasses the principle of secularism which accords with the constitutional order of the Italian state. On the other hand, Mrs Lautsi claimed that secularism constitutes the duty of the state to remain impartial in its actions, in particular in the field of education. This duty of the state enfolds its obligation to ensure religious pluralism, equal treatment of all religious groups and faiths forming its society, and demonstration of its secular nature by refrainment

its public sphere should be imposed. As a result, it declined to interfere in the national law of a member state as it would amount to an unlawful intervention in a state's jurisdiction, thus trespassing the authority of the ECHR.

In the context of outweighing interests, criticism was raised that both instances, the Second and the Grand Chamber ignored the aspect of the right of the Lautsi children to education *per se*, irrespective of their right to believe or not to believe.[1594]

b) Individual Symbols

aa) Dahlab v Switzerland

Similar to national case laws, the wearing of religious symbols worn by individuals in the public school system were brought for resolution before the judicial instances in Strasbourg in two salient events. First, applications submitted when the legal right holder was a student or pupil, and, second, submission when the legal right holder was a teacher.

Since the focus of this analysis is restrained to examination of the cases relating to religious symbols worn by teachers, an emphasis will be put on this set of conflicts.

The most famous case concerned with a teacher wearing a headscarf in public schools system was *Dahlab v Switzerland.*[1595]

(1) Factual Background

The case involved a complaint of a schoolteacher against Swiss school authorities, challenging the ban as an unlawful restriction on her fundamental right to manifest religious freedom. The teacher, who converted to Islam subsequent to her admission to school, started wearing loose cloths and hijab. She was able to appear at school like that for several years without any objection

---

from display of religious symbols in its public institutions. In that sense, Mrs Lautsi rejected the interpretation of the Italian government that it should uphold an atheist approach which carries an anti-religious character. She claimed for her part that the Italian state should provide pupils with a neutral educational environment keeping out any religious influence and at the same time safeguarding all religions and beliefs by deployment of even-handed treatment. See in *Lautsi* and others *v Italy*, Appl. no. (2011) ECHR 30814/06, 18 March 2011 (ECtHR), para 44.

1594 *Temperman, Lautsi* Papers 2012 Volume 11, 143, 152; *Lautsi and others v Italy* (2011) ECHR 30814/06.

1595 *Dahlab v Switzerland*, Appl. no. 42393/98, 15 February 2001 (ECtHR).

on part of the pupils or their parents. After an inspection by the district director of public education, she was ordered to remove the headscarf for the reason that it runs counter to the strict adherence of the Swiss state to the obligation of religious neutrality and the guarantee of public, secular (laic) education system imprinted by this secularist approach. The teacher claimed for a breach of her right under Article 9 ECHR. Her claim was rejected by the Swiss Federal Court, which considered her special duty as a teacher subjecting her to a different rule of conduct based on a provision in public school legislation (Art. 6 of the law from 6.1.1940). It was due to her duty as a teacher that yielded according to Swiss law special relation with pupils and parents. This duty obliged her to refrain from any political or religious manifestation, which may appear disrespectful towards the religion or belief the latter hold. Further, the Swiss Court took reference as to the considerable influence a teacher may have, in particular with respect to pupils of a young age. The teacher then submitted a complaint to the ECtHR, claiming a breach of both her right to freedom of religion under Art. 9 and a breach of her right to equality under Art. 14 ECHR.

(2) Leading Legal Aspects

Justification for interference according to Art. 9 para 2 ECHR:

The ECtHR held that freedom of thought, conscience, and belief prescribed in Art. 9 para 1 ECHR constitutes an absolute right which cannot be restricted. Nonetheless, the right to manifest a religion or belief stipulated in Art. 9 para 2 ECHR can be restricted or limited only if the prohibition or ban on an individual to appear with a headscarf is legitimized by fulfilling several conditions. These criteria were outlined by the ECtHR as follows:

(a) Prescribed by Law

The notion that underlies this requirement aimed to ensure that a state or its public authorities are prevented from imposing a restriction on the right of an individual to freely manifest a religion if it was made arbitrary, it is not foreseeable and accessible to all and without any legal basis in domestic law.[1596] In this case, however, the ECtHR was convinced that the law banning teachers in public schools from appearing with religious symbols constituted an adequate legal basis for the alleged infringement on the teacher's right to manifest her

1596 *Howard*, p. 104.

religion.[1597] Further, the provisions in the law (Art. 6 and Art. 120 para 2 of the law from 6.1.1940) were accessible and sufficiently specified.

(b) Necessary in a Democratic Society

The ECtHR recognizes at the outset that Art. 9 ECHR applies also to teachers since they act within their capacity as civil servants. It determines that civil servants are subject to a neutrality duty emanating from their special status, which obliges them to refrain from any manifestation of ostentatious religious symbols in public. Nonetheless, the ECtHR acknowledges that teachers as civil servants are also individuals who are entitled to enjoy the right to freedom of religious manifestation as safeguarded to them in Art. 9 ECHR. This freedom, however, can be confined if the state pursues the protection of legitimate interests that are 'necessary in a democratic society'. The requirement to prove the necessity of limitation on Art.9 ECHR in order to protect pre-eminent values in a democratic society enables the court to outweigh between the competing rights. On the one hand, the right of a teacher to freely manifest his/her religion and, on the other hand, the ability of a state to confine the right of the latter only in the case it pursues the protection of a legitimate aim associated with a democratic society.

In the case of *Dahlab*, the ECtHR upheld that the ban was necessary in Switzerland's democratic society[1598].

A legitimate aim is considered to be one of the aims enumerated in Art. 9 para 2 ECHR.[1599]

(c) Legitimate Aim – The Protection of Public Safety, Public Health, the Protection of Rights, and Liberties of Others

Art. 9 para 2 ECHR denotes that as a legitimate aim justifying the curb of the fundamental right to religious freedom can count one of the following: the protection of public safety, public order, public health, or morals. The ECtHR generally examines not only if one of the aims has been recognized, but also if the means to achieve the legitimate aim was proportionate. This will require the ECtHR to assess whether less intrusive means were available and still provide for the necessary safeguarding of a legitimate aim.[1600]

1597 *Dahlab v Switzerland*, Appl. no. 42393/98, 15 February 2001 (ECtHR).
1598 *Dahlab v Switzerland*, Appl. no. 42393/98, 15 February 2001 (ECtHR).
1599 Appl. no. 65500/01, 24 January 2006 (ECtHR).
1600 *Howard*, p. 107

(d) Public Order and Public Safety

The protection of public order has been used in cases where the ban on the wear of religious symbols was necessary in order to ensure the peaceful co-existence in school. In addition, the need to preserve the secular nature of the state has been included as a justification that falls within the protection of public order.[1601]

(e) The Rights and Freedoms of Others

The protection of the 'rights and freedoms of others' can be used as a ground for limitation of the right to manifest religious freedom as stipulated in Art. 9 para 2 ECHR. This ground is upheld in order to justify state restriction on the exercise of the teachers' right to religious freedom as guaranteed under Art. 9 para 1 ECHR.[1602]

In that case, the negative right of pupils not to be exposed to a teacher with a headscarf qualifies as a justified ground for curtailment of her fundamental right to appear with the Islamic headscarf. Though the ECtHR was aware of the fact that the appearance of the teacher with a headscarf at school for several years had generated no complaints on part of the pupils or their parents, it concluded that the headscarf is a visible salient sign that could not be denied to have some impact on the pupils. The ECtHR established that the age of the children is a distinctive factor to be taken into account in this respect, as an influence on young aged pupils cannot be compared to the possible effect on mature pupils who are less likely to be influenced. The assumption behind it is that mature pupils have already developed self-independence and conscious opinions. It was held that since the children were aged between four and eight, a tender age, it can influence their young minds, and a proselytizing effect cannot be denied outright.[1603]

Further, the ECtHR determined that it is difficult to assess the impact of an external, powerful symbol like the headscarf on the freedom of religion and belief of young children.[1604] Nevertheless, since its proselytizing effect cannot be negated completely, preference should be given to the negative right of pupils within the outbalance of competing rights.

1601 *Howard*, p. 108.

1602 Freedom of Religion, UN and European Human Rights Law and Practice, p. 161.

1603 *Dahlab v Switzerland*, Appl. no. 42393/98, 15 February 2001 (ECtHR)).

1604 The identification of the headscarf as a powerful external symbol obtained support also in the legal literature. See *Wittinger*, VBlBW 2001, 425, 428.

(f) Gender Equality

Finally, the ECtHR ascribes the headscarf a character of a symbol that stands for women oppression and runs counter to the notion of gender equality.[1605] This argument played a significant role in the Court's judgement that proclaimed its degrading characteristic may carry a proselytizing effect, which influences the behaviour and views of young girls and cannot be reconciled with the equality of women.

The Court decided that due to the perception of the headscarf as a symbol which stands for women oppression and which is imposed on women on the basis of a religious precept in the Koran, it cannot be aligned with the principle of gender equality, non-discrimination, tolerance, and respect for others. These values, according to the ECtHR, are a message that teachers are obliged to convey to their pupils in a democratic society.[1606]

Foremost, it was explained that the headscarf was a symbol which negates the free, liberal democratic values underpinning the Western world. The fear of the headscarf was especially perceived in the context of contravening gender equality due to its association as a symbol of women oppression. The Court captured the societal apprehension of the headscarf and what it symbolizes as follows:

> ... It cannot be denied outright that the wearing of the headscarf might have some kind of proselytising effect. Seeing that it appears to be imposed on women by a precept, which is laid down in the Koran and which ... is hard to square with the principle of gender equality. It therefore appears difficult to reconcile the wearing of an Islamic headscarf with the message of tolerance, respect for others and above all, equality and non-discrimination that all teachers in a democratic society must convey to their pupils.[1607]

(g) The Proportionality Test

Pursuant to this requirement, the Court is required to exercise a balance test according to which it outweighs whether the violating party, in that case the

---

1605 *Dahlab v Switzerland*, Appl. no. 42393/98, 15 February 2001 (ECtHR), 7.

1606 *Dahlab v Switzerland*, Appl. no. 42393/98, 15 February 2001 (ECtHR), 446, 463.

1607 *Dahlab v Switzerland*, Appl. no. 42393/98, 15 February 2001 (ECtHR), 13 or 446, 463. The same approach was held by the ECtHR in the Sahin case. Though the Islamic headscarf was worn by a student and not a teacher, the interpretation attached to it associated the headscarf as a symbol of women oppression and derogation as it presented the submission of women to men and by that conflicted with the right to gender equality. See *Leyla Sahin v Turkey*, 10 November 2005, ECtHR, no. 44774/98, para 115.

Swiss state, was pursuing a legitimate aim so as to justify the curtailment of the teacher's right to religious freedom (i.e., wearing a headscarf while teaching in classrooms). In addition, the Court will identify whether the means used was proportionate to the aim sought to be achieved or other less harsh means were available.

In this case, however, the ECtHR took reference not only to the aims prescribed under Art. 9 para 2 ECHR, but rather provided statements as to the principle of neutrality and the importance it established under Swiss law. Surprisingly, the ECtHR makes specific references to pronouncement provided in the national Swiss Court with respect to the special role of a teacher. This obliges her as a state representative to adhere to the principle of neutrality, especially as mandated under Geneva's public education law.

The fact that the ECtH R ascribes the Swiss state a strict application of state neutrality was regarded controversial in the legal literature as up till then the aspect of state neutrality was rarely discussed as an own standing ground for justification.[1608] Legal scholars rejecting the inclusion of state neutrality as a justifying ground for limitation of religious rights proclaimed, on the one hand, that the neutrality principle does not constitute an own standing ground for justification as enumerated in Art. 9 para 2 ECHR.[1609] On the other hand, others contended that the principle of neutrality establishes the basis for all other grounds of justification.[1610] It was explained that the adherence of the state to remain neutral in aspects of religion, especially in public education, is significant. The reason is that it guarantees the protection of religious rights (positive and negative) of parents and pupils (the protection of liberties and interests of others prescribed in Art. 9 para 2 ECHR). This serves as well the maintenance of the peaceful co-existence within school realm (the protection of public order and public safety).

(h) Margin of Appreciation

The ECtHR concluded that there was an interference with the teacher's right to manifest her religion according to Art. 9 para 1 ECHR. However, it held that it

1608 *Wittinger*, VBlBW 2001, pp. 425, 430. Others claimed that the ECtHR included many times the principle of neutrality and secularity as additional exceptions to those already prescribed in Art. 9 para 2 ECHR. See in this respect, *Davies*, (European Constitutional Law Review, 2005) 1 EuConst, 3; 511, 519.

1609 *Davies*, (European Constitutional Law Review, 2005) 1 EuConst, 3; 511, 518.

1610 *Clayton/Tomlison*, p. 248. In this respect it was held that the ban pursued the legitimate aim of ensuring the neutrality of state education. *Flauss*, RDP 2004, 317, 321.

was justified under Art. 9 para 2 and proportionate in order to achieve the pronounced aim, namely, the protection of the rights and freedom of pupils and parents not to be exposed to any kind of religious influence. The ECtHR mentioned also the 'margin of appreciation' which is conferred to member states and enables them to use their own discretion when deciding what will be regarded as a legitimate aim worth protection. This will require the European judicial instances to review whether the measures taken are justified and, if so, whether the grounds for justification were adequate and substantive to achieve the aim pursued.[1611]

In similar cases subsequent to the *Dahlab* case, the Court did not deviate from its general approach, keeping in line with the wider discretion, granted to member states in matters relating to Art. 9 ECHR.[1612] Especially in cases concerning religious symbols, the supervisory bodies acknowledged that national authorities are in a better position to assess the necessity of interference with individual right.[1613] As a result, it acknowledged the 'special importance to be given to the role of national decision-making'[1614] and took it into account in assessing the width of the margin of appreciation.

(i) Discrimination Based on Grounds of Religion or Gender Art. 14 ECHR

The ECtHR did not go into details of the discriminatin claim based on religious grounds pursuant to Art. 14 ECHR. It reviewed only the infringement of the gender equality principle.

It determined that no discrimination on gender grounds was established, as the same ban would also be applicable to a man who in similar circumstances wore clothing that would clearly identify him as a member of a different faith.[1615] The ECtHR also refrained from examining whether the ban of the headscarf can qualify as indirect discrimination based on religious grounds.

1611 ECtHR decision from 15.2.2001, *Dahlab v Schweiz*, 42393/98, 2001-V, 446 (462).

1612 See *Kurtulmus v Turkey*, Appl. no. 65500/01, ECtHR, 24 January 2006; *Fatma Karaduman and Tandogan v Turkey*, Appl nos. 41296/04 et 41298/04, ECtHR, 3 September 2008.

1613 *Evans*, (2001), p. 143.

1614 *Leyla Sahin v Turkey* (Appl. no. 44774/98 ECtHR (Grand Chamber), 10 November 2005), para 109.

1615 *Vakulenko*, p. 46; *Howard*, p. 116.

bb) Kurtulumus v Turkey

(1) Factual Background

In the case of *Kurtulumus v Turkey*[1616] the applicant, a professor at Istanbul University, lodged a complaint against her dismissal from the teaching post emanating from her refusal to refrain from wearing the headscarf and abide by the dress code for civil servants. The applicant's reluctance to refrain from wearing the headscarf in order to comply with dress regulations had been the subject of disciplinary measures and resulted ultimately in her dismissal. The applicant asserted that her dismissal due to her refusal to comply with the dress regulations imposed on civil servants in the performance of their duties violated her fundamental right to religious freedom (Art. 9 ECHR).

(2) Leading Legal Aspects

(a) Inadmissible According to Art. 9 ECHR

The Court dismissed the claim and concluded that there was an interference in the applicant's right to religious freedom guaranteed in Art. 9 ECHR; however, this could have been justified on the ground that it pursued a legitimate aim. The Court determined that though Art. 9 applies also with respect to public servants, their right to behave in accordance with their religious beliefs is not unlimited, as this right would have to be set back should the state substantiate a legitimate interest as enumerated in Art. 9 para 2 ECHR. Following application of the proportionality test, the Court decided that the right of a democratic state to prescribe a dress code which applies to its whole public service as necessary for its proper function will prevail the individual's right to religious freedom as long as legitimized grounds for justification exist. In that case, the restriction on the Islamic headscarf worn by the applicant clashed with the aim of the state to ensure the negative religious rights and freedoms of others and the prevention of disorder. The Court perceived the legitimate interest of a state to regulate dress code in the public service as aimed to ensure adherence to the principles of secularism and neutrality of civil servants, especially in the context of state education.

Finally, it concluded that Turkey had not overstepped its margin of appreciation and found dress regulations, especially with respect to public officials as acceptable since they are obliged by virtue of their special status to adhere to the

---

1616 *Kurtulmus v Turkey* (Appl. no. 65500/01 ECtHR 24 January 2006).

constitutional principles of secularism. This emanates that university professors are subject to an obligation of discretion in public, which imposes on them a duty to neutral appearance.[1617]

(b) Inadmissible According to Art. 14 ECHR

The complaint was also declared to be inadmissible under the anti-discrimination provision. Since the applicant was not dismissed due to her religion nor because she was a woman, no discrimination took place on ground of Art. 14.

c) Assessment of Case Laws

Several aspects arise within the context of the admissibility of religious symbols in state schools and provide for discrepancy points between the two types of case laws discussed above: first, institutional display of symbols and, second, individual display of symbols. Albeit differentiation between the two categories of case laws the implementation of similiar assessment criteria in the analysis, demonstrate that the ECtHR follows a relatively determined line when examining whether an interference with Art. 9 ECHR can be justified. Thence, member states that are alleged to violate Convention rights need to meet identical requirements which establish a minimum standard they have to observe.

As a general principle, the demonstration of the case laws depicted above necessitates that the ECtHR should take careful consideration under the special circumstances of each case that the interference in a fundamental right of an individual to religious freedom corresponds with the following requirements: first, a prohibition on endorsement of religious symbols in state schools must be prescribed by law; second, the alleged infringement on the right to practice religious freedom may be justified by a relevant reason: to establish a pressing social need implied by the notion of 'necessity'; and, third, the protection of rights that are necessary in a democratic society must be proportionate to the legitimate aim pursued.

The distinction drawn in the judgements of the contested cases has been established based on these requirements; however, they have been elaborated on the basis of several criteria and examined extensively, taking into account general principles that have been gradually evolved in previous jurisprudence of the ECtHR.

1617 *Kurtulmus v Turkey* (Appl. no. 65500/01 ECtHR 24 January 2006), 5.

Thence, following criteria have been considered by the Court in order to assess whether the requirements for the justification of limitations on an individual's freedom to manifest religion have been met.

aa) The Nature of the Symbol

It was asserted by the ECtHR that the display of a crucifix in a classroom does not pose the same endangerment of unfavourable effect on pupils as in the case of a teacher wearing a headscarf. As grounds for segregation the ECtHR referred, first, to the nature of the symbol; differentiation was made between 'essentially passive symbols'[1618] as opposed to 'powerful external symbols'.[1619] It was held in the Lautsi's judgement that the crucifix is regarded as a passive symbol due to its affixation on a classroom wall. In contrast, the headscarf is perceived as a strong, external, powerful, and political symbol. Second, the manner of the display or manifestation was claimed to play an important role with respect to the influence it may incur on children. It was determined that the crucifix by virtue of its passiveness cannot have the same proselytizing effect compared to that of a 'didactic speech or participation in religious activities'. Since Mrs Dahlab did not wear the headscarf for other purposes than teaching, it was criticized that the conclusion of the ECtHR is odd and cannot be reconciled by virtue of its obligation to guarantee fundamental human rights to individuals like their right to exercise religious freedom.[1620] Third, the type of observance taking into account that the crucifix was viewed by pupils also during teaching hours, and the assumption that a crucifix hanged on the wall is excluded *a priori* as a sign deemed to have an influence on pupils, was criticized as being dubious in itself.[1621] In that sense, the ECtHR discerned between the two case laws, explaining that even if there is a difficulty to assess the extent of its impact on children of young age, the fact that some kind of influence occurring due to their exposure to a teacher wearing a headscarf cannot be completely denied.[1622]

1618 *Lautsi and others v Italy*, Appl. no. 30814/06, 18 March 2011 (ECtHR), para. 72.

1619 'The Court accepts that is very difficult to assess the impact that a powerful external symbol such as the wearing of a headscarf may have on the freedom of conscience and religion of very young children. The applicant's pupils were aged between four and eight, an age at which children wonder about many things and are also more easily influenced than older pupils. In those circumstances, it cannot be denied outright that the wearing of a headscarf might have some kind of proselytising effect…'

1620 See also *Temperman*, in: Temperman, The Lautsi Papers 2012 Volume 11, 143, 154.

1621 *Temperman*, in: Temperman, The Lautsi Papers 2012 Volume 11, 143, 155.

1622 *Dahlab v Switzerland*, Appl. no. 42393/98, 15 February 2001 (ECtHR) p. 10.

bb) Burden of Proof

It was demonstrated that in cases involving the display of institutional symbols the ECtHR presupposes that no negative effect exists and, hence, places the burden of providing evidence to the contrary of some negative or detrimental effect of a symbol on the individual applicant. Individuals like a teacher as wearers of religious symbols will be regarded at the outset for the detrimental effect they have on the viewers and will be compelled to prove that no negative effect or intent of indoctrination of pupils took place de facto.

cc) Establishment of Legitimate Aim for the Ban on Religious Symbols

The right of an individual to freely manifest his/her religion is regarded a pre-eminent fundamental human right so that any state measure interfering with this freedom will need to be substantiated based on potential legitimate grounds. These are listed in the second paragraph of Article 9 and include the following: the protection of public safety or public order, health or morals, and the protection of the rights and freedom of others. The restriction placed on the right of the teacher, Mrs Dahlab, to appear with a headscarf to school amounted to infringement with the *forum externum*. From a human rights law perspective, this requires that the state will provide some minimum of proof that the fundamental right of others is endangered. An abstract ground delivered on part of the state determining it was necessary in order to achieve the pronounced aim (i.e., the negative rights of pupils and their parents not to be exposed to its display) would normally not suffice.[1623] Surprisingly, in the *Dahlab* case, no evidence was submitted to the ECtHR that the teacher with a headscarf triggered objection on part of the minority of pupils and parents. Nonetheless, the inclusion of an abstract ground (i.e., proselytizing effect) on the part of the teacher sufficed the ECtHR in *Dahlab* in order to conclude that the limitation on a teacher's fundamental right to religious freedom was justified.

dd) Presumption of Abstract Indoctrinating or Detrimental Effect

The ECtHR considers that when a religious symbol like the crucifix is placed by the state in a classroom, one can assume that in the absence of proof to the contrary, such a display will not have an adverse effect on the right of other pupils

1623 *Temperman*, in: Temperman, The Lautsi Papers, 2012 Volume 11, 143, 158, 159.

and parents (believers and non-believers). Whereas, when a teacher appears with a garment like a headscarf to school then as long as no proof to the contrary provides that no indoctrinating effect (even potential) has taken place, the assumption is that indoctrinating effect took place. The ECtHR holds that there is an initial assumption that a powerful symbol, like the headscarf does have a detrimental effect on the viewers, i.e., the pupils.[1624] It is worth to note that in the case of *Dahlab*, the ECtHR legitimized the prohibition on the ban merely based on the fact that its indoctrinating effect on the minds of young pupils could not be negated outright. In that sense, it satisfied the requirement of an indoctrinating effect even if only abstract endangerment existed. In the *Lautsi* case, however, it rejected the applicant's complaint that the visibility of the crucifix exposes the children to an indoctrinating effect. An abstract endangerment did not suffice in the case of *Lautsi* to satisfy the Court which adversely sought a concrete proof of some proselytizing effect to be substantiated by the applicants.

ee) The Neutrality of State

It was decided by the GC in the *Lautsi* case that there is no agreed threshold among the European states relating to the presence of religious symbols in state schools and their safeguard. Since this practice is still mixed among the European states, the court itself cannot develop a higher level of protection if there is no clear indication of a tendency to an increased protection on the European level.[1625]

In order to apply the proportionality test in an adequate manner, the GC reiterates measures adopted in its previous case laws as a guidance for the correct balance to be made between the religious rights of the minority group not to be exposed to the crucifix and the majority right to maintain the crucifix on state schools' walls as reflecting the predominant (Christian) religion of a state.

The Court underscores the responsibility of the European states to impartiality and neutrality in the exercise of various religions, faiths, and beliefs.[1626]

1624 *Temperman*, in: Temperman, The Lautsi Papers, 2012 Volume 11, 143, 154.

1625 *Lautsi and others v Italy*, Appl. no. 30814/06, 18 March 2011 (ECtHR), para. 60 in the concurring opinion of Judge Rozakis and Judge Vajic.

1626 *Lautsi and others v Italy*, Appl. no. 30814/06, 18 March 2011 (ECtHR), para 60 in the concurring opinion of Judge Rozakis and Judge Vajic: 'States have responsibility for ensuring neutrally and impartially, the exercise of various religions, faiths and

Though it admits that the display of a crucifix in state schools clearly impacts the obligation of the state to neutrality, it reaches the conclusion that unlike the headscarf there are enough grounds to 'neutralise' the religious symbolic meaning of the crucifix. First, the GC asserts that there is nothing in a cross hanged on the wall that associates it with compulsory teaching about Christianity. Moreover, the applicants themselves did not assert that the presence of crucifix in their classroom had encouraged teaching practices with a proselytizing effect. The nature of the symbol, in that sense, the passiveness of the crucifix detracts its indoctrinating effect.[1627] Second, the school encouraged religious pluralism in its environment as it demonstrated a liberal and tolerant approach towards manifestation of other religious convictions; alternative arrangements to minorities' religious practice and optional religious education were offered to 'all recognised religious creeds'.[1628] Third, there was nothing to suggest that the mother as an applicant was prevented from fulfilling her duty as an educator conveying her children with the precepts of her own philosophical conviction.[1629]

ff) Gender Equality

In the case of *Dahlab*, the ECtHR has interwoven between the proselytizing effect of the headscarf and the notion of gender equality. It was mostly criticized in the legal literature for this association.[1630] Moreover, critics raised the forbearance of court to deliver of a clear judgement with respect to what it will consider as a 'proselytising effect' of religious symbols.

The ECtHR held that since the headscarf is imposed on women by a precept laid down in the Koran, its proselytizing effect cannot be denied. Therefore,

---

beliefs. Their role is to help maintain public order, religious harmony and tolerance in a democratic society, particularly between opposing groups'.

1627 *Lautsi and others v Italy*, Appl. no. 30814/06, 18 March 2011 (ECtHR), para 71 & 72.

1628 *Lautsi and others v Italy*, Appl. no. 30814/06, 18 March 2011 (ECtHR), para 39 & 74.

1629 *Lautsi and others v Italy*, Appl. no. 30814/06, 18 March 2011 (ECtHR), para 75 (the GC supports its conclusion by reference to its former judgement delivered in *Kjeldsen, Busk Madsen and Pedersen and Valsamis* (Application no. 5095/71; 5920/72; 5926/72, para. 54 & 31).

1630 *Temperman*, Hum. Rts. Q. 2010, 32 (4), 865, 894; *Evans*, Melbourne Journal of International Law 2006, Vol 7, 52, 4, 13; *Vakulenko*, Human Rights Law Review, 2007, 7 (4), 717, 733.

it is especially difficult to equalize the headscarf with the principle of gender equality.[1631] It was asserted that the restriction on a teacher to appear with a headscarf was imposed purely in the educative context resulting in her activities as a teacher and not in her private life. This assertion can be justified by the need to ensure that school pupils in a democratic society will be educated in an environment of denominational neutrality. Other legitimate aims considered for that purpose were the negative right of pupils to religious freedom and the right of pupils' parents not to be exposed to such a proselytizing effect, even if only abstract danger persists.[1632]

In addition, it was declared as a symbol which is difficult to reconcile with fundamental values of a democratic liberal state, such as tolerance, respect of others, the principle of equality, and non-discrimination. This determination that the headscarf as a religious symbol contradicts the fundamental values which are essential in a democratic society strengthened the opinion of the ECtHR for its indoctrinating effect. In the Court's opinion that by wearing the headscarf the teacher cannot transfer those values that all teachers in a democratic society must convey to their pupils. This perception of the ECtHR has also been the subject of criticism in the legal literature.[1633]

The importance assigned to the gender equality argument by its proponents in the legal literature claims for its legitimacy by virtue of its double disposition. First, as a supplementary affirmative argument, the gender equality precept may be used for reinforcement of the claim for 'proselytising effect' on the right of pupils not to be exposed to any religious influence that contravenes with fundamental liberal values (i.e., tolerance, respect for others, equality and non-discrimination). Second, as an independent ground, it can stand by its own as an additional ground for justification when implementing the proportionality test. However, it remains doubtful in the legal literature whether the gender equality argument would appear 'relevant and sufficient' for fulfilment of the proportionality test.[1634] The measure would need to substantiate that it was proportionate for observing state neutrality.

1631 42393/98 *Dahlab v Switzerland*, Appl. no. 42393/98, 15 February 2001 (ECtHR) para 1.

1632 *Wittinger*, VBlBW 2001, 425, 428.

1633 *Martínez-Torrón*, in: Hill, Religious Liberty and Human Rights, 2002, 99, 121.

1634 *Ganz*, p. 264.

4. Compliance of National Laws and Jurisdiction with the ECtHR Jurisprudence

a) Germany

aa) Institutional Symbols

As far as comparison of the *Lautsi* case against the decision of the BVerfG in the Crucifix[1635] demonstrates, the effect the ECtHR induces with respect to safeguarding of religious rights in Germany is rather minor.

It was even proclaimed that the decision of the ECtHR could not serve as a guideline for future decisions of the BVerfG. The reason is that the protection offered to fundamental rights under the Grundgesetz as demonstrated in decisions of the BVerfG, is much more reflected and ample in scope than those offered by the ECtHR.[1636]

The prerequisites laid down in Art. 9 para 2 ECHR and which were progressively evolved by the ECtHR constitute the criteria measure according to which interference in an individual's right to manifest religious freedom will be considered.[1637] As presented earlier, application of the criteria measure will be similar with respect to both cases: first, state-displayed symbol and, second, individually displayed symbol. However, albeit application of similar verification scheme it is demonstrated that the standard of protection offered under German constitutional law provides to a great extent a more comprehensive and durable guarantee of fundamental human rights than featured in the ECHR. Through application of the Conventions' requirements, the following will attempt to evaluate whether the legal order practiced in each of the compared states conforms on the national level to Convention law and its interpretation by the highest European jurisdiction supervising its enforceability, the ECtHR. The assessment will relate to both types of cases conjointly as same the measures of proof come into consideration.

bb) Individual Symbols

The opinion held in the legal literature with respect to conformity of Germany (i.e., the individual federal states) imposing in inner legislation the ban on the

---

1635 BVerfGE 93,1.

1636 *Lock*, in Hunter-Henin, Law, Religious Freedoms and Education in Europe, 2011, 347, 355.

1637 Krimphove, EuR 2009, 330, 336.

headscarf to Art. 9 para 1 ECHR is that it is unlikely to be held in violation to the ECHR. This is based on judgements delivered by the ECtHR in similar cases (e.g., *Dahlab*, *Sahin*) which demonstrated the ample margin of appreciation conferred upon the states and the reluctance of the ECtHR to interfere in the discretion of the MS. It is proclaimed, therefore, that the possibility that the judgements delivered by the European jurisdictions will have some impact on the legal situation in Germany is very minor and unpredictable.[1638]

(1) Legal Criteria

(a) Prescribed by Law

In the case of *Ludin*, the BVerfG determined that an infringement on the teacher's right to appear with a headscarf during school occurred without having sufficient legal basis in the Public Service Code (BBG).[1639] The regulation of religious symbols and their endorsement into public schooling took place only following delivery of the BVerfG's judgement. In contrast to the *Ludin*'s case, the requirement of prescription by law had been satisfied in the case of the Bavarian Crucifix as its display in state classrooms walls was embodied in the Bavarian constitution as well as in the BayEUG (Art. 59).

(b) Legitimate Aim

German jurisprudence deviates from the prescription of justification grounds enumerated in Art. 9 para 2 ECHR as legitimate aims pursued by the state when implementing a measure that interferes in the right of individuals to exercise their religious freedom (e.g., the prohibition on a teacher to appear with headscarf to school). By doing so, the German judicator makes use of the margin of appreciation delegated to it by the ECtHR.

In *Ludin*'s case the majority of the BVerfG decided that the measure employed, a prohibition on a teacher to appear with a headscarf to school was compatible with the aim sought to be realized, namely, the negative right of pupils to religious freedom, the parental right to ensure that the education of their children conforms with their religious conviction, the duty of the state to religious neutrality in state schools, and the observance of peaceful co-existence in school.[1640]

1638 *Zacharias* KuR 2006, 189 (199).

1639 *Ludin v Baden-Württemberg* (Ludin II, BVerfG), 24 September 2003, 2 BvR 1436/02 = NJW 56 (2003), 3111, para 54 and 72.

1640 *Ludin*, BVerfG, NJW 2003, 3111, para 56. BVerfGE 108, 282.

Nonetheless, if the headscarf is worn by a teacher simply as a fashionable accessory detached from any religious motivation, then it will not be considered to be violating the (negative) right of pupils to religious freedom. In the Crucifix decision, the BVerfG underscored mainly the negative religious rights of the minority pupils not to be exposed to the crucifix. In addition, it emphasized the duty of the state to remain neutral and impartial, especially in the field of public education as a result of the special importance attributed to schools in society.

(c) Proportionality

The proportionality test requires that the means pursued is proportionate to the aim sought to be achieved. So far, the approach held by the German jurisprudence when applying the balance test ('practical concordance') has conferred considerable weight, especially with respect to the safeguarding of the negative right of pupils to religious freedom. This was reasoned by virtue of possible abstract endangerment to a proselytizing effect the teacher may have on pupils. This goes hand in hand with the acceptance by the ECtHR in the *Dahlab* case that it suffices for the purpose of burden of proof that a teacher with a headscarf merely poses an abstract jeopardy of some indoctrinating effect the pupils are exposed to in order to justify interference in the teacher's fundamental right to religious freedom. The ECtHR sustained that abstract fear from proselytizing or adverse effect would suffice in its opinion to legitimize the headscarf ban. Surprisingly, in contrast to the case of *Dahlab*, the contention raised in the *Lautsi* case by the GC sought to dismiss the applicants' complaint due to their inability to demonstrate a concrete endangerment of an adverse influence or proselytizing effect that took place with respect to the pupils as a result from their constant exposure to the crucifix hanging in their classroom. It determined instead that no concrete evidence was brought before the ECtHR for the indoctrinating influence of the crucifix on the pupils (regarded as a 'passive' symbol). This raises the question whether the ECtHR would require in cases involving state-imposed symbols a higher evidential standard on part of the pupils or parents as legal right holders since the substantiation of an abstract endangerment to the indoctrinating effect would not suffice, as the *Lautsi* case clearly demonstrates.

In contrast to this approach, it was recently held by the BVerfG in the new headscarf case that mere abstract endangerment would not avail to justify a harsh encroachment on a teacher's right to religious freedom.[1641] The precedence

1641 1 BvR 471/10, 1 BvR 1181/10 27.1. 2015 para (3)b).

of BVerfG in the delivery of this judgement turned the burden of proof upside down and required the proof of a concrete endangerment to indoctrinate the pupils or to have an adverse effect on them. In the absence of such concrete endangerment on part of the teacher so as to justify that the negative religious right of pupils or other eminent rights, such as the duty of the state to religious neutrality, the peaceful co-existence ('religious harmony') in school, or the educative task of parents to supervise the education of their children, there exists no legal justification to the headscarf ban.

(2) Compliance of Federal States' Legislation with Art. 9 ECHR

In the perspective of the various legislative amendments adopted by the different federal states in Germany following *Ludin*'s case, one should consider compatibility of the ban imposed on teachers to refrain from manifestation of religious symbols as outlined in their regional legislation with the right to religious freedom as guaranteed in Art. 9 ECHR. The compatibility will be reviewed also in relation to the anti-discrimination provision (Art. 14 ECHR). Thence, the conformity of amended laws prohibiting the endorsement of religious symbols into state school system to the ECHR will be considered separately with respect to the respective federal states compared in this analysis.

(a) Bavaria – Art. 59 BayEUG

(aa) Prescribed by Law and Necessary in a Democratic Society

The prohibition on teachers as prescribed in Art. 59 para 2 BayEUG forbids them from display of any garments or symbols that express a religious or ideological creed that runs counter to the neutrality of state or its constitutional values while on duty. The demand that the prohibition will be regarded as necessary in a democratic society is likely to comply with the interpretation of the ECtHR as proved in the *Dahlab* case. The duty of teachers as public servants to abide by the precept of religious neutrality obliges them, especially by virtue of their role as state representatives, to appear impartial in order not to impart to the public their affinity to a particular religion. The precept of neutrality was acknowledged by the ECtHR as a prominent principle that should be observed in a democratic society. In this respect, it is worth to note that all federal states in Germany are obliged by the Grundgesetz to maintain the democratic nature of the state (Art. 20 GG). As a result, the presumption is that the legislators in the individual federal states will endeavour to enact legislation with protected interests that are necessary in a democratic society.

(bb) Legitimate Aim

As legitimate interference in the fundamental right of a teacher to religious freedom the legislation includes any religious symbol that would be regarded as running counter to pre-eminent values prescribed in the constitution or any other educational objectives of the constitution. Though Art. 59 para 2 BayEUG does not exclude specifically Islamic symbols like the headscarf it gives preference to Christian symbols within public education, as it outlines that an educational objective will include the Christian-occidental tradition and values. It is very likely that within the wide margin of appreciation granted to member states a prohibition on a headscarf may be approved in order to ensure the educative task of the state (Art. 7 para 1 GG), as it may fall within 'public order' or 'public safety' as a legitimate aim. The Islamic headscarf may be regarded as contradicting the educative task of the state whose aim is to maintain and foster the Christian tradition and values imprinted by the salient Christian nature of the Bavarian state and the affinity of its majority to the Christian faith.

(cc) Proportionality

Taking into consideration the decision of the ECtHR in the case of *Dahlab*, it is likely that the headscarf ban on Muslim teachers if established on Art. 59 para 2 BayEUG would be regarded as proportionate to the aim pursued (i.e., ensuring the duty of the state to religious neutrality in public education [Art. 137 para 1 WRV]; negative religious freedom of pupils [Art. 4 GG]; the educative task of the state [Art. 7 para 1 GG]; and promotion of equality and gender equality [Art. 3 para 3 and Art. 33 para 3 GG]). The peaceful operation of school lessons and other legislative educative preferences taken into account by the Bavarian lawmaker may fall within the margin of appreciation granted to MS.

Accordingly, Art. 59 para 2 BayEUG will be regarded as complying with the prerequisites laid down in Art. 9 para 2 ECHR.

(b) Berlin – Sec. 2 of the Act to Art. 29 BlnLV

(aa) Prescribed by Law and Necessary in a Democratic Society

The legal situation in the state of Berlin prescribes the general exclusion of all religious symbols from the public service without any segregation (Sec. 2 of the Act to Art. 29 BlnLV).

(bb) Legitimate Aim

The ban itself establishes the existence of a legitimate aim, that is, the significance imparted in the state of Berlin to the duty of civil servants to abide by the neutrality principle. The obligation applies equally with respect to all of its public officials as state representatives to appear impartial and unbiased while on duty.

(cc) Proportionality

It is very likely that an all-embracing ban on all religious symbols would be regarded as disproportionate. However, the ban applies equally with respect to all religious groups and faiths and all office holders in the public service without any segregation. As a result, the ban imposed by the state of Sec. 2 of the Act to Art. 29 Berlin cannot be held to defy the principle of equality prescribed in Art. 14 ECHR. In addition, the protection of the duty of the state to religious neutrality as a protected aim may well be held proportionate since the ban applies equally to the public service as a whole. A careful consideration of individual cases can prove to be compatible with the aims prescribed in Art. 9 para 2 ECHR.

Notably, the prohibition prescribed by the state of Berlin excludes political or ideological insignias from within its confinement. As a result, the headscarf may still be banned by virtue of its identification as a political symbol associated with extremist, fundamentalist groups. Thence, a substantiation of the real incentive of the wearer, whether religious or political, may be very difficult to prove as it is a subjective matter that cannot be assessed by the viewers (i.e., pupils, teachers, or school authorities). Nonetheless, the prohibition of the headscarf due to its political symbolism may amount to count as unlawful indirect discrimination since the motivation for banning the headscarf may be wrongly implemented, disguising the real intention of the legislator. Though the ban applies to all religions equally, it places female teachers who are members of the Muslim faith at disadvantage in comparison to other religions.

As a result, it is likely that the ban imposed by the state of Berlin can be regarded on a case-by-case basis, on condition that no foreign factors were taken into account as conforming to the prerequisites prescribed in Art. 9 para 2 ECHR.

(c) North Rhine-Westphalia

Previously, in the aftermath of *Ludin*'s case the legislators of Baden-Württemberg and NRW introduced similar amendments into their education laws prohibiting teaching staff the display of conspicuous symbols that express outwardly a religious, political, or philosophical affiliation. However, the NRW legislator has taken initiative following the recent decision of the

BVerfG,[1642] declaring Sec. 57 para 4 SchulG NRW to be incompatible with the constitution and as null and void. Accordingly, it amended its Sec. 57 para 4 and replaced it with a new provision, Sec. 2 para 8 SchulG NRW.[1643] The following will examine the conformity of the new Sec. 2 para 8 SchulG NRW with Art. 9 ECHR.

(aa) Prescribed by Law and Necessary in a Democratic Society

Sec. 2 para 8 SchulG NRW declares and sustains the prohibition on teachers to refrain from any manifestation of insignias that by their outward appearance express a religious, political, or ideological affiliation. The new ban is prescribed by law and may well be considered to be necessary in a democratic society if introduced for the protection of democratic values. According to the phrasing of Sec. 2 para 8 SchulG NRW, there remains little doubt as to its necessity in a democratic society.

(bb) Legitimate Aim

The NRW legislator still emphasizes the same legitimate aims it used in its former Sec. 57 para 4 SchulG NRW with the only difference that the stipulation in Sec. 2 para 8 SchulG NRW refrains from any expression that indicates application of the ban if abstract endangerment exists to constitutional protected values. This was enumerated in Sec. 2 para 8 SchulG NRW as neutrality of state, peaceful school operation, human dignity, non-discrimination precept, democratic order of the state, and constitutional rights and freedoms of others. The peaceful school operation may well be classified within the protection of the public order or public safety as prescribed in Art. 9 para 2 ECHR. This classification may be successful, as the intention of the NRW legislator was to reduce conflicts and controversies arising in the public school system provoked on religious-ideological grounds, while inducing the formation of religious groups, and pressure imposed on other pupils to obey by religious precepts and discrimination. The duty of the state to religious neutrality had also been recognized by the ECtHR in both decisions delivered in the cases of *Lautsi* and *Dahlab*. Other constitutional protected values may fall within the margin of appreciation granted to member states. The guarantee of the non-discrimination principle stipulated in Art. 3 GG conforms to the anti-discrimination provision pursuant to Art. 14 ECHR.

1642 BVerfGE 138, 296 = NJW 2015, 1359.

1643 See in Chapter III 2. C) dd) (b) (aa) & (bb).

(cc) Proportionality

The proportionality test needs to evaluate whether the measure imposed pursues a legitimate aim and there is no alternative that may achieve the same goal without curbing so harsh on an individual's right to exercise his right to religious freedom. It well may be that following the prerequisites established in the recent NRW headscarf decision determining that an all-inclusive ban is forbidden[1644] and that the examination will be made on a case-by-case basis that Sec. 2 para 8 SchulG NRW will be regarded as satisfying the proportionality test since the all-inclusive ban is negated in the first place. This means that the test will be satisfied if the legislator proves that no other, less harsh measures were at hand in order to prevent the curtailment on a teacher's right to wear the headscarf.

(d) Baden-Württemberg

Art. 38 para 2 of the SchG BW is subject to doubts regarding its conformity with Art. 9 ECHR and will be reviewed for its compliance in accordance with the following requirements.

(aa) Prescribed by Law and Necessary in a Democratic Society

The legislative ban was meant explicitly to capture the headscarf within its scope. However, the phrasing of Art. 38 para 2 SchG BW prohibiting symbols that *prima facia* are capable of posing some danger to pre-eminent constitutional values was meant to capture other symbols than the headscarf which may either: (i) pose danger to highly minded values or freedoms inscribed in the BW constitution, or (ii) that contradict the Christian-occidental educational values. The prohibition is extensively stipulated to encompass as much as possible Islamic symbols that may contradict constitutional values and pillars of the Christian-Western tradition.

(bb) Legitimate aim

The specification of legitimate goals outlined in Art. 38 para 2 SchG BW complies with the denotation of legitimate aims enumerated in Art. 9 para 2 ECHR. For instance, the protection of rights and freedoms of others as a recognized legitimate ground for limitation will suffice for the purpose of justifying the restrictive measure adopted by BW in its respective legislation. Having regard to the jurisprudence of the ECtHR in similar cases, further legitimate grounds will be accepted: the right of other pupils to (negative) religious freedom, as well as the peaceful co-existence or as termed by the ECtHR 'religious harmony' in school,

---

1644 BVerfGE 138, 296 para 82= NJW 2015, 1359, 1360.

the parental educative right not to have their children adversely influenced by the precepts of a religion other than their own, gender equality, and state duty to religious neutrality. Though the state's obligation to denominational neutrality in public schooling is not explicitly mentioned in Art. 9 para 2 ECHR, it will still be regarded as legitimate aim for interference in an individual's right to religious freedom that is in accordance with the development of the neutrality principle by the ECtHR.[1645]

(cc) Proportionality

Taking into consideration the decision of the ECtHR in *Dahlab v Switzerland*, the ban imposed on a teacher to wear a headscarf would be regarded as proportionate to the aim sought to be achieved, that is, the negative right of pupils not to be exposed to a daily view of a teacher with a headscarf. The negative right of pupils to religious freedom was even given special consideration by the ECtHR in *Dahlab*, explaining that pupils of a tender age they are more likely to be influenced by the teacher's view during lessons. This assumption of an indoctrinating effect cannot be negated completely and as a result should confer prevalence to negative religious freedom of pupils. Consequently, pursuant to the prerequisites established in Art. 9 ECHR and the jurisprudence of the ECtHR in its similar case laws granting the member states a wide margin of appreciation regarding special considerations, it is likely that Art. 38 para 2 SchG BW would pass the proportionality test.

So far, the ECtHR, similarly to German jurisdiction, did not examine in detail whether the headscarf posed influence de facto on the pupils as viewers. However, by delivery of the new headscarf case the constitutionality of the abstract endangerment test becomes dubious in German constitutional law. In its new judgement, the BVerfG determined that an abstract endangerment of some proselytizing effect will no longer suffice for interference in a teacher's right to wear a headscarf.[1646] Instead, it ascertained the need to prove a concrete danger of an adverse or negative effect the pupils are likely to suffer. The recent decision of the BVerfG declines previous determinations made with respect to the Islamic headscarf in *Ludin*'s as well as in *Dahlab* case, as in both jurisdictions the presumption held that insofar as the subject of the ban relates to external powerful symbols like the headscarf, the need to examine an actual impact on the pupils disposes itself.

1645 *Dahlab v Switzerland*, Appl. no. 42393/98, 15 February 2001 (ECtHR) para 1.

1646 BVerfGE 138, 296 para. 100, 101 = NJW 1359, 1362.

(3) Compliance of the Legislation of Federal States with Art. 14 ECtHR

The right to equality and non-discrimination is set forth in Article 14 and Protocol 12 ECHR. Article 14 prohibits discrimination in the enjoyment of rights and freedoms set forth in the ECHR. The prohibited grounds for discrimination are diverse and include: sex, race, colour, language, religion, political or other opinion, national or social origin, association with a national minority, property, birth, or other status. A ban on an individual to wear religious symbol or garment may amount to discrimination on ground of religion but may also conjoin other discriminatory heads like discrimination on ground of gender. This would normally be the case given that a ban on religious dress may apply only with respect to women (e.g., the headscarf), giving rise to a claim of indirect discrimination on grounds of gender as men are not likely to be captured under the same restrictive measure. Notably, the prohibition of discrimination under Art. 14 ECHR does not apply specifically to discrimination in employment law if conducted on grounds of religion or belief, but rather applies to discrimination in enjoyment of other Convention rights.[1647] Due to this reason, the submission of a claim cannot invoke the infringement of Art. 14 ECHR solely but needs to support itself with a main claim based on a fundamental human right provision (e.g., Art.9 or Art. 10 ECHR).

(a) Bavaria

It is due to the formulation of Art. 59 para 2 BayEUG which grants preferential treatment to Christian symbols as opposed to Islamic emblems that it is likely to be declared as incompatible with Art. 14 ECHR. This may substantiate a claim of an indirect discrimination established on religious grounds.

A claim of discrimination on grounds of gender is also likely to succeed since according to the Bavarian legislation Art. 59 para 2 relates to preference granted to Christian symbols. On the one hand, this does not aim to segregate between men and women as the ban grants prevalence to Christianity irrespective of the public official's gender. On the other hand, the Islamic headscarf is worn predominantly by women and not men. From this perspective, Art. 59 para 2 BayEUG could also allege a violation on grounds of gender discrimination since it places women in an equal position to that of men.

1647 *Harte*, in Hill, Religious Liberty and Human Rights, 2002, 159, 161.

(b) Berlin

The conformity of the ban inscribed in Sec. 2 of the Act to Art. 29 BlnLV to the anti-discrimination provision, Art. 14 ECHR, would be difficult to challenge as the ban applies equally to the whole public service and to all religious symbols. Hence, a claim of direct discrimination on religious grounds cannot be established, as the ban did not aim to discriminate against a specific religious group but rather applies equally with respect to all religions; nor can the ban substantiate a claim of indirect discrimination as the law did not purport to apply different measures to a particular religion or faith.

Further, the ban imposed by the state of Berlin gives no rise to a claim of discrimination based on gender equality as it was not directed solely at female teachers and it could similarly be applied to a man should he wear clothing that can associate him with a different faith.

(c) North Rhine-Westphalia

The conformity of Sec. 2 para 8 SchulG NRW with the obligation to equality prescribed in Art. 14 ECHR is very likely to succeed as the ban prescribed in it applies equally to all religions. The former Sec. 57 para 4 SchulG NRW was reamended due to an explicit declaration of the BVerfG towards the NRW legislator to preclude the privilege granted to Christian tradition.[1648] This former provision impaired teachers' right to equal access in the public service as it potentially discriminated her right to religious profession in comparison to other teachers, members of the Christian or Jewish faith. According to previous legislation, Christian or Jewish Teachers were more likely to get away from the ban and wear religious garments by virtue of their notional proximity to Christian-Western tradition and values.

Albeit the new phrasing of the ban in Sec. 2 para 8 SchulG NRW, I assume that it still carries a dubious phrasing in particular in its second part, enabling endorsement of unequal treatment directed towards the Islamic headscarf from the back door. This can be inferred from the wording in Sec. 2 para 8 SchulG NRW declaring that 'particular illegitimate is a behaviour of a … teacher … that can appear to pupils or parents a demonstration against human dignity, discrimination according to Art. 3, the rights and freedom and the democratic constitutional order'.

1648 BVerfG 1 BvR 471/10, 1 BvR 1181/10.

(aa) Discrimination Based on Religious Grounds

The new formulation of Sec. 2 para 8 SchulG NRW may not be declared to constitute a forbidden direct discrimination established on religious grounds as it does not explicitly discriminate against Islamic symbols. However, it may still pose a forbidden indirect discrimination, as clearly the headscarf is grasped as a symbol that runs counter to fundamental constitutional values, such as equality of women and men, the democratic order of a state, and human dignity and as such may fall within the confines of a ban.

(bb) Discrimination Based on Gender Grounds

The prohibition is very likely to fall within the confines of unlawful indirect discrimination based on grounds of gender, as a female Muslim teacher is more likely to suffer a violation of her right to manifestation of religious freedom by wearing the headscarf since it is a symbol worn by in particular by Muslim women. Nonetheless, the ban applies also to men in general and, as a result, it still may be that religious symbols worn by members of other faiths may fall within the confinement of the ban, as they may be regarded as contradicting constitutional values such as human dignity, the neutrality of state, or disturbance of the peaceful operation of schools.

(d) Baden-Württemberg

A determination of the compatibility of Art. 38 para 2 SchG BW with Art. 14 ECHR is difficult to assess for two reasons. First, the ECtHR has not been confronted so far with case laws invoking solely the anti-discrimination provision. Second, the ECtHR has not been required so far to review the legitimacy of a legislative ban which aims specifically to exclude the Islamic headscarf like in the case of Art. 38 para 2 SchG BW. In practice, the inequality provision was always conjoined with the fundamental right to religious freedom (Art. 9 ECHR) so the ECtHR took marginal reference with respect to Art. 14 ECHR.

In principle, applications submitted to the ECtHR were reviewed with respect to a general ban which did not intend to capture a specific religion within its scope. A ban would be reviewed by the ECtHR as long as it is claimed to violate against a fundamental human right like the right to religious freedom, as safeguarded under the ECHR. As a result, since jurisprudence of the ECtHR in such cases is scarce, it would be difficult to follow a scheme of proof that the ECtHR is likely to adopt. In the following, assessment will be provided with respect to the conformity of Art. 38 para 2 SchulG BW to the anti-discrimination provision (Art. 14 ECHR).

(aa) Discrimination Based on Religious Grounds

Art. 38 para 2 SchG BW explicitly discriminates in favour of Christian and occidental symbols and tradition. It therefore constitutes a direct discrimination advancing Christian and Jewish symbols. Thus, the provision contravenes the non-discrimination precept stipulated in Art. 14 ECHR, as the German legislature in BW does not treat all religious groups evenly. If at all such legislation will be challenged before the ECtHR it remains uncertain how this is likely to be reconciled with the Convention rights. In addition, it constitutes indirect discrimination as it applies an equal ban to all religions; however, it places a Muslim teacher in a disadvantaged position in comparison to a Christian teacher. The reason is that a religious symbol like the Islamic headscarf is very demonstrative and conspicuous by nature whereas, a cross necklace worn by a Christian teacher can remain discreet beneath a pullover and will not connote outwardly her religious affiliation.

Several aspects may be taken into account when applying the proportionality test within the balance of competing rights. It was decided in *Dahlab* that for the purpose of Art. 14 ECHR in order to declare a difference in treatment as discriminatory in nature it must either pursue a legitimate aim or fulfil the proportionality test that may tilt towards justification of the ban. Accordingly, following aspects will be considered by the ECtHR.

(bb) Margin of Appreciation

Taking into account the margin of appreciation conferred to the member states, it is possible that such a ban will find a justified ground which would be approved by the ECtHR as long as the means employed pursues a legitimate aim and is proportionate to the aim sought to be achieved.

It is possible, therefore, that given the margin of appreciation conferred upon the member states and the individual proximity in the state of BW to Christian faith and tradition that the ECtHR would perceive itself refrained from stating a clear opinion with respect to such a sensitive topic. Similar to the case of *Dahlab* where the ECtHR upheld the right of the Swiss authorities to maintain secularism in its educational system, it may acknowledge the right of the BW state to prescribe in its domestic law the nexus between religion and its educational system.

Nevertheless, it may be claimed that the safeguarding of the negative right to religious freedom of pupils cannot justify the ban only with respect to symbols of a particular religion.

(cc) Exception to Christian and Jewish Symbols Adhering to Western-Liberal Values

In the context of the judgement of the ECtHR in *Dahlab*, the headscarf was perceived at the outset as a symbol which contravenes Western values and principles since it stands for a symbol of women oppression and underscores the inequality between men and women. Such a justification is not likely to be regarded as discriminatory and would constitute a sufficient ground for differentiation in treatment. However, the ban should not be supported merely on the inequality principle but should demonstrate intertwining with other pre-eminent values and principles.

It is worth to note that German jurisprudence overruled so far attempts to challenge the laws on grounds of religious discrimination. The prohibition directed at Muslim teachers to appear with a headscarf while on duty was challenged against the decision to allow nuns to appear with their habits. Though such a ban amounts to indirect discrimination founded on religious grounds as it clearly disadvantage teachers of Muslim religion in comparison to other religions and faiths, such a segregation was objectively justified. Not only the German judicator upheld the advancement of symbols stemming from Christianity to be constitutional, but also the reason for privileging Christian and Jewish symbols was argued to be a result of their adhesion to Western-liberal values and traditions rooted by Christianity.[1649] The acceptance of an exception that will apply solely with respect to conveyance of Christian values and tradition, however, is not likely to be regarded as pursuance of a legitimate aim. Therefore, in the comparison with a nun teaching while wearing her habit, it is likely that the ECtHR would decide that the ban violates Art. 14 ECHR.

Consequently, neither direct nor indirect discrimination established on religious grounds is likely to pass the proportionality test.

The Bavarian Constitutional Court confirmed as well that the display of Christian symbols advances Christianity and its precepts not in its pure religious meaning but as culture formed in the historical tradition of the European nations.[1650] Many German states accepted the exception for Christian occidental symbols.

1649 Staatsgerichtshof des Landes Hessen, 10 December 2007 – PSt 2016, 33 and 53.

1650 Bayerischer Verfassungsgerichtshof, 15 January 2007, 60,1; *Mancini*, Cardozo L. Rev. 30, 2009 (6), 2629, 2654.

(dd) Voluntariness of the Teacher and Alternatives

In the second revision of *Ludin*'s case before the BVerwG[1651] it had to consider the possibility that Art. 38 para 2 of the BW SchG may indirectly discriminate against Muslim teachers and thus stands in violation to the constitutional principles of equality and equal treatment in access to the public service (Art. 3 para 3 and 33 para 3 GG). The BVerwG reached the conclusion that Art. 38 para 2 BW SchulG does not infringe against the equality percepts prescribed in the GG. The reasons given were firstly, the teacher has entered her job voluntarily whereas the pupils had no option of deviation due to compulsory schooling. The argument of voluntariness of the teacher was reiterated also in the case of *Dahlab*. Second, other options were available for her, for instance, employment in private schools so she was not placed at a particular disadvantage in comparison to other teaching staff. In addition, the right of a teacher to religious manifestation is not excluded to her in private life.

(4) Discrimination Based on Grounds of Gender Equality

The aspect of gender equality as a justifying ground for the ban of the headscarf according to Art. 14 ECHR and its compliance with the proportionality test had been approved by the ECtHR in the *Dahlab* case. The ECtHR emphasized even that the headscarf not only contradicts gender equality as a prominent value in a democratic system but also runs counter to the applicant's role as a teacher whose task it is to convey these values. It underscored that the advancement of the equality of sexes serves nowadays a major goal of the member states.

The compatibility of Art. 38 SchG BW with the aspect of gender equality was left unresponsive by the German judicator in the second revision of *Ludin*'s case. However, taking into consideration that the gender equality ground would have been reviewed as an additional argument to the main claim, there is a probability that it would be regarded as legitimate, similar to *Dahlab*, since the means employed is proportionate to the aim sought to be realized.[1652]

In addition, the claim that the prohibition on the Islamic headscarf amounts to discrimination on grounds of sex since a man pertaining to the Islamic faith

1651 BVerwG, NJW 2004, 3581.

1652 The gender equality will be adequate for examination of proportionality when the subject of the ban is the Islamic headscarf. However, this test will not be applicable with respect to all other religious symbols that are not viewed as contradicting the gender equality principle.

would not be subject to the same prohibition as a Muslim woman who would need to forbear her religious practice in order to teach had been also rejected by the ECtHR. It was explained that the prohibition could also apply to a man who in similar circumstances wore clothing that identify him as a member of a different faith.[1653] Therefore, according to the decision of the ECtHR in *Dahlab*, no violation on grounds of gender equality can be established with respect to the compatibility of Art. 38 SchG BW with Art. 14 ECHR. The reason is that the ban is formulated comprehensively and may apply equally to both men and women respectively.

cc) Conclusion

Since no uniform guidelines were provided in the European jurisprudence in order to enforce unity among the European states in the context of admissibility of religious symbols in public education, it is not clear what would be ascertained by the ECtHR with respect to compliance of the amended School Education Acts (Art. 38 para 2 SchG BW, Art. 57 para 4 SchulG NRW and Art. 59 para 2 BayEUG) with the ECHR.

Following implementation of a compatibility test of the ECtHR judgement in *Dahlab* with the ECHR there is a probability that the ban would not be held to contravene the requirements prescribed in Art. 9 para 2 ECHR.

An assessment of the amendments made by the specified federal states with respect to their School Education Acts identified the following:

(1) Margin of Appreciation

The prohibition on ostentatious religious symbols employed in Bavaria, BW, and NRW may fall within the 'margin of appreciation' conferred to the member states and which enables them sole discretion with respect to the goals or aim they seek to achieve (e.g., religious harmony, peaceful co-existence, denominational neutrality, or negative right of pupils to religious freedom). In the case of a crucifix, a legitimate aim will be regarded as the positive right of the majority of pupils and parents that the state will foster and perpetuate the tradition of the Christian faith as sustained in the *Lautsi* case.[1654]

1653 *Dahlab v Switzerland*, Appl. no. 42393/98, 15 February 2001 (ECtHR) para 2.

1654 *Lautsi and others v Italy*, Appl. no. 30814/06, 18 March 2011 (ECtHR) para 64, 65 and 68.

(2) The Age Group of Pupils as a Factor Determining a Proselytizing Effect

In contrast to the emphasis given by the ECtHR in the *Dahlab* case to the age group of pupils as a significant factor justifying a ban on a teacher's headscarf due to the potential indoctrinating effect on the young mind of pupils, the German jurisprudence does not find it necessary to make a differentiation between the age group of pupils. The ECtHR, however, holds the view that an encroachment on the teacher's right to religious freedom can and should be justified, especially when pupils of tender ages from four to eight are involved, as the probability of a proselytizing effect is higher than in a situation where pupils are of mature age.

Such a differentiation may be of importance when considering the incompatibility of the headscarf ban in the respective states, BW and NRW. The indoctrinating effect on pupils of tender age was considered also with respect to the display of a crucifix on classrooms walls.

(3) Discrimination Based on Religious Grounds

Such a discrimination, which is prohibited according to Art. 14 ECHR may give rise to direct or indirect discrimination. The ban on manifestation of ostentatious religious symbols prescribed in Art. 38 para 2 SchG BW as well as in Art. 57 para 4 SchulG NRW may be regarded as permissible as long as the ban does not aim towards the outward manifestation of a specific religion or belief, as otherwise this would amount to a direct discrimination which is forbidden pursuant to Art. 14 ECHR. Accordingly, the ban prescribed under the Education Act of all three federal states (SchG BW, SchulG NRW, BayEUG) may pass the compatibility test if they are to prove that the ban on manifestation of signs or symbols did not aim to exclude a particular religion (Islam) while privileging a preferred religion (i.e., Christianity). In this context, an assertion of a Muslim teacher that Art. 38 para 2 SchG BW/Art. 57 para 4 SchulG NRW does not discriminate against other religions and consequently gives rise to a claim of indirect discrimination based on religious grounds would be difficult to substantiate: first, if a legitimate aim is established and regarded as proportionate to the aim sought to be realized; second, lack of sufficient jurisprudence relating specifically to admissibility of religious symbols in the educational context, as there are scarcely case laws challenging its enforceability against other faiths.

Since so far the permissibility of a nun to appear with a habit has not been challenged in front of the European jurisdictions, it is difficult to anticipate what their respective resolution would be. In addition, Art. 38 para 2 SchG BW does not explicitly specify the garment of a nun to be permissible;

consequently, it remains doubtful whether it would be regarded as incompatible with Art. 14 ECHR.

The only state in this analysis whose prohibition on the manifestation of religious symbols raises no doubts as to its compatibility with Art. 14 ECHR is the state of Berlin. This is because Art. 29 BlnLV which prescribes the ban on religious manifestation applies it equally with respect to all offices in the public service and all religions and denominations without exclusion.

(4) Discrimination Based on Political Opinion

Though the headscarf may provide no ground for a discrimination claim based on religious grounds, whether direct or indirect, it may still contravene Art. 14 ECtHR based on another discriminatory head. The headscarf can be banned in the state of Berlin due to its political meaning. This, nonetheless, would still be regarded an unlawful discrimination based on Art. 14 ECHR.

(5) Discrimination Based on Gender Grounds

An assertion that Art. 38 para 2 SchG BW/Art. 57 para 4 SchulG NRW purports to discriminate on grounds of gender was not substantiated; this is because, parallel to *Dahlab*, the law was not directed solely at the teacher due to her being a member of the female gender. The ban could similarly be applied to a man if he wore clothing that can identify him as a member of a different faith.[1655] Finally, the legislators of BW and NRW did not intend to create a differentiation between men and women with regard to the application of the ban.

b) England

aa) Institutional Symbols

The state education system in England, which is divided mainly between Christian state schools ('voluntary controlled' or 'voluntary aided') and independent faith schools ('voluntary schools') leaves the imposition of organization and thereof religious practices to the discretion of the state through municipal authorities.[1656] According to public education law, denominational schools – whether of the Church of England, the Roman Catholic Church, or other faith bodies – act as partners of the state.[1657] Consequently, there is no general law

---

1655 *Dahlab v Switzerland*, Appl. no. 42393/98, 15 February 2001 (ECtHR) para 2.
1656 *Harte*, in: Hill, Religious Liberty and Human Rights, 2002, 159, 177–178.
1657 *Harte*, in: Hill, Religious Liberty and Human Rights, 2002, 159, 176.

imposing the display of the crucifix in all state classroom walls; subsequently, unlike the case in Germany, controversies surrounding removal of the crucifix were not subject to a heated societal debate. Further, due to the liberal approach mandated in England towards religious minorities, tolerance demonstrated towards their religious practice, and effort to accommodate their need on part of the general government's policy, sensitiveness to feelings of members of minority faith groups is higher in comparison to other states in this analysis.

bb) Individual Symbols

The ECHR was incorporated through the HRA 1998 into English law. This requires British courts to take account of the jurisprudence emanating from the ECtHR and to use it as guidance when reviewing the compatibility of its primary and subordinate legislation with the Convention.[1658] This means that British courts will follow the same scheme of proof laid down by the ECtHR, when contested with the question whether interference in the right to religious freedom pursuant to Art. 9 or Art. 14 ECHR took place. This will require a proof of the prerequisite as laid down in Art. 9 para 2 ECHR (i.e., first, prescribed by law; second, necessary in a democratic society; third, fulfilment of the proportionality test).

In addition, the HRA reinforced the existing legal place of religion in schools. The relevant laws which regulate and guarantee freedom of religion in public education system with respect to teachers, other employees, and parental rights to supervise the religious education of their children are the SSFA 1998 and the Education Act 1996. Notably, these legislations did not prescribe a general rule as to the permissibility of teachers to appear with distinguishable religious insignia and the extent to which they will be regarded as admissible in school, as this issue was left to sole discretion of the district council.

(1) Compliance of British Law with Art. 9 ECHR

(a) Prescribed by Law and Necessary in a Democratic Society

The prohibition on the *niqab* was not prescribed by law, however, the protection of pupils' rights and interests will definitely be regarded as worth of protection in a democratic society. Especially the protection of pupils' rights and interests gains significance when these are to be outweighed against the role of the teacher.

1658 *Hill*, in: Hill, Religious Liberty and Human Rights, 2002, 1, 8.

The teacher, as a state representative, should not affect the pupils with daily confrontation of the *niqab*, a powerful external symbol in itself. The negative effects, namely, fear and social pressure by the surroundings on schoolgirls to imitate the teacher as their role model cannot be negated.

Taking reference to the judgement of the ECtHR in *Dahlab*, it can be reasonably inferred that if a symbol like the headscarf was held to be a powerful symbol that emphasizes gender inequality then there is no doubt that the same assumption may be provided also with respect to a face covering such as the *niqab*.

(b) Legitimate Aim

There is no doubt that the ban of the *niqab* in the case of *Azami*[1659] will not be regarded as incompatible with Art. 9 ECHR. Eminently, school authorities could justify the ban claiming to pursue the protection of a legitimate aim (i.e., the safeguarding of the interests and rights of the pupils).

It was established by the EAT that the appearance of a teacher with a *niqab* which covered most of her face affected her work due to lack of comprehensibility, as the pupils were unable to understand her facial expressions.

(c) The Proportionality Test

The prohibition on the teacher to appear with the *niqab* during school lessons will stand the proportionality test. First, it stands in proportion to the aim which considers the interests and right of pupils not to be negatively affected by the *niqab* as protection-worthy. Second, the ECtHR will always examine whether other less harsh alternatives were at hand. In that case, the teacher was not refrained from wearing the *niqab* outside the classroom. In addition, employment in private schools was still left as an option for her.

(2) Compliance of British Law with Art. 14 ECHR

Although the prohibition of discrimination embodied in Art. 14 ECHR does not specifically relate to discrimination in employment law, it applies to cases of tension between Convention rights which may arise in the course of employment; for instance, rejecting a teaching candidate for employment or his/her dismissal on the basis of religious grounds (e.g., the wearing of a distinguishable religious insignia). In England, the relevant legislation that regulates differentiation of treatment in employment and which includes all grounds of discrimination, direct or indirect, is the Equality Act 2010.

1659 Appeal no. UKEAT/0009/07 *Azmi v Kirklees Metropolitan Borough Council* (2007).

(a) Discrimination Based on Religious Grounds

Since the wearing of the headscarf in public schools has not been challenged in British jurisprudence, it is difficult to sustain that the ban of the *niqab* poses a direct discrimination on religious grounds, as other religious symbols can also be excluded by a ban. Even if a direct discrimination were substantiated, then the same grounds of justification used for Art. 9 ECHR would be applicable also with respect to Art. 14 ECHR.

It is worth to note that the admissibility of religious symbols other than those worn by teachers had been reviewed by British jurisprudence, which did not hesitate to overrule their presence in other employment sectors.[1660]

(b) Discrimination Based on Gender Grounds

It is unlikely that a claim based on gender discrimination would be successful since the ban on religious symbols applies to men and women equally. First, there are case laws relating to other employment sectors which impose the ban of wearing religious symbols also with respect to men (especially members of the Sikh faith).[1661] Second, even if discrimination on grounds of gender were proved, then the ban of the *niqab* could be still justified. As a ground for justification of differentiation it can be explained that the *niqab*, in comparison to the *turban* of a Sikh worn by men of the Sikh faith, symbolizes inequality of men and women and stands as a symbol for women oppression.

c) France

aa) Institutional Symbols

The strict application of the secularist approach in France's public sphere, guided and imprinted by the main constitutional pillar of *laïcité* prescribes no official affinity of the state with a particular religion or faith. It determines, in fact, the strict adhesion to religious neutrality of the state and the avoidance of manifestation of religious symbols that may associate the state with a particular religion. In addition, as explained above (Chapter III), the notion of separating religion from state was prominent and essential – in particular with respect to education – as the idea of secularism was anticipated at the outset to take place in the public school system.

1660 *Eweida v British Airways plc* [2010] EWCA Civ 80; *Chaplin v Royal Devon & Exeter Hospital NHS Foundation Trust* [2010] ET 1702886/2009.

1661 *Mandly v Dowell Lee*, [1983] 2 AC 548.

bb) Individual Symbols

The particularity of the Convention under France law is that it obtains a constitutional stand within its hierarchy of norms. This should argue for the highest protection offered to enjoyment of fundamental human rights. This legal status enables French citizens who wish to invoke their right to religious freedom due to a state interference a direct access to French courts. On the part of the state it will be obliged to a higher standard of proof as an infringement in individuals' right to religious freedom will need to be balanced only against the retrenched list of justification grounds as specifically prescribed in the Conventions' provision (i.e., Art. 9 ECHR).

(1) Compliance of the Law 2004–228 with Art. 9 ECHR

The Law of 2004 contains an explicit general prohibition on pupils to refrain from the display of conspicuous symbols or garbs in state schools. The ban extends its scope also to other symbols that by their outer manifestation and the manner they are worn (e.g., at all times and without exception) connote to the surroundings of their religious motivation.

A number of cases brought before the ECtHR[1662] challenged the conformity of the Law 2004 with the ECHR, invoking Art. 9 in conjunction with Art. 14 ECHR (hereafter 'the decisions relating to the 2004 Law'). The cases emerged around the same period of 2008–2009 and surrounded the legitimacy of the school headmaster to order the expulsion of several pupils from school due to their refusal to remove their conspicuous accessories by virtue of the prohibition prescribed in the 2004 Law. The challenge was brought by groups of religious minorities, for instance: Muslim girls who substituted their head coverings with a bonnet, and several Singh (Sikh) boys wearing under-*turban*. Surprisingly, though the claims did not involve directly the wearing of a religious head covering but rather alternative, modest forms of accessories, the Court decided in all these cases that the claims were inadmissible. One of the main reasons submitted by the ECtHR for discharge of the pupils' claim was attributed to the wide margin of appreciation granted to member states in regulating their state-church affairs, in particular with respect to educational matters. Relying on its previous case laws,

---

1662 *Gamaleddyn v France*, Appl. no. 18527/08; *Aktas v France*, Appl. no. 43563/08; *Bayrak v France*, Appl. no. 14308/08; *Ghazal v France*, Appl. no. 29134/08; *J. Singh v France* Appl. no. 25463/08; *R. Singh v France*, Appl. no. 27561/08, 17 July 2009 (ECtHR). The cases concerned the expulsion of pupils from French schools for wearing conspicuous symbols of religious affiliation.

the Court emphasized the extensive leeway of discretion it grants to member states enabling them to impose a high or low standard of protection based on the accommodated state-church model adopted by each respectively.[1663] In that sense, the ECtHR kept in line with its previous judgements.

The question whether the Law of 2004 complies with the requirements prescribed under Art. 9 para 2 ECHR will be considered based on the decisions relating to the 2004 Law.

(a) Prescribed by Law

The prohibition on pupils to abstain from wearing religious symbols in the public – school system is sufficiently outlined and prescribed in domestic legislation, the Law 2004–228 of March 15, 2004.

(b) Necessary in a Democratic Society and Pursuing a Legitimate Aim

As a justification of the ban on the alternative modes of dress as raised under the Law of 2004, the French state can claim the pursuance of one of the legitimate aims as enumerated in Art. 9 para 2 ECHR. The pre-requisite that an interference was necessary in a democratic society will be examined together with the establishment of a legitimate aim. The reason is that, normally, the pronouncement of a legitimate aim such as secularism was upheld by the jurisprudence to justify the restriction on individuals' right to religious manifestation. At the same time, secularism is claimed to be necessary for preserving the democratic system of a state. The argument justifying religious state neutrality or secularism was acknowledged by the ECtHR that reiterated and relied on its previous case laws (*Dahlab v Switzerland*, *Kurtulumus v Turkey*, *Kaaraduman v Turkey*), underscoring that conforming to the secular nature of the state is a legitimate aim necessary for the democratic state. Other legitimate aims considered are: the protection of public order emanating from the need to apply the rule of law in all state schools, and peaceful school operation by applying the ban equally with respect to all religions. The protection of public health will also be regarded as a legitimate aim since the ban was confined to sport lessons.

1663 This was asserted by the ECtHR in *Lautsi v Italy* in the concurring opinion of Judge Rozakis and Judge Vajic who refrained from adopting an increased level of protection to minorities' religious rights if no tendency existed among the European states to justify the Court's interference in their discretion.

(c) Proportionality

It was evident that the school applied the rules equally to all pupils and without any distinction. In that sense, the measure applied is proportionate and is not excessive. In addition, the efforts on parts of the school prior to expulsion of the pupils (e.g., placing them in separate study rooms, further consultation how to continue their studies on part of the headmaster school) sufficed to rest the Court's opinion that other alternatives were taken into consideration by the school directors. Though the principle of neutrality or *laïcité*, as entrenched in France's constitutional system, does not exist as an own ground of justification according to Art. 9 para 2 ECHR, it will be reviewed in conjunction with the other aims, similarly to the *Dahlab* case, when adduced by the proportionality test.

In such a case, the principle of secularism fortifies other legitimate aims, as secular education protects the negative religious right of others not to be exposed to other conspicuous signs and, at the same time, contributes to the protection of public order and public safety in school.

Consequently, the confinement of the right to religious freedom by the principle of secularism will not only be considered as a legitimate aim in light of the values underpinning the ECHR, but it will also be proportionate to the aim it sought to achieve (secular education free of any religious influence).

Accordingly, the compatibility of the French Law of 2004 with Art. 9 ECHR and the jurisprudence delivered in the series of 'decisions relating to the 2004 Law' had been established.

(2) Compliance of the Ban on Teachers Pursuant to Art. 9 ECHR

The prohibition on teachers' right to religious manifestation is likely to be held compatible with Art. 9 ECHR. Since the pre-requisites were extensively elaborated earlier demonstrating the general approach of the ECtHR also with respect to teachers, this will be briefly covered here as follows:

Firstly, *prescribed by law* – though there is no explicit codification in statutes as to a ban on religious symbols, the principle of laicité as laid down in the Charter of laicité applies equally with respect to the whole public service. In addition, the obligation to observe the principle of laicité in public education, according to Art. 141-5 of the Education Code, should as well comply with this requirement.

Secondly, necessary in a democratic society and pursuant to a legitimate aim – it is very likely that having due regard to previous case laws of the ECtHR (Dahlab v Switzerland; Kurtulumus v Turkey, Sahin v Turkey; Kaaraduman v Turkey), the imposing of a ban will be upheld as a measure that is justified for the purpose of safeguarding the principle of secularism and that is necessary in a democratic society.

Thirdly, *fulfilment of the proportionality test* – given again the cases of *Dahlab* and *Kaaraduman*, it is very likely that the ECtHR would reach the conclusion that the safeguarding of *laïcité* justifies the ban on teachers and would not be regarded as excessive interference in their right to religious freedom, as the purport is to preserve the secular nature of the state. Nonetheless, it is notable that this approach of the ECtHR will not hold water when contested with the permissibility of a small cross necklace worn by a teacher. It may be that under these circumstances the Court would find the ban disproportionate and that other, less restrictive measures could be adopted by the state.

Notably, the French ban on teachers can be segregated from the case of *Dahlab* based on several key points that will be outlined here in short:

(a) Comprehensive General Ban

The French ban on teachers to refrain from religious manifestation relates to all religious symbols regardless of size and form, unlike the prohibition in *Dahlab*. In France, the impartiality of public servants is sacrosanct and absolute; as a result, even the ban on the wearing of a small necklace may be justified on grounds of the special duty of public servants to appear impartial.

In the *Dahlab* case, the ECtHR referred merely to symbols as the headscarf, which were assigned the title of 'external powerful symbols'. Therefore, it is unlikely that a small cross necklace worn by a teacher would be recognized as proportional to the aim sought to be achieved. Nonetheless, it may well be that France would not held to be in breach with Art. 9 para 2 ECHR due to the wide margin of appreciation the ECtHR grants to member states in educational matters, and also by virtue of stark adherence to the principle of *laïcité* – especially in the public service –that had also been recognized by the Court.

(b) The Equal Treatment Principle

The contention made by the ECtHR in the *Dahlab* case upheld that the wearing of the headscarf as a sign of women oppression is made according to a religious precept in the Koran and cannot be aligned with gender equality and the principle of equal treatment. In addition, it was upheld that the headscarf contravenes against pre-eminent democratic values such as equality between men and women; as a result, the teacher as a state representative cannot convey these values if she was to wear the headscarf herself. However, this point was left undebated in French discourse mainly because the French ban relates to all religious symbols, and the necessity to differentiate between the headscarf and other symbols remained redundant.

(c) The Age of Pupils

The age of pupils was not considered in the French jurisprudence as a detrimental point with respect to the ban of the headscarf. In contrast, the ECtHR took special reference to the age of pupils, especially in relation to the proselytizing effect of the headscarf. The ECtHR held that the age of pupils is a pivotal factor when conducting the proportionality test, as the headscarf's effect as a powerful symbol on the tender minds of young children aged four to eight cannot be denied.

(d) Conclusion

The French takeover on the ban imposed on teaching staff as civil servants to religious manifestation makes no segregation in admission of religious symbols into the public service in terms of form, size, and type. Due to its lack of explicit codification in law and the fact that it applies strictly and equally with respect to the whole public service, it is very difficult to establish fulfilment of the requirements in order to prove its compatibility with Art. 9 ECHR, also given the respective case law delivered by the ECtHR in *Dahlab.*

If France substantiates enough grounds for justification of the ban as outlined in Art. 9 para 2 ECHR, and if these are supported by the principle of secularism as an admissible ground within the 'margin of appreciation' granted to the member states, then it is likely to pass the proportionality test.

The outcome of the case would also depend on the age of the pupils as viewers and, as already demonstrated in the *Dahlab* case, this would be given a considerable weight when examining whether the ban was proportionate and adequate to the aim pursued (the protection of the negative religious right of the pupils).

The position of the ban on pupils, as was demonstrated by the ECtHR was acknowledged in the series of 'decisions relating to the 2004 Law'.

To conclude, the ECtHR, based on the 'margin of appreciation' conferred upon the member states, acknowledged their right to decide individually on the delicate relations between state and church. This entails that in some member states, such as France or Switzerland (Turkey in the past) there is an obligation to adhere to the constitutional principle of secularism which contemplated and conformed to their political regime. In this respect, *laïcité*, or the principle of secularism was regarded as protection-worthy. In France, it is considered as a prominent founding principle of the Republic to which the entire population must adhere. It is due to its national importance and sacrosanct position in the historical evolvement as a constitutional pillar of the Republic that it will be protection-worthy, especially in public schools.

(3) Compatibility with Art. 14 ECHR

(a) Discrimination Based on Religious Grounds

The compatibility of the Law of 2004 prescribing the ban on religious manifestation in primary and higher education will be tested against the equality provision of the Convention. Taking into consideration the rulings of the ECtHR in the series of 'decisions relating to the 2004 Law',[1664] it is unlikely that the ban would constitute a breach as a direct or indirect discrimination on religious grounds. This is because it applies equally to both faiths: Muslim girls and Sikh boys. Insofar, it is likely to be held compatible with Art. 14 ECHR.

Insofar as the French ban on religious manifestation through signs or dress relates to teachers, it is not likely to violate a teacher's right not to be discriminated on religious ground pursuant Art. 14 ECHR.

Since the ban applies equally to all religious symbols when worn by teachers, it raises no claim of direct discrimination nor of an indirect discrimination. No direct discrimination on religious ground takes place as it applies to all teachers equally regardless of their religious affiliation. A claim of indirect discrimination may only be applicable if a teacher will challenge the 2011 Act, as it did purport to impose a ban that discriminates indirectly against a particular religious group, the Muslim community, by virtue of their manifold head coverings.

Notably, the ability of pupils – unlike teachers – to appear with small discrete signs or necklaces to school may establish the claim of indirect discrimination based on religious grounds. Such a claim of indirect discrimination may be successful as it places mainly Muslims at disadvantage. For instance, Muslim females would clearly feel disadvantaged compared to members of other religions (e.g., Christians wearing a small necklace cross). Clearly, Muslim women by reason of the ostentatious character of their dress or donning (the headscarf, *niqab*, or *jilbab*) are predestinated at outset. Symbols like the hijab, niqab, or jilbab are not only considered as visible but are perceived as conspicuous demonstrative

1664 *Gamaleddyn v France*, Appl. no. 18527/08; *Aktas v France*, Appl. no. 43563/08; *Bayrak v France*, Appl. no. 14308/08; *Ghazal v France*, Appl. no. 29134/08; *J. Singh v France* Appl. no. 25463/08; *R. Singh v France*, Appl. no. 27561/08, 17 July 2009 (ECtHR).

symbols. These, in contrast to a small cross necklace that can be hidden beneath a shirt or a pullover.

It is worth to note that a claim of indirect discrimination may be substantiated on the same grounds of justification as prescribed in Art. 9 para 2 ECHR. As far as pupils are concerned, it remains however dubious whether such a justification would stand the proportionality test.

In the case of a teacher, since the exclusion of all signs, whether discreet or conspicuous, applies equally to all religions then the ban may be regarded as proportional to the aim sought to be achieved. So a teachers claim of indirect discrimination established on religious grounds is unlikely to be successful. The reason is that the law fulfills its aim through equal application with respect to all religions regardless of visibility of the sign or dress.

(b) Discrimination Based on Gender Grounds

It is unlikely that a claim for discrimination on gender grounds would be successful taken the experience demonstrated in the Law of 2004. The Law of 2004 did not intend to preclude men from its confines as it applied also to Sikh male pupils who wore the *turban* as head covering. Thence, the prohibition on appearance with ostentatious religious symbols in school applies equally in terms of gender.

In this respect, the Law of 2004 will be regarded as compatible with Art. 14 ECHR.

Also in the case of the ban on teachers it is due to its comprehensive, absolute application on all office holders in the public service without deviation, it is unlikely that the ban on teachers will be regarded to be discriminatory on gender grounds as the ban may be applied equally to a Sikh (male) teacher wearing a *turban*.

5. Conclusion

Due to the fact that there is no common European model on state-church relations and no general accommodation of religious pluralism on the national level, the outcome relating to the permissibility of religious symbols or attire in public education will vary according to the entanglement of religion with state affairs prevailing in each of the individual European states.

The two different types of case laws brought before the ECtHR as an exemplary in this regard were *Dahlab v Switzerland* (a teacher with a headscarf) and *Lautsi v Italy* (a cross hanged on a classroom wall). These judgements had to account for the divergence in the rulings of the ECtHR, especially since both dealt with the admissibility of religious emblems in the state school system; however, they resulted in a different outcome. Whereas in the earlier case the headscarf was held to be impermissible and non-conform to the Convention, the latter declared the crucifix to be admissible and compatible with the Convention.

The discrepancy between two of the case laws was addressed by the ECtHR itself which explained that the earlier decision of *Dahlab* cannot be compared with the *Lautsi* case as it 'cannot serve as a basis in this case (*Lautsi v Italy*) because the facts of the two cases are entirely different'.[1665]

The segregation made between the different display of religious symbols in the context of public education; that is, state-displayed symbol versus individual-displayed symbol underscored following identifying criteria: first, the type of religious symbol and, second, its mode or form of display.

In principle, in all cases involving the Islamic veil the ECtHR has held that the prohibition of the headscarf is consistent with the Convention. The reasoning provided was that member states are in a better position than the Court for estimating possible justifications for interference in the right to religious freedom. This discretion granted to member states by the Court is known as the margin of appreciation. The wide margin of appreciation granted to the member states enables them to exercise an ample discretion as far as confinement of religious freedom is concerned. The Court holds the view that member states must be granted a wide margin of appreciation due to their ability to assess better which values and rights are to be safeguarded in a democratic society.

The ban on religious symbols or garments in the public school system and its classification as a recognized interference in the fundamental right to religious freedom differs in the compared states in this analysis. An evaluation of legitimacy of the ban will take the following criteria into account: first, *prescribed by law* – the existence of a legislative order prohibiting the display of religious emblems in the state school system will need to be established; second, *scope of ban* – the extent to which such a ban applies (i.e., an all-embracing ban as common in France or a limited ban with exceptions as common in Germany).

This naturally results in different outcomes and, as will be demonstrated, excludes any possibility for a unified formula to apply equally in all legislative systems of the compared states.

Thence, the following judicial aspects will be considered in the assessment of the compatibility of religious symbols in state school systems with the ECHR:

1665 *Lautsi and others v Italy*, Appl. no. 30814/06, 18 March 2011 (ECtHR) para 73, 29.

a) The Fundamental Right to Religious Freedom (Art. 9) Scope of Protection

aa) ECHR

As a general practice, infringement upon the positive right of an individual to religious freedom, in other words, a restriction on an individual's liberty to manifest his/her belief in the educational system will trigger application of Art. 9 ECHR. This means that applications made to the ECtHR relating to the admissibility of religious symbols or attire in the education context were submitted on ground of infringement upon the right to religious freedom based on Art. 9 ECHR, and in cases involving pupils as aggrieved applicants also in conjunction with the right to education (Art. 2 of Protocol 1 ECHR).[1666]

(1) Pupils

As far as the negative right of pupils to religious freedom is at stake, then in principle Art. 9 ECHR was invoked in conjunction with the right to education as guaranteed in Art. 2 of Protocol 1.

(2) Parental Educative Right

This safeguards not only an irrevocable right of pupils to public education but ensures also the parental right to decide on the education of the children so as to conform to the precepts of their own faith.

Moreover, a violation of religious rights may often establish a claim against a measure which is of a discriminatory nature, an infringement of Art. 14 ECHR (anti-discrimination provision). Art. 14 forbids discrimination on different grounds, inter alia, religious grounds. A discrimination on grounds of religion under Art. 14 involves negative religious freedom, in that sense, the liberty of an individual not be discriminated on grounds of one's religion or belief.

It is worth to note that a claim which is merely established on the anti-discrimination provision cannot prove to be successful if it was not submitted in conjunction with a substantive provision (e.g., Art. 9 ECHR).

Thence, from a fundamental human right perspective, cases involving an interference with a teacher's right to appear with a headscarf in school, as a general rule, will establish an application based on Art. 9 in conjunction with Art. 14 ECHR.

1666 *Stinnett*, B.C. Intl. & Comp. L. Rev, 429, (2005), 429, 441.

In the case of a state-displayed symbol like the crucifix on classrooms walls, the legal right holders are the pupils and their parents who can establish a claim for infringement of their negative right to religious freedom (Art. 9 ECHR) in conjunction with their right to education as safeguarded in Art. 2 of Protocol 1.

The parental right to decide on the education of their children can also constitute a ground for a claim; however, this will be only marginal to the main claim and will be taken into consideration when the children are minors and under the age of legal maturity.

bb) Germany

According to German constitutional law, an interference in an individual's right to religious freedom can be substantiated based on the right to religious freedom safeguarded in Art. 4 GG. Therefore, the right of a Muslim teacher to wear a headscarf is principally worth protection by the Grundgesetz as it falls within Art. 4's scope of protection.

In the German jurisprudence and legal literature, high importance is attributed as to application of a test which will try to identify the true motivation of an individual displaying a religious symbol. The test laid down for determination of the true motivation (religious grounds or other) of the legal right holder will be subject to a subjective test. The test will check the sincerity of the aggrieved person in a strict manner that attempts to track the individual's real motivation. However, so far no defined criteria can be identified in the German jurisprudence for application of such a sincerity (credibility) test.

Taking into consideration the jurisdiction of the ECtHR with respect to the prohibition on a state schoolteacher to appear with a headscarf while on duty, it seems that the ban imposed by the federal states on the Islamic veil is likely to comply with the judicial test established in Art. 9 para 2 ECHR. In accordance it must satisfy the following: first, prescribed by law; second, necessary in a democratic society; and, third, proportionate to the aim it pursues to achieve.

(1) Prescribed by Law

Many German federal states amended their legislation following *Ludin*'s decision in order to regulate a prohibition on a teacher to appear with a headscarf (i.e., the manifestation of ostentatious symbols) and interweave this ban with the possible endangerment to high-minded values and rights. The ban is thence inclusive; however, its legitimacy will be subject to a judicial review of the legislative order in the concerned respective state.

(2) Necessary in a Democratic Society

As a possible ground for justification, the following values and rights have been often considered in the German jurisprudence: the safeguarding of public order (i.e., peaceful co-existence in school, ordinary flow of school lessons) and the safeguard of the rights and freedoms of others (i.e., negative religious right of pupils, their parents, or other teaching personnel) and other pre-eminent values that had been recognized and elaborated by the ECtHR, such as the principle of neutrality, religious pluralism, and tolerance.

(3) The Proportionality Test

The proportionality test may pose some difficulty to some of the federal states' amended legislation, as they will be under a duty to prove that an interference was necessary to pursue the aim it sought to achieve. This was for instance the case in states like BW and previously NRW (prior to the recent modification of their School Act) which introduced exceptions to the general ban on religious emblems in state schools. The current legal situation in the state of BW is likely to encounter difficulties to comply with the proportionality test.

From a constitutional perspective, the delivery of the recent headscarf case by the BVerfG raises a difficulty to reconcile some of the legislative bans amended by the federal states, as it declared the prohibition on a teacher to appear with an Islamic veil while on duty *prima facie* to be unconstitutional.

Germany does not include a general ban prohibiting pupils from manifestation of religious symbols since this will *de facto* constitute a violation of their constitutional right to religious freedom (Art. 4 GG).

cc) England

The British legal system maintains the most liberal approach among the compared states with respect to the position of teachers to endorse religious symbols in its state school system. In principle, teachers are not prohibited from wearing religious garments while on duty. Therefore, the Islamic veil is permitted for teachers in public education on a general level. However, deviation from such general admittance is possible in specific cases where the display will be banned due to genuine occupational requirements. This was the case in *Azmi* where the headscarf as a religious symbol hindered the teacher's performance at school (e.g., teacher assistant with the *niqab* who was claimed to hinder communication with the pupils due to the inability of pupils to understand her properly because the garment covered her face). Therefore, British jurisprudence will declare a ban to be justified in cases of indirect discrimination if there are practical considerations arguing against the religious symbol in question. British courts will normally disregard justification for a ban on a religious symbol if established plainly by virtue of its religious connotation.

Teachers who encounter interference in their religious right and are prohibited from wearing a religious garb while on duty will be able to establish their claim on anti-discrimination law (i.e., Equality Act 2010). The reason is that equality/anti-discrimination laws are more protective in scope under British law as oppose to a fundamental right complaint lodged under the HRA.

In fact, though the right of a teacher to manifest her religious freedom through the display of a religious garment falls within the scope of the fundamental right to religious freedom protected under the HRA 1998, it will be difficult in practice to establish an infringement of the right. The reason is that a British court will take two factors into consideration: first, *voluntariness* – if a teacher took upon himself voluntarily to work in a public school, it would be regarded as a factor for dismissal of a claim for infringement in a person's religious right. The reason is that the teacher entered his/her profession voluntarily. Second, *alternative school* – the possibility to exchange to a private Muslim school where the wearing of the religious garment in question would be possible may discharge any claim for infringement. This raises criticism in legal literature which contends that the job opportunities for teachers are decreased in a locality where a large proportion of schools are faith schools or that a faith school is the only maintained school in the area.[1667]

Pupils – a legal ban with respect to the permissibility of pupils to wear a religious symbol while on school premises does not exist in legislation, as in general all public schools subject pupils to school uniform rules. Exceptional cases will be admitted but rather in a very individual form, enabling each school to decide on the acceptance of different religious symbols that accord with the respective school uniform rules. Nonetheless, even within the boundaries of such a liberal approach an exclusion of specific religious symbols with a distinctive religious character will be regarded as justifiable (e.g., the *jilbab*). A justification ground for the prohibition of powerful religious symbols like the *jilbab was* explained in the British jurisprudence by their ability to influence other pupils to dress up so as to comply with stricter religious precepts placed by their religious communities and the formation of groups within school. This social peer pressure on pupils who are not religiously motivated was explained

1667 *Vickers*, in Hunter-Henin, Law, Religious Freedoms and Education in Europe, 2011, 87, 94.

to be a sound ground since it is capable of distorting the peaceful co-existence in school.

dd) France

France stands at the other end of the scale in this analysis as an extreme model of its well-known state-church separation. The entrenched principle of *laïcité* provides introspection as to the constitutional status of religious freedom and the admissibility of individuals to manifest religious symbols in state education. The fundamental right to manifest religious freedom is safeguarded in the constitution and, in principle, may also apply with respect to the Islamic veil. A major difference that plays a significant role with respect to the other compared states in this analysis is the basic notion of *laïcité* which is grounded in France's constitutional history and is characterized by the alienated approach of France towards religion.

France applies a general strict ban with respect to all religious symbols in the public office. Therefore, teachers are included under this general ban and no form of visible religious signs would be permitted. The 2011 Act prohibits explicitly the wearing of face veils – not only in public institutions but also in the public space in general. As a result, pupils are also included under the ban and the manifestation of any visible ostentatious religious symbols will be consequently prohibited.

Nonetheless, the demonstration of an infringement on the right of an individual to manifest his religious freedom can still be justified if argumentation grounds exist and if it satisfies the proportionality test.

Teachers, as public officials, fulfil the voluntariness requirement when entering freely the public school system. Likewise, their alternative option to apply for a teaching vacancy in a private Muslim school will be taken into consideration within application of the proportionality test so as to dismiss a claim of infringement on the teacher's right to religious freedom.

Taking into consideration the interpretation delivered by the ECtHR with respect to religious freedom (Art. 9) and the justification arguments prescribed in Art. 9 para 2, it is likely that the French legislation will stand in conformity to the Convention. It is however doubtful whether the comprehensive form of the ban which entirely excludes display of the headscarf would pass the proportionality test.

In this regard, even the ECtHR admitted already that 'not every act inspired by religion or belief gets protected under the Convention'.[1668] Public officials,

1668 *Leyla Sahin v Turkey* 2005, ECtHR, no. 44774/98, para. 105.

like other individuals, can be limited in the exercise of their right to religion or belief. It is therefore of relevancy to differentiate between manifestation of an individual's right to religion or belief conducted in private or in public. The relevancy is known since manifestation of religious right in public, as opposed to the private sphere, may trigger encroachment upon the personal right of others and may justify the imposition of limitations on those who wish to invoke it while exercizing their public function. This emanates that the right to freedom of religion does not protect at all times the right to manifest a religion in public.[1669]

b) The Neutrality Concept and Its Impact on Manifestation of Religious Symbols in the Education

aa) ECHR

The principle of neutrality is not enshrined in the Convention but was rather gradually elaborated by the ECtHR in case laws concerning manifestation of religious freedom (Art. 9) to the extent that it has become a general important principle of the Court.[1670]

The member states were granted by the ECtHR a wide leeway to impose limitations on teachers' right to display religious symbols. The preclusion of a particular religious manifestation from falling within the ambit of Art. 9 will be assessed based on the states' ability to establish justification for the interference in the individual's right to religious freedom. The justifications for limitation are prescribed in Art. 9 para 2 ECtHR and do not include state neutrality. However, since the ECtHR enabled the states a large margin of appreciation the duty of the state to religious neutrality has been read into Art. 9 and was developed gradually by it so as to keep compatibility with the Convention.

Especially in cases relating to display of religious symbols in state teaching, it was often the case that the ECtHR interlinked the duty of the state to be neutral and impartial with other high-minded values, such as pluralism, tolerance and broadmindedness. By that association, the Court has assumed not only the duty of the state to safeguard neutrality but also religious pluralism and tolerance as pursued aims of the Convention.[1671]

1669 *Westerfield*, Am. J. Comp. L. 637 (2006), 637, 641.

1670 *Van Ooijen*, in Temperman, The Lautsi Papers, 2012 Volume 11, 219, 221.

1671 *Evans*, Manual on the Wearing of Religious Symbols in Public, p. 51; *Van Ooijen*, in Temperman, The Lautsi Papers, 2012 Volume 11, 219, 220.

A major critic point was raised especially with respect to individuals' right to manifest religious freedom in state schooling, as the ECtHR refused to find a ban on a teacher to appear with a headscarf as a far-reaching interference in her fundamental right to religious manifestation. On the contrary, it was justified by virtue of her public official's duty to abide by state neutrality,[1672] declaring it as incompatible with the Convention. This was contrasted on the background of the later *Lautsi* case, where the ECtHR held that display of a religious symbol like the crucifix by the state[1673] stands in no contradiction to the neutral appearance of the state.

In the legal literature, this approach remained odd, foremost given the religious meaning attached to the cross and its display in public schools. It was argued that state neutrality as possible justification for limitation on institutional manifestation of religious symbols was not implemented properly due to the reluctance of the ECtHR to perceive the display of the crucifix in Italian public schools as a pure religious symbol which contravenes the duty of the state to religious neutrality.[1674]

Finally, the ECtHR upheld in the *Lautsi* case that due to lack of consensus among the European states as to the concept of religious pluralism in general and as to the display of the cross in public institutions (as a salient Christian symbol) in particular, there is no general apprehension regarding the neutral image of the state. Thus, it refrained from interference in the domestic discretion of the state (Italy), leaving it for the individual self-determination of each state to decide on the nexus to religious neutrality that varies according to the constitutional state-church model adopted by each member state.

bb) Germany

An application of the neutrality principle as a justification ground for interference in the right to religious freedom takes place with respect to state-displayed symbols as well as individually displayed symbols. The difficulty, however, arises due to lack of consent in the German literature and jurisprudence as to its exact meaning and application (strict or liberal).

1672 *Dahlab v Switzerland*, Appl. no. 42393/98, 15 February 2001 (ECtHR).

1673 *Lautsi and others v Italy*, Appl. no. 30814/06, 18 March 2011 (ECtHR).

1674 *Van Ooijen*, in Temperman, (2012), pp. 223-224, 237-238; *J. Temperman* , 2012 pp. 153-155; *Arthur* British Journal of Education Studies 60.2 (2012), 129 (141-142).

Nonetheless, in both given situations the neutrality principle does not constitute an own standing justification ground for limitation but is conjoined in principle with other constitutional rights such as pupils' negative right to religious freedom (Art. 4 para 1 and para 2 GG), parental right to decide on the education of their children (Art. 6 para 2 GG), and the educative task of the state (Art. 7 para 1 GG).

The new headscarf case delivered by the BVerfG[1675] turned down the strict application of the neutrality principle which thence far tilted towards permissibility of the ban given that other rights were at stake, for instance, the disturbance of peaceful co-existence in school and the possibility to indoctrinate the pupils. In the new headscarf case, it was determined that the duty of the state to remain neutral and the special obligation of the teacher as state representative emanating from her position as a public servant do not justify encroachment on the teacher's right to wear a headscarf in such all-embracing manner, as this would fail to comply with the proportionality test.

On the other side of the token, the legitimacy provided to Christian and Jewish symbols in state schools as an exception to the general ban on religious symbols – as was introduced in the states of Baden-Württemberg and previously NRW – remains questionable. Especially since such an exception would probably not stand the proportionality test of Art. 9 para 2 and may further constitute a violation of the anti-discrimination provision prescribed in Art. 14 ECHR. Thence, the permissibility of Christian and Jewish symbols would give rise to a declaration of incompatibility with the ECHR. This demonstrates, therefore, constitutional difficulty for the state of BW to justify the admittance of Christian and Jewish symbols, especially if Islamic symbols are to be completely out-factored from school teaching. If the state of BW wishes to abide by a strict application of the neutrality principle which would prohibit all religious emblems from schools, it should apply the ban equally to all religious symbols in order to satisfy the proportionality test and the equality principle.

cc) England

England is the only state that does not acknowledge the notion of state neutrality in its legal system. Albeit decrease in the position of the Anglican Church, there is no total separation between these two entities and the special privileged position can still be recognized today.[1676] Therefore, the neutrality principle cannot

1675 1 BvR 471/10, 1 BvR 1181/10 27.1. 2015.

1676 *Van Ooijen*, p. 217.

be invoked in the English legal system as a justification ground for interference in religious freedom.

dd) France

The principle of *laïcité* is very unique to France's constitutional system and is very complex to define and conceptualize.[1677] In the French discourse, the principle of *laïcité* has been constantly interwoven with the neutrality principle. It is regarded as the equivalent to the English definition of the neutrality principle, though not fully covered by it, and constitutes a paramount constitutional principle in France's legal system.

Its significant position as a fundamental constitutional pillar emphasizes its difference to other legal systems in this analysis. Two central elements can be recognized: first, the ability to stand on its own as a justification ground for encroachment on individuals' right to religious freedom; and, second, the fact that France adopts a strict model of state-church separation enables it to deploy a strict application of the neutrality principle.

The obligation of the teacher to conform to the neutrality principle and her duty as a state representative to refrain from manifestation of any visible religious signs when at school will serve as a justification of the ban to appear with conspicuous symbols to school. As a result, the prohibition on a teacher to appear with a headscarf to school will probably not be regarded as incompatible with the ECHR. The reason is that as a potential ground for the teachers' dismissal can serve not only the obligation to obey by the principle of *laïcité* but also other justifying aims may be available, such as the negative rights of pupils and the safeguarding of public order.

Due to the endorsement of the 2011 Act which prohibits the wearing of ostentatious religious symbols in public, a justification can also be used with respect to a ban imposed on pupils' right to appear with religious symbols to school. It is worth to note that if so far a prohibition was justified on ground of the necessity to safeguard the public order in school, nowadays a ban will be able to satisfy conformity to the ECtHR based on the obligation to respect the religious neutrality of the state.

Nonetheless, a critical point may rise as to the difficulty to establish compliance with the ECHR, in particular since such a general ban to refrain from the display of religious symbols in public may fail to satisfy the proportionality principle, especially as far as religious rights of pupils are concerned.

1677 *Rogoff*, p. 336 et seq.

c) Neutrality and Its Impact on the Conception of Public Officials

The position favouring a refrainment of the teacher as public official from displaying a religious symbol argues for the imposition of a duty to religious neutrality.

The permissibility of public officials to manifest religious symbols has been subject to two contention points within the state-public officials relations.[1678] First, *the personification argument* – this emanates from the special status of public officials which perceives them as representatives of the state.[1679] Second, this personification of public officials imposes on them a duty of allegiance to the state, the duty of religious neutrality, which requires them as representatives of the state to appear neutral in their function.

aa) Germany

The personification argument has been often used in Germany and France to dispel the teachers' right to display religious symbols while on duty. The notion underlying the personification argument underscores that teachers as public officials are perceived as representatives of the state and are, therefore, under a special obligation to appear neutral and unbiased. The German jurisprudence accepted this argument especially in cases involving young pupils, upholding that there exists a presumption of a proselytizing effect which cannot be completely negated.

bb) England

The personification argument with respect to teachers as representatives of the state is not considered in English law since public officials are not perceived as personifying the state.[1680] Public officials, including teachers, are not subject to a duty to appear neutral and impartial while in office and, as a result, the personification argument is not applicable.

cc) France

France applies specific principles and obligations with respect to the whole public service which differ substantially from those relating to the private sector.[1681]

1678 *Mancini*, Cardozo Law Review, 30, 2009, 2629, 2632.

1679 *Dahlab v Switzerland*, Appl. no. 42393/98, 15 February 2001 (ECtHR).

1680 *Vickers* in: Hunter Henin, pp. 88 et seq.

1681 *Vickers* in: Hunter Henin, pp. 89 et seq.

Public officials are part of the public service and are subject to a different legal regime which compels them to abide by several recognized principles emanating from their special status as *agent public*. This means that when public officials had entered the public service they were voluntarily subjecting themselves to certain duties that apply only within their function.[1682] Public officials are subject to the duty of neutrality[1683] which obliges them to refrain from any expression or manifestation of their religious belief whether by conduct, verbal expression, or the wearing of religious garb or garment.[1684] The underlying aim of the duty of neutrality is that public officials appear impartial and neutral; the state would thus effectively guarantee equal access of individuals to the public service, as it would not appear biased and could not be accused for preferential treatment of a specific religion or belief.[1685]

The same view was held by the ECtHR in the case of *Dahlab*. It was explained that such possible improper influence on the young mind of pupils, coupled with its interpretation as a symbol which runs counter to the principle of gender equality and non-discrimination would tilt following application of the proportionality test towards limitation on the teacher's right to wear the headscarf.

Accordingly, this positive duty to religious neutrality, limiting the right of a teacher to religious freedom was justified based on the need to protect the right and freedoms of others according to Art. 9 para 2 ECHR.

Following justifications were considered by the ECtHR while evaluating the proportionality of the headscarf ban: jeopardy to the negative right of pupils to religious freedom, its message as a symbol which is incompatible with the equality principle, contrasting with the notion of gender equality, and the fact that it repeals the notion of respect for others.

Second, *the policy of equal treatment* – mandates that all public officials are to be treated equally and no disparities between individuals are to be taken into consideration.

1682 *Van Ooijen*, p. 181.

1683 *Van Ooijen*, p. 180; *Berthoud*, p. 1142.

1684 *McGoldrick*, pp. 73, 75; *Berthoud*, p. 1144.

1685 *Van Ooijen*, p. 180; *Zauberman/Lévy*, Criminology 41(4) 2003, 1065, 1081; *Bedouelle/Costa*, Les laïcités à la française, 1998, pp. 118–119; *Guimezanes*, Introduction au droit français, 2nd edition, p. 124; *Gaudu*, Comp. Lab. L. & Pol'y J. 2009 (3), 507, 517.

d) Protection of Public Order

The argument of safeguarding public order is familiar in the legal system of all compared countries and its application is normally interwoven with the protection of the (negative) religious rights of others (i.e., pupils and parents who claim for an adverse effect). The protection of public order has been often used as a justification argument for the endangerment of the peaceful co-existence in school and the operation of ordinary course of lessons. Since the display of religious symbols by individuals may trigger religious peer pressure adduced by the community or other classmates, the aim invoked is the safeguarding of public order that may be endangered due to building of religious groups within school and result in clash of rights.

In the case of a teacher wearing a headscarf, the need to protect the public order will be used with respect to the proselytizing effect such a symbol may have on pupils who will feel pressured by her appearance or otherwise may be adversely affected by her view.

A similar clash of rights may occur also when other pupils wearing an ostentatious religious symbol or garment may deploy negative influence on their school fellows and subject them to peer pressure.

It is worth to note that in the legal literature the view held is that accordance with fundamental human rights mandates that the state needs to establish an evident clash of rights, especially in cases involving limitation of individual religious manifestation, as well as imminent effect so as to warrant state interference.[1686]

e) The Policy of Equal Treatment

The policy of equal treatment has its roots in the general principle of equality which forbids unequal treatment based on various grounds (race, ethnic, gender, religion, belief etc.). This also prescribes an obligation of equal treatment in the process of access and hiring requirements in employment to the public service.

Accordingly, a prohibition on public officials to refrain from manifestation of religious symbols should be inclusive and apply to all public officials without segregation. This contention point which pursues the equal treatment policy prefers to follow a formal conception of equality rather than a substantive conception.[1687]

An encroachment on public officials' religious freedom will be legitimized by the ECtHR insofar as: (i) the teacher took upon herself voluntarily to enter

---

1686 *Temperman*, in Temperman, The Lautsi Papers 2012 Volume 11, 143, 159.
1687 *Van Ooijen*, pp. 155–156.

the job and comply with the contractual duties (e.g., dress code requirements) imposed on her by virtue of her function; (ii) the teacher had a free choice to dismiss herself from public schooling and apply for a vacancy in private schools.

aa) Germany

The right of an individual (e.g., a teacher wearing a headscarf) is open to submit a complaint for a breach of the equality principle. Nonetheless, even in the German jurisprudence a discrimination claim established on religious grounds (Art. 3 and 33 GG) will be subsidiary to the main application and will not stand on its own.

In federal states like BW and NRW, where the ban is not inclusive in nature and makes an exception with respect to Christian and Jewish symbols, there exists a difficulty to establish its constitutional conformity with the equality principle prescribed in the Grundgesetz (Art. 3 and 33). Unlike BW and NRW, the Bavarian legislator does not explicitly declare an exclusion of ostentatious religious symbols (e.g., the headscarf) with respect to teachers. Nonetheless, the amended legislation demonstrates favouritism towards Christian tradition and heritage (e.g., the crucifix hanged on classroom walls) as an inseparable bond between the state and its people. Accordingly, the scope of the ban and its extent will be subject to judicial review and the interpretation bestowed to the amended legislation.

Under the Convention aspect, it will be difficult, however, to reconcile the prohibition imposed by the federal states with the exception of the state of Berlin with the anti-discrimination provision (Art. 14 ECHR).

The only federal state that did not introduce an exception for Christian and Jewish symbols is the state of Berlin. The ban on religious symbols is general and inclusive with respect to all offices in the public sector. Such a strict comprehensive ban exists also in France and, at least from an anti-discrimination perspective, is likely to be held as compatible with the jurisdiction of the ECtHR as so far delivered with respect to the Islamic headscarf.

bb) England

The opportunities for teachers who wish to invoke their right to religious freedom are open either through: (i) lodging a fundamental human right claim based on the HRA 1998; (ii) a claim established on discrimination on grounds of religion or belief based on the Equality Act 2010. It is worth to note that a substantiation of an anti-discrimination claim within the framework of the equality legislation which relates specifically to the employment sector will be easier to prove than to pass the strict application of the proportionality test mandated under a fundamental human right claim.

cc) France

France is the only state that adopts a strict general comprehensive prohibition with respect to manifestation of religious symbols. The Law of 2004 applies a general ban on all religious symbols without any segregation and is valid with respect to all office holders in the public sphere.

f) Gender Equality

The question of the permissibility of the Islamic headscarf in public schooling was often challenged on the background of its association with notion of women repression, their subordination to men, and its contradiction with the principle of gender equality (equality between men and women).[1688]

The gender equality argument has been used in all compared states and establishes a recognized justification argument for the interference in an individual's right to display the Islamic headscarf. Though it still remains controversial whether a religious symbol can be deprived of its legitimacy merely by virtue of its attachment with a notion that repeals the gender equality principle, it was often invoked by the states when interwoven with the need to protect the right of others. Thus, states underscored the need to safeguard the right of other pupils or their parents (pertaining to the religious majority group) or even other teaching staff.

As far as the ban imposed on teachers to appear with a headscarf is concerned, then all compared states – whether Germany, England, or France –find it easier to legitimize such a prohibition, as it is perceived as an inherent duty of state education to promote Western liberal values and principles such as the equality between men and women.

The problematics raised relates to the justification of the headscarf ban with respect to pupils since they, unlike teachers, are under no obligation to promote the principle of gender equality. Whereas in France this argument may still be justified in conjunction with the perception enshrined in the principle of laïcité that schools should remain a neutral place where no exertion of unnecessary pressure is allowed, it is likely to fail in Germany and England.[1689]

1688 *Shadid/Van Koningsveld*; Journal of Islamic Studies, 16:1 (2005), 35, 46.

1689 In Germany, the headscarf ban on pupils would be difficult to align with gender equality since it does not substantiate a justification ground, unlike with respect to

g) Abstract Endangerment

The abstract endangerment argument has been used in all compared countries as a justification ground for interference in the right to religious freedom.

Strikingly, the ECtHR applied the abstract endangerment test in both of the exemplary case laws in order to examine whether the display of a teacher with a headscarf or the display of a cross in a classroom would pose a concrete endangerment to other high-minded values, such as the negative right of pupils to religious freedom, the peaceful course of school lessons, public order, public safety, gender equality (equality of men and women), or other fundamental morals that are worth protection in a democratic society.

In the case of *Dahlab*, the ECtHR did not look into a concrete endangerment that may occur with respect to the rights of others (negative religious freedom of pupils and their parents) due to their confrontation with the teacher. On the contrary, the ECtHR ignored the fact that the teacher appeared for years in school with a headscarf without any problem or complaint,[1690] and accepted grounds for restrictions although the alleged 'proselytising effect' was too abstract as it was established on groundless fears.[1691]

However, in the *Lautsi* case the ECtHR presupposed arbitrarily that an 'essential passive symbol' like the crucifix could not have an adverse or proselytizing effect on pupils.[1692] This narrow indoctrination test applied by the Grand Chamber in the *Lautsi* case was criticized in the legal literature[1693] as a

---

teachers. Mainly since they are under no duty to do so and due to the significance known to Art. 4 as a constitutional fundamental right. In England, the situation is remarkable since an all-inclusive ban exists with respect to symbols like the *jilhab* and *niqab*; however, not with respect to the headscarf. At the outset these symbols were regarded to be more 'powerful' by far than the headscarf due to their oppressive nature and political extremism with which they are associated. Thence, their ban would be justified based on the ground of safeguarding the (negative) religious right of pupils from unnecessary pressure exerted by other fellow pupils to accord with the wearing of these garments which stand for women suppression and inequality between men and women. *Ganz*, p. 312.

1690 *Dahlab v Switzerland*, Appl. no. 42393/98, 15 February 2001 (ECtHR), p. 13.

1691 *Temperman*, in Temperman, The Lautsi Papers 2012 Volume 11, 149, 154,157,158, 161, 162.

1692 *Lautsi and others v Italy*, Appl. no. 30814/06, 18 March 2011 (ECtHR), concurring opinion of Judge Bonello, para. 2.8–2.9; *Temperman*, in Temperman, The Lautsi Papers, 2012 Volume 11, 149, 154,155, 163, 165, 168.

1693 *Temperman*, in Temperman, The Lautsi Papers 2012 Volume 11, 149, 164.

deviation from other state education case laws in which the Court adopted the 'non-proselytism' test.[1694] Criticism contended that in the case of a state-imposed symbol a 'misplaced proselytism' is rather easily *prima facie* established.[1695] This, however, was negated by the Court that denounced indoctrination on part of the state providing that 'no evidence' was brought by the pupils or their parents to prove the contrary. It sufficed the Court to decide that no necessity was posed by the applicants relating to the invoked ground for limitation (their negative right to religious freedom, their exposure to adverse proselytizing effect), at least not due to an abstract ground so as to justify the seizure of the majority right to religious freedom (i.e., proportionality test was not established).

From a human right law perspective, the assumption at the outset should be that a restriction on the right of an individual, whether a teacher or a pupil, to manifest a religion both in public or private should be safeguarded. This inherited fundamental right cannot legitimate any ground for interference on part of the state.[1696] It was already established by the ECtHR that any measure affecting even minimally the right to religious freedom amounts to an interference with the *forum externum.*[1697] A substantiation of a risk to potential, recognized and legitimated grounds which are necessary for interference should be presented by the state.

Nonetheless, despite the conclusion that even individuals in their capacity as teachers are entitled in principle to exercise their undisturbed fundamental right to religious freedom,[1698] the European jurisprudence finds that the special position of a teacher bears a duty which justifies a restriction. Thence, in case of a teacher as a symbol displayer the ECtHR acknowledged that teachers represent the state and must abide by certain professional duties.[1699] Accordingly, odd as it seems, state interference was warranted in the case of individual display of religious symbol whereas in the case of state-displayed symbol it had been rejected.

1694 In the case of *Folgero* (Appl. no. 1547202) the ECtHR decided that the curriculum in public schools must be applied by the competent authorities at utmost care to pupils' and parents' religious convictions and are not substituted by misplaced proselytism.

1695 *Temperman*, in Temperman, The Lautsi Papers 2012 Volume 11, 149, 165.

1696 *Temperman*, in Temperman, The Lautsi Papers 2012 Volume 11, 149, 158–159.

1697 *Dahlab v Switzerland*, Appl. no. 42393/98, 15 February 2001 (ECtHR), pp. 11–12.

1698 *Temperman*, in Temperman, The Lautsi Papers 2012 Volume 11, 149, 162.

1699 *Temperman*, in Temperman, The Lautsi Papers, 2012 Volume 11, 149, 162–163.

aa) Germany

The abstract endangerment argument is not unfamiliar in the German jurisprudence. This argument has often served as a core of controversy in the jurisprudence and legal literature as to whether the interference in an individual's right to manifest a religion can be justified based on a concrete or abstract endangerment posed to other rights and values. So far, the perception held by the BVerfG was that abstract endangerment suffices; however, with the delivery of the new headscarf judgement it determined that an abstract endangerment constitutes an encroachment too severe on a teacher's fundamental right to religious freedom.

bb) England

Though in general the legal situation is that teachers are not confined in their right to manifest their religion through wearing of religious dress, there are exceptions to this general permission. In these exceptional cases (i.e., an assistant teacher with a *niqab*) the establishment of an abstract endangerment will suffice.

cc) France

As far as teachers and pupils are concerned, the general ban that exists in France with respect to manifestation of religious symbols in public education will substantiate a justification for interference in the right to manifest religious freedom even if the symbol in question pose a mere abstract endangerment to other constitutional freedoms. Hence, the French constitutional system, which adopts a strict approach, would not even look into the establishment of a concrete endangerment.

V Ending Conclusion

1. The Legal Framework and Constitutional Elements for Safeguarding of Human Rights

Germany – the legal system is a centralized civilian system prescribed in the highest source of law, the 1949 German Constitution (Grundgesetz). The codification of fundamental human rights and constitutional values in a fully fledged 'Bill of Rights' is unique to the German legal system, as such a comprehensive written document for the safeguarding of fundamental human rights does not exist in the other compared legal systems of England and France. Germany's written constitution embodies the core essence of its legal framework and constitutes a distinguishable characteristic for differentiation in the perception of fundamental rights, their guarantee, and its legal status within the federative hierarchy of norms. The organizational structure of the state is established as a federal system which employs a co-operation between the federal states to act together for the benefit of the central state, and which determines allocation of powers and legislative competencies between the federation and the central state unless the latter is assigned exclusively in the constitution to act in a particular legal matter, known also as the principle of federalism (*Bundesstaatsprinzip*) prescribed in Art. 20, 30 and 70 GG. Accordingly, the power to legislate in education and school system is granted to the individual federal states in the constitution as part of the competency conferred to them to regulate their inner affairs at their sole discretion. Since each region differs from the other by virtue of historical–cultural identifications and political power, this naturally influences the educational school system which varies from one federal state to the other. The educative mandate of the state is one of the most significant constitutional provisions, establishing the exclusive supervision of the state in educational matters and is prescribed in Art. 7 para 1 GG. It is very extensive in nature and includes the power to govern the formation, organization, establishment, administration, and supervision of the federal states over their individual school system.

England – a distinctive characteristic of England's legal system in that it pertains to the countries governed by a common law system. This is in sharp contrast to civilian law systems, as practised, for instance, in Germany and France. This means that the English legal system does not rely on codification of law through legislative procedure; but rather, the development of law is subject to decisions and case laws delivered by the judiciary (courts and tribunals) and by its precedential effect on evolvement of future case laws. In addition, an identifiable, pre-eminent feature of England's constitutional order is the absence of a written constitution that designates state-power relations and enshrines the safeguarding of fundamental human rights. This entails that liberty rights, inter alia the protection of the right to religious freedom are more likely to suffer abuses either by state authorities or individuals as they are not laid down in a single written document. The right to religious freedom can be found in the old systems of common law and equity, Acts of Parliament, and its obligations undertaken on the international level to abide by human rights treaties to which it assigned. Eminently, the constitutional principle of 'parliament supremacy' which enables British Parliament to change any law so that it can potentially override other statutes or regulations increases the danger for disregard or abuse of fundamental human rights. These comparative segregation points constitute a key element in the perception of fundamental human rights, their origin, and the options of effective mechanisms offered for their protection when compared against the background of the legal framework existing in the different countries depicted in this analysis.

France – the French legal system is classified as a civil law system, which means that its basis can be found in the codification of rules and laws. In addition, further sources of law constitute its legacy of constitutions, jurisprudential decisions, and several international human rights and instruments that France has ratified, all of which prescribe the guarantee of fundamental and civil rights and comprise a part of French law and its structural hierarchy of norms.

The guarantee of individual rights through the state is an approach particular to the French republican tradition. In the history of France, this even dates back to a major historical event which in its aftermath ensued the period of the First French Republic; the time of the French Revolution, influenced by social upheaval, introduced one of the most fundamental documents in the protection of human rights, the Declaration of the Rights of Man and of the Citizen from 1789. Further, the safeguarding of liberty rights can be traced both in the preamble of the 1946 Constitution and in the 1958 Constitution of the Fifth Republic and indicates that their attachment in these documents is reminiscent of their importance also in the legal history of France. Another considerable element to be taken into account is the obligations of France under EU law and its commitments to respect fundamental human rights in international conventions to which France is a signatory. Their significance under French law can be attached to: first, their self-executing force, which enables French citizens to rely on them directly in domestic courts; second, the prevalence of EU and international treaties over national legislation, whether enacted prior to or after domestic legislation, grants French citizens assurance and reliance when invoking liberty rights before national courts.

Finally, the status of case laws – in general, case laws delivered by the jurisprudence do not have a binding effect; they are more declaratory in nature since the role of judges is perceived to apply rather than develop rules of law. This again contrasts sharply with the jurisprudential approach practised in the legal systems of Germany and England. However, the authoritative status of decisions delivered by the CE or the Cons. Const. in administrative law is a vital source of reference and in the development of the law. Nonetheless, they do not have a formal binding status as precedents for the lower courts and, in fact, the latter remain free to reject them. On the same token, the importance known to doctrinal legal writing in contrast to the authority of judicial decisions and their precedential force underscores another key element for its distinctiveness in relation to the compared legal systems of Germany and England. This is reflected in the relative superior position they have in the constitutional hierarchy of norms in comparison to juridical decisions, even those delivered by the highest instances.

To sum up, the essence of French domestic law, distinguishing it from the British and German legal systems can be attributed to several facts: the structure and variety of French court institutions are elementary in the perception of its judicial system and the way it functions, as France has a dual legal system dividing strictly public from private law and accordingly operates a different judicial system. Further divisiveness originates in the process of decision-making policy, the formation of legal rules, the special bond of France with its republican notion, and the values interlinked with the idea of a unified national state: 'Liberty, Equality and Fraternity' inscribed also in its constitution. All of these serve as distinctive features of France's legal system and identify its uniqueness as opposed to the common law heritage of the English system and the nature of civilian system dominating in the German tradition.

In addition, the juridical instances in Germany and England were particularly confronted with the question whether aspects relating to religious manifestation in public education should be left to decision makers (i.e., school/public authorities) or should remain within legislative supervision. The problematic with the first option is to empower the administrative with a wide discretion where it is not apt to balance between fundamental human rights. Nonetheless, it is a common practice in England that LEAs are delegated with the discretion to regulate dress code rules and uniform policies to state schools within their region. In Germany, educational matter remain within the exclusive competency of the individual lands' legislators.

2. Decision-Making Policy Analogous to the Legal System Governed in the States

Germany – the organization and administration of inner affairs are conferred to the supervision of federal states and include their legislative powers with respect to the framework of their school system to be decided at sole discretion (Art. 30 and 70 GG). This yields that education and the proximity of religion to public affairs, including religious influence and conveyance of religious content in schools curricula are dealt on a regional level. The lawmakers in the respective individual *Länder* (federal states) are responsible for enactments regulating the appearance or display of religious insignias in public schools. This varies to a large extent between the federal states and is affected by the position religion acquires in each state as enshrined and prescribed in the respective land's constitution and the degree of piety of the population to influence of the church. Thence, state-church entanglement can differ from strong adherence to the Catholic Church, as known in Bavaria and BW, to integrative and respective approach to the Christian faith and tradition as incorporated in NRW, or a strong secularist–separationist approach as adopted in the state of Berlin.

It is worth to note that the recent decision of the BVerfG upholding the headscarf ban in NRW as unconstitutional indicates that the German judicator acknowledges a shift of responsibility with respect to bans imposed on religious symbols from the legislative to the administrative level, in a very similar manner to the British concept.

England – under British law, the wearing of school uniform is subject to school authorities' policy and may vary among schools in the same region. It had been often underscored that local authorities or school administrators are in a better position to assess the necessity of imposing regulations restricting the appearance of pupils with religious garments in school. The reason is that school authorities may take advice from the religious communities involved and attain better estimation as to which garments are concluded as accepted mainstream even within the respective religious community itself. As such, the ability of school authorities to approve only certain religious symbols while excluding others would not be regarded as harsh interference in an individual's right to wear other extreme forms of head coverings, as school authorities took advice from the religious community itself. In the absence of written regulations which apply also to schoolteachers as civil servants, it seems that this argument can work well also with respect to teachers who wish to appear with a *niqab* or *jilbab* to school.

A critical point should be raised when taking into consideration consultation with the relevant religious community; even within a religious community, it is very difficult to achieve consensus as to what will be regarded as appropriate religious dress that coincides with the mainstream view. In other words, also within a religious group, there exists divisiveness and lack of uniformity as to what will be regarded as religious dress that conforms to the precepts of that particular faith. Radical groups within a religious community may assume that a normal headscarf is insufficient and inadequate for women or girls for their appearance in public, as they will require compliance with a more conservative form of dress as appropriate. As a result, they may pressurize female members of their community to abide by a stricter religious dress code in order to keep their modesty and morals and thus conform to their restrictive-extremist apprehension.

In addition, British courts prefer deference to the executive insofar as the admissibility of religious symbols and their classification is called into question. In addition, they would most likely not even accept a ban on religious symbols as interference but would rather find them to be objectively justified.

This method of argumentation had been evident foremost in considerations brought by the HL in the famous case of *Begum*.

France – a distinguishable feature of France's education system in contrast to Germany and England is attributed to the fact that its organization, structure, establishment, and operation is highly centralized. Regulation or management of religion and religious expression in public education is subject to governmental intervention that due to its tedious historical-religious-political controversies wishes to maintain a national, secular education system in France. In addition, in the legal history of France, great significance is attached to the supremacy of laws as Acts of Parliament (*loi*), meant to fortify abidance of the French people and adherence to legislative acts and their high status in the pyramid of norms. A further characteristic of its legal system relates to its being a system of codification of rules. The necessity to consolidate different areas of law and adapt them in order to achieve a coherence of the legal system, accessibility, and simplification of the law to its citizens dates back to the earliest attempt to codify civil law through Napoleon in 1804. The Napoleonic Code or Civil Code established among others the obligations and rights of the citizens. Following this codification, consolidations in other fields of law emerged and alongside this legislative process also the Code of Education (*code de léducation*).

There is no explicit prohibition on public servants, prescribed in a codified law, to refrain from religious manifestation. The general rule to a duty of strict religious neutrality is absolute and applies with respect to the public service as a whole without differentiation. The obligation to refrain from any outward manifestation that indicates a teacher's religious affiliation can be inferred from case laws as well as from the earlier laws on education that envisaged the laicization of the education system, such the Ferry laws from 1882 and Goblet law from 1886.

Art. L-141-5-1 of the 2004 Law outlines explicitly the prohibition on pupils to overt manifestation that by virtue of their outer apparel, the wearing of a dress, or insignia may indicate their religious affiliation. The law includes public elementary schools, colleges, and public high schools. All this demonstrates that decisions on dress code and inadmissibility of religious nuances, whether relating to educational content or by their display or apparel, are dealt on the national level and are not subject to administrative discretion. Unlike the legal situation in England where school uniform policy is resolved on a regional level by the relevant LEAs or school administrators, the French law discerns from its counterpart by virtue of its being an Act of Parliament (e.g., the law prohibiting conspicuous signs in public schools from 2004 and the law banning manifestation of ostentatious symbols in the public from 2011) which one cannot simply override.

3. Constitutional Protection of the Right to Religious Freedom

Germany – under the German legal system, the protection of fundamental human rights includes the right to religious freedom as safeguarded in its constitution, the German Basic Law (GG). The right to religious freedom is guaranteed in Art. 4 which determines its pre-eminent status as an absolute right due to its non-reservation clause (Art. 4 para 2 GG). This means that the right to religious freedom cannot be limited by any regular laws but only against another constitutional right that is prescribed specifically in the constitution itself.

Thence, the right to hold, to have a religion, or not to have a religion (*forum internum*) is safeguarded and unconditioned (Art. 4 para 1 GG), whereas the right to manifest a religion outwardly in public (*forum externum*) is subject to limitations under specific requirements (Art. 4 para 2 GG). The limitation of Art. 4 scope of protection is subject to judicial review and had been developed by the German jurisprudence under the principle of 'practical concordance' ('*praktische Konkordanz*'). This jurisprudential mechanism can be described as a 'checks and balances' form of the judicator to make sure that one fundamental constitutional right would not override another; rather, through interpretation of the judiciary, both rights will exist and attain maximum efficiency.

Teachers' right to religious manifestation – the right of a teacher to outwardly manifest her religion through religious apparel while on duty is safeguarded under Art. 4 GG. However, the right would be subject to limitations and would not be exerted by an individual and ensured to him/her at their own wish and unlimitedly. This will be especially the case when other protected constitutional rights are at stake (i.e., negative right of pupils not to be exposed to the view of a teacher with a headscarf). According to the classic definition of interference (*'klassischer Eingriffsbegriff'*) in a constitutionally protected right, there has been no doubt, as laid down in the German jurisprudence,[1700] that the ban on teachers to refrain from manifestation of their religion through overt insignias or garments will be classified as an interference in the freedom to practise a religion. An infringement on another constitutional right can be concluded also with respect to the teachers' right to freedom of profession as safeguarded in Art. 12 GG. Nonetheless, a violation of the right to religious freedom can be justified only subject to fulfilment of several requirements.

Pupils' right to religious manifestation – the right of pupils to religious manifestation within school realm is constitutionally ensured and protected. A challenge of this legal protection against the right of pupils has not been required so far under German jurisprudence. It is very unlikely that such a challenge to invoke the right protected under Art. 4 GG – if ever made – would be successful, as such an interference is perceived as extremely harsh as far as pupils' rights are concerned and would likely have to be supported by other constitutional precepts and not only by Art. 4 GG (e.g., the right to self-dignity and autonomy of a person prescribed in Art. 2 GG).

England – in the absence of a written constitution, the right to religious freedom as a fundamental human right does not achieve a sacred constitutional protection as in other legal systems, namely, Germany and France. As such, in theory one would assume that due to the fact that religious rights did not achieve the highest legal ranking in the hierarchy of norms and statutes of a state, they are more likely to suffer breaches and interferences as opposed to states with an organized constitutional order and tradition of entrenched protection of fundamental rights. However, legal practice in jurisprudential decisions, as was demonstrated above, does not correspond with the legal situation and cannot be said to reflect the status of individual right holders invoking enforcement of their religious rights. The evolvement of religious rights in the legal history of Britain has taken place in a piecemeal manner. Fundamental human rights, inter alia the

---

1700 BVerfGE, 108, 282; BVerfGE 138, 296 = 1 BvR 471/10 1 BvR 1181/10.

right to religious freedom achieved statutory protection with the incorporation of the Convention rights into the HRA 1998. Until the promulgation of the HRA 1998, religious rights were recognized in the system of common law and other statutory provisions such as the Race and Relations Act 1976 which actually provided protection to racial and ethnic minorities; however, rights of religious groups were not recognized by the 1976 Act. In similar to French law, the right to religious freedom had been recognized as a negative right that contributed to its longsome piecemeal development under British law. The endorsement of the right to religious freedom in the HRA 1998 was the first step to acknowledge it as a positive right.

France – the guarantee of fundamental rights and liberties is not to be found under a single comprehensive catalogue of rights; rather, they are scattered in several constitutions and statutes. The right to religious freedom receives a constitutional protection and is specifically mentioned in several constitutional documents; thus, it ranks high in France's legal history and its hierarchical pyramid of norms. It was first mentioned in the Declaration of the Rights of Man and of the Citizen from 1789, followed then by the Constitutions of 1946 and 1958. It is also safeguarded in several statutory provisions; for instance, the law of 1905 establishing formal separation between state and religion is regarded as the cornerstone establishing the protection of the freedom of conscience as well. Notably, in contrast to the monolithic phrasing of the term 'freedom of religion' under German and English law, the French law differs in the analogous references made in various constitutions and enactments to the term 'freedom of religion' (i.e., freedom of conscious, freedom of opinion, freedom of belief, etc.). The different terminology confers in part an identical, overlapping or diverse meaning of its synonyms and indicates an extensive or retrenched scope of protection; for instance, the term 'freedom of conscience' (used in Art. 1 of the 1905 law) refers mainly to the right of a person to hold a religion or belief or the right to not have a religion at all, i.e., the *forum internum* of 'freedom of religion' (inscribed in the preamble of the 1946 Constitution). The right of an individual to religious manifestation, i.e., *forum externum* is regarded as a form of the right to 'freedom of expression' (Art. 10 of the 1789 Declaration). Two contributing factors can explain this lack of consistency: first, the vast terminology used for capturing the right to religious freedom is interlinked with the fact that religious manifestation is apprehended by French society as a matter that should be confined solely to the private sphere by virtue of the adherence of the citizens to its republican ideology. Second, the French judicator lacked consistency regarding the construction of the right to religious freedom and its scope of protection.

4. Prescription of Legislative Bans

Germany – education laws and enactments have been subject to a great deal of amendments and were closely taken under the loop since the delivery of the judgement in *Ludin's* case. The gradual development can be conceptualized as follows: first, *demand for existence of a legal basis for a ban* – in Germany, legislative bans on teachers to appear with religious symbols were prompted in the aftermath of *Ludin's* case due to the absence of their legal basis. The rush to promulgate legislation that will confer the federal states a legislative leeway to ban the headscarf with respect to their teaching staff was not prescribed in their respective Public Service Laws. The ban on public servants has been initiated through modifications into states' existing School Education Acts. This legislative course has taken place swiftly following the pronouncement of the BVerfG in *Ludin's* appeal that the state of BW could not ban the teacher's headscarf without any legal basis in its inner regulations. Accordingly, most of the federal states have taken immediate initiatives by virtue of the constitutional right conferred to them under the Grundgesetz to decide on inner affairs, inter alia educational matters, on sole discretion (Art. 30 and 70 GG).

Second, *introduction of a legal ban* – all federal states (Bavaria, NRW, and BW) with the exception of the state of Berlin implemented a prohibition on teachers' outer appearance while on duty, which was meant to exclude the Islamic headscarf and, by the wording of their legislation, to confer prevalence to the Christian-Judeo tradition. This kind of preference is forbidden according to the German Constitution, as it infringes upon the equality before the law precept and the freedom of free access to the public service without segregation of any kind or type (Art. 3 para 1 and 3 in tandem with Art. 33 para 3 GG).

The state of Berlin is the only state where the ban applies widely and includes an equal prohibition that applies to many roles in the public service, including public school teachers to refrain while on duty from any manifestation of religious or political symbols as prescribed in the law relating to Art. 29 BlnLV.

The legislative bans had been challenged before German courts as was evidenced in the states of BW and NRW. Only the NRW legislator resumed subsequent modifications. Other lands' legislators may need to take in a future perspective necessary amendments into account.

In the period post *Ludin's* case, the states of BW and NRW implemented similar prohibitions on a teacher's right to appear with a headscarf; however, in order for the prohibitions not to appear so obviously directed towards the Islamic faith and symbols, the wording of the legislation choose the term display of 'ostentatious religious symbols'. The consequence thereof was the legal challenge of some education acts before the BVerfG and the request for judicial review by reason of their non-conformity with the German Constitution as was the case in the states of BW and NRW.

Third, *legal bans challenged in courts* – this was demonstrated in a significant recent decision of the BVerfG declaring the relevant former provision in NRW SchulG to be unconstitutional and void (Art. 57 para 4). Fourth, the prerequisites for a legislative ban had been extensively examined and proved and thoroughly developed. The guidelines provided by the German Constitutional Court can be summarized as follows: (i) no all-inclusive ban; (ii) concrete endangerment to other constitutional rights or values needs to be substantiated, as abstract endangerment will no longer suffice; (iii) examination of legitimacy of a symbol should be made on a case-by-case basis; (iv) equal application – the ban should apply equally to all religions without any differentiation or favouritism towards a particular religion (i.e., Christian-Judeo symbols); (v) no strict apprehension of state duty to religious neutrality.

Following this decision, the NRW legislator prompted hastily necessary amendments in its education act, currently envisaged in Art. 2 para 8 SchulG NRW. So far, the education act of BW has neither been judicially challenged in court, nor any initiatives for amendments of the respective Art. 38 para 2 BWSchG has been yet taken by its lawmaker. The education act of the state of Bavaria (Art. 59 BayEuG) is also likely to be contested before courts for its incompatibility with the constitution due to its declared preference of Christian tradition and values made by reference to provisions in its inner constitution (Art. 131 para 2 & Art. 135 BayVerfG).

England – following elements can be identified with respect to bans of religious symbols in public schooling under English legal system: first, *no legislative prescription* – there is no explicit statutory prohibition on teachers nor on pupils to refrain from outer appearance which suggests or indicates the religious affiliation of an individual or his association with a group of religious or ethnical minorities. The second ground emanates actually as an indirect consequence of the latter and relates to the extensive competency conferred to local authorities.

In the absence of a legislative ban that applies both with respect to teachers and to pupils to refrain from manifestation of religious symbols, the legal considerations are complicated in comparison to Germany and France. First, educational matters are being resolved on the regional level and no uniform resolution can be achieved on a national level. Second, the difficulty is even political, as British policy was characterized by its accommodative-liberal openness towards its religious minorities, so it would hesitate to enforce stricter disciplinary measures in case of non-compliance with school uniform policy and thus expose its municipalities and school governors to the risk of stark, offensive objections headed by their religious communities.

Third, *examination of infringement* – in the British legal system, unlike the German one, there are no clear guidelines for application of a constitutional test to determine whether an infringement of fundamental human right has taken place or not. Whereas under German constitutional law, examination will take place as to: (i) scope of protection; (ii) infringement; and (iii) justification, the British law does not make a clear segregation and no rules or guidelines were developed for determining what will be regarded as an infringement. Thence, it was often the case that the HL in its decisions concluded that no infringement with respect to a complainant's right to religious manifestation had taken place. If so, it went on to decide whether justification grounds were at hand in order to decline unlawfulness of infringement even if it were theoretically substantiated.

Fourth, *no clear judicial delineation* – criticism in the literature argued for the rather inconsistency and inability of the British jurisprudence to deliver a clear path that would consider carefully the parties' respective interests. It was argued that this emanated from lack of apprehension of the Convention and case laws delivered by the ECtHR.[1701]

France – albeit the fact that from a constitutional point of view religious rights are entrenched and safeguarded in France's legal framework, in practice their legal position is doubted and criticized mostly in legal literature. This has been intensified following the promulgation of several enactments intending to exclude Islamic symbols such as the veil (*foulard*) from educational institutes, and subsequently aiming to diminish its display completely from the public sphere. Therefore, considerable milestones in the development of the right to religious freedom and its strict application under French law will be set forth: first, *an absolute ban by law* – the Law of 2004, which bans appearance with conspicuous religious symbols and the 2011 Act, which bans the wearing of ostentatious religious symbols in public that had been argued to pose the harshest interference in individuals' right to free exertion/practice of religion and one's right to live in accordance with precepts dictated by one's faith. Second, *no conferment of discretion to school authorities or administrators* as to the admittance of religious symbols into schools through inner regulation. This excludes the power to incur disciplinary measures on the pupil to be conducted among school authorities, the pupil, and his parents by way of consultation. Therefore, legislative bans will be imposed only on a national level and will include all public schools in order

1701 *Howard, Erica*, Law and the Wearing of Religious Symbols, 2012, p. 69–70.

to maintain coherence and equal application of the law and eliminate any form of divisiveness between citizens.

Third, *the principle of laïcité* – this unique principle is particular to French law and no identical equivalent exists in other legal systems. As a result, its interpretation is very confined since it may be understood only in the context of France's legal history and the meaning attached to it in the French language. It was even crowned to constitute a paramount cornerstone of French republicanism. The French people are very proud of their republican tradition and require from their immigrants to assimilate to French culture and society and expect adhesion and conformity to its constitutions and values. The principle of *laïcité* does not mean plainly secularism, although the secular nature of the state is a salient feature forming a part of its unique national character. *Laïcité* envisages rather the conceptualization of two elements: first, neutrality of religious power – embracing the negative approach of separation between state and church in the sense that no delegation of powers between these two institutions would be accepted. Second, the positive approach of the state to ensure on its part the right of individuals to free exercise of religion. This suggests by no means that the state would act in favour or to the detriment of a specific religion. Thence, the apprehension of the principle of laïcité plays a major role in the perception of religious rights and the position religion acquires in the public sphere.

The considerations taken with respect to pupils' right to religious manifestation should be segregated between two periods, in this regard: first, prior to enactment of the Law of 2004 and following its promulgation. The jurisprudence was reluctant to deliver a clear-cut decision until the enactment of the Law of 2004 whether a ban imposed on pupils within inner school regulations to refrain from religious manifestation would be regarded as an infringement on their right to religious freedom. In practice, the CE acknowledged the right of pupils to religious manifestation prior to publication of the 1989 Circular and even in its aftermath (the Ministerial Circular together with the CE Advice from 1989 aimed to serve as guidelines for school authorities with respect to limitations on religious manifestation of pupils, in particular by wearing conspicuous symbols or signs). Second, following publication of the Law of 2004, the courts took account not only of the nature of the symbol as 'conspicuous' but of whether the symbol was worn with the intent to demonstrate manifestation of religious affinity (i.e., the context in which it is worn). The notion of the legislator was to capture as many symbols as possible within the scope of the ban. Thence, the objective apprehension by a third party will be considered rather than the subjective intention of the wearer in order to cast doubts as to the true declared motivation of the wearer.

Teachers – in principle, the position of teachers as public servants and the application of different set of rules as office holders in the public service impose on them a strict duty to religious neutrality and allegiance to the constitutional principle of *laïcité*. Their duty to appear impartial and unbiased since under French perception, they work in service for the people, is highly observed, and prohibits them from any external manifestation of religious insignias which may indicate their affiliation with a particular religion. In addition, their obligation to religious neutrality engenders by virtue of their function as state representatives.

Pupils – as far as pupils are concerned, the ban prohibiting the wearing of religious symbols gains a different focus since its prescription in legislation makes its challenge in court or request for annulment more difficult as opposed to inner school regulation. In addition, the ban prescribed in the Law of 2004 is difficult to align with pre-eminent constitutional values. Accordingly, the differentiation between the two periods will be depicted as follows. First, *until promulgation of the Law of 2004* – the decisions delivered by the CE, especially due to increase of controversies towards end of the nineteenth to beginning of the twentieth century were rather accommodative and accepting the right of pupils to religious manifestation. Albeit prohibitions on part of school authorities, mainly directed at Muslim female pupils to refrain from appearing with the headscarf or veil to school, the CE held this would be permissible unless the outfit posed a disturbance to public order (i.e., the peaceful and ordinary operation of the school). Second, *following promulgation of the Law of 2004* – the problematics that has been raised with respect to the Law of 2004 focused on specification of the ban directed at conspicuous signs. This entails that the Muslim veil is included within the scope of the ban as a conspicuous sign. Consequently, the ban is much likely to be held in breach with the constitutional precept of equality, as other discrete signs like a small cross necklace will be excluded from it. It is worth to note that in the French jurisprudence the prohibition does not include mainly symbols which carry a purely religious meaning but also signs that indicate from the circumstances that the reason they are worn by the wearer is religiously motivated. This interpretation of 'conspicuous signs' is very similar to the approach held in the German jurisprudence, which confers considerable weight to the manner and circumstances in which a symbol is worn, also within the balancing of rights. The reason is that some symbols may transfer the viewer a religious connotation by way of their wearing. Thence, for instance, the case of a female pupil wearing a kerchief or 'keski' as a head covering was recognized in France as a forbidden manifestation of religion (*Gamaleddyn v France and others*). Similarly, also in German jurisprudence, the real motivation of the wearer was called into question in order to exclude any disguised intent on part of the teacher who by virtue of her outer appearance, displaying a garment that is not religious in nature, still may have some proselytising effect on the pupils due to its presentation (e.g., the German case of teacher with a *Basque,* a wool cap worn at all times). In practice, German courts will have a careful look of the general circumstances as a whole in order to exclude any abuse of the ban by display of symbols that allegedly are not religiously motivated.

On another level, heavy criticism was raised as to the constitutionality of the ban inscribed in the 2011 Act. This criticism was waved by the French government declaring the compatibility of the 2011 Act with the constitution. The 2011 Act was explained by the French government to be justified on grounds of public order and general values of the French Republic. However, critics suggested that the difficulty to constitutionally justify the 2011 Act relate mainly to two different aspects: (i) the general all-inclusive formulation which bans head coverings from the whole public sphere and does not merely exclude their display within the boundaries of public institutions; (ii) the constitutional justification by application of the *laïcité* principle and the duty to religious neutrality with respect to pupils as individuals. The interference in the pupils' *forum externum* is in itself contradictory to the constitution as one cannot appropriate its citizens in sharp contrast to public servants, any duty, or obligation to religious neutrality.

5. Equality and Non-discrimination Laws

Germany – equality rights under German law will always be ancillary to the substantial claim which is established on the constitutional fundamental right to religious freedom (Art. 4 GG). Thus, a teacher with a headscarf who wishes to challenge the ban on manifestation of religious symbols at court may invoke in parallel to her human right claim an anti-discrimination claim pursuant to the equality precepts prescribed in Art. 3 para 1 and 2 and 33 para 3 GG. The equality precepts provide protection against direct and indirect discrimination. In addition, the EU Anti-Discrimination Directives (EU 2000/78, EU 2000/73 and EU 2000/43) had been transferred into German domestic law within Germany's obligations to respect and give due regard to EU law by way of its implementation. The Anti-Discrimination Directives were meant to achieve a uniform European standard of equal treatment and anti-discrimination in hiring and employment practices and impose a special protection against discrimination on religious grounds. The general ban on discrimination was phrased to encompass an ample scale of grounds, especially in employment relations as pronounced in Sec. 1 AGG. Sec. 24 AGG, extends its validity, and prescribes its application also with respect to civil servants in the public sector.

In principle, the scope of protection under the AGG is much more extensive than the basic precept to equality of treatment prescribed under the German Constitution (Art. 3 para 1 and 3 and 33 para 3 GG) as it covers various discriminatory features and a large number of participants. However, since the EU Directives enable exceptions for unequal treatment, the position of teachers is not safeguarded better under the AGG than by the constitutional protection offered to them. This explains why complainants hardly ever establish their claim on the AGG provisions in addition to their main claim, which would be founded on their constitutional right to religious equality and the right not to be discriminated in access to the public service.

England – the analysis demonstrated a preference under English law of claimants to submit claims against bans on religious manifestation as contravening non-discrimination rights as opposed to fundamental human rights. The substantiation of an anti-discrimination claim was alleged to be more successful in comparison to a fundamental human rights claim.

This preference may be attributed, first, to the fact that Britain has no written constitution and, thus, the perception of fundamental human rights is less entrenched in its legal system. Second, anti-discrimination legislation is more extensive and wide in scope under the British legal system. The current applicable legislation that covers a wide list of grounds in claims of discrimination is the Equality Act 2010. Third, this reason emanates from the second and associates the relative ease of establishing an anti-discrimination claims, as they are much developed under British law and its jurisprudence. In addition, justification grounds for discriminatory bans are not likely to be regarded as objectively legitimate as the case with fundamental human rights claims would be.

Discrimination on religious grounds in the area of education was not subject to legal protection until coming into force of the Equality Act 2006.

A much enforceable mechanism was envisaged and sought in the equality duty imposed on public authorities in Britain as established by the Equality Act 2010. It prescribes the need to eliminate unlawful discrimination, advance equality of opportunity, and foster good relations at work in general and includes, inter alia the education sector.

France – the notion of equality of all citizens is regarded as one of the three pre-eminent constitutional pillars of the French nation. The obligation of the Republic to treat all its citizens equally without divisiveness is also unique to the republican doctrine and is starkly entrenched in the historical period ensuing the French Revolution and the establishment of the First Republic in its aftermath. The principle of equality is thence engraved in the 1789 Declaration of the Rights of Man and of the Citizen, in the preamble to the 1946 Constitution and in the first article of the 1958 Constitution. The idea that all French people are alike and that no differentiation should exist was meant to fortify the republican doctrine of nationalism and a unified nation. It is the strong adherence of the French people to its Republic, the idea of one undivided nation that is regarded as a significant element in the lack of anti-discrimination laws under French laws, as well as the lacking jurisprudential development in that field of law. This is another pivotal segregation point that stands in sharp contrast to the importance and reliance of complainants on equality laws both under the English and German system insofar as bans on manifestation of religious symbols in public education are concerned.

6. State-Church Interplay as a Pivotal Factor for Development of Religious Rights

The place of religion and its position in the compared states depends to a large extent on historical influence of the church on European societies and their population. This state-church interplay differs considerably in each of the compared states. In addition, institutional links between the church and the state which remained in force in several countries to a certain degree, especially in the field of education, played a major role in the development of religious rights. For instance, in England, it was the protestant Anglican Church; in Germany – the spatial division between Catholicism and Protestantism varied from one federal state to the other, France had in its history a dominance of the Catholic Church till complete disentanglement in the events of the 1789 French Revolution. Lastly, the relationship between religion and state normally derives from the structural state-church model adopted within a state's system (Germany – a cooperationist model, England – formal unification, France – strict separation). The continuous ongoing efforts to endorse religious influence in public education till date demonstrate the significance attributed to achievement of religious dominance, especially because schools are perceived as a place that forms future society not only through education but also by conveyance of tradition, moral, and values.

In the following, several landmarks and orientation points will be set forth and provide a benchmark for estimation of a balanced approach that legitimizes and ensures liberalism, secularism, equality, and religious neutrality, in particular in public education, as prevalent values contravening the right to religious manifestation in future disputes.

a) Keeping in Line Religious Pluralism

Religious pluralism and acceptance of all religious symbols, especially in public education, cannot be conclusive and accepting at all times, as also here the legal praxis and jurisprudence raised fear and concerns of peer pressure, the building of religious groups within school boundaries, undue influence or coercion, segregation and ostracism, lack of tolerance, and absent willingness for integration. This has a double-sided effect on all school participants: both pupils pertaining to religious and ethnical minorities as well as the group of religious majority in school. This is because, on the one hand, the demand to accommodate the religious practices of an individual pupil belonging to a minority group may trigger other pupils, members of the same ethnical minority, the feeling of coercion to act in accordance with the same religious dress code or even a more extreme form of donning such as *jilbab* or *burqa* in order not to be rejected by their religious communities. On the other hand, the accommodation of rather milder forms of religious insignias may trigger the expectation in extremist movements to enforce further the demand for other head coverings or even full body coverings in order to fulfil their religious agenda. This may lead to the danger of a 'slippery slope' from which there is no end.

From another perspective, it was mentioned in the analysis that England has a tradition of school uniform to which pupils should abide. Under these circumstances, the position of Christian pupils or atheists cannot be equated with that of ethnical minorities who will be allowed to not conform strictly to school dress code; following, the boundaries to admittance of religious insignias would become blurred. This contention supports again the claim that the outcome would be an increase of conflicts on religious grounds in school realm and an overload pressure on administrative and regional level, as these issues are left to discretion and resolution of LEAs and, finally, even a burden on the jurisdictional instances.

b) Pressure or Coercion within Religious Groups in Schools

This argument has been often raised by the judiciary in all three states, Germany, England, and France, in order to downplay and reduce the visibility of ostentatious religious symbols in schools. It was accredited in the *Begum* case that other Muslim girls in the same school feared that they would be pressurized into wearing the *jilbab* if school authorities were to allow it. In addition, a heavy doubt was casted over the question whether the pupil Begum reached the decision to wear the *jilbab* out of an autonomous consideration derived from a purely true belief in the precepts of her religion, or whether she was negatively influenced into it. The HL supported its view by reference to the well-known fact that her brother was a radical Islamic activist and the fact that she could have been influenced by his views could not be denied.

c) Fortifying Arguments of Public Safety or Public Order

The English jurisprudence accepted the justification of public safety or order as an argument to curtail an individual's right to religious manifestation as was the case in *Begum*. In *Begum*, the HL reached the conclusion that no interference in the pupil's right to manifest a religion had taken place. The prevention of school premises from becoming a place of religious indoctrination, or where undue pressure is exerted on pupils belonging to other religious groups or even of the same religious minority presiding in the same educational institute can be successful if argued to protect highly minded values (e.g., gender equality, protection of public safety or order). Insofar, refusal to accept an amplified, extensive apprehension of religious insignias into public education should be fortified and supported by the arguments that schools should support liberalism and enable pupils of all religions a peaceful environment, fortify gender equality by demonstration and not merely by conveyance as a written value, conform to the duty of religious neutrality by virtue of its educational task, and ensure it will be an institute free from any fears or pressure of religious indoctrination by reason of the need to keep educational institutions free from potential conflicts and controversies surrounding religious symbols. The increase of religious symbols in public education may only intensify future conflicts and endanger the peaceful operation of schools.

d) Character of Symbols – Objective or Subjective Plausibility Test

Germany – in the German jurisprudence, the question whether the wearing or display of insignias which, by their character, do not carry a salient religious meaning (e.g., *bandana*, *basque*) was also included by the headscarf ban and had been subject to an objective viewer test. The jurisprudential approach delivered by the German Federal Labour Court (BAG) upheld that the character of a symbol does not have to ensue from the garment itself but from the impression it raises in a third party and its surrounding (pupils, other teachers, parents, etc.). For instance, in the famous *Ludin* case, the teacher claimed that she was wearing the headscarf purely out of religious motivation and the strong belief dictated by the precept of her faith. In contrast, the teacher wearing a *basque* (woollen hat) to school was not successful with her claim in court, as it rejected the claimant's pretension that it was worn as a fashionable accessory (*modisches Accessoire*). The BAG held that the culmination of facts demonstrated incontestably that the teacher was driven by her religious motivation in sharp contrast to her claim that she decided to appear to school with a hat as a fashionable garment. For this purpose, the Court applied the objective viewer test since it was evident that pupils and other teaching personnel did recognize her wearing the *basque* as a head covering. In particular, the fact that the teacher wore the hat at all times and without any exception of yearly seasons, the fact that she took care to cover also other body parts such as ears and her neckline, and the proximity to the release of the legislative headscarf ban constituted a distinctive indicator that the wool hat was meant to conceal the real intent to wear it purely as a religious garment. These, in addition to the fact that cannot be undermined that the teacher identified herself as a practicing Muslim sufficed for the BAG to discharge her claim.

England – since in England there is no legislative prohibition on the wearing of religious symbols in public education, the religious character per se of wearing a garment, whether by teachers or by pupils, will not be called into question; rather, it is the act or practice itself which is regarded or perceived as a form of religious manifestation worth protection according to Art. 9 para 1 ECHR. In addition, in contrast to the situation in Germany and France, the headscarf itself was never disputable in the English legal debate. For instance, in the case of *Azmi*, both the Employment Tribunal and the EAT declared the wearing of a *niqab* as a religious manifestation; nonetheless, the interference was justified since the observance of school authorities on her performance while on duty demonstrated that due to the fact that her face was covered her communication with the pupils was impinged. Eventually, it was not the objective perception by the pupils of the head covering as an indoctrinating religious symbol that was taken into account by the Court, but the fact that it hindered an effective educational performance of the pupils.

France – it is due to strong adherence and allegiance to the principle of *laïcité* and the special duty of public servants to religious neutrality by way of their outer apparel that the approach is strictly upheld with respect to teachers who under French public law are bound by their public function and act in service of the state. Accordingly, taking into consideration the Law of 2004, the emphasis was on conspicuous religious signs. The determination of conspicuousness of a sign does not really disclose which signs would be apprehended as conspicuously religious. However, in general, the intention was to prohibit signs assumed of having a proselytising effect or of posing a threat to neutrality by their visibility. Nonetheless, similar to the view held by German jurisprudence, the jurisprudential approach by reference to decisions of the CE demonstrates that even symbols which by their nature are not outstanding for their religiosity such as bonnets and hats would still be included in the ban since they may be attributed a religious character albeit their 'irreligiosity'. This was considered by the CE in the *Marteaux* case where the Court opined that it would eventually be the nature and degree of conspicuousness of a symbol that will determine whether it carries a proselytising character.

e) Jurisprudential Approach

Germany – in earlier decisions of the BVerfG and BVerWG up to the Crucifix decision, there was a tendency to embrace a rather open, religion-friendly approach that was accommodative and welcoming towards conveyance of the Christian religion and practices in the state school system. The situation has changed abruptly with the delivery of the Crucifix decision which, not unsurprisingly, caused a turmoil when the BVerfG ordered the removal of the cross from elementary school classrooms and accepted the claim of atheist pupils and their parents invoking the infringement of their negative right to religious freedom (Art. 4 para 1 and 2 GG in tandem with Art. 6 para 2 GG). Following this, the decision in the famous *Ludin* case was shattered when the BVerWG first decided that an expulsion of a teacher from her post due to wearing a headscarf would be permissible but was reversed by the BVerfG, not on merits of the case but rather due to lack of sufficient legal basis for her dismissal from school. These decisions constitute a core element in the jurisprudential-legal debate of this analysis, as eventually the German Federal Constitutional Court, FCC, will attempt to give careful consideration and balance between all involved, constitutional, and competing rights.

In the recent BVerfG decision,[1702] a dismissal of a teacher from her duty in the state of NRW due to her appearance with a headscarf to school was regarded to be unconstitutional, and the relevant legislative provision in the School Education Act of the state NRW was declared to be unconstitutional and void. The decision gains significance due to the fact that it made precedent in several aspects relating to manifestation of religious symbols by teachers: first, *the prohibition to apply an all-inclusive ban*, a general ban will not be allowed; rather, the demand is for examination to be made on a case-by-case basis. Second, *abstract endangerment will not suffice* – so far it was sufficient for school authorities to exempt a teacher wearing a headscarf from her post by virtue of an abstract endangerment she poses by her religious manifestation to other constitutional freedoms and values. The reference to other constitutional freedoms includes: the peaceful school operation, state neutrality, other constitutional rights or freedoms prescribed in the constitution, such as the right to equality, gender equality, or values upheld in democratic society like public safety or the public order. Following this recent

1702 BVerfGE 138, 296 = NJW 2015, 1359.

judgement, an abstract endangerment will not suffice as the BVerfG demands a higher threshold for interference in the fundamental right of an individual to religious freedom, i.e. the substantiation of a concrete endangerment to other fundamental rights.

Third, *no prevalence to Christian faith and symbols* – the preference conferred so far to conveyance of the Christian tradition and values poses, first, a breach of the constitutional right to religious equality based on Art. 3 GG and equality in application to the public service according to Art. 33 para 3 GG. Second, the BVerfG upheld that this unlawful advancement of a specific religion is contradictory to the constitutional principle of 'no state-church' prescribed in Art. 137 1 para 1 WRV, which prohibits identification of the state with religion. Fourth, no strict apprehension of the state's duty to religious neutrality but rather a liberal, comprehensive approach enabling all religions enough room to flourish would eliminate the risk of unnecessary interference in a teacher's right to religious manifestation and would not contradict with the educative task of the state according to Art. 7 para 1 GG.

England – it is noticeable that the Islamic headscarf was not subject to legal debate and fierce controversies as in Germany and France, both with respect to teachers and to pupils. Since the general approach of the state towards religion is of co-operation and the approach towards religious-ethnical minorities was very accommodative and accepting, the subject of dispute involved extreme forms of head coverings, such as *jilbab* and the *shalwar kamiza* in the case of pupils, or the *niqab* involving a teaching assistant. It is surprising that in the case of *Begum* the HL found no interference in the pupil's right to manifest her religion under Art. 9 para 1 ECHR. However, albeit dismissing the claim already at this point, it went on to examine whether the prohibition can be justified and finally reached the conclusion that even if it had decided that there was an interference, this would have been justified since it was brought as evidence that school authorities went a long way towards the pupil, e.g., initiating consultation with the relevant involved parties (the pupil, parents, school authority, and religious community), and had considered carefully ways to a compromise that were refused by the pupil.

As far as pupils' right to manifest religion as guaranteed under Art. 9 ECHR is concerned, the British jurisprudence was reluctant to accept interference at all if two requirements were fulfilled:

Alternative schooling – if the pupil had access to a nearby alternative schooling and no excessive difficulty for her to reach it existed, and if, in addition, she could still in practice manifest her religion at her own choice in the new school, then the expulsion of the pupil would not be regarded as an infringement in her right to religious freedom. This was demonstrated in the cases of *Begum* and *X v Headteacher and Governors of Y School* where school authorities were not held to breach the pupil's right to manifestation of her religion.

Consultation and considerations – the efforts made on part of school authorities to accommodate the religious needs of the pupil by reference to the specific religious community are considered a significant factor, as demonstrated in case laws. British jurisprudence has given due regard to initiatives taken by school authorities, whether by consultation with the relevant Muslim community or taking advice as to the appropriateness of wearing an ostentatious symbol like the *niqab*. This, for instance, was verified in the case of *Begum*, as discussion and inquiries initiated by school authorities together with parents and pupils proved the sensitiveness of school authorities. This very accommodative approach of school had established the ground for the HL to dismiss the claimants' allegations that her right to profess her religion has been violated. It was pronounced by the HL as a justification ground that it was sufficient on part of the school to try through consultations to accommodate to the pupils' religious needs and accept different forms of religious symbols. It was demonstrated that school had 'gone to great lengths to work out its policy on uniform…' so no interference in the pupils' right to religious manifestation had been established.

Teachers – the case laws surrounding a teacher's right to religious manifestation are relative scarce. There are no case laws involving directly a ban on a teacher wearing a headscarf. The famous case of *Azmi* involved a teacher assistant who was prohibited from wearing a *niqab* to school. In contrast to the legal position of teachers as civil servants in Germany and France, teaching staff in England are not considered public servants. Several reasons can be identified with respect to teaching personnel and sparse case laws in regard to their right to religious manifestation in education. First, there is neither codification of public law under English law nor are teachers protected under the shield of the civil service as they are not considered to be public officials. Second, there is no general duty to religious neutrality that applies with respect to the public service, unlike in Germany and France. Third, there is no uniform application of permissibility to display religious symbols that applies equally to all capacities in the public service but rather each sector may prescribe its own rules. This point is distinguishable, as in contrast to the general rule to strict duty of neutrality which is practised under French law with respect to all office holders in the public sphere without any exception, there is no comprehensive obligation of neutrality under English law. Fourth, equality and non-discrimination rights are more developed under English law. This was demonstrated in the case of *Azmi* as the jurisprudence concentrated mainly on dismissing the complainant's claim to indirect infringement of her right to religious equality rather than examining the breach of her fundamental right to religious freedom based on Art. 9 ECHR. Fifth, other justifying grounds available – even had the EAT decided in the case of *Azmi* that an infringement in her right to religious freedom under Art. 9 ECHR took place, the reasons for dismissal would not consider the mainstream justifying limitations as recognized by the ECtHR, such as the breach in the negative right of pupils to religious freedom. English jurisprudence upholds rather that the religious symbol in question impinged her professional aptitude to work as a teacher since the head covering hindered her proper communication with the pupils who could not understand her. This was specifically underscored with respect to the fact that she was employed as an English teacher and the fact that her mouth and mimics were disguised by her face covering and detracted her performance.

France – in a similar manner to the situation in England, laws and decisions of the French judicator are very rare as far as the eligibility of teachers to display religious symbols is concerned. However, unlike the relative liberal legal position of teachers in England, where this outcome can be mainly reasoned by lack of legal codification and the general comprehensive duty to equality in employment, the major difference under French law can be attributed to its outstanding adhesion to its constitutional ideal of *laïcité* and strongly ordained codified system.

Teachers – in principle, the legal position of teachers as public officials and their freedom to manifest religion by way of outer external appearance deem to collide with their strict duty to neutrality while acting within their function. The prohibition on state school teachers to refrain from religious manifestation by outer apparel is absolute, as it stemmed originally from the notion of disempowering the church from the educational sphere. It was contemplated by the laicization of education, which imposed the duty of *laïcité* with respect to teaching personnel. The duty to neutral appearance extends not only to wearing or display of religious symbols but also verbal expression and conduct. This strongly held approach had been fortified by the decisions of the CE with respect to teachers' freedom to religious manifestation in the cases of *Barel* from 1957 and the *Marteaux* decision from 2000. The idea is twofold: (i) *voluntariness* – public officials are regarded to subject themselves voluntarily to the duty of neutrality by virtue of entering the public service at their own will. The element of voluntariness is a strong factor which is highly taken into consideration by all juridical instances in the compared countries Germany, England, and France. In addition, this element had been emphasized by decisions of the ECtHR as will be demonstrated below; (ii) *impartial and unprejudiced* – within their function vis-á-vis the citizens, public officials work for the public and must appear and demonstrate their impartiality. It is worth to note that unlike the legal position of public servants in Germany and England, French law takes a different stand with respect to its public sector. In that sense, French law considers its public officials under a duty to carry some responsibility in their private sphere. So although outside their function as public servants they may manifest their religion or belief, they are still subject to a milder form of duty which obliges them to act in a manner that would not undermine the image of the public service.

Pupils – the jurisprudential approach with respect to pupils is more complex, taking into consideration: first, the fact that they are not subject to a duty of neutrality and, second, any excessive interference in their right to religious manifestation poses a breach of France's obligation to safeguard fundamental human rights according to its obligation on the European and international level to respect international treaties to which it is a signatory.

Nonetheless, a segregation between two periods of time is necessary as a benchmark: (i) prior to promulgation of the Law of 2004, decisions of the CE were characterized by a liberal-accommodative approach realizing no infringement of the *laïcité* principle insofar as pupils were wearing religious symbols in the narrow sense of an act of religious manifestation. This approach was demonstrated in the famous case from 1989 involving the expulsion of three Muslim girls who refused to remove the headscarf during classes and in the *Kherouaa* decision from 1992. In principle, the guidelines published by the CE in 1989 with respect to admittance of religious symbols in schools determined that a prohibition would be justified if: first, the nature of the symbol is conspicuous or protesting; second, the symbol has an effect of proselytization, propaganda, or coercion with respect to other pupils; and third, the symbol clashes against other interests or rights, such as the proper functioning of the public service (this would normally be encompassed by the endangerment to public order), public health, public safety, or if it undermines the human dignity of another pupil.

(ii) Following promulgation of the Law of 2004 – the CE held the view that not only conspicuous religious symbols will fall within confine of this legislation. It was explained that it is the nature of the symbol and the circumstances under which it is worn that will establish whether it is prohibited or not. Thence, even if a symbol is not conspicuous by itself but rather the context in which it is worn indicates that the symbol was worn purely out of religious motivation; and in addition the wearing of a conspicuous sign was disguised by the true intent of the wearer, it will still be regarded as falling within the confine of a prohibited symbol (e.g., *Aktas v. France, Gamaleddyn v. France and others*).

It is worth to note, the CE held over the years a steady approach as to the exclusion of conspicuous symbols from schools insofar as they aim to promote religion. This was demonstrated in its famous advice from 1989, its support of promulgation of the Law of 2004, and the acknowledgement that the face veil contradicts the precept of gender equality. Surprisingly, albeit this approach, the CE refused to deliver its acceptance to the passing of the 2011 Act in French Parliament.

7. The European Mechanism for Safeguarding Fundamental Human Rights (ECHR)

On the European level, there are several instruments aiming to reinforce the protection of fundamental human rights such as the EU Charter and the ECHR. However, due to the fact that the EU Charter offers a weaker mechanism for the protection of human rights the analysis focused on the enforcement mechanism inscribed in the ECHR and the accountability of the MS to comply with its provisions under their respective domestic law.

Though the ECHR subjects the MS to transpose convention rights into inner legislation, it does not prescribe the manner in which convention rights are supposed to be conveyed into the domestic law of the respective MS. Thence, the status of the ECHR within the hierarchy of norms of each respective state varies as its position is determined on the basis of its implementation into the respective legislative system. *Germany* inserted a provision into its constitution which actually confers the ECHR the highest position within its constitutional framework (Art. 23 GG). Nonetheless, fundamental human rights receive better protection under the German GG by virtue of its extensive scope of protection. *England* promulgated the HRA 1998 and actually transposed the rights in the convention to its inner legislation; in that sense, it is approved as Act of Parliament and naturally enjoys under the principle of parliament supremacy the special status that it may be abolished, changed, or repealed only by the British Parliament and, moreover, it is regarded as a constitutional statute. *France* subordinates itself to its obligations on the international level. Accordingly, given the constitutional hierarchy of its legal system, the ECHR equals in rank to an international treaty obligation and, as a result, human rights and liberties enshrined in it possess the highest legislative rank. This position confers priority to international law over domestic law and, as submitted within its constitutional provision (Art. 55 of the 1958 Constitution), the supremacy of international treaties over its national legislation.

The question of how effective the ECHR as an enforcement mechanism is, and what ability it has to confine MS to its supervision had been examined by reference to leading case laws reviewing complaints of individuals submitted against their states in matters of religious expression in public education.

Interpretation and application of the relevant Convention provisions, mainly Art. 9 (the right to religious freedom) in conjunction with Art. 2 of Protocol 1 ECHR (the general right to education), had been laid down by the ECtHR and established pre-requisites and tests to be applied both with respect to manifestation of religious symbols – whether displayed by an individual or in the buildings of public institutions. Some appellants submitted conjoined claims of a breach of their fundamental rights according to Art. 9 and anti-discrimination pursuant to Art. 14 ECHR; however, the ECtHR did not go in detail to examine whether discrimination on religious grounds was substantiated, and whether in fact dismissal of the main claim (Art. 9) would have sufficed to disregard examination of the latter. How some of the tests and principles developed by the ECtHR were implemented to segregate between the two forms of symbols' manifestation, and which justification grounds were concluded and outweighed by the Court will be set forth in the following.

a) Jurisprudence in Case Laws

The key guidelines to be inferred from the decisions of the ECtHR, though not all directly involve the countries depicted in this analysis, have an effect on national legislation of the MS, and the juridical instances are bound to have due regard to decisions submitted by the Strasbourg instances. The essence thereof will be summarized as follows:

b) Manifestation of Symbols by Individuals

Observance of the legal practice delivered by the ECtHR demonstrates that the wearing of ostentatious symbols like the headscarf – whether worn by pupils or teachers – had been perceived as infringement on the guarantee of the right to religious freedom as safeguarded in Art. 9 ECHR. Nonetheless, the justification grounds for infringement were mostly accepted by the Court due to the wide margin of appreciation granted to the states.

Teaching staff – as a general principle, the right of teachers as public officials to manifest their religion or belief by displaying a symbol was not negated outright in decisions of the ECtHR, as they are still held to be individuals who are entitled to invoke their right to religious freedom under the Convention (Art. 9). However, by virtue of their special status as state representatives they may be subject to several duties, like abidance by the state neutrality precept. This may entail conforming to dress code regulations incumbent on them since they are obliged to appear impartial and unbiased while working with the public. Essentially, even if the outcome is a restricted access to the public service, cases challenged before the ECtHR may not be held incompatible with the ECHR if a justification ground was at hand. For instance, in *Dahlab v Switzerland*, the ECtHR decided that there was an interference in the teacher's right to religious manifestation; however, this was justified on several grounds: the protection of public order (often intertwined with the peaceful operation of school), the negative right of pupils and their parents to religious freedom, gender equality (perceived as the obligation of a female teacher to convey these paramount values of equality and non-discrimination to her pupils), and state neutrality that accords with the secular nature of the state (will be acknowledged by the ECtHR especially with respect to countries like Switzerland with a separationist state-church model upholding strict denominational state neutrality in its public education and constitutional secularism). The same approach was affirmed later in the subsequent case of *Kurtulumus v Turkey* leading the ECtHR to conclude again that preserving the secular nature of the Turkish state was important to sustain democracy, and this required discretion of its civil servants as to manifestation of their religious affiliation in public. The judgement was supported by its earlier decision in *Dahlab*, confirming the discretion of a member state to impose restrictions on dress regulations even with respect to university professors if this complied with the constitutional principle of secularism (*laïcité*). Hence, the right of teachers as public officials to religious manifestation is not absolute, and MS may interfere in the right but not held to be in violation of the ECHR, as long as certain pre-requisites are met and substantiate a justifying limitation. The pre-requisites and justifying grounds are prescribed and listed in Art. 9 para 2 ECHR, and the Court will examine whether they were fulfilled on the basis of tests and standards laid down by the Court.

Pupils – the status of pupils or student cannot be aligned with the position of teachers since they act merely as individuals and do not carry special obligations by virtue of their function as state representatives, and no duty of abidance to the precept of religious neutrality is incumbent on them. In practice, even in earlier decisions relating to manifestation of symbols by religious affiliation brought before the competent judicial instance, the Commission, it was held that Art. 9 ECHR does not confer an absolute right to religious manifestation in the public sphere that prevails at all times. In addition, a strongly upheld view of the Commission contended that not every act motivated by a religious precept worth protection under Art. 9 ECHR (e.g., *Karaduman v Turkey*). In the case of university students, as was demonstrated in the case of *Karaduman*, the element of transparency and willingness of the students were given heavy weight by the Commission, as they were aware of the university regulations and subjected themselves willingly to them. This position was preserved and reiterated years later in the famous case of *Leyla Sahin v Turkey* where the GC – although it acknowledged an interference in the applicant's right to religious manifestation – concluded in its final verdict that the interference (university dress code regulations prohibiting appearance with the headscarf within its premises) was justified. At that time (1998), the political regime and agenda pursued by the Turkish government were to advance secularism and state neutrality in the public sphere. These paramount values were considered by the ECtHR to be compatible with the spirit of the Convention and its underpinning values and necessary for the safeguarding of a democratic regime in Turkey. Other legitimate aims that justified the interference were the protection of the rights and freedoms of other students who did not pertain to the majority religion and might have felt pressurized and intimidated by the presence of the headscarf. Aligned with it, the Court will assess the protection of public order as a possible justification ground which prescribes the need to keep the interests of various religious groups in society: tolerance, equality, the proper functioning of democratic society, and state impartiality.

Remarkably, even in cases purporting to challenge the strict secular approach that is upheld under French law, especially in the education context, it is not too difficult to observe that the ECtHR found no reason to conclude the incompatibility of the Law of 2004 prohibiting manifestation of conspicuous religious signs with the Convention (e.g., *Dogru v France*). Similarly, the challenge of the 2004 Law was unsuccessful also with respect to symbols which did not classify under the category of a pure religious symbol but were worn indirectly as a head covering, such as the case of Muslims schoolgirls, who arrived at different schools wearing a kerchief or a headscarf. The complaints were held to be inadmissible (see *Gamaleddyn v France, Aktas v. France, Bayrak v. France and Ghazal v. France)*. In the same application to the ECtHR, the right of Sikh boys to wear a 'keski', a smaller headwear than the traditional turban, was rejected. The ECtHR declared that the interference in the pupils' freedom to religious manifestation based on Art. 9 ECHR was justified and proportionate to the aim pursued (see *J. Singh v. France and R. Singh v. France*). The ECtHR explained that the Law of 2004 pursued a legitimate aim of protecting the rights and freedoms of others and public order and recognized the right of the state to remain neutral and impartial[1703].

c) Manifestation of Symbols in Institutions

Similar to the *Bavarian Crucifix* case in Germany, the ECtHR had to deliver a decision in a complaint brought before it against the state of Italy regarding the legitimacy of mandatory affixation of crosses in public schools. It was challenged by a complainant on behalf of her minor children who requested the removal of the crucifix from all classrooms which her children attended, and supported her action by claiming for violation of Art. 9 para 2 ECHR (the right to religious manifestation) in conjunction with Art. 2 of Protocol 1 (the general right to education). The underlying outcome, following reversal of the decision of the upper chamber, which ruled in favour of the complainant by the GC demonstrates the acceptance of institutional symbols. The general approach of the ECtHR is to refrain from interference in the inner affairs of a state. This indicates the reluctance of the ECtHR to overrule the discretion conferred to states by employing an extensive margin of appreciation. The considerations within the balancing of rights in a country like Italy, where the majority adheres strongly to Catholicism, may be different than in a laic state like France. Since a decision requiring the removal of a cross from all public schools' classrooms may offend the right and feeling of the majority of its population who wish to preserve their religious tradition. In the *Lautsi* case, the passiveness of the crucifix was argued to negate its proselytising effect and established the grounds for its justification by the ECtHR. To sum up, challenging the obligatory affixation of crucifixes on classroom walls was proved unsuccessful.

d) Bans on Religious Symbols as Grounds for Equality and Non-discrimination Claims

As far as challenges made before the ECtHR which are engaged in prohibition on the wearing of religious symbols in state schools are concerned, it was demonstrated above that anti-discrimination claims based on Art. 14 ECHR do not confer claimants an independent, freestanding right; rather, these will always be subsidiary to the main claim which will rest upon another essential provision

---

1703 *Gamaleddyn v France*, Appl. no. 18527/08; *Aktas v France*, Appl. no. 43563/08; *Bayrak v France*, Appl. no. 14308/08; *Ghazal v France*, Appl. no. 29134/08; *J. Singh v France* Appl. no. 25463/08; *R. Singh v France*, Appl. no. 27561/08, 17 July 2009 (ECtHR).

of the Convention (e.g., Art. 9 or Art. 10). The list of discriminatory grounds listed in Art. 14 ECHR is extensive; yet from its wording, it indicates to be an open-ended list so that other grounds may fall within its ambit. As relevant grounds for a claim challenging the unlawfulness of a ban on religious symbols in public education, the following or their combination may be relevant: religion or belief, ethnic or race, political or other opinion (depending on how a headscarf or other face veiling will be interpreted by the Court), or association with a national minority.

Claimants may submit a claim that a ban on their right to manifest a religious symbol is discriminatory in nature and contravenes against the right established in Art. 14 ECHR which prohibits direct or indirect discrimination and falls within the following grounds: religion or belief, race, ethnic origin, gender, or even combination of these grounds.

In general, claims that were successful based on the substantial provision had exempted the ECtHR from dealing with a prohibition of unlawful discrimination based on Art. 14 ECHR. Further, the ECtHR makes no distinction between direct and indirect discrimination, and, in practice, a declaration of unlawful prohibition on religious symbols will not succeed if the MS is able to establish an adequate justification and prove that it was proportional to achieve a legitimate aim (e.g., the list provided in Art. 9 para 2 ECHR).

The justification grounds to be established before the ECtHR in anti-discrimination claims will be similar to those used in the test laid down by Art. 9 para 2 ECHR. Similarly, in cases invoking the violation of human rights to free practice of religion (Art. 9 para 2), it is most likely that the ECtHR would dismiss claims of indirect discrimination based on Art. 14 ECtHR and would find them to be justified based on the grounds provided under Art. 9 para 2 ECHR.

The jurisprudence delivered by the ECtHR so far demonstrates that claims of violation of Art. 14 ECHR, such as *Dahlab v Switzerland*, *Karaduman v Turkey*, *Sahin v Turkey*, *France and Kurtulmus v Turkey*, were not considered carefully. Even to the extent that those claims are well considered, it is most likely that the ECtHR will find no violation of Art. 14 ECHR and the alleged breach will be held legitimate and justified. As a result, discrimination-based claims are not likely to be successful.

In practice, the ECtHR exempted itself from considering alleged violations of equality and non-discrimination under Art. 14 ECHR if it had found a breach of other substantive articles of the Convention.

To sum up, the legal basis for submitting a claim that will be rather founded on a fundamental – human rights claim or equality anti-discrimination – depends on the right holder himself.

Human rights claims are generally open to everyone – individuals as well as public authorities or educational institutions, whereas claims for a breach of the equality duty will be applicable with respect to violations or breaches of anti-discrimination measures conducted by public authorities or schools.

e) Inferring Guidelines

aa) Religious Neutrality of the State

At the outset, the principle of state neutrality was not enshrined in the ECHR but was actually alluded to Art. 9 ECHR and read into it, so it developed to be one of the Court's general principles. As was exemplified, there is no single apprehension or construction of the state neutrality precept even within the legal system of each of the compared states. The ambiguous interpretation of neutrality was reflected also in decisions of the ECtHR that refrained from conferring it a rigid formulation or any attachment to a particular state-church model. In the absence of unanimous apprehension as to its interpretation, the outcome is that the admissibility of religious symbols in education-related cases were and still are left dubious. The problematics with respect to the neutrality principle is the lack of consensus as to its construction. While in principle the ECtHR upheld that neutrality indicates the duty of MS to stay impartial and unbiased with respect to religious matters interlinking it with pre-eminent values of pluralism, mutual tolerance, and religious equality, the MS used acknowledgement of the neutrality principle by the ECtHR to ascribe to it a stricter application so as to fit to the particular circumstances of a state. In the case of *Dahlab v Switzerland,* for instance, the Swiss interpretation of state neutrality adopted a secular perception of the term, favouring a separationist approach between the state and the church. By this method of interpretation, the Swiss state was able to claim that the headscarf worn by a teacher infringes on the duty of the state to non-identification and coupled it with other constitutional values, such as the gender equality precept, the negative right of the pupils to religious freedom, and the non-proselytising effect of the headscarf especially emphasized with respect to minor children. So eminently all of these could not be equated with the duty to neutrality of the state. In a slightly different context, the case of *Lautsi v Italy* referring to a state-imposed symbol is a further demonstration that the manifold use of the state neutrality precept had often served the ECtHR in delivering a decision that does not conflict with the margin of appreciation granted to the MS. In this case, the GC upheld that the display of a crucifix cannot be estimated by its pure religious meaning as ascribed to it in Christianity, but rather its passiveness in addition to its association with Western-liberal values, such as mutual tolerance, compassion, and respect of others conferred enough weight so to negate its religiosity. To sum up, the construction of the principle of state neutrality has been often used as a justification ground standing on its own. However, the reading of other high-minded values, (e.g., tolerance) into it concealed the fact that it was meant to support additional justification grounds other than those prescribed under the limited list of Art. 9 (2) ECHR.

bb) Alternative Mode of Dress

Similar to the jurisprudential approach held in Germany and France, the ECtHR will not rule specifically as to the admissibility of symbols that directly qualify as religious in nature. The Court will consider carefully the circumstances as a whole, and if it is to conclude that within the context the manifestation of a garment is religiously motivated though by its nature it does not qualify as such (e.g., a bonnet), it will not hesitate to dismiss a complaint established on Art. 9 ECHR as inadmissible.

cc) Concrete or Abstract Endangerment

In *Dahlab v Switzerland*, one of the most pivotal case law regarding limitations placed on teachers' right to religious manifestation, it was proclaimed by the ECtHR that an abstract or potential proselytising effect on the young mind of pupils will suffice to render the interference in a teacher's right to wear a headscarf as a justified limitation. In this case, the Court determined that the potential impact on the pupils could not be repudiated by virtue of the overt powerful display of the headscarf. The decision remained controversial in the legal literature, mainly since the Court concluded that abstract endangerment on the negative right of pupils not to be disturbed by the view of a teacher with a headscarf will suffice to justify the override of a teacher's right to religious manifestation.

dd) Margin of Appreciation

In the revision of several case laws brought before the ECtHR with respect to the display of religious symbols in education and the construction of justification grounds as established in Art. 9 para 2 ECHR, it is noticeable that the Court grants MS – especially within the context of education – an ample room for discretion, the so called 'margin of appreciation'. The reason is that the ECtHR considers MS to be in a better position to assess the 'pressing social needs' in their society that will justify interference in individual rights to religious manifestation; as a result, with application of the proportionality test, it will examine whether the measures used justified the aim pursued or other less harsh alternatives were at hand. In addition, the place religion acquires in a state will also influence the construction of 'pressing social needs', as this will assist in the adequate process of weighing colliding interests. The fact that each MS operates differently and confers religious rights a disparate level of protection by virtue of their legal status in their respective constitutional framework argues for different balancing of competing constitutional rights and values. The term 'pressing social needs' is variable and what may be perceived in one state to be a pressing social need may change its context in another state where other interests will be considered. Finally, the fact that there is no European consensus of religion and its adequate place in society enables the states a relative wide leeway of discretion; as a result, the ECtHR will be rather reluctant to decide against legislative prohibition of religious symbols applied by a member state. This was exemplified, for instance, in the cases *Dahlab v Switzerland*, *Kurtulumus v Turkey*, or *Lautsi v Italy* where the GC reversed the decision of the Upper Chamber.

8. Development of Thesis

The manner claims engaged with the prohibition of religious symbols in education were resolved whether established plainly on the basis of a breach of fundamental human rights under Art. 9 para 2 ECHR, or in support of equality anti-discrimination claim under Art. 14 ECHR. This demonstrated that the ECtHR was inclined to recognize an extensive margin of appreciation of the MS. While judgements tilted mostly towards recognition of an infringement on an individual's right to religious manifestation, the establishment of justifying grounds for limitations were acknowledged by the Court. Cases invoking anti-discrimination rights were normally dismissed on the same ground as the main claim. The question whether the ECtHR would enable a member state an extensive margin of appreciation without having to deliver clear criteria as to the permissibility of religious symbols, especially in public education, is doubtful. In particular, the religious-cultural-societal changes occurring in Europe recently indicate that the balance of competing rights would no longer be the same. This is also true with respect to the apprehension shared mainly by Western tradition as to pre-eminent values, such as gender equality, liberalism, tolerance, or religious neutrality and the regard of constitutional rights that are not shared as general, common acceptances by all.

It was demonstrated that the scrutiny implied by national courts as well as the ECtHR in order to find out the gravity of interference in individuals' right to manifestation of their religion was assisted by applying a proportionality test which balanced and outweighed the competing rights at stake.

In light of the societal change Europe has encountered recently due to the large influx of immigrants into the European continent, one must consider that this balance and outweigh of rights would change, and that the effect of religious manifestation and the exposure to conspicuous religious insignias are likely to have a greater impact than being the case so far. Taking a future perspective, there is a danger of increased controversies and disputes on the background of symbols' manifestation by religious affiliation, especially in the context of public education and teaching personnel that are under a special duty to appear impartial and neutral by virtue of their function as state representatives and their work in service of the public. The tendency should be heading towards clear regulations as to teachers' dress code and a rigorous application of state neutrality. This holds true also with respect to potential increase of challenges before courts as to the display of religious symbols like the crucifix in public school classrooms. The reasons advocating identifiable pre-requisites to be underlined by the ECtHR will be provided as follows:

a) Overturn of the Balancing of Rights

Within application of the proportionality test, there is no difference whether the ECtHR deals with a claim based on Art. 9 or Art. 14 ECHR, as it is very similar in implementation. As had been argued in different case laws, the Court will scrutinize whether the prohibition serves a legitimate aim and that the means used is proportionate and necessary to achieve the aim sought to be realized. In this respect, several interests were considered as legitimate aims in case a curtailment of individual religious rights were at stake. These were religious neutrality, the peaceful operation of school, proper function of a democratic society (mainly interlinked with public order or public safety), the protection of rights and freedom of others (e.g., negative religious freedom of pupils and parents), gender equality, and public safety or public order (in some cases public health, as e.g., the experience in French case laws showed that the prohibition of especially Islamic garments was perceived as hazardous to public health in gymnastic/sport lessons). Given the case that the majority of Christian pupils, for instance in some schools or districts, may become a minority and the group of what is known to be pertaining to religious or ethnic minority would become the majority, which religious interest should override in such a case? Is the general tendency of accommodating religious practices practicable and realistic? If so, to which extent? Would Christian Europe agree, for instance, to accept a demand for removal of crucifixes in public schools in order to accommodate to religious demands of a majority of Muslims in a school since they feel disturbed by its view? In such a case where the balance had been distracted or overturned, the aim to achieve a peaceful school operation will probably need to be handled differently, as it is obvious that the benefit of the majority will be differently construed. Taking into consideration the majority's interest will tilt in favour of allowing or permitting the headscarf or other extreme forms of head covering; or accepting a demand for removal of the cross will necessarily indicate that the means for achieving a peaceful school operation will be differently construed. The conclusion, therefore, is that the balance of competing rights can no longer be the same and will overturn.

b) Absolute Accommodation of All Religions and Beliefs Is Not Practical

In both German and British jurisprudence, the fact that school authorities or regional administration cannot adjust to and accommodate all religious needs of all religious groups and faiths had been recognized and confirmed. There is no obligation on school authorities or school administrations to accept at all times every request for religious accommodation. In the famous *Begum* case, Lord Hoffmann had already announced that Art. 9 ECHR does not confer a person the right to manifest one's own religion at any given time and any chosen place. The tests as applied so far in Britain and the ECtHR examined whether there had been efforts on part of the school authorities or MS to reasonably accommodate the religious practices of religious minorities without causing undue hardship or laying financial burden on the states or school administrations when doing so.

c) Factual Situation Varies According to Type of Educational Institution

A further difficulty that may arise in the attempt to accommodate religious practices is associated with the fact that the majority of religious groups within one educational institute in the same region may vary immensely (e.g., different streams within the same religion expect different dress code rules). In such a situation, taking either a centralized system like in France or a regional one like in Germany and England which are responsible for educational matters, a duty to accommodate to religious needs of minorities will still involve undue hardship for lands' lawmakers or school governors to adopt a uniform school dress policy. As on the one hand, in a school with a majority of Muslim pupils, the wearing of a *jilbab* or *niqab* would be welcomed and appreciated, on the other hand, in a school with a majority of Christians, atheists, or Jewish pupils, the presence of other religious symbols (e.g., Crucifix, yarmulka) or no display of religious symbols may be anticipated. In addition, the situation in England where school authorities make efforts to find an exception to the general dress code policy if requested to do so by a pupil does not seem to be practicable. The reason is that if school authorities will be under a duty to take consultation with the relevant religious community in every single case so as to find an adequate solution, then such a duty will impose a disproportionate burden on educational institutions and will not necessarily stand the reality test. Especially in light of the current situation, it is not reasonable to assume that school authorities would consult with all involved parties (pupils, parents, teachers, and school authorities) in every single case, as a case-by-case examination and efforts to make an exception may lead to a counterproductive solution where the exception may rapidly become the general dress code rule. In such a situation, one should take into account the religious interests of other pupils involved and consider whether this effect is indeed desired. The jeopardy is that this would lead to undue, massive burden on the administration (teachers, school authorities, or governors) and to an increase in complaints submitted to court that will only be cumbersome and adding to the overload of the judicial system.

d) Increased Potential of Conflicts

An overview of the case laws reflected especially by the jurisprudential approach in Germany and England leads to a conclusion that the current problematics and its complexity is actually underestimated and remains ignored. There is a refusal of acceptance that the real situation in public education requires a feasible solution with clear understanding of the consequences offered in the legal literature or the jurisprudence relying on efforts to be made on part of the school authorities to accommodate the religious practices of individuals, foster good relations and atmosphere in school, and promote religious equality. It is necessary also to be confronted with the question whether the same tolerance, mutual respect, the fostering of good atmosphere, and implementation of religious equality would be applicable in a situation where the ethnical or religious minority of today becomes the majority in another educational institution.

e) Undue Coercion or Pressure

This aspect had often been raised in the legal literature and also considered carefully by the judicator in all three countries as an argument in favour of a prohibition on religious symbols in public schooling. The argument assumes that permissibility of religious symbols in schools introducing Islamic head coverings such as *niqab* or *jilbab* may bear the risk that other female Muslim pupils would feel pressurized into wearing these religious garments albeit the fact that the school offers them a place of escape from any religious coercion or traditional precepts adhered vehemently by their family members, religious community, or close surrounding.

f) Delegation of Powers to the Administration Is Not Feasible

This aspect gains importance especially when analysing a country like Germany. The discretion in educational matters and regulation of school dress code, including of public servants, is left on the regional level to the respective lawmaker of the federal states. In several federal states, such as Bavaria, BW, and NRW, which uphold and foster Christian tradition and values, it is not a mere aspect of tradition but rather an explicit pronouncement in their lands' constitutions as an educational goal to be fostered and preserved. Should the authority of determination be delegated to school administration, it remains doubtful to which extent the Islamic majority would agree to preserve or support the conveyance of Christian precepts and tradition in public schools. Here again, it will be necessary to consider carefully the impact of this shift of majority–minority power when weighing the interests at stake. In England, a similar proposal was raised by the HL in the *Begum* case, suggesting that school authorities should be given some leeway of discretion. However, this has been criticized as conferring too much power to the administrative.

g) Fostering Religious Pluralism or Advancing Religious Neutrality in Public Schooling

The interpretation of state neutrality had been the source of manifold legal controversies and criticism debated in legal literature as to the justified interpretation method. On the one side of the scale, proponents of the liberal interpretation proclaimed inclusive neutrality as phrased in the legal literature,[1704] which anticipates a full and equal enclosure of all religious symbols to the extent that no segregation between different religions or faiths is made, as all religious insignias will be equally permitted. On the other side, opponents of the all-embracing, accepting approach supported the notion of irreligious neutrality which implies a strict application of the neutrality principle, advocating a

1704 *Howard*, Law and the Wearing of Religious Symbols, p. 155

strict separation between religion and public education. The societal change with which European states are confronted demands rather a strict interpretation of religious state neutrality in order to achieve cohesive uniformity established on discipline, educational effectiveness, and the safeguarding of democratic constitutional rights upheld in Western societies, namely, gender or sex equality, religious equality, the respect of rights and freedoms of others, and state neutrality.

h) An Extensive Obligation to Religious Neutrality on Public Servants

Given the last socio-economical changes as discussed and mentioned briefly in the introduction (Chapter I), it is worth to consider whether these challenges embarking upon the European countries and their societies should not justify implementation of a strict obligation to refrain from religious manifestation of any form as far as the outer appearance of teaching personnel is concerned. This would be the same situation as practised in the state of Berlin and would apply equally to all religions and beliefs; as such, it will not contravene the German Basic Law and the spirit of its provisions. The ban should apply as long as the teacher acts within his/her position in state schools; however, the teacher may be free to manifest outwardly his/her religious belief by wearing religious insignias or garments outside school premises at his/her own will or within his/her function in private faith schools.

This approach is appropriate and adequate taking several factors into consideration:

First, no-unanimity under German law as to the neutrality principle – the opinions in German legal literature as well as the jurisprudence are not clear-cut as to its application, whether strict or liberal. As such, a stricter approach which is established on the wording of Art. 137 para 1 WRV would not be regarded as incompatible with the German Constitution.

Second, as far as the experience from other countries demonstrates, there is no legal apprehension and acceptance that individuals are entitled to practise or manifest their religion at every given time and in every chosen place as pronounced by Lord Hoffmann in the famous *Begum* decision.

Third, the jurisprudential instances in Strasbourg were relatively reluctant to decide that a ban on religious manifestation demonstrates unlawful interference in an individual's right to religious manifestation according to Art. 9 ECHR. Even if it did find that there was an interference, it would normally find it objectively justified based on the list of measures prescribed in Art. 9 para 2 ECHR. In addition, the extensive margin of appreciation granted to the MS enables them an ample leeway to take their domestic considerations into account when outweighing grounds for justifications and their appropriateness. Evidentially, the ECtHR adopted the Swiss construction of the neutrality principle in the *Dahlab* case recognizing the laic form of its educational system. Abidance by the strict neutrality precept obliged its teaching personnel to refrain from any religious apparel as it may have an indoctrinating effect on pupils.

Teachers in vocational training – the permissibility of teachers in vocational training must also be taken into consideration as they are yet to be subject to the special duty incumbent on public servants and, as a result, cannot be simply obliged to remove religious symbols if worn by them based on the argument that they must conform to a different set of rules applicable to office holders in the public sphere. Therefore, they cannot invoke the right to equal access to the public service according to Art. 33 para 2 GG; rather, the way to establish a constitutional claim should rely on the right to freedom of profession (Art. 12 para 1 GG) as well as the general right to equality and non-discrimination which prescribes among other things the right to religious equality (Art. 3 para 1 GG).

i) Application of the Proportionality Test

Within considerations of the proportionality test and its implementation, the courts will normally examine whether alternatives and less discriminatory measures are at hand (this will be applicable both to claims established on Art. 9 and Art. 14 ECHR). In this respect, the court will prove whether the measure was necessary to achieve the declared aim and if other less intrusive or restrictive alternatives for obtaining the same aim were available. The notion behind this application of examination was meant to explore whether a harsh interference in an individual's right to religious manifestation was necessary to achieve the declared aim. The finding of less intrusive measures will assist in the evaluation whether it is possible to accommodate religious practice of individuals applying an absolute ban or whether a partial one would have sufficed to achieve the stated aim. A very salient example for the efforts made on part of the school to accommodate sensibly to pupils' special religious practices by devising its uniform school policy was demonstrated in the *Begum* case as part of the school's policy to find less intrusive measures than prohibition of the *jilbab*. These efforts were highly perceived and recognized by the HL which explained that school authorities have gone a long way in considering how the religious requirements of the pupil, Begum, could be met, especially since the school had even taken advice and consulted the Muslim community in order to achieve appeasement that would conform with its school's uniform policy. In addition, it was provided that the appellant had an alternative as she could have applied to other schools in her living area which accepted the wearing of the *jilbab*. This served the HL as sufficient evidence to decide that the interference in the pupil's right to religious manifestation was proportionate and as a result also justified.

The problematics this examination evokes is two-fold: on the one hand, it was criticized in the legal literature that alternative nearby schooling or even home schooling for pupils is no option since the right to education is elementary and free access should be offered to all. For teachers, it is the right to equal access in employment, freedom of profession, and the fundamental right of religious freedom that were argued against alternative schooling. On the other hand, finding a compromise or appeasement instead of a general applicable rule risks an ample scale of 'eligible symbols' and may even aggravate tension and strife between different religious groups in schools. This is because no general consensus as to appropriate religious dress code can be achieved even within the same religious community. The same application of the *Begum* decision was followed in another case involving a pupil, the case of *X (R (on the application of X) v Headteacher and Governors of Y School)* where a Muslim girl appeared with a *niqab* to school, contradictory to the school's uniform policy. Similarly to the *Begum* case, the fact that the school authorities were able to demonstrate that they sought alternatives to adjust to the religious preferences of the pupil by seeking advice from the relevant religious community, conducting a full consultation process with parents and pupils prior to adoption of a new uniform policy, and the existence of alternative schools were sufficient to decide that no infringement on the right to religious manifestation under Art. 9 ECHR was found.

In the *Azmi* case, for instance, the teaching assistant insisted on wearing the *niqab* since she refused to appear without her garment in close proximity to her male colleagues. As a result, she could have alternatively abstained from wearing the *niqab* during school lessons. It was due to her refusal to accept any deviation from the observance of her religious manifestation that the EAT refused to accept her claim for unlawful indirect discrimination.

j) Individual v Institutional Displayed Symbols

A significant difference between individual-displayed symbol and institutional-displayed symbol, as pronounced by decisions of the ECtHR in the *Lautsi* case on the background of the headscarf teacher in the case of *Dahlab* had been underscored with respect to the nature of the symbol and its mode of display. The crucifix in the case of *Lautsi* had been conceptualized as 'an essentially passive symbol', whereas the headscarf in *Dahlab* as an 'external powerful symbol'. Undoubtedly, there is room for segregation between the two types of displayed symbols by virtue of several factors to be taken into account: their nature, their size, their mode of display, the manner in which they are displayed, their perception or acceptance in society and, finally, the effect they have on their viewers. First, the crucifix is indeed hanged on a classroom wall and by its mode of display is rather passive, whereas the headscarf is worn by a teacher who has an interactive role with pupils or students since she needs to be in constant communication with them. Therefore, the impact on pupils is more likely to be significant within their encounter with the teacher. Second, it can be said that a crucifix, when hanged on one classroom wall, will definitely have a different impact dependent on its size. A small crucifix cannot be said to be as prominent and distinguishable as a large-scaled one and is likely to cause less resentment or raise objections. A head covering or any other full body garment are overt and will not be estimated by their size since by their nature they are demonstrative and eye-catching. Third, the affixation of a cross in the corner of a classroom or not in a central visible place of a classroom is presumed to be a display in a modest and not provoking manner and imply sensitiveness towards non-believers and other religious minorities. In contrast, an ostentatious religious garment worn by a teacher enables pupils no room to escape as they are exposed to its constant observation because of mandatory schooling. Fourth, the perception of the crucifix as a symbol that is compatible with the democratic, Western nature of the European states embraces by far a wider acceptance than the headscarf and in some sense is regarded as a consensus. The headscarf, in contrast, was often criticized in national jurisdictions, the ECtHR, and legal literature to be non-compatible with Western-liberal values. It is rather perceived as a religious symbol associated with religious extremism, starkly interlinked with fundamentalist political regimes, women inferiority, and inequality between men and women.

Lastly, when taking into consideration the balance between all involved parties, the emphasis should be directed to the impact these symbols have by their display on their viewers. It was, therefore, rightfully concluded in the *Dahlab* case that the proselytising effect of such a powerful symbol like the headscarf when worn by an elementary school teacher cannot be denied outright, especially when the rights of pupils of tender age are at stake, and in particular since they are more likely to be influenced by the view of their teacher as they are not in a position to reach an independent thinking by themselves.

In the jurisprudential legal debate, the compatibility of these symbols with religious neutrality and their potential proselytising effect stood to question and had been a key element in the process of examination and weighing competing interests. Therefore, the teacher, by virtue of her role as state representative, should be inclined to conform to a special duty deriving from her status as civil servant. This includes the duty of the state to appear neutral and impartial in its actions and even more so in educational matters. This special duty of a teacher to appear neutral and impartial by virtue of her function as a civil servant supports the conclusion that the teacher's right to religious manifestation should be set back, when clashing against the negative right of pupils to religious freedom.

As to the crucifix, it can be contended that the symbol does not completely conform to the perception of religious neutrality and the obligation of the state to appear impartial. Nonetheless, as had been outlined by the descending judgement in the famous *Crucifix* case, the crucifix should be interpreted in a manner which goes beyond its pure religious meaning. This manner of construction negates the indoctrinating effect of the crucifix on pupils of religious minorities. It was explained that albeit the fact that the cross is a central symbol of the Christian faith, it is also associated with Christian-occidental tradition and values, as it stands for human dignity, tolerance, mercy, and mutual understanding. The same notion was conceptualized by the ECtHR in the *Lautsi* case, declaring eventually the crucifix to be a symbol that conforms to Western-liberal values regardless of the church-state model a state adopts. Eminently, its passiveness and its construction as a symbol that fosters harmony and spirit of tolerance served the GC with the basis for its verdict and enabled the crucifix as a symbol and its affixation in public school classrooms. The display of the crucifix coincides with the wish of the majority of Christians and fits to the political model of the European democratic societies that are party to the Convention.

Literature List

Achour, Christiane, The Quest for Identity: Proper Names and Narrators in Algerian Life-Histories, in: *Hargreaves, Alec G./Heffernan, Michael J.* (eds.), French and Algerian Identities from Colonial Times to the Present: A Century of Interaction, Lewiston 1993, pp. 203–216.

Addison, Neil, Religious Discrimination *and* Hatred Law, London 2007.

Adrian, Melanie, France, the Veil and Religious Freedom, Religion, State and Society 37(4) (2009), pp. 345–374.

Ahdar Rex, Leigh Ian, Religious Freedom in the Liberal State, Oxford 2005.

Alder, John, Constitutional and Administrative Law, 6th edn., Hampshire 2007.

Alloway, Lark E., The Crucifix Case: Germany's Everson v. Board of Education?, Dickinson Journal of International Law 15(2) (1997), pp. 361–383.

Alston, Philip/Megret Frederic, The United Nation and Human Rights: A critical Appraisal, Oxford 1995.

Anger, Thorsten, Was bedeutet und wie wichtig ist der "Schulfrieden"? Zur Lösung religiöser Konflikte in der Schule, KritVJ 2005, pp. 52–66.

Arthur James/Holdsworth, Michael, The European Court of Human Rights, Secular Education and Public Schooling, British Journal of Education Studies 60(2) (2012), pp. 129–149.

Auslander, Leora, Bavarian Crucifixes and French Headscarves – Religious Signs and the Postmodern European State, Cultural Dynamics 12(3) (2000), pp. 283–309.

Avenarius, Hermann, The Case of Germany, in: *López-Muniz, Martinez/Luis, Josè/De Groof, Jan/Lauwers, Gracienne* (eds.), Religious Education in Public Schools: Study of Comparative Law, Yearbook of the European Association for Education Law and Policy 6, Dordrecht 2006, pp. 143–153.

Bacquet, Sylvie, Manifestation of Belief and Religious Symbols at School: Setting Boundaries in English Courts, Religion and Human Rights 4(2) (2009), pp. 121–135.

Baer, Susanne/Wrase, Michael, Staatliche Neutralität und Toleranz in der "christlich-abendländischen Wertewelt" – Zur aktuellen Entwicklung im Streit um das islamische Kopftuch, DÖV 2005, pp. 243–251.

Bailey, Stephen, Henry/Harris, David, John./Jones, B. L, Civil Liberties: Cases and Materials, 5th edn., London 2001.

Baillie, Lauren C., Protection of Religious Minorities in Europe: The Council of Europe's successes and Failures, American University International Law Review 23 (2007), pp. 617–645.

Baker, Christina A., French Headscarves and the US Constitution: Parents, Children, and Free Exercise of Religion, Cardozo Journal of Law & Gender 13 (2007), pp. 341–368.

Barbibay, Yael, Citizenship Privilege or the Right to Religious Freedom, Cardozo Journal of International and Comparative Law 18 (2010), pp. 159–206.

Baubérot, Jean, The Place of Religion in Public Life: The Lay Approach, in: *Lindholm, Tore/Durham W. Cole Jr./Tahzib-Lie, Bahia. G.* (eds.), Facilitating Freedom of Religion or Belief: A Deskbook, Leiden 2004, pp. 441–453.

Beatty, David M., The Forms and Limits of Constitutional Interpretation, American Journal of Comparative Law 49(1) (2001), pp. 79–120.

Bell, John, French Constitutional Law, Oxford 1992.

Bell, John/Boyron, Sophie/Whittaker, Simon, Principles of French Law, 2nd edn., Oxford 2008.

Bedouelle, Guy/Costa, Jean Paul, Les laïcités à la française, Paris 1998.

Benhabib, Seyla/Post, Robert (ed.), Another Cosmopolitanism: Hospitality, Sovereignty, And Democratic Iterations, Oxford 2006.

Bergmann, Jan, Vom Umgang des deutschen Rechtsstaats mit dem Islam, ZAR 2004, pp. 135–141.

Berthou, Katell, The Issue of the Voile in the Workplace in France: Unveiling Discrimination, International Journal of Comparative Law and Industrial Relations 21(2) (2005), pp. 281–320.

Bethge, Herbert, Der Grundrechtseingriff, VVDStRL 57 (1998), pp. 7–56.

Betten, Lammy, The Human Rights Act 1998 – What It Means – The Incorporation of the European Convention on Human Rights into the Legal Order of the United Kingdom, The Hague, Boston 1999.

Birnbaum, Pierre, On the Secularization of the Public Square: Jews in France and the United States, Cardozo Law Review 30 (2008/2009), pp. 2431–2443.

Blair, Ann/Aps, Will, What Not to Wear and Other Stories: Addressing Religious Diversity in Schools, Education and the Law 17(1–2) (2005), pp. 1–22.

Bloß, Lasia, European Law of Religion – Organizational and Institutional Analysis of National Systems and Their Implications for the Future European Integration Process, in: *Weiler, Josef H. H.*, Jean Monnet Working Paper 13/03, New York 2003.

Bloß, Lasia, Cuius religio - EU ius regio? Berlin/Brüssel 2008.

Böckenförde, Ernst-Wolfgang, Die Entstehung des Staates als Vorgang der Säkularisation, in: *Ebracher Studien*, Säkularisation und Utopie, Festschrift für Ernst Forsthoff zum 65. Geburtstag, Stuttgart, Berlin, Köln, Mainz 1967, pp. 75–94.

Böckenförde, Ernst-Wolfgang, Vorläufige Bilanz im Streit um das Schulgebet, DÖV 1974, pp. 253–258.

Böckenförde, Ernst-Wolfgang, Kreuze (Kruzifixe) in Gerichtssälen? Zum Verhältnis von staatlicher Selbstdarstellung und religiös-weltanschaulicher Neutralität des Staates, ZevKR 1975, 119–142.

Böckenförde, Ernst-Wolfgang, Staat, Gesellschaft, Freiheit, Frankfurt am Main 1976.

Böckenförde, Ernst-Wolfgang, Zum Ende des Schulgebetsstreits, DÖV 1980, pp. 323–327.

Böckenförde, Ernst-Wolfgang, "Kopftuchstreit" auf dem richtigen Weg?, NJW 2001, pp. 723–728.

Böckenförde, Ernst-Wolfgang, Anmerkung zu BVerwG v. 24.6.2004, Das islamische Kopftuch in Baden-Württemberg, JZ 2004, pp. 1178–1184.

Borowski Martin, Die Glaubens- und Gewissensfreiheit des Grundgesetzes, Tübingen 2006.

Bowen, John R, Why the French Don't Like Headscarves: Islam, the State, and Public Space, Princeton 2007.

Brenner, Michael, Staat und Religion, VVDStRL 59 (2000), pp. 264–297.

Breuer, Marten, Karlsruhe und die Gretchenfrage: Wie hast du's mit Straßburg?, NVwZ 2005, pp. 412–414.

Britz, Gabriele, Kulturelle Rechte und Verfassung, Tübingen 2000.

Brown, Neville L./Bell, John S, French Administrative Law, 5th edn., Oxford 1998.

Brownlie, Ian, Basic Documents in International Law, 5th ed., Oxford, 2002.

Brownlie, Ian/ Goodwin-Gill, Guy S., Basic Documents on Human Rights, 4th ed., 2002.

Brugger, Winfried, On the Relationship between Structural Norms and Constitutional Rights in Church – State – Relations, in: *Brugger, Winfried/ Karayanni Michael* (eds.), Religion in the Public Sphere: A Comparative Analysis of German, Israeli, American and International Law, Beiträge zum ausländischen öffentlichen Recht und Völkerrecht 190, Berlin, Heidelberg, New York 2007, pp. 21–86.

Campenhausen von, Axel, Kruzifixe und religiöse Symbole in der öffentlichen Schule, in: *Stammen, Theo/Oberreuter, Heinrich/Mikat, Paul* (eds.), Politik – Bildung – Religion, Hans Maier zum 65. Geburtstag, München, Oldenburg 1996, pp. 661–671.

Campenhausen von, Axel, Zur Kruzifix - Entscheidung des Bundesverfassungsgerichts, Archiv des Öffentlichen Rechts 121 (1996), p. 448–464.

Campenhausen von, Axel, The German Headscarf Debate, Brigham Young University Law Review 2004, pp. 665–699.

Campenhausen von, Axel/de Wall, Heinrich, Staatskirchenrecht, 4th edn., München 2006.

Campenhausen von, Axel, Kruzifixe und religiöse Symbole in der öffentlichen Schule, in: *Munsonius Hendrik/Heinig Hans Michael* (eds.), Gesammelte Schriften II, Tübingen 2014.

Chelini-Pont, Blandine, Religion in the Public Sphere: Challenges and Opportunities, Brigham Young University Law Review, 2005, pp. 611–627.

Choudhury, Nusrat, From the Stasi Commission to the European Court of Human Rights: l`affaire du foulard and the challenge of protecting the rights of Muslim girls, Columbia Journal of Gender an Law 16(1) (2007), pp. 199–234.

Classen, Claus Dieter, Religionsrecht, 2nd edn., Tübingen 2015.

Clayton, Richard/Tomlinson, Hugh: The Law of Human Rights, 2nd edn., Oxford 2009.

Coons, John E., Of Crucifixes and Community, in: *Burmeister, Joachim* (ed.), Verfassungsstaatlichkeit, Festschrift für Klaus Stern zum 65. Geburtstag, München 1997, pp. 927–937.

Coppel, Jason, The Human Rights Act 1998: Enforcing the European Convention in the Domestic Courts, New York 1999.

Coumont, Nina, Muslimische Schüler und Schülerinnen in der öffentlichen Schule, Köln 2007.

Cumper, Peter, Freedom of Thought, Conscience, and Religion, *in:Harris, David/Joseph Sarah* (eds.), The International Covenant on Civil and Political Rights and United Kingdom Law, Oxford 1995, pp.355- 389.

Cumper, Peter/Lewis, Tom, "Taking Religion Seriously?" Human Rights and Hijab in Europe – Some Problems of Adjudication, Journal of Law and Religion 24(2) (2008/2009), pp. 599–627.

Currie, David P., The Constitution of the Federal Republic of Germany, Chicago 1994.

Curtit, Françoise, Égalité vs Non-Discrimination, in: *Hill, Mark* (ed.), Religion and Discrimination Law in the European Union = La Discrimination en matière religieuse dans l'Union européenne, Proceedings of the 23rd Congress of the European Consortium for Church and State Research, University of Oxford, 29th Sept.-2nd Oct., Trier 2012, pp. 145–154.

Czermak, Gerhard, Öffentliche Schule Religion und Weltanschauung in Geschichte und Gegenwart der Bundesrepublik Deutschland, in: *Muckel, Stefan* (ed.), Kirche und Religion im sozialen Rechtsstaat, Festschrift für Wolfgang Rüfner zum 70. Geburtstag, Berlin 2003, pp. 79–109.

Czermak, Gerhard, Zur Rede von der religiös-weltanschaulichen Neutralität des Staats, NVwZ 2003, pp. 949–953.

Danchin, Peter G., Suspect Symbols: Value Pluralism as a Theory of Religious Freedom in International Law, Yale Journal of International Law 33(1) (2008), pp. 1–61.

Davie, Grace, Is Europe an exceptional case?, The Hedgehog Review 8 (2006), pp. 5–177.

Davies, Gareth, Banning the Hijab: Reflections on Restricting Religious Clothing in the Light of the Court of Appeal, European Constitutional Law Review 1(3) (2005), pp. 511–530.

Davis, Britton D., Lifting the Veil: France's New Crusade, Boston College International & Comparative Law Review 34(1) (2011), pp. 117–145.

Debus, Anne, Das Verfassungsprinzip der Toleranz unter besonderer Berücksichtigung der Rechtsprechung des Bundesverfassungsgerichts, Frankfurt am Main 1999.

Decherf, Dominique, French Views of Religious Freedom, U.S.-France Analysis Series, July 2001 available at http://www.brookings.edu/fp/cusf/analysis/relfreedom.htm.

Degenhart, Christoph, Die allgemeine Handlungsfreiheit des Art. 2 Abs. 1 GG, JuS 1990, pp. 161–169.

Delmas, Clémence, Das Kopftuchverbot in Frankreich, Frankfurt am Main 2006.

Debbasch, Charles/Pontier, Jean-Marie, Les Constitutions de la France, Paris 1983.

Dietlein, Max, Föderative Schulhoheit und Religionsfreiheit in der Schule – zur Auslegung des Art. 12 Abs. 6 Landesverfassung NRW, in: *Burmeister Joachim* (ed.), Verfassungsstaatlichkeit, Festschrift für Klaus Stern zum 65. Geburtstag, München 1997, pp. 443–456.

Doe, Norman, Law and Religion in Europe – A Comparative Introduction, Oxford 2011.

Donald, Alice/Gordon, Jane/Leach, Philip, The UK and the European Court of Human Rights, Equality and Human Rights Commission Research Report 83, London 2012.

Dörr, Oliver/*Grote, Rainer/Marauhn, Thilo*, EMRK/GG Konkordanzkommentar zum europäischen und deutschen Grundrechtsschutz, 2nd edn., Tübingen 2013.

Dreier, Horst, Grundgesetz, Volume I – Artikel 1-19, 3rd edn., Tübingen 2013.

Dreier, Horst, Grundgesetz, Volume III – Artikel 83-146, 2nd edn., Tübingen 2008.

Durand–Prinborgne, Claude, La Laïcité, Paris 1996

Eberle, Edward J., Free Exercise of Religion in Germany and the United States, Tulane Law Review 78 (2004), pp. 1023–1088.

Eckhoff, Rolf, Der Grundrechtseingriff, Köln 1992.

Edge, Peter W., Legal Responses to Religious Difference, The Hague, London, New York, 2002.

Ev. Kirchenamt der EKD, Zusammenleben mit Muslimen in Deutschland, 2000, to download under https://www.ekd.de/glauben/44716.html.

Evans, Carolyn, Freedom of Religion under the European Convention on Human Rights, Oxford 2001.

Evans, Carolyn, The "Islamic Scarf" in the European Court of Human Rights, Melbourne Journal of International Law 7 (2006), pp. 52–74.

Evans, Malcolm D., Religious Liberty and International Law in Europe, Cambridge (UK) 1997.

Evans, Malcolm D., Manual on the Wearing of Religious Symbols in Public Areas (Council of Europe Manuals: Human Rights in Culturally Diverse Societies), Leiden, Boston 2008.

Ferrari, Alessandro/Pastorelli, Sabrina, The Burqa in Europe: European Institutions and the Comparative/Interdisciplinary Approach, The Burqa Affair across Europe, Burlington, 2013, pp. 225–248.

Fetzer, Joel S./Soper, Christopher J., Muslims and the State in Britain, France, and Germany, Cambridge, New York 2005.

Fiedler, Wilfried, Staat und Religion, (VVDStRL) 59 (2000), pp 199–230.

Fischer, Erwin, Volkskirche Ade! Trennung von Staat und Kirche, 4th edn., Berlin, Aschaffenburg 1993.

Flauss, Jean-François, Laïcité et Convention européenne des droits de l'homme, RDP 2004, pp. 317, 324.

Fogel, Ruben Seth, Headscarves in German Public Schools: Religious Minorities Are Welcome in Germany, Unless – God Forbid – They Are Religious, New York Law School Law Review 51(3) (2006/2007), pp. 618–651.

Fornerod, Anne, The Burqa Affair in France, in: Ferrari, Alessandro/Pastorelli, Sabrina (eds.), The Burqa Affair across Europe, 2013, Burlington, pp. 59–76.

Franzke, Hans-Georg, Die Laizität als staatskirchenrechtliches Leitprinzip Frankreichs, DÖV 2004, pp. 383–387.

Freedland, Mark/Vickers, Lucy, Religious Expression in the Workplace in the United Kingdom, Comparative Labor Law and Policy Journal 30 (2009), pp. 597–625.

Frowein, Jochen Abraham/Peukert, Wolfgang, Europäische Menschenrechtskonvention EMRK-Kommentar, 3rd edn., Kehl am Rhein, 2009.

Gaelle Le Roux, Anti-Veil law Risks Being Shot Down by Constitutional Council, France 24 (July 8, 2010), http://www.france24.com/en/20100708-anti-veil-law-risks-being-shot-down-france-constitutional-council-burqa-ump-party-government/.

Ganz, Sarah, Das Tragen religiöser Symbole und Kleidung in der öffentlichen Schule in Deutschland, Frankreich und England, Berlin 2009.

Gaudu François, Labor Law and Religion, Comparative Labor Law & Policy Journal 30(3) (2009), pp. 507–528.

Germann, Michael/ Cornelius Wiesner, Schule und Religion in der Entwicklung des Schulwesens in Deutschland. Recht der Jugend und des Bildungswesen, (2013) pp. 396–424.

Gerstenberg, Oliver, Germany: Freedom of Conscience in Public Schools, International Journal of Constitutional Law 3(1) (2005), pp. 94–106.

Giegerich, Thomas, Freedom of Religion as a Source of Claims to Equality and Problems for Equality, Israel Law Review 34 (2000), pp. 211–259.

Goerlich, Helmut, Distanz und Neutralität im Lehrberuf - zum Kopftuch und anderen religiösen Symbolen, NJW 1999, pp. 2929–2933.

Goerlich, Helmut, Religionspolitische Distanz und kulturelle Vielfalt unter dem Regime des Artikels 9 EMRK, NJW 2001, pp. 2862–2863.

Goggins, Paul, in Hansard, 6 December 2005, col 171.

Grabenwarter Christoph/Pabel, Katharina, Europäische Menschenrechtskonvention, 6th edn. München, Basel, Wien 2016.

Guimezanes, Nicole, Introduction au droit français, 2nd edn., Baden-Baden 1999.

Gunn, Jeremy T: Religious Freedom and Laicité: A Comparison between the United States and France, Brigham Young University Law Review 2004, pp. 419–506.

Gunn, Jeremy T., Under God but Not the Scarf: The Founding Myths of Religious Freedom in the United States and Laïcité in France, Journal of Church and State 46 (2004), pp. 7–24.

Häberle, Peter: Erziehungsziele und Orientierungswerte im Verfassungsstaat, Freiburg, München 1981.

Hale, Brenda, Religious freedom and the law, in: *Cranmer, Frank, Hill, Mark, Kenny*, Celia, ua. (eds.),The Confluence of Law and Religion, Cambridge 2016, p. 218–231.

Hambler, Andrew, Religious Expression in the Workplace and the Contested Rule of Law, Abington, Oxon 2015.

Hamdan, Amani, The Issue of Hijab in France: Reflections and Analysis, Muslim World Journal of Human Rights 4(2) (2007), pp. 1–27.

Harris, David, The International Covenant on Civil and Political Rights and the United Kingdom, in: Harris, David/Joseph, Sarah (eds.), The International Covenant on Civil and Political Rights and UK Law, Oxford 1995, pp. 1-67.

Harris, David/O'Boyle Michael/Bates, Edward/Buckley, Carla: Law of the European Convention on Human Rights, 3rd edn., Oxford 2014.

Harte J. David C., The Development of the Law of Employment and Education in; *Hill, Mark* (ed.), Religious Liberty and Human Rights, Cardiff 2002, pp 159–194.

Hassemer, Winfried/*Hömig*, Dieter, Rechtsprechung des Bundesverfassungsgerichts im Bereich der Bekenntnisfreiheit, EuGRZ 1999, pp. 525–536.

Hatzis, Nicolas, Personal Religious Beliefs in the Workplace: How Not to Define Indirect Discrimination. Modern Law Review 74(2) (2011), pp. 287–305.

Häußler, Ulf, Muslim Dress-codes in German State Schools, European Journal of Migration and Law 3(3) (2001), pp. 457–474.

Häußler, Ulf, Leitkultur oder Laizismus, ZAR 2004, pp. 6–14.

Häußler, Ulf, Rahmenbedingungen und Gestaltungsmöglichkeiten für die Einrichtung islamischen Religionsunterrichts, ZAR 2000, pp. 255–265.

Healey, M. Robert, The Year of the Debre Law, Journal of Church and State 12(2) (1970), pp. 213–235.

Heckel, Martin, Das Kreuz im öffentlichen Raum, DVBl 1996, pp. 453–468.

Heckel, Martin: Religious Human Rights In Germany, Emory International Law Review 10(1) (1996), pp. 107–114.

Heckel, Martin, The Impact of Secular Modern Law on Church and State in Germany, Tel-Aviv Uni. Studies In Law 13 (1997), pp. 187–204.

Heinig, Hans Michael, Religionsfreiheit oder Neutralitätsgebot? Das Kopftuch in der rechtstaatlichen und juristischen Debatte, Bundeszentrale für politische Bildung, http://www.bpb.de/politik/innenpolitik/konfliktstoff-kopftuch/63259/einstieg-in-die-debatte

Heinig, Hans Michael, The Headscarf of a Muslim Teacher in German Public Schools, in: *Brugger, Winfried/Karayanni, Michael* (eds.), Religion in the

Public Sphere: A Comparative Analysis of German, Israeli, American and International Law, Beiträge zum ausländischen öffentlichen Recht und Völkerrecht 190, Berlin, Heidelberg, New York 2007, pp. 181–197.

Hennecke, Frank J., Rechtsprobleme religiöser Minderheiten im öffentlichen Schulwesen der Bundesrepublik Deutschland, in: *Ellwein, Thomas/Grimm, Dieter/Hesse, Joachim Jens/Folke Schuppert, Gunnar* (eds.), Jahrbuch zur Staats- und Verwaltungswissenschaft 8 (1995), Baden-Baden 1996, pp. 83–105.

Hesse, Konrad, Grundzüge des Verfassungsrechts der Bundesrepublik Deutschland, 20th edn., Heidelberg 1999.

Heun, Werner, Die Religionsfreiheit in Frankreich, ZevKR, 49 (2004), pp. 273–284.

Hill, Mark, Church Autonomy in the United Kingdom, in *Robbers Gerhard* (ed.) Church Autonomy: A Comparative Study, Frankfurt, 2001, pp. 267–283.

Hill, Mark, Religious Liberty and Human Rights, Cardiff 2002.

Hill, Mark, Bracelets, Rings and Veils; The Accommodation of Religious Symbols in the Uniform Policies of English Schools, in: *Hunter-Henin*, Myriam (ed.), Law, Religious Freedoms and Education in Europe (Cultural Diversity and Law), Farnham 2011, pp. 307–327.

Hill, Mark, Religion and Discrimination Law in the European Union, Trier 2012.

Hill, Mark, Legal and Social Issues Concerning the Wearing of the Burqa and Other Head Coverings in the United Kingdom, in: *Ferrari, Alessandro/Past orelli, Sabrina* (eds.), The Burqa Affair across Europe, Burlington, 2013, pp. 77–100.

Holzke, Frank, Die „Neutralität" des Staates in Fragen der Religion und Weltanschauung, NVwZ 2002, pp. 903–913.

Howard, Erica, School Bans on the Wearing of Religious Symbols: Examining the Implications of Recent Case Law of the UK, Religion & Human Rights 4(1) (2009), pp. 7–24.

Howard, Erica, Bans on the Wearing of Religious Symbols in British Schools: A Violation of the Right to Non-discrimination? Religion and Human Rights 6(2) (2011), pp. 127–149.

Howard, Erica, Law and the Wearing of Religious Symbols, London 2012.

Hübner, Ulrich, Constantinesco Vlad, Einführung in das französische Recht, 4th edn., München 2001.

Hufen, Friedhelm: Die kulturintegrative Kraft der Verfassung, in: *Däubler-Gmelin, Herta* (ed.), Gegenrede. Aufklärung - Kritik – Öffentlichkeit, Festschrift für Ernst Gottfried Mahrenholz, Baden-Baden 1994, pp. 115–132.

Hufen, Friedhelm, Aktuelle Probleme der Religionsfreiheit im schweizerisch-deutschen Rechtsvergleich, in: *Hänni, Peter* (ed.), Mensch und Staat / L'homme et l'Etat, Festschrift für Thomas Fleiner, Fribourg 2003, pp. 343–360.

Humphrey, John Peter, Political and Related Rights in: *Meron, Theodore* (ed.), Human Rights International Law, Oxford 1985, pp. 171–203.

Hunter-Henin, Myriam, Law, Religious Freedoms and Education in Europe (Cultural Diversity and Law), London 2011.

Hunter-Henin, Myriam, Why French Don`t Like the Burqa: Laicité, National Identity and Religious Freedom, International and Comparative Law Quarterly 61(3) (2012), pp. 613–639.

Hunter-Henin, Myriam/Howard, Erica, Law and the Wearing of Religious Symbols: European Bans on the Wearing of Religious Symbols in Education, International Journal of Discrimination and the Law 12 (2012), pp. 243–250.

Huster, Stefan, Die ethische Neutralität des Staates, Eine liberale Interpretation der Verfassung, Tübingen 2002.

Huster, Stefan, Warum die Lehrerin (k)ein Kopftuch tragen darf. Zum Verhältnis von gesellschaftspolitischen Zielen und verfassungsrechtlicher Argumentation, in: *Häberle, Peter/Morlok, Martin/Kouris, Vassilios* (eds.), Festschrift für Dimitrios Th. Tsatsos zum 70. Geburtstag, Baden-Baden 2003, pp. 215–230.

Huster, Stefan, Die ethische Neutralität des Staates: Eine liberale Interpretation der Verfassung, in: Beiträge zum Öffentlichen Recht, Bd. 90, Bochum 2017.

Idriss, Mazher Mohammad, Laicité and the Banning of the "Hijab" in France, Legal Studies 25(2) (2006), pp. 260–295.

Isak, Axel, Selbstverständnis der Kirchen und Religionsgemeinschaften und seine Bedeutung für die Auslegung staatlichen Rechts, Berlin 1994.

Isensee, Josef/Kirchhof, Paul, Handbuch des Staatsrechts, Volume VII – Freiheitsrechte, 3rd edn., München 2009.

Isensee, Josef/Kirchhof, Paul, Handbuch des Staatsrechts, Volume IX – Allgemeine Grundrechtslehren, 3rd edn., München 2011.

Janz, Norbert/Rademacher, Sonja, Islam und Religionsfreiheit - Die religiöse und weltanschauliche Neutralität des Staates auf dem Prüfstand, NVwZ 1999, pp. 706–713.

Janz, Norbert/Rademacher, Sonja, Das Kopftuch als religiöses Symbol oder profaner Bekleidungsgegenstand? – BayVGH, NVwZ 2000, 952 und VG Stuttgart, NVwZ 2000, 959, JuS 2001, pp. 440–444.

Jarass, Hans/Pieroth, Bodo, Grundgesetz für die Bundesrepublik Deutschland Kommentar, 14th edn., München 2016.

Jellinek, Georg, System der subjektiven öffentlichen Rechte, 2nd edn., Tübingen 2011.

Jeuffroy, Bernard/Tricard, François, Liberté religieuse et régimes des cultes en droit francais 1237–1038 Paris, 1996.

Kästner, Karl-Hermann, Hypertrophie des Grundrechts auf Religionsfreiheit?, JZ 1998, pp. 974–982.

Kästner, Karl-Hermann: Religiös akzentuierte Kleidung des Lehrpersonals staatlicher Schulen. Verfassungsrechtliche Erwägungen zum Wunsch einer Muslimin, den Dienst als Lehrerin an öffentlichen Schulen des Landes Baden-Württemberg aus religiösen Gründen ausschließlich mit Kopftuch zu versehen, in: *Kästner, Karl-Hermann/Nörr, Knut Wolfgang/ Schlaich, Klaus* (eds.), Festschrift für Martin Heckel zum 70. Geburtstag, Tübingen 1999, pp. 359–372.

Kanger, Helle, Human Rights in the UN Declaration, Uppsala 1984.

Kommers, Donald P., Miller, Russell A.,The Constitutional Jurisprudence of the Federal Republic of Germany, 3rd edn., Durham, London 2012.

Krimphove, Dieter, Europäisches Religions- und Weltanschauungsrecht, EuR 2009, pp. 330–348.

Krüger, Herbert, Allgemeine Staatslehre, 2nd edn., Stuttgart 1966.

Krüper, Julian, Die grundrechtlichen Grenzen staatlicher Neutralität: Zum Inhalt eines Verfassungsprinzips – aus Anlaß des Kopftuchstreits, Jahrbuch des Öffentlichen Rechts 53 (2005), pp. 79–109.

Kühling, Jürgen, Christliche Neutralität – Eine Zwischenbilanz im Kopftuchstreit, in: Vorgänge - Zeitschrift für Bürgerrechte und Gesellschaftspolitik 2004, pp. 127–132.

Ladeur, Karl-Heinz/Augsberg, Ino, Toleranz - Religion - Recht. Die Herausforderung des "neutralen" Staates durch neue Formen der Religiosität in der postmodernen Gesellschaft, Tübingen 2007.

Ladeur, Karl-Heinz, Symposium: Constitutionalism and Secularism in Age of Religious Revival: The Challenge of Global and Local Fundamentalism: Religion and Secularism in Theory: The Myth of the Neutral State and the Individualization of Religion: The Relationship between State and Religion in the Face of Fundamentalism, Cardozo Law Review 30 (2009), pp. 2445–2471.

Langenfeld, Christine, Integration und kulturelle Identität zugewanderter Minderheiten, Tübingen, 2001.

Langenfeld Christine/Mohsen Sarah, Germany: The Teacher Headscarf Case, International Journal of Constitutional Law 3(1) (2005), pp. 86–94.

Lanzerath, Sonja, Religiöse Kleidung und öffentlicher Dienst – Zur Zulässigkeit dienstrechtlicher Bekleidungsverbote in Schule, Gerichtsbarkeit und Polizei, Frankfurt 2003.

Lecheler, Helmut, Kirchen und staatliches Schulsystem, in: Listl Joseph/Pirson Dietrich (eds.), Handbuch des Staatskirchenrechts der Bundesrepublik Deutschland, Bd. II, 2nd edn., Berlin 1995, pp. 415–437.

Levine, Mark A., The Modern Crusade: An Investigation of the International Conflict between Church and State, California Western School of Law, 2009, pp. 33–52.

Liederman-Molokotos, Lina, Pluralism in Education: The display of Islamic Affiliation in French and British Schools, Islam and Christian -Muslim Relations 11(2) (2000), pp. 105–117.

Lindholm, Tore/Durham W. Cole Jr./Tahzib–Lie, Bahia. G., Facilitating Freedom of Religion or Belief: A Deskbook, Leiden 2004.

Listl, Joseph, Die Konkordate und Kirchenverträge in der Bundesrepublik Deutschland, Vol. I, Berlin 1987.

Listl, Joseph/Pirson, Dietrich, Handbuch des Staatskirchenrechts der Bundesrepublik Deutschland, 2nd edn., Vol. I, Berlin 1994.

Lochak, Danièle, La condition des minorités en France. Les minorités et le droit public francais: du refus des différences à la gestion des différences' in: *Fenet, Alain/Soulier, Gérard* (eds.), Les minorités et leurs droits depuis 1789, Paris 1989, pp. 111–185.

Lock, Tobias, Religious Freedom and Discrimination in Germany and the United Kingdom: Towards a Common European Standard?, European Law Review 38(5) (2013), pp. 655–676.

Lock, Tobias, Of Crucifixes and Headscarves; Religious Symbols in German Schools, in: *Hunter-Henin*, Myriam (ed.), Law Religious Freedoms and Education in Europe (Cultural Diversity and Law), Farnham 2011, pp. 347–369.

López-Muniz Martinez, Luis, Josè/De Groof, Jan/Lauwers, Gracienne (eds.), Religious Education in Public Schools: Study of Comparative Law, Yearbook of the European Association for Education Law and Policy 6, Dordrecht 2006.

Lübbe-Wolff, Gertrude, Die Grundrechte als Eingriffsabwehrrechte, Baden-Baden 1988.

Magen, Stefan, Staatskirchenrecht als symbolisches Recht, in: *Lehmann, Hartmut* (ed.), Koexistenz und Konflikt von Religionen im vereinten Europa, Göttingen 2004, pp. 30–54.

Mager, Ute, Der Kopftuchstreit vor dem Bundesverfassungsgericht, Religion – Staat – Gesellschaft, 2004, pp. 275–303.

Mahlmann, Matthias, Religious Tolerance, Pluralist Society and the Neutrality of the State: The German Constitutional Court's Decision in the Headscarf Case, German Law Journal 4(11) (2003), pp. 1099–1116.

Mahrenholz, Ernst Gottfried, Ein Kopftuch, aber ach, kein Kopftuch nur, wie fass ich Dich, unendliche Kultur, in: *Michael Brenner* (ed.), Der Staat des Grundgesetzes - Kontinuität und Wandel, Festschrift für Peter Badura zum siebzigsten Geburtstag, Tübingen 2004, pp. 749–763.

Mancini, Susanna, The Power of Symbols and Symbols as Power: Secularism and Religion as Guarantors of Cultural Convergence, Symposium: Constitutionalism and Secularism in an Age of Religious Revival: The Challenge of Global and Local Fundamentalism: Religious Symbols in the Public Space: Cardozo Law Review 30(6) (2009), pp. 2629–2668.

Mancini, Susanna, The Cruzifix Rage: Supranational Constitutionalism Bumps against the counter – Majoritarian-Difficulty, European Constitutional Law Review 6 (2010), pp. 6–27.

Mangoldt von, Hermann/Klein, Friedrich/Starck, Christian, Kommentar zum Grundgesetz, 6th edn., München 2010.

Mann, Suzanne, Das Kopftuch der muslimischen Lehrerin (Lehramtsanwärterin) als Eignungsmangel im Beamtenrecht, Frankfurt am Main 2004.

Manterfeld, Norbert, Die Grenzen der Verfassung. Möglichkeiten limitierender Verfassungstheorie des Grundgesetzes am Beispiel E.-W. Boeckenfoerdes, Berlin 2000.

Marré, Heiner, Der Islam in Deutschland – Historische, politische und rechtliche Überlegungen zu einem komplexen Thema, in: *Muckel, Stefan* (ed.), Kirche und Religion im sozialen Rechtsstaat, Festschrift für Wolfgang Rüffner zum 70. Geburtstag, Berlin 2003, pp. 552–591.

Martinez-Torrón, Javier, Religious Liberty in European Jurisprudence in Religious Liberty and Human Rights, in: *Hill, Mark* (ed.), Religious Liberty and Human Rights', Cardiff 2002, pp. 99–127.

Martinez-Torrón, Javier, Limitations on Religious Freedom in Case Law of the European Court of Human Rights, Emory International Law Review 19(2) (2005), pp. 587–636.

Martinez-Torrón, Javier, The (Un-)protection of Individual Religious Identity in the Strasbourg Case Law, Oxford Journal of Law and Religion 1(2) (2012), pp. 363–385.

Maunz, Theodor/*Dürig*, Günter, Kommentar zum Grundgesetz, Loseblattsammlung, München 2015.

Mawhinney, Alison, Coercion, Oaths and Conscience in: *Cranmer, Frank, Hill, Mark, Kenny*, Celia, ua. (eds.),The Confluence of Law and Religion, Cambridge 2016, pp. 205–217.

McGoldrick, Dominic, The Human Rights Committee: Its Role in the Development of the International Covenant on Civil and Political Rights, Oxford 1994.

McGoldrick, Dominic, Human Rights and Religion: The Islamic Headscarf Debate in Europe, Oxford 2006.

McGoldrick, Dominic, Religion in the European Public Square and in European Public Life – Cruzifixes in the Classroom? Human Rights Law Review 11(3) (2011), pp. 451–502.

McCrea, Ronan, The Ban on the Veil and the European Law, Human Rights Law Review 13(1) (2013), pp. 57–97.

Meder, Theodor/Brechmann, Winfried, Die Verfassung des Freistaats Bayern, 5th edn., Stuttgart 2014.

Meredith, Paul, Educational Reform, Modern Law Review 52(2) (1989), pp. 215–231.

Meredith, Paul, Religious Education and Collective Worship in State Schools: England and Wales, in: *López-Muniz, Martinez/Luis, Josè/De Groof, Jan/Lauwers, Gracienne* (eds.), Religious Education in Public Schools: Study of Comparative Law, Yearbook of the European Association for Education Law and Policy 6, Dordrecht 2006, pp. 155–169.

Merten, Detlef: Der Kruzifix Beschluß des Bundesverfassungsgerichts aus grundrechtsdogmatischer Sicht, in: *Burmeister, Joachim* (ed.), Verfassungsstaatlichkeit, Festschrift für Klaus Stern zum 65. Geburtstag, München 1997, pp. 987–1009.

Messner, Francis/Prélot, Pierre-Henri/Woehrling, Jean Marie, Traité de droit français des religions, Litec, Paris 2003.

Meyer-Teschendorf, Klaus, Religionsfreiheit in der Staatsschule, ZevKR 23 (1978), pp. 202–230.

Morange, Jean, Droits de l'Homme et libertés publiques, PUF, 5th edn., 2000.

Morlok, Martin, Selbstverständnis als Rechtskriterium - Vorkommen, Funktionen und dogmatische Bedeutung, Tübingen 1993.

Mückl, Stefan, Religionsfreiheit und Sonderstatusverhältnisse – Kopftuchverbot für Lehrerinnen?, Der Staat 40 (2001), pp. 96–127.

Muckel, Stefan, Reiner, Tillmanns, Die religionsverfassungsrechtlichen Rahmenbedingungen für den Islam, in: *Muckel, Stefan* (ed.), Schriften zum Öffentlichen Recht, Berlin 2010, pp. 234–272.

Muckel, Stefan, Pauschales Kopftuchverbot an öffentlichen Schulen verletzt die Religionsfreiheit, Juristische Arbeitsblätter 6 (2015), 476–478.

Müller, Christoph, Religionskritische Anmerkungen zu Fragen des Verhältnisses von Christentum und Rechtsstaat, in: *Behrendt, Ethel Leonore* (ed). Rechtsstaat und Christentum 1 (1982), pp. 443–484.

Müller-Volbehr, Jörg, Das Grundrecht der Religionsfreiheit und seine Schranken, DÖV 1995, pp. 301–310.

Münch von, Ingo/Kunig, Philip, Grundgesetz-Kommentar, Vol. I – Präambel, Art. 1 bis Art. 69, 6th edn., München 2012.

Münch von, Ingo/Kunig, Philip, Grundgesetz-Kommentar, Vol. II – Art. 70 bis Art. 146 und Gesamtregiste, 6th edn., München 2012.

Murdoch, Jim, Freedom of Thought, Conscience and Religion. A Guide to the Implementation of Art.9 of the European Convention on Human Rights, Human Rights Handbooks, 9 (2007), Strasbourg.

Nathwani Nira, Islamic Headscarves and Human Rights: A Critical Analysis of the Relevant Case Law of the European Court of Human Rights, Netherlands Quarterly of Human Rights 25(2) (2007), pp. 221–254.

Nowak, Manfred, UN Covenant on Civil and Political Rights. CCPR Commentary, 2nd rev. edn., Kehl am Rhein, 2005.

Oliva, Javier Garcia, Religious Symbols in the Classroom: A Controversial Issue in the United Kingdom, Brigham Young University Law Review, (3) 2008, pp. 877–896.

Oliva Javier Garcia/Cranmer, Frank: Education and Religious Symbols in the United Kingdom, Italy and Spain: Uniformity or Subsidiarity? European Public Law 19(3) (2013), pp. 555–582.

Opsahl, Torkel, The Human Rights Committee, in: *Alston, Philip* (ed.), The United Nation and Human Rights: A Critical Appraisal, Oxford 1995, pp. 369–443.

Palandt, Kommentar zum Bürgerlichen Gesetzbuch, bearb. v. Bassenge, Peter/ Brudermüller, Gerd/ Ellenberger Jürgen ua, 75th edn., München, 2016.

Palmer, Edith, Religious Liberty: The Legal Framework in Selected OSCE Countries, Washington 2000.

Papier Hans-Jürgen, Umsetzung und Wirkung der Entscheidungen des Europäischen Gerichtshofes für Menschenrechte aus der Perspektive der nationalen deutschen Gerichte, EuGRZ 2006, pp. 1–3.

Papier, Hans-Jürgen, Aktuelle Herausforderungen im Verhältnis zwischen Staat und Kirche unter besonderer Berücksichtigung der staatlichen Neutralitätspflicht, in: *Pitschas, Rainer/Uhle, Arnd* (eds.), Wege gelebter Verfassung in Recht und Politik, Festschrift für Rupert Scholz zum 70. Geburtstag, Berlin 2007, pp. 1123–1139.

Pieroth, Bodo/Schlink, Bernhard: Grundrechte, 31th edn., Heidelberg 2015.

Poggeschi, Giovanni, Religion in France: A Juridical Approach, European Yearbook of Minority Issues, 3 (2003–2004), pp. 263–271.

Pottmeyer, Maria, Religiöse Kleidung in der öffentlichen Schule in Deutschland und England, Tübingen 2011.

Poulter, Sebastian, Muslim Headscarves in Schools: Contrasting Legal Approaches in England and France, Oxford Journal of Legal Studies 17(43) (1997), pp. 43–74.

Poulter, Sebastian, Ethnicity, Law and Human Rights: The English Experience, Oxford 1998.

Püttner, Günter, Toleranz als Verfassungsprinzip – Prolegomena zu einer rechtlichen Theorie des pluralistischen Staates, Berlin 1976.

Puza, Richard, The Headscarf Issue: A German Perspective, in: *Durham Jr, Cole W./Torfs, Rik/ Kirkham, David M./Scott, Christine* (eds.), Islam, Europe and Emerging Legal Issues, Burlington 2012, pp. 185–206.

Radačić, *Ivana*, Religious Symbols in Educational Institutions, Jurisprudence of the European Court of Human Rights, Religion and Human Rights, 7(2) (2012), pp. 133–149.

Rademacher, Sonja, Das Kreuz mit dem Kopftuch: Wieviel religiöse Symbolik verträgt der neutrale Staat?, Baden-Baden 2005.

Rayner Julie/Williams Helen M./Lawton Alan/Allinson Christopher W., Public Service Ethos: Developing a Generic Measure, Journal of Public Administration Research and Theory, Oxford 2010.

Rémond, René, Evolution de la notion de laicité entre 1919 et 1939, Cahiers d'histoire Tome IV n°1 1959, pp. 71–89.

Renck, Ludwig, Staatliche Religionsneutralität und Toleranz - BVerfGE 35, 366 und 52, 233, JuS 1989, pp. 451–455.

Renck, Ludwig, Zum Stand des Bekenntnisverfassungsrechts in der Bundesrepublik, BayVBl 1999, pp. 70–77.

Reuter Astrid/Kippenberg, *Hans. G.*, Religionskonflikte im Verfassungsstaat, Göttingen 2010.

Richburg, Keith B, French President Urges Ban on Headscarves in Schools; Chirac Confronts Spread of Islam, Wash. Post, Dec. 18, 2003, at A1.

Richter, Birgit, Religious Garments in Public Schools in Separation Systems: France and the U.S.A., in: *Brugger, Winfried/Karayanni, Michael* (eds.), Religion in the Public Sphere: A Comparative Analysis of German, Israeli, American and International Law, Beiträge zum ausländischen öffentlichen Recht und Völkerrecht 190 (2007), Berlin, pp. 199–242.

Riddell, Sheila/Ahlgren, Linda/McCluskey, Gillean/Weedon, Elisabet, Religious Education in a Multicultural Society: Scotland National Report, Edinburgh 2009, http://www.docs.hss.ed.ac.uk/education/creid/Reports/17ii_REMC_ScotNatRpt.pdf.

Riley, Alan, Headscarves, Skull Caps and Crosses – Is the proposed French Ban Safe from European Legal Challenge?, Centre for European Policy Studies, Brief no. 49, 2004, pp. 1–7.

Robbers, Gerhard, Religious Freedom in Germany, Brigham Young University Law Review, 2001, pp. 643–668.

Robbers, Gerhard, Muslimische Lehrerinnen, das Kopftuch und das deutsche Bundesverfassungsgericht, Österreichisches Archiv für Recht & Religion 2003, pp. 405–417.

Robbers, Gerhard, Religion in der öffentlichen Schule, RdJB 51(2003), pp. 11–22.

Robbers, Gerhard, Staat und Kirche in der Europäischen Union, 2nd edn., Baden-Baden, 2005.

Robbers Gerhard, Religion in Public Education - La religion dans l'éducation publique, European Consortium for Church and State Research - Tagungsband, Trier 11.-14. November 2010, Trier, 2011.

Robert, Jaques, La liberte' Religieuse, R.I.D.C. 46 (1994); pp, 630–644, available at http://www.persee.fr/web/revues/home/prescript/article/ridc_0035-3337_1994_num_46_2_4893.

Robert, Jaques, Religious Liberty and French Secularism, Brigham Young University Law Review, 2003, pp. 637–660, available at http://digitalcommons.law.byu.edu/lawreview/vol2003/iss2/8-

Robert, Jacques/Duffar, Jean, Droits de l'homme et libertés fondamentales, Paris 2009.

Robert, Paul/ Rey, Alain, 5 Le Grand Robert De La Langue Francais, 1992, p.915.

Rogoff Martin A., French Constitutional Law: Cases and Materials, (Carolina Academic Press Comparative Law Series) Durham, 2011.

Rorive, Isabelle, Religious Symbols in the Public Space: In Search of a European Answer, Cardozo Law Review, 30(6) (2009), pp. 2669–2698.

Sachs, Michael, Grundgesetz, 7th edn., München 2014.

Sandberg, Russel, Law and Religion, Cambridge 2011.

Sandberg, Russell, A Uniform Approach to Religious Discrimination? The Position of Teachers and Other School Staff in the UK, in: *Hunter-Henin, Myriam* (ed.), Law Religious Freedoms and Education in Europe (Cultural Diversity and Law), Farnham 2011, pp. 327–346.

Saunders, David, France on the Knife-Edge of Religion: Commemorating the Centenary of the Law of 9 December 1905 on the Separation of Church and State, in: *Levey, Geoffrey Brahm, Modood, Tariq* (eds.), Secularism, Religion and Multicultural Citizenship, Cambridge 2008, pp. 56–81.

Saxena, Mukul, The French Headscarf Law and the Right to Manifest Religious Belief, University of Detroit Mercy Law Report 2007, pp. 765–827.

Schlaich, Klaus, Neutralität als verfassungsrechtliches Prinzip, Tübingen 1972.

Schmidt-Bleibtreu Bruno/Hofmann, Hans/Henneke, Hans-Günter, Kommentar zum Grundgesetz, 13th edn., München 2014.

Ségur Philippe, Le principe constitutionnel de laicité, Annales de l'Université des Sciences Sociales de Toulouse, 1996, pp. 117–34.

Seifert, Achim, Religious Expression in the Workplace: The Case of the Federal Republic of Germany, Comparative Labor Law and Political Journal 30 (2009), pp. 529–568.

Selbmann, Frank, Developments in German Case Law Regarding the Freedom of Religion, European Yearbook of Minority Issues 3 (2003), pp. 199–216.

Sherlock Ann/Williams Kate, Islamic Dress, Institutions of Education and Freedom of Religion under the ECHR: A UK Perspective, Wales Journal of Law and Policy 4 (2005), pp. 214–230. RAE2008.

Shadid W/van Konigsfeld P.S., Muslim Dress in Europe: Debates on the Headscarf, Journal of Islamic Studies 16(1) (2005), pp. 35–61.

Silverman, Max, Rights and Difference: Questions of Citizenship in France, in: *Hargreaves Alec G./Leaman Jeremy* (eds.), Racism, Ethnicity, and Politics in Contemporary Europe, Aldershot 1995, pp. 256–264.

Skjeie, Hege, Headscarves in Schools: European Comparisons, in: *Loenen, M. L. P, Goldschmidt, Jenny E.* (eds.), Religious Pluralism and Human Rights in Europe: Where to Draw the Line?, Antwerp 2007 pp. 129–145.

Spotts, Frederic: The Churches and Politics in Germany, Journal of Church and State 18 (1976).

Ssenyonjo, Manisuli, Limits on the Freedom to Manifest Religion in Educational Institutions in Uganda and the United Kingdom, International Journal of Constitutional Law 7(2) (2009), pp. 275–305.

Stern, Klaus, Das Staatsrecht der Bundesrepublik Deutschland, Volume I – Grundbegriffe und Grundlagen des Staatsrechts. Strukturprinzipien der Verfassung, 2nd edn., München 1984.

Stern, Klaus, Das Staatsrecht der Bundesrepublik Deutschland, Volume III/2 – Allgemeine Lehren der Grundrechte, München 1994.

Stinnett Nathaniel, Defining Away Religious Freedom in Europe: How Four democracies Get Away with Discriminating against Minority Religions, Boston College International & Comparative Law Review 28(2) (2005), pp. 429–451.

Straw Jack/Boateng Paul, Bringing Rights Home: Response to Labours' Plans to Incorporate the European Convention on Human Rights into United Kingdom Law, European Human Rights Law Review 1 (1997), 71-80.

Sydow, Gernot, Religiöse Symbole im Öffentlichen Dienst. Eine verfassungs- und Europarechtliche Kritik gegenwärtiger Restriktionstendenzen, ZG 2004, pp. 313–330.

Taylor, M. Paul, Freedom of Religion UN and Human Rights Law and Practice, Cambridge 2005.

Temperman, Jereon, State Neutrality in Public School Education: An Analysis of the Interplay between the Neutrality Principle, the Right to Adequate Education, Children's Right to Freedom of Religion or Belief, Parental Liberties, and the Position of Teachers, Human Rights Quarterly 32(4) 2010, pp. 865–897.

Temperman, Jereon, The Lautsi Papers: Multidisciplinary Reflections on Religious Symbols in the Public School Classroom, Studies in Religion, Secular Beliefs and Human Rights 11 (2012) Leiden, Boston, pp. 143–200.

Thielmann, Jörn/Vorholzer, Kathrin, Burqa in Germany – Not Really an Issue, in: *Ferrari, Alessandro/Pastorelli, Sabrina* (eds.), The Burqa Affair across Europe, Burlington 2013, pp. 189–196.

Traub, Thomas, Der Islam im Völker -und Europarecht, in: *Muckel, Stefan* (ed.), Schriften zum Öffentlichen Recht, Berlin 2010, p. 273–298.

Traulsen, Christian, Distanzierende Neutralität an Baden-Württembergs Schulen?, RdJB 2006, pp. 116–132.

Triebel, Matthias, Kopftuch und staatliche Neutralität, BayVBl 2002, pp. 624–627.

Troper, Michel, French Secularism, or Laicité, Cardozo Law Review 21(4) (2000), pp. 1267–1284.

Troper, Michel, The Problem of the Islamic Veil and the Principle of School Neutrality, in: *Sajo, Andras* (ed.), The Law of Religious Identity/Models for Post Communism, The Hague 1999, pp. 89–102.

Troper Michel, Constitutional Law in: *Bermann, George A./Picard, Etienne* (eds.), Introduction to French Law, Alphen aan den Rijn 2008.

Troper, Michel, Sovereignty and Laicite, Cardozo Law Review 30(6) (2009), pp. 2561–2574.

Tyndale, William, Junior and Infants School Public Inquiry: A Report to the Inner London Education Authority, ILEA, London 1976.

Vaisse, Justin, Veiled Meaning: The French Law Banning Religious Symbols in Public Schools, Washington D.C. 2004.

Vakulenko, Anastasia, Islamic Dress in Human Rights Jurisprudence: A Critique of Current Trends, Human Rights Law Review 7(4) (2007), pp. 717–739.

Vakulenko, Anastasia, Islamic Veiling in Legal Discourse, London 2012.

Van Dijk, Pieter/Van Hoof, Fried/Van Rijn, Arjen/Zwaak, Leo, Theory and Practice of the European Convention on Human Rights, 4th edn., Antwerp/Oxford 2006.

Van Ooijen, Hana M.A.E, Neutrality and Displaying Religious Symbols, in: *Temperman, Jereon* (ed.), The Lautsi Papers: Multidisciplinary Reflections on Religious Symbols in the Public School Classroom, Studies in Religion, Secular Beliefs and Human Rights 11 (2012), Leiden, Boston, pp. 219–238.

Van Ooijen, Hana M.A.E, Religious Symbols in Public Functions, Unveiling State Neutrality: A Comparative Analysis of Dutch, English and French Justifications for Limiting the Freedom of Public Official to Display Religious Symbols, Cambridge (UK) 2012.

Vickers, Lucy, Religion and Belief Discrimination and the Employment of Teachers in Faith Schools, Religion and Human Rights 4 (2009), pp. 137–156.

Vickers, Lucy, Religious Discrimination and Schools: The Employment of Teachers and the Public Sector Duty in: *Hunter-Henin*, Myriam (ed.), Law, Religious Freedoms and Education in Europe (Cultural Diversity and Law), Farnham 2011, pp. 87–107.

Ungern- Sternberg von, Antje, Religionsfreheit in Europa, Tübingen 2008.

Wallach Scott, Joan, The Politics of the Veil. Princeton, Oxford 2007.

Walter, Christian/Ungern-Sternberg von, Antje, Transformation of Church and State Relations in Great Britain and Germany, Heidelberg 2013.

Walter, Christian, Religionsverfassungsrecht in vergleichender und internationaler Perspektive, Tübingen 2006.

Ward, Richard/Wragg, Amanda, Walker & Walker's English Legal System, 9th edn. Oxford, 2005.

Weber, Albrecht, Religiöse Symbole in der Einwanderungsgesellschaft, ZAR 2004, pp. 53–60.

Weil, Patrick, Why the French Laicite is Liberal, Cardozo Law Review 30(2) (2009), pp. 2699–2715.

Westerfield, Jennifer M., Behind the Veil: An American Legal Perspective on the European Headscarf, The American Journal of Comparative Law 54(3) (2006), pp. 637–678.

Wick, Volker, Die Trennung von Staat und Kirche, Beiträge zum evangelischen Kirchenrecht und zum Staatskirchenrecht 81 (2007), pp. 29–78.

Wiese, Kirsten, Lehrerinnen mit Kopftuch, Zur Zulässigkeit eines religiösen und geschlechtsspezifischen Symbols im Staatsdienst, Berlin 2008.

Wiles, Ellen, Headscarves, Human Rights, and Harmonious Multicultural Society: Implications of the French Ban for Interpretation of Equality, Law and Society Review 41(3) (2007), pp. 699–736.

Winter, Bronwyn, Uncovering The French Headscarf Debate, New York 2008.

Wittinger, Michaela, "Kopftuchstreit auf europäisch": Aspekte des europäischen Grund- und Menschenrechtsschutzes, VBlBW 2001, pp 425–430.

Youngs Raymond: English, French & German Comparative Law, 3rd edn. Routledge NY 2014.

Zacharias, Diana, Schutz vor religiösen Symbolen durch Art.4 GG?, in: *Muckel, Stefan* (ed.), Kirche und Religion im sozialen Rechtsstaat, Band 42, Festschrift für Wolfgang Rüfner zum 70. Geburtstag, Berlin 2003, pp. 987–1007.

Zacharias, Diana, Das Kopftuch vor internationalen Gerichten, Kirche & Recht 2006, pp. 189–199.

Zacharias, Diana, Der postmortale Schutz religiöser Freiheit, Neuere Entwicklungen im Religionsrecht europäischer Staaten 61 (2013), pp. 859–880.

Zaubermann, Renée, Levy René: Police, Minorities and the French Republican Ideal, Criminology 41(4) (2003), pp. 1065–1100.

Ziegler, Janine, Republik ohne Gott – Zur französischen Vorstellung eines religionsneutralen Staates in: *Kink, Markus*; *Ziegler, Janine* (eds.), Staatsansichten und Staatsvisionen – Ein Politik- und Kulturwissenschaftlicher Querschnitt. Münster 2013, p. 319–340.

Zezschwitz von, Friedrich, Staatliche Neutralitätspflicht und Schulgebet, JZ 1966, pp. 337–344.

Internet Sources

Europe

European Court of Human Rights	http://www.echr.coe.int
European Union	http://europa.eu.int

England

Legislation	http://legislation.gov.uk
	http://www.education.gov.uk
Judgments	http://www.bailii.org
Supreme Court Judgments	http://supremecourt.gov.uk

France

Legislation	http://legifrance.gouv.fr
	http://www.assemblee-nationale.fr
Judgments	http://conseil-constitutionnel.fr
	http://conseil-etat.fr
	http://courdecassation.fr
Studies in comparative Law	http://www.senat.fr/elc
French laws and regulations	http://lexisnexis.co.uk

Germany

Legislation	http://gesetze-im-internet.de
Judgments	http://BVerfG.de
	http://bverwg.de
	http://bundesarbeitsgericht.de

www.ingramcontent.com/pod-product-compliance
Ingram Content Group UK Ltd.
Pitfield, Milton Keynes, MK11 3LW, UK
UKHW021847100926
8556IPUK00020B/1101

9 783631 769607